CHANGING LIVES

CHANGING LIVES

Studies in Human Development and Professional Helping

Edited by
Martin Bloom

Rutgers,
The State University of New Jersey

UNIVERSITY OF SOUTH CAROLINA PRESS

Published in Columbia, South Carolina, by the
University of South Carolina Press

Printed in Canada

Library of Congress Cataloging-in-Publication Data

Changing lives : studies in human development and professional helping
    / edited by Martin Bloom.
        p.   cm.
    Includes bibliographical references and indexes.
    ISBN 0–87249–755–0   (pbk. : acid-free)
    1. Social service.   2. Developmental psychology.   3. Social
service—United States.   4. Developmental psychology—United States.
I. Bloom, Martin, 1934–   .
HV40.C429   1991
155—dc20   91–18482

Contents

IX. THEORIES OF HUMAN BEHAVIOR AND DEVELOPMENT

Contents:

SELECTED TOPICS

I. THEORIES

A. Ecological Models: Carel Germain (chapter 46); systems approaches in chapters 38, 42

B. Behavioral Theories: Bruce Thyer (chapter 47); behavioral methods discussed in chapters 22, 23

C. Cognitive Theories: Albert Bandura discussed in chapters 17, 38; Lawrence Kohlberg discussed in chapter 23; Jean Piaget discussed in chapters 13, 23; problem solving theories discussed in chapters 10, 16, 23

D. Communication Theory: Virginia Satir discussed in chapters 4, 7; persuasion, chapters 6, 38

E. Social Development Model: discussed in chapter 39 (J. David Hawkins and Joseph G. Weis)

F. Psychodynamic Theories: discussed by Sophie Freud, chapter 48; Erik Erikson discussed in chapters 13, 42, 48; Daniel Levinson discussed in chapters 42, 46

G. Genetic Theories: discussed in chapters 1, 20

H. The Community Mental Health Model: discussed in chapter 21

I. Theories or Programs Considering Cultural Factors: discussed in chapters 5, 10, 11, 16, 21, 34, 38, 43

II. MODES OF PRACTICE

A. Primary Prevention or Actions Before a Problem Emerges: discussed in chapters 1, 4, 6, 10, 13, 16, 17, 21, 22, 32, 38, 39, 41

B. Treatment or Social Intervention with Existing Problems: discussed in chapters 1, 7, 18, 19, 20, 23, 24, 33, 43, 45

C. Rehabilitation or Restitution after a Problem Has Been Resolved as far as Possible: discussed in chapters 1, 8, 11, 18, 23, 28, 30, 32, 45

III. STAGES OF THE LIFE COURSE

A. Infancy—discussions regarding:
1. Conception, Pregnancy, and Birth: chapters 1, 2, 3, 7, 13
2. The First Year of Life: chapters 7, 8, 12

B. Childhood—discussions regarding:
1. Toddler Stage Through Preschool Period: chapters 2, 3, 7, 8, 9, 10, 12, 22, 27, 28, 32, 33, 36
2. Elementary-School Period to Puberty: chapters 2, 3, 4, 5, 7, 8, 12, 16, 17, 19, 27, 28, 32, 34, 36, 40, 44, 45

C. Adolescence—discussions regarding: chapters 2, 3, 4, 6, 8, 11, 12, 13, 14, 17, 19, 28, 29, 32, 37, 38, 39, 44, 45

D. Adulthood—discussions regarding:
1. young adults (approximately aged 21 to 40): chapters 1, 2, 3, 7, 8, 9, 12, 18, 19, 20, 21, 23, 25, 27, 28, 32, 33, 41, 44, 45
2. middle-aged adults (approximately aged 40 to 65): chapters 2, 3, 7, 8, 12, 18, 19, 20, 21, 23, 24, 25, 27, 30, 35, 41, 42, 44, 45

E. The Elderly (including the young-old, approximately ages 65 through 74; the mid-elderly, approximately ages 75 through 84; the old-old, approximately ages 85 and over)—discussions regarding: chapters 2, 15, 25, 30, 31, 34, 35, 36, 44, 45

F. Issues Related to the Family: discussed in chapters 1, 2, 3, 7, 8, 9, 12, 14, 15, 18, 20, 21, 23, 27, 28, 30, 31, 32, 33, 35, 41

G. Issues Related to Women: discussed in chapters 1, 6, 7, 8, 9, 12, 13, 14, 20, 23, 24, 25, 27, 28, 29, 30, 31, 32, 33, 35, 41

H. Issues Related to Minority Concerns: discussed in chapters 5, 6, 10, 11, 12, 13, 21, 26, 34, 37, 38, 41, 43

CHANGING LIVES

PREFACE

I am standing on a threshold about to enter a room. It is a complicated business. In the first place I must shove against an atmosphere pressing with a force of fourteen pounds on every square inch of my body. I must make sure of landing on a plank traveling at twenty miles a second around the sun—a fraction of a second too early or too late, the plank would be miles away. I must do this whilst hanging from a round planet head outward into space, and a wind of aether blowing at no one knows how many miles a second through every interstice of my body.

(A. S. Eddington,
The Nature of the Physical World, 1929, p. 342.)

Nothing is as abstract as concrete behavior. Consider your decision to enter the room in which you now reside. Or your decision to enter your chosen helping profession. Eddington identifies the complexity of the physical world, but that is hardly anything compared to the ordinary events in your bio-psycho-social-cultural world. Consider what goes into a social act:

• your internal thoughts and feelings—the hopes, expectations, and fears—stemming from your memory of past comparable situations and your consciousness of the present situation;
• your genetic inheritance that enables you to perform some actions, while limiting you in the performance of others;
• your value system that determines the correctness of the means you use and the rightness or goodness of the ends you seek by means of this action;
• the social pressures exerted by formal or informal communications and actions by members of your primary groups, family members, close friends and the like;
• the sanctions and the demands exerted by representatives of secondary groups active in your life, such as your work associates or because of your civic roles and responsibilities;
• the subcultural and cultural pressures you experience, especially the conflicts between some dominant group and your membership in one or another of some minority group;

• as well as the overall definition of the situation from your historical age and place, as contrasted with another time and location in which the very act that you are performing may have been forbidden or enjoined.

Yet, as in Eddington's example about the physical world, while we know all of the above is "true" about our bio-psycho-sociocultural behavior, we nonetheless act smoothly and deftly. We enter rooms, and we enter upon some profession. We are not, like the centipede who is asked how it knows to lift which leg in which order, petrified into immobility. How can this be? Why should we as students of the helping professions study human behavior and development if we already live it without any effort?

• Because if we are to know accurately what a given piece of behavior is,
• because if we are to understand how that given behavior came to be as it is,
• because if we are to predict how it is likely to change—and thereby, to be potentially able to affect that behavior in some desired direction,

then we must look to theories and research about human behavior and development in the social and physical contexts for this active knowledge base of professional helping.

In short, as helping professionals, we must know the underlying structures and dynamics of human behavior and development if we are to offer efficacious and humane helping. This anthology offers one set of approaches to this knowledge base.

In this preface, let me indicate the underlying principles by which I constructed this book. First, I selected materials from a wide range of authors, from the social sciences to the helping professions, on grounds that we all seek to understand and affect human behavior. However, we come to this task from varying directions, each with its special insights from which other helping professionals might well benefit. Thus, you will find readings by writers in social work, psychology, sociology, nursing, medicine, public health, epidemiology, education, and economics.

1

Second, any anthology on human development must be selective, but I have tried to find interesting, self-contained, and recent papers on significant topics, which also offer many points of departure for additional study through their references. I have also tried to be comprehensive on special topics. For example, on abuse, I have offered selections on child sexual abuse, date rape, spousal abuse, and elder abuse. On AIDS, I have provided information directly dealing with this most devastating new epidemic, but I also offer supporting materials in the areas of drugs, homosexuality, and adolescent explorations in adult-like behavior that put them at risk for sexually transmitted diseases of all sorts. On the topic of stress and stress management, I have presented papers indicating the varied ways stress affects human behavior at home, at school, and at work. A scan of the topic headings and the particular papers will illustrate the other themes that are presented in this book.

Third, I have tried to give equal attention to each of the developmental stages, infants and children, adolescents, young adults, middle-aged, and older adults. I have also given special attention to the family as a source of problems as well as an important resource in the helping process. Papers include discussion of the effects of family size, of siblingship over the life cycle, of working parents and their concerns on raising their families, of single-parent families, of alternative life style families, of the effects of unemployment on families, of homelessness that is now appearing as a family experience, of the problems of divorce and of stepparenting, and to the end of life, how experiences in hospices help to unify the family as one member approaches death.

Fourth, I have grouped these readings around eight elemental human experiences that all must face in the act of living. We all grow (physically) and develop (psycho-socially). We all communicate and form intimate attachments. We all work and play, adapt to our several environments, and deal with conflicts, and so on. For each of these elemental experiences, I have offered readings that span the life course.

For example, young people learn to form intimate attachments, but older persons maintain or change these intimate attachments as well. We will learn how depression, the most frequently occurring of the mental illnesses, appears in children, adolescents, and in adults. There will be eight iterations of the life course in which we examine particular content areas for how these same contents are experienced by persons of different ages and in different contexts. (If you prefer your human development served in the traditional categories of children, adolescents, adults, and aged, this arrangement is also provided by an alternative table of contents.)

Another conscious decision involved including papers that provide illustrations of all the modes of helping—primary prevention, treatment, and rehabilitation—so as to expand the vision of helping that our students receive. I have also included the major theoretical orientations of our day, as special papers directed exclusively on this topic—the ecological perspective, the behavioral approach, and psychodynamic theories. In addition, I illustrate many other focused theories as parts of papers dealing with specific contents. For example, Bandura's social learning principles are displayed on a paper on health education; Kohlberg's model is used as the basis for dealing with wife batterers; Piaget and Erikson are discussed in considering a developmental approach to pregnancy prevention.

In addition to the half dozen specific research reports, and the five times that number of papers that review literatures on their content area, I have included some ''I-witness'' reports, for example, a paper written by a homeless woman, and some case studies involving clinical and protective situations.

Most of the topics considered here should be familiar to readers, but some new issues are raised that may be surprising. I suspect that we will be seeing some serious discussions soon about intergenerational equity—how shall we distribute limited social resources between children and elders without detracting from either? I think that creativity, and particularly the loss of creative potential in women and minorities, will surface as a significant social concern in the face of world competition. And I believe that the implications of the rapid growth of knowledge in biology and genetics will become so important that all helping professionals will have to have a clearer understanding of these matters.

The only certainty we face in the helping professions is constant change. The knowledge we learn today must be not only relevant for the immediate context, but it must lead to critical thinking for the future. Knowledge is power, as Bacon wisely noted, but for the helping professional in times of rapid change, knowledge about knowledge is an equally appropriate power. This anthology introduces readers to the wide and penetrating scope of contemporary knowledge, just as it raises critical questions about what we know and how we might best apply this knowledge in practice.

INTRODUCTION

Anthologies are like smorgasbords, arrays of possible delights to the intellectual palate, but which are capable of producing cognitive indigestion if devoured unwisely. This introduction is a guide to the nine parts of which this anthology is composed, so that they may yield up their proper feast.

Several dimensions went into the planning of this book. First is the concept most central to social work and the helping professions, that the person must always be viewed within relevant sociocultural and physical environments. Thus, when we view some particular human behavior or aspect of development, we must consider not only the events internal to the person—thoughts, feelings, and the working out of genetic and physiological structures—but also external events. These external events include experiences in primary groups such as family and peers, secondary groups such as work and school, and the socio-cultural and physical environments of everyday life set within some historical context.

The life history of an individual as he or she moves over the life course is a complex affair. It is no longer possible, as earlier theorists had suggested, to look merely at the internal experiences of an individual to understand the twists and turns a life may take. Nor is it useful to inquire only about the external forces creating opportunities and barriers. I will argue that the most useful perspective for the analysis of any social behavior is the whole configuration, the actions and reactions of the individual, primary and secondary groups, and sociocultural and physical environmental contexts. Ignore any segment of this configuration at your own risk.

However, it is difficult to grasp this complex whole all at once, and so we use theories as guides to action with regard to portions of reality. This is the second dimension that went into the construction of this anthology—the provision of information for use. Each of these articles can be read as the basis for one or more modes of scientific helping, although some are more direct than others.

There are three general modes of helping: primary prevention, treatment, and rehabilitation. Briefly described, primary prevention involves actions taken (a) to prevent predictable problems to persons at risk; (b) to protect existing states of health and healthy functioning; and (c) to promote or enhance the desired possibilities. All of these actions occur before the specific problem has taken place, or before the potential has been fulfilled.

Treatment involves actions directed to an existing problem for a given individual or group. It can include crisis intervention, which involves immediate response to the emergence of a problem. Treatment can also involve ongoing efforts to resolve an existing problem.

Rehabilitation is the third form of helping. This involves helping treated persons reestablish their lives to the highest levels possible, given the effects of the problem. This form of helping involves putting the pieces back together again, so to speak. This involves the mutual rehabilitation of the person and the relevant environment.

For all of these modes of helping, theories may be useful guides to professional action. An alternative table of contents focusing on selected topics (pp. ix–x) identifies more than a dozen theories that are described or illustrated in the articles in this anthology. Any theory provides us with hypotheses, informed guesses about the way events will happen if we take certain actions. These practice hypotheses require objective testing to ascertain whether or not the desired results occurred as predicted.

This anthology also employs the concept of elemental human experiences, those classes of experiences that are universally present in the lives of people at all times and places. These elemental human experiences are terms identifying patterned ways people move through the life course, each culture, each group, and each individual having some similar and some different patterns. Everyone who survives as a human being must:

- grow (physically) and develop (psychosocially);
- must communicate in some fashion;
- must feel and express that form of connectedness that some call love or attachment;

3

• must adapt to the inner and outer demands in the ways one becomes a unique individual and a member of social groupings;

• must face the various similarities and differences they encounter in the act of being a member of a pluralistic society;

• must relate to the conflicts and the cooperative situations that constitute all of social living;

• must work in order to survive, and no less urgent, must play in order to survive work; and

• must face an inevitable death just as one has faced the inevitable tasks of living.

Thus, each elemental human experience has both personal and interpersonal aspects.

The individual is conceived as if at a center of multiple concentric circles each representing types of groups, organizations, community, culture, and the physical environment at this time in history. To understand any individual or group requires that we understand as well the enveloping and interacting circles.

As John Muir, the great American environmentalist said, "When we try to pick out anything by itself, we find it hitched to everything else in the universe." This is the ultimate expression of the systems thinking that is probably the predominant view currently in the helping professions. It is the underlying theme of this volume as well (*See also* Bloom, 1984, 1990).

However, systems thinking is a difficult task master. It demands that we see the universe in each atom of human behavior. How people decide to act in any given situation—whether or not to have a baby, change jobs, or just to stay home and read a good book—depends on their assessment of the alternatives, the pros and cons pushing and pulling them in one direction or another. It is difficult to assign specific numbers as weights to these pros and cons, but in fact people act as if they have done this. Even "impulsive" actions may be interpreted as rapid weighing and valuing one direction over another. Whether or not an action is wise or produces good results is another question entirely. This decision making is often done rapidly. Like the centipede walking, if we had to think about which foot to lift in what order, we might never be able to walk at all.

When helping professionals seek to understand a client's situation so as to help the client help him or herself, this process of decision making is slowed down and the alternatives are more explicitly considered. The helping process may consist in just this, helping the client to think through the weightings of alternatives. Or, the helping process may consist of guidance on ways to make changes in these conditions so as to change the weightings in a direction more favorable to the client, without imposing problems for others.

What helps us to think through this decision making process more carefully and deliberately are the guidelines offered by various theories. Each theory tells us, in effect, to pay special attention (and give extra weight) to certain factors that may be part of the client's situation. Another theory dealing with the same set of events may tell us to pay attention to another set of factors. As we will see in the last part of this anthology, how we make decisions and translations from theories to the world of action is a special topic unto itself.

The reasons we go through this exercise in dissection of human actions are threefold. First, the sheer description of what an action consists of, and what are its probable component pieces, may help us to see that action better. A given client behavior becomes less mysterious—to the client as well as to the practitioner—when we can describe it clearly, accurately, and fully.

Second, a thorough description of a human action may allow us to understand it. That is, we may come to understand what calls that action into being, what sustains that action, and what terminates it. We are probably driven to seek understanding because it is the very basis of social life. We live in a sea of social options, of possible actions and reactions, and unless we understand how social events work, we are at the mercies of these various forces and structures around us.

The third reason we engage in these detailed studies of human behavior in social environments is to predict what will happen. This is the ultimate aim of a life that a person seeks to call his or her own: Based on a thorough description of social reality, and an understanding of its beginnings and endings, we seek to predict the life course of particular happenings that most concern us. As we predict (and test our predictions for accuracy), so we come to control some portions of that world. Existentialist philosophers and social scientists assert that it is by making choices, especially risky choices for which we may have only partial information, that we truly construct our lives and ourselves.

Description, understanding, and prediction—the three dimensions of theory—are also the rationale for taking apart significant pieces of human experience. However, it is the special task of helping professionals to try to put the pieces together again. Thus, the goals I seek in this anthology are to present many interesting and important writings about human experience from across the broad spectrum of the social and health sciences. These selections are presented as examples to be dissected, to be carefully pulled apart to study what they say, and how they explain the workings of their subject. Then we can learn about predicting and controlling these events, that is, we can learn the knowledge base and skills needed as helping professionals.

Every anthology is finite and limited. Thus, it is not my intention to be comprehensive on every subject, but rather, I wish to provide the opportunity for picking out important points on a topic, examining them, and then realizing that they are indeed "hitched to everything else in the universe." We cannot act on everything in the universe, that is, we cannot plan our professional response to a client to take account of every possible event in his or her life. But we can come to realize that every act we perform does in fact affect every significant part of the client's situation. So we must consider to the extent possible the various repercussions of professional helping.

This is where theories and frames of reference are helpful in categorizing the major topics to be considered. So too in this anthology, I call your attention to the configuration of events—the elemental human experiences—that involve these questions:

• Human growth and development of the person in environments: At what stages of life are your client and his or her significant others, such as family, friends, work associates, and the like? How does the configuration of one person's life fit in with, or not fit in with, the configurations of the lives of the others?

• Communication: In what ways does the individual communicate or not communicate significant information and values to the people important in his or her life? In what ways do the groups (such as families, peers, work associates) communicate or not communicate vital information? What are the barriers to significant communications?

• Love, sexuality, pregnancy: How does the individual attach him or herself to significant others,

and they to him or her? Granted that human attachment is needed, probably at every portion of life, then what form does this attachment take? What are the forms of loving (not merely genital forms) that individuals partake in or lack? How do these experiences shape those individual lives?

• Adaptation: If life consists of coping with and mastering the continuous flow of events, large and small, then we have to ask how these adaptations occur. What is the price we pay for adapting by denial or avoidance, for example, as contrasted with working with or changing events to make the world a more agreeable place in which to live. In the phrase of William Faulkner, how are we not merely to survive, but to prevail?

• Similarities and differences: As the anthropological truism states, we are like ALL other people in some ways, like SOME others in other ways, and like NO other person in yet different ways—ALL AT ONCE. The question for helping professionals is to recognize this fundamental sameness even in the face of extreme differences, as well as the differences among us, even when we appear to be "the same kind." What are the implications of similarities and differences among people, and especially between the professional helpers and the people who need help? What are the moral bonds that exist between and among people?

• Conflict and cooperation: Do not be surprised that your most benign act of helping meets with negative responses at times, for what you intend to be good and helpful may appear—and be!—unhelpful or harmful to the client in ways that you do not yet understand. The social configuration of which life is composed is filled with cooperative and conflicted elements, each at different levels. Successfully treat a problematic child, and discover that the resolved problem now creates unexpected difficulties for the parents who may have been held together only because of that child's "bad" behaviors.

• Work and play: Why is it that children work so hard at play? And why do adults sometimes "play" at working? Or, more likely in a Type A society, why are some adults unable to play—at risk of their lives? We have much to learn about the play of children and adults. We have also much to learn about how children learn to work—or do not learn to work—and what effects these have on the individuals involved as well as the society.

• Life and living, dying and death: The great sociologist Emile Durkheim pointed out that suicide, that wholly personal and unique act, is powerfully influenced by the social structures and forces in which the individual lives and dies. This is yet another perspective on John Muir's ecological axiom, or the configural perspective that bids us examine carefully all the levels of a person's life to determine what are the significant forces acting on him or her. We must examine as well the forces acting on the groups and communities of which our clients are one part. Even in death we are part of the human configuration. We all owe nature a death, but we use our "borrowed time" to invest in life, in ourselves, in others including those whom we procreate. Thus, the cycle continues, reflected in our novels and poems, our bibles, our mythologies and ideologies. Let us begin to study changing lives.

PART I

GROWTH AND DEVELOPMENT OF THE PERSON IN ENVIRONMENTS

INTRODUCTION

The readings in this section sample the many contexts of human growth and development, from our genetic inheritance to the families in which that inheritance is expressed. Although each paper has its own focus—such as Julia Rauch's description of modern genetics, Ann Goetting's analysis of sibling developmental relationships, or Mazie Earle Wagner and her colleagues' paper on the effects of family size—all of the papers may be dissected by the careful reader to discover a configuration of factors. There will always be involved:

• **A person on whom we focus attention for a time.** This focal person may change as circumstances direct, but we must always be aware of the history and current makeup of the individuals with whom we are interacting.

• **A primary group, one with whom that individual has intimate and ongoing associations.** Probably the focal individual will be a member of more than one primary group, such as a family, peer groups, close work or play groups, etc. These groups may or may not be in agreement on influencing the individual in one given direction.

• **A secondary group, one with whom that individual has functional relationships in a division of societal labor.** Again, the focal individual may be a member of more than one secondary group, such as in a work situation, or as a member of a religious institution. And again, the individual may or may not receive a consistent message from these several large groups about valued goals of action.

• **A cultural group, one with whom that individual shares a common language, traditions, life style, and values.** In modern society, it is likely that each individual belongs to several cultures such as the primary culture of the family, and a secondary culture of the larger society. The messages provided by these different cultures may not only represent contrary values, but may include oppressive conditions for some minority group members making it difficult to succeed in attaining the commonly held values.

• **A community and society, large sociophysical arenas within which all of the other events take place, and which are influenced by their collective pressures.** The laws of the community and society are one visible way in which these collective pressures are manifested, but there are also shared values of loyalty and patriotism—and their opposites for those who are poorly integrated into a community or badly controlled by it.

• **The physical environment and the historic time period also stimulate and set limits on social behavior even though it is sometimes difficult to be aware of these pervasive aspects of the configuration.** While we have "conquered time and space" with our modern transportation and communication systems, tell that to the long-suffering driver trying to get through the daily traffic jam, or to the rural elderly trying to get some basic medical assistance from a distant location. We are and remain passengers on the increasingly crowded spaceship Earth.

These six aspects of the social configuration are the ingredients about which we must be concerned as we seek to understand any client situation. The knowledge base begins with how individuals grow physically and develop socially. It continues with the understanding of how groups, especially families, change over time, how the expected and the unexpected shape the development of these basic contexts of the human experience.

The specific articles in this section reflect this entire range of human growth and development. Each should be read not only for what is directly discussed, but also for what are the implications for the other parts of the human configuration. For example, in Julia Rauch's paper on the genetics revolution, it is clear that the focus is on the new knowledge modern genetics provides social workers and other helping professionals, but implied is that this knowledge be shared with marital partners and

9

others making fundamental decisions concerning procreation and other life-making or unmaking decisions that affect the family and ultimately the community and society.

Ann Goetting explores with us the tasks of siblingship over the entire life cycle. As each sibling in the family grows and develops into his or her own person at first within the family, and then outside of it, so the tasks of siblingship change. They never cease, but rather expand in different directions depending on the social contexts of the life course.

Mazie Earle Warner, Herman Schubert, and Daniel Schubert present information of the effects of family size on members of that family. There are powerful effects, often invisible to the members of the family, that influence individual member's life chances. At the same time, society itself stands to gain or lose depending on parental decisions regarding family size. Cultural values for or against large families are another factor in this complex equation of simple numbers.

In each of these papers, we find evidence for the interactions between aspects of the person (physiological, cognitive, affective, behavioral) and the social environments (both the social pressures and the concrete objects in a physical environment). Some of these changes over time are more or less regular for all human beings, such as the sequence of physical growth in a standard environment. (However, when the environment is not "standard," when persons begin life with genetic or constitutional handicaps, when basic resources are unobtainable, or when oppressive forces limit the expression of behavior, then deviations may appear even in the expected universal patterns of growth.) Other psychosocial changes that occur to human beings are far less predictable, and depend on the set of forces and structures that enable or inhibit a person's development. Theorists have proposed certain uniformities in these psychosocial changes (such as Sigmund Freud, Erik Erikson, and Jean Piaget), while other theorists dispute such social uniformities (such as the behaviorists and the ecologists or systems theorists). All agree that human behavior is complex. Indeed, to understand any aspect of social life, whether it is the inner private feelings one holds or the sprawling urban reality, we must ultimately consider each aspect of the human configuration for its contribution to understanding, and possibly, to control. Here again are the three functions of theory: description, explanation, and control. Thus it is that we must share the knowledge-building of theorists who have proceeded us, and where suitable theories do not exist, we must contribute to knowledge-building as we grapple with the problems and potentials of living.

1

SOCIAL WORK AND THE GENETICS REVOLUTION: GENETIC SERVICES

Julia B. Rauch

School of Social Work and Community Planning
University of Maryland at Baltimore

More than half a century ago, Mary Richmond (1917) recognized the value to social workers of obtaining a family genetic history:

> He must aim to get at facts of heredity. . . . The pertinent data would cover the condition of health and cause of death of parents, grandparents, brothers and sisters, uncles and aunts. The items should be especially clear and detailed whenever, in any of these relatives, there seems to be a question of consanguineous marriage, of miscarriages, or tuberculosis, alcoholism, mental disorder, nervousness, epilepsy, cancer, deformities or abnormalities, or of any exceptional ability. (p. 187)

Guided by a biopsychosocial perspective, social workers always have used family and developmental histories to assess problems in an individual or the environment. This perspective includes awareness that genetic factors often contribute to psychosocial dysfunction. Historically, social workers have provided services to individuals and families affected by developmental disabilities, handicapping conditions, and chronic illnesses—conditions often of genetic etiology. Thus social work will be affected by current developments in human genetics.

Better understanding of the etiology, causes, risks of inheritance, course, prognosis, and treatment of genetic disorders now is available to people with genetic concerns. A network of specialized clinical genetic services is available throughout the United States (U.S. Department of Health and Human Services, 1986). Because of these new information and service capacities, clients' genetic questions can be answered more fully and accurately than previously was possible. This important new resource is enhancing traditional areas of social work. In addition, the meaning of the term "genetic disorder" is broadening, the number and proportion of clients with genetic concerns is expanding, and new practice sites are proliferating.

This article is intended to stimulate readers to consider the significance of changing genetic knowledge and services for social work. The author reviews basic genetic concepts, briefly describes genetic services, and discusses the ramifications of both concepts and services for the profession.

GENETICS AND GENETIC DISORDERS

In its broadest sense, human genetics deals with those qualities that distinguish human beings from other species and with those that differentiate human populations, families, and individuals. The study of genetic processes includes the causes of hereditary similarities and differences among humans, the ways in which they are transmitted from generation to generation, and those factors, both internal and external, that affect gene action and outcome. One subspecialty, medical genetics, is concerned with the etiology, prevention, diagnosis, and treatment of genetic disorders; another, behavioral genetics, examines genetic contributors to variations of conduct that range from innate temperament to major psychiatric disorders.

There are four types of genetic disorders: those associated with (1) single gene inheritance, (2) multifactorial inheritance, (3) chromosome aberrations, and (4) exposure to harmful environmental agents (Nagle, 1984; Riccardi, 1977; Schild & Black, 1984; Singer, 1985). The word *genetic* connotes "of, relating to, or being a gene" (*Webster's Ninth New Collegiate Dictionary*, 1987, p. 511). "Genetic" is not equivalent to "inherited" or "congenital."

GENES AND CHROMOSOMES

Genes, the basic units of inheritance, are packaged in units called chromosomes. Humans normally

---

From *Social Work*, 1988, *33*(5): 389–395. Copyright © 1988. National Association of Social Workers, Inc. Reprinted with permission of the publisher and the author.

have 23 pairs of chromosomes, or a total of 46. Twenty-two of the pairs are *autosomes,* a term derived from the roots for *auto* (meaning "self") and *soma* (meaning "of the body") (*Webster's Ninth New Collegiate Dictionary,* 1987). Autosomal pairs have identical structures, with matching genes located in the same sequence at identical sites. Thus, each person has two copies of each gene located on an autosome. Although the partners in each pair of genes usually are identical, about one-third of human genes have variants, as is evident in the diversity of human eye, skin, and hair color.

The sex chromosomes are located in the twenty-third pair. Females have two copies of the female X chromosome (XX). Males have one copy each of the female X chromosome and the male Y chromosome (XY). As is the case with autosomal genes, not all genes on the sex chromosomes are identical.

SINGLE GENE INHERITANCE

All humans carry abnormal, or mutant, potentially harmful genes of which they are unaware. These "hidden" genes are *recessive;* if only one recessive gene is present, the more powerful, or *dominant,* partner conceals its existence.

However, if two people who carry the same abnormal, autosomal recessive gene reproduce with each other, then the chances are one in four with each conception that both parents will pass the gene on to the child. As a result, the child will have two copies of the abnormal gene and will have its associated inherited disorder, which is called a *single-gene disorder* because the condition is associated with a specific abnormal gene and *autosomal recessive* because the gene is carried on an autosome but is not evident if a dominant gene partner is present. The condition is *inherited* because it is caused by genes that are transmitted from the parents to the child. Examples of autosomal recessive diseases are cystic fibrosis, sickle-cell anemia, and Tay-Sachs disease.

A second form of single gene inheritance is *autosomal dominant.* Again, a mutant gene is located on an autosome, but it is dominant and will manifest itself whenever it is present. In this case, the parent with the gene has the associated disorder. With each conception, a 50-percent chance exists that the affected parent will transmit the gene to the child, who also will be affected. Examples of autosomal dominant conditions are Huntington's disease and neurofibromatosis.

A third form of single-gene inheritance is that of *X-linked recessive.* In this pattern, a recessive gene is carried on the female X chromosome. Because the carrier woman's second X chromosome carries a dominant partner, the presence of the recessive gene is hidden. A 50-percent chance exists that any child conceived will inherit from the mother the X-chromosome that bears the recessive gene. A daughter who inherits the recessive gene will be another carrier of the disorder. A son who inherits the recessive gene also inherits from the father a Y gene, which has no dominant gene partner. Consequently, the son will have an X-linked (carried on the X chromosome) recessive disorder. Examples of X-linked disorders are hemophilia and Duchenne's muscular dystrophy. *Codominance,* in which the partner genes have equal power, also occurs, as in the case of a wavy-haired child born to parents who have straight and curly hair, respectively.

MULTIFACTORIAL INHERITANCE

Multifactorial inheritance involves the additive effect of interaction between genes and the environment. Examples include variations in height, weight, and intellect, each of which is affected by nutrition and general health. Many relatively common disorders involve multifactorial inheritance: asthma, cleft lip, cleft palate, club foot, congenital scoliosis, diabetes mellitus, some types of mental retardation, and spina bifida.

Important to understanding multifactorial inheritance is the concept of *genetic liability.* Children of the same parents, or within the same extended family, may be more or less likely—that is, liable—to be affected by a familial condition, depending on which specific genes they inherit. Theoretically, one child could inherit all of the parents' potentially harmful genes, and another child could inherit none. Thus, the vulnerability of different children to equivalent, potentially damaging environments would differ. A child with high liability might be affected negatively; a child with low liability might thrive. A high-liability child also might develop symptoms even in a relatively benign environment.

Behavioral dysfunctions that once were thought to be environmental in origin now are known to have, or are suspected of having, genetic roots. A prominent example is alcoholism (Russell, 1985; Schuckit, 1985; Smith 1982). Genes for two types of manic depression have been identified (Schmeck, 1986a, 1986b). Although it is debated, evidence also suggests that other affective disorders and schizophrenia are aggregations of distinct disorders with diverse causes, including single gene and multifactorial inheritance (Group for the Advancement of Psychiatry, 1984; Lykken, 1987; McGruffin & Gottesman, 1985; Tsuang & Vandermey, 1980). A possibly genetic basis for Alzheimer's disease has been identified; like schizophrenia, Alzheimer's disease also may be more than one condition (Heston, 1974; Schmeck, 1987a, 1987e, 1987f). Mental retardation is a prominent example of a condition that often has genetic determinants (Abuelo, 1983; Dickerson, 1981; Drew, 1984; Petrie, 1985; Russell, 1985).

CHROMOSOMAL ABERRATIONS

Some genetic disorders are associated with too few or too many chromosomes or with abnormal chromosome structure. Most autosomal chromosome aberrations prevent survival. One exception is Down's syndrome, an important cause of mental retardation, which is caused by an extra chromosome 21. Evidence also shows that specific structural faults are linked to certain learning disabilities (Ludlow & Cooper, 1983; Rossi, 1972).

Sex chromosome anomalies, in which an individual has one or too many sex chromosomes, are relatively common (Berch & Bender, 1987; Money, 1968). These include single-X (XO) females (Turner's syndrome), triple-X (XXX) females, double-X (XXY) males (Klinefelter's syndrome), double-Y (XYY) males, and other combinations.

Chromosomal aberrations usually result from accidents during *meiosis,* the process of chromosome replication and cell division that produces sperm and eggs. Thus, aberrations are not inherited. However, because these aberrations are associated with abnormalities of amounts or misplaced genetic material, they are genetic. Chromosomal aberrations also are *congenital,* which means they are present at birth.

EXPOSURE TO HARMFUL ENVIRONMENTAL AGENTS

At any life stage, exposure to certain environmental agents can damage genes, alter chromosomes, and disrupt normal genetic processes (Avers, 1984; Cain, 1984; Elkington, 1987; Mange & Mange, 1980; Norwood, 1980; Nyhan, 1976; Riccardi, 1977; Stern, 1973). If this exposure occurs during prenatal development, miscarriage or neonatal death may occur or the baby may have birth defects. For example, the baby of a woman who abuses alcohol during pregnancy may have fetal alcohol syndrome, which is characterized by mental retarda-

tion, facial deformity, and other problems (Little, 1982; Wright, 1981). Fetal alcohol syndrome is genetic because it is associated with disruption of normal genetic processes and is congenital, but it is not inherited.

Other dangerous prenatal agents include certain therapeutic and recreational drugs; infections, such as Rubella (German measles); acquired immune deficiency syndrome and other sexually transmitted diseases; nuclear radiation; and poor maternal physiology. For example, women with phenylketonuria (PKU)—a condition which, if not treated by a special diet, leads to mental retardation—are at risk for giving birth to mentally retarded offspring even though they themselves, having been treated effectively, have normal intelligence.

In adulthood, exposure to radiation and some chemicals may harm sperm or ova before conception, which can result in infertility, multiple miscarriages, and birth defects (Rauch & Tivoli, 1988). Cardiovascular disease, hypertension, and diabetes are multifactorial conditions derived from the combination of genetic liability with an unhealthy lifestyle. One theory of cancer holds that some genes that are carried by all people (oncogenes) cause cancer if activated by a carcinogen (Bishop, 1982; Rubsenthal, 1985; Schmeck, 1987b, 1987c, 1987d). Vulnerability to specific infections also varies (Stern, 1973).

VARIABLE EXPRESSIVITY, GENETIC HETEROGENEITY, AND PLEIOTROPY

The principle of *variable expressivity* asserts that a given gene may manifest itself differently in different individuals. (This principle is analogous to the systems concept of multifinality.) For this reason, no genetic disorder is identical from person to person. For example, one child with cystic fibrosis may be severely ill at birth and die within six months; another may have no symptoms until adolescence, when a few mild symptoms develop. An individual with mild symptoms may live to adulthood and live a relatively normal life that includes working and marrying.

The principle of *genetic heterogeneity* (equifinality) asserts that a single characteristic, such as mental retardation or deafness, may have different genetic etiology in different individuals. According to another principle, *pleiotropy,* a single gene may affect different, apparently unrelated systems. For example, PKU, which if untreated causes mental retardation, also is associated with blond hair, blue eyes, and skin problems.

As can be seen, the scope of human genetics is broad, and the concept of genetic disorders is broadening as growing knowledge reveals the contribution of genetic factors to conditions once believed to have environmental causation only. This expanding definition likely will increase the number and proportion of social work clients who have genetic concerns and might benefit from referral to genetic services.

GENETIC SERVICES

The 1976 National Genetic Diseases Act authorized federal support of a national genetic diseases testing, counseling, and education program and mandated that those services be made available to all individuals on a voluntary basis (Hormuth, 1977). Public and voluntary genetic services, including comprehensive clinical genetic centers, now exist throughout the United States (U.S. Department of Health and Human Services, 1986). In addition, networks of genetic service providers coordinate services, research, and education within each region of the U.S. Department of Health and Human Services. Thus, an array of programs exist, many of which were not available even a decade ago (Burney, Walker, & Dumars, 1985; Fuchs, 1980; Nyhan, 1976; Riccardi, 1977; Schild & Black, 1984).

GENETIC SCREENING

The clinical purposes of genetic screening are to determine whether a person needs remedial or preventive health care and to obtain information for use in reproductive decision making. Four types of genetic screening are available: (1) carrier, (2) prenatal, (3) neonatal, and (4) presymptomatic.

CARRIER SCREENING. Carrier screening detects the presence of genes or abnormal chromosomes that might be harmful to potential offspring. Most often, carrier screening is offered on a voluntary basis to persons of reproductive age who plan to have children and who meet criteria for risk of carrying a deleterious gene. One important criterion is membership in a population with high frequency of a specific abnormal gene. For example, the gene for Tay-Sachs disease, which is rare in the general population, is more common in Ashkenazi Jews (one in 30 carriers). Similarly, the gene for sickle-cell anemia is more common in Americans of west African, Mediterranean, south Indian, and south Chinese descent. A family history of an autosomal recessive disorder is another criterion, among others.

PRENATAL SCREENING. Prenatal screening detects the possible presence of a genetic disorder in a fetus. Testing for elevated levels of alpha-fetoprotein (AFP) in the blood of pregnant women usually is a routine part of prenatal care; elevated levels of AFP are associated with certain birth defects and signal a need for additional evaluation. Sonography, which is a means of visualizing the fetus, also is used in prenatal screening. If any of the screening results are positive, prenatal diagnosis then is recommended.

NEONATAL SCREENING. Neonatal screening identifies the possible presence of serious genetic diseases shortly after birth, even if the baby is asymptomatic. If the results are positive, diagnostic evaluation and treatment can be initiated expeditiously. Newborn screening has had major successes. For example, most mental retardation caused by PKU has been eliminated, because early identification has made it possible to institute preventive treatment before brain damage occurs.

PRESYMPTOMATIC SCREENING. In some cases, presymptomatic screening promotes health by enabling individuals to take preventive action. For example, the person who is predisposed genetically to alcoholism can abstain from drinking. In other cases, presymptomatic screening facilitates accurate diagnosis and appropriate treatment when symptoms appear. Unfortunately, in many instances, presymptomatic screening can do little more than relieve or confirm anxiety. For example, many children of parents with Huntington's disease can learn whether or not they have inherited the gene, but effective prevention or treatment is not yet available. For this reason, children of affected parents may prefer not to know, rather than risk losing hope.

PRENATAL DIAGNOSIS

Prenatal diagnosis has been available for about 15 years (Kolata, 1987). The number of diagnosable conditions is increasing steadily. Amniocentesis is the most commonly used procedure; a needle is inserted into the sac surrounding the fetus and some amniotic fluid is withdrawn. Ideally, the sample is taken between 15 and 17 weeks of pregnancy, when sufficient fluid exists to allow safe withdrawal. The fluid contains fetal cells, which are grown and processed for laboratory studies. Another procedure being used increasingly is chorionic villi sampling (CVS), in which a small amount of placental tissue is removed and examined. CVS can be performed between 8 and 11 weeks of pregnancy, which is an advantage because the earlier in the pregnancy that a procedure can be performed, the more options may be available. When AFP screening suggests the presence of spina bifida or other neural tube defects, sonography can provide information about the nature and severity of the defect.

If parents learn that the fetus has a genetic disorder, they have several options, depending on the specific condition, their individual situation, and their values. Options include intrauterine treatment, obtaining specialized perinatal care, preparing emotionally and materially for the baby's birth and homecoming, or termination of the pregnancy.

DIAGNOSIS

More accurate differential diagnosis now is possible, and to the degree that it affects prognosis and treatment, improved diagnosis is beneficial. In addiiton, knowledge about the etiology of a disorder often is critical to family members, who may be concerned about inheritance risks to themselves, to their children, or to other loved ones. Diagnosis may shape reproductive decisions. A genetic evaluation includes taking detailed genetic and medical family history, a task that, for nonphysicians, requires specialized training through master's programs in genetic counseling. Depending on the situation, other components of a genetic evaluation may include a pregnancy and health history, developmental assessment, physical evaluation, and laboratory tests.

TREATMENT

Advances in medical treatment have extended life expectancy significantly for people with genetic conditions, especially infants and children. Individuals who once would have died by early childhood are surviving into adolescence and even adulthood. Anticipated breakthroughs in gene therapy and genetic engineering undoubtedly will affect the course and outcome of genetic disorders and will provide affected people with longer, more active, and more fulfilling lives.

Depending on the individuals, the specific disorders, and the services locally available, people with genetic disorders may obtain medical care from a community provider, from a clinic for people with a specific disorder, or from a clinical genetics center. Clinical geneticists act as consultants to other health care professionals, serve on specialty clinic interdisciplinary teams, and provide ongoing care, especially to persons with very rare disorders.

GENETIC COUNSELING

Genetic counseling has medical and psychosocial aspects. Medical specialists or genetic counselors provide clients with information about the disorder—the way in which heredity contributes, risks of recurrence, and reproductive or treatment op-

tions. Such specialist-counselors also support clients in choosing a course of action appropriate to them. Social workers focus on the psychosocial aspects of genetic counseling, both as members of genetic center teams and as community-based practitioners (Golden, Davis, & Leavy, 1981; Hall & Young, 1977).

Social workers involved in genetic counseling can assess social service needs, make appropriate referrals, and act as case managers. By providing individual, family, and group counseling, social workers can enable individuals and families to cope with the demands posed by genetic disorders. Social workers also offer crisis intervention during exacerbations of disorders, and, if needed, during the terminal stages of life and to the bereaved.

Because of their long-term involvement, community-based social workers are in a position to identify when genetic service provision needs change. For example, social workers may learn that the information provided initially was not absorbed and that reiteration may be necessary. Maturing children with genetic disorders may wonder about their fertility or the chances that a child of theirs would inherit the condition. Also, changing knowledge and technology may outdate earlier information. Particularly because changes in the field of human genetics occur so rapidly, genetic counseling should not be considered a one-time event. Social workers will need to know how, and when, to refer different members of genetically affected families to genetic centers as their needs change.

SOCIAL WORK AND GENETICS

INCREASING NUMBERS OF CLIENTS WITH GENETIC CONCERNS

Social worker involvement with people who have genetic concerns and with the provision of genetic services likely will increase. The general public is learning about human genetics through the media; as clients and potential clients become more knowledgeable, they will raise genetic issues with social workers. Clinical genetic services are proliferating, and the use of those services is increasing as both the public and members of the helping professions become more aware of recent developments. In addition, both the number and size of specialty clinics have increased as more effective treatments have developed and life expectancy has increased. Because these facilities may not have adequate social work staff or may be located far from clients' homes, they may refer clients to community agencies for counseling, support services, and case management.

The policy of deinstitutionalization is maintaining many developmentally delayed or otherwise handicapped people in the community. Such individuals come to the attention of social workers and bring genetic concerns and concerns of their families. The increased life expectancy for children with genetic disorders is generating demand for flexible, community-based social services appropriate for different stages of the life cycle, including adulthood. The value that impaired children, youths, and adults should live as normally as possible within the constraints of their conditions is bringing these individuals into schools and other mainstream institutions.

As Schild (1977) noted, social workers use generic knowledge and skills to work with chronically ill or disabled people and their families. However, a genetic diagnosis is distinctive; the condition generally is "permanent, chronic, familial, complex, labeling and threatening" (Schild, 1977, pp. 34–35). Genetic diagnoses touch on intimate, deeply personal areas of life: sexuality, decisions to conceive, and decisions to terminate pregnancy for genetic reasons. A genetic diagnosis also may reveal family secrets, such as incest or adultery.

Although social workers can apply generic skills, genetically affected individuals and families confront unique adaptive demands. Involved practitioners need to be familiar with specific disorders and their burdens, able to empathize with their psychological and familial effects, competent in assessing service needs, and skilled in making what may be emotionally charged referrals, including referrals to genetic centers.

CHANGING PRACTICE EXPECTATIONS

The specific requirements of social work practice that involves genetics are changing, as illustrated by adoptions. In 1983, the President's Commission for the Study of Ethical Problems in Medical and Biomedical Behavioral Research recommended that adoption records include genetic histories and that procedures be established for postadoption release of information about genetic risk to biological families and to adoptees (National Committee for Adoptions, Inc., 1984; President's Commission for the Study of Ethical Problems in Medical and Biomedical Behavioral Research, 1983). The Wisconsin legislature, in response to lobbying by organized groups of adoptees, already had enacted such a provision effective in 1982 (Simanck, 1983). A special project is underway in Wisconsin to train child welfare workers to take formal family genetic histories (Black, 1983; Burns, 1984; Cook, 1955; Omenn, Hall, & Hansen, 1980; Schulz & Motulsky, 1971). These events suggest that adoption agencies will face expectations to provide a full and competent family genetic history, genetic evaluation of the potential adoptee, and genetic counseling for the adopting parents when warranted. Similar expectations also may hold for children in long-term out-of-home care.

Adoptions will not be the only area to have such changes. As genetic services are used more widely, genetic risks identified more often, and genetic disorders diagnosed more accurately, genetic questions will become more prevalent. Documentation of the relationship between prenatal exposure to alcohol and other agents and miscarriage, stillbirth, and birth defects indicates the importance of preventive intervention. The harmful effects of prenatal exposure to certain environmental agents raises the question of fetal abuse (Abel, 1984; Bonavoglia, 1987; Chambers, 1986; McKenzie, Collins, & Popkin, 1982). If legislatures or the courts decide that prenatal abuse is possible, social workers will need to be prepared to refer to protective services which, in turn, will need to accept this new responsibility. Health and reproductive problems associated with exposure to environmental toxins in workplaces and communities have advocacy implications for community organizers and occupational social workers (Avers, 1984; Bowman, 1984; Cain, 1984; Elkington, 1987; "Job Site Hazards," 1985; Mange & Mange, 1980; Norwood, 1980; Nyhan, 1976; Riccardi, 1977; Stern, 1973).

Evidence of genetic substrates to some behavioral dysfunctions suggests that formal genetic evaluation may become an accepted part of assessment and treatment planning. If clients have had genetic counseling, social workers will need to assess whether faulty comprehension of the information, life-cycle changes, or new developments in genetic knowledge or technology warrant additional genetic evaluation and counseling. When clients raise genetic concerns, social workers will need to provide accurate information, know the limits of their knowledge and skills, obtain consultation, and refer appropriately.

The definition of "appropriate referral" is likely to change. For example, the discovery that genetic liability and single-gene inheritance are factors in some psychiatric disorders has led to genetic counseling in psychiatry (Crowe, 1978; Hamovit,

1984; Kay, 1980; Schulz, 1982; Stancer & Wagener, 1984; Targum & Gerson, 1981; Targum & Schulz, 1982). In South Carolina, genetic counseling regularly is provided to patients and their families at community mental health centers (R. Abramson, personal communication, September 23, 1984). As this capability becomes more widely known, social workers in various fields will be obligated to ensure that clients' psychiatric genetic questions are answered by the results of competent evaluation and counseling.

CONCLUSION

Social work clients include people with genetic concerns. The ways in which these concerns can be addressed are being transformed by advances in human genetics knowledge and the proliferation of genetic services. Developments in human genetics are broadening the definition of genetic disorders, increasing the number of social work clients with genetic concerns, and adding to the requisites of social work practice. The professions must confront the challenge.

References

Abel, E. L. (1984). Fetal alcohol syndrome: A case of prenatal abuse? In E. L. Abel (Ed.), *Fetal alcohol syndrome and fetal alcohol effects* (pp. 213–217). New York: Plenum.

Abuelo, D. N. (1983). Genetic disorders. In J. L. Matson and J. A. Mulick (Eds.), *Handbook of mental retardation* (pp. 105–126). New York: Pergamon.

Avers, C. (1984). *Genetics* (2nd ed.). Boston: Willard Grant.

Berch, D. B. and Bender, B. G. (1987). Margins of sexuality. *Psychology Today, 21,* 54–57.

Bishop, J. M. (1982). Oncogenes. *Scientific American, 246,* 81–92.

Black, R. B. (1983). Genetics and adoption: A challenge for social work. In M. Dinerman (Ed.), *Social work in a turbulent world* (pp. 193–205). Silver Spring, MD: National Association of Social Workers.

Bonavoglia, A. (1987). Reproductive rights: The ordeal of Pamela Rae Stewart. *Ms, 16,* 92f.

Bowman, J. E. (1984). Identification and stigma in the workplace. In J. O. Weiss, B. A. Bernhardt, and N. W. Paul (Eds.), *Genetic disorders and birth defects in families and society: Toward interdisciplinary understanding* (pp. 223–228). White Plains, NY: March of Dimes Foundation.

Burney, L., Walker, A. P., and Dumars, K. W. (1985). Prenatal diagnosis: The state of the art. In H. R. Chamberlin and E. M. Eklund (Eds.), *Developmental handicaps: Prevention and treatment II,* (pp. 1–25). Silver Spring, MD: American Association of University Affiliated Programs for Persons with Developmental Disabilities.

Burns, J. (1984). *Genetic family history: An aid to better health in adoptive children.* Washington, DC: National Center for Education in Maternal and Child Health.

Cain, L. S. (1984). Prenatal causes of atypical infant development. In M. J. Hanson (Ed.), *Atypical infant development* (pp. 27–56). Baltimore, MD: University Park.

Chambers, M. (1986, November 16). Are fetal rights equal to infants? *New York Times,* p. C2.

Cook, R. C. (1955). Genetics and adoption practice. In M. Shapiro (Ed.), *A study of adoption practice* (pp. 59–65). New York: Child Welfare League.

Crowe, R. (1978). Is genetic counseling appropriate for psychiatric illness? In J. P. Brady and H. L. Brodie (Eds.), *Controversy in psychiatry* (pp. 763–775). Philadelphia, PA: W. B. Saunders.

Dickerson, M. U. (1981). *Social work practice with the mentally retarded.* New York: Free Press.

Drew, C. J. (1984). *Mental retardation: A life cycle approach.* St. Louis, MO: Times Mirror/Mosby College.

Elkington, J. (1987). *The poisoned womb.* New York: Penguin Paperbacks.

Fuchs, F. (1980). Genetic amniocentesis. *Scientific American, 242,* 47–53.

Golden, D., Davis J. G., and Leavy, L. (1981). The contribution of long-term psychosocial services to the genetic counseling process. In S. R. Applewhite, D. L. Busbeck, and D. S. Borgaonkar (Eds.), *Genetic screening and counseling: A multi-disciplinary perspective* (pp. 123–130). Springfield, IL: Charles C Thomas.

Group for the Advancement of Psychiatry. (1984). *Research and the complex causality of the schizophrenias* (Research Report 116). New York: Brunner/Mazel.

Hall, W. T., and Young, C. L. (Eds.). (1977). *Proceedings: Genetic disorders: Social service interventions.* Pittsburgh, PA: University of Pittsburgh, Graduate School of Public Health, Public Health Social Work Program.

Hamovit, J. (1984). Genetics, genetic counseling and psychiatric disorders. In J. B. Rauch (Ed.), *Educating for practice in a changing world* (pp. 91–100). Baltimore, MD: University of Maryland School of Social Work and Community Planning.

Heston, L. L. (1974). Genetic counseling and the presenile dementias. *Social Biology, 23,* 135–141.

Hormuth, R. P. (1977). Current legislation in genetic disorders. In W. T. Hall and C. L. Young (Eds.), *Proceedings: Genetic disorders: Social service interventions* (pp. 3–9). Pittsburgh, PA: University of Pittsburgh, Graduate School of Public Health, Public Health Social Work Program.

Job site hazards imperil workers health. (1985, November). *NASW News,* pp. 13–16.

Kay, D. W. (1980). Assessment of familial risks with functional psychoses and their application in genetic counseling. *Advances in Family Psychiatry, 2,* 335–365.

Kolata, G. (1987, September 22). Tests of fetuses rise sharply amid doubts. *New York Times,* pp. C–1, C–10.

Little, R. E. (1982). Maternal alcohol use during pregnancy: A review. In E. L. Abel (Ed.), *Fetal alcohol syndrome II: Human studies* (pp. 47–64). Boca Raton, FL: CRC.

Ludlow, C. L., and Cooper, J. A. (Eds.). (1983). *Genetic aspects of speech and learning disorders.* New York: Academic.

Lykken, D. T. (1987, August). Schizoaffective disorder. *Harvard Medical School Mental Health Newsletter, 4,* 4–6.

Mange, A. P., and Mange, E. J. (1980). *Genetics: Human aspects.* Philadelphia, PA: Saunders College.

McGruffin, P., and Gottesman, I. I. (1985). Genetic influences on normal and abnormal development. In M. Rutter and L. Hersov (Eds.), *Child and adolescent psychiatry: Modern approaches* (pp. 17–33). Oxford, England: Blackwell Scientific.

McKenzie, T. B., Collins, N. M., and Popkin, M. E. (1982). A case of fetal abuse? *American Journal of Orthopsychiatry, 52,* 699–703.

Money, J. (1968). *Sex errors of the body.* Baltimore, MD: Johns Hopkins University.

Nagle, J. J. (1984). *Heredity and human affairs* (3rd ed.). St. Louis, MO: Times Mirror/Mosby College.

National Committee for Adoptions, Inc. (1984). *An act to establish a mutual consent voluntary adoption registry to provide for the transmission of nonidentifying information on the health history and the genetic and social history of adoptees.* Washington, DC: Author.

National Genetic Diseases Act. P. L. 94–278. Title IV, sec. 403(b)(c), April 22, 1976, 90 Stat. 409, 42 U.S.C.

Norwood, C. (1980). *At highest risk: Protecting children from environmental injury.* New York: Penguin Books.

Nyhan, W. (1976). *The heredity factor.* New York: Grosset & Dunlap.

Omenn, G. S., Hall, J. G., Hansen, and K. D. (1980). Genetic counseling for adoptees at risk for specific inherited disease. *American Journal of Medical Genetics, 5,* 7–64.

Petrie, G. (1985). Biological and physical causes of handicap. In E. Stanley (Ed.), *Mental handicap: A handbook of care* (pp. 23–43). Edinburgh: Churchill Livingstone.

President's Commission for the Study of Ethical Problems in Medical and Biomedical Behavioral Research. (1983). *Screening and counseling for genetic conditions: The ethical, social and legal implications of genetic screening, counseling, and educational programs.* Washington, DC: U.S. Government Printing Office.

Rauch, J. B., and Tivoli, L. (1988). *Social workers' knowledge and utilization of genetic services.* Unpublished manuscript.

Riccardi, V. M. (1977). *The genetic approach to human disease.* New York: Oxford University.

Richmond, M. (1917). *Social diagnosis.* New York: Russell Sage Foundation.

Rossi, A. O. (1972). Genetics of learning disabilities. Journal of Learning Disabilities, 5, 489–496.

Rubsenthal, L. (1985). Creating cancer. *Science 85, 6,* 54–56.

Russell, M., Henderson, M. A., and Blume, S. (1985). *Children of alcoholics: A review of the literature.* New York: Children of Alcoholics Foundation, Inc.

Russell, O. (1985). *Mental handicap.* Edinburgh, England: Churchill Livingstone.

Schild, S. (1977). Social work interventions with genetic problems. In W. T. Hall and C. L. Young (Eds.), *Proceedings: Genetic disorders: Social service interventions* (pp. 33–39). Pittsburgh, PA: University of Pittsburgh, Graduate School of Public Health, Public Health Social Work Program.

Schild, S., and Black, R. B. (1984). *Social work and genetics: A guide for practice.* New York: Haworth Press.

Schmeck, H. M. Jr. (1986a, February 26). Defective gene tied to form of manic-depressive illness. *New York Times,* pp. A1, B7.

Schmeck, H. M., Jr. (1986b, March 19). Second genetic defect linked to illness. *New York Times,* p. A20.

Schmeck, H. M., J. (1987a, March 13). Genetic abnormality seen as link with Alzheimer's. *New York Times,* p. A14.

Schmeck, H. M., Jr. (1987b, October 6). Young science of cancer genes begins to yield practical applications. *New York Times,* pp. C1, C4.

Schmeck, H. M., Jr. (1987c, October 8). Scientists link an activated gene to lung cancer. *New York Times,* p. A28.

Schmeck, H. M., Jr. (1987d, October 20). Venereal virus strongly implicated in several cancers. *New York Times,* pp. C1, C4.

Schmeck, H. M., Jr. (1987e, October 29). Blood abnormality may predict Alzheimer's. *New York Times,* p. A23.

Schmeck, H. M., Jr. (1987f, November 17). Experts voice hope in Alzheimer's fight. *New York Times,* pp. C1, C10.

Schuckit, M. A. (1985). Genetics and the risk for alcoholism. *Journal of the American Medical Association, 254,* 2614–2617.

Schulz, P. M. (1982). Patient and family attitudes about schizophrenia: Implications for genetic counseling. *Schizophrenia Bulletin, 3,* 504–513.

Schultz, A., and Motulsky, A. G. (1971). Medical genetics and adoption. *Child Welfare, 50,* 4–17.

Simanck, S. E. (1983). Adoptions records reform: Impact on adoptees. *Marquette Law Review, 67,* 110–146.

Singer, S. (1985). *Human genetics: An introduction to the principles of heredity* (2nd ed.). New York: W. H. Freeman.

Smith, M. (1982). The genetics of alcoholism. *Advances in Alcohol and Substance Abuse, 1,* 127–146.

Stancer, H. C., and Wagener, D. K. (1984). Genetic counseling: Its need in psyvhaitry and the directions it gives for future research. *Canadian Journal of Psychiatry, 29,* 289–294.

Stern, C. (1973). *Principles of human genetics* (3rd ed.). San Francisco: W. H. Freeman.

Targum, S. D., and Gerson, E. S. (1981). Pregnancy, genetic counseling and the major psychiatric disorders. In J. Schulman and J. Simpson (Eds.), *Genetic diseases in pregnancy* (pp. 413–438). New York: Academic Press.

Targum, S. D., and Schulz, C. S. (1982). Clinical applications of psychiatric genetics. *American Journal of Orthopsychiatry, 52,* 45–87.

Tsuang, M. R., and Vandermey, R. (1980). *Genes and the mind: Inheritance of mental illness.* Oxford: Oxford University.

U.S. Department of Health and Human Services, Public Health Service, Health Resources and Services Administration, Division of Maternal and Child Health, National Center for Education in Maternal and Child Health. (1986). *Comprehensive clinical genetic services centers: A national directory—1985* (DHHS Publication No. HRS–D–MC 86–1). Washington, DC: Author.

Webster's ninth new collegiate dictionary. (1987). Springfield, MA: Merriam-Webster.

Wright, J. M. (1981). Fetal alcohol syndrome: The social work connection. *Health and Social Work, 6,* 5–10.

2

THE DEVELOPMENTAL TASKS OF SIBLINGSHIP OVER THE LIFE CYCLE

Ann Goetting

Department of Sociology, Anthropology, and Social Work
Western Kentucky University

One component of the family system in the United States that has been underrepresented in sociology journals and family textbooks is the sibling relationship. Those researchers who have considered siblingship generally have limited the scope of their work to children and have taken a psychological perspective, concentrating on sibling rivalry and on personality outcomes as they relate to sibling possession, sibling gender status, birth order, and family size. No direct attention has been focused on the patterns of activities that bind siblings throughout the life cycle.

Bowerman and Dobash (1974: 48) attribute the dearth of research attention devoted to siblings when compared with that directed toward the husband-wife and parent-child relationships to the fact that the husband-wife relationship rates a higher priority for both theoretical and practical purposes, since it is more central to family process and continuity, and to the fact that the parent-child relationship also has a more critical influence on family interaction as well as significant consequences for the socialization process. Bank and Kahn (1975: 313) relate the discrepancy to our current cultural emphasis within the nuclear family on the conjugal and parent-child dyads rather than the sibling dyad. Whereas historical-cultural and economic conditions associated with some preindustrial cultures, including preindustrial Western society, have fostered an emphasis on primogeniture and fraternal solidarity, modern Europeans and North Americans, with a very different set of such conditions, assign great importance to the romantic component of family life, namely, the husband-wife relationship and the direct product of that union, the parent-child relationship.[1]

In spite of its secondary significance, siblingship remains recognized as unique and influential, and perhaps gaining in importance with the development of modern trends in family norms. It is unique among close human relationships by virtue of its long duration and also because participants share a common genetic and social heritage, a common cultural milieu, and common early experiences within the family. Furthermore, the relationship between siblings is highly egalitarian (Cicirelli, 1982; 268). Bank and Kahn (1982: 12–15) outline a series of cultural transformations over the last hundred year that may be lending greater relevance to the sibling relationship. First, family size has diminished to where today the average child has only one sibling, thus creating the potential for greater interdependence and intensity in that relationship. Further, our more extensive life spans may act to deepen such interdependence and intensity by virtue of time alone. Certain forms of dislocation that accompany modernity may also serve to strengthen the sibling bond. A distinct increase in geographic mobility and in divorce and subsequent remarriage may cause people, young and old alike, to cling rather tightly to the constancy and permanency a brother or sister can provide. Finally, the ineffectiveness and sometimes absence of parents due to general stress, employment, and marital tension and dissolution may invite young siblings to band together as a mutual support system. Bank and Kahn (1982: 15) state:

> Children are biologically propelled by these vital needs [contact, constancy, and permanency]—what some psychologists call "object constancy"—to turn for satisfaction to any accessible person. In worried, mobile, small-family, high-stress, fast-paced, parent-absent America, that person can be a brother or sister.

The purpose of this article is to explore the developmental tasks of siblingship in the United States over the life cycle. The term *developmental task* is used here to signify prosocial observed and expected

From *Journal of Marriage and Family,* 1986, *48* (4): 703–714. Copyright 1986 by the National Council on Family Relations. Reprinted by permission.

behaviors.[2] Derived from a review of selected research on siblings, the present analysis is organized in a framework of three successive life-cycle stages: childhood and adolescence, early and middle adulthood, and old age. The information outlined here allows us to anticipate those activities or tasks that will be expected of us and of our children as we relate to siblings through the progression of our own lives. To the extent that these expectations are accurately predicted, we are further advised of the gratifications due us by virtue of our siblingship status.

CHILDHOOD AND ADOLESCENCE

In childhood and adolescence, the sibling relationship is perhaps more intense than at later stages because it is at this point in the life cycle that the incumbents are in direct daily contact and must compete for and share common resources. Relationships are more typically marked by intimacy during these formative times, and siblings seemingly play a more critical role in one another's lives. As a result, demands made on siblings during childhood and adolescence may be more intense, tasks more pressing. The limited available research reported in this section suggests that the exchange patterns of companionship, emotional support, caretaking, and direct services that are so characteristic of the sibling relationship in later years are securely anchored during childhood and adolescence.

COMPANIONSHIP AND EMOTIONAL SUPPORT

Perhaps the most important task of siblingship throughout the life cycle is that of providing companionship, friendship, comfort, and affection. It has been well documented that humans, from infancy on, require human social support. In order to maintain a sense of well-being and even to remain physically healthy, people must have a network of loyal friends and trusted confidants (Lynch, 1977). In childhood and adolescence, siblings are in a unique position to fill these crucial roles. By the very nature of our contemporary family and social structures, home-reared children provide the most and often only regular source of same-age companionship to their brothers and sisters. When age-compatible peers are not available in the child's neighborhood or when contact with peers is limited, the sibling relationship becomes of ultimate importance.

Research verifies what perhaps most of us have observed to be true: that young siblings play together often and happily (Bossard and Boll, 1956;

168), and that throughout their years of living together they view one another as friends. Home observations suggest that while infant and childhood siblings show the full range of affective behaviors, most of their interactions are of a positive nature, and furthermore, the same-sex sibling pairs (particularly sisters) demonstrate a higher concentration of prosocial behavior than do opposite-sex pairs (Abramovitch, Pepler, and Corter, 1982: 70, 73). From their clinical observations, Bank and Kahn (1975: 323) report that a "conspiracy of silence," a powerful bond of loyalty, may exist among young siblings, from which parents are excluded. The sibling commitment to emotional support during early childhood years is further demonstrated by laboratory observations of preschool children with their infant siblings. Gaining results consistent with Stewart's earlier findings and with the work of Dunn and Kendrick (1982: 91, 114), Stewart and Marvin (1984: 1327–1328) discovered that within 10 seconds of the mother's departure from the room (in each case causing infant stress), 51% of the older siblings responded to the stressed infant with comfort, nurturance, and consolation. Forty-three percent of the remaining preschoolers offered such solace after the 10-second interval.

In his overview of sibling relationships across the lifespan, Lamb (1982: 5) observes that siblings commonly become primary sources of emotional support in preadolescence, and that these bonds typically persist well into adolescence and young adulthood. He suggests further that during adolescence, when parents and children characteristically have difficulty communicating about emotionally laden issues such as sexuality and the use of recreational drugs and when friends of both sexes prove fickle and unpredictable, siblings provide the most consistently supportive relationships. Though Lamb's observations are not backed by solid research, they are consistent with the work of Shapiro and associates (1984), who found that nearly three-quarters of their 8-to-16-year old respondents reported confiding in siblings during times of stress. Like Abramovitch and associates (1982; 73) and Dunn and Kendrick (1982: 44), these researchers found sisters to be more confiding than brothers.

DELEGATED CARETAKING

While the delegation of child-caretaking responsibilities to older siblings[3] seems to be less prevalent in the United States than in other cultures (Whiting and Whiting, 1975, cited by Weisner and

Gallimore, 1977: 174), it apparently remains an important consideration in many American families.[4] The only data available describing the prevalence of sibling child-caretaking in this country are reported by Bossard and Boll (1956: 148–150). From their 6-year observation of 100 large families, they report that 91 indicated sibling participation in childrearing, and in 82 of these families siblings were important in that capacity. In fact, in a third of these 82 cases, siblings carried on the entire childrearing function because of the abdication or incapacitation of parents.

Bossard and Boll (1956; 166) note that older siblings were more likely to serve as parent substitutes in those families with the largest number of children and where the children were spaced over the longest time period. Also, in accordance with traditional gender role expectations, it was most commonly the oldest daughter who assumed responsibility for siblings (Bossard and Boll, 1955: 72). This latter finding is congruent with laboratory observations on mother-child and sibling-sibling interactions surrounding a problem-solving task, which suggest that mothers relinquish a portion of their helping role toward a given child when the child has an older sister but not an older brother. Mothers delegate the role, and older sisters accept the role and function in it effectively enough that the mothers feel less need to help this child, even in the absence of the older sister. The study showed that mothers tended to provide personal help to the child with an older brother, but tended to delegate the help where the child had an older sister (Cicirelli, 1976: 594).

Several conditions have been suggested as antecedent to greater sibling responsibility for younger children (Essman, 1977: 259–260). A lack of parental involvement in and/or commitment to parenthood may be conducive to sibling adoption of a parent-surrogate role. And of course, the incapacitation of parents due to illness, disability, institutionalization, and death must be contributing factors. It is probably true that single-parent families, low-income families, and families where both parents participate in the labor force are more likely to delegate caretaking responsibility to siblings, as are families burdened with many children or with children who are in some way handicapped and therefore needful of close supervision.

Available information confirms the notion that children who assume delegated responsibilities for the care of siblings demonstrate caretaking styles distinguishable from those of adults.[5] Cicirelli

(1976) discovered that mothers provided more explanations and feedback to children than did older siblings, and also that the children related to their mothers with more help-seeking and help-accepting behaviors and with fewer independence-seeking behaviors than they did to their sibling caretakers. This suggests that children may influence differences in caretaking styles between their parents and siblings. Bryant (1979) explored possible differences between parents and siblings as child caretakers by comparing how children aged 7 and 10 described their parents and siblings on six caretaking dimensions. She found that children differentiated caretaking styles more clearly as a function of generation than as a function of gender of caretaker, and that parents were rated as more active on five of the six dimensions—nurturance, instrumental companionship, achievement demands, control and principled discipline. The sixth dimension, physical punishment, was seen to be more actively carried out by sibling caretakers. Older siblings were perceived as meting out more physical punishment than parents.

In a somewhat similar later research endeavor, Bryant (1981) factor-analyzed children's descriptions of their parents' and siblings' caretaking styles, using 14 caretaking dimensions. As in her earlier work, she found the factor structures of the older brothers and older sisters to be entirely congruent with one another and only partially overlapping with parental factors. Mothers demonstrated the most integrated underlying caretaking style. It should be noted that in this latter study, Bryant (1981) found the punishment factor to be similar for parent and sibling caretakers. Bryant and Crockenberg (1980) observed mothers with their first- and later-born daughters in a "seminaturalistic" game-playing setting, and once again discovered few similarities between parent and older sibling caretaker style when that older sibling was assigned the role of helper. A finding of particular interest is that children with mothers who gave them much unsolicited help, encouragement, and approval had older sisters who gave them unsolicited disapproval. This phenomenon is interpreted by the researchers as suggestive that the older child may adopt the directive strategy of the mother but lack the skill to implement it positively. Another plausible explanation, in my view, is that such discrepancy in caretaking style may result from the older child's rivalrous tendencies toward the maternally indulged younger sibling.

The overall desirability of delegating child-caretaking responsibilities to older siblings is debatable. The consequences appear to be mixed.

Consider first the advantages. It can be argued that sibling caretaking is in some ways advantageous to all parties involved. In addition to the obvious benefits accrued to the younger child who is the recipient of this supplementary source of attention and care, there are perhaps two latent benefits to that child. First, it has been suggested that sibling caretaking weakens attachment to the mother while strengthening bonds with sibling caretakers. Such shifting and redistribution of attachment are believed to reduce stress associated with maternal separation and to offer children the opportunity to fortify relationships with siblings (Weisner and Gallimore, 1977: 177). A second latent benefit to the younger child relates to the more rounded socialization experience provided by caretaker diversity; sibling caretaking may serve to check parental oppression through exclusive or near-exclusive monopoly of the child's intake of information (McMurty, 1977: 7). The primary caretaker, usually the mother, may also reap benefits from sibling child-caretaking. Relief from exclusive caretaking must certainly enhance role flexibility, parental satisfaction, personal freedom, and ultimately an overall sense of well-being (Weisner, 1982: 310; Weisner and Gallimore, 1977: 180). In addition to the benefits derived by the younger siblings and by the mother, there may be advantages, often less apparent in nature, for the sibling caretaker. Weisner and Gallimore (1977: 176) and Essman (1977: 260) testify to the value of hierarchical sibling relationships as anticipatory socialization for parenthood. Also, such caretaking responsibilities are viewed as promoting the development of social skills in children in the form of prosocial, responsible, and nurturant behaviors (Weisner and Gallimore, 1977: 177).

The practice of delegated sibling caretaking is not without its costs. Bossard and Boll (1956: 158–59, 162, 263–265) note the hardships imposed upon sibling caretakers especially during the "courtship years" when other adolescents are out socializing. The well-being of this usually oldest daughter may be sacrificed to the needs and/or comforts of other family members. Another important drawback to sibling child-caretaking centers around the likelihood that siblings are less effective in the caretaking role than are parents. Essman (1977: 260–61) attributes such ineffectiveness to several factors. First, the lack of clarity associated with the sibling caretaking role and the disagreement among family members regarding role expectations may decrease satisfaction and effectiveness. Second, siblings who are likely to be delegated parent-surrogate responsibilities may

be the least likely to demonstrate attributes elicitous of desirable behavior on the part of their young charges. For example, literature on the subject relates children's desirable behavior to parental empathy, and research suggests that firstborns may be less empathetic than other siblings. Third, parents may impose unreasonable expectations on sibling caretakers such as heavy responsibilities without the authority to set down and enforce rules. Other factors include the general immaturity and intolerance for young children that is associated with typical adolescence, and the adolescent's romanticized notions of parenthood.

AID AND DIRECT SERVICES

The limited information on the subject suggests that siblings remain available to one another throughout their childhood and adolescence as a general source of support, providing various kinds of aid and services. A considerable portion of material in this area focuses on siblings supporting one another in their relationship with their parents or in the absence of parental effectiveness. Bank and Kahn (1975: 322–324) describe a significant and pervasive task of siblingship—the formation of sibling coalitions for the purpose of dealing with parents. Children can and do benefit their siblings by managing relationships in various ways between those siblings and the parents. First, a child can protect a sibling from involvement in a confrontation with the parent by distracting one of the parties from the potentially destructive or explosive situation. In the example provided by Bank and Kahn (1975: 322), whenever a particular alcoholic father would become abusive toward his son, the sister would suggest that she and her brother play cards or engage in some other activity. Second, siblings can join forces with one another against the parent for at least two reasons: to strengthen resources for negotiation with the parent ("We would *both* use the new computer for our homework"), and to reduce the perceived seriousness of an act of misbehavior by joining the sibling in the misbehavior ("I'm not the *only* one who did it").

A third way that siblings form coalitions for the purpose of dealing with parents is through providing various types of translation services. One of these types is applied when children translate and interpret to their parents the behavior of their siblings, perhaps representing such behavior in a light beneficial to the sibling ("He stole money at school because his friends threatened him"). Also, siblings translate and predict parental behavior for one another. They alert one another to forthcoming punishment, signal each other about parents' moods and attitudes, and warn one another regarding the consequences of transgressing against the parents. A third kind of translation service is referred to as "educational pressure tactics." In this case, children educate their parents in the ways of a broader culture from which the parents may have been isolated. Siblings join forces bringing educational pressure to bear on parents to the advantage of each child ("Everyone out there smokes marijuana, so she's just acting like her friends. We've all smoked it. Besides, it's not as dangerous as alcohol and cigarettes").

In addition, there are sibling support systems of a more extreme nature precipitated by parental inefficacy, which may occur in various degrees ranging from minimal incapacitation, perhaps due to both parents working, to total absence, typically due to divorce or death. Research suggests that when parents do not or cannot carry out their responsibilities, siblings may unite to provide needed resources for one another. From a review of literature of the previous forty years and from their own work, Bank and Kahn (1982) conclude that parental hostility, weakness, or absence in conjunction with other factors can promote intense loyalty among siblings, and that such loyalty is characterized by cooperation, sympathy, and mutual aid through childhood years and into various stages of adulthood. In an earlier study of underprivileged families, Minuchin and associates (1967: 223) observed similar patterns. Bryant and Crockenberg (1980), in their previously cited laboratory observations, consistently found that when mothers ignored (because of helplessness rather than negativism) their younger daughter's request for help and attention, the child often turned to her sibling for that help and frequently got it.

Sibling solidarity may also be related to family structure. Johnson (1982: 164) discovered that children of Italian parents were more likely to be embedded in active kinship networks than were children with only one Italian parent or children of European Protestant descent. In these Italian-American families, older siblings took over the physical care of younger children, brothers supervised the behavior of sisters outside the home, and older children assumed an active role in socializing their siblings into American culture.

Other studies show forms of sibling aid and direct services similar to those found to be outstanding in Italian-American families. Bank and Kahn (1975: 321–322) report that siblings lend each other money,

physically protect one another, supply friendship networks, and teach each other skills. Consistently, Marra (unpublished work cited in Bowerman and Dobash, 1974: 49) discovered friendship networks to be shared among siblings, and Bryant (1982: 107) found that the majority of later-born children in her study indicated having siblings who would help them with homework. She determined this to be as true for first graders as fourth graders, males as females, children from small families as well as those from large families, and whether the older sibling was a brother or a sister. With reference to siblings teaching one another, it should be noted that, while no information is available lending direct insight into the structure and dynamics of teaching and learning among siblings in their natural settings, Cicirelli (1985b: 202–203) has conducted a series of laboratory studies of sibling teaching and learning on a concept-teaching task in middle childhood, the results of which may be suggestive of true-life sibling interaction. He found that girls teaching their siblings tended to use a deductive teaching method, while boys used an inductive method; both sexes taught differently with nonsiblings. Also, girls were more effective as teachers. Younger siblings were more likely to accept direction from an older sister than from an older brother, and from one 4 rather than 2 years older.

EARLY AND MIDDLE ADULTHOOD

This second life-cycle stage is defined here to include those years when a person no longer resides with his or her parents and siblings and has become actively involved with his or her family of procreation and/or with economic endeavors. Sibling contact becomes voluntary and ties become loosened and diffused. Relationships are increasingly mediated by marriage, parenthood, and economic roles—and by geographical distance. Though the sibling support system characteristic of childhood and adolescence appears to persist, albeit with decreased intensity (Bank and Kahn, 1975: 331, 1982: 16; Cummimg and Schneider, 1961: 501; Ross and Milgram, 1982: 231), throughout early and middle adulthood, it necessarily must be expressed differently. Siblingship tasks of nurturance, caretaking, and teaching must be transformed into tasks addressing adult needs as persons become spouses, parents, and children of aging parents.

Research on sibling relationships in adulthood is very limited, even in comparison with the body of sibling research in childhood and adolescence. Consider first what we know about young adults who have recently left the parental home. Available information suggests that they continue to participate in significant patterns of exchange with their siblings. Cicirelli (1980a) found that college women perceived as much emotional support from the sibling whom they rated as "closest" as they did from their mother. The researcher concludes that when a young woman needs a family member to serve as confidant, she apparently seeks out either her mother or her sibling, perhaps depending upon whether topics are more or less peer-oriented. These college women also indicated that they could turn to this closest sibling when in need of help and guidance, though to a lesser extent than they felt toward either their mother or their father. Finally, the respondents felt protected by their sibling against difficulties and dangers, though with less intensity than indicated for these other tasks, and once again to a lesser extent when compared with either parent. Like Cicirelli (1980b), Bossard and Boll (1956: 157–158, 171) found sibling support among young adults who recently had left the family of orientation—this time in the form of economic aid to those still at home and to those in school.

In light of the fact that sibling interaction becomes volitional during adult years, perhaps one cursory index of general socioemotional sibling support lies in the pattern and frequency of contact. The potential for contact between sibling pairs varies, of course, with such factors as the age, health, income level, available sources of transportation, travel time and costs, and the nature of competing activities and responsibilities. To the extent that these factors limit accessibility, they also limit potential for performing siblingship tasks.

Contact between siblings in early and middle adulthood has been measured on the basis of frequencies of the visiting, telephoning, and letter writing of married and previously married subjects. In his study of young adults in Greensboro, North Carolina, Adams (1968: 100) discovered that some form of monthly contact occurred between 93% of his subjects and their age-nearest siblings who lived in the same city. That proportion was reduced to 65% when that sibling lived outside the city but within 100 miles, 38% when living beyond 100 miles away in a three-state area, and 39% when beyond that. Cicirelli (1982: 271) studied middle-aged adults and found that 19% of all siblings were seen at least weekly and 41% were seen at least monthly.

The modal visiting pattern, reported for 36% of all siblings, was several times a year but less often than once a month. Only 3% of the siblings had not been seen over the last two years, and they were living outside of the country. From their sample of middle-aged and elderly working-class Philadelphians, Rosenberg and Anspach (1973: 110) discovered that 70% of the middle-aged respondents had siblings residing in that city, and that in the 45–54 age range, 68% saw that sibling during the week preceding the interview, compared with 58% in the 55–64 age range. These data suggest a decline in frequency of sibling visiting with increasing age.

While this information on contact frequency suggests that sibling relationships remain intact and supportive through early and middle adulthood, it provides no hint of the particular forms or intensity of sibling exchange. It leaves unspecified those activities that bind siblings at these stages in their life cycle. Though no research has probed in any depth the patterns of behavior between adult siblings, scattered sources allow us to construct a tentative picture of siblingship tasks during early and middle adulthood. We turn now to those sources.

Adams (1968: 104–105, 164) discovered most age-nearest sibling contact to be in the form of telephone and letter communication and home visits; very little reflected the exchange of aid. He characterizes the age-nearest sibling relationship with the terms "interest" and "comparison." To him, "interest" signifies a passive concern for how the other is getting along, and "comparison" refers to the reciprocal viewing of one another as a yardstick for success. In the words of Adams (1968: 105-106):

> The overall pattern is simply one of keeping in touch, and even this is not uniformly frequent. There are a minority who share social, organizational, and ritual interaction with moderate frequency, but the exchange of aid is to a great extent idiosyncratic. From the sharing of clothes or baby-sitting by adult sisters living close to each other to the loaning of $2,000 to a brother to invest in his business, it is the particular situation which elicits the help of a sibling. To speak of "patterns" of mutual aid between age-near siblings would be presumptuous.

The earlier work of Sussman (1959: 336) reflects a clear consistency with these observations of Adams. In his survey of adult members of lower-middle and working-class Cleveland families, Sussman (1959: 336) discovered that just less than half of the respondents provided some form of help to siblings over the previous year: 42% provided help during illness,

30% provided child care, 10% provided financial help, 3% provided personal or business advice, and 2% provided valuable gifts. Adams (1968: 118–120) considers the sister relationship to be the most supportive of the sibling dyads, but he perceives the adult sibling relationship in general as one high in perseverance but low in intensity. Cicirelli (1982: 275) found results similar to those of the Adams study. He discovered that while over three-quarters of his respondents expressed positive sentiments toward their siblings, far fewer viewed these siblings as confidants (fewer than half felt that they could discuss intimate topics; 8% talked over important decisions frequently or almost always).

Except for the global tasks of reserved companionship and socio-emotional support (Cicirelli, 1985b; 202; Ross and Milgram, 1982: 232), the most commonly cited tasks of siblingship during early and middle adulthood relate to cooperation in the care of elderly parents and later in the dismantling of the parental home (Bank and Kahn, 1975: 331, 1982: 16; Cicirelli, 1980b: 460, 1982: 268; Cumming and Schneider, 1961: 501; Matthews and Rosner, 1985). Typically, it is the diminution of the parents' health and independence that reactivates the sibling relationship during the middle years. The sibling bond may be reactivated initially to manage a particular crisis but may then continue to serve as a "fundamental axis of socio-emotional interaction" throughout the process of parental decline and death (Cumming and Schneider, 1961: 501). It is at this point in their adult life cycles that siblings must turn to one another in a spirit of unity in order to adequately carry out critical responsibilities to their parents. In this sense, what is perhaps the most singularly important developmental task of siblingship in early and middle adulthood is concomitant with the final development task of childhood.

As was suggested to be true during childhood and adolescence, sibling relationships and task performance in adulthood may well vary with circumstances. Family structure, for example, may affect sibling solidarity in adulthood as well as during earlier years. In the Italian-American context, Johnson (1982: 164) found that frequent contact after marriage set a lifelong pattern of sociability and mutual aid. Within this particular family structure, one is as likely to go to a sibling as to a spouse when problems arise. Another factor that may enhance sibling interaction and support is marital disruption. Rosenberg and Anspach (1972: 112) report that a slightly higher proportion of maritally disrupted than maritally intact respondents had interacted with a sibling

within the previous week, suggesting sibling solidarity to become operative in a compensatory manner. Additionally, Cicirelli (1984: 620) observes that his maritally disrupted respondents depended more on siblings in their provision of aid to elderly parents. They were more likely than were their maritally intact counterparts to view the burden of helping elderly parents as one that should be shared with their own siblings. Consistent with Rosenberg and Anspach (1973: 112) and Cicirelli (1984: 620), Weiss (1975: 142–143) suggests a special form of sibling solidarity to be associated with marital disruption in his observation that sometimes the adult brother of a woman serves as a male role model for her children when she has no husband. Another variable that may influence the sibling relationship in adulthood is social mobility. Adams (1968: 107) discovered that while upwardly mobile men kept in close touch with their fathers, they maintained less contact with their brothers than did their stable counterparts. Blood and Blood (1978: 344) attribute this particular weakening of the siblingship bond between mobile and nonmobile brothers to sibling rivalry. Even in adulthood, siblings react negatively to losing out in competition.

Cicirelli (1980b: 460) effectively summarizes the developmental tasks of siblingship during early and middle adulthood:

> In early adulthood siblings offer mutual support in establishing themselves socially and psychologically as independent persons in the community. They assist, if only through interest and psychological support, in the rearing of nieces and nephews. . . . A major task of middle-aged siblings is the care and support of their parents during the periods of their decline and death and the achievement of the division of parental property (or the settlement of parental obligations) without rancor and bitterness. [Finally,] siblings may offer support to each other as they face the problems of [their own] aging.

OLD AGE

The final stage in the life cycle is defined here to include what are typically the postretirement years, when an individual no longer is actively involved with economic endeavors and when the family of procreation no longer is intact. While sibling relationships continue to be mediated by geographical distance as they are during early and middle adulthood, they are to a lesser extent interceded by marriage (in the case of widowhood), parenthood, and economic roles. Perhaps this partially explains the finding that despite reduced contact with siblings

(Rosenberg and Anspach, 1973: 110), older adults express sentiments of greater closeness and compatibility with siblings when compared with younger cohorts (Cicirelli, 1985a: 97, 1985b: 200; Scott, 1983: 49). It has become apparent that although older people sometimes disengage from their roles outside their families, they rarely disengage from family involvements. Troll, Miller, and Atchley (1975: 6) observe that the elderly disengage *into* rather than *from* their families. As their worlds shrink, their kinship networks, including their siblings, become more important to them.

Of the three life-cycle stages analyzed in these pages, it is the last—old age—that has stimulated the least scholarly inquiry into the sibling relationship. While this relative paucity of research relating to sibling interaction among older adults might seem reasonable, the facts remain that most elderly Americans have at least one living sibling and perform siblingship tasks until the relationship is terminated by death (Scott, 1983: 47).

Because of health decline and mobility limitations associated with advanced age, the pattern and frequency of contact may provide a less accurate index of socio-emotional support for older siblings than for their younger adult counterparts. Cicirelli (1985a: 95) demonstrates that although somewhat over half of siblings of the elderly live within 100 miles, and a quarter of them are to be found in the same city, the typical pattern of contact is several visits and several telephone calls per year. Furthermore, the exchange of aid seems to remain minimal, as it does among siblings in earlier adulthood. Scott (1983: 54) reports that though the proportion represents a sizable increase from Adams's (1968) sample of young adults, fewer than 40% of his respondents had received assistance from the most contacted sibling (residing within an hour of the respondent) over the previous year. Children and grandchildren were the primary sources of aid. If one were to judge by contact and assistance alone, the relationship between elderly siblings could not be described as a close one for most sibling pairs. Interestingly, however, as mentioned above, research suggests that older siblings experience a sense of enhanced closeness and compatibility when compared with younger cohorts. Perhaps this sense of intensified closeness is at least partially a *function* of diminished contact! Furthermore, it may mean that the relatively few sibling contacts in old age are richer in socio-emotional support than are the more frequent contacts of earlier years, yielding an overall increased quality of support in the final stage of the life cycle.

It appears that siblingship in old age is similar to siblingship in young and middle adulthood in the sense that basically it requires a rather inert form of involvement. Interaction is sporadic and assistance is reflective of situational demands rather than patterned commitment. The essence of the relationship lies in a reserved form of companionship and socio-emotional support that is expressed mostly through the sharing of ritual occasions, brief visits, and commercial and home recreation. Assistance, when offered, is supplied in the form of aid when ill; financial support; and help with critical decisions, business dealings, homemaking, home repairs, transportation, and shopping (Cicirelli, 1982: 279, 1985a: 100; Lopata, 1973: 157; Ross and Milgram, 1982: 232; Scott, 1983: 60).

Perhaps the single most important siblingship task associated with this particular place in the life cycle relates to shared reminiscence and ultimately to perceptual validation. While this task is undertaken to some extent throughout the life cycle, it reaches its pinnacle of value during these declining years as individuals undergo the life review process. Cicirelli (1985b: 206) examined communication topics of older people and discovered that discussion of old times together was more common with siblings than with adult children, indicating the more important role of siblings in reminiscing. He notes that because of their common biographies, siblings can use reminiscences to validate and clarify earlier events and relationships, and to place them in mature perspective. Ross, Dalton, and Milgram (1980: 14) emphasize the importance for the elderly of maintaining self-esteem and control over their lives and, to that end, stress the critical nature of social contact that validates perceptions of self and reality. Siblings can provide that form of contact. From their observations of white middle-class older adults, Ross and Milgram (1982: 232) report that the sharing of happy childhood experiences and rewarding interactions in adulthood (both of which, in my view, may involve selective or even distorted perception) appeared to be a major source of comfort and pride. Being able to do so seemed to confer a sense of integrity—one had lived one's life in harmony with one's own values and with those of one's family.

Another important task of siblingship in old age may be the resolution of sibling rivalry (Ross, 1982: 22). Such rivalry, whether having been initiated in childhood or later, whether by adults (usually parents) or by the siblings themselves, persists for some into old age (Ross and Milgram, 1980). While having its benefits, sibling rivalry may prove destructive, especially in the later years when shared reminiscence and perceptual validation, both of which require relaxed and harmonious interaction, come into play as important sources of well-being.

As has been suggested earlier, sibling relationships and task performance may vary with contextual circumstances. One thread of consistency over the life cycle that becomes apparent in this review relates to the gender composition of the sibling dyad. With a single exception (Scott, 1983: 61), research demonstrates the sister-sister relationship bond among the elderly to be stronger than the other combinations (Farber and Smith, 1985: 4; Troll, 1971: 281). This finding of outstanding sister-sister solidarity throughout the life cycle conforms to the principle of female linkage observed in studies of other kinship attachments.

Another factor reflecting congruency with earlier life cycle stages becomes evident in the work of Rosenberg and Anspach (1973: 112), who discovered a higher frequency of sibling interaction among the maritally disrupted than the maritally intact for both their middle-aged and elderly respondents. This observation suggests that sibling solidarity becomes operative in a compensatory manner. Other forms of support for this "compensation" thesis, originated by Shanas and associates (1968: 166), are derived from their own discovery that old people who had remained single maintained closer relationships with siblings than did those who had married and had children. Furthermore, they found that married persons without children resumed closer sibling solidarity upon the death of a spouse but, interestingly, not as close as single persons. Consistently, the more recent work of Scott (1983: 61) suggests that sibling relations increase in significance among the elderly when no child is available to provide support. It is important to note that the compensatory nature of sibling solidarity may not be uniform across sibling pairs. Farber and Smith (1985) discovered that how an older person conceptualized kinship ties had a significant effect on the comparative frequency of both contact and assistance granted to children and siblings.

SUMMARY: THE DEVELOPMENTAL TASKS OF SIBLINGSHIP

This review has outlined the obligations and activities binding siblings throughout the life cycle here in the United States. In light of the very limited information on the subject, the developmental tasks delineated herein must be viewed as tentative. We must assume exceptions to the generalizations stated; their application may be limited to particular segments of the population and/or to special circumstances. Still, they suggest some patterns and insights that may prove instructive to us in our personal lives as behavior guidelines and to researchers who are inclined to explore the topic further.

In the tradition of Havighurst (1966) I have prepared a listing of developmental tasks of siblingship over the life cycle on the basis of the research reviewed here. The following organizational scheme of siblingship tasks may serve as a tentative descriptive model of prosocial observed and expected behaviors associated with the three stages of the life cycle.

CHILDHOOD AND ADOLESCENCE

1. COMPANIONSHIP AND EMOTIONAL SUPPORT. Children and adolescents are in a unique position to provide to their siblings the inherent human need of social support. Throughout their years of living together, they act as close friends and confidants.

2. DELEGATED CARETAKING. Many families, especially single-parent families, low-income families, and large families, expect children and adolescents, particularly older daughters, to contribute to caretaking responsibilities for their siblings. Although the overall desirability of such a practice is debatable, it is worldwide in scope.

3. AID AND DIRECT SERVICES. As they confront the challenges associated with the early stages of maturation, children and adolescents provide to their siblings a myriad of direct services:

a. the formation of sibling coalitions for dealing with parents. Children and adolescents can and do benefit siblings by managing relationships between those siblings and the parents. This may be accomplished in several ways: by distracting one party from a potentially destructive situation; by joining forces with one another against the parent; and by translating and predicting parental behavior for one another.

b. The formation of sibling coalitions as compensation for parental inefficacy. When parents fail to carry out responsibilities, siblings may unite to provide needed resources to one another. Parental inefficacy may promote intense sibling loyalty, which could persist through adulthood.

c. Miscellaneous services. Children and adolescents provide both patterned and situational services to their siblings, including money lending, physical protection, sharing of friends, teaching of skills, and helping with homework.

EARLY AND MIDDLE ADULTHOOD

1. COMPANIONSHIP AND EMOTIONAL SUPPORT. Siblings continue to relate to one another as friends and confidants, albeit with decreased intensity, throughout these adult stages when family of procreation and economic activities command priority, and when sibling interaction has become voluntary. The level of companionship and emotional support between siblings reflects a passive concern for how the other is getting along.

2. COOPERATION IN THE CARE OF ELDERLY PARENTS AND ULTIMATELY IN THE DISMANTLING OF THE PARENTAL HOME. The sibling bond may be reactivated initially to manage a particular parental crisis but may then continue to serve as a "functional axis of socio-emotional interaction" throughout the process of parental decline and death, and through the dismantling of the parental home.

3. AID AND DIRECT SERVICES. The general tendency for young and middle-aged adult siblings is to exchange help as situations require; patterns of mutual aid are the exception, rather than the rule. Forms of sibling aid associated with these stages in the life cycle include help during illness, babysitting, sharing of clothes, and lending of money.

OLD AGE

1. COMPANIONSHIP AND EMOTIONAL SUPPORT. During postretirement years the sibling support bond appears to intensify, though contact may become less frequent. Perhaps the expressed sentiments of greater closeness during these final years is at least partially explained by the need to compensate for other kinship and friendship losses.

2. SHARED REMINISCENCE AND PERCEPTUAL VALIDATION. Because of their common biographies, older siblings are in a unique position to validate and clarify earlier events and relationships, and to place them in mature perspective. This process may be an important source of comfort and well-being in later years.

3. RESOLUTION OF SIBLING RIVALRY. It is during this final stage in the life cycle that any unresolved sibling rivalries must be laid to rest, allowing more constructive elements of siblingship to come into play.

4. AID AND DIRECT SERVICES. During old age, the aid and direct services supplied by siblings remain basically unchanged from earlier adult years. They are reflective of situational demands rather than patterned commitment, and occur in such forms as aid when ill; financial support; and help with crit-

ical decisions, business dealings, homemaking, home repairs, transportation, and shopping.

CONCLUDING STATEMENT

Although there is a wide variation in sibling commitment and support, it appears that the sibling support bond typically persists throughout the life cycle, manifesting its rewards in a variety of forms. Some siblingship tasks are constant, weaving threads of consistency from birth to death, while others stand out as idiosyncratic to the context of the particular stage of the life cycle. Over separations of time and distance, as they come to share fewer and fewer of life's circumstances, brothers and sisters persist in caring for one another and remaining on call as a source of aid. Their common heritage binds them in a truly unique relationship.

The study of siblingship tasks is sorely in need of development. This review divulges a multitude of knowledge gaps, perhaps generating more questions than answers. One research priority lies in discovering the important antecedent variables of sibling help. It appears that many siblings provide aid to one another throughout their lives, yet no firm predictors of such behavior have been established. What categories of persons offer what kinds of help, and under what circumstances?

We also need insight into the helping process itself. How is aid elicited, initiated, and received? What are the reactions of the sources and recipients of such exchanges? Studies that employ direct participation and/or observation of siblings in their natural settings would address these questions. Such research might be particularly helpful in understanding interactions between young children, since their natural setting places them together.

Another research priority centers around the need to understand siblingship tasks in the context of the larger family system. It would be of interest to know, for example, how families of orientation and procreation operate to encourage and discourage sibling solidarity and the performance of siblingship tasks. Network analysis could be applied here.

Still another valuable contribution to family studies would probe ways in which sibling task performance is affected by changing family patterns. Does reduced family size (i.e., having only one sibling) influence the frequency and quality of siblingship task performance? The recent influx of divorce and its resultant alternative lifestyles involve relationships between half- and stepsiblings. Do patterns of biological siblingship extend to include these variations? Does the presence of these half- and stepbrothers and sisters and their parents affect the biological sibling bond?

Consider finally that our largest minority group is virtually ignored in available studies on sibling relationships. It would be of value to understand the dynamics of siblingship in the black family structure. In her analysis of support systems in black families, Manns (1981: 245) observes, "The older sibling has been more critical to Black family life than has been recognized in either research or literature, and merits study." It is time to heed her suggestion.

Knowledge and insights yielded by these forms of research could prove instructive in efforts to promote and maintain the sometimes crucial support system that binds siblings throughout the life cycle.

Notes

1. For a detailed account of the development of importance of romantic love in modern Western culture, see Goode (1963).
2. According to Bryant and Crockenberg (1989: 530), the term *prosocial behavior* refers conceptually to activity undertaken for the well-being of others, and operationally to a cluster of behaviors: comforting, sharing, helping, defending, rescuing, cooperating, etc.
3. Delegated sibling caretaking refers to activities ranging from complete and independent full-time care of a child by his or her older sibling to the performance of specific tasks under the direct supervision of a parental figure. The concept is global, including all kinds of socialization, training, and routine responsibilities delegated to a child to benefit his or her sibling. It includes verbal or other explicit training and direction of the child's behavior, as well as simply "keeping an eye out for" younger siblings (Weisner and Gallimore, 1977: 169).
4. In addition to those outlined by Weisner and Gallimore (1977: 173–176), at least two other factors operate to limit sibling child-caretaking in the United States today. The fact that women are having on the average somewhat less than two children (National Center for Health Statistics, 1984), and are spacing them an average of three years apart (U.S. Bureau of the Census, 1984), suggests that only a moderate proportion of children now and in the near future will occupy a position where they are old enough to care for a younger sibling. A second factor relates to an ideology popular among American middle classes and referred to by Lerner (1957: 560–570) as the "cult of the child." This ideology views the family as a "child-centered anarchy" and dictates that the "fragile" child should be coddled—a perspective that may be interpreted by many to preclude delegation to a child of such adult responsibilities as child-caretaking.
5. This discussion of sibling caretaking styles is derived from Bryant's (1982: 109–113) more detailed coverage of the studies cited herein.

References

Abramovitch, Rona, Debra Pepler, and Carl Corter. 1982. "Patterns of sibling interaction among preschool-age children." Pp. 61–86 in Michael E. Lamb and Brian Sutton-Smith (eds.), Sibling Relationships: Their Nature and Significance across the Lifespan. Hillsdale, NJ: Lawrence Erlbaum Associates.

Adams, Bert. 1968. Kinship in an Urban Setting. Chicago: Markham.

Bank, Stephen, and Michael D. Kahn, 1975. "Sisterhood-brotherhood is powerful: Sibling subsystems and family therapy." Family Process 14: 311–337.

Bank, Stephen, and Michael D. Kahn. 1982. The Sibling Bond, New York: Basic Books.

Blood, Bob, and Margaret Blood. 1978. Marriage. New York: Free Press.

Bossard, James H. S., and Eleanor Stoker Boll. 1955. "Personality roles in the large family." Child Development 26: 71–78.

Bossard, James H. S. and Eleanor Stoker Boll. 1956. The Large Family System. Philadelphia: University of Pennsylvania Press.

Bowerman, Charles E., and Rebecca M. Dobash. 1974. "Structural variations in inter-sibling affect." Journal of Marriage and the Family 36: 48–54.

Bryant, Brenda K. 1979. "Siblings as caretakers." Paper presented at the annual meeting of the American Psychological Association, New York (September).

Bryant, Brenda K. 1981. Middle Childhood Experiences of Stress and Support. Manuscript in preparation.

Bryant, Brenda K. 1982. "Sibling relationships in middle childhood." Pp. 87–121 in Michael E. Lamb and Brian Sutton-Smith (eds.), Sibling Relationships: Their Nature and Significance across the Lifespan. Hillsdale, NJ: Lawrence Erlbaum Associates.

Bryant, Brenda K., and Susan B. Crockenberg. 1980. "Correlates and dimensions of prosocial behavior: A study of female siblings with their mothers." Child Development 51: 529–544.

Cicirelli, Victor G. 1976. "Mother-child and sibling-sibling interactions on a problem-solving task." Child Development 47: 588–596.

Cicirelli, Victor G. 1980a. "A comparison of college women's feelings toward their siblings and parents." Journal of Marriage and the Family 42: 111–120.

Cicirelli, Victor G. 1980b. "Sibling relationships in adulthood: A life span perspective." Pp. 455–462 in Leonard W. Poon (ed.), Aging in the 1980s. Washington, DC: American Psychological Association.

Cicirelli, Victor G. 1982. "Sibling influence throughout the lifespan." Pp 267–284 in Michael E. Lamb and Brian Sutton-Smith (eds.), Sibling Relationships: Their Nature and Significance across the Life Span. Hillsdale, NJ: Lawrence Erlbaum Associates.

Cicirelli, Victor G. 1984. "Marital disruption and adult children's perception of their siblings' help to elderly parents." Family Relations 33: 613–621.

Cicirelli, Victor G. 1985a. "The role of siblings as family caregivers." Pp. 93–107 in W. J. Sauer and R. T. Coward (eds.), Social Support Networks and Care of the Elderly, New York: Springer.

Cicirelli, Victor G. 1985b. "Sibling relationships throughout the life cycle." Pp. 177–214 in Luciano L'Abate (ed.), The Handbook of Family Psychology and Therapy. Homewood, IL: Dorsey Press.

Cumming, Elaine, and David M. Schneider, 1961. "Sibling solidarity: A property of the American kinship." American Anthropologist 63: 498–507.

Dunn, Judy, and Carol Kendrick, 1982. Siblings: Love, Envy, and Understanding. Cambridge, MA: Harvard University Press.

Essman, Clifford S. 1977. "Sibling relations as socialization for parenthood." Family Coordinator 26: 259–262.

Farber, Bernard, and Karen Smith. 1985. "Ties with children and siblings among residents of Sun City." Paper presented at the annual meeting of the American Sociological Association, Washington, DC (August).

Goode, William J. 1963. World Revolution and Family Patterns. New York: Free Press.

Havighurst, Robert J. 1966. Developmental Tasks and Education. New York: David McKay.

Johnson, Colleen Leahy. 1982. "Sibling solidarity: Its origin and functioning in Italian-American families." Journal of Marriage and the Family 44: 155–167.

Lamb, Michael E. 1982. "Sibling relationships across the life span: An overview and introduction." Pp. 1–11 in Michael E. Lamb and Brian Sutton-Smith (eds.), Sibling Relationships: Their Nature and Significance across the Lifespan. Hillsdale, NJ: Lawrence Erlbaum Associates.

Lerner, Max. 1957. America as a Civilization. New York: Simon and Schuster.

Lopata, Helena Znaniecki. 1973. Widowhood in an American City. Cambridge, MA: Schenkman.

Lynch, James J. 1977. The Broken Heart: The Medical Consequences of Loneliness. New York: Basic Books.

Manns, Wilhelmina. 1981. "Support systems of significant others in black families." Pp. 238–251 in Harriette Pipes McAdoo (ed), Black Families. Beverly Hills, CA: Sage Publications.

Matthew, Sarah H. and Tena Tarler Rosner, 1985. "Explanations for the division of filial responsibility between daughters in older families." Paper presented at the annual meeting of the American Sociological Association, Washington, DC (August).

McMurty, John. 1977. "Monogamy: A critique." Pp. 3–13 in Roger W. Libby and Robert N. Whitehurst (eds.), Marriage and Alternatives. Glenview, IL: Scott Foresman. Reprinted from the Monist 56 (1972): 4.

Minuchin, Salvador, Braulio Montalvo, Bernard G. Guerner, Jr., Bernice L. Rosman, and Florence Schumer. 1967. Families of the Slums. New York: Basic Books.

National Center for Health Statistics. 1984. "Advance report of final natality statistics." Monthly Vital Statistics Report 33(6): Supplement.

Rosenberg, George S., and Donald F. Anspach. 1973. "Sibling solidarity in the working class." Journal of Marriage and the Family 35: 108–113.

Ross, Hegola G. 1982. "Perceived sibling rivalry: A threat to personal relationships." Paper presented at the International Conference on Personal Relationships, Madison, WI (July).

Ross, Hegola G., Mary Jo Dalton, and Joel L. Milgram. 1980. "Older adults' perceptions of closeness in sibling relationships." Paper presented at the 33rd Annual Scientific Meeting of the Gerontological Society, San Diego (November).

Ross, Hegola G., and Joel I. Milgram, 1980. "Rivalry in adult sibling relationships: Its antecedents and dynamics." Paper presented at the annual meeting of the American Psychological Association, Montreal (September).

Ross, Hegola G., and Joel I. Milgram. 1982. "Important variables in adult sibling relationships: A qualitative study." Pp. 225–249 in Michael E. Lamb and Brian Sutton-Smith (eds.), Sibling Relationships: Their Nature and Significance across the Lifespan. Hillsdale, NJ. Lawrence Erlbaum Associates.

Scott, Jean Pearson. 1983. "Siblings and other kin." Pp. 47–62 in Timothy H. Brubaker (ed.), Family Relationships in Later Life. Beverly Hills, CA: Sage Publications.

Shanas, Ethel, Peter Townsend, Dorothy Wedderburn, Hennig Friis, Poul Milhoj, and Jan Stehouwer. 1968. Old People in Three Industrial Societies. London: Routledge and Kegan Paul.

Shapiro, Edna K., et al. 1984. "Sibling relationships and family structure." Paper presented at the annual meeting of the American Psychological Association, Toronto (August).

Stewart, Robert B., and Robert S. Marvin. 1984. "Sibling relations: The role of conceptual perspective-taking in the ontogeny of sibling caregiving." Child Development 55: 1322–1332.

Sussman, Marvin B. 1959. "The isolated nuclear family: Fact or fiction." Social Problems 6: 333–340.

Troll, Lillian E. 1971. "The family of later life: A decade review." Journal of Marriage and the Family 33: 263–290.

Troll, Lillian E., Sheila J. Miller, and Robert C. Atchley. 1975. Families in Later Life, Belmont, CA: Wadsworth.

U.S. Bureau of the Census. 1984. "Child spacing among birth cohorts of American women: 1905 to 1959." Current Population Reports, Series P-20, No. 385 (Table 10). Washington, DC: Government Printing Office.

Weisner, Thomas S. 1982. "Sibling interdependence and child caretaking: A cross-cultural view." Pp. 305–327 in Michael E. Lamb and Brian Sutton-Smith (eds.), Sibling Relationships: Their Nature and Significance across the Lifespan. Hillsdale, NJ: Lawrence Erlbaum Associates.

Weisner, Thomas S., and Ronald Gallimore. 1977. "My brother's keeper: Child and sibling caretaking." Current Anthropology 18: 169–190.

Weiss, Robert S. 1975. Marital Separation. New York: Basic Books.

Whiting, B., and J. W. M. Whiting. 1975. Children of Six Cultures. Cambridge, MA: Harvard University Press.

3.

FAMILY SIZE EFFECTS: A REVIEW

Mazie Earle Wagner
Herman J. P. Schubert
Department of Student Counseling
State University College at Buffalo

Daniel S. P. Schubert
Case Western Reserve Medical School
Cleveland Metropolitan General Hospital

Sibling constellation effects is a voluminous field. Effects of family size is its largest subdivision and the one of greatest importance. This review is a synthesis of earlier research (Wagner, Schubert, & Schubert, 1979) with a fuller description of recent findings.

The purpose of this article is to clarify the effects of family size on the intelligence, academic achievement, occupation, personality, adjustment, morbidity and mortality, as well as on the parents' health, happiness, and adjustment. The interaction with socioeconomic status (SES), family ideology, race, and spacing of children are detailed.

FAMILY SIZE AND SOCIOECONOMIC STATUS

Of all the sibship-variable effects, those of family size are the most difficult to isolate. Socioeconomic status is probably most interrelated. The family of six is living at a lower SES level, farther down the poverty line with severely limited resources (unless, indeed, the husband's income is quite substantial) than are smaller families. Baird (1974), in his comprehensive paper on birth rate and perinatal death, states that children are the most common cause of poverty.

Page and Grandon (1979), in their statistically sophisticated paper with a sample of about 12,000 high school U.S. graduates, detail the SES-family size relationship very succinctly. When they use their total population, a significant relation between family size and intelligence is found. However, for the top 25 percent by SES, they find that sibship size shows only a very slight relation to mental ability. For the middle 50 percent SES, the relation between family size and mental ability increases to a moderate and significant level. For the lowest 25 percent by SES, the relationship increases to a very significant size, with each family size level increase showing a definite decrease in mental ability. In ad-

dition, they show that almost 75 percent of those in the top 25 percent SES are from families of two, three, and four, whereas less than one-half (44 percent) of the bottom 25 percent SES are from these family sizes (approximately 5 percent of each SES classification are onlyborns). With a difference of this magnitude, it is obvious that combining the SES groups would lead to a heightened relationship between family size and mental ability. Belmont et al. (1977), for some 200,000 19-year-old males in the Netherlands, gives similar relationships between mental ability and family size, consistent with Page and Grandon.

Given a stated paternal income, with each additional child, the effective social class level actually decreases in money for nutrition, medical attention, educational facilities, and leisure time activities (the hidden educators of sightseeing, travel, musical instruments, sophisticated toys, and, most recently, computers). As experienced functionally, family size is an extension and modification of SES, at the lower levels of this latter measurement.

FAMILY SIZE AND PARENTAL ATTITUDES

Parental attitudes and treatment of children change as the number of children increases. Positively, the larger sibship is more family centered, with more family socialization and family-developed entertainment, and the father increases his role (see Wagner et al. 1979 for a comprehensive review). However, with a larger number of children, rules become more authoritarian (Bartow, 1961), with more corporal punishment (Nye, Carlson and Garrett, 1970), and discipline becomes more restrictive and punitive. There is poorer performance on IQ tests, lack of spontaneity, giving up quickly (Kent and Davis, 1957; Ojha and Sinha, 1982), and more authoritarian parental control with more power assertion,

From the *Journal of Genetic Psychology*, 1985, *146*(1): 65–78. Reprinted by permission.

criticism, and control by parents (Bartow, 1961). All children are treated more alike, despite individual needs and differences. Such child-rearing practices result in poorer development of inductive reasoning, poorer self-esteem, less self-differentiation, and low ego identity. Parents are less interested in children's school work (Douglas, 1964; Warburton and Fraser, 1964). In addition there is low basic acculturation, language usage, control of violence, and ego strength (Pavenstadt, 1967). Girls are less harshly treated and more protected than boys. Earlierborn girls have heavy household chores while older boys are withdrawn from school to help support the family (Assmen, 1981). Family size has a somewhat stronger negative effect on girls and blacks than on boys and whites (Blau, 1981).

Parents show poorer marital relations (Bossard and Ball, 1956) with each succeeding child (Hurley and Palonen, 1967; Rutter and Madge, 1976). Farber and Blackman (1956) found lack of ability to control the number of their children leads to pronounced marital dissatisfaction.

Blau (1974) concludes that among white children socioeconomic level is the strongest predictor of IQ and achievement scores while family size also has a definite negative effect. Among black children, both family size and socioeconomic level have strong effects.

Blau (1981) emphasizes that a pattern of high maternal ambition for her children, coupled with heavy investment of resources, results in high intellectual aptitude. A strategy of high investment of resources and low use of aversive authoritarian discipline optimizes the scholastic achievement of both black and white children. High investment with high aversive discipline is counterproductive. Mothers who use high aversive discipline with low investment of resources have children with the lowest achievement.

Sex differences by socioeconomic level and race vary, with high investment and aversive discipline directed more to boys than to girls. Where education for girls is more highly valued and aversive control more used for boys, the girls are better than the boys in intellectual pursuits (Blau, 1974). Firstborns, for whom parents, on the average, have higher ambitions and in whom more parental time and interest are invested rate higher on intelligence and achievement tests.

Crowding, with lack of special space for each child, leads to tension, nervousness, and hypertension (Blau, 1981). In enumerating the advantages of being an only child, those without siblings frequently mention having a room to oneself as well as going places with parents and special training advantages such as musical instruments and special classes.

Other complicating factors are cultural ideology and religion. Blau (1974) reports that black and white children of both Catholic and Baptist mothers score lower on IQ than do those born to undenominationals, Episcopalians, or Presbyterians. Her findings are presumably confounded by sibship size and socioeconomic level. Of her black Baptists, 46 percent derived from sibships of five or more versus 29 percent of black Methodists.

These results support the general hypothesis that those from large sibships are less intelligent and achieving than those from smaller families (Berent, 1952; Breland, 1974; Marjoribanks, 1976; Olneck and Bills, 1979; Olneck and Wolfe, 1980). In large families one finds authoritarian and rule-dominated treatment of children.

FACTORS INFLUENCING SIBSHIP SIZE

Factors which tend to reduce family size, in addition to ideology and religion, are industrialization, more education for women, and more employment of women outside the home (Abrams, 1980).

McKenna, Null and Ventis (1979) found firstborns in two-child families had significantly higher IQs when their parents were married at a later age. This supports the usual finding that firstborns of older parents have higher IQs (1929). Such children also, on the average, have higher self-esteem.

To examine the effects of early fertility Anderson and Smith (1975) studied 1,028 women in Atlanta, 15 to 44 years of age. Adolescent fertility was found more frequent among blacks. Because of such early pregnancies, black women are at risk of child bearing for a longer period, resulting in a higher fertility rate. They found little efficient or rational fertility control among the teenagers, and that fertility control increased with age.

The length of the period between marriage and the birth of the first child and the spacing between the first and second child are both negatively related to the final sibship size. For example, Stewart and Barber (1963) report concerning 3,751 births that of the 1,319 onlyborns, the period between marriage and the birth of this first child averaged 2.5 years; for the elder of sibships of two, the period averaged an even 2 years; for siblings of three, 1.7 years, with decreasing lengths to one year or less for sibships of 10 and over. The spacing between the first and second birth in sibships of two was found to be 4.1 years; for sibships of three and four, 3.0 years; and 2.4 or less for larger sibships, decreasing steadily to a 1-year interval between the first and second for a sibship of 15. Similar data are reported by Davidson (1970) and by Zajonc (1976).

Regarding family size preference. Clay and Zuiches (1980) found that wives conform to the two-child ideal depending on the extent to which they are exposed to it via reference group interaction and on size of family of origin. Husbands were influenced only by size of family of origin.

PERSONALITY AND FAMILY SIZE

The effects of sibship size on personality are less well documented than those on intelligence, achievement, and occupational success. Sibship size effects on personality are smaller, therefore requiring more sophisticated statistics, larger samples, and generally more effort and expertise on the part of researchers.

Individuals from larger families tend to have less ideational flexibility, to be less able to face ambiguity, are more distrustful of others, more frequently suicidal, more discouraged as youths, and more in need of approval than those from smaller sibships. They average a poorer self-concept and are more resentful. They value conformity rather than independence, self-control over self-expression, and highly value organization and leadership (Wagner et al., 1979).

Diagnostically, different psychological maladjustments appear for individuals from small versus larger sibships. For the small family, anxiety is greater, especially among male offspring, and neurosis among the eldest. Delinquency is more frequent among those from large families with findings in Australia (Ogden, De and Horne, 1976), in Germany (Ostapiuk, Morrison and Porteous, 1974), in Glasgow (Ferguson, 1952), and in Canada (Jones, Offord and Abrams, 1980). Delinquents come from larger families, have more brothers than controls do; delinquent brothers are more antisocial than the control brothers, and sisters seem to reduce delinquency and antisociability (Jones, et al., 1980). Others (Blakely, Stephenson and Nichol, 1974; Miller, Court, Knox, and Brandon, 1974; West and Farrington, 1977) report large families are over-represented among delinquents without attention to socioeconomic status.

Large families more frequently produce those who commit more serious crimes, have school problems, do poor school work, and commit antisocial behavior (Rutter, Tizard and Whitmore, 1970; Wagner et al., 1979; West and Farrington, 1977); are child abusers (Jensen, 1977); are more risk taking (Wagner et al., 1979); and are at more risk of smoking and alcoholism (Conley, 1978; Wagner et al., 1979). Research needs to be done to separate the proportion of effects due to family size, SES, parental value of and investment in the child, types of reward and punishment, and other variables.

Middleborn college girls from closely spaced large sibships (four and over), especially when between like-sexed siblings, were more maladjusted than middleborn girls from families of three (Wagner, Schubert, and Schubert, manuscript submitted for publication).

Elementary school boys from large families were less verbally and physically aggressive than those from smaller families among Hispanic lower-class normal children (Bone and Montare, 1979) and among children referred for adjustment problems (Searcy-Miller, Cowen, and Terrell, 1977). These researches did not examine change in aggressiveness with age, the relation of ordinal position to family size differences, nor the generalizability of such findings to those for older children, adolescents, and adults. Michael (1977), using a sample of 2,708 parents and 100 school classes, found parental involvement in children's learning activities decreased both with the number of children in the family and decrease in the SES level.

Robertson (1971) attempted to separate the effects of SES and family size on personality, using 14- and 15-year-old boys, 114 from the upper SES, 95 from the middle, and 88 from the working class, all from intact homes. He used the Cattell Personality Questionnaire, an objective personality test, rather than observation of behavior as done by Michael (1977). His findings showed interaction of SES and personality variables. He found that among firstborns introversion and anxiety were highest among lowest social class and lessened progressively as class increased. On the other hand, among later-born boys anxiety and introversion increased as social class increased. Boys from low-skilled homes are most group-activity oriented and those from upper middle-class homes best able to work with adults (authority figures). Boys from highly skilled homes seem a bit closer to those from the upper middle class in these regards.

In large families, laterborns are more accident prone (Krall, 1951), as 14- to 19-year-olds are more likely to attempt suicide (Angel, Taleghani, Choquet, and Courteouisse, 1978), and generally are more risk taking (Jensen, 1977).

Hogan and Sitagawa (1982), in a very sophisticated study of fertility among 690 very low SES and 388 average SES black adolescent girls, showed both initial sexual intercourse and first pregnancy were earlier for those from sibships over five in size, especially if a sister had had a pregnancy. Other factors contributing to early sexual experience and pregnancy were lack of intactness of home and parental supervision of dating.

PSYCHIATRIC DISORDERS AND FAMILY SIZE

Schizophrenia is found more frequently among laterborns from large families (Wagner et al., 1979). Schooler (1972) warns that these findings may be attenuated by declining birthrate which increases the proportion of laterborns. Alkire (1974) and Wahl (1956) investigated by reviews and surveys the familial backgrounds of schizophrenics. They conclude that a large number of siblings (a) increases difficulty with self-identification due to little time with parents, and consequently poor differentiation between siblings and the self, and (b) increases sibling rivalry for the limited parental time. Rutter and Madge (1976) explain such findings as due to "inadequate family resources," mentioning over-crowding, poor nutrition, reduced parental supervision, and increased stress on the mother. There is evidence that many of the above described findings regarding large sibships do not hold for upper-middle and upper social classes and rural populations (Breland, 1974; Kennett and Cropley, 1970).

MORBIDITY, MORTALITY, AND LONGEVITY

A large number of sophisticated studies using very large samples present data concerning the effects of family size on health, morbidity, and mortality. As sibship size increases, the morbidity and mortality rates of children rise. Wray (1971) points out that with increased parity (number of live births per woman) there is an increase in low birth weight (prematurity). Prematurity is associated with higher rates of perinatal deaths and congenital malformations. Laterborns from large sibships are at risk of greater exposure to contagious diseases from older siblings. Family size is undoubtedly the most impor-

tant variable in morbidity and mortality during the first three years of life (Lowe and McKeown, 1954; McKeown and Rećard, 1978) due to exposure to contagious diseases at an age when they are more vulnerable to complications. The increasing age of the mother as her family grows in number also increases prenatal, perinatal, and early infancy mortality and morbidity.

Birth weight increases steadily with both parity and with mother's height (Barron and Vessey, 1966; Grossman, Handlesman and Davies, 1974) for U.S. and Israeli infants. Mothers under age 20 have a higher frequency of infants of less than 2,500 grams. Such low birth weight decreases for mothers 25 to 29 years of age, and then steadily increases with mother's age and parity. Using a sample of 32,649 East Indian babies (Nanboodiri and Balakrishnan, 1958–59), low birth weight also was found to increase with parity and mother's age.

Bongarts (1980) summarized effects of malnutrition on fertility and found no evidence that infant mortality was increased. Famine did temporarily reduce population by increasing infant deaths and by reducing women's fertility about 50%.

Also higher in larger sibships are spontaneous abortions (James, 1974; Warburton and Fraser, 1964), stillbirths (James, 1968; Duncan, Baird and Thomson, 1952), Down's syndrome (Hay and Barbano, 1972; Somasundaram and Papakumari, 1981), Rh factor complications, and risk of congenital malformation (atrial septal defects, especially in parities 0 and 5 plus) (Stewart, Kray and Smith, 1969).

Sudden Infant Death Syndrome (SIDS) increases in frequency with number of children born to the mother. Children born to mothers under 20 years of age, illegitimates, blacks and American Indians are also at high risk of SIDS (Kraus, Franti and Borhani, 1972). Lead poisoning (Chisolm and Harrison, 1957; Mellins and Jenkins, 1955), lack of immunization (Markland and Durand, 1976), protein malnutrition (Wray and Aquirre, 1969), and accident rate (Kraus et al., 1972; Wagner et al., 1979) are all higher in large families. Ordinal ranks of five and over are more at risk of coronary heart disease (Lind and Theorell, 1973; Antonowsky, 1968). Patients who present multiple physical complaints and those on psychosomatic wards are more frequently laterborns from large sibships (Meiners, 1978). Also more frequently from large families are patients with diabetes, peptic and duodenal ulcers (Miller et al., 1974), arthritis, contagious diseases, and increased sensitivity to physical pain (Wagner et al., 1979).

On the other hand, some difficulties are more frequent among members of small sibships. These include obesity, ulcerative colitis, autism in childhood (Wagner et al., 1979), and Hodgkins disease (Gitehsohn and Cole, 1981).

FAMILY SIZE EFFECTS ON PARENTAL HEALTH

Women who have many children more frequently develop hypertension, stress symptoms, gall bladder disease, diabetes, and postpartum depression. Women with many children are at higher risk for cancer of the cervix, digestion organs, and peritoneum, but are at less risk for breast cancer (LeShan and Risnikoff, 1960; Zimmerman and Hartley, 1982). Heightened blood pressure, both diastolic and systolic, is at no greater frequency among mothers with large than with small families (Feldstein, Harburg and Hauenstein, 1980). Marital adjustment becomes poorer with increase in family size (Bossard and Ball, 1956; Hurley and Palonen, 1967; Rossi, 1972). Neal and Groat (1980) report that many women experience pregnancies as occurrences, happenings, or unintended events within a social-psychological context of social drift. Fathers of large families are at greater risk of hypertension and peptic ulcers (Monson, 1970; Wagner et al., 1979).

Hinshaw, Pyeatt and Habicht (1972) found that extended lactation extends amenorrhea and that causes greater spacing among children with reduced fertility in Guatemala. Salber, Feinleib, and MacMahon in 1966 reported that Massachusetts women who lactated six months or more had amenorrhea extended by about six months (Hinshaw et al., 1972).

Finally, people from small families, especially with wide sibling spacing, live longer (Beeton and Pearson, 1901). Again, SES has its confounding effect in that average longevity increases as income and occupational level increases (Wagner et al., 1954).

DISCUSSION

The first consideration is the validity and reliability of the results reviewed: Sibship constellation variables are among the most accurate of retrospective data. Most of the interrelating reviewed measures (e.g., IQ, level and quality of academic attainment, weight at birth, age at death, and incarceration in mental or penal institutions) are accurate as well. These reviewers tried to exclude studies with faulty design and biased samples. As researchers subdivide their samples, for instance by sex or SES, using actual appropriate subsamples or sophisticated statistics, results regarding family size effects are providing new generalizations.

RESEARCH NEEDS

The need is for both innovative research and for use of broader, relatively unresearched target populations. We shall try to illustrate both from the literature, hoping our selections will be heuristic. The first consideration is unusually innovative research.

Davis, Cahan and Bashi (1977) studied 191,993 Israeli eighth graders, dividing them into those whose fathers emigrated from Europe, U.S., and South Africa with those from the Far East, Near East, and North Africa. The mothers of the former had a modicum of schooling while only a minimum of the latter had ever had any schooling at all. Family size still had an effect on IQ and schooling in the manner consistent with usual findings for those whose mothers had had some schooling. Ordinal position effects were inverse for children whose parents came from the Near and Far East and Northern Africa where the mothers mostly had had no education. Here the youngest child, on the average, was superior to the next to last who had a better school record than his predecessor. When queried about source of help with school work, the children whose mothers had some schooling said their parents; the children from Near and Far East parentage said their older siblings. This research does not greatly contribute to the issue of family size, but is quoted for its innovativeness.

Page and Grandon's study (1979) makes the point that for the three SES levels, the relationship between family size and ordinal rank with academic performance is considerably higher for the lowest SES.

An exception to the middle-class white suburb as sample studied is that of Pavenstadt et al. (1967) who studied children of multiple-problem lowest-SES families. Another exception to the mode is the recent study by Hogan and Kitagawa (1982) who compare very impoverished black female adolescents with all Chicago black female youth for family factors affecting fertility. (Comparable white statistics are also included.) Their sophisticated statistical procedures indicate that both low SES and large sibships increased early sexual experience and pregnancy. More research at this lower SES level is needed.

Blau (1981), in her exhaustive study of 579 black and 523 white 11-year-old children, does some research regarding ideology and SES on effect of family size. She found such effects varied with race, religion, and ideology. The usually used SES levels might well be further subdivided for study of sibship variable effects. Belmont and Marolla (1973), for example, subdivided their large sample into farmers and farmworkers, manual and nonmanual workers.

Studies of sibships by specific size might well throw additional light on the processes of development. Effects of sex of and spacing between siblings need careful control since they may have interacting effects. The sibship of two has been the source of much research on intellect and various personality characteristics. Such data needs collation and new research regarding sibships of two is needed to test the general supposition that two is the best number. Except for intellect, studies of effects of being one of three is limited.

TYPES OF ERROR

By now the reader will have become aware of some of the errors that plague the researcher on sibling constellation effects including sibship size. But lest some be overlooked, a list is herewith discussed with examples.

The first consideration is sampling errors: The researcher must guard against truncating his sample in respect to the dependent variable, for example, IQ, or academic achievement. In a table of family size by ordinal position, a recent investigator filled in the average entrance test score for each cell for college students. This is not a complete population from the point of view of academic ability, since many of the age peers of these college entrants had withdrawn in their progress up the academic ladder. By eliminating all the less able, the results showed little difference by either ordinal position or family size in academic ability.

Berglin (1981) emphasizes that year(s) of birth of the study sample and control sample must be identical to make the two samples comparable. Using volunteers is another cause of sampling error since volunteers, particularly when not reimbursed (Schubert, Patterson, Miller, and Brocco, 1984) or given other tangible reward, differ from nonvolunteers. They are more educated and more likely to be female, younger, married, and Jewish or Protestant. They are also more cooperative and differ in other areas of personality. Many samples collected by mail are especially likely to be self-selected (volunteer) samples.

A second group of errors occurs in research design. To illustrate, despite emphasis by Adler and others of the ill effects of early "dethronement" (displacement as number one) by a younger sibling, only children and other firstborns have too often been placed in a single category. Also, despite known interaction of sex with various personality traits, the two sexes are studied as a single class. Such combinations result in lack of significant differences, whereas if the sexes were studied separately differences might indeed be considerable. When two groups are found not to differ, they may be combined.

Perhaps the most frequent and most pervasive error is generalization of findings beyond similar samples: Conclusions regarding middle-class white, two-child sibships are generalized to all SES groups, all races, and all ideologies. When results differ from the usual findings, progress will be made by seeking the cause of the lack of conformity, as illustrated by the research of Davis, Cahan and Bashi (1977) described above.

Finally, a word regarding the meaning of differences, statistically significant or otherwise. Subdividing large samples into subgroups by additional classification may bring large differences for one such subgroup and none for another, thus adding understanding to the field. Small samples may yield large differences that are not statistically significant. Here the next step is clear: more subjects or another study. The size of sibship variable effect is frequently large and findings consistent.

References

Abrams, D. (1980). *Women's Educational Attainment and Fertility.* Presented at the American Psychological Association Meeting, Montreal.

Alkire, A. A., Brunse, A. J. and Houlihan, J. P. (1974). Avoidance of nuclear family relationships in schizophrenia. *Journal of Clinical Psychology, 30,* 398–400.

Anderson, J. E. and Smith, J. C. (1975). Planned and unplanned fertility in a metropolitan area: Black and white differences. *Family Planning Perspectives, 7,* 281–285.

Angel, P., Taleghani, M., Choquet, M., and Courteouisse, N. (1978). An epidemiological approach to suicide attempts in adolescence: Some responses to the environment. *Evolution Psychiatrics, 43,* 351–367.

Antonowsky, A. (1968). Social class and the major cardiovascular diseases. *Journal of Chronic Diseases, 21,* 59–73.

Assman, J. S. U. (1981). The overloaded parent; results and reasons in family size effects on parenting. B. C. Rollins (Ed.), in *Family Structure and Process in Socialization of Children*, Provo, UT.: Brigham Young University Press.

Baird, D. (1974). Epidemiology of congenital malformation of the central nervous system in (a) Aberdeen and (b) Scotland. *Journal of Biosocial Science, 6*, 113–137.

Barron, S. L., and Vessey, M. F. (1966). Birth weight of infants born to immigrant mothers. *British Journal of Preventive Social Medicine, 20*, 127–134.

Bartow, J. (1961). Family size as related to child-rearing practices. *Dissertation Abstracts International, 22*, 5581.

Beeton, M., and Pearson, K. (1901). Inheritance of the duration of life and the intensity of natural selection in men. *Biometrika, 1*, 50–89.

Belmont, L., and Marolla, F. A. (1973). Birth order, family size, and intelligence. *Science, 182*, 1096–1101.

Belmont, L., Wittes, J., and Stein, Z. (1977). Relation of birth order, family size, and social class to psychological function. *Perceptual and Motor Skills, 45*, 1107–1116.

Berent, J. (1952). Fertility and social mobility. *Population Studies, 5*, 244–260.

Berglin, C. G. (1981). Regular skewness of birth order distribution. *Scandinavian Journal of Social Medicine*, supplement 23, pp. 1–138.

Blakely, R., Stephenson, P. S., and Nichol, H. (1974). Social factors in a random sample of juvenile delinquents and controls. *International Journal of Social Psychiatry, 20*, 203–217.

Blau, Z. S. (1974). The strategy of the Jewish mother. In M. Sklar (Ed.), *The Jew in American Society*. New York: Behrman House.

Blau, Z. S. (1981). *Black children, white children: Competence, socialization and social structure*. New York: The Free Press.

Bongarts, J. (1980). Does malnutrition affect fecundity? A summary of evidence. *Science, 208*, 564–569.

Boone, S. L., and Montare, A. (1979). Aggression and family size. *Journal of Psychology, 103*, 67–70.

Bossard, J., and Ball, E. (1956). *The large family system: An original study in the sociology of family behavior*. Philadelphia: University of Pennsylvania Press.

Breland, H. M. (1974). Birth order, family configuration, and verbal achievement. *Child Development, 43*, 1011–1019.

Chisolm, J. J., and Harrison, H. E. (1957). The treatment of acute lead encephalopathy in children. *Pediatrics, 19*, 2–20.

Clay, D. C., and Zuiches, J. J. (1980). Reference groups and family size norms. *Population and Environment: Behavioral, Environmental and Social Issues, 3*, 262–279.

Conley, J. J. (1978). Ordinal position, personality, and alcoholism. *Dissertation Abstract International*, Microfilm No. 7907050, 168.

Davidson, M. (1970). Social and economic variations in child spacing. *Social Biology, 17*, 107–113.

Davis, D. J., Cahan, S., and Bashi, J. (1977). Birth order and intellectual development: The confluence model in the light of cross-cultural evidence. *Science, 196*, 1470–1472.

Douglas, J. W. B. (1964). *The home and the school*. London: Macgibbon and Kee.

Duncan, E. H. L., Baird, D., and Thomason, A. M. (1952). Causes and prevention of stillbirths and first week deaths. *Journal of Obstetrics and Gynecology: British Empire, 59*, 183–196.

Farber, B., and Blackman, L. (1956). Marital role tension and number and sex of children. *American Sociological Review, 21*, 596–601.

Feldstein, A. L., Harburg, E., and Hauenstein, L. (1980). Parity and blood pressure among four race-stress groups of families in Detroit. *American Journal of Epidemiology, 111*, 356–366.

Ferguson, T. (1952). *The young delinquent in the social setting*. London: Oxford University Press.

Gitehsohn, N., and Cole, P. (1981). Childhood social environment and Hodgkin's disease. *New England Journal of Medicine, 304*, 135–140.

Grossman, S., Handlesman, Y., and Davies, A. M. (1974). Birth weight in Israel 1968–70. Effects of birth order and maternal origin. *Journal of Biosocial Science, 5*, 43–58.

Hay, S., and Barbano, H. (1972). Independent effects of maternal age and birth order on the incidence of selected congenital malformations. *Annals of Human Genetics, 6*, 371–379.

Hinshaw, R., Pyeatt, P., and Habicht, J. P. (1972). Environmental effects of child-spacing and population increase in Highland Guatemala. *Current Anthropology, 13, 216–230*.

Hogan, D. P., and Kitagawa, E. M. (1982). *Family Factors and Fertility of Black Adolescents*. Population Research Center, University of Chicago. Unpublished.

Hurley, J., and Palonen, D. (1967). Marital satisfaction and child density among university student parents. *Journal of Marriage and the Family, 29*, 483–484.

James, W. H. (1968). Stillbirth and birth order. *Annals of Human Genetics, 32, 151–162*.

James, W. H. (1974). Spontaneous abortions and birth order. *Journal of Biosocial Science, 6*, 23–41.

Jamieson, H. D. (1969). The influences of birth order, family size, and sex differences on risk-taking behavior. *British Journal of Social and Clinical Psychology, 8*, 1–8.

Jensen, D. E. (1977). Child abuse in a court referred inner city population. *Journal of Clinical Child Psychology, 6*, 59–62.

Jones, M. B., Offord, D. R., and Abrams, N. (1980). Brothers, sisters and antisocial behavior. *British Journal of Psychiatry, 136*, 139–145.

Kennett, K. F., and Cropley, A. J. (1970). Intelligence, family size and socioeconomic status. *Journal of Biosocial Science, 2*, 227–236.

Kent, N., and Davis, D. R. (1967). Discipline in the home and intellectual development. *British Journal of Medical Psychology, 30*, 27–33.

Krall, V. (1951). Personality characteristics of accident-prone children. *Journal of Abnormal and Social Psychology, 48,* 99–108.

Kraus, J. F., Franti, C. E., and Borhani, N. O. (1972). Discriminatory risk factors in post-neonatal sudden unexplained death. *American Journal of Epidemiology, 96,* 328–333.

LeShan, L., and Risnikoff, M. (1960). A psychological factor apparently associated with neoplastic disease, *Journal of Abnormal and Social Psychology, 60,* 439–440.

Lind, E., and Theorell, T. (1973). Sociological characteristics and myocardial infarctions. *Journal of Psychosomatic Research, 17,* 59–73.

Lowe, C. R., and McKeown, T. (1954). Incidence of infectious disease in the first three years of life, related to social circumstance. *British Journal of Preventive Social Medicine, 8,* 24–28.

Marjoribanks, K. (1976). Sibsize, family environment, cognitive performance, and affective characteristics. *Journal of Psychology, 94,* 195–204.

Markland, R. E., and Durand, D. E. (1976). An investigation of socio-psychological factors affecting infant immunization. *American Journal of Public Health, 66,* 168–170.

McFadden, J. H. (1929). A further note on the different IQ's of siblings. *Journal of Applied Psychology, 13,* 86–91.

McKenna, V. V., Null, C. B., and Ventis, L. (1979). *Marital age and the spacing of children: Influence on children, parents, and family interaction.* Contract R01 MD 42844, NICHD, Center Population Research.

McKeown, T., and Record, R. G. (1978). Relationship between childhood infections and measured intelligence. *British Journal of Preventive Social Medicine, 39,* 101–106.

Meiners, G. (1978). Sibling constellation and psychosomatic disease in adults. *Zeitschrift fur Psychosomatische Medisin und Psychoanalyse, 24,* 90–99.

Mellins, R. B., and Jenkins, C. D. (1955). Epidemiological and psychological study of lead poisoning in children. *Journal of American Medical Association, 158,* 15–20.

Michael, C. B. (1977). The relationship between teacher's self-concept and the extent of parental involvement in children's learning activities. *Dissertation Abstracts International, 37,* 4917.

Miller, F. J. W., Court, S. D. M., Knox, E. G., and Brandon S. (1974). *The School Years in Newcastle upon Tyne.* London: Oxford University Press.

Monson, R. R. (1970). Familial factors in peptic ulcer. II: Family structure in duodenal ulcer. *American Journal of Epidemiology, 91,* 460–465.

Nanboodiri, N. K., and Balakrishnan, V. (1958–59). On the effect of maternal age and parity on the birth weight of the offspring (Indian infants). *Annual of Human Genetics, 23,* 189–203.

Neal, A. G., and Groat, M. T. (1980). Fertility decision making, unintended births, and the social drift hypothesis: A longitudinal study. *Population: Behavioral, Social and Environmental Issues, 3,* 221–235.

Nye, F., Carlson, J., and Garrett, G. (1970). Family size, interaction, affect and stress. *Journal of Marriage and the Family, 32,* 216–226.

Ogden, E. J. D., De, L., and Horne, D. J. (1976). An Australian residential youth training centre: Population study. *Australian and New Zealand Journal of Criminology, 9,* 49–54.

Ojha, M., and Sinha, M. (1982). Family structure and parental behavior. *Psychologia: An International Journal of Psychology in the Orient, 25,* 107–114.

Olneck, M. R., and Bills, D. B. (1979). Family configuration and achievement effects of birth order and family size in a sample of brothers. *Social Psychological Quarterly, 42,* 135–148.

Olneck, M. R., and Wolfe, B. L. (1980). Intelligence and family size: Another look. *Review of Economics and Statistics, 62,* 241–247.

Ostapiuk, E., Morrison, N., and Porteous, M. A. (1974). A brief numerical summary of some family variables among boys in an assessment centre. *Community Schools Gazette, 67,* 571–580.

Owen, E., (1982). Family size, birth order, and test performance. *South African Journal of Psychology, 12,* 24–30.

Page, E. B. and Grandon, G. M. (1979). Family configuration and mental ability. Two theories contrasted with U.S. data. *American Educational Research, 16,* 257–272.

Pavenstadt, E. (ed.) (1967). *The Drifters: Children from Disorganized Lower-Class Families.* Boston: Little Brown.

Robertson, A. (1971). Social class differences in the relationship between birth order and personality development. *Social Psychiatry, 6,* 173–178.

Rossi, A. S. (1972). Family development in a changing world. *American Journal of Psychiatry, 128,* 108.

Rutter, M., and Madge, N. (1976). *Cycles of disadvantage,* London: Heinemann.

Rutter, M., Tizard, J., and Whitmore, K. (1970). *Education, health and behavior.* London: Longman.

Schooler, C. (1972). Birth order effects: Not here, not now! *Psychological Bulletin, 78.* 161–175.

Schubert, D. S. P., Patterson, M. S., Miller, F., and Brocco, K. J. (1984). Informed consent as a source of bias in clinical research. *Psychiatry Research, 12,* 313–320.

Searcy-Miller, M., Cowen, E. L., and Terrell, D. L. (1977). School adjustment problems of children from small and large families. *Journal of Community Psychology, 5,* 319–324.

Somasundaram, O., and Papakumari, M. (1981). A study of Down's anomaly. *Child Psychiatry Quarterly, 14,* 85–94.

Stewart, A., and Barber, R. (1963). Data on parental age, sibship size and twins. *Annals of Human Genetics, 27,* 1.

Stewart, A., Kray, A. J., and Smith, P. G. (1969). Congenital malformations: A detailed study of 2,500 liveborn infants. *Annals of Human Genetics, 32,* 353–360.

Terhune, K. W., and Pille, R. J. (1974). *A review of the actual and expected consequences of family size.* Department of Health, Education, and Welfare Publication (NIH) 760779. Washington, D.C.: US Government Printing Office.

Wagner, M. E., Schubert, H. J. P., and Schubert, D. S. P. *Effects of sibling spacing on psychosocial adjustment of middleborn girls.* Manuscript submitted for publication.

Wagner, M. E., and Schubert, H. J. P. and Schubert, D. S. P. (1954). Comparative longevity of physicians and of general population. *New York Journal of Medicine, 64,* 1849–1850.

Wagner, M. E., Schubert, H. J. P., and Schubert, D. S. P. (1979). Sibship-constellation effects of psychosocial development, creativity, and health. In H. W. Reese and L. P. Libsitt (eds.), *Advances in Child Development and Behavior, 14,* 58–155. New York: Academic Press.

Wahl, C. W. (1956). Some antecedent factors in the family histories of 568 male schizophrenics in the U.S. Navy. *American Journal of Psychiatry, 113,* 201–210.

Warburton, D., and Fraser, F. C. (1964). Spontaneous abortion rates in men: Data from reproduction histories collected in a medical genetics unit. *Human Genetics, 16,* 1–25.

West, D. J., and Farrington, D. P. (1977). *The delinquent way of life.* New York: Crane Russak

Wray, J. D. (1971). *Population pressure on families: Family size and child spacing.* Reports on Population, No. 9. New York: Population Council.

Wray, J. D., and Aguirre, A. (1969). Protein-caloric malnutrition (PCM) in Candeloria, Columbia. I. Prevalence, social and geographic causal factors. *Journal of Tropical Pediatrics, 14,* 76–90.

Zajone, R. R. (1976). Family configuration and intelligence, *Science, 192,* 227–236.

Zimmerman, M. K., and Hartley, W. S. (1982). High blood pressure among employed women: A multifactor discriminant analysis. *Journal of Health and Social Behavior, 23,* 205–220.

PART II

COMMUNICATION

INTRODUCTION

The readings in this part of the book involve various types of communications, from how language is used in spoken and written forms (including laws and mass media), to the ways communications are used to socialize children into society, to the formal modes of education. Although you and I speak and write in the first person singular, language itself is intrinsically sociocultural; it is our inheritance from our ancestors and contemporaries; it is our gift to our progeny through which we transmit the wisdom or the follies of our experience so that they may benefit appropriately. Language is also an end unto itself; songs soothe the savage breast, poems and puns amuse and amaze, and gossip greases the gears of the social machine.

Let us then understand and praise communication, but understanding comes first. Paula Englander-Golden, Joan Elconin, and Virginia Satir describe their studies with middle school–aged children who are facing the dilemmas of saying "no" to alcohol or drugs while maintaining their friendships in the face of peer pressure. The lessons they learn are applicable to the entire range of social communications.

Sandra H. Fradd introduces the complex topic of bilingual education. In spite of being a society composed historically of many diverse peoples, Americans have usually imposed English (that is to say, American-English) as the one standard language for everyone as a means of unifying the nation. When a significant proportion of people were not being well-integrated by this means, some educators experimented with various forms of using the child's "mother tongue" (the language spoken at home) as a tool for teaching him or her the language of the dominant culture. Critics argue that this weakens rather than strengthens the ability to communicate in the dominant language, and thus imposes further handicaps on minorities. Fradd reports the experiences of other nations in dealing with this same issue.

Ronald M. Davis opens the window on a little-known aspect of mass communication that powerfully affects growth and development. Billions of dollars are silently being spent in advertising and marketing cigarettes, even though some 350,000 deaths are attributed to cigarette smoking each year as well as $65 billion dollars expended annually for smoking-related health costs and lost productivity. Particularly interesting are the directed advertising campaigns aimed at special targets like women, blacks, Hispanics, blue-collar workers, and children and adolescents. Such mass media communications are overwhelming bombardments as compared to the Surgeon General's warning messages on cigarette packages.

We next turn to a section on child rearing, which consists largely of verbal and nonverbal communications attempting to shape our offspring to fit into the modern world. But this contemporary society imposes many barriers to child rearing, as when both parents have to work outside the home in order to provide basic resources for surviving, or for a quality of life that comes from exercising native talents and being recompensed for that work. Dr. T. Berry Brazelton reviews some basic issues for working parents and their at-risk children. He offers some important suggestions for strengthening these family ties within the context where both parents are working. Brazelton also introduces the complex issue of the various forms that substitute care can take.

Elizabeth J. Susman, Penelope K. Trickett, Ronald J. Iannotti, Barbara E. Hollenbeck, and Carolyn Zahn-Waxler present a study on the child-rearing patterns that depressed, abusive, and normal mothers exhibit in the areas of discipline, the regulation of emotions, and how the task of separation from parent and development of an individual identity was carried out. Some important patterns emerged that differentiated these three groups.

It is not the family alone that influences the education of the nation's children. Howard V. Hayghe points out in his paper that employers have some part to play in child care when both parents (or a single parent) work (works). Whether or not employers are in fact fulfilling a substantial role in child care for working parents is an important question, as increasing numbers of mothers join the work force.

A third section of this part concerns formal education. Lawrence J. Schweinhart and David P.

Weikart review early childhood development programs, including their own highly acclaimed High/Scope Foundation's Perry Preschool Project, and conclude that early educational programs may help prevent children's later failure in schools, drop out, and the vicious cycle of welfare dependence. However, they point out that only high-quality programs are successful; there is no free lunch anywhere in society. Schweinhart and Weikart describe some basic characteristics of these high-quality programs.

José Cárdenas and Joan McCarty First consider children at risk, particularly those who are disadvantaged because of race, class, cultural and sexual discrimination. As we shortchange these minority groups in the name of short-run economies, we actually shortchange the nation as these children become adults with less-than-useful skills in an increasingly complex society. Likewise, there are problems in the way we label and educate "handicapped students," which include misusing standardized achievement tests. All of these public discussions and decisions communicate social values that affect the self-esteem of individuals and the well-being of society, now and in the future.

One-parent families have grown in significant numbers in the last several decades due to changes in patterns of divorce as well as parenthood without marriage. This pattern has become a major challenge for educators as well as welfare officials. Oliver Moles reviews the school performance of children from one-parent families, and the planning needed to provide social services for these people. Children of one-parent families tend to have lower school performance (especially grades, achievement scores, and attendance records), but this is more often due to the family's socioeconomic status than from the mere absence of the father.

Overall, we communicate in many ways. We make children social and civil through our formal and informal communications. Or else we fail to do so. We encourage children to make healthy decisions with regard to the challenges of everyday life, from cigarettes to drugs to unsafe sexuality. Or else we fail to do so. We provide children with the healthy loving environments in which they may grow to maturity. Or else we fail to do so. In these failings, we not only fail our children; we fail ourselves and our society.

PART II

A. Language

4

ASSERTIVE/LEVELING COMMUNICATION AND EMPATHY IN ADOLESCENT DRUG ABUSE PREVENTION

Paula Englander-Golden
Institute for Studies in Addictions
University of North Texas

Joan Elconin
Virginia Satir

Assertiveness training techniques are part of many school-based programs designed to prevent the onset of smoking or alcohol/drug abuse among adolescents (Botvin and Eng, 1982; Englander-Golden, Elconin, and Miller, 1985; Evans, Rozelle, Maxwell, Raines, Dill, and Guthrie, 1981; Evans, Rozelle, Mittelmark, Hansen, Bane, and Havis, 1978; Horan and Williams, 1982; Hurd, Johnson, Pechacek, Bast, Jacobs, and Luepker, 1980; McAlister, Perry, Killen, Slinkard, and Maccoby, 1980; McAlister, Perry and Maccoby, 1979; Perry, Killen and Slinkard, 1980). Satir's clinical observations suggest that youngsters prefer strategies which enhance their self-esteem and elicit respect from their peers. Since youngsters may find themselves saying "yes" when their feelings tell them to say "no," it is important to allow them to explore such conflicts. This opportunity is provided in the SAY IT STRAIGHT (SIS) training program described in Englander-Golden et al., 1985; 1986. Through role playing and guided imagery youngsters learn to recognize explicitly the ways they respond in different interactions, as well as the feelings which accompany these responses. They explore feelings which emerge when they use various communication styles to role play saying "yes," saying "no," saying "I have quit," and talking to a friend about whose behavior they are concerned. Finally, they receive feedback from their peers concerning their effectiveness. Thus, saying "no" to an offer of drugs could be role-played in the following ways: "I don't want it; if I get caught my parents will kill me," or "No. I'm hungry. Let's go eat," or "That's stupid, you jerk!" Intervention with a friend might be explored as: "This is killing you. Don't be stupid," "Don't you have anything better to do?" "If I had your troubles I'd do it too," or "We are friends. I care about you and it scares me to see what you are doing," or "I'll stick by you, let's go to the counselor." Although the focus of SIS training is drug abuse prevention, youngsters are allowed to explore other situations which are salient to them. Satir's body sculpting techniques (Satir, 1972) are used to maximize the experience and expression of feelings associated with the different communication styles.

Rather than telling youngsters the most effective means of communicating, SIS training gives them the opportunity to discover this for themselves in their own interactions. The success of this approach is reflected in the significantly lower frequency of alcohol/drug related school suspensions incurred during the 1983–84 school year by the 1,564 6th–9th graders who have been trained since September of 1982 as compared to the 1,295 remaining 6th–9th graders in the same city who did not receive this training. A detailed description of SIS training methodology along with behavioral and attitudinal effects is provided in Englander-Golden et al., 1985; 1986. The present paper reports the feelings surfaced by the 5th–8th graders who participated in SIS training described in Englander-Golden, et al., 1986.

The results reported in this paper are based on feedback from 5th–8th graders who participated in SIS training in 1983–84. This information, collected on the last day of training, concerned how it felt to be the sender and receiver of the following communication styles: passive/placating (we don't stand up for ourselves, we feel we are nothing without the other person's approval); aggressive/blaming (we push others around, we ridicule, threaten or blame); super-reasonable (we lecture without ever expressing

From the *Journal of Primary Prevention*, 1986, 6 (4): 231–243. Copyright © 1986. Human Sciences Press. Reprinted by permission.

our feelings); irrelevant (we discount ourselves by not sticking to the issue, we distract or change the subject), and assertive/leveling (we respect our rights and the rights of others, we honestly express our thoughts and feelings rather than only telling others what we think they feel). The hybrid terminology used to define these communication styles reflects the pooling of concepts from assertiveness training (Lange and Jakubowski, 1978) and Satir's communication work (Satir, 1972; Satir, 1976).

In SIS training, the expression "positive peer pressure" describes an intervention with a friend in which assertive/leveling communication is used to express friendship, concern, support and a gentle yet firm request that the friend seek help. This positive use of peer pressure gives youngsters the opportunity to develop empathy, to discover its effects, and to compare such effects with those of blaming, lecturing, or never taking the risk of addressing the problem. By assuming both the role of the intervener and the friend with the problem, youngsters develop out of their own experience an understanding of the other person's perspective. These role plays also provide youngsters with the opportunity to respond to each other affectively. The development of empathy is most directly addressed within positive peer pressure role plays, and is reinforced through further exploration and dialogues in other role plays. In all role plays youngsters are given the opportunity to exchange roles, so that they experience and express feelings from different vantage points. Thus, youngsters develop the capacities to identify another's emotional state, to assume the other's perspective, and to respond affectively, the three components Feshbach conceptualized as making up the experience of empathy (Feshbach, 1983).

Results reported here underscore the importance of empathy training for young people and indicate that assertive/leveling communication is the style most frequently associated with high self-esteem, respect from others, and greatest effectiveness. These results are congruent with Satir's communication work (Satir, 1972; Satir, 1976), as well as the Johnson Institute's highly successful model of intervention with chemically dependent people (Johnson, 1980). Within this model, significant others (family members, employers, friends, etc.) of the chemically dependent person express their deep concern in a non-judgemental fashion, sticking to specific incidents with the goal of getting the person to treatment.

METHOD

SUBJECTS

The subjects were the same 5th–8th graders described in Englander-Golden, et al., 1986 as school A. The information reported here was obtained from youngsters who were present on the last day of training and who were members of classes in which feedback was collected on all communication styles. Thus, subjects include 65 eighth graders, 118 seventh graders, 95 sixth graders, and 71 fifth graders.

PROCEDURE

During the last session of SIS training youngsters were asked how they felt when they were senders or receivers of passive/placating, aggressive/blaming, irrelevant, super-reasonable and assertive/leveling communication, either in role plays in which they had just participated or in real life. They were also asked what was most effective in talking to a friend about whose behavior they were concerned. This feedback was collected in 5 groups of 8th graders (N = 65), 7 groups of 7th graders (N = 118), 6 groups of 6th graders (N = 95) and 3 groups of 5th graders (N = 71). When students used different labels to describe similar feelings, such as "weak" and "not so strong," both were recorded on the chalkboard. However, each descriptive label was recorded only once, regardless of how many students endorsed it in a particular group. This method of data collection was made necessary by time constraints in the classroom.

Following are examples of the communication styles which were processed:

PASSIVE/PLACATING COMMUNICATION

Mary: Want to smoke a joint after school?
Susan: No, we might get caught.
Mary: Don't worry. I know a place, no one will see us.
Susan: If my parents find out, they'll kill me.
Mary: Don't be a baby! I do it all the time and I haven't been caught.
Susan: Oh, all right.

The above is an illustration of role plays developed by youngsters in which their passive/placating attempt to say "no" became increasingly difficult or failed completely.

AGGRESSIVE/BLAMING COMMUNICATION

Sam: Here, Bart, take one of these. The team is counting on you tonight.

Bart: What are you trying to do, mess me up?

Sam: What's the matter, are you chicken?

Bart: Watch who you're calling chicken, junkie!

Sam: You couldn't complete a pass to save your life . . .

IRRELEVANT COMMUNICATION

Margaret: Tom, come to my house and we'll sneak my parents' beer.

Tom: Did you see that new show last night?

Margaret: Yes. Are you going to come over?

Tom: Man, that science test was rough!

Margaret: Answer me! Are you coming over or not?

Tom: Let's go get a coke.

Margaret: Are you deaf or just stupid? Forget it!

SUPER-REASONABLE COMMUNICATION

George: Want to get high?

Ralph: No, thanks. Did you know smoking causes cancer in laboratory rats?

George: Who cares? I'm not a rat.

Ralph: That could seriously injure your health, and the penalties if you get caught are very severe. You shouldn't . . .

George: What are you, the encyclopedia? Get lost!

ASSERTIVE/LEVELING COMMUNICATION

Louise: Janet, come drink this with me.

Janet: No, I don't want it.

Louise: Please, you're my best friend. I've done lots of things for you.

Janet: I don't want it (and walks away).

POSITIVE PEER PRESSURE

Bret: Hi, Bill. We want to talk to you.

Mike: We're worried about your drinking.

Bill: Leave me alone. It's none of your business.

Bret: You keep falling asleep in class and you threw up yesterday.

Mike: We're your friends and we want to help.

Bill: I'm fine. I'll see you later.

Bret: Wait. Come see the counselor. We'll stick by you (gently takes Bill's arm).

Bill: O.K.

Often, a role play which is initially an assertive/leveling "no" to an offer of alcohol or other drugs becomes a positive peer pressure role play. For example, in the previous illustration of assertive/leveling communication, Janet's response might have been "I don't want it and it scares me to see what you are doing. You're my best friend."

[Editor's Note: The authors present five tables in the original paper containing examples of feelings reported by senders and receivers of five types of communications—passive/placating, aggressive/blaming, irrelevant, super-reasonable, and assertive. These five tables are omitted in this version, but the sixth table included here summarizes the most and the least effective ways mentioned by these youngsters to talk to a friend about whose behavior they are concerned. This information is presented by grade, and the numbers in parentheses indicate the number of groups in which the specific statement was made.]

DISCUSSION

The results reported here open up conceptual issues relevant to assertiveness training and alcohol/drug abuse prevention programs. Although the definition of assertiveness (Lange and Jakubowski, 1978) is comparable to Satir's leveling (Satir, 1972; Satir, 1976), in practice there are at least two major differences. First, as has been recognized, some assertiveness trainers advocate the use of countermanipulations as part of being assertive (Lange and Jakubowski, 1978). This is never the case with leveling. Second, in assertiveness training people are often taught to express what they think the other person feels rather than revealing their own feelings, whereas the hallmark of leveling is the expression of one's own feelings (Satir, 1976). As assertiveness is meant to convey a feeling of respect for the other person as well as for oneself, perhaps the best way to discover whether a communication is assertive or countermanipulative is to discover its effect on the sender and the receiver.

The results reported here indicate that changing the subject, which is taught as an assertive strategy in some adolescent substance abuse prevention programs (Resnik, 1983; National Institute on Drug Abuse, 1983), elicited overwhelmingly angry and frustrated feelings in the receiver and feelings of being pressured, scared and stupid in the sender. Although in the previously mentioned example of irrelevant communication the subject may have been changed more times than is taught in adolescent substance abuse prevention programs, it is clear that caution must be exercised in training youngsters to respond in this manner.

TABLE 6. Reported Most and Least Effective Ways to Intervene with a Friend, by Grade

8th Grade Most Effective: showing caring (4), touch (3), concern (2), saying you'll stick with them (2), straight talk, being nonjudgmental, persistence, friendly force, eye contact, logical reasons, being assertive/leveling, friendship, being at same level

8th Grade Least Effective: blaming (3), yelling (3), putting them down, lectures, being super-reasonable, anger, being irrelevant, name calling, saying "I heard...", talking about self, forcing, not giving a choice, giving logical reasons, saying "you've got a problem"

7th Grade Most Effective: friendship (6), touch (5), express caring (4), concern (3), be at eye level (2), trusting, respect, low voice, trying to find out what the problem is, not denying the problem, offering to go with them, expressing feelings, being reasonable about alternatives, empathy, sincerity

7th Grade Least Effective: name calling (5), forcing (3), not showing concern, hard touch, towering over, standing high above, not enough friends, making them feel dumb, putting them down, being aggressive, ignoring, lecturing, being irrelevant, ridiculing, blaming, saying that others know

6th Grade Most Effective: express caring/concern (5), touch (3), saying you'll stick with them (3), friendship (2), stating facts, expressing feelings, being helpful, being assertive, express worry, want them to feel better

6th Grade Least Effective: blaming (4), yelling (2), ridicule (2), being super-reasonable, lecturing, hitting, pushing, arguing, guilting, anger, aggression, trying to control, saying "go get help"

5th Grade Most Effective: show caring (2), touch (2), respect (2), friendship (2), show concern, be on eye level, honesty, trusting feelings, being nice, being close, caring voice

5th Grade Least Effective: blaming (2), ordering, jerking, ridiculing, forcing, backing off, being above them, telling on them, threatening, screaming, not expressing feelings, saying "you need..."

A similar note of caution is relevant when training youngsters in the strategy of giving excuses (Fairfax County School Board Department of Student Services and Special Education, 1983). In SIS training this strategy can be labeled as passive/placating when the reasons given are such as "we will get caught," "my parents will kill me," "I have to do chores," or "I have a lot of homework to do"; or as super-reasonable when reasons given are such as "this is not good for you," "this is dangerous," "this can give you cancer," etc. Passive/placating communication results in feelings of powerlessness and low self-esteem in the sender. In our experience with over 1,500 youngsters, saying "no" in a passive/placating manner was almost invariably followed by further pressure. The youngster who originally said "no" almost always finished by saying "yes." Youngsters who said "no" in a super-reasonable way elicited so much anger from the recipients of such communication that these role plays ended very much like the ones which illustrated aggressive/blaming communication, i.e., in name calling. The speed with which super-reasonable role plays changed into aggressive/blaming ones reminded us of Satir's observation that the "teaching finger" is closely related and easily confused with the "blaming finger." In contrast, youngsters who were assertive/leveling were not only effective in refusing, they also reported feeling good and feeling high self-respect. Receivers of assertive/leveling communication, although they reported feeling anger, also felt respect for the sender and an understanding that the anger might be short-lived. Indeed, eighth graders mentioned feelings of acceptance and nonviolence.

The possibility of underlying developmental changes in moral reasoning (Rest, 1973; Kohlberg, 1964) and empathy (Hoffman, 1975) are suggested by differential self-reports of guilt and positive peer pressure behaviors as a function of grade. Sixth through eighth grade pushers reported feeling guilty when receiving a passive/placating response. Fifth graders did not. Furthermore, although all youngsters discovered they were most effective in convincing a friend to seek help when they showed caring and friendship and used touch, fifth graders had much more difficulty in producing such behaviors. Although most youngsters required some verbal coaching to eliminate blaming, lecturing and irrelevancy, these were the only youngsters who consistently required trainer modeling of positive peer pressure. The main concern they expressed was with the illegality of substance use and the consequent punishment. In one instance in which the trainer did not model, the intervention was not effective. When asked why he did not respond to the request to seek help, the fifth grader answered "I did not feel cared for." Thus, even though fifth graders did not spontaneously produce the behaviors which are defined as positive peer pressure, their responses were the same as the older students' when they were the objects of such interventions. This indicates that they understood the meaning of such behaviors even though these were not yet part of their spontaneous repertoire. The effectiveness of training youngsters in straightforward communication and empathy is reflected in the significantly lower incidence of "users" among trained youngsters as reported in the preceding paper and in the paper by Englander-Golden et al. (1985). It is further demonstrated by school counselor reports that self-referrals increase not only among trained youngsters, but also among their siblings (S. Barker, personal communication, 1984).

As mentioned previously, due to time constraints, youngsters' responses were recorded only once per group. Although this is an obvious limitation, the information obtained from the youngsters is of great importance to the conceptual framework of prevention programs for adolescents, as well as for empathy training programs. In future research the frequency of occurrence of responses for all youngsters will have to be recorded. Such data will reveal more accurately the prevalence of responses reported in this paper as a function of communication.

References

Barker, S. (1984). Personal Communication.

Botvin, G. J. and Eng, A. (1982). The efficacy of a multicomponent approach to the prevention of cigarette smoking. *Preventive Medicine, 11,* 199–211.

Drugs and You (1983). Department of Student Services and Special Education, County School Board of Fairfax County.

Englander-Golden, P., Elconin, J., and Miller, K. J. (1985). SAY IT STRAIGHT: Adolescent substance abuse prevention training. *Academic Psychology Bulletin, 7,* 65–79.

Englander-Golden, P., Elconin, J., Miller, K. J., and Schwarzkopf, A. B. (1986). Brief SAY IT STRAIGHT training and follow-up in adolescent substance abuse prevention. *Journal of Primary Prevention, 6,* 219–230.

Evans, R. I., Rozelle, R. M., Maxwell, S. E., Raines, B. E., Dill, C. A., and Guthrie, T. J. (1981). Social modeling films to deter smoking in adolescents: Results of a three-year field investigation. *Journal of Applied Psychology, 66,* 399–414.

Evans, R. I., Rozelle, R. M., Mittlemark, M. B., Hansen, W. B., Bane, A. L., and Havis, J. (1978). Deterring the onset of smoking in children: Knowledge of immediate physiological effects and coping with peer pressure, media pressure, and parent modeling. *Journal of Applied Social Psychology, 8,* 126–135.

Feshbach, N. D. (1983). Learning to care: A positive approach to child training and discipline. *Journal of Clinical Child Psychology, 12,* 266–271.

Hoffman, M. L. (1975). Developmental synthesis of affect and cognition and its implications for altruistic motivation. *Developmental Psychology, 11,* 607–622.

Horan, J. J., and Williams, J. M. (1982). Longitudinal study of assertion training as a drug abuse prevention strategy. *American Educational Research Journal, 19,* 341–351.

Hurd, P. D., Johnson, C. A., Pechacek, T., Bast, L. P., Jacobs, D. R., and Luepker, R. V. (1980). Prevention of cigarette smoking in seventh grade students. *Journal of Behavioral Medicine, 3,* 15–28.

Johnson, V. (1980). *I'll Quit Tomorrow.* CA: Harper & Row.

Kohlberg, L. (1964). The development of moral character and ideology. In M. Hoffman (ed.), *Review of child psychology.* New York: Russell Sage Foundation.

Lange, A. J. & Jakubowski, P. (1978). *Responsible assertive behavior.* IL: Research Press.

McAlister, A., Perry, C., Killen, J., Slinkard, L. A., and Maccoby, N. (1980). Pilot study of smoking, alcohol, and drug abuse prevention. *American Journal of Public Health, 70,* 719–721.

McAlister, A. L., Perry, C., and Maccoby, N. (1979). Adolescent smoking: Onset and prevention. *Pediatrics, 63,* 650–658.

Peer pressure: It's OK to say no. (1983). National Institute on Drug Abuse, DHHS Publication No. (ADM) 83-1271.

Perry, C. L., Killen, J., and Slinkard, L. A. (1980). Peer teaching and smoking prevention among junior high students. *Adolescence, 15,* 277–281.

Resnik, H. (1983). Saying no programs. Prepared for the Prevention Branch, Division of Prevention and Technology Transfer, National Institute on Drug Abuse.

Rest, J. R. (1973). The hierarchical nature of moral judgement: A study of patterns of comprehension and preference of moral stages. *Journal of Personality, 41,* 86–109.

Satir, V. (1972). *Peoplemaking.* CA: Science and Behavior Books, Inc.

Satir, V. (1976). *Making Contact.* CA: Celestial Arts.

5

GOVERNMENTAL POLICY AND SECOND LANGUAGE LEARNING

Sandra H. Fradd
Bilingual Multicultural Education Program
University of Florida

Over past several years the public has heard much about educational excellence.[1] At the same time educators have become aware of the special learning needs of the growing number of minority language students. In the desired educational renaissance, goals of universal quality education cannot be realized unless language minorities are included in the overall master plan for educational improvement.[2] Data from a variety of sources indicate that populations of limited English proficient (LEP) students in the United States are expanding at a faster rate than the English speaking majority.[3] Both higher fertility rates and immigration patterns have produced a continuous increase in the number of children whose first language is not English. The overall numbers of children in need of special language instruction appear to have been largely underestimated by the 1980 Census.[4] Limited English proficient children are found in every state in the country. Fourteen states have over 50,000 LEP students each, while six (Texas, California, New York, Florida, Illinois, and New Jersey) have more than 200,000 each. These estimates include children who speak only English at home but whose parents and other household members speak a language other than English. By the year 2000 the non-English language background population in the United States is projected to increase from the 1976 base year measurement of 28 million to 39.5 million.[5]

Although language learning and maintenance may appear to be a straightforward matter of ethnic origin and environmental experience, the simplicity of this perception is belied by a complex set of political and social forces. For example, in the U.S. since the civil rights movement of the 1960s, various ethnic groups have viewed language education as the vehicle by which to obtain economic parity with those living within the mainstream cultural and economic system.[6] As a result of this movement and other political and economic factors, the second language acquisition, or bilingual education, policy has been primarily compensatory, designed to enable disadvantaged groups to gain educational and economic advantages. While seeking to remedy the plight of minority language populations, legislation and political attitude have fostered a series of related learning problems. Contrasting U.S. bilingual or minority language education policy with those of other countries provides a means for understanding the effects of divergent bilingual language policies on children's language acquisition and on academic learning. The following analysis of the influence of governmental policies on language acquisition highlights the fact that historical traditions as well as economic and social expectations have influenced governmental policy and hence educational outcomes.

U.S. BILINGUAL EDUCATION POLICY

The bilingual education policy in the United States, by legislative definition, has focused almost exclusively on educating children for whom English is not the first language, that is, minority language children.[7] These children are provided English as a second language, and in some states instruction in their first language, until they acquire sufficient English to be transitioned into regular, monolingual classrooms. After this transition is made, rarely is any further consideration given to the continued development or maintenance of the first language. At the school level the use of the first language is often viewed as detrimental to academic achievement and social integration.[8] Parents of language minority children are sometimes advised to stop speaking to their children in the first language.[9]

Governmental funding of special programs for children who enter school with little English has resulted in public backlash against bilingual education.

From *The Educational Forum*, 1985, *49*(4): 431—443. Reprinted by permission.

This sentiment has been fanned by inflammatory media presentations. Such as pronouncements as " . . . the anti-assimilationist theory has become accepted practice—Miami's youth can take 12 years of bilingual public schooling with no pretense made that the program is transitional toward anything,"[10] exemplify the concern which many citizens feel toward bilingual education.[11] Combined with concern for social fragmentation and political unrest are fears of emotional instability and other nonspecific learning disabilities.[12]

SUBTRACTIVE LEARNING.

Research indicates that it is not the use of two languages that causes emotional and educational problems, but the social and economic perceptions of the language users which are at the root of the difficulties.[13] Transitional bilingual education results in the acquisition of a second language and often the eventual loss of the first language. As the second language is acquired, the first language is less frequently used. This can be seen as the subtraction of the first language and its replacement with the second, hence the term *subtractive bilingualism*.[14]

For some children a balancing of the two languages occurs, namely, increased competence in the second language with decreased competence in the first.[15] The subtractive process may result in mastery of neither language.[16] The term, *semilingualism*, or the lack of native proficiency in any language, has been applied to this type of bilingualism.[17] The detrimental consequences of such lack of linguistic development are obviously related to academic progress in school, as well as to general cognitive development and social acceptance. Children who speak only English but whose home language is not English may be classified as semilingual and in need of special language instruction. Their spoken language, English, may not be sufficiently native-like or well-developed to enable them to benefit from regular classroom instruction in English.[18] The difficulties of semilingualism, or lack of native proficiency within appropriate age expectations, is not confined to the United States. In many industrialized countries where immigration and migration have produced populations that do not speak the language of the host or majority group, evidence of this problem exists.[19]

LANGUAGE LEARNING IN OTHER COUNTRIES

Language shelter programs have been established in Scandinavian countries to alleviate learning problems. Although the use of the first language combined with the promotion of the second may appear to be similar to the initial aspects of transitional bilingual programs of the United States, the goals and assumptions of the Scandinavian programs are quite different.[20] Conceptual development is promoted in both languages, and personal identity is reinforced through use of the first. Consequently children acquire and maintain both languages.[21]

A variation of the language shelter program is found in the second language programs in some parts of Australia. Parallel multimedia instructional modules are prepared in both English and the community languages. Learners have the option of selecting instruction in either or both languages. This type of instruction has proven to be successful with both aborigines and immigrant children.[22]

There are a number of inherent problems which exist in providing literacy instruction to populations of immigrant or transient people, as evidenced by programs for the educationally disadvantaged in Germany.[23] The language learning needs of immigrants can be categorized in three groups, each requiring different instructional approaches. Those who arrive after several years of successful schooling and literacy instruction in their first language make the transition to German literacy most easily. The second group, those who arrive as preschoolers, may acquire a bicultural perspective. Some, however, do not ever make the transition to German and do not succeed in school. The third group arrive as babies or are born in Germany. As they develop, German becomes their first language. These young people serve as interpreters for their families and make the shift toward assimilation within the German economic and social systems. Children from the later two groups are at high risk of semilingualism.

In many cases these children must acquire three languages in order to become literate in the majority language. First, they master the oral language of the home. As a result of language shift, the influence of the second language and culture, the home language becomes different from the standard version. Children often encounter difficulty learning to read and write the home language because of the disparity between the home and the standard version. When presented with the majority language, they are in effect learning three languages. The language learning problems immigrants encounter in German schools are not unlike those of immigrants in the U.S. educational system. Intuition would dictate that direct instruction in the majority language would be the most appropriate approach. However, research from all over the world indicates that literacy skills in the home language facilitate literacy acquisition in other languages.[24]

Language shift is also related to sociocultural and economic differences at the community level. When children see that the majority language is the language of prestige and power, they are often reluctant to be identified with the language of the minority group.[25] This reluctance in effect cuts them off from both cognitive and cultural advantages advanced through the maintenance of the home language and the acquisition of the second.[26]

CANADIAN BILINGUAL EDUCATION POLICY

Canadian bilingual education policy encourages English-speaking children (Anglophones) to become French-speaking (Francophones). Encouragement of bilingualism at the national level does not end with public education. Since 1971 bilingualism has been accepted as a national heritage. It is viewed as a criterion for promotion within federal civil service and considered an asset in private sector employment as well.[27] Bilingual education in Canada has been successful. One of the best indicators of success is the continued increase in bilingual program enrollments in spite of a decline in general school enrollment. In fact, successful bilingual programs suffer from other problems such as overcrowding, lack of adequate staffing, and difficulties in providing transportation for all who wish to participate.[28]

The primary factor promoting bilingual education in Canada is economic. Parents believe that by obtaining bilingual literacy, their children will have increased options within the labor market.[29] Promotion of biculturalism and national unity are secondary factors that motivate second language acquisition.[30] Bilingualism in Canada may also promote a type of elitism not observed in the United States.[31]

ADDITIVE LEARNING.

In contrast to the U.S. policy, the notion of *additive* bilingualism is often associated with Canadian language education policy.[32] Research indicates that, in this form, children can acquire a second language without detrimental effects. Until the early 1960s, however, most studies comparing bilingual and monolingual children found in favor of the monolinguals and documented problems of mental confusion, linguistic handicaps, and emotional instability for bilinguals.[33] Frequently the participants in these studies were children of immigrant or guest workers and were experiencing subtractive bilingualism.

Peal and Lambert[34] were among the first researchers to document the cognitive advantages of being bilingual. They compared English-French bilinguals in Montreal with both English and French monolinguals there. Their findings initiated an increased interest in research associating the acquisition of two languages with a variety of cognitive advantages. Although the more recent work has controlled for factors such as age of acquisition, IQ, socioeconomic level, which were not always considered in earlier research, these positive findings are still open to question because of the obvious difficulties in comparing two unequal populations.[35] In any case, the favorable results reported have been instrumental in encouraging Canadian parents to request bilingual education for all children. Large-scale immersion programs have been initiated to teach kindergarten and first-grade Anglophones to function entirely in French. The term, *immersion,* is applied because the children are completely surrounded by French for the entire school day. Native Francophones, fluent in English, are used in these programs. Although all interactions between the teachers and students are in French, the teacher can address specific student needs in English, should such needs arise. Other forms of immersion in the later grades have also been developed, and these have proven to be successful as well. After children acquire literacy in the second language, in this case French, literacy skills are introduced in the first language (English). By sixth grade, immersion students are performing as well as their monolingual counterparts in both English and French as measured by nationally normed tests.[36] They have effectively added a second language without losing the first.

COMPARISONS BETWEEN THE CANADIAN AND U.S. PROGRAMS

Comparisons between the Canadian and U.S. bilingual programs reveal that the language policies established within the two countries were designed to meet historically different needs. In Canada, the rights of both the French minority and English majority are guaranteed. All ethnic groups are encouraged to continue to maintain their cultural heritage.[37] Quite the opposite is true in the United States; English has consistently been affirmed to be the only language. In Canada, economically advantaged children have largely been the participants in the second language immersion programs; in the U.S. economically disadvantaged immigrant children have been the focus of transitional bilingual efforts.

Neither policy is viewed here as being intrinsically superior, since each has produced certain limitations in terms of available resource allocations. Table 1 compares the characteristics of the two types of bilingual education.

After two to three years of first language instruction, LEP students in the United States are transitioned into regular school programs. After about the same time period in Canada, students immersed in French begin literacy instruction in English. It was Canadian parents who initiated immersion programs, while U.S. bilingual programs have a parent participation, and sometimes a parent training, component to stimulate parental involvement. The Canadian programs are viewed as forms of educational enrichment and confer an advantaged status; U.S. bilingual education is conceptualized as a remedial program for children who are disadvan-

taged. Canadian programs include a large proportion of children from upper and middle classes, but U.S. programs are primarily for low socioeconomic groups. In the United States, first language literacy instruction stops after the second language is learned, while it continues in both languages in Canada. In Canada the second language is added while the first language is maintained—in the U.S. the second language is acquired while the first language is lost. In Canada bilingualism is viewed positively; here bilingualism is not seen as an advantage; rather as a disadvantage.

While both Canada and the United States are nations of immigrants, the migration patterns of the two countries have also been different. Canada has not been faced with the extensive immigration which the U.S. has experienced over the past three decades,[38] and until recently children of immigrants

TABLE 1. Comparison of Canadian Immersion and U.S. Transitional Bilingual Education Programs

Canada	United States

Public Perspective
  a) Programs provide enrichment
  b) Bilingualism is advantageous
	Public Perspective
	  a) Programs are remedial
	  b) Bilingualism has no advantage, may be viewed by some as negative

Parental Status
  a) Socioeconomic level is generally middle to high
  b) Parents initiate programs, and are highly motivated
	Parental Status
	  a) Socioeconomic level is generally low
	  b) Parental component requires parent participation as part of federal funding

Program Components
  a) Students expected to learn two languages
  b) All students begin at same level
  c) Literacy is emphasized in second language first
  d) Literacy in first language is emphasized and continues to develop
	Program Components
	  a) Students study home language until second language is learned
	  b) LEP students expected to perform at same level as native speakers
	  c) Literacy is emphasized in second language
	  d) Literacy in first language is emphasized only until second language is acquired

Outcome
  a) First language maintained while second language is added
	Outcome
	  a) Second language added, first language not usually maintained, may be lost

in Canada as a whole achieved at or above national norms.[39] Not all Canadian educators or politicians are in accord, but a policy of maintaining ethnic identity still remains the official government position. Both federal and provincial policy toward heritage language instruction acknowledges, either implicitly or explicitly, the value of Canada's ethnic and linguistic resources. In some sections of Canada heritage language programs (i.e., first language instruction in languages other than English or French) have been enthusiastically accepted. In other areas this policy has been the focus of acrimonious debate. Some Canadian bilingual programs use a transitional model similar to the one used in the United States. Most bilingual education is based on the maintenance and enrichment models for the acquisition and maintenance of both the first language and English. In contrast, the notion of language and culture maintenance is anathema to many educators and policy makers in the U.S.[40]

LINGUISTIC INTERDEPENDENCE

Haste in placing students in instructional programs where English is the only language may be detrimental to the mastery of English as well as academic achievement.[41] An intuitively reasonable argument can be made that if students are to master English, they need intensive instruction exclusively in English. This argument implies that competence in two different languages is based on separate underlying proficiencies, but research indicates that a common underlying proficiency exists among all languages.[42] Language learning environments that promote additive second language learning build on this underlying factor, and instruction in the second language combined with that in the first maximizes cognitive and linguistic skills in both languages. That is to say, competence in the first language is significantly correlated with acquisition in the second.[43]

In conjunction with the theory of linguistic interdependence, Cummins[44] suggests that there are three thresholds of bilingual competence over which children may potentially, but do not necessarily, pass in the process of attaining linguistic competence. The first threshold is that of semilingualism. As previously stated, bilingual children whose linguistic development in at least one language does not progress at a rate equal to that considered appropriate for normal children are classified as semilingual. Semilinguals may be balanced, equally proficient in both languages, or they may have one language in

which they are dominant. However, if they are unable to express themselves with native-like proficiency in at least one of the languages, they may suffer from the cognitive deficiencies of semilingualism. The second threshold which children may pass is the attainment of native-like proficiency in at least one language. The child at this threshold may be in the process of adding or subtracting a language. The third threshold is passed when the child achieves balanced, native-like proficiency in both languages. Research indicates that children functioning in this range have specific intellectual advantages over their monolingual peers.[45]

The cognitive and academic advantages of acquiring and maintaining two languages is not always observed in early childhood. Thus, for example, Flores[46] found that students who were provided an additive environment in which to maintain Spanish skills while learning English performed at a higher level of achievement on English measures of reading than did students from the same socioeconomic levels who had English-only instruction. During elementary and junior high school, achievement scores for the two groups were equal. Not until the 11th grade did the students receiving instruction in Spanish and English as elementary students surpass their English-only instructed counterparts. The bilingually instructed group had maintained Spanish and was more proficient in both English and Spanish than was the English-only Hispanic group at the time both groups graduated from high school.

A variety of studies conducted within North America and other parts of the world indicate that creativity, mental flexibility, and greater skill in problem solving are associated with additive bilingualism.[47] Other studies find that bilingual children perform significantly better on tasks of concept formation that do their monolingual peers matched for age, socioeconomic level, and intelligence.[48] One explanation offered for this difference in achievement is that the bilingual child is exposed to a wider social experiences than is the monolingual child. The cognitive dissonance which the bilingual child experiences in different social and linguistic environments may encourage concept development and mental flexibility.[49]

While many industrialized countries view second language learning as an option that should be be available to most, if not potentially all, of the educated citizenry, the United States continues to be embroiled in controversy over the notion that speaking a language other than English is unpatriotic and unnecessary.[50] Perhaps the time has come to reconsider the implications of linguistic isolation. By denying limited English proficient children the opportunity to maintain their first language as they acquire English, educational policy makers may be increasing the possibility that many potentially bilingual children never realize their maximum intellectual development. By not offering second language programs to children for whom English is the first language, educational policy makers are also denying the language majority children an opportunity for increased cognitive growth and divergent thinking skills. Most important of all, bilingualism enhances the possibility for effective communication and cultural understanding with a larger population of the world's community. Perhaps educational policy makers should consider bilingual education as a curricular model for general education, rather than a remedial model for minority children.

References

1. George H. Gallup, "The 16th Annual Gallup Poll of the Public's Attitudes Toward the Public Schools," *Phi Delta Kappan* 66 (September 1984): 23–28.
2. Cathaleen Brawer, "Report to the Governor's Florida State Commission on Hispanic Affairs." Paper presented as Commission Testimony, October 24, 1984, Tallahassee, Florida.
3. Rebecca Oxford-Carpenter, Louis Pol, David Lopez, Paul Stupp, Murray Gendell, and Samuel Peng, *Demographic Projections of Non-English-Language-Background and Limited-English-Proficient Persons in the United States to the Year 2000 by State, Age, and Language Group.* (Rosslyn, Va.: Inter-America Research Associates, 1984).
4. National Clearinghouse for Bilingual Education, "Study Finds 3.6 Million School-age Children Are LEP," *Forum* (June/July 1979): 102; J. Michael O'Malley, *Children's English and Services Study, Language Minority Children with Limited English Proficiency in the United States* (Rosslyn, Va.: National Clearinghouse for Bilingual Education, 1984); Dorothy Waggoner, "The Need for Bilingual Education: Estimates from the 1980 Census," *Journal of the National Association for Bilingual Education* 8 (Winter 1984):1–14.
5. Waggoner, "The Need for Bilingual Education."
6. Henry T. Trueba, Grace P. Guthrie, and Katheryn H. Au, eds., *Culture and the Bilingual Classroom* (Rowley, Mass.: Newbury House Publishers, 1981); United States Commission on Civil Rights, *A Better Chance to Learn: Bilingual-Bicultural Education* (Publication 51) (Washington, D.C.: U.S. Government Printing Office, 1975).
7. U.S. Commission on Civil Rights, *A Better Chance to Learn.*
8. Clem Adelman, "Language, Culture and Bilingual Schooling—Reflections After a Case Study of a School," *Journal of Multilingual and Multicultural Development* 2 (No. 4 1981): 259–268.
9. Richard Rodriguez, *Hunger of Memory: The Education of Richard Rodriguez* (Boston: David R. Godine, 1982).
10. William A. Henry, "Against a Confusion of Tongues," *Time* (June 13, 1983): 30, 31.
11. K. Anderson, "The New Ellis Island," *Time* (June 13, 1983): 18–22, 24–25; M. Carrison, "Bilingual No!" *Principal* 62 (1983): 41–44; Henry, "Against a Confusion." Paul Simon, "Is America Tongue-tied?," *Academe: Bulletin of the American Association of University Professors* 69 (March/April 1983): 9–12; Rudolph Troike, "Bilingual Si!" *Principal* 62 (1983): 46–50.
12. Tove Skutnabb-Kangas, *Language in the Process of Cultural Assimilation and Structural Incorporation of Linguistic Minorities* (Rosslyn, Va.: National Clearinghouse for Bilingual Education, 1979).
13. James Cummins, "Empirical and Theoretical Underpinnings of Bilingual Education," *Journal of Education* 162 (Winter 1981): 16–29.
14. G. Richard Tucker, "Implications for U.S. Bilingual Education: Evidence from Canadian Research," *Focus* 2 (February 1980); 1–4.
15. James Macnamara, *Bilingualism and Primary Education* (Edinburgh: Edinburgh University Press, 1966).
16. Arturo Tosi, "Bilingual Education Problems and Practices," in *Bilingualism and Language Disability,* ed. Niklas Miller (San Diego College-Hill Press, 1984), 199–219.
17. Ibid. Also see footnote 45.
18. Waggoner, "The Need for Bilingual Education."
19. Tosi, "Bilingual Education Problems."
20. James Cummins, "The Language and Culture Issue in the Education of Minority Language Children," *Interchange* 10 (1979–80): 72–88.
21. Ibid.
22. Ibid.
23. Hans G. Lingens and Barbara Lingens, *Education in West Germany: A Quest for Excellence* (Bloomington, Ind.: Phi Delta Kappa, 1980).
24. Cummins, "The Language and Culture Issue," Sandra Fradd, "Reading Instruction for Non-English Speakers: When and How?," *Florida Reading Quarterly* 18 (June 1982): 35–37.
25. Carlos Sole, "Language Usage Patterns among a Young Generation of Cuban-Americans," in *A Festschrift for Jacob Ornstein,* eds. E. L. Blansitt and R. V. Teschner (Rowley, Mass.: Newbury House Publishers, 1980).

26. Niklas Miller, "Language Use in Bilingual Communities," in *Bilingualism and Language Disability,* ed. Niklas Miller (San Diego: College-Hill Press, 1984).

27. James Cummins, *Bilingualism and Special Education: Issues in Assessment and Pedagogy* (Avon, England: Multilingual Matters, 1984).

28. Paul Olson and George Burns, "Politics, Class and Happenstance: French Immersion in a Canadian Context," *Interchange* 14 (1983): 1–16.

29. Ibid.

30. Ibid.

31. Ibid.

32. Tucker, "Implications for U.S. Bilingual Education."

33. Natalie T. Darcy, "A Review of the Literature on the Effects of Bilingualism upon the Measurement of Intelligence," *Journal of Genetic Psychology* 82 (March 1953): 21–57.

34. Elizabeth Peal and William E. Lambert, "The Relationship of Bilingualism to Intelligence," *Psychological Monographs* 76 (1962): 546.

35. Grace L. MacNab, "Cognition and Bilingualism: A Reanalysis of Studies," *Linguistics* 17 (1979): 231–255.

36. Tucker, "Implications for U.S. Bilingual Education."

37. Cummins, *Bilingualism and Special Education.*

38. American Council for Nationalities Service, "Statistics," *Refugee Reports* 3 (November 1982): 25.

39. Cummins, *Bilingualism and Special Education.*

40. Ibid.

41. James Cummins, "The Entry and Exit Fallacy in Bilingual Education," *NABE Journal* 6 (Spring 1980): 25–59.

42. James Cummings, et al., "Linguistic Interdependence among Japanese and Vietnamese Immigrant Students," in *The Measurement of Communicative Proficiency: Models and Applications,* ed. Charlene Rivera (Washington, D.C.: Center for Applied Linguistics, 1982).

43. Sandra H. Fradd, "Language Acquisition of 1980 Cuban Immigrant Junior High School Students" (Doctoral dissertation, University of Florida, 1983).

44. James Cummins, *"The Cognitive Development of Bilingual Children: A Review of Recent Research"* (Eric Document No. 145 727, 1977).

45. Ibid. However, he has since taken the position that it is preferable to consider only the latter two thresholds (See Cummins, *Bilingualism and Special Education*). Semilingualism is a definable pedagogical construct. Many of us who work with bilingual children in the United States know children who appear to be without other handicapping conditions, but who have not developed written or oral proficiency within age-appropriate norms in either of their two languages. Cummins cautions against the application of the term *semilingual* with respect to these children because the label has been used as a pedagogical or psychological explanation for the child's failure to acquire native proficiency in at least one language. The term *semilingual* is used in this paper for purposes of research and planning rather than an explanation of behavior.

46. Dorothy J. Flores, "An Investigation on the Long-term Effects of Bilingual Education upon Achievement, Language Maintenance, and Attitudes" (Doctoral dissertation, University of Florida, 1981).

47. Dennis C. Carringer, "Creative Thinking Abilities of Mexican Youth," *Journal of Cross-cultural Psychology* 5 (December 1974): 492–503; Richard G. Landry, "A Comparison of Second Language Learners and Monolinguals on Divergent Thinking Tasks at the Elementary School Level," *Modern Language Journal* 13 (January/February 1974): 10–15; E. Paul Torrance et al., "Creative Functioning of Monolingual and Bilingual Children in Singapore," *Journal of Educational Psychology* 61 (February 1970): 72–75.

48. E.g., W. W. Liedke and L. D. Nelson, "Concept Formation and Bilingualism," *Alberta Journal of Educational Research* 14 (1968): 225–232.

49. Carringer, "Creative Thinking Abilities"; Cummins, "Cognitive Development"; Landry, "Comparison of Second Language Learners."

50. Andersen, "Ellis Island"; Henry, "Against a Confusion of Tongues"; Simon, "Is America Tongue-tied?"

6

CURRENT TRENDS IN CIGARETTE ADVERTISING AND MARKETING

Ronald M. Davis
Office on Smoking and Health
Center for Health Promotion and Education
Centers for Disease Control
Rockville, Maryland

According to the U.S. Surgeon General, cigarette smoking is "the chief, single avoidable cause of death in our society and the most important public health issue of our time."[1] Estimates of the effects of cigarette smoking on mortality in the United States range from approximately 270,000 deaths[2] to 485,000 deaths[3] per year. A middle estimate by the U.S. Public Health Service puts the toll at about 350,000 deaths per year,[1,4,5] or about one sixth of deaths from all causes. Smoking-related diseases annually account for an estimated $22 billion in health care costs and $43 billion in lost productivity.[6]

Because of the impact of smoking on the nation's health, the widespread promotion of tobacco products has come under intense scrutiny. On July 18 and August 1, 1986, the U.S. House of Representatives Committee on Energy and Commerce, Subcommittee on Health and the Environment, held hearings on tobacco advertising. More than 40 witnesses gave testimony, representing health organizations, the tobacco and advertising industries, and several other groups.

Federal legislation was introduced in the last Congress that would ban all tobacco-product advertising and promotion (H.R. 4972) or disallow the deduction of tobacco-product advertising costs as business expenses (H.R. 3950 and S. 1950). These bills have been reintroduced in the new Congress.

The purpose of this article is to analyze, from a public health perspective, current trends in cigarette advertising and marketing. The analysis focuses on the extent of cigarette advertising and on special themes and targets of advertising and promotional activities.

THE EFFECTS OF CIGARETTE ADVERTISING

The influence that cigarette advertising has on smoking behavior is a matter of current debate. Representatives of the tobacco and advertising industries maintain that the only purpose and effect of cigarette advertising is to promote brand loyalty and brand switching. Others believe that cigarette advertising may perpetuate or increase cigarette consumption by recruiting new smokers, inducing former smokers to relapse, making it more difficult for smokers to quit, and increasing the level of smokers' consumption by acting as an external cue to smoke. These effects may be exerted by direct or indirect means. Indirect mechanisms would include the influence of cigarette advertising revenues in discouraging media coverage of issues related to smoking and disease, and the possible effect of advertising, by its mere existence, in fostering the notion that smoking is socially acceptable or at least "not really all that bad." The evidence on this issue has been reviewed elsewhere,[7,8] and extensive testimony on the subject was presented at the recent Congressional hearings mentioned above.[9]

The possible effects of cigarette advertising on overall cigarette consumption could be attributed to the language and imagery used in cigarette advertisements, which tend to undermine the effectiveness of the Surgeon General's warnings. In its report to Congress for the year 1978, the Federal Trade Commission (FTC) noted that "some ads use language which directly contradicts the required health warning and scientific evidence that smoking is dangerous to health and perhaps to life itself. . . . A

From the *New England Journal of Medicine, 316* (March 19, 1987): 725–732. Copyright © 1987 by the Massachusetts Medical Society. Reprinted by permission.

number of campaigns imply that smoking a particular brand solves the health dilemma or at least minimizes the problem." The FTC drew attention to the advertising slogan, "Alive with pleasure," which is still in prominent use today.[10] The brand advertised by this slogan—Newport—is touted as "the fastest growing brand in America" in an industry trade journal.[11] (The use of trade names in this article is for identification only, and does not constitute endorsement by the Department of Health and Human Services or any of its agencies.) The Commission concluded that cigarette advertisements "may have the capacity to create misimpressions of the safety and desirability of smoking."[10]

A British study of cigarette sponsorship of televised sporting events provides evidence that promotional activities have effects similar to those of traditional print advertising.[12] Many of the promotional activities for cigarettes, such as distributing non-tobacco products bearing cigarette brand names, do not include the Surgeon General's health warnings that are required on print advertisements. Moreover, cigarette sponsorship of sporting events allows cigarette brand names to be shown or mentioned on television and radio, despite the ban on broadcast cigarette advertising.

THE EXTENT OF CIGARETTE ADVERTISING

According to an FTC staff report on cigarette advertising, "cigarettes are the most heavily advertised product in America."[13] Total cigarette advertising and promotional expenditures reached $2.1 billion in 1984.[14] From 1974 through 1984, total advertising and promotional expenditures increased approximately sevenfold, or threefold after adjustment of expenditures according to the consumer price index (all items) to constant 1974 dollars (Fig. 1). In 1974 dollars, total advertising and promotional expenditures increased from 1.0 cent per pack sold in 1974 to 3.3 cents per pack sold in 1984 (assuming all cigarettes were sold in 20 cigarette packs).

The 100 companies with the highest advertising expenditures in 1985 included all 6 major cigarette manufacturers: Philip Morris Companies, No. 2; RJR/Nabisco (R. J. Reynolds Tobacco Company), No. 3; Grand Metropolitan plc (Liggett & Myers Tobacco Company), No. 43; Batus (Brown & Williamson Tobacco Corporation), No. 44; American Brands, No. 51; and Loews Corporation (Lorillard Division), No. 54.[15] Of the 100 most heavily advertised brands of all products and services in the major media in 1985, 8 were cigarette brands[16] (despite the absence of the cigarette brands' advertising from 4

FIGURE 1. Cigarette Advertising and Promotional Expenditures, United States, 1974–1984

Adjusted expenditures are adjusted according to the consumer price index (all items), to constant 1974 dollars.

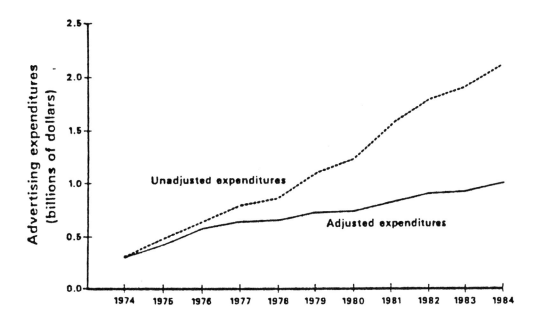

of the 8 media because of the ban on broadcast cigarette advertising).

The FTC classifies cigarette advertising and promotional expenditures into 11 categories in (Table 1). Traditional forms of print advertising are the first five categories in Table 1; promotional activities are those that fall into the remaining categories. In 1984, newspaper, magazine, and outdoor advertising accounted for 43.2 percent of total expenditures.[14]

TABLE 1. Cigarette Advertising and Promotional Expenditures According to Category (FTC Classification), United States, 1984[*]

Category	Expenditures
	$ millions (%)
Newspapers	193.5 (9.2)
Magazines	425.9 (20.3)
Outdoor media	285.0 (13.6)
Transit[†]	25.8 (1.2)
Point of sale	167.3 (8.0)
Promotional allowances[‡]	363.2 (17.3)
Sampling distribution[§]	148.0 (7.1)
Distribution bearing name[¶]	128.0 (6.1)
Distribution not bearing name[‖]	12.4 (0.6)
Public entertainment[**]	60.0 (2.9)
All others[††]	286.0 (13.7)
	2095.2

[*]Source: Federal Trade Commission.

[†]Advertising in or on public transportation facilities.

[‡]Paid to retailers and any other persons (other than full-time company employees involved in cigarette distribution and sales) in order to facilitate the sale of cigarettes.

[§]Includes the costs of the cigarettes and the costs of organizing, promoting, and running sampling efforts.

[¶]Net costs of distributing all items, other than cigarettes, including the cost of such items, distributed to consumers by sale, redemption of coupons, or otherwise, bearing the name or depicting any portion of the package of any variety of cigarettes sold by the company.

[‖]Net costs of distributing all items, other than cigarettes, including the cost of such items, distributed to consumers by sale, redemption of coupons, or otherwise, not bearing the name or depicting any portion of the package of any variety of cigarettes sold by the company.

[**]Promotion and sponsorship of sporting, musical, and other public entertainment events bearing or otherwise displaying the name of the company or any of its cigarettes.

[††]Includes direct mail, audio-visuals, and endorsements and testimonials. The category "endorsements and testimonials" includes, but is not limited to, all expenditures made to procure cigarette use; the mention of a cigarette product or company name; the appearance of a cigarette product, name, or package; or other representation associated with a cigarette product or company, in any situation (e.g., motion pictures, stage shows, or public appearance by a celebrity) in which such use, mention, or appearance may come to the public's attention.

The proportion of total expenditures devoted to promotional activities has steadily increased, from 25.5 percent in 1975 to 47.6 percent in 1984 (Table 2). This shift parallels a similar shift from advertising to promotional spending by the packaged-goods industry in general,[17] although the shift has been more rapid in the case of cigarettes. One cigarette company, RJR/Nabisco, sponsored more than 1600 events in 200 cities in 1985.[18]

Data are available from several sources on advertising expenditures in different media. Figures vary slightly from one source to another because different methods are used to estimate expenditures and because some sources include both media costs (e.g., charges for broadcast time, magazine space, or billboard rental) and production costs, whereas others include only media costs. The data presented in Table 3 show that cigarette advertising expenditures in 1985 accounted for 0.8, 7.1, and 22.3 percent of total advertising expenditures in newspapers, magazines, and outdoor media, respectively. These proportions underestimate the true proportions because the figures for cigarette advertising expenditures include only media costs, whereas the figures for total media advertising expenditures include media and production costs. The proportions in 1984 were 1.0 percent (newspapers), 8.4 percent (maga-

TABLE 2. Cigarette Advertising and Promotional Expenditures. United States, 1975–1984[*]

Year	Advertising Expenditures[†]	Promotional Expenditures[‡]
	$ millions (percent of yearly total)	
1975	366.2 (74.5)	125.1 (25.5)
1976	430.0 (67.3)	209.1 (32.7)
1977	552.1 (69.1)	247.4 (30.9)
1978	600.5 (68.6)	274.5 (31.4)
1979	748.9 (69.1)	334.5 (30.9)
1980	829.9 (66.8)	412.4 (33.2)
1981	998.3 (64.5)	549.4 (35.5)
1982	1040.1 (58.0)	753.7 (42.0)
1983	1080.9 (56.9)	819.9 (43.1)
1984	1097.5 (52.4)	997.7 (47.6)

[*]Source: Federal Trade Commission.

[†]Includes advertising in newspapers and magazines and outdoor, transit, and point-of-sale advertising (see Table 1 for definitions).

[‡]Includes promotional allowances, sampling distribution, distribution bearing name, distribution not bearing name, public entertainment, and "other" (see Table 1 for definitions).

TABLE 3. Estimated Tobacco Advertising Expenditures in Five Media, United States, 1985*

Medium	All Advertising†	Cigarette Advertising‡	Advertising of Other Tobacco Products and Accessories‡
	millions of dollars		
Newspapers	25,170	199.8	4.2
Magazines	5,155	367.1	8.1
Television	20,770§	0	23.5¶ ‖
Radio**	6,490	0	4.7 ‖
Outdoor	945	210.8	0.2
Other††	36,220	NA	NA
	94,750	777.7	40.7

*Source: Newspaper Advertising Bureau, New York City, based on data from Media Records, Leading National Advertisers, Spot Radio Report, and McCann Erickson Inc. NA denotes data not available.
†Includes media and production costs.
‡Includes media costs but not production costs.
§Includes network and spot television, and network and local cable television.
¶Includes network and spot television and network cable television, but not local cable television.
‖Pursuant to the Comprehensive Smokeless tobacco Health Act of 1986(Public Law 99–252), advertising of smokeless tobacco products (chewing tobacco and snuff) on electronic media was prohibited after August 27, 1986.
**Includes network and spot radio.
††Includes farm publications, direct mail, business papers, transit, point-of-sale, yellow pages, weekly newspapers, "shoppers," "penny-savers," and others.

zines), and 21.1 percent (outdoor). The relative decrease in cigarette advertising in newspapers and magazines may reflect the gradual shift from advertising to promotional activities during the past decade (Table 2).

The three major types of advertising are national advertising (e.g., by manufacturers), retail advertising, and classified advertising. Data are available for national-advertising expenditures that allow comparisons of advertising expenditures for different products and services. According to the Media Records classification system, national advertising expenditures are classified into major categories (e.g., alcoholic beverages, automotive products, foods, tobacco, and transportation) and subcategories (e.g., beer, passenger cars, dairy products, cigarettes, and airlines). In 1985, the subcategory of cigarettes was the most heavily advertised in outdoor media, the second most heavily advertised subcategory in magazines (after passenger cars), and the third most heavily advertised subcategory in newspapers (after passenger cars and airlines)

(Newspapers Advertising Bureau [New York]: unpublished data).

Of the seven companies with the largest advertising expenditures in outdoor media in 1985, six were cigarette companies.[15] Cigarette advertisements accounted for 14.6 percent of transit-shelter advertisements in 1984, second only to liquor advertisements (19.4 percent).[19] In 1985, tobacco advertising expenditures for eight-sheet (5 by 11 ft [1.5 by 3.4 m]) billboards were $7.8 million—about half the total expenditures for this medium ($15.6 million).[20]

SPECIAL THEMES

The major advertising themes for 1982 and 1983, according to the FTC, associated cigarette smoking with high-style living, healthy activities, and economic, social, and professional success.[21] The FTC did not report any changes in advertising themes for 1984.[14] The advertising and marketing themes discussed below are especially likely to increase cigarette consumption.

LOW-TAR CIGARETTES

Sixty-four percent of total advertising and promotional expenditures in 1984 were for cigarettes yielding 15 mg or less of "tar." These cigarettes accounted for 54 percent of the domestic market share in the same year.[14] During the past decade, the proportion of total advertising and promotional expenditures devoted to cigarettes yielding 15 mg or less of tar has increased substantially, but this proportion has consistently exceeded the domestic market share of these cigarettes (Fig. 2). This suggests that cigarette companies are seeking to expand this market. An article in *Business Week* explains why the industry may be motivated to try to do so: "Some [industry executives] suggest that the explosion in low-tar brands . . . has finally done the job of stopping health-conscious smokers from quitting."[22]

One advertisement for a low-tar cigarette included the headline, "Vantage is changing a lot of my feelings about smoking," and the following statement:

> I like to smoke, and what I like is a cigarette that isn't timid on taste. But I'm not living in some ivory tower. I hear the things being said against high-tar smoking as well as the next guy. And so I started looking. For a low-tar smoke that had some honest-to-goodness taste. . . .[23]

FIGURE 2. Domestic Market Share and Proportion of Total Advertising and Promotional Expenditures Related to Cigarettes Yielding 15 mg or Less of "Tar," United States, 1975–1984

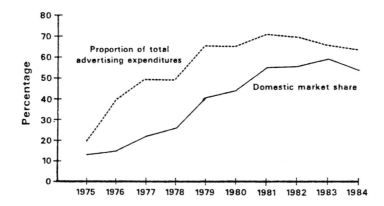

Another advertisement for True cigarettes contained this testimonial from a woman smoker: "Considering all I'd heard, I decided to either quit or smoke True. I smoke True."[13] According to the FTC, advertising that emphasizes tar and nicotine content may "contain the implied representation that low 'tar' and nicotine cigarettes are 'safe.' Such implied representations may mislead the reader about the safety of smoking reduced 'tar' and nicotine brands."[10]

Although today's filter-tipped "low-yield" cigarettes are associated with lower rates of lung cancer than their higher-yield predecessors, their effect on the incidence of cardiovascular disease, chronic obstructive lung disease, and fetal damage is unclear. In some ways, low-yield cigarettes may even increase the health risk, since smokers who switch to these cigarettes may compensate for the lower intake of nicotine by smoking more cigarettes per day, inhaling more deeply, puffing more frequently, or smoking cigarettes to a shorter butt length. Moreover, cigarette additives are more commonly introduced into lower-yield cigarettes to enhance their "taste"; the identity of these additives is not disclosed to consumers, and they present unknown risks to the smoker.[24]

Other cigarette brands are designed and advertised in ways that suggest a lower exposure to tar. These too may mislead consumers about the dangers of smoking. For instance, Parliament Lights have a "recessed" filter that is claimed to "keep your lips from touching the tar that builds up on the filter."[25] Concord has a "flavor control filter," which can be twisted to "adjust the taste from a rich, flavorful

low tar to a light, mild ultra low tar, or anyplace in between."[26]

DISCOUNTED BRANDS

Several discounted name brands (e.g., Doral and Stride) were introduced in 1984, reportedly to compete with the less expensive, nonbrand ("generic") cigarettes. Doral was offered at a price competitive with the prices of generic varieties, approximately 30 percent below the cost of regular brands. The market share of discounted brands has increased from 5.5 percent in 1984 (approximately twice the share in 1983) to 7.2 percent in 1985. More than 80 percent of the discounted-brand share in 1984 was attributed to generic cigarettes.[14,27]

This trend has important public health implications since cigarette sales are inversely related to price. Teenagers appear to be especially price-sensitive in their purchase of cigarettes.[28]

PACKAGES WITH 25 CIGARETTES

Another fast-growing market includes brands with 25 cigarettes per pack, which were virtually nonexistent in the United States before 1983. Five of the six major U.S. cigarette manufacturers now sell brands in packs of 25 cigarettes, some at the regular, "value-added" price, and others at a premium price. By the end of 1985, three of these brands (Richland, Century, and Players Lights 25s) accounted for 1.4 percent of the domestic cigarette market.[29]

John C. Maxwell, Jr., a tobacco-industry analyst, refers to marketing of the 25-cigarette pack as the "consumption goes up to availability" strategy.[30] In other words, a person usually smoking one pack per day would be inclined to finish the pack by the end of the day, whether it contained 20 or 25 cigarettes. The advertising slogan for Marlboro 25s is consistent with this strategy: "5 more smokes for the long working day."[31] Since the health effects of smoking are dose-related, switching to 25-per-pack brands would increase the risk of disease if daily consumption increased. On the other hand, persons smoking 30 or 40 cigarettes per day might reduce their daily cigarette consumption by switching to 25-cigarette packs[32] (although compensatory changes, such as an increased frequency of puffing, might offset the benefits).

SPECIAL TARGETS

In response to the decline in cigarette sales and the proliferation of brands, the U.S. cigarette market has become increasingly segmented. According to industry analysts, new cigarette brands must target specific segments of the market in order to succeed.[33] As a result, marketing campaigns have targeted women, minorities, blue-collar workers, and several other groups.

WOMEN

Since 1968, several cigarette brands marketed specifically for women have been introduced, including Virginia Slims, Silva Thins, More, Eve, Satin, and Ritz. A number of "brand extensions," such as Newport Slim Lights and Salem Slim Lights, are also targeted toward women. The cigarette paper and package are often designed to appeal to women. For instance, Eve has a flower design on its filter tip; Satin has a satin-like paper tip; and Ritz, billed as the first "designer cigarette," bears the logo of the fashion designer, Yves Saint Laurent, on its package and filter tip.[34–36]

Although the current prevalence of smoking among women (28 percent) is nearly as high as that among men (33 percent),[37] women's brands account for only 5 to 10 percent of the total cigarette market.[35,38] This suggests that the majority of female smokers purchase sex-neutral (or male-oriented) brands instead of women's brands, perhaps as a sign of equality.

The use of such words as "slim" and "thin" in the brands' names and advertisements may suggest the weight-losing effect of smoking, which is likely to have special appeal to women. Indeed, advertisements for women's brands appear prominently in *Weight Watchers Magazine.* Similarly, Silver Lights cigarette paper is advertised with the slogan, "Keep thin and light."

Cigarette advertising in women's magazines had grown substantially.[39,40] Of the 20 magazines receiving the most cigarette advertising revenue in 1985, 8 were women's magazines *(Better Homes and Gardens, Family Circle, Woman's Day, McCall's, Ladies' Home Journal, Redbook, Cosmopolitan,* and *Glamour).*[41] The themes in these advertisements are typically designed to attract women. The slogan for Virginia Slims—"You've Come a long way, baby"—associates smoking with women's liberation. Similarly, Brown and Williamson Tobacco Corporation is test-marketing a new slim cigarette, KIM 25s, using the advertising slogan: "For women who know the meaning of free."[42] Ritz, according to an R. J. Reynolds spokesperson, is aimed at women in their 20s and 30s who are "more independent, probably tending to be single rather than married, and who spend more of their income on fashion and fashion accessories."[43]

Women's products are offered free or at discounted prices when some women's brands are purchased. During the introduction of Newport Slim Lights, a free package of Aziza eye shadow came with the purchase of two packs of cigarettes.[36] Empty packs of Eve Lights were redeemable for a free pair of Silkies panty hose or a discounted Anne Rothschild chemise.

During the past 20 years, the rate of smoking among women has declined much more slowly than among men.[37,44] Among adolescents, females have surpassed males in terms of smoking rates. In 1985, a higher proportion of women than men were daily cigarette smokers among graduating high-school students (21 percent and 18 percent, respectively) and college students (18 percent and 10 percent, respectively).[45]

The American Cancer Society predicted that by the end of 1985, lung cancer would surpass breast cancer as the most common cause of death from cancer in women.[46] By contrast, the incidence of lung cancer among men is now declining.[47]

BLACKS

Several cigarette brands have been promoted specifically to the black community, including Kool, Winston, More, Salem, Newport, and Virginia Slims.[48,49] In one study, Newport, Kool, and Salem accounted for 60 percent of cigarettes purchased by blacks. Blacks (65 percent) were more likely than whites (24 percent) to smoke menthol cigarettes, and menthol brands were more commonly advertised in black-oriented than in white-oriented magazines (Cummings KM, Giovino G, Mendicino AJ: unpublished data).

Cigarettes are advertised heavily in black-oriented publications such as *Ebony, Jet,* and *Essence.* Cigarette advertisements account for 12 percent of total advertising revenue in *Essence,* billed as "The magazine for today's black woman."[48] In 1985, cigarette companies spent $3.3 million for advertisements in *Ebony.*[41] Philip Morris has published "A Guide to Black Organizations," filled with cigarette advertisements featuring black models.[48]

An effective advertising medium for targeting ethnic groups is the eight-sheet billboard, which is small (5 by 11 ft) and usually placed low and close to the street. In 1985, tobacco companies spent $5.8 million for advertisements on eight-sheet billboards in black communities, accounting for 37 percent of total advertising in this medium. The most commonly advertised brands in these markets were Newport ($2.0 million), Kool ($1.4 million), Salem ($911,000), and Winston ($622,000).[20]

Other promotional methods targeted to blacks include sponsorship of athletic, civic, cultural, and entertainment events by cigarette brands or companies. Examples include the 40th anniversary gala of the United Negro College Fund, the Kool Achiever Awards (presented to "outstanding adults who are working to improve the quality of life in inner city communities"), an *Ebony* fashion show, and a forum for publishers of black newspapers on preserving freedoms in American life.[49–51]

From 1965 to 1983, smoking rates among black males consistently exceeded those among white males by 8 to 10 percentage points, whereas rates among black females and white females were similar.[52] Correspondingly, black males have had a 45 percent excess mortality rate from lung cancer as compared with non-minority males, whereas the mortality rates among black and non-minority females are about the same. Death rates associated with heart disease are higher in blacks than whites, among both males and females.[53]

HISPANICS

Three cigarette brands with Spanish names have been introduced in recent years (Rio, Dorado, and L&M Superior) and are reportedly aimed at Hispanics.[33,54,55] Of the top 10 companies advertising in Hispanic markets, 2 are cigarette compa-

nies—Philip Morris (No. 1) and R. J. Reynolds (No. 10).[56] In 1985, tobacco companies spent $1.4 million for advertisements on eight-sheet billboards in Hispanic areas—more than twice the amount spent for the next most heavily advertised product (liquor). In these markets, the brands most commonly advertised were Newport, Winston, Camel, and Salem.[20] Since 1981, Philip Morris has published a directory of national Hispanic organizations, filled with cigarette advertisements in English or Spanish. Cigarette brands and companies have sponsored cultural and entertainment events in Hispanic communities, often accompanied by free-sample campaigns.[49,57]

The Behavioral Risk Factor Surveys for 1981–1983 showed that smoking rates were somewhat lower in Hispanic males than in white and black males, but markedly lower in Hispanic females than in white and black females.[58] According to the National Health Interview Survey for 1980, Hispanic men had a smoking rate (38 percent) intermediate between that of white men (36 percent) and black men (42 percent).[59] Local surveys have shown a marked increase in smoking among Mexican-American youths, to a rate above those among their black and white peers.[53]

BLUE-COLLAR WORKERS

Recently, cigarette companies have increased their emphasis on advertising in "blue-collar" magazines (e.g., *Popular Mechanics*). The number of pages with cigarette advertising in the top 10 "upscale" magazines (e.g., *Vogue* and *U.S. News & World Report*) fell 23 percent in 1984 and 17 percent in 1985, whereas the number of pages in the top 10 blue-collar magazines fell only 7.1 percent in 1984 and 9.5 percent in 1985.[60] Blue-collar workers are also targeted in other media. According to an R. J. Reynolds executive:

> Blue-collar people read the sports pages, and we will make every effort to place Winston in newspapers. We also know that they're impressed with out-of-home advertising because that gives them comfort when they see their brand in the marketplace.[22]

Smoking rates among blue-collar male workers (47 percent) exceed those among white-collar male workers (33 percent),[61] and smoking rates generally increase with decreasing education.[58] Tobacco-industry executives are no doubt aware of these trends. The executive director of the Tobacco Merchants Association (New York) has attributed the higher smoking rates among blue-collar workers to their relative lack of education (presumably regarding the health hazards of smoking): "Certainly a lot of data indicate that smoking is becoming a more blue-collar activity, partly because of increased education, at the other end."[60] This contradicts the usual assertion by the industry that consumers are universally aware of the "claimed health risks" associated with smoking.

CHILDREN AND ADOLESCENTS

Whether adolescents are the target of, or at least exposed to, cigarette advertisements is an important question, since most smokers acquire the habit as minors. According to the National Health Interview Survey for 1978–1980, 79 percent of male smokers and 70 percent of female smokers born between 1940 and 1949 began to smoke before they were 20.[37]

The tobacco industry denies that it advertises to children.[62] The Tobacco Institute states that "In 1969, the industry offered to end radio and television advertising because of its substantial audience of young people."[63] However, cigarette advertisements continue to appear in publications with large teenage readerships. In *Glamour,* one fourth of whose readers are girls under 18 years of age,[64] cigarette advertising expenditures were $6.3 million in 1985.[41] In *Sports Illustrated,* one third of whose readers are boys under 18 years of age,[64] cigarette advertising expenditures were $29.9 million in 1985.[41] R. J. Reynolds is the exclusive advertiser in *Moviegoer,* a "customized" magazine distributed free in hundreds of movie theaters nationwide.[65,66] About half of those who attend movies today are less than 21 years of age.[67] *TV Guide,* which receives more cigarette advertising revenue than any other magazine ($36 million in 1985),[41] informs its advertising clients that each issue reaches 8.8 million teenagers 12 to 17 years old.[68,69] Themes in cigarette advertising that emphasize youthful vigor, sexual attraction, and independence are likely to be especially appealing to teenagers and young adults grappling with these issues.

Cigarette brands are promoted indirectly to children as candy cigarettes. Many have names, logos, and packaging identical or similar to those of real cigarette brands.[70–72] Although not manufactured by tobacco companies, they have remained on the market for years despite obvious copyright infringement.

More important than the issue of whether tobacco advertising targets children and adolescents is the question of whether the advertisements actually reach these groups. Studies have shown that ciga-

rette advertisements and promotional activities do indeed reach teenagers. In a study involving 1195 Australian schoolchildren, subjects were presented with cigarette advertisements from which all identifying writing had been removed. A large proportion of smokers and nonsmokers were able to identify the brand names and slogans correctly.[73] Similar results were obtained in a study of 306 high school students in Georgia (Goldstein AO, et al.: unpublished data). A survey of 880 children in Great Britain showed that their recognition of cigarette brands varied according to which brands had recently sponsored televised sporting events.[12]

Although daily cigarette smoking among high school seniors fell from 29 percent in 1976 to 20 percent in 1981, the rate has remained at 19 to 21 percent through 1985.[45]

MILITARY GROUPS

Members of military services have long been targets of cigarette advertising campaigns.[74] Numerous cigarette advertisements continue to appear in publications aimed at those in the military, such as *Army Times, Navy Times,* and *Air Force Times.* For the six-month period from March through August 1986, each weekly issue of *Army Times* carried an average of 2.3 pages of color cigarette advertisements, including 14 of 26 back covers. Park Avenue Tobacco Company (Richmond, Va.) was reported to have introduced a cigarette brand named 1776, aimed at those in the military. Its advertising slogan is "The flavor says 'Attention.' The price says 'At ease.' "[75,76] Philip Morris has tested Cambridge, a discounted brand, on U.S. military bases.[77]

Smoking rates in the military are among the highest reported for any group—47 percent of military-service members in 1985. Smoking-related costs to the military health care system in fiscal year 1984 were an estimated $210 million.[78]

MISCELLANEOUS GROUPS

There are probably many other unrecognized cigarette advertising campaigns that have targeted various groups. Two unusual targets are religious groups and prisoners. Cigarette advertisements have appeared in the Jewish-oriented publications *Hadassah Magazine* and *Jewish World* (Long Island, N.Y.), and cigarette companies have sponsored several religious events.[79]

Lorillard has offered free athletic equipment to prison inmates who save empty packages of Newport cigarettes and Beech-Nut chewing tobacco. Correctional institutions were supplied with collection bins for the empty packages and with posters to alert inmates to the promotion.[80] Smoking rates have been reported to be 80 to 85 percent in various prison populations.[81–83]

CONCLUSION

The advertising of tobacco products promises to be the subject of ongoing discussion and debate. While these discussions proceed, the study of trends in cigarette marketing will be useful in several ways. Marketing data may assist health officials in identifying and predicting patterns of cigarette use. Groups targeted by advertising campaigns are likely to face greater problems with cigarette smoking in the future. The heavy promotion of low-yield brands will continue to undermine the message that there is no safe cigarette.

The study of cigarette advertising may be useful in developing effective health promotion programs. Anti-smoking counteradvertisements that parody cigarette advertisements have been developed. "Ad-spoof" competitions among schoolchildren have been used to enhance their understanding of the messages in cigarette advertisements as well as the health and cosmetic consequences of smoking.[84–89] An entire school curriculum project has been developed around the film *Death in the West*. The film, featuring six cowboys in the American West who were dying of lung cancer or emphysema, was designed to counter what is generally regarded as the most successful cigarette advertising image ever created: the Marlboro cowboy.[90]

References

1. Department of Health and Human Services. The health consequences of smoking: cancer: a report of the Surgeon General, 1982. Rockville, Md.: Office on Smoking and Health, 1982:v, xi. (DHHS publication no. (PHS) 82–50179.)
2. Rice DP, Hodgson TA, Sinsheimer P, Browner W, Kopstein AN. The economic costs of the health effects of smoking, 1984. Milbank Q 1986; 64:489–548.
3. Ravenholt RT. Tobacco's impact on twentieth-century U.S. mortality patterns. Am J Prev Med 1985; 1(4):4–17.
4. Department of Health and Human Services The health consequences of smoking: cardiovascular disease: a report of the Surgeon General, 1983. Rockville, Md.: Office on Smoking and Health, 1983:iv. (DHHS publication no. (PHS) 84–50204.)
5. Department of Health and Human Services. The health consequences of smoking: chronic obstructive lung disease: a report of the Surgeon General, 1984. Rockville, Md.: Office on Smoking and Health, 1984: viii. (DHHS publication no. (PHS) 84–50205.)
6. Smoking-related deaths and financial costs. Washington, D.C.: United States Office of Technology Assessment, September 1985.
7. Warner KE. Selling smoke: cigarette advertising and public health. Washington, D.C.: American Public Health Association, 1986.
8. Chapman S. Cigarette advertising and smoking: a review of the evidence. In: Smoking out the barons: the campaign against the tobacco industry. New York: John Wiley, 1986:79–97.
9. Popper ET. Oversight hearings on tobacco advertising. Subcommittee on Health and the Environment, Committee on Energy and Commerce, United States House of Representatives, July 18 1986.
10. Federal Trade Commission. Report to Congress pursuant to the Public Health Cigarette Smoking Act, for the year 1978. Washington, D.C.: Federal Trade Commission. Dec. 1979:6–10.
11. We're the fastest growing brand in America. US Tobacco Candy J 1986; 213(27):5.
12. Ledwith F. Does tobacco sports sponsorship on television act as advertising to children? Health Educ J 1984; 43:85–8.
13. Myers ML, Iscoe C, Jennings C, Lenox W, Minxky E, Sacks A. Federal Trade Commission staff report on the cigarette advertising investigation. Washington, D.C.: Federal Trade Commission, May 1981:3,12.
14. Federal Trade Commission, Report to Congress pursuant to the Federal Cigarette Labeling and Advertising Act, 1984. Washington, D.C.: Federal Cigarette Labeling and Advertising Act, 1984. Washington, D.C.: Federal Trade Commission, July 1986.
15. 100 leading national advertisers. Advertising Age. September 4, 1986: 1,116.
16. The top 200 brands, Marketing and Media Decisions (New York). July 1986.
17. Edwards PL. Sales promotion comes into its own. Advertising Age. July 28, 1986:65.
18. Giges N, Freeman L. ANA hears talk of better days. Advertising Age. November 3, 1986:1, 106.
19. Drug ads could fill in for smokes. Advertising Age. December 16, 1985: 1,68.
20. National advertising report of eight-sheet outdoor: 4th quarter and 1985 summary. Independence, Mo.: Eight-Sheet Outdoor Advertising Association, 1986:31–2.
21. Federal Trade Commission. Report to Congress pursuant to the Federal Cigarette Labeling and Advertising Act, for the years 1982–1983. Washington, D.C.: Federal Trade Commission, June 1985.
22. Cigarette sales keep rising. Business Week, December 15, 1980:52, 57.
23. Vantage is changing a lot of my feelings about smoking. Time Magazine. November 7, 1977:86–7.

24. Department of Health and Human Services. The health consequences of smoking: the changing cigarette: a report of the Surgeon General. Rockville, Md.: Office on Smoking and Health, 1981. (DHHS publication no. (PHS) 81–50156.)

25. Open invitations. Chicago Tribune Magazine. April 25, 1982:23.

26. Twist and shout. Advertising Age. August 12, 1985:2.

27. Maxwell JC. Cigaret sales smolder below 600 billion. Advertising Age. November 18, 1985:61.

28. Warner KE. Smoking and health implications of a change in the federal cigarette excise tax. JAMA 1986; 255:1028–32.

29. Maxwell JC. Maxwell report: sales estimates for the cigarette industry. New York: Furman Selz Dietz Mager & Birney, February 3, 1986.

30. Gloede WF. New menthol cigaret brands battle in Pa. Advertising Age. January 20, 1986:36.

31. 5 more smokes for the long working day. Time Magazine. April 21, 1986:44–5.

32. Kozlowski LT. Pack size, reported cigarette smoking rates, and public health. Am J Public Health 1986; 76:1337–8.

33. Hollie PG. Segmented cigarette market. New York Times. March 23, 1985:29, 31.

34. Gloede WF. RJR stumps tobacco industry with Ritz plan. Advertising Age. February 24, 1986:4.

35. Abrams B, Guyon J. Lorillard tries to lure women with a Satin cigarette fantasy. Wall Street Journal. February 17, 1983.

36. Gloede WF. Newport has slim chance. Advertising Age. February 10, 1986:72.

37. Department of Health and Human Services. Smoking and health: a national status report. Rockville, Md.: Centers for Disease Control, Office on Smoking and Health, 1986:19, 21. (DHHS publication no. (CDC) 87–8396.)

38. Gloede W. B & W's Capri answers women's quest for slim. Advertising Age. December 8, 1986:76.

39. Ernster VL. Mixed messages for women: a social history of cigarette smoking and advertising. NY State J Med 1985; 85:335–40.

40. Jacobson B, Amos A. When smoke gets in your eyes: cigarette advertising policy and coverage of smoking and health in women's magazines. In: Smoking out the barons: the campaign against the tobacco industry. New York: John Wiley, 1986:99–137.

41. Gorog WF. Oversight hearings on tobacco advertising. Subcommitte on Health and the Environment, Committee on Energy and Commerce, United States House of Representatives, August 1, 1986.

42. Tompor S. Brown & Williamson to test cigarette brand designed for women. Louisville Courier Journal. May 23, 1986:B9.

43. Puffing up the Ritz. Time Magazine. February 4, 1985:46.

44. Department of Health and Human Services. The health consequences of smoking for women: a report of the Surgeon General. Rockville, Md.: Office on Smoking and Health, 1980.

45. Johnson LD, O'Malley PM, Bachman JG. Drug use among American high school students, college students, and other young adults: national trends through 1985. Rockville, Md.: National Institute on Drug Abuse, 1986:37, 202. (DHHS publication no. (ADM) 86–1450.)

46. Cancer facts and figures, 1985. New York: American Cancer Society, 1985:8.

47. Decrease in lung cancer incidence among males—United States, 1973–1983. MMWR 1986; 35:495–6, 501.

48. Cooper R, Simmons BE. Cigarette smoking and ill health among black Americans. NY State J Med 1985; 85:344–9.

49. Blum A. Selling cigarettes: the blue-collar, Black target. Washington Post. May 18, 1986:F1, F4.

50. Williams L. Tobacco companies target blacks with ads, donations, and festivals. Wall Street Journal. October 6, 1986. 2:1.

51. Rowan CT. Making a mint by selling cigarettes and booze to blacks. Chicago Sun-Times. October 8, 1986:33.

52. Department of Health and Human Services. Health, United States, 1985. Hyattsville, Md.: National Center for Health Statistics, 1985:72. (DHHS publication no. (PHS) 86–1232.)

53. Department of Health and Human Services, Report of the Secretary's Task Force on Black and Minority Health. Washington, D.C.: Office of Minority Health, 1985; 1:108, 1986; 3:14, 4:69–70.

54. Gloede WF. RJR puts on the Ritz; PM goes to Rio. Advertising Age. January 21, 1985:1, 78.

55. Gardner F. Smoke with a Spanish accent. Marketing and Media Decisions. July 1984:176.

56. Fitch E. Hispanic marketing: prime space available at low rates. Advertising Age THURSDAY. February 27, 1986:11.

57. Delgado JL. Oversight hearings on tobacco advertising. Subcommittee on Health and the Environment, Committee on Energy and Commerce, United States House of Representatives, July 18, 1986.

58. Remington PL, Forman MR, Gentry EM, Marks JS, Hogelin GC, Trowbridge FL. Current smoking trends in the United States: the 1981–1983 behavioral risk factor surveys. JAMA 1985;253:2975–8.

59. Marcus AC, Crane LA. Smoking behavior among US Latinos: an emerging challenge for public health. Am J Public Health 1985; 75:169–72.

60. Englander TJ. Cigarette makers shift ad strategies. US Tobacco Candy J 1986; 213:1, 46.

61. Department of Health and Human Services. The health consequences of smoking: cancer and chronic lung disease in the workplace: a report of the Surgeon General, no. 21, 1985. Rockville, Md.: Office on Smoking and Health, 1985:25. (DHHS publication no. (PHS) 85–50207.)

62. R. J. Reynolds Tobacco Company. We don't advertise to children. Time Magazine, April 9, 1984:91.

63. Voluntary initiatives of a responsible industry. Washington, D.C.: Tobacco Institute, 1983 (brochure).

64. Hutchings R. A review of the nature and the extent of cigarette advertising in the United States. In: Proceedings of the National Conference on Smoking or Health. New York: American Cancer Society, 1981:241–62.
65. Levin G. Tailoring medium to marketers' needs. Advertising Age THURSDAY. October 3, 1985:38.
66. R. J. Reynolds reaches kids with "Moviegoer." Tobacco Youth Rep 1986: 1(1):13–4.
67. International motion picture almanac. New York: Quigley Publishing, 1981:32A.
68. Next time you're in the checkout line, look around: that's your intermarket. Wall Street Journal. May 25, 1982:5.
69. Not all marketing decisions are made at the office. Adweek (Eastern Ed.). April 25, 1983:47.
70. Blum A. Candy cigarettes. N Engl J Med 1980; 302:972.
71. Idem. Aiming at children—"Who, us?" Med J Aust 1983; 1:235–6.
72. School bans "cigarettes" after parents' complaints. Med J Aust 1983; 1:248.
73. Chapman S, Fitzgerald B. Brand preference and advertising recall in adolescent smokers: some implications for health promotion. Am J Public Health 1982; 72:491–4.
74. Blake GH. Smoking and the military. NY State J Med 1985; 85:354–6.
75. Hall T. Smokers in military are firm's market for 1776 cigarette. Wall Street Journal. February 12, 1985:1.
76. Epidemic of new cigarette brands plagues U.S. Smoking Health Rep 1985: 2(3):5.
77. Tobacco marketers on new-product roll. Advertising Age. February 3, 1986:56.
78. Department of Defense. Department of Defense report on smoking and health in the military. Washington, D.C.: Office of the Assistant Secretary of Defense (Health Affairs) and Office of the Assistant Secretary of Defense (Force Management and personnel), 1986.
79. Blum A, Fitzgerald K. How tobacco companies have found religion. NY State J Med 1985; 85:445–50.
80. Gloede WF. Hey, Louie! Save da pack. Advertising Age. November 18, 1985:98.
81. Miller RE, Cappiello LA. Relationships between inmates' past drug practices and current drug knowledge and attitudes. Int J Addict 1983; 18:881–90.
82. Bell DS, Champion RA. Deviancy, delinquency and drug use. Br J Psychiatry 1979; 134:269–76.
83. Biener K. Genussmittel-und Drogenprobleme Strafgefangener. Off Gesundheitswes 1980; 42:55–8.
84. Blum A. Medicine vs Madison Avenue: fighting smoke with smoke. JAMA 1980; 243:739–40.
85. What's up DOC? Med J Aust 1983; 1:246–7.
86. Bittoun R. A tracheostomy for the Marlboro man. Med J Aust 1982; 2:69–70.
87. Blum A. Wodak A, Grigor J, et al. A tracheostomy for the Marlboro man. Med J Aust 1982; 2:459–60.
88. Battle of the billboards. American Medical News. September 26, 1986:2.
89. Spoofing the 'joy of smoking.' American Medical News. December 5, 1986:1, 29.
90. Glantz SA. Death in the West curriculum project. NY State J Med 1985; 85:470–1.

PART II

B. Child Rearing

7

ISSUES FOR WORKING PARENTS

T. Berry Brazelton

Children's Hospital and Harvard Medical School
Boston

In 1981, more than half the mothers in the United States were employed outside the home.[29] By 1990, it is predicted that 70 percent of children will have two working parents. The number has been increasing each year since World War II, and ten times as many mothers of small children work now as did in 1945. No longer is it culturally unacceptable for mothers to have jobs. In fact, the practice has become so widespread that many mothers at home feel that they "should" be working. There is a general feeling that *(a)* unless she works, a woman is missing out on an important part of life, and *(b)* taking care of a home is not sufficiently rewarding work. These feelings create unspoken pressures on women today, making new mothers wonder when they should return to their job or begin to look or train for one. At each domestic frustration, at each spurt in their baby's independence, young mothers are apt to question whether their baby's need to have them at home still outweighs their own need for an occupation outside the home.

Countering these various pressures on women to work, there is still a strong bias against mothers leaving their babies in substitute care unless it is absolutely necessary. Since society does not yet wholeheartedly support working mothers and their choices about substitute care, in the back of young mothers' minds a nagging question tends to persist: Is it really all right for mothers to work? Indeed, this troubling question may reflect the age-old, commonly cherished image of the "perfect mother"—at home taking care of her children.

In addition, the loss of the extended family has left the nuclear family unsupported. Strong cultural values are no longer available to new parents, while broad social issues such as nuclear war, ecological misuse, and overpopulation parallel the more personal issue of changing roles for women and for men. As each sex begins to face squarely the unforeseen anxieties of dividing the self into two important roles—one geared toward the family, the other toward the world—the pressures on men and women are enormous and largely uncharted by past generations. It is no wonder that many new parents are anxiously overwhelmed by these issues as they take on the important new responsibility of creating and maintaining a stable world for their baby.

We do not have enough studies yet to know about the issues for the infant. The studies we do have are likely to be biased, or based on experiences in special, often privileged populations.[19,23] We need to know when it is safest for the child's future development to have to relate to two or three caregivers; what will be the effects on a baby's development of a group care situation; when babies are best able to find what they need from caregivers other than their parents; when parents are best able to separate from their babies without feeling too grieved at the loss. In a word, we need information on which to base general guidelines for parents. For it could be that the most subtle, hard-to-deal-with pressure on young adults comes indirectly from society's ambivalent and discordant attitudes, which create a void of values in which the building and nurturing of a family becomes very difficult.

Another serious threat to the new family is posed by the very instability of its future as a family. Largely because of divorce,[29] 48 percent of children in the U.S. will have spent a significant part of their lives in a single-parent home. Half of the marriages of the 1970s will split up in the 1980s. The U.S. family is in serious trouble.

A new baby can be seen as an opportunity for strengthening relationships within the family. Because of the realignments that necessarily will occur around the advent of the new member, the old ties and the previous adjustments to the family's integrity are likely to be shaken—for better or for worse. The work of pregnancy for each parent has been documented by Bibring[5] and others.[9] The powerful

From *American Journal of Orthopsychiatry,* 1986, *56* (1): 14–25. Copyright © 1986. The American Orthopsychiatric Association, Inc. Reprinted by permission.

ambivalence of pregnancy represents parental efforts to reshape their previous adjustment to their lives and to their partners. The self-questioning that leads to worry about having an impaired baby is common to women and represents the depth of their anxious ambivalence as they attempt to "make it" to the new level of nurturing and caring for the coming baby. This anxiety and the force of their ambivalence can, however, be channeled into a positive adjustment to accepting and nurturing the baby. Similarly, these forces can serve to strengthen relations with other members of the family. But this cannot be left to chance. Supportive, sensitive interventions during pregnancy must be offered to stressed, high-risk parents.

We have seen that relatively minor, relatively inexpensive adjustments on the part of the medical system—such as prepared childbirth, father participation, presenting the baby to the mother and father at delivery[24]—can increase the opportunities for "bonding" to the baby. Although this is likely to be only a first step toward fostering attachment and significantly enhancing the possibilities for the baby's optimal developmental, it is a most important step. In my own work with the Newborn Behavioral Assessment,[8,13] I have found that presenting a baby's behavior to eager parents gives them a better chance to understand their infant *and themselves* as nurturers at a sensitive point in their development as adults.[3] These simple interventions in an otherwise rather unwelcoming pathological medical system seem to enhance the parents' image of themselves as vital to their baby and to each other. Thus, they further the likelihood that the parents' positive self-image will be passed on to the baby.

In my work in pediatric primary care, the parents I see in a prenatal interview are generally predisposed to share their concerns about themselves and the well-being of their future baby. As they talk to me, they share the passion and the work of making the future adjustment to parenthood with either the hoped-for normal or the dreaded impaired infant. However, when both parents anticipate the pressures of having to return to work "too early" (in their own words, "before three months"), they seem to guard against talking about their future baby as a person and about their future role as parents. Instead, their concerns are expressed in terms of the instrumental work of adjusting to time demands, to schedules, to lining up the necessary substitute care. Very little can be elicited from them about their dreams of the baby or their vision of themselves as

new parents. Perhaps they are already defending themselves against too intense an attachment in anticipation of the pain of separating prematurely from the new baby.

Efforts to involve the father in the birth process, to enhance his sense of paternity and empowerment as he adjusts to his new role, should be increased. Having the father involved in labor and delivery can significantly increase his sense of himself as a person who is important to his child and to his mate. Several investigators have shown that increased participation of fathers in the care of their babies, increased sensitivity to their baby's cues at one month, and significantly increased support of their wives can result from the rather simple maneuver of sharing the newborn baby's behavior with the new father at three days, using the Neonatal Behavioral Assessment Scale (NBAS).[3] In light of these apparent gains, we would do well to consider a period of paid paternity leave, which might serve both symbolically and in reality as a means of stamping the father's role as critical to his family. Ensuring the father's active participation is likely to enhance his image of himself as a nurturing person and to assist him toward a more mature adjustment in his life as a whole.

Supporting the mother in her choices about delivery and in adjusting to the new baby seems even more critical for those new mothers who must return to work. If the mother can be awake and in control of delivery, if she can have the thrill of cuddling her new infant in the delivery room, if she can have the choice of rooming in with her baby and of sharing her baby's behavior with a supportive professional, she is likely to feel empowered as a new mother.

WORK OF ATTACHMENT

The efforts of the medical system to enhance parental "bonding" to a new baby are certainly important to parents who must return to work. But bonding is not a magical assurance that the relationship will go well thereafter. The initial adjustment to the new baby at home is likely to be extremely stressful to any set of new parents. Most have had little or no prior experience with babies or with their own parents as they nurtured a smaller sibling. They come to this new role without enough knowledge or participational experience. The generation gap makes it difficult for them to turn back to parents or extended family for support. Professional support is expensive and difficult to locate. The mother (and father) is likely to be physically exhausted and emotionally depressed for a period after delivery. The baby is unpredictable and has not developed a reliable day-night cycle of states of sleep and waking. Crying at the end of the day often serves as a necessary outlet and discharge for a small baby's nervous system after an exciting but overwhelming day. This crying can easily be perceived as a sign of failure in parenting by harassed, inexperienced parents, and the crying that starts as a fussy period is then likely to become a colicky, inconsolable period at the end of every day over the next three months. Any mother is bound to feel inadequate and helpless at this time. She may wish to run away and to turn over her baby's care to a "more competent person." If she *must* go back to work in the midst of this trying period, she is unlikely to develop the same sense of understanding and competence with regard to her baby as she might if she had been able to stay at home and to "see it out." When this period of regular crying at the end of the day mercifully comes to an end at 12 weeks, coincident with further maturation of the nervous system, mothers tell me they feel relieved and as if they had finally "helped" the baby learn to adjust to its new environment. They claim to have a sense of having learned to cope with the baby's negativism over these months; their feelings of anger, frustration, and inadequacy during the infant's fussy period are replaced by a sense of mastery at this time. Since the baby is now vocalizing, smiling, and cooing responsively at this same time at the end of every day, they report that they feel they have "taught" the baby to socialize in more acceptable ways. They feel that "at last the baby is mine, and is smiling and vocalizing for *me*." There is likely to be a significant difference in a mother's feelings of personal achievement and intimacy with her baby if she has had to leave this adjustment to another caregiver in order to return to work before the end of the three-month transition.

In our own research on the development of reciprocal communication between parents and small babies, we have been impressed with the necessity for the development of a reciprocal understanding of each other's rhythms of attention and nonattention, which develops between a mother and her baby over the first four months. At least four levels of behavioral organization in the communication system between parents and their small infants develop at this time.[11] Based on a rhythmic interaction of attention and nonattention that is critical to the homeostatic controls necessary to the immature organism, par-

ents and infant can learn to communicate more and more complex messages in clusters of behavior. Such behavior does not demand verbal communication, but involves important elements of affective and cognitive information and forms the base of the infant's learning about the world.[12] Thus, in an important period of intense communication between parent and infant, the parent provides the baby with affective and cognitive information, and with the opportunity to learn to exert controls over the internal homeostatic systems needed to pay attention to its surroundings. The four stages of learning about these controls provide infants with a source of learning about themselves and provide the mother or father with an important opportunity for learning the ingredients of a nurturant role with their baby. These early experiences of learning about each other are the basis for their shared emotional development in the future, and are critical as anlages for the infant's future ego.

MOTHER'S ROLE

The most important role of the adult interactants seems to be that of helping infants to form a regulatory base for their immature psychological and motor reactions.[2,13]

The most important rule for maintaining an interaction seems to be that a mother develop a sensitivity to her infant's capacity for attention and the infant's need for withdrawal—partial or complete—after a period of attending to her. Short cycles of attention and inattention seem to underlie all periods of prolonged interaction. Although in the laboratory setting we thought we were observing continuous attention to the mother on the part of the infant, stop-frame analysis subsequently revealed the cyclical nature of the infant's looking and not-looking. Looking-away behavior reflects the need of infants to maintain some control over the amount of stimulation they can take in during such intense periods of interaction. This is a homeostatic model, similar to the type of model that underlies all the physiological reactions of the neonate, and it seems to apply to the immature organism's capacity to attend to messages in a communication system.[12]

Basic to this regulatory system or reciprocal interaction between parent and infant is the basic rhythm of attention-inattention that is set up between them.[12] A mother must respect her infant's needs for the regulation that this affords or she will overload the infant's immature psychophysiological system and the infant will need to protect itself by turning her off completely. Thus, she learns the infant's capacity for attention-inattention early, in order to maintain her infant's attention. Within this rhythmic, coherent configuration, mother and infant can introduce the mutable elements of communication. Smiles, vocalizations, postures, and tactile signals all are such elements. They can be interchanged at will as long as they are based on the rhythmic structure.[13] The individual differences of the baby's needs for such a structure set the limits on it. The mother then has the opportunity to adapt her tempo within these limits. If she speeds up her tempo, she can reduce the baby's level of communication. If she slows down, she can expect a higher level of engagement and communicative behavior from her infant.[12,28] Her use of tempo as a means of entraining the baby's response systems is probably the basis of the baby's learning about his* own control systems. In this process of variability, the baby learns the limits of his control systems. As the baby returns to a baseline, he learns about basic self-regulation. The feedback systems that are set up within this process afford the baby a kind of richness of self-regulation or adaptation.

Built on top of this base is the nonverbal message. By using a systems approach to understand this, we find that each behavioral message or cluster of behavior from one member of the dyad acts as a disruption of the system, which must then be reorganized. The process of reorganization affords the infant and the parent a model for learning—learning about the other as well as learning about oneself within this regulatory system. An "appropriate" or attractive stimulus creates a disruption and reorganization that is of a different nature from those that are the result of an intrusive or "inappropriate" stimulus. Each serves a purpose in this learning model.[9]

An inspection of the richness of such a homeostatic model, which provides each participant with an opportunity to turn off or on at any time in the interaction, demonstrates the fine-tuning available and necessary to each partner of the dyad for learning about "the other." The individual actions that may be introduced into the clusters of behavior that dominate the interaction become of real, if secondary, importance. A smile or a vocalization may be couched within several other actions to form a signaling cluster. But the individual piece of behavior is not the necessary requirement for a response: the cluster is. The basic rhythm, the "fit" of clusters of behavior, and the timing of appropriate clusters to produce responses in an expectable framework become the best prediction of real reciprocity in parent-infant interaction.[13]

STAGES OF REGULATION

We have identified four stages of regulation and of learning within this system over the first four months of life:[11]

1. Infants achieve homeostatic control over input and output systems (*i.e.*, they can both shut out and reach out for single stimuli, but then achieve control over their physiological systems and states).
2. Within this controlled system, infants can begin to attend to and use social cues to prolong their states of attention and to accept and incorporate more complex trains of messages.
3. Within such an entrained or mutual reciprocal feedback system, infants and parents begin to press the limits of (a) infant capacity to take in and respond to information, and (b) infant ability to withdraw to recover in a homeostatic system. Sensitive adults press infants to the limits of both of these and allow infants time and opportunity to realize that they have incorporated these abilities into their own repertoires. The mother-infant "games" described by Stern[28] are elegant examples of the real value of this phase as a system for affective and cognitive experiences at three and four months.
4. Within the dyad or triad, the baby is allowed to demonstrate and incorporate a sense of autonomy. (This phase is perhaps the real test of attachment.) At the point where the mother or nurturing parent can indeed permit the baby to be the leader or signal-giver, when the adult can recognize and encourage the baby's independent search for and response to environmental or social cues and games—to initiate them, to reach for and play with objects, etc.—the small infant's own feeling of competence and of voluntary control over its environment is strengthened. This sense of competence is at a more complex level of awareness and is constantly influenced by the baby's feedback systems. We see this at four to five months in normal infants during a feeding, when the infant stops to look around and to process the environment. When a mother can allow for this and even foster it, she and the infant be-

---

*"His" or "he" is used here as a shortened form of his/her in referring to the baby.

come aware of the baby's burgeoning autonomy. In psychoanalytic terms, the infant's ego development is well on its way![9]

This model of development is a powerful one for understanding the reciprocal bonds that are set up between parent and infant. The feedback model allows for flexibility, disruption, and reorganization. Within its envelope of reciprocal interaction, one can conceive of a rich matrix of different modalities for communication, individualized for each pair and critically dependent on the contribution of each member of the dyad or triad. There is no reason that each system cannot be shaped in different ways by the preferred modalities for interaction of each of its participants, but each *must* be sensitive and ready to adjust to the other member in the envelope. And at successive stages of development, the envelope will be different; richer, we would hope.

I regard these observations as evidence for the first stages of emotional and cognitive awareness in the infant and in the nurturing "other." A baby is learning about himself, developing an ego base. The mother and father who are attached to and intimately involved with this infant are both consciously and unconsciously aware of parallel stages of their own development as nurturers.[9]

These four stages of learning about each other constitute a kind of entrainment of developmental processes for each participant with those of the other participant. Thus, they are learning as much about social communication as they are about themselves in the process. Learning about the internal control system becomes the experimental base for internalizing a kind of early ego function for the small infant. As infants achieve homeostasis and then go on to learn about a less-than-balanced state of expectation and excitement within a nurturant envelope, they learn about the control systems and the capacities for emotional experience with which they are endowed. They are experiencing emotion. As they learn to elicit and then to reply to the nurturant adults around them, they learn the importance of communication and even the experiencing of emotion in "the other." Thus, they are experiencing the ingredients of affect within themselves and learning to demonstrate and to enrich their responses to the external world in order to elicit affect in others.

As they engage, respond to, and enlarge upon the adult's responses, infants learn from adults how to produce an appropriate affective environment—one that is appropriate and necessary for learning about themselves and about their world. Thus, infants are learning to fuel both sources of energy—that from within and that from without. They learn about causality within the emotional sphere. They begin to internalize controls that are necessary for experiencing emotion but also learn what is necessary for producing emotional responses from others. By the end of the fourth month, infants can "turn on" or "turn off" those around them with an actively controllable set of responses. They have begun to learn how to manipulate their own experience and their own world. The emotions that they are experiencing and registering unconsciously by this age can be consciously manipulated as well. They have been learning about their own emotions within the envelope of attachment.[6,9] The anlages for detachment and autonomy are surfacing and the precursors for the infant's superego are already apparent.

In summary, the precursors for ego function, the anlages of emotional experience in an older child, are observable in the behavior of the fetus and infant. The experience of completing an anticipated act of social communication closes a feedback cycle, creating a sense of mastery that confirms children's sense of self and fuels them toward further development. By entraining the nurturant environment around them, infants add a further source of fuel as it provides an envelope within which they can learn more quickly a sense of self and the mastery of complex inner control mechanisms as well as social response systems that will assure them of future nurturance. Thus, early experience provides the base for precursors of future emotion.

What if the infant is deprived of this opportunity for learning about himself? We can now begin to conceptualize how experience can be represented in the memory of infants and how it can shape them toward future responses. These early experiences, when they are repeated, and when they are accompanied by a behavioral representation of recognition in the infant, must be considered as potential anlages (or precursors) of future ego development or as precursors of cognitive patterns, shaping the infant toward preferred psychomotor patterns. These early reactions are likely to become, as Greenacre[20] put it, the "precursors for future response patterns." If they are successful patterns in early infancy, the chances are that they will be repeated, be learned, and eventually become preferred patterns in the older infant. In this way, behavior that represents reactions of the infant becomes a precursor for future development.

An understanding of the infant's development within any particular developmental line—such as that of affect or emotional development—must include the interaction between this and other developmental lines. The immaturity of cognitive neuro-motor and psychophysiological equipment of the baby limits the infant's potential for developing clearly definable emotions in the early months. The responses of the infant's neurological and physical systems are at the core of any development of emotions. The immaturity of these systems places obvious restraints on development, but their experiential maturation forms the base for future emotional experience. As infants learn to cope with a stimulus from the outside world, they experience a sense of achievement, and the feedback system that is activated may give them an inner representation of mastery.[31] Although this terminology is "adulto-morphic" and probably represents mechanisms that are more consciously experienced in an older child or adult, it seems to me that the concepts of mastery and learning do fit the anlage of experiences on which the infant begins to build.

The central nervous system (CNS), as it develops, drives the infant toward maturation and mastery of self and world. Any internal equilibrium is tested and upset by the imbalance that is created as the CNS matures. Hence, maturation and an increase in differentiation of infant skills and potential become a force that drives the infant to reorganize and "relearn" control systems. Each step is a new opportunity for mastery and for learning new feedback systems.

There are two sources fueling this maturation. Feedback loops that close on completion of an experience after an anticipated performance affect the baby from within. Our concept is that, as each step is mastered, anticipation has generated energy that becomes realized and is available as the step is completed. In this way, a sense of mastery[31] is incorporated by the developing infant, and this liberated energy drives the infant toward the next developmental achievement. Meanwhile, there is a second important source of energy that fuels infant development and enhances each experience. The environment around the infant, when it is nurturant, tends to entrain responsive behavior to the behavior of the infant. Not only do parents register recognition and approval of an infant's achievement, but they add a salient, more developed signal to their approval. This signal, coupled with the positive reinforcement, both fuels the infant and leads the child to match the adult's expectation. For example, when an infant vocalizes with an "Ooh," a parent couples an added

experience with open approval of the infant's production. Thus parents offer the infant positive reinforcement and an added stimulus to reach for. This fuels the infant to go on.[2]

These two sources of energy—one from within, the other from without—are in balance under ideal conditions, and both provide the energy for future development. The infant's recognition of each of these sources, as he or she masters a developmental step, is often unconscious, but it adds to a preconscious recognition of mastery. This internal representation, coupled with the closure of feedback loops of mastery of steps in autonomic and CNS control, must become the precursors of emotional as well as of cognitive recognition and contribution toward the infant's developing ego.

When either of these are deficient, the infant's development of affective and cognitive stages can be impaired. This occurs when (a) an infant is at risk for CNS or autonomic deficits (such as one whose autonomic system is too labile or too sluggish, or one whose threshold for intake of stimuli is too low and is thus overwhelmed by each stimulus); or (b) when the environment is inappropriately responsive to the infant (either under or over). Thus, the internal and external feedback systems become intertwined from the first. Since each is dependent on the infant's endowment and capacity for overt and internalized reactions, the infant's genetic capacities determine the kind of internal and external feedback systems that are available. They both fuel the infant's development and place limits on it.

When parents are deprived too early of this opportunity to participate in the baby's developing ego structure, they lose the opportunity to understand the baby intimately and to feel their own role in development of these four stages. The likelihood that they will feel cheated of the opportunity for their own development as nurturing adults is great.

When a new mother must share her small baby with a secondary caregiver, she will almost inevitably experience a sense of loss. Her feelings of competition with the other caregiver may well be uppermost in her consciousness. But beneath this conscious feeling of competition there is likely to be a less-than-conscious sense of grief. Lindemann[25] described a syndrome, which he labeled a grief reaction, that seems to fit the experiences that mothers of small babies describe when they leave them in substitute care. They are apt to feel sad, helpless, hopeless, inadequate to their babies. They feel a sense of loneliness, of depression, of slowed down physical responses, and even of somatic symptoms. To protect themselves from these feelings, they are likely to develop three defenses.[10] These are healthy, normal, and necessary defenses, but they can interfere with the mother's attachment to her baby if they are not properly evaluated. The younger the baby and the more inexperienced the mother, the stronger and more likely are these defenses. They are correlated with the earliness with which she returns to work:

1. *Denial.* A mother is likely to deny that her leaving has consequences—for the child or for herself. She will distort or ignore any signals in herself or in the baby to the contrary. Mothers who obviously know better will not visit their baby's day care center "because it is too painful." The denial may be a necessary defense against painful feelings but it may distort a mother's capacity to make proper decisions.
2. *Projection.* Working parents will have a tendency to project the important caregiving issues onto the substitute caregivers. Responsibility for both good and bad will be shifted, and often sidestepped.
3. *Detachment.* Not because she doesn't care but because it is painful to care and to be separated, the mother will tend to distance her feelings of responsibility and of intense attachment.

These three defenses are commonly necessary for mothers to handle the new feelings engendered by separating from a small baby. For example, imagine the feelings of a mother who returns to pick her baby up from the day care center at the end of a working day. The baby has saved up all his important feelings and now blows up in a temper tantrum when the mother arrives. At that point, someone in the day care center turns to her and says, "He never cries like that with me, dear."

These conflicting emotions need to be faced by new parents and understood by them in order to prevent costly adjustments which are not in the family's best interests. We need to prepare working parents for their roles in order to preserve the positive forces in strong attachments—to the baby and to each other. We certainly must protect the period in which the attachment process is solidified and stabilized by new parents. With the new baby, this is likely to demand at least four months in which the new mother can feel herself free of competing demands of the workplace. Since most young families cannot afford a period of unpaid leave, and since the workplace is not inclined to provide such a period without sanc-

tions against the new family, it seems critical at this time to work toward a nationally subsidized policy for paid leave at the time of a new baby. Such national recognition of the importance of the family could become symbolic recognition of the value of the family. It might serve to heighten the emphasis on strong ties within the family, at a time when the national trend toward divorce and instability of attachments has proven especially costly to our children.[21,30] As a nation, we can no longer afford to ignore our responsibilities toward children and their families.

SUBSTITUTE CARE

Obviously, it is critical that parents be provided the opportunity for optimal substitute child care. If a mother is to be free emotionally to realize her potential in the workplace, she must be confident that her baby is in good hands. And, of course, it is critical for children to grow and develop in a caring, stimulating environment. The younger the child, the more critical is environment for the future of his or her emotional and cognitive development.

Results of the research that has looked into outcomes for infants and toddlers who have been in substitute care have ranged from citing the dangers and potential emotional damage[1,16–19,27] to reporting potential emotional gains. Most studies to date have not found negative consequences,[4,14,15,22] but these studies tend to be biased in one of several ways. They have investigated short-term outcomes, they have studied middle-class, supervised day care, and their outcome measures may not have been aimed appropriately at the total child's development. Certainly, for millions of children, substitute care may not be optimal and we shall not understand fully the consequences for another generation.

We must have adults who can relate individually to each baby with an appropriate amount of time and the energy to assure reciprocal, sensitive, caring responses. Safety and intellectual stimulation are elemental to such care. In order to provide this for each baby, we cannot tolerate ratios of more than one adult to every three infants, or one adult for every four toddlers.[22,26] In addition, these adults need to be mature and well trained in such areas as the necessary requirements of social, intellectual, and physical parameters of infant development. The training for caregivers must be required and supervision for quality assurance be mandated at local, state and national levels.[32,33]

Optimal day care would include parents in the curriculum. Not only could parents be urged to participate actively in their babies' care but the centers could provide opportunities for education, for peer support groups, and for the nurturing comforts for parenting that have been lost by nuclear families. Thus, with quality day care, both families and their small children could benefit.

Our future generations are at stake. Throughout the last 40 years, Spitz, Bowlby, Harlow, and many subsequent researchers have pointed to the importance of providing a nurturing environment for small children. At present, infant caregivers are too often untrained, unsupervised, and grossly underpaid. But until we provide them with the salaries necessary for professionals, we cannot expect training or supervision to be successful. Even under the present conditions, the choices in child care for over 50 percent of working mothers are grossly inadequate. Poor, vulnerable people are unable to find care of any quality and must leave their small children in dangerously inadequate circumstances. Physical abuse and neglect, as well as sexual abuse, are inevitable under such conditions.

We must provide vital safeguards if we mean to protect the future development of small children of working parents. These are costly, and cannot be paid for by parents alone. Our responsibility as mental health and child care professionals requires that we work toward development of a national policy with national subsidy.

References

1. Ainsworth, M. 1979. Attachment as related to mother-infant interaction. *In* Advances in the Study of Behavior, Vol. 9. J. Rosenblatt et al, eds. Academic Press, New York.
2. Als, H. 1978. Assessing an assessment. *In* Organization and Stability of Newborn Behavior: Commentary on the Brazelton Neonatal Behavioral Assessment Scale, A. Sameroff, ed. Mongr. Soc. Res. Child Devlpm. 43(177):14–29.
3. Beal, J. 1984. The effect of demonstration of the Brazelton Neonatal Assessment Scale on the father-infant relationship. Presented to the International Conference in Infant Studies, New York.
4. Belsky, J., Steinberg, L., and Walker, A. 1982. The ecology of day care. *In* Childrearing in Nontraditional Families. M. Lamb, ed. Erlbaum, Hillsdale, N.J.
5. Bibring, G., Dwyer, T. and Valenstein, A. 1961. A study of the psychological processes in pregnancy. Psychoanal. Stud. Child 16:9–72.
6. Bowlby, J. 1973. Attachment and Loss, Vol. 2. Basic Books, New York.
7. Braun, S. and Caldwell, B. 1973. Emotional adjustment of children in day care who enrolled prior to or after the age of three. Early Child Devlpm. Care 2:13–21.
8. Brazelton, T. 1973. The Neonatal Behavioral Assessment Scale. Spastics International Medical Publications, Heinemann, London. (Lippincott, Philadelphia, 1984)
9. Brazelton, T. 1983. Precursors for the development of emotions in early infancy. *In* Theory, Research and Experience, Vol. 2, R. Pluchik, ed. Academic Press, New York.
10. Brazelton, T. 1985. Working and Caring. Addison-Wesley, Boston.
11. Brazelton, T. and Als, H. 1979. Four early stages in the development of mother-infant interaction. Psychoanal. Stud. Child 34:349–369.
12. Brazelton, T., Koslowski B. and Main, M. 1974. The origins of reciprocity: the early mother-infant interaction. *In* The Effect of the Infant on Its Caregiver. M. Lewis and L. Rosenblum, Eds., John Wiley, New York.
13. Brazelton, T. et al. 1975. Early mother-infant reciprocity *In* Parent-Infant Interaction, Ciba Foundation Symposium 33. Elsevier, Amsterdam.
14. Caldwell, B. et al. 1970. Infant day care and attachment. Amer. J. Orthopsychiat. 40:397–412.
15. Clarke-Stewart, K. et al. 1980. Development and prediction of children's sociability from 1 to 2½ years. Devlpm. Psychol. 16:290–302.
16. Egelund, B. and Sroufe, L. 1981. Attachment and early maltreatment. Child Devlpm. 52:44–52.
17. Farber, E. and Egelund, B. 1982. Developmental consequences of out-of-home care for infants in a low income population. *In* Day Care: Scientific and Social Policy Issues, E. Zigler and E. Gordon, eds., Auburn House, Boston.
18. Fraiberg, S. 1977. Every Child's Birthright: In Defense of Mothering. Basic Books, New York.
19. Gamble, T. and Zigler, E. 1986. Effects of infant day care: another look at the evidence, Amer. J. Orthopsychiat. 56:26–42.
20. Greenacre, P. 1941. The Predisposition to Anxiety: Trauma, Growth, and Personality (Parts I and II). International Universities Press, New York.
21. Hetherington, M. 1981. Children and Divorce, *In* Parent-Child Interaction: Theory, Research, and Prospect, R. Henderson, ed. Academic Press, New York.
22. Kagan, J. 1982. Psychological Research on the Human Infant: An Evaluation Summary. W. T. Grant Foundation Publications, New York.
23. Kessen, W., Haith, M. and Salapatek, P. 1970. Human infancy: a bibliography and guide. *In* Charmichael's' Manual of Child Psychology (Vol. 1), W. Mussen, ed. John Wiley, New York.

24. Klaus, M. and Kennell, J. 1970. Mothers separated from their newborn infants. Pediat. Clin. N. A. 17:1015.

25. Lindemann, E. 1944. Grief. Amer. J. Psychiat. 101:141.

26. Rutter, M. 1981. Social-emotional consequences of day care for preschool children. Amer. J. Orthopsychiat. 51:4–28.

27. Schwartz, P. 1983. Length of day care attendance and attachment behavior in eighteen-month-old infants. Child Devlpm. 54:1073–1078.

28. Stern, D. 1974. The goal and structure of mother-infant play. J. Amer. Acad. Child Psychiat. 13:402–421.

29. U.S. Senate. 1982. American Families: Trends and Pressures. Joint Hearings before the Subcommittee on Children and Youth and the Committee on Labor and Public Welfare (Sept.).

30. Wallerstein, J. and Kelly, J. 1975. The effect of parental divorce: experiences of the preschool child. J. Amer. Acad. Child Psychiat. 14:600–616.

31. White, R. 1959. Motivation reconsidered: the concept of competence. Psychol. Rev. 66:297–333.

32. Zigler, E. and Butterfield, E. 1968. Motivational aspects of changes in IQ test performance of culturally deprived nursery school children. Child Devlpm. 39:1–14.

33. Zigler, E. and Trickett, P. 1978. IQ, social competence, and evaluation of early childhood intervention programs. Amer. Psychol. 33:789–798.

8

CHILD-REARING PATTERNS IN DEPRESSED, ABUSIVE, AND NORMAL MOTHERS

Elizabeth J. Susman
Penelope K. Trickett

Ronald J. Iannotti
Barbara E. Hollenbeck
Carolyn Zahn-Waxler

National Institute of Mental Health
Bethesda, Maryland

Several studies have identified links between depression in parents and emotional problems in their offspring. Children of depressed parents are reported to have a relatively high incidence of depression.[4] They also exhibit other disturbances in their social interactions and emotional functioning, such as social isolation, aggression, anxiety, and dysregulation of emotion following stress.[19,28,32,37] Attempts to unravel the etiology of intergenerational transmission of depression and related affective disturbances have focused on both biological and behavioral explanations.[3,12,15] Systematic research on those specific characteristics of heredity and environment that could predispose an individual to emotional problems is, however, quite new.

The present research was designed to explore characteristics of the child-rearing environments created by parental depression which could, in turn, influence the social and emotional development of the offspring. Clinically depressed mothers were compared with diagnosis-free mothers, as well as with mothers who physically abused their children. Clinical accounts of abusive parents frequently contain references to their high levels of depression. But, by definition, their primary presenting symptoms or emotional dysregulation are manifested in overt expressions of hostility and anger that culminate in physical harm to the child. Pure depression, on the other hand, more characteristically is viewed as reflecting sadness, anhedonia, and an internalizing of angry impulses. The extent to which parental depression and abuse are similar or different entities and hence result in overlapping or unique problems in child rearing is an unresolved empirical question.

Information regarding depressed parenting styles derives from many clinical observations and from few investigations. Mostly lower-class populations of depressed women have been studied. Hence, little is known about the rearing of depressed middle-class mothers and the extent to which their children may be buffered by protective factors that higher socioeconomic status makes possible. In parent-child interaction, the depressed parent has been variously described as hostile, critical, and rejecting;[5,14,24,33-35] as emotionally withdrawn from the child[16,33] and as having unrealistic expectations and standards regarding the child.[12,39] In some of these studies, depressed mothers have also been characterized as inconsistent and disorganized; high levels of conflict between the spouses have been reported as well.

Anthony[1,2] has described the potentially deleterious consequences for the child of the depressed parents' preoccupation, immaturity, deficits in empathy, and failures in the capacity to achieve mutuality and reciprocity in interpersonal relations. Such problems might be expected to foster impairments in affectional bonds between parent and child and parental encouragement of autonomy and separation-individuation. There is virtually no corresponding systematic research on specific dimensions of the child-rearing practices of physically abusive parents.

From *American Journal of Orthopsychiatry,* 55 (2): 237–251. Copyright © 1985. The American Orthopsychiatric Association, Inc. Reprinted by permission.

[Editor's Note: I have excerpted portions of this paper by Dr. Susman and her colleagues, emphasizing the research question and the answers that emerged. Omitted from this selection is the discussion of research methods. Ninety-four mothers involved in ongoing investigations of atypical child-rearing environments were studied. The specific procedures and the detailed tables of results are also omitted. Students interested in these aspects are directed to the original article.]

Several of the same hypothesized characteristics of depressed parents would seem equally applicable to abusive parents, especially the hostility. There have been, for example, some suggestions of connections between depression and child abuse, which may be a function, in part, of the degree of hostility that exists between a depressed mother and her child.[22]

An assumption of this study was that many of the symptoms of depression become reflected directly in the child-rearing attitudes and practices of depressed mothers in the arenas of teaching, discipline, and social-emotional development. Symptoms of depression such as sadness, irritability, social withdrawal, rumination, low self-esteem, guilt, and cognitive confusion would seem especially likely to influence parent-child interactions. That depression reflects physiological as well as psychological disturbance suggests that themes of pain and suffering, too, may become deeply entrenched in the interactions of depressed parents with their children. In conjunction with the heightened capacity for guilt of depressed individuals, this parental vulnerability to pain and fatigue may produce a special sensitivity to issues of blame, hurting, suffering, and feelings of responsibility. Such sensitivity, in turn, may make these mothers prone to emphasize self-sacrifice and use guilt-inducing techniques with their children.

Still other characteristics of the parenting patterns of depressed adults could be identified that might create disturbances in parent-child interaction. While it is usually suggested that parental affective illness creates problems for the offspring, it is also important to recognize that emotional illness has sometimes been shown to create special opportunities for children.[10,21] Deviance or divergence from the norm need not always be seen as a sign of maladaptation or psychopathology. Hence, there are many complexities of research design and interpretation to be considered. There is still a considerable distance between hypotheses and theories of depression, and systematic empirical data on child-rearing patterns of depressed and nondepressed mothers. Studies are needed in which parent-child interaction is carefully observed.[25] There is a need, as well, for systematic surveys in which parents are queried about child-rearing patterns, using standardized research instruments that minimize the likelihood of obtaining socially desired responses. Information is also needed regarding the extent to which child-rearing practices are influenced (a) by the severity and type of the parental depression, (b) by the recency of the illness, and (c) by the diagnostic entity

of depression as opposed to some other form of parental emotional difficulty (e.g., schizophrenia, alcoholism, anxiety or hostility, etc.).

This investigation was designed to begin to examine some of these issues. Variations in the child-rearing values in mothers with different kinds of diagnosed unipolar depression were assessed using the Block Child-Rearing Practices Report,[6] a standardized instrument that has been employed in a number of studies to assess child-rearing attitudes, values, philosophies, and practices. It covers a wide range of psychological issues that confront all parents. Recently it revealed atypical rearing patterns regarding the socialization, expression, and control of emotion in families with a manic-depressive parent.[13] Middle-class mothers with (1) past major depression, (2) current major depression, (3) past minor depression, and (4) current minor depression were seen in the present study. The psychiatric assessments were based on Research Diagnostic Criteria. These mothers were compared with diagnosis-free, middle-class mothers and also with a sample of women who had physically abused one of their children. The maltreating group was lower in socioeconomic status (SES), hence a second matched SES comparison group was included. The primary research foci involved comparisons of mothers having different types of depression with normal and abusing mothers. Separate examination of the two control groups, however, also permitted examination of the relationship between socioeconomic status (which might be conceptualized as a depressogenic experience) and child-rearing patterns.[24] Differences in mothers rearing of boys and of girls[7] were also examined. The possible link between the higher incidence of depression among women than among men may have origins in early socialization experiences. Environments may be fashioned in childhood that permit more striving, achievement, and independence in males[7] and hence more real and perceived control over their lives. . . .

RESULTS

Normal middle-class mothers expressed emotions openly with their children, encouraged similar openness in their children, and experienced a preponderance of positive rather than negative emotions toward their children. With regard to their role as an authority figure, these mothers expressed conviction in discipline practices that emphasize reasoning and rational guidance in contrast to techniques that are authoritarian, arbitrary, unnecessarily strict or repressive, or that are fraught with worries. Finally, these mothers were especially likely to value the child and to encourage the kind of parent-child separation that is presumed necessary for the development of sense of self, autonomy, and independence; correspondingly, they were unlikely to be overly protective, holding the child back from the kinds of new experiences that permit and promote intellectual and interpersonal growth.

Atypicalities in rearing practices were most apparent in mothers who physically abused their children. These data indicate that child abuse is part of a much larger constellation of parenting problems that pervade the entire socialization system, including motives and goals as well as behavior. This generalization is, however, at odds with conclusions of several others who have studied the etiology of child abuse,[27] particularly from a behavior modification perspective. Thus it has been argued that abusive families and normal families do not differ on the great majority of their interactions with their children; rather, abuse is largely the product of particular discipline situations in which coercive cycles become established and escalate to levels that provoke the abuse. These contrasting generalizations have very different implications for treatment and intervention; one would suggest a primary focus on the behavior in the discipline encounters; the other would suggest a much wider focus on modification of motives, goals, and values, as well as aversive behavior.

The problems of middle-class depressed mothers paralleled the problems of abusive mothers on those dimensions consistent with earlier studies indicating that depressed mothers are hostile, rejecting, and conflictual about their children. Recently, for example, Weisman[34] has described the high levels of anger and conflict that depressed women express toward their children and husbands in the family setting, yet which tend to remain hidden from the therapist who sees the depressed, compliant, self-deprecatory side of the individual. It is important to recall, however, that the deviations seen here in the rearing practices of depressed women were not as strong or as pervasive as those of abusive mothers. Furthermore, mothers whose depression was neither severe nor current responded very much like normal middle-class mothers. When deviations in the rearing practices of depressed mothers appeared, they were reflected in differences in the domains of emotion regulation and separation-individuation more than in the domains of discipline and encouragement

of achievement. Differences in discipline patterns that did occur, namely high guilt-induction and high anxiety induction coupled with inconsistency, are illustrative of how specific symptoms of depression may affect child-rearing processes. For example, the items that defined inconsistency concerned (a) threatening punishment but then not giving it and (b) forgetting promises that were made to the child. Such behavior may reflect the helplessness, lowered social competence, impairment of memory function, or self-preoccupation and rumination that commonly accompany depression.

High guilt induction and high anxiety induction characterized the abusive mothers as well as the currently seriously depressed mothers. But the implications for the child must be very different if these techniques are accompanied by harsh, authoritarian, sometimes abusive actions. If guilt-induction attempts are successful, the guilt experienced by the child of an abusive parent, more than of a depressed parent, may be linked with high levels of fear and anger as well. The Block Q-sort procedure does not make it possible to determine precisely how each of the different child-rearing practices are experienced by the child and the extent to which they occur. Observational studies will be needed to address these issues. One might hypothesize that for some children, particularly those of depressed mothers, depending on how the guilt-induction is dispensed, it could represent a relatively benign, educational influence of (a) sensitizing a child to the negative emotional experiences of others and (b) the development of feelings of responsibility to ease the difficulties of others. Or it could draw the child too far into the realm of parental suffering and be counterproductive. One recent study has found that toddlers of mothers who were diagnosed with depression, but who were not seriously ill, were especially *unlikely* to show physical aggression toward their playmates.[38] Similarly, exposure to parental depression has been described in the clinical literature as an incentive to later entry into the mental health professions. This may result, in part, from early lessons about the importance of not hurting others, which in turn may be very much linked to parental reliance on techniques that attempt to induce feelings of responsibility in the child.[36] The points at which these rearing methods technically become labeled as guilt-induction, and at which the techniques (a) become so strong as to induce unrealistic feelings of responsibility for the problems of others or (b) backfire to produce resentment and reactance, is an important empirical issue.

Consistent with previous research,[9,17,23,24] lower-class parenting attitudes and values were suggestive of greater punitiveness and restrictiveness, a reliance on authoritarian disciplinary practices, and an emphasis on traditional values more than on values of self-reliance, eagerness for learning, and growth as a person. The partial overlap of some rearing practices of depressed mothers with those of abusing and lower SES mothers may be illustrative of "depressogenic" environmental conditions, in addition to those that derive from formal psychiatric diagnoses which result in some rearing problems. Many of these depressogenic experiences may, in turn, be the result of living in highly stressful and sometimes dangerous environments which are also characterized by a real lack of control over (aversive) life circumstances.

In 1973, Block[7] reported that parents of girls, more than parents of boys, were likely to exert constraints on the development of autonomy, achievement, and independence. Other studies, too, have indicated that parents allow males more freedom from adult supervision than they do females, and that females are more sheltered.[20] The findings from the present study suggest that little has changed in this respect, with parents still adhering to values and practices with their girls that are likely to interfere with the development of assertiveness, competence, independence, and positive control over life events—and hence, perhaps, to facilitate the development of dependency, helplessness, and hopelessness. Thus, the higher incidence of depression in females than in males could result, in part, from the very different environments in which they have been reared. Mother of females, in turn, may be less open to providing new experiences for these children, and may enjoy their parental role less because of realistic concerns about the long-term welfare of their female children, particularly regarding their ability to become self-sufficient and to earn an adequate in-

come. This negative cycle of socialization experiences is likely to be difficult to alter. That the sex differences in the socialization experiences reported here were less true of middle-class than lower-class mothers suggests, however, that significant cultural changes have already been set into motion.

There are many research questions left unanswered. It is not possible, within the design of this study, to determine exactly the independent contributions of different conditions—such as parental depression, parental hostility, socioeconomic status, or rearing a female child—to deviations in child-rearing practices. Sorely needed, too, is research that examines the connections between parents' stated child-rearing values and their actual behavior in interaction with the child.[26] It is possible, for example, that the self-reports of a depressed mother may be biased against herself: the guilty and self-deprecatory stance that commonly accompanies depression could lead the mother to view her parenting as worse than it really is.[10] The self-report items also may be subject to various interpretations by different parents, depending on other characteristics of their environments, their personalities, and their children's personalities. The children of emotionally disturbed parents may already be functioning in nonoptimal ways that are contributing to the parenting problems. Observations of the actual child-rearing practices would aid in determining whether certain patterns should be viewed as adaptive or maladaptive. Many of the "maladaptive" practices identified in this study may, in fact, be finely tuned and adaptive to the particular social-cultural climate in which the child is reared. Additional information on child-rearing in conjunction with other data on the biological and familial backgrounds of these parents and on the child's social-emotional development is needed to bring us closer to understanding the impact on the developing child of emotional illness in the parent.

References

1. Anthony, E. 1975, The influence of a manic-depressive environment on the developing child. *In* Depression and Human Existence, E. Anthony and T. Benedek, eds. Little, Brown, Boston.
2. Anthony, E. 1983. An overview of the effects of maternal depression on the infant and child. *In* Children of Depressed Parents: Risk, Identification and Intervention, H. Morrison ed. Grune and Stratton, New York.
3. Akiskal, H. and McKinney, W. 1975. Overview of recent research in depression: integration of ten conceptual models into a comprehensive clinical frame. Arch. Gen. Psychiat. 32:285–305.
4. Beardslee, W. et al. 1983. Children of parents with major affective disorder: a review, Amer. J. Psychiat. 140:825–832.
5. Belle, D. 1979. Mothers and their children: a study of low income families. *In* The Evolving Female, C. Heckerman, ed. Human Sciences Press, New York.
6. Block, J. 1965. The Child Rearing Practices Report, Institute of Human Development, University of California, Berkeley.

7. Block, J. 1973. Conception of sex roles, Amer. Psychol. 28:512–526.
8. Block, J. 1980. The Child-Rearing Practices Report (CRPR): A Set of Q Items for the Description of Parental Socialization Attitudes and Values. Institute of Human Development, University of California, Berkeley.
9. Bronfenbrenner, U. 1958. Socialization and social class through time and space. In Readings in Social Psychology (3rd Ed.), E. Maccoby, T. Newcomb and E. Hartley, eds. Holt, Rinehart and Winston, New York.
10. Cohler, B. et al. 1983. Social adjustments among schizophrenic, depressed and well mothers and their school age children. In Children of Depressed Parents: Risk, Identification and Intervention, H. Morrison, ed. Grune and Stratton, New York.
11. Conners, C. et al. 1979. Children of parents with affective illness. Amer. Acad. Child Psychiat. 18: 600–607.
12. Davenport, Y. et al. 1979. Manic depressive illness: psychodynamic features of multigenerational families. Amer. J. Orthopsychiat. 49:24–35.
13. Davenport, Y. et al. 1984. Early childrearing practices in bipolar families. Amer. J. Psychiat. 141: 230–235.
14. Fabian, A. and Donohue, J. 1956. Maternal depression: a challenging child guidance problem. Amer. J. Orthopsychiat. 26:400–405.
15. Fieve, R., Mendlewicz, J. and Fleiss, J. 1973. Manic-depressive illness: linkage with the hg blood group. Amer. J. Psychiat. 130:1355–1359.
16. Grunebaum, H. et al. 1978. Children of depressed and schizophrenic mothers. Child Psychiat. Hum. Devlpm. 8:219–229.
17. Hess, R. and Shipman, V. 1965. Early experience and the socialization of cognitive modes in children. Child Devlpm. 34:869–886.
18. Hollingshead, A. 1975. Four Factor Index of Social Status, Department of Sociology, Yale University, New Haven, Conn.
19. Hops, J. et al. 1983. Direct observation study of family processes in maternal depression. Presented to the American Psychological Association, Anaheim, Calif.
20. Huston, A. 1983. Socialization personality and social development. In Handbook of Child Psychology, P. Mussen, ed. John Wiley, New York.
21. Kauffman, C. et al. 1970. Superkids; competent children of psychotic mothers. Amer. J. Psychiat. 11:1398–1402.
22. Kinard, E. 1980. Child abuse and depression: cause or consequence? Presented to the American Public Health Association, Detroit.
23. Kohn, M. 1959. Social class and parental values. Amer. J. Sociol. 64:337–351.
24. Longfellow, C., Zelkowitz, P. and Saunders, E. 1982. The quality of mother-child relationships. In Lives in Stress: Women and Depression, D. Belle, ed. Sage Publications, Beverly Hills, Calif.
25. Orvaschel, H., Weissman, M. and Kidd, K. 1980. Children and depression: the children of depressed parents; the childhood of depressed patients; depression in children. J. Affect. Disord. 2:1–16.
26. Radke-Yarrow, M. et al. NIMH Research Protocol, Clinical Project Number 79–M–123, Bethesda, Md.
27. Reid, J. Social-interactional patterns in families of abused and non-abused children. In Altruism and Aggression: Social and Biological Origins, C. Zahn-Waxler, E. Cummings and R. Iannotti, eds. Cambridge University Press, New York. (in press)
28. Rolf, J. 1976. Peer status and the directionality of symptomatic behavior: social competence predictors of outcome for vulnerable children. Amer. J. Orthopsychiat. 46:74–88.
29. Sears, R., Maccoby, E. and Levin, M. 1957. Patterns of Child-Rearing. Row, Patterson, Evanston, Ill.
30. Spitzer, R. and Endicott, J. 1978. Schedule for Affective Disorders and Schizophrenia—Lifetime Version, New York State Psychiatric Institute.
31. Trickett, P., Susman, E. and Lowrie, I. The impact of the child-rearing environment on the social and emotional development of the physically abused child. NIMH Research Protocol, Clinical Project Number 80–CM–112.
32. Weintraub, S., Prinz, R. and Neale, G. 1978. Peer evaluations of the competence of children vulnerable to psychopathology. J. Abnorm. Child Psychol. 6:461–473.
33. Weissman, M. and Paykel, E. 1974. The Depressed Woman, University of Chicago Press, Chicago.
34. Weissman, M. 1983. The depressed mother and her rebellious adolescent. In Children of Depressed Parents: Risk, Identification and Intervention, H. Morrison, ed. Grune and Stratton, New York.
35. Weissman, M., Paykel, E. and Klerman, G. 1972. The depressed woman as a mother. Soc. Psychiat. 7:98–108.
36. Zahn-Waxler, C., Radke-Yarrow, M. and King, R. 1979. Child-rearing and children's prosocial initiations toward victims of distress. Child Devlpm. 50:319–330.
37. Zahn-Waxler, C., et al. 1984. Altruism, aggression, and social interactions in young children with a manic-depressive parent. Child Devlpm. 55:112–122.
38. Zahn-Waxler, C. et al. 1984. Young offspring of depressed parents: a population at risk for affective problems. In New Directions for Child Development; Developmental Approaches to Childhood Depression, D. Cicchetti and K. Schneider-Rosen, eds. Jossey-Bass, San Francisco.
39. Zelkowitz, P. 1982. Parenting philosophies and practices. In Lives in Stress: Women and Depression, D. Belle, ed. Sage Publications, Beverly Hills, Calif.

9

EMPLOYERS AND CHILD CARE:
WHAT ROLES DO THEY PLAY?

Howard V. Hayghe
Division of Labor Force Statistics
Bureau of Labor Statistics
Washington, D.C.

As more and more mothers are joining the ranks of the employed, child care has become one of today's most widely debated social and political issues. Awareness of the problem has spread dramatically, as demonstrated by the recent report by the Secretary of Labor and by child-care initiatives presently in the Congress.[1] Employers, too, are beginning to be involved in the search for solutions.

As in the past, American employers on the whole still do not play an active role in the care of their workers' children. However, with mothers becoming a more important part of the work force, some employers are coming to realize that the difficulties that their employees face in arranging care for their children may result in absenteeism, tardiness, low morale, and productivity problems. This may be exacerbated in some areas by worker shortages. Consequently, there is some evidence that employers are looking at steps they can take to help their employees who are parents.[2]

To determine what employers were doing, the Bureau of Labor Statistics conducted a special nationwide survey of approximately 10,000 business establishments and government agencies in the summer of 1987.[3] Results from this survey show that direct aid to working parents is still very limited. Only about 2 percent, or 25,000, of the Nation's 1.2 million nonagricultural establishments with 10 or more employees actually sponsored day-care centers for their workers' children while an additional 3 percent provided financial assistance towards child-care expenses.[4] But, as this report will show, employers are doing a number of other things to aid employees with growing children.

SCOPE OF THE ISSUE

The potential demand for child care is immense. As of March 1987, there were 10.5 million children under the age of 6 whose mothers were in the labor force—more than half of all children these ages.[5] In addition, there were 15.7 million youngsters ages 6 to 13 whose mothers were in the labor force and who required some sort of care or supervision before or after school or on school holidays. A total of 26.1 million children under age 14 lived in homes where both parents or the lone parent was in the labor force.

How are these children being cared for? The following tabulation, which is based on data collected by the Bureau of the Census in the winter of 1984–85, shows a percentage distribution of children under age 15 in terms of the institution or person *primarily* responsible for their supervision while their mothers worked:[6]

Percent Total	100.0
In own home	17.8
In others' home	14.4
Day-care facility	9.1
School	52.2
Child cares for self	1.8
Parent	4.7

The survey also showed that there were more than a million children ages 5 to 14 who cared for themselves after school—the so-called "latch-key" children.[7] These data simplify the actual complexity of today's child-care arrangements: parents working different shifts; transporting the children to and from the day-care providers; and coping with breakdowns

---

From *Monthly Labor Review*, 1988, *111* (9): 38–43.

[Editor's Note: Three tables from the original paper are omitted. The main points of the data are summarized in the article.]

in the arrangements or other emergencies. However, child-care arrangements are not the concern solely of parents, children, and day-care providers; employers are also affected in terms of worker reliability and productivity.[8]

WHAT EMPLOYERS REPORTED

In the survey conducted in the summer of 1987, about 11 percent of the establishments with 10 employees or more reported that they provided at least some employees such direct benefits as employer-sponsored day care, financial assistance toward it, or information and referral services to guide employees to child-care providers in their communities. Typically, large establishments (250 employees or more) were far more likely than small ones to offer such child-care benefits to their employees. Private employers in the service sector and government agencies were much more likely than goods-producing establishments to offer child-care benefits to their employees.

About three-fifths of the establishments reported that at least some of their workers could take advantage of indirect benefits in the form of work-schedule or leave policies that could aid them in fulfilling their family obligations including child care. Such policies—which include flexitime, flexible leaves, and voluntary shifts to part-time work schedules—may or may not have been initiated with child care in mind.

Small establishments were just as likely as the large ones to provide such "liberal" work-schedule/leave policies, while private service sector establishments (which include day-care providers) were more likely than either goods-producing firms or government agencies to have them in place. Moreover, when both industry and size of establishment are taken in account, flexible work-schedule/leave policies were more prevalent among large private service sector establishments and government agencies than among large goods-producing establishments. One reason for this difference may be that in order to coordinate the production processes and maximize efficiency, large establishments in goods-producing industries are more likely to adhere to rigidly standardized work schedules.[9]

Work force composition—especially the proportion of women—is undoubtedly a major factor underlying the extent of child-care assistance (either benefits or work-schedule policies) by industry. In the summer of 1987, 53 percent of payroll employees in private service-producing establishments were women, as were 51 percent in government agencies.

In contrast, just 28 percent of the workers in goods-producing establishments were women, including only 11 percent in mining and construction (combined).

DIRECT BENEFITS

The direct child-care benefits that some employers provide fall into five basic categories: employer-sponsored day care; assistance with child-care costs; information and referral to community child-care resources; counseling services; and a variety of miscellaneous benefits. Employer-sponsored child care includes a variety of arrangements such as onsite day care or care at a nearby location and consortia (that is, several employers joining together to establish a day-care center for use by their employees). Also included are day-care providers that accept their own employees' children.

Likewise, employer assistance with child-care costs comes in many different forms. These include flexible spending accounts, contractual arrangements with day-care providers that allocate space for employees' children or give them discounts, or giving employees vouchers (or checks) to defray their expenses. The voucher method may be included as part of the regular benefits package or may be an option in a "cafeteria" or flexible compensation plan.

Child-care information and referral services provided by employers can range from something as simple as maintaining a list of child-care providers all the way up to staff assistance in locating and evaluating the providers and even matching the employees with the most appropriate provider. Counseling services include advice and information on parenting and parenting problems, while the "other" or miscellaneous category includes each disparate—and often informal—benefits as payment for extra child-care expenses incurred because of overtime or illness of the child to bringing the child to work (school bus drivers are an example of the latter).

As already noted, relatively few employers provide such direct benefits. The most frequently provided—10 percent of the establishments—are information, referral, and counseling services. Only 2 percent of establishments provided day-care facilities (either onsite or through a consortium); some of these employers turned out to be day-care businesses which made their facilities available to the children of their employees. An additional 3 percent of the establishments, while not providing day-care facilities, assisted with child-care expenses.

There are several reasons why employers seldom provide day care. One is, of course, cost. The employer has to be able to make a determination that a day-care center will increase productivity sufficiently—by, for example, reducing absenteeism, boosting morale, or improving recruitment and retention—to offset its cost. Another is that establishing a day-care center requires dealing with issues of legal liability as well as a thicket of state and local regulations governing such undertakings. Finally, a firm may not believe that it has a sufficient number of employees with day-care needs to justify the benefits at all.

Providing financial assistance to employees who are parents also presents problems. Employers as well as employees may not be very familiar with the methods of setting up flexible spending accounts as permitted by the Economic Recovery Tax Act of 1981.[10] Another method for assisting employees with child-care expenses are so-called "cafeteria" style, flexible compensation plans under which employees are allowed to select from a "menu" of benefits those that they feel are most appropriate to their life-cycle stage. Such plans were authorized under Section 125 of the Internal Revenue Code in 1978. However, the Internal Revenue Service subsequently challenged some versions of this arrangement, and, perhaps because of this, or because many employers may still be unfamiliar with such plans, relatively few establishments aid their employees with their child-care expenses.[11]

As might be expected, the type and frequency of child-care benefits varies by firm size. Relatively few establishments with less than 50 employees (10 to 49) offered any benefits: 2 percent sponsored day care, another 2 percent gave financial assistance, and 8 percent provided information, referral, or counseling services (or a combination of these). In contrast, 14 percent of those with at least 250 employees sponsored day care or provided financial assistance toward it, and 31 percent provided information, referral, or counseling services (or a combination).

Child-care support benefits appear to be almost unheard of in goods-producing establishments. Undoubtedly, this reflects the fact that relatively few women work in these industries. Among private service-producing establishments, 2 percent sponsored day care, and 4 percent gave some form of financial assistance, while about 10 percent provided information, referral, or counseling.

Among government agencies (federal, state, and local), however, the proportion supporting some form of day care and information, referral, or counseling was much higher than was the case in private industry, largely because of legislative and executive initiatives. For instance, California has mandated its agencies to provide information and referral services to state employees, as well as the general public. Michigan has established a pilot day-care program to serve the children of state employees, while New York State, in conjunction with its state employee unions, has created 30 day-care centers and is planning on establishing 50 or more by the end of 1988.[12] Meanwhile, the General Services Administration of the federal government has appointed an official with the specific task of creating more child-care facilities at federal agencies.[13]

When both the number of employees and the type of industry are taken into account, some interesting patterns in the availability of child-care benefits emerge. Among goods-producing industries, the proportion of establishments with day-care centers remains very low regardless of the number of employees, but the larger the firm the more likely it was to offer information, referral, and counseling services. Among service-producing establishments, the availability of all four major benefit categories also increases with size. It is notable, however, that in finance, insurance, and real estate, in which only 1.5 percent of establishments with 250 employees or more had day care, about 25 percent had at least one of the following: financial assistance, information and referral, and counseling benefits. Trade establishments, however, despite having a high proportion of female employees, were infrequent providers of benefits. Instead they offered a great deal of schedule flexibility. Service industry establishments with 250 employees or more had the highest proportion providing day-care services.

INDIRECT BENEFITS

Work-schedule policies that can aid parents in meeting their child-care responsibilities are far more common than child-care support benefits. One obvious reason is that their perceived cost, if any, is less than that of direct benefits. Moreover, such policies do not involve the legal and technical complexities of establishing and maintaining day-care centers or financial assistance benefits.

Flexitime and flexible leave are the most common forms of work-schedule/leave policies cited by employers as being of possible aid to workers with child-care problems. About 43 percent of the establishments maintained flexitime policies and an equal proportion had flexible leave arrangements.

Under flexitime, employees can vary the beginning and end times of their work day; under one version, they can work extra hours on some days so they can work fewer hours on others. Although there is surprisingly little variation in the frequency of this kind of work schedule by size of establishment, it is obviously not appropriate for all industries. Flexitime in private industry is most likely to be found in retail trade establishments and least likely to be found in mining, construction, and manufacturing, in which the close coordination of tasks and workers makes such scheduling difficult.

The retail trade industry is unique in relation to other industry categories. Seventy-two percent of retail establishments offer their employees some sort of flexible work-schedule/leave policy benefit. This is not surprising, given the seasonal peaks and troughs in demand for specific types of goods, for example, Christmas, Easter, and summer. Peaks and troughs even occur on a weekly or daily basis. Hence, it is critical for the industry to maintain highly flexible staffing patterns.[14] To attract a flexible work force, retail establishments must be prepared to offer a wide variety of work schedules. This, in turn, represents an ideal situation for persons with off-worksite responsibilities—such as mothers or students—to find employment.

Examples of flexible leave are personal leave, or sick or annual leave flexibly administered—that is, not restricted to a specific time of the year or to periods of illness (some employers allow workers to use sick leave to take care of an ill child) or vacations. Like flexitime policies, the availability of flexible leave varies little by size of establishment but does differ by industry, ranging from 37 percent in manufacturing to 47 percent in retail trade.

About 35 percent of all establishments allowed full-time employees to shift temporarily to part-time jobs on a voluntary basis with corresponding cuts in pay and benefits. The employees might work fewer hours at their usual job or be transferred to a part-time position. This practice is more prevalent among small than large establishments. It was also much more prevalent among the retail trade (50 percent) and services industries (39 percent).

Job sharing, which is the division of one full-time job into two part-time ones held by different people, was offered by about 16 percent of establish-

ments. There was very little variation in the extent of this policy by establishment size; it was more prevalent in government agencies than in industry.

The information collected in the Survey of Employer-Provided Child Care Benefits shows that employers as a group have yet to respond in a significant way to the child-care needs of their workers. About 90 percent of establishments with 10 or more employees do not provide direct benefits such as day care or financial assistance. While it is true that 60 percent allow employees to alter their work schedules in ways that might help them with child care, it must be kept in mind that these policies serve a variety of purposes and may not have been formulated with child care in mind. Thus, they do not necessarily indicate that employers are focused specifically on the child-care needs of their workers.

Great care must be taken in generalizing from these data about employers' motivations and attitudes regarding child care. Many employers, especially those with few employees, may deal with child-care problems of their workers on an *ad hoc* basis as they arise, rather than offering specific child-care benefits or establishing work-schedule policies with child care in mind. Also, although child-care benefits are sometimes used as a tool for recruitment or retention purposes, many firms may have no problems of this type.[15]

Because the 1987 survey was a one-time effort, it is difficult to extrapolate future trends from these data. It found that only 2 percent of the 442,000 establishments that reported no child-care benefits or flexible work-schedule policies said they were "considering" doing something in the future. This appears to contradict more optimistic reports and comments by experts in the field of child care which indicate that employers are generally becoming more supportive of the child-care needs of their workers.[16] However, these reports are more often than not based on anecdotal evidence rather than surveys with consistent methodologies and definitions, and so it is very difficult to derive accurate estimates of the trends in employer policies regarding child care.

Notes _____

1. See U.S. Department of Labor, Report of the Secretary's Task Force. *Child Care: A Workforce Issue.*
2. See, for example, Beth E. Hoffman, "Employee surveys spark decision to establish child care," *Quirk's Marketing Research,* August—September, 1987, p. 34; or "California makes business a partner in day-care," *Business Week,* June 8, 1987, p. 100.

3. For more information on the survey methodology, see Technical Note in "BLS Reports on Employer Child-Care Practices," USDL *News,* 88–7, Jan. 15, 1988.

4. According to the BLS *Handbook of Methods,* an establishment is defined as an economic unit which produces goods or services, such as a factory, mine, or store. It is generally at a single location and engaged predominantly in one type of economic activity. Where a single location encompasses two or more distinct activities, these are treated as separate establishments, provided that separate payroll records are available and certain other criteria are met. See Bulletin 2285 (Bureau of Labor Statistics, 1988), p. 13.

5. For further information of children and mothers, see "Over half of mothers with children one year old or under in labor force in March 1987," USDL *News,* 87–345, Aug. 12, 1987.

6. U.S. Bureau of the Census, Current Population Reports, Household Economic Studies, Series P–70, No. 9, *Who's Minding the Children? Child Care Arrangements: Winter 1984–85* (U.S. Government Printing Office, Washington, 1987), p. 3, table B.

7. *Ibid.,* p. 10, table F.

8. See M. Purnell and P. Proctor, *Industry Sponsored Child Care: A Question of Productivity,* 1977 (Texas, Industrial Commission, 1977); or P. Voydevoff, *Implications of Work-Family Relationships for Productivity* (White Plains, NY, Work in America Institute), Studies in Productivity, Vol. 13 (New York, Pergamon Press, 1982).

9. See Sheila B. Kamerman and Alfred J. Kahn, *The Responsive Workplace: Employers and a Changing Labor Force* (New York, Columbia University Press, 1987), p. 236.

10. This law created a new Section 129 of the Internal Revenue Code that provides that employees may exclude from their gross income amounts paid by employers under qualified dependent care assistance programs. Employers, in turn, may deduct as an employee fringe benefit all amounts paid into the plan, See *Employees and Child Care: Development of a New Employee Benefit,* BNA special Report (Washington, The Bureau of National Affairs, Inc., 1984), p. 13. In effect, the federal government is providing the benefit, because employees' federal income tax obligations are reduced and these savings partially offset child-care expenses.

11. *Ibid.,* pp. 14–16.

12. Statement of Shirley Dennis, director, Women's Bureau, U.S. Department of Labor, before the Subcommittee on Government Operations, U.S. House of Representatives, September 9, 1987.

13. For an overview of Federal efforts to establish day-care centers for Federal employees, see Lesley Barnes, "Agencies Open Doors to On-Site Sitting," *Government Executive,* vol. 20, No. 3, p. 50.

14. See Steven E. Haugen, "The employment expansion in retail trade, 1973–85," *Monthly Labor Review,* August 1986, p. 13.

15. *Employees and Child Care,* pp. 6–7.

16. *Ibid.,* 5.

C. Education and Dropout from Education

10

EARLY CHILDHOOD DEVELOPMENT PROGRAMS:
A PUBLIC INVESTMENT OPPORTUNITY

Lawrence J. Schweinhart
David P. Weikart
High/Scope Educational Research Foundation
Ypsilanti, Michigan

The raising of young children is changing dramatically in our time. Parental roles are shifting as unprecedented numbers of mothers are joining the work force. Single-parent families and poverty among children are both on the increase. Amid these changes, early childhood development programs have emerged as a response to immediate family needs, as well as a potential public investment that can improve the quality of life for the next generation of children.

Early childhood development programs, providing education or supplemental care, have increased dramatically in recent years. Between 1970 and 1984, the percentage of three- and four-year-olds enrolled in programs identified as "nursery schools" or "kindergartens" increased from 21 to 36 percent, serving 2.6 million of the nation's 7.2 million three- and four-year-olds in 1984 (U.S. Bureau of the Census 1985). The percentage of families using supplemental child care arrangements, while difficult to estimate directly, is closely tied to the labor force participation rate of mothers. Between 1950 and 1985, the percentage of mothers in the labor force with children under 18 increased from 14 to 62 percent, with similar rates for mothers of three- and four-year-olds (U.S. Bureau of the Census 1983 and unpublished updates). Thus, 4.3 million three- and four-year-olds today require supplemental child care arrangements while their mothers and fathers are working. Nursery schools and kindergartens serve about one-third of these children, providing some or all of the supplemental care that they need.

Public schools serve 85 percent of kindergarten children and 91 percent of students in grades 1–12 (U.S. Bureau of the Census 1985). In contrast, only one out of three nursery school enrollments is in a publicly funded program. The primary source of public funding for programs for three- and four-year-olds is the federal government, which provides at least 85 percent of the total public funds for these programs while spending only about 7 percent of the total public funds for elementary and secondary schools (National Center for Education Statistics 1985, p. 36). Federal spending includes about $1 billion a year for Project Head Start and about $1 billion a year for various other education and supplemental care programs for young children (Schweinhart 1985). Also, the federal dependent care tax credit leaves parents with about $2 billion a year to cover expenses of supplemental care for young children.

State, county, and municipal governments and school boards have recently renewed their interest in public investment in early childhood programs prior to kindergarten. State funding for these programs has grown to over a quarter-billion dollars annually. In the past two years, 19 states have initiated, maintained, or expanded their own investments in early childhood programs—Alaska, California, Florida, Illinois, Louisiana, Maryland, Maine, Massachusetts, Michigan, Minnesota, Missouri, New Jersey, New York, Oklahoma, Pennsylvania, Rhode Island, South Carolina, Texas, and Washington. Large cities—such as Chicago, New York, Philadelphia, and Washington, D.C.—are making significant investments of their own in early childhood programs. County and municipal funding is widespread, since school districts and local agencies, in the process of administering federal and state funds, often contribute their own funds.

Early childhood programs are particularly valuable for young children living in poverty. One of every four children under six is poor (U.S. Bureau of the Census 1984). Early childhood poverty is ram-

From *Educational Leadership 44* (3): 4–13 (September 1986). Reprinted with the permission of the Association for Supervision and Curriculum Development. Copyright © by ASCD. All rights reserved.

pant among minorities, extending to half of all black children and two of every five Hispanic children. Figure 1 illustrates the growth in the poverty rate from 1969–1983. This growth, over and above the general poverty rate, may be attributed largely to the growth in single-parent families, resulting from the high divorce rate and the growing rate of never-married mothers.

Early childhood poverty often leads to children's failure in school (e.g., see Education Commission of the States 1984), which in turn often results in their dropping out of high school (National Center for Education Statistics 1983) and eventual socioeconomic failure and poverty in adulthood. In this country, continuing poverty from generation to generation is not inevitable, but the connection remains strong. Two out of five children from the

poorest fifth of families remain in the poorest fifth as young adults; seven out of ten remain in the poorest two-fifths (Hill and Ponza 1983). Poverty and school failure are also correlated to some extent with high rates of both juvenile delinquency (Loeber and Dishion 1983) and teenage pregnancy (Guttmacher Institute 1981).

POTENTIAL BENEFITS OF EARLY CHILDHOOD DEVELOPMENT PROGRAMS

The 1960s saw a renaissance of interest in early childhood education as a means of addressing the consequences of poverty for children. Martin Deutsch in New York, Susan Gray in Tennessee, and David Weikart in Michigan initiated the first of this new wave of experimental early childhood pro-

FIGURE 1. U.S. Poverty Rates, 1969–1983, Overall and for Children under Age 6

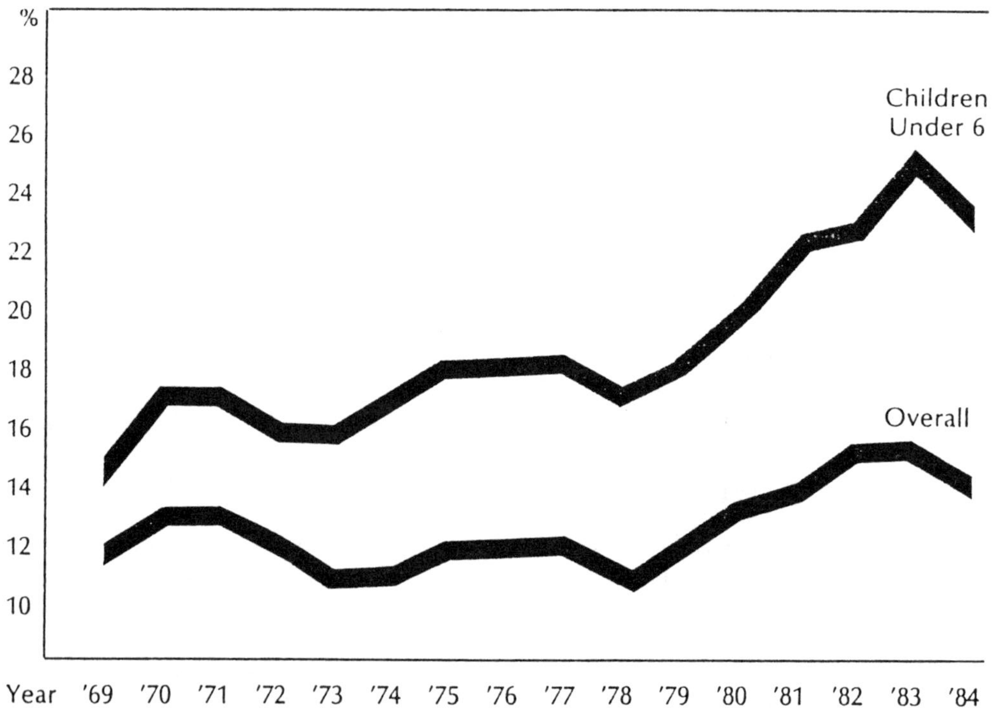

Year	'69	'70	'71	'72	'73	'74	'75	'76	'77	'78	'79	'80	'81	'82	'83	'84
Under 6 (%)	15	17	17	16	16	17	18	18	18	17	18	20	22	23	25	24
Overall (%)	12	13	13	12	11	11	12	12	12	11	12	13	14	15	15	14

Note: Figures for children under six and for 1984 are from unpublished data of the U.S. Bureau of the Census. Figures for the overall poverty rate are from U.S. Bureau of the Census. Money Income and Poverty Status of Families and Persons in the United States: 1983, Current Population Reports, Series P-60, No. 145. Washington, D.C.: U.S. Government Printing Office, 1984, p. 20.

grams for children from low-income families. The designers of these experimental programs all employed curriculum approaches specifically geared to the perceived needs of young children living in poverty. They also used research methods to evaluate their programs and continued these evaluations for some years after children had completed the programs. Thus, the fortunes of early childhood education for children from low-income families became linked to longitudinal research findings.

As might be expected, many studies have addressed the short-term effects of early childhood programs, while only a handful have been able to examine effectiveness ten years or more after program completion. Yet, the weight of the evidence from carefully designed studies suggests that effective programs help children from low-income families do better in school and avoid the later problems that have their roots in school failure.

Table 1 summarizes the findings of some of the better-designed studies, most with random assignment of subjects to program and comparison groups. Each study compared two groups of children from low-income families. One group was placed in some type of early childhood program; the other group attended no program. These studies found that the early programs help improve children's intellectual performance as school begins, though this advantage appears to be temporary. The programs also reduce the need for children to be placed in special education programs or to repeat grade levels because they are unable to do the work expected of them. Third, participation in these programs leads to a lower high school dropout rate. Additional evidence, largely from the High/Scope Foundation's Perry Preschool study, indicates that good early childhood programs can lead to consistent improvement in poor children's achievement throughout schooling, reduced rates of delinquency and arrest and teenage pregnancy; an increased employment rate at age 19; and a decreased rate of welfare dependency at age 19.

To understand how early childhood experiences can affect children throughout their lives, look at life as a series of interactions between persons and setting, with performance and experience in one setting affecting access to the next setting, and so on. For example, successful performance in first grade leads to second grade, while failure may lead to repetition of first grade. Success occurs not only from year to year, but day to day, and even minute to minute. Early childhood experiences stand at the gateway of schooling—a formal cultural system with clear

norms of right and wrong activities. Good early childhood experiences help a child to acquire an interest in learning, a willingness to try new things and to trust adults, a strong sense of independence. They also help children avoid negative behaviors such as misconduct, rejection of school and adults, and an inability to respond properly to adult requests.

In seeking to understand the long-term effects of early childhood development programs for at-risk children, we proposed and tested a causal model of early childhood program effects over time (Schweinhart and Weikart 1980, Berrueta-Clement et al. 1984). The model builds on a simple framework that links short-, mid-, and long-term preschool effects:

1. Poor children who attend a good early childhood development program are better prepared for school, intellectually and socially.

2. A better start in school helps children achieve greater school success, as demonstrated by a decreased need for attending special education classes or repeating a grade.

3. Greater school success leads to greater success in adolescence and adulthood, as demonstrated by lower rates of delinquency, teenage pregnancy, welfare, and unemployment.

The evidence for short-term effects of good early childhood programs is abundant (e.g., see McKey et al. 1985, the final report of the Head Start Synthesis Project). The evidence for mid-term effects comes largely from the Consortium for Longitudinal Studies (Lazar et al. 1982, Consortium 1983), a collection of follow-up studies of early childhood programs that operated in the 1960s. The evidence for long-term effects comes from High/Scope's Perry Preschool study and a few other studies. We anticipate more of this same pattern—many studies identifying short-term effects, a modest number of studies establishing mid-term effects, and a few studies indicating long-term effects.

An economic cost-benefit analysis was conducted with data from the High/Scope Perry Preschool study (Berrueta-Clement et al. 1984, Barnett 1985). Since the data from this study are consistent with other studies, the economic findings may well apply to some extent to other good early childhood programs for low-income children.

The analysis indicated that, strictly in financial terms, such programs can be an excellent investment for taxpayers. One way to represent the program's investment potential is its internal rate of return, equivalent to the real interest rate that the investment earns. This rate was 8 percent for the two-year

TABLE 1. Documented Effects of Good Preschool Programs for Poor Children

Finding Study	Program Group	Control Group	Probability of Error[a]
Intellectual ability (IQ) at school entry			
Early Training	96	86	<.01
Perry Preschool	94	83	<.01
Harlem	96	91	<.01
Mother-Child Home	107	103	—
Special education placements			
Rome Head Start	11%	25%	<.05
Early Training	3%	29%	<.01
Perry Preschool	16%	28%	<.05
New York Prekindergarten (age 9)	2%	5%	<.01
Mother-Child Home (age 9)	14%	39%	<.01
Retentions in grade			
Rome Head Start	51%	63%	—
Early Training	53%	69%	—
Perry Preschool	35%	40%	—
Harlem	24%	45%	<.01
New York Pre-Kindergarten	16%	21%	<.05
Mother-Child Home	13%	19%	—
High school dropouts			
Rome Head Start	50%	67%	<.05
Early Training	22%	43%	<.10
Perry Preschool	33%	51%	<.05
Additional Perry Preschool findings			
Functional competence			
(average or better score)	61%	38%	<.05
Postsecondary enrollments	38%	21%	<.05
Detentions and arrests	31%	51%	<.05
Teenage pregnancies per 100 girls	64	117	<.10
19-year-olds employed	50%	32%	<.05
19-year-olds on welfare	18%	32%	<.05

Note: Adapted from John R. Berrueta-Clement; Lawrence J. Schweinhart, W. Steven Barnett, Ann S. Epstein, and David P. Weikart. *Changed Lives: The Effects of the Perry Preschool Program on Youths through Age 19,* (Monographs of the High/Scope Educational Research Foundation, 8.) Ypsilanti, Mich.: High/Scope Press, 1984, pp. 2 and 102.

[a]Statistical likelihood that the difference between the groups could occur by chance; "<.01" means that a particular group difference could occur by chance less than 1 time out of 100.

program and over 11 percent for the one-year program. (The two-year program had the same effects as the one-year program, but its operational costs were about twice as much.)

Another way to represent the returns to taxpayers of the Perry Preschool program is to depict its per child profits in constant dollars over and above some reasonable standard of investment profitability. Figure 2 presents the value of the program investment in constant 1981 dollars discounted at 3 percent annually. The 3 percent discount rate is equivalent to the long-term growth rate of the U.S. economy. The major cost of the program was the initial investment of about $5,000 per participant

FIGURE 2. Perry Preschool Program Per-Child Costs and Benefits to Taxpayers

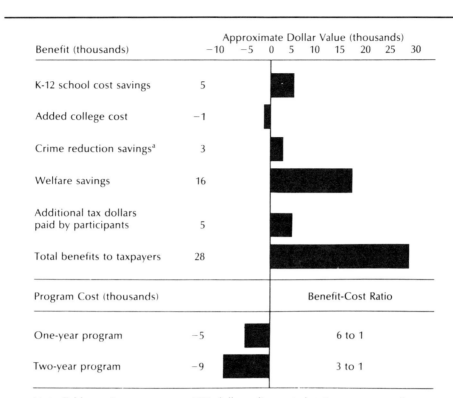

Benefit (thousands)	Approximate Dollar Value (thousands)
K-12 school cost savings	5
Added college cost	-1
Crime reduction savings[a]	3
Welfare savings	16
Additional tax dollars paid by participants	5
Total benefits to taxpayers	28

Program Cost (thousands)		Benefit-Cost Ratio
One-year program	-5	6 to 1
Two-year program	-9	3 to 1

Note: Table entries are constant 1981 dollars, discounted at 3 percent annually. Adapted from John R. Berrueta-Clement, Lawrence J. Schweinhart, W. Steven Barnett, Ann S. Epstein, and David P. Weikart. *Changed Lives: Effects of the Perry Preschool Program on Youths through Age 19*, Monographs of the High/Scope Educational Research Foundation, 8 (Ypsilanti, Mich.: High/Scope Press), 1984, p. 91.

[a]Savings to citizens as taxpayers and as potential crime victims.

per program year. Major benefits to taxpayers were reduced costs of about $5,000 per preschool participant for special education programs, $3,000 for crime, and $16,000 for welfare assistance. Additional postsecondary education of preschool participants added about $1,000 to costs. Participants were expected to pay $5,000 more in taxes because of increased lifetime earnings resulting from their improved educational attainment.

Thus, total benefits to taxpayers amounted to about $28,000 per participant, nearly six times the initial cost of the one-year program or three times the cost of the two-year program. The return is large enough that even a two-year program that was only half as cost-effective as the program studied would still yield a positive return on investment at the 3 percent discount rate.

WHO SHOULD BE IN PUBLIC PRESCHOOL PROGRAMS?

In responding to the demonstrated potential of good early childhood programs, policymakers and administrators must decide whether to provide these programs for all children or only for some—and, if only for some, which children shall be eligible.

Some educational leaders have advocated that publicly funded preschool programs should be made available to all four-year-olds. Serving everyone of a certain age has obvious appeal. The age criterion is widely accepted, and no one protests that they have been unjustly or improperly excluded. The public schools select this option for older students almost exclusively. When they do serve special populations, such as the handicapped, schools provide the service in lieu of another service received by the rest of children.

Evidence from the Brookline Early Education Project (BEEP) in Massachusetts indicates that the school problems of middle-class children are lessened somewhat by experience in good early childhood programs. At the end of grade two, 14 percent of BEEP participants exhibited inappropriate classroom learning behaviors, as compared to 28 percent of a control group: 19 percent of BEEP participants had difficulty in reading, as compared to 32 percent of the control group (Pierson et al. 1984). These are certainly significant, but not as profound in magnitude or in economic effect as the positive impact of early childhood programs for children living in poverty.

Ironically, nursery school enrollment rates are lower for children living in poverty than for more affluent children. One national survey found that the preprimary enrollment rate for three-and four-year-olds was only 29 percent for families with annual incomes below $10,000 but that it was 52 percent for families with annual incomes above $20,000. Parents' educational level also plays a role: the enrollment rate for three- and four-year-old children of elementary school dropouts was 23 percent, but for children of college graduates it was 58 percent (National Center for Education Statistics 1982).

A possible policy alternative is to offer early childhood programs that are open to all children, but to provide funding only for low-income children at special risk of school failure. This option conserves public funds while maintaining universal enrollment opportunity. The prekindergarten programs in Texas exercise a variation on this approach, making state funds for four-year-olds universally available, with districts required to provide programs if they contain 15 or more four-year-olds who are either "unable to speak and comprehend the English language" or "from a family whose income . . . is at or below subsistence level" (Texas House Bill 72, Section 1).

If all children are not served or do not receive funding, they must be selected for the program or for funding by some criteria. These criteria generally focus in some way on risk of school failure, for

example, children living in poverty or those identified by a screening test as being at risk. Perhaps the best option is to use the poverty criterion supplemented by screening test information.

However, screening tests should only be used if they meet the psychometric criteria of reliability and validity, particularly the ability to predict accurately which children will later fail in school and which will succeed. One recent review of screening instruments recommends only four of the many that are on the market—Denver Developmental Screening Test, Early Screening Inventory, McCarthy Screening Test, and Minneapolis Preschool Screening Instrument (Meisels 1986).

ONLY HIGH-QUALITY PROGRAMS ARE A GOOD INVESTMENT

Unless program quality is carefully defined and maintained, an early childhood program is just another place for a child to be. There is no intrinsic value in a young child's leaving home for a few hours a day to join another adult and a group of children. If an early childhood program is to promote healthy child development, research and experience show that it must be conducted to high standards of quality by competent child development professionals who establish an environment that supports active learning by the child (see Epstein et al. 1985). To achieve this goal, a program should have a child development curriculum, proper staffing, and adequate attention to child and family needs.

A CHILD DEVELOPMENT CURRICULUM

Unlike a solely academic approach that does not take full advantage of the potential for positive influence on long-term habits of social behavior, a child development curriculum enhances social, intellectual, and physical development. There are many kinds of early childhood curriculum models based on principles of child development, particularly the notion that children learn actively from their surroundings. Roopnarine and Johnson (1986) have recently complied a book of curriculum models for young children, containing at least eight variations of the child development curriculum approach.

The High/Scope Educational Research Foundation has developed its own version of a child development curriculum. The fundamental premise of the High/Scope curriculum (Hohmann et al. 1979), which is based on Piaget's ideas, is that children are active learners who learn best from activities that they plan and carry out themselves. The teachers arrange interest areas in the classroom and maintain a daily routine that permits children to plan and carry out their own activities. During these activities, the teachers ask children questions that encourage them to think. The teachers encourage various key experiences that help children learn to place things in categories, rank things in order, predict consequences, and generally engage in thinking at their own levels of development.

Teachers who use the High/Scope curriculum must be committed to providing settings in which children learn actively and construct their own knowledge. Their knowledge comes from personal interaction with the world, from direct experience with real objects, and from the application of logical thinking to this experience. The teacher's role is to supply experiences with real objects and to help children think about them logically. In a sense, children are expected to learn by the scientific method of observation and inference, at their own level of understanding, something that even very young children can do.

Child progress in the curriculum is reviewed around a set of key experiences that include active learning, using language, representing experiences and ideas, classification, seriation, number concepts, spatial relations, and time. These categories help teachers organize their interaction with children, just as children organize their activities through the daily routine of the plan-do-review sequence. Those key experiences help the teacher to support and extend the child's self-designed activities. They provide a way of thinking about curriculum that frees the teacher from schedules of teacher-imposed activities, as well as promoting the growth of rational thought in children.

Unlike many curriculum models, the High/Scope curriculum does not require any special materials; the only cost is that of equipping the classroom, as would be typical of any good nursery school program. The High/Scope curriculum lends itself to training and supervision and shares its emphasis on the child as active learner with historic early childhood methods like those of Froebel and Montessori. It differs from them in its use of cognitive-developmental theory to place primary emphasis on problem solving and independent thinking, instead of focusing primarily on social development and relationships. In social development approaches, the child's active learning occurs because the teacher stands out of the way and permits it to take place, not because the teacher encourages

it to happen. In some Montessori programs, for example, teachers view themselves almost as guests in the child's classroom environment. Using the High/Scope model, teachers continuously gauge the child's development status and present intellectual challenges to stretch awareness and understanding.

Teachers or caregivers cannot maintain a child development curriculum without a support system. The administrators to whom they report are the key individuals in providing that support, both personally and institutionally. Above all, those administrators must be curriculum leaders who understand and agree with program goals and who communicate these beliefs to staff and parents.

Further, the evaluation techniques and inservice training provided must support and enhance the child development curriculum. It is essential to evaluate the progress of children and the success of the program with observational and testing techniques that are sensitive to children's developmental status and needs. Teaching staff should be able to use the feedback from evaluations in developing their teaching strategies. The program of inservice training provided to all the teaching staff should be directly applicable to the early childhood curriculum in use. As more and more staff are required for growing early childhood programs, a sound inservice training program in child development and early childhood education is absolutely essential to program quality.

STAFFING

A second characteristic of quality programs pertains to the number and qualifications of their staff members. Smaller classroom group sizes were found to be associated with desirable classroom behavior and improved cognitive performance in the National Day Care Study conducted by Abt Associates in the 1970s (Ruopp et al. 1979). This large-scale study found the most favorable outcomes for groups with fewer than 16 preschool-age children enrolled, with positive outcomes extending to groups of up to 20 children enrolled; larger groups had negative outcomes. Study findings also led to a recommendation of two adults per group. The only teacher characteristic found to predict program processes and effectiveness in the National Day Care Study was amount of early childhood training. No other teacher characteristic was found to be related to effectiveness—*not* college degrees and *not* amount of experience, whether in teaching or in child care.

If teaching young children is to be a valued and stable function in our society, we must create a hierarchical profession that permits viable careers. Teaching assistants making lower wages should see the promise of salaries for master teachers that permit them to support their families at a reasonable standard of living. If this is an issue for the teaching profession in general, it is much more of an issue for early childhood teachers. The average annual salary of Head Start staff members in 1985 was $7,700, substantially below the average *starting* public school salary of $14,500 and a mere one-third of the average public school salary of $23,546 (quoted by Hymes, 1986). While some of this disparity is attributable to a greater use of teaching assistants in Head Start, much of it is due to an undervaluing of the early childhood teaching specialization. This specialization has been accorded very low stature because of society's failure to recognize the vast potential of early childhood development programs, when properly implemented, to contribute to preventing educational and social problems.

CHILD AND FAMILY SERVICES

Third, a good relationship between teaching staff and parents in early childhood development programs is crucial to program success. Parents placing their children in these programs retain primary responsibility for their children and have unique and profound psychological influence over them. In terms of sheer contact time, most children spend the majority of their waking hours with their parents, even if their parents work full-time.

Parents are best viewed as partners or colleagues of early childhood teachers, with both parent and teacher having their own areas of responsibility and expertise. The parent-teacher relationship should be built on mutual respect and a pooling of knowledge about individual children and child development principles. For example, if a parent tells the teacher to teach a three-year-old reading skills for which the child is not ready, the teacher should explain to the parent why the child is not ready to learn those skills and identify for the parent the skills that the child can and will be developing.

Maintaining a broad focus on the whole child rather than a narrow focus on academics has long been a rallying cry for early childhood educators. The phrase has implications not only for classroom curriculum but for support services needed by children and families. As the number of U.S. children living in poverty increases, so does the need for early childhood educators who are sensitive to children's health and nutrition needs and to their families' needs for various social services. Head Start has proven that such needs can be met in the context of early childhood programs. But even if the services are not integrated into the early childhood program delivery system, educators should know how to gain access to them.

Today the majority of families with young children need supplemental child care services. Some early childhood programs are designed to partially meet the need by providing programs either part-day (2–3 hours) or full-school day (5–6 hours). Families needing full-time supplemental child care (typically 8–9 hours a day) must make additional child care arrangements, which frequently call for transportation by someone other than the parent. The supplemental child care needs of families must somehow be met, and the quality of these services will have a significant effect on the children we are raising.

NEW HOPE FOR YOUNG CHILDREN AT RISK

High-quality early childhood programs offer new hope to children at risk. With the help of these programs, they can avoid to some extent the school failure that may otherwise plague their lives. Since school failure is at the root of many of our social problems, preventing it can benefit our society as well as the children involved. The research and experience of the past two decades has given us the knowledge we need to make these programs work. All that we need is the political will to invest the necessary resources to serve all children at risk of school failure and the abiding commitment to do the programs well—with proper staffing, sufficient attention to child and family needs, and a well-implemented child development curriculum.

References

Barnett, W. Steven. *The Perry Preschool Program and Its Long-Term Effects: A Benefit-Cost Analysis.* High/Scope Early Childhood Policy Papers, No. 2, Ypsilanti, Mich.: High/Scope Press, 1985.
Berrueta-Clement, John R., Lawrence J. Schweinhart, W. Steven Barnett, Ann S. Epstein, and David P. Weikart. *Changed Lives: The Effects of the Perry Preschool Program on Youths through Age 19.* (Monographs of the High/Scope Educational Research Foundation, 8.) Ypsilanti, Mich.: High/Scope Press, 1984.

Congressional Research Service and Congressional Budget Office. *Children in Poverty.* Washington, D.C.: U.S. Government Printing Office, 1985.

Consortium for Longitudinal Studies. *As the Twig is Bent . . . Lasting Effects of Preschool Programs.* Hillsdale, N.J.: Lawrence Erlbaum Associates, 1983.

Education Commission of the States, National Assessment of Educational Progress. *The Third National Mathematics Assessment Results, Trends, and Issues.* Denver: Education Commission of the States, 1983.

Elliott, D. S., S. S. Ageton, and R. J. Canter. "An Integrated Theoretical Perspective on Delinquent Behavior." *Journal of Research in Crime and Delinquency* 16 (January 1979).

Epstein, Ann S., Gwen Morgan, Nancy Curry, Richard C. Endsley, Marilyn R. Bradbard, and Hakim M. Rashid. *Quality in Early Childhood Programs: Four Perspectives.* (High/Scope Early Childhood Policy Papers, No. 3.) Ypsilanti, Mich.: High/Scope Press, 1985.

Guttmacher Institute, *Teenage Pregnancy: The Problem that Hasn't Gone Away.* New York: Guttmacher, 1981.

Hill, Martha S., and Michael Ponza. "Poverty and Welfare Dependence Across Generations." *Economic Outlook USA.* Institute for Social Research (Summer 1983): 61.

Hohmann, Mary, Bernard Banet, and David P. Weikart. *Young Children in Action: A Manual for Preschool Educators.* Ypsilanti, Mich.: High/Scope Press, 1979.

Hymes, James L., Jr. *Early Childhood Education: The Year in Review: A Look at 1985.* Carmel, Calif.: Hacienda Press, 1986.

Lazar, Irving, Richard Darlington, Harry Murray, Jacqueline Royce, and Ann Snipper. "Lasting Effects of Early Education." (Monographs of the Society for Research in Child Development, 47) (1–2, Serial No. 194, 1982).

Loeber, Rolf, and T. Dishion, "Early Predictors of Male Delinquency: A Review." *Psychological Bulletin* 94, 1 (1983).

McKey, Ruth H., L. Condelli, H. Ganson, B. Barrett, C. McConkey, and M. Plantz. *The Impact of Head Start on Children, Families and Communities* (Final Report of the Head Start Evaluation, Synthesis and Utilization Project). Washington, D.C.: CSR, Inc., 1985.

Meisels, Samuel J. *Developmental Screening in Early Childhood: A Guide.* Rev. ed. Washington, D.C.: National Association for the Education of Young Children, 1985.

National Center for Education Statistics. *The Condition of Education: 1985 Edition.* Washington, D.C.: U.S. Government Printing Office, 1985.

National Center for Education Statistics. *Preprimary Enrollment 1980.* Washington, D.C.: National Center for Education Statistics, 1982.

National Center for Education Statistics. *Two Years in High School: The Status of 1980 Sophomores in 1982.* Washington, D.C.: National Center for Education Statistics, 1983.

Pierson, Donald E., Deborah Klein Walker, and Terrence Tivnan. "A School-Based Program from Infancy to Kindergarten for Children and Their Parents." *The Personnel and Guidance Journal* (April 1984): 448–455.

Roopnarine, Jaipaul L., and James E. Johnson, eds. *Educational Models for Young Children.* Columbus, Ohio: Charles E. Merrill Co., in press.

Ruopp, Richard, Jeff Travers, F. Glantz, and Craig Coelen. *Children at the Center: Summary Findings and Their Implications* (Final Report of the National Day Care Study, Volume 1). Cambridge, Mass.: Abt Associates, 1979.

Schweinhart, Lawrence J., *Early Childhood Development Programs in the Eighties: The National Picture.* (High/Scope Early Childhood Policy Papers, No. 1) Ypsilanti, Mich.: High/Scope Press, 1985.

Schweinhart, Lawrence J., and David P. Weikart. *Young Children Grow Up: The Effects of the Perry Preschool Program on Youths Through Age 15.* (Monographs of the High/Scope Educational Research Foundation, 7.) Ypsilanti, Mich.: High/Scope Press, 1980.

Schweinhart, Lawrence J., David P. Weikart, and Mary B. Larner. "Consequences of Three Preschool Curriculum Models through Age 15." *Early Childhood Research Quarterly* 1, 1 (1986): 15–45.

U.S. Bureau of the Census. *Child Care Arrangements of Working Mothers: June 1982* (Current Population Reports, Series P-23, No. 129). Washington, D.C.: U.S. Government Printing Office, 1983.

U.S. Bureau of the Census. *Money Income and Poverty Status of Families and Persons in the United States: 1983.* (Current Population Reports, Series P60, No. 145.) Washington, D.C.: U.S. Government Printing Office, 1984.

U.S. Bureau of the Census. *School Enrollment—Social and Economic Characteristics of Students: October 1984 (Advance Report).* (Current Population Reports, Series P-20, No. 404.) Washington, D.C., U.S. Government Printing Office, 1985.

Weikart, David P., Ann S. Epstein, Lawrence J. Schweinhart, and James T. Bond. *The Ypsilanti Preschool Curriculum Demonstration Project: Preschool Years and Longitudinal Results.* (Monographs of the High/Scope Educational Research Foundation, 4.) Ypsilanti, Mich.: High/Scope Press, 1978.

11

CHILDREN AT RISK

José Cárdenas
Joan McCarty First
Intercultural Development and Research Associates
San Antonio, Texas

The doors to public schools are more open than they were 20 years ago to low-income persons, blacks, Hispanics, and the learning disabled. The bad news is that there is a lack of commitment to making those students successful once they are in school. These are the findings of an independent Board of Inquiry[1] commissioned by the National Coalition of Advocates for Students (NCAS) to investigate the status of children of greatest need in public schools. NCAS is a network of child advocacy organizations that address public school issues at the federal, state, and local levels. These groups share a commitment to public education, maximum student access to appropriate educational experiences, and state and local advocacy as a constructive approach to school improvement.

As part of its year-long study, the Board held 15 days of public hearings in 10 cities[2] during late 1983 and throughout 1984. At these hearings, students, dropouts, parents, educators, and other citizens shared their experiences with and worries about public schools in their communities. Based on information gathered from these hearings and a review of recent research, the Board prepared a report, *Barriers to Excellence: Our Children at Risk.*[3] Here we summarize the Board's findings and present some of their recommendations for change.

RACIAL DISCRIMINATION

In 1985, more than 30 years after the *Brown* decision, 63 percent of America's school children still attend predominantly minority schools. The study found that, compared with white students:

• Black students are three times more likely to be suspended from high school, often for trivial reasons.

• Black students are three times more likely to be placed in classes for mildly mentally handicapped.

• Black students drop out of school at a rate more than twice that of white students.

CLASS DISCRIMINATION

The income level of a child's family is still the major determinant of the quality and quantity of the education a child receives. The average child from a bottom quarter income family receives four fewer years of education than a child from a top quarter income family.

Many of the testimonies at the public hearings concerned the various forms that class discrimination takes in schools. For example:

• Many districts allocate fewer resources to schools in poor neighborhoods than to schools that serve primarily middle- and upper-income level students.

• Only half of the almost ten million children eligible to receive Chapter 1 services actually receive those services.

• Teachers often alter expectations on the basis of students' social class.

CULTURAL DISCRIMINATION

Only half of the 2.7 million students with limited-English proficiency receive the special help they need. That figure falls to 10 percent for Hispanic students. Only 3 percent of teachers are adequately prepared to instruct limited-English-proficient students, although 25 percent of all teachers have such children in their classrooms. Special language-responsive programs are made available to only a small segment of the non-English-proficient population, and existing programs suffer from untrained teachers, inadequate instructional materials, invalid testing, and a lack of administrative support.

SEX DISCRIMINATION

Female students experience lowered expectations in public schools and by high school often function well behind male students in reading, science, social studies, and mathematics. Vocational education programs are often segregated by sex, with females clustered in programs that prepare them for the lowest paying jobs.

Pregnant and parenting teens are the young women most discriminated against in schools. Of the over one million teens who become pregnant each year, 10,000 are under age 15. A disproportionate number of these young women are minority students. Teens who are parents are much more likely to drop out of school than are teens who are not, and young, single mothers face almost certain poverty.[4]

SPECIAL EDUCATION

Handicapped students, their parents and concerned educators described both problems of limited access to special services and problems related to children being inappropriately labeled as handicapped.

When PL 94–142 was passed, Congress assigned high priorities to identifying and serving out-of-school handicapped children and to meeting the needs of the severely handicapped. The Board of Inquiry concluded that schools appear to have met these objectives fairly well with regard to elementary-age children. However, large numbers of three- to five-year-olds, secondary students, 18- to 22-year-olds, and emotionally disturbed children of all ages remain underserved, as well as children of migrant families, military dependents, adjudicated and incarcerated youth, and foster children.

On the other side of the coin, many children who are not handicapped end up in the special education system. Sometimes a lack of adequate regular education options designed to meet the needs of children with diverse learning styles results in this misplacement. Biased assessment and evaluation tools may support discriminatory referrals. Poorly defined criteria for entrance into categorical special programs, inferior curriculum, and failure to estab-

lish exit criteria that clarify what the child must accomplish to qualify for return to the regular classroom also contribute to inappropriate placements.

The children most likely to be misclassified are minority youngsters who perform adequately in a variety of family and community roles but experience difficulty in school. They are often assigned to special education, having experienced academic failure in the regular classroom, a failure that is routinely ascribed to the child, rather than to the classroom setting or the school environment.

The processes by which school districts are usually reimbursed under PL 94–142 require them to declare students handicapped and then determine their needs for special services. Thus, the service delivery system that attaches labels to children in or-. der to ensure that money is spent on students of greatest need also acts as an incentive to school districts to place more children in special classes, often inappropriately.

With its emphasis on higher standards, the current education reform movement may increase the risk of many low-achieving minority and disadvantaged students being inappropriately labeled as handicapped. Unless higher academic standards in public classrooms are accompanied by additional resources directed toward strengthening mainstream programs, an increasing number of children may be placed in double jeopardy by being assigned handicapped status in addition to their minority status.

MISUSES OF TESTING

Over-reliance on standardized achievement tests as a basis for making educational decisions may have far-reaching effects on students. In districts where testing is in widespread use, the Board urged that the relationship of testing practices to three major, interrelated concerns be carefully examined: (1) the availability of additional resources to assist children who are labeled "failures" as the result of their poor performance on tests; (2) the effects of testing on *what* is being taught and *how* it is being taught; and (3) the effect of tests on school exclusion rates.

The Board of Inquiry found particularly troublesome policies that require school districts to label children as handicapped or academically deficient in order to receive funds needed to provide services to them. The Board considers funding mechanisms of this type to be a contributing factor in the disproportionate placement of minority students in classes for the educable mentally handicapped and in the growing number of students being classified as learning disabled. Nationally, the learning disabilities category grew by 125 percent between 1976 and 1982.

Finally, there is a great need for school districts and state departments of education to collect data concerning the effects that intensive testing programs and other school reform strategies have on exclusion rates. Reform legislation does not have monitoring provisions in some states, while other states require the collection of extensive data, but do not require that they be collected by race, sex, or ethnicity.

That school exclusionary practices have always had a disproportionate effect on minority children has been well documented by Office of Civil Rights Elementary and Secondary School Surveys carried out during the last decade. Failure at the school, school district, and state level to document that reality is certain to diminish the likelihood of remedy. Because the roots of the problem of disproportionate impact of school suspensions on minority students rest in the ways that teachers make referrals, collection of referral data is an important part of any local self-monitoring effort. Finally, the absence of a uniform system for collecting dropout data is a widely acknowledged problem.

Despite the fact that there is no reliable body of evidence indicating that grade retention is more beneficial than grade promotion for students with serious academic or adjustment difficulties, retention at grade level is a widely employed remedial strategy. Even before the beginning of the national movement to raise academic standards, more than an estimated one million students each year were being retained at grade level.[5]

SCHOOL FINANCE

The quality of education a child receives is profoundly affected by the accident of whether the child lives in a high tax wealth or low tax wealth school district. Testimony documented vast differences in per-pupil expenditures among states, among school districts inside states, and among school buildings inside school districts. Despite efforts in many states to equalize education expenditures, property taxes are still the primary source of funding for public education. This results in special problems for property-poor districts. Since Robin Hood approaches to equalization are doomed to failure, the most practical solution requires the allocation of massive amounts of state money to districts at lower

tax wealth levels. Achieving a satisfactory remedy to the lack of adequate financing for public education is made extraordinarily difficult by the fact that while 90 percent of the nation's children attend public schools, only 27 percent of American adults have children in public schools.

SUMMARY OF RECOMMENDATIONS

Barriers to Excellence: Our Children at Risk identifies 104 strategies for achieving public schools that are both excellent and fair. The following recommendations, excerpted from the report, note appropriate changes in policy and practice that are needed if academic excellence is to be defined in a way that embraces equity issues.

We call for continued, rather than diminished, federal, state, and local attention to the rights of the disadvantaged and those discriminated against because of race, language, sex, or handicapped condition.

We seek:

• To minimize discrimination in the schools by restoring and expanding support for programs serving economically disadvantaged students, recognizing that it is false economy to cut programs which work for poor children.

• To reaffirm commitments to non-discrimination by race by vigorously pursuing efforts to eliminate racially identifiable educational programs and altering school practices which result in minority children dropping out, becoming "push outs" or staying in the educational system but failing to learn.

• To minimize discrimination against students from linguistic minorities by recognizing the importance of bilingual education as a technique which supports their academic development and by moving towards an acceptance of bilingualism as a means of enriching our society.

• To renew commitment to the ideals embodied in Title IX (Education Amendments of 1972) sex discrimination legislation, thereby assuring that female students will have an opportunity to develop their talents and skills fully.

• To promote changes in special education which will improve services for children with moderate and severe handicaps while developing more regular education options for children with milder learning difficulties so that they can attend school without being labeled handicapped.

We call for greater willingness on the part of those in positions of responsibility to adjust schools to the diverse needs of all students who attend them.

We seek:

• To end tracking and rigid ability grouping, recognizing that such practices work against the best interests of both the most vulnerable and the most able students in the schools.

• To eliminate the use of inappropriate testing practices as a basis for making educational decisions which have far-reaching effects upon the futures of young people.

• To broaden curriculum and teaching practices so that they better meet the needs of diverse student populations, based upon the proposition that individual children have differing needs and abilities.

• To move vocational education programs away from the current narrow focus upon job skills and toward the broader goal of preparing young people for a changing world of work.

We call for more democratic governance of schools which assures parents a significant role in making decisions about the education of their children and teaches children principles of democratic participation and the exercise of constitutional rights.

We seek:

• To reinstate federal mandates for parent involvement in local programs.

• To remove barriers to parental involvement and create opportunities for parents to participate in decisions about school staffing, education programming, school discipline and resource allocation.

• To assure students of their due process rights in such matters as school suspension and expulsion.

We call for the establishment of comprehensive early childhood education, day care programs, and in-school support services for children and youth as a means of preventing school failure.

We seek:

• To recognize the usefulness and cost effectiveness of high quality early childhood education and child care programs as a means of preventing school failure.

• To respond to the needs of an increasing number of young people whose chances of remaining in school would be increased if they had help with serious personal and social problems.

We call for the enactment of more equitable and adequate systems for financing schools, so that the quality of education available does not depend upon where a child lives.

We seek:

• To increase tax equity through state systems of raising revenues that are not dependent on regressive taxes and that insulate property poor districts against excessive local taxes.

• To eliminate inequality in educational access, resulting from disparities in funding for schools.

• To raise funding levels for programs serving children at risk, so that every eligible child is assured of adequate services.

We call for more systematic attention to the problems of jobs for youth and drop-outs by federal, state, and local education authorities.

We seek:

• To ensure that a comprehensive school-to-work transition program is available for all youth.

• To strengthen counseling services for noncollege-bound youth and develop job-placement services in high schools.

• To encourage broadly based community councils charged with responsibility for examining what could be done locally to revitalize the local economy and create jobs for youth.

Neither the Board of Inquiry nor the advocacy community is naive enough to assume that the changes urged in *Barriers to Excellence* can be accomplished quickly or easily. In all likelihood their achievement may require collaborative energies of more than one generation of educators and concerned citizens. Why is it important for that effort to begin now? Paul Ylvisaker, former dean of the Harvard Graduate School of Education and co-chair of the National Commission on Secondary Schooling for Hispanics, has answered that question simply: "Because we are confronted with a generation of children too precious to waste."

Notes

1. The Board of Inquiry was co-chaired by Harold Howe, a former U.S. Commissioner of Education, who is now senior lecturer at the Harvard Graduate School of Education, and Marian Wright Edelman, President, The Children's Defense Fund.
2. The ten cities were Boston, Louisville, Chicago, Lansing, New York, Atlanta, Columbus, Cleveland, Seattle, and San Antonio.
3. Unless otherwise noted, documentation for facts and opinions expressed in this article is contained in *Barriers to Excellence: Our Children at Risk*. Copies are available for $5.50 each (prepaid) from: NCAS, 76 Summer St., Suite 350, Boston, MA 02110.
4. The Children's Defense Fund, *Teenage Pregnancy: Some Facts* (Washington, D.C., 1985).
5. Gregg C. Jackson, "The Research Evidence on the Effects of Grade Retention," *Review of Educational Research* 45, 4 (Fall 1975): 613–635.

12

SCHOOL PERFORMANCE OF CHILDREN FROM ONE-PARENT FAMILIES

Oliver C. Moles

Office of Educational Research and Improvement
U.S. Department of Education
Washington, D.C.

This paper will review research on the relationship between living in a one-parent family (divorced, separated, widowed or never married) and children's school performance (academic achievement, attitudes toward school, attendance and conduct). It will also draw some implications for school personnel who interact with such children and their parents.

Recent years have witnessed a dramatic increase in divorce and children living in single-parent families in this country as documented by the Select Committee on Children, Youth and Families of the U.S. House of Representatives (1989). Almost half of all marriages today end in divorce, and more than a million children per year see their parents become divorced. From 1960 to 1975 the number of divorces and the number of children whose parents divorced each year more than doubled. The peak came in 1979. Since then divorce rates have stabilized, but they remain at very high levels. In view of this situation, it behooves us to learn as much as possible about the circumstances of children in one-parent families, and whatever effects their living conditions may have on their educational and social development. Further information on these remarkable changes in family living patterns may help to set the stage for this discussion.

In 1960 only 9 percent of children were living in single-parent families, while the proportion climbed to 24 percent in 1988. The vast majority of such children (88 percent) reside with their mothers. As of 1988 about 38 million of the 63 million children in the United States, or 60 percent, lived with both of their biological parents. More than 15 million, almost a quarter, lived in single-parent families at that time.

While the majority of single parents will remarry, almost 60 percent of all children will spend at least part of their childhood in one-parent homes (Norton and Glick, 1986). Black and Hispanic children in 1988 were more likely than non-minority children to live with only one parent—51 percent of black children compared to 27 percent of Hispanic children and 16 percent of white children lived with just their mothers (U.S. House of Representatives, 1989). One sixth of all *families* and over 40 percent of black families are headed by women, and one-third of these female-headed families are poor (*Washington Post*, 1988).

A generation ago many more children lived with widowed parents. From 1970 to 1988 the number of children living with a widowed mother dropped by 39 percent, but those living in other kinds of one-parent families increased markedly: divorced mothers up 119 percent, separated mothers up 24 percent, and never-married mothers up a huge 678 percent. In 1988 4.3 million children lived with a never-married mother, 5 million lived with a divorced mother, 2.9 million with a separated mother, and .8 million with a widowed mother (U.S. House of Representatives, 1989). Unfortunately, there has been little study of never-married parents and their children as compared to other kinds of one-parent families.

REVIEWS OF ONE-PARENT FAMILY STUDIES

Over the past two decades there have been a number of reviews of research bearing on the effects of divorce and one-parent family status on children. Three comprehensive reviews of such households will be discussed below. This approach was taken in-

This paper was written for this anthology; an earlier version was presented at the 1988 meetings of the National Association of Social Workers. Views expressed in this paper do not necessarily represent the position or policy of the U.S. Department of Education, and no official endorsement should be inferred.

stead of trying to review individual studies. There are simply too many, even when those of poor quality are put aside.

A review by Shinn (1978) on father absence and children's cognitive development summarizes 54 studies. Shinn highlighted those studies of nonclinical populations which had comparison groups of father-present children and which controlled for socioeconomic status (SES) in some way. She noted that among the 28 studies with adequate methodology, 16 showed detrimental effects of father absence and nine found no reliable differences. Children from fatherless families were disadvantaged in achievement tests, IQ and aptitude, and grades in school compared to children from two-parent families, but the effects were often not so large as those due to SES.

Few studies identified the reason for father absence, but where this was done divorce was among the most damaging reasons in all cases. Children with a father surrogate or stepfather scored between father-present and father-absent children on achievement and IQ tests. Shinn (1978) concluded that father absence is not a unitary variable, and that future research should consider the cause, onset, duration and degree of father absence, and access to father surrogates.

A second review carried out by Hetherington, Featherman and Camara (1981) also depends on a count of relevant studies, and eliminated ones which do not meet standards of methodological adequacy. Regarding IQ this review concluded that the differences found in studies are usually small (3–4 points favoring two-parent children) and reduced further when SES is taken into account. On aptitude and standardized achievement tests, differences were usually less than one year but nevertheless favored the two-parent families. Most studies did not furnish information on SES or ethnic background of students, and other factors that might be related to test performance such as time of onset, reasons for and length of parental separation, or the nature of family relations after separation.

A sharper pattern emerged when teacher evaluations were considered: students from one-parent homes received lower teacher-assigned grades. The authors suggest this poorer performance in the classroom may be due to a complex interaction of student attitudes and behavior, teacher attitudes, and home conditions. The studies summarized report more absenteeism, truancy, and tardiness among children from one-parent families, and describe them as be-

ing more disruptive, aggressive, immature, and less self-controlled than children from two-parent households. As the authors observed, absence from class may limit learning time as well as create disruptions for teachers and signify to them a lack of motivation and interest on the part of students and parents. Such a state may in turn affect the teacher's evaluation of students and create lower expectations for performance which become translated into less assistance to students (Hetherington, Featherman and Camara, 1981). This review concluded that despite their lower grades children reared in one-parent homes are unlikely to be experiencing any serious intellectual deficit.

In the latest review, Salzman (1987) identified 137 studies from 1925 to 1986 on effects of father absence on cognitive performance which employed comparisons between father-absent and father-present samples. The overall effect size of $-.26$ in this meta-analysis reflects a .26 standard deviation advantage of the father-present children. The effect size is $-.19$ for intelligence texts, $-.21$ for academic aptitude, $-.30$ for academic achievement tests, and $-.29$ for school grades. For academic achievement tests, this means that the average father-present child scored higher than about 60 percent of the father-absent children. Effects for the death of the father ($-.21$) were smaller than for divorce, separation or desertion ($-.31$). As with the other reviewers, Salzman (1987) notes that many studies have methodological problems including the lack of large samples, the failure to identify reasons for father's absence, inattention to other aspects of family life and the child's development, a focus on potential problems and weaknesses rather than positive effects, and inadequate control for comparability of father-absent and father-present samples.

The preponderance of evidence from these three reviews is that there are some negative effects of father absence on children's school performance, more so in grades, achievement tests, and attendance patterns. But the effects are generally small, and not as large as those for SES. All the reviewers lament the poor quality of many studies.

In view of these limitations, it is worth examining studies which look at major subgroups of children in one-parent families—those with different socioeconomic status, age, race and gender—to see where the effects are more or less pronounced. Subsequently, relationships in one-parent families which might influence students' school performance will also examined.

CHILD AND FAMILY STATUS CONDITIONS

SOCIOECONOMIC STATUS (SES)

As noted in the reviews, the effects of one-parent families on school performance are not as large as those of SES. A recent study not included in any of the reviews examined white and black families in broadly representative samples: all students in first through sixth grade in 242 randomly selected elementary schools, and sophomores in the national High School and Beyond study (Milne, Myers, Rosenthal and Ginsberg, 1986). Family income, a principal component of SES, was the most important mediator of one-parent family status for both white and black elementary students, and for white high school students' reading and math achievement test scores. It is quite likely that detrimental effects of separation and divorce are due in no small part to reduced income of the custodial parent after the break. A country-wide survey shows that as high a proportion of single-parent children finished high school as those in two-parent families once economic disadvantage was taken into account (Mueller and Cooper, 1986). And it has been found that low income has a greater effect on child-rearing practices than father absence among divorced mothers (Colletta, 1979).

The drop in income can be precipitous. In a national longitudinal study of families, when women were separated or divorced and retained custody of the child, their ratio of income to needs fell by 35 percent (Hill and Hoffman, 1977). Part of the problem is the frequent lack of reliable support payments. When fathers retain custody, the financial problem is much less severe. It is also well established that divorce is more common among families with low and unstable incomes (Bane, 1979; Hetherington, 1980). Whether effects on school performance are caused by low initial income or a drop in income is difficult to disentangle.

Low income is associated with stresses which make household upkeep and child care more difficult such as poor quality of housing and neighborhoods, the need for the mother to work, child care, and moving (Colletta, 1978; Hodges, Wechsler and Ballantine, 1978). Many divorced women lack the education and job skills to obtain good-paying jobs and quality child care. The social isolation following divorce may be intensified for children by moving and the loss of friends, neighbors, families and schools. The new home is more likely to be in an area with higher risks to personal safety, fewer recreational fa-

cilities, and less adequate schools (Hetherington, 1980).

RACE AND ETHNICITY

While there are much higher proportions of one-parent families among blacks and Hispanics than whites, Hispanic families have been little studied regarding the present topic. In an exception, Bianchi (1984) found that Hispanic children living in one-parent families were much more likely to be enrolled below the modal grade for their age than those in two-parent families. The differences for black and white children were not as large. In a national study looking at the level of schooling attained when white women had lived with a single parent there was no effect on high school completion once the generally lower income of single parents was taken into account. For black women, both living with a single parent and income independently contributed to the probability of dropping out of school (Shaw, 1982).

Comparing black children from one- and two-parent families, Hetherington et al. (1981) found only small differences. Shinn (1978) observed more studies favoring two-parent families among whites than blacks. But Milne et al. (1986) noted larger differences for blacks than for whites in elementary and high school. Why these racial differences occur is not altogether clear and the evidence for differences in school performance between races is uneven.

GENDER

Several studies have shown that girls are better adjusted and have higher achievement than boys in one-parent families (Guidubaldi, 1985; Zimiles and Lee, 1988; Hetherington, 1980; Wallerstein and Kelly, 1980), although Shinn (1978) found little evidence of gender differences. The Hetherington, Featherman and Camara (1981) review concluded that boys from one-parent families score lower on verbal and quantitative tests than do boys in two-parent families, but there were no differences for girls.

Differences may become larger with age. Guidubaldi (1985), working with school psychologists in 38 states, collected extensive information on the school performance, behavior and attitudes of 700 first, third and fifth grade children and their families. Besides overall differences favoring the children of two-parent over divorced parents on both social-emotional and academic-intellectual criteria, girls in divorced family households were consistently better adjusted than boys. There were also more significant relationships between marital status and criteria for boys than for girls, especially regarding academic achievement. But the profiles of boys and girls were more similar in first grades. In third and fifth grade, two-parent and divorced family boys showed increasing numbers of adjustment differences, whereas girls became increasingly alike. Two years later, the differences persisted. When family income was controlled, however, the academic differences virtually disappeared both initially and in the two-year follow-up.

Wallerstein and Kelly (1980), in their study of children after divorce, observed that girls were treated with greater consideration by their mothers, except for 5–7 year old boys whose strong yearning for their fathers may have forced their mothers to attend to their distress. Nearly twice as many girls as boys improved their overall functioning by eighteen months after parents' separation. More boys felt stressed and were depressed at that time, even though boys were initially very similar to girls in their adjustment and responses. The boys needed to adjust to a greater change with the absence of their fathers than did the girls.

In a study of 3rd to 6th graders, Hammond (1979) explored self-concept, achievement, school behavior and attitudes of children from two-parent and one-parent separated and divorced families. Teachers indicated no significant differences in reading or math achievement, or self-concept between the groups. They did rate the sons of divorced parents higher on school behavior problems of ''acting out'' and ''distractibility'' but no differences were found for daughters. Boys from divorced families also rated their families as less happy, but again for girls there was no difference.

Moving to the high school grades, Zimiles and Lee (1988), analyzing the national High School and Beyond data, found that sophomores from one-parent families as well as those from reconstituted families had lower achievement test scores and grades than students who lived with their natural parents, even after adjusting for social class differences. In this study the probability of dropping out of school also depended on the relationship between the sex of the single parent and the sex of the child. Boys were more likely to drop out when living with their mothers, and girls when living with their fathers, even after adjustments for social class and sophomore achievement level. Thus the situation may be more complex than it would appear from the

generally poorer performance of boys. Since the vast majority of one-parent households are headed by women, the boys' performance may reflect difficulties in cross-sex interaction with their mothers.

AGE

In her review, Shinn (1978) noted that researchers have linked father absence to poor cognitive performance all the way from infancy to college with about the same proportion of studies showing effects at the elementary, high school and college ages. But Shinn concluded that the father-absence effects may not emerge among young children. Three studies she cites found no cognitive effects of father absence in kindergarten to second grade, but the same children in later grades experienced significant detrimental effects. On the other hand, a national study of young men (age 28) which controlled for race, family income, mother's employment and other family characteristics showed that years of school completed was only affected by living in a one-parent family during the preschool years and not later. These children had over ¾ of a year less education than those who lived with both parents during the preschool period (Krein, 1986).

The study by Milne and others (1986) concluded that there are more benefits of having two parents in the home for elementary than for high school students. Salzman's (1987) review showed that eight independent variables contributed to effect sizes, among them age at the time of the study (high school) and age at onset of the parent's departure (middle years—the 7–12 years olds). This raises the question of what age really means. The older children will in general have experienced more years living with only one parent, since more divorces occur early in marriage. So duration of single-parent experience is confounded with the child's age. This may account for the lack of effects in many studies with younger children. On the other hand, several studies have found that the first year after divorce is the hardest for children, and that their behavior and school performance improve afterward (Hetherington, 1980; Wallerstein and Kelly, 1980). This would suggest that older students will show fewer effects since they are more likely to have had a longer time since the parent's departure.

FAMILY RELATIONSHIPS

Since the research reviews have shown some detrimental effects of father absence, some explanation for the effects should be sought beyond the child's age, gender, or race, and the family's SES. These statuses merely categorize students who may be experiencing more or less difficulty in school, and do not suggest the processes which may affect their performance. The relationship between parents and their children is one potential arena for investigation. Another arena to be considered is the school and classroom. A brief review of family relationships with the best established effects follows.

As noted in Shinn's (1978) review, divorce was among the most damaging causes in all studies which compared reasons for father absence. Citing evidence from clinical studies, Longfellow (1979) reports more aggressive and antisocial behavior among children of divorce, and more anxiety, moodiness and neurotic symptoms among children of widows. Studies of nonclinical samples also demonstrate the same pattern, Longfellow observes in an excellent short analysis of research on the impact of divorce on children.

Closely tied to the reason for father absence is the question of conflict between spouses. This area of investigation dates from Nye's (1957) comparison of high school students from happily married, conflict-ridden and divorced families. He found no difference in reported school adjustment between children from one-parent homes and those from unhappy and conflict-ridden two-parent homes. But children from single-parent families reported fewer psychosomatic symptoms and less delinquent behavior than those from unhappy two-parent homes. The findings held up at all socioeconomic levels. More recent studies described by Longfellow (1979) and by Hetherington (1980) make the same point: that conflict is more important than number of resident parents in producing antisocial behavior, psychiatric symptoms and other adjustment problems.

Conflict in divorcing families may have different effects. Wallerstein and Kelly (1980) in their follow-up of 60 middle class families who had divorced found that conflict prior to the divorce was not related to post-divorce adjustment among normal preschool children. But if conflict between parents continued after the divorce, children were harmed.

There is evidence that poor parent-child relations in intact families are associated with child behavior problems, and that the probability is increased dramatically when poor parent-child relations are coupled with a poor marriage (Rutter, 1971). In their long-term study of coping with divorce, Wallerstein and Kelly (1975) estimated that two-thirds of the mother-child relationships deterio-

rated during the year after divorce. This meant less cooperation, more anger, less trust and more disorder and tension in daily living. A number of the children developed more serious psychological problems than before. However, young children, especially preschoolers, were given special attention, whereas those eight and older often felt that mothers had been almost entirely withdrawn. Girls were also treated with more consideration than boys (Wallerstein and Kelly, 1980). These findings may help to explain the better cognitive and school performance of girls and preschoolers.

Household routine, authoritative control, nurturance and maturity demands are important for the adjustment of preschool children. Parents turn to older children and adolescents more for emotional support and assistance with household functioning. If her demands for emotional support are not excessive, greater communication of concerns and plans can lead to more companionship between a divorced mother and her children. The greater participation of young people in family decision making and household chores may also lead to accelerated self-sufficiency in children (Weiss, 1978). But too much independence and responsibility can also make youngsters feel overwhelmed, incompetent and resentful.

Friends, neighbors, relatives, organizations and institutions may provide supports for parents and children experiencing divorce. A number of studies indicate that support from family and friends promotes positive attitudes toward self and one's circumstances, and enhances the parenting role among women (see Hetherington, 1980). While contact with the noncustodial parent and grandparents appear in general to be beneficial to the child, other supports among peers, school, the neighborhood, church and other groups have received little attention. Where relations with teachers, peers and neighbors are positive, they help lessen the impact of family stress (see Hetherington, 1980). One recent study has shown that higher achieving students have more social supports, such as being active in Scouts, sports, religious activities, Big Brother or Big Sister, and time with playmates, the other parent, and other relatives (Roy and Fuqua, 1983).

SCHOOL EXPERIENCE

Difficulties in school performance—achievement test scores, grades, attendance, and behavior—among children from one-parent families have been discussed earlier. The contrast with much smaller or nonexistent differences in standardized tests of ability and aptitude noted by Hetherington, Featherman and Camara (1981) poses an interesting problem. Are there features of the school environment or the child's behavior in the classroom which contribute to this discrepancy between ability and performance, and to low performance in general?

Multiple demands and stresses on divorced mothers, we have seen, may prevent their family life from having the regularity which helps children to come to school well prepared and on time. The stress of divorce itself seems most critical in the first year. During this period children respond best to a relatively structured and predictable school environment. Positive adjustment also depends on qualities of the teacher—attentiveness, warmth, supportiveness and assignment of responsibilities. (Hetherington, Cox and Cox, 1979). Such an environment may be more important to young children who cannot structure their own environments as older children can, and those experiencing more stress at home.

The difficulties of children from one-parent families may be at least partly in the eyes of the beholders. In a study by Santrock and Tracy (1978), two groups of teachers viewed a videotape showing social interaction of an eight-year-old boy. One group was told the boy's parents were divorced; the other group that he lived with both natural parents. Teachers rated the "divorced" child more negatively on happiness, emotional adjustment, and coping with stress. In another study, teachers were observed to direct more negative behavior toward children of divorce in the first year following the divorce, but by the second year there were no differences (Hetherington, Cox and Cox, 1979).

Elementary teachers perceive more school behavior problems in children from one-parent families (Fuller, 1986; Touliatos and Lindholm, 1980). But teachers 35 and under were more favorable in their perceptions of children from one-parent homes than older teachers (Fuller, 1986), suggesting they may be less influenced by preconceptions.

The teacher's influence can extend beyond the classroom to contact with parents. In a statewide survey, single parents felt more pressure to assist their children at home and spent more time on home learning activities, but still felt unable to help as the teachers expected. Teachers who were active in trying to stimulate parent-child home learning activities worked equally with single- and two-parent families, whereas relatively inactive teachers believed that one-parent families would not be helpful even after parent education, parent involvement at school, the child's achievement and other important variables were taken into account. Teachers active in parent involvement were more positive about the assistance received from all parents (Epstein, 1984). Teachers' beliefs about one-parent children and their parents can thus influence their own behavior, and probably child and parent behavior also, thus contributing to a self-fulfilling prophecy.

From the parent's viewpoint, a number of complaints can be heard. Clay (1980) solicited information from over 1200 single parents across the country regarding experiences with their children's schools. Over one-third of the parents had heard school personnel make specific negative comments about one-parent families, and almost half had heard them mention "broken homes" or other stereotypes. Over half said they had to take time off work for conferences with teachers. Few schools provided care for younger children during school activities. Less than ten percent reported that noncustodial parents received report cards or notices of school activities, although one-third noted that noncustodial parents may attend parent-teacher conferences.

The disparities between schools and families also show up in a comparison of junior high school personnel, PTA groups and single parents (Earls, 1981). The school personnel and PTA respondents thought that the children of single parents had more behavioral and academic problems, but that school conference times, programs, and assistance for single parents were adequate. Single parents strongly disagreed on all these points. All groups agreed, however, that training to help them work with children from one-parent families was essentially nonexistent. Thus, in recent years there remain serious shortcomings in the responses of teachers, the schools, and parent associations to the needs of single parents.

IMPLICATIONS FOR SCHOOL PERSONNEL

School systems are beginning to recognize the need, and to develop procedures to prepare teachers and other school staff to work more effectively with children experiencing separation and divorce, and those living in one-parent families. Yet stereotypic talk of "broken" families, prejudicial treatment, and lack of understanding still abound. Schools, educators, and school social workers can do a number of things to help children of single parents in the classroom through training, counseling and other approaches. The following suggestions are adapted from a joint publication of the National PTA, Boys Town, and the National Association of Elementary School Principals entitled *Single Parents and Their Families* (1983).

RECORD KEEPING

For teachers and counselors to be responsive to the needs of children, they must be informed when a change or crisis occurs in the family. A standard form updated at regular intervals might provide names, addresses, and telephone numbers of both parents, and who is authorized to pick up the child from school. This form could also help schools inform noncustodial parents of students' progress and school events.

CLASSROOMS

School personnel need to avoid pejorative language about separation, divorce, and single-parent status, and any assumptions that children from one-parent families will necessarily have lower school performance. Staff expectations may play a significant role in student motivation and achievement. Teachers should also be made aware of symptoms that may accompany severe stress at home such as weight change, lack of concentration, attention seeking through negative behavior, and falling grades or attendance. If changes are sudden or prolonged, students may need more personal attention, and possibly referral to a guidance counselor, school social worker, or support group. But many school problems will be temporary, and children need to feel accepted, not different. In time, the distress surrounding separation from a parent should subside for many children. Wherever possible, children from one-parent families, especially boys, might be placed with male teachers.

TRAINING

Training programs will have to present an accurate picture of when children from one-parent families are likely to be unhappy or poorly adjusted, and conditions in their lives with parents and support systems which can create better functioning among these children. Staff development programs need to help school personnel examine their own values, attitudes, and stereotypes regarding divorce, unmarried mothers, and single parents; identify signs of stress in children; learn ways to provide support and understanding and respond to the needs of distressed children; and use community resources.

CURRICULUM AND INSTRUCTION

Courses or workshops in family life and parenting can be created for discussion on changing family patterns and personal experiences of students. Nonjudgmental class discussion can also help children feel more secure in their own families. Books and other educational materials can be selected for classroom use which depict various family forms including one-parent families and stepfamilies.

COUNSELING

Although many children can handle the loss of a parent with support from family and friends, others may benefit from some form of counseling. Programs for counseling groups of children of divorce have been developed in various places. Avoiding any sense of being singled out or stigmatized is important. Individual teachers can also encourage students to talk. Listening with understanding in a nonjudgmental way can be very supportive.

ACTIVITIES FOR PARENTS

Evening programs and support groups for parents can help develop better child discipline and communication between single parents and their children, and help parents trying to cope with new lifestyles. Child care, car pools, and low fees can help families with young children and those with limited income and transportation to attend.

Sponsoring "parent" activities instead of "mother" or "father" events can show schools' responsiveness to variations in family structure. Addressing school correspondence to the parent instead of to parents also recognizes this. When there is joint custody, schools can send correspondence to both parents, and find out if both want to attend parent-teacher conferences, receive newsletters, etc.

Conferences before school and in late afternoons and evenings help employed parents avoid missing work and pay. Keeping the school open for occasional evening and weekend meetings with the principal and counselors can let these parents talk with them more easily. The main point is to help parents keep in touch with their children's education.

OTHER RESOURCES

A resource library of books, audio and visual materials on aspects of one-parent families and their relationships with schools may also be helpful to staff, students and parents. Many books have been written for school-aged children living in one-parent families. The library might also arrange a parent resource center. In addition, descriptions of community resources can be compiled and distributed to parents. Staff need to stand ready to refer parents to sources of financial aid, health care, legal advice, child care, and emotional support.

CONCLUSIONS

Evidence from the three reviews of research indicate that children in one-parent families have somewhat lower school performance—especially their grades, achievement test scores, and attendance—but that the family's socioeconomic status has a much larger influence on school performance than the absence of a father. Divorce usually exacerbates family income problems and is a period of crisis for children, but with time the effects of divorce diminish for many.

Much of the research on divorce has been of poor quality and focused on investigating anticipated problem behavior among children. This assumption of deficits is gradually being replaced by inquiries into a deliberately broad range of parent-child interactions and child outcomes. Some are even paying special attention to the potential strengths and benefits of life in one-parent families, and have found

that more responsible behavior by children, more authority to women over their family life, and improved self-concepts can be documented (Kohen, Brown and Feldberg, 1979; Weiss, 1975).

Our understanding of the effects of divorce will only be deepened when characteristics of the child (e.g., age, sex, personality traits, concepts of family life) and characteristics of the family itself before and after separation (e.g., demography, income level, extent of conflict, coping strategies, custodial arrangements) become dimensions of investigation. The specification and testing of family processes by which marital disruption and living in one-parent families affect children's lives is essential to understand the facets of family life which might be altered to assist parents and children. This will require more longitudinal studies which begin near the point of separation rather than divorce and follow families for some time, as well as more in-depth analyses (see also Levitin, 1979).

The studies of recent years have opened the door to many intriguing aspects of children living in one-parent families. Hopefully the years to come will see these avenues of inquiry expanded to gain fuller knowledge of this complex phenomenon and provide further guidance to workers in the helping professions.

References

Bane, M. J. 1979. Marital disruption and the lives of children. In G. Levinger and O. C. Moles, eds., *Divorce and separating: Context, causes and consequences*. New York: Basic Books.

Bianchi, S. M. 1984. Children's progress through school: A research note. *Sociology of Education, 57* (3), 184–192.

Clay, P. 1980. Single parent families: How do the public schools treat them? A preliminary report. Columbia, MD: National Committee for Citizens in Education,.

Colletta, N. D. 1978. Divorced mothers at two income levels: stress, support and child-rearing practices. Unpublished thesis, Cornell University, Ithaca NY.

Colletta, N. D. 1979. The impact of divorce: Father absence or poverty? *Journal of Divorce* 3:27–34.

Earls, P. 1981. The perceptions of single-parents, junior high school personnel and parent-teacher groups related to problems experienced by children in single-parent families. *Dissertation Abstracts International* 45 (03–A), 926.

Epstein, J. L. 1984. Single parents and the schools: The effects of marital status on parent and teacher evaluations. Report No. 353. Baltimore: Johns Hopkins University Center for Social Organization of Schools.

Fuller, M. L. 1986. Teachers' perceptions of children from intact and single-parent families. *School Counselor*, (May), 365–374.

Guidubaldi, J. 1985. Age-sex differences in children's divorce adjustment. Summary of paper in conference on the impact of divorce, single-parenting and stepparenting on children. Bethesda, MD: National Institute on Child Health and Human Development.

Hammond, J. M. 1979. Children of divorce: A study of self-concept, school behaviors, attitudes, and situational variables. Unpublished dissertation, University of Michigan.

Hetherington, E. M. 1980. Children and divorce. In R. Henderson (ed.), *Parent-child interaction: Theory, research and prospect*. New York: Academic Press.

Hetherington, E. M., Cox, M., and Cox, R. 1979. Family interaction and the social, emotional and cognitive development of children following divorce. In V. Vaughn and T. B. Brazelton (eds.), *The family: Setting Priorities*. New York: Science and Medicine Publishing Co.

Hetherington, E. M., Featherman, D. L., and Camara, K. A. 1981. Intellectual functioning and achievement of children in one-parent households. Washington, D.C.: National Institute of Education.

Hill, D., and Hoffman, S. 1977. Husbands and wives. In G. J. Duncan and J. N. Morgan (eds.), *Five thousand American families: Patterns of economic progress* vol. 4. Ann Arbor: Institute for Social Research.

Hodges, F. H., Wechsler, R. C., and Ballantine, C. 1978. Divorce and the preschool child: cummulative stress. Paper presented at the American Psychological Association meetings, Toronto, Canada.

Kohen, J. A., Brown, C. A., and Feldberg, R. 1979. Divorced mothers; The costs and benefits of female family control. In G. Levinger and O. C. Moles (Eds), *Divorce and separation: Context, causes and consequences.* New York: Basic Books.

Levitin, T. E. 1979. Children of divorce: An introduction. *Journal of Social Issues 35* (4), 1–25.

Longfellow, C. 1979. Divorce in context: Its impact on children. In G. Levinger and O. C. Moles (eds.), *Divorce and separation: Context, causes and consequences.* New York: Basic Books.

Milne, A. M., Myers, D. E., Rosenthal, A. S., and Ginsberg, A. 1986. Single parents, working mothers, and the educational achievement of school children. *Sociology of Education, 59* (July) 125–139.

Mueller, D. P., and Cooper, P. W. 1986. Children of single parent families: How they fare as young adults. *Family Relations,* 35 (1), 169–175.

Norton, A. J., and Glick, P. C. 1986. One parent families: A social and economic profile. *Family Relations,* 35 (1), 9–18.

Nye, F. I. 1957. Child adjustment in broken and in unhappy unbroken homes. *Marriage and Family Living.* 19, 356–360.

Rutter, M. 1971. Parent-child separation: Psychological effects on the children. *Journal of Child Psychology and Psychiatry,* 12, 233–260.

Roy, C. M., and Fuqua, D. R. 1983. Social support systems and academic performance of single-parent students. *School Counselor* (January) 183–192.

Salzman, S. A. 1987. Meta-analysis of studies investigating the effects of father absence on children's cognitive performance. Paper presented at the meeting of the American Educational Research Association, Washington, D.C.

Santrock, J. W., and Tracy, R. L. 1978. Effects of children's family structure status on the development of stereotypes by teachers. *Journal of Educational Psychology,* 70, 754–757.

Shaw, L. B. 1982. High-school completion for young women—effects of low income and living with a single parent. *Journal of Family Issues, 3* (2), 147–163.

Shinn, M. 1978. Father absence and children's cognitive development. *Psychological Bulletin,* 85, 295–324.

Single parents and their families 1983. Chicago: National PTA, Boys Town, and National Association of Elementary School Principals.

Touliatos, J., and Lindholm. B. W. 1980. Teachers' perceptions of behavior problems in children from intact, single-parent, and stepparent families. *Psychology in the Schools, 17,* 264–269.

U.S. House of Representatives. 1989. *U.S. children and their families: Current conditions and recent trends, 1989.* Washington, D.C.: U.S. Government Printing Office.

Wallerstein, J. S., and Kelly, J. B. 1980. *Surviving the breakup: How children and parents cope with divorce.* New York: Basic Books.

Wallerstein, J.Š., and Kelly, J. B. 1975. The effects of parental divorce: Experiences of the preschool child. *Journal of the American Academy of Child Psychiatry,* 14, 600–616.

Washington Post. 1988. The poverty figures. Editorial, Sept. 1, 1988, A22.

Weiss, R. 1978. Single-parent households as settings for growing up. Paper presented at the National Institute of Mental Health Conference on Divorce, Washington, D.C.

Weiss, R, 1975. *Marital separation.* New York: Basic Books.

Zimilies, H., and Lee, V. E. 1988. Educational development among adolescents from single-parent, remarried and intact families: Impact on academic performance and educational persistence. Paper presented at the meeting of the American Educational Research Association, New Orleans, La.

PART III

LOVE, SEXUALITY, AND PREGNANCY

INTRODUCTION

Few topics have as much fascination for students (and teachers) of human development as love and sexuality, and for good reasons. For the individual, love and attraction to another (or others) involves some of the most pleasurable and sustaining feelings a person can experience; it is what makes the struggle for life worth the effort for many people. For families, the network of affective relationships provides a bonding that appears vital to the healthy development of infants, to the maintenance of the family grouping itself, and as sustenance to the elderly.

However, for society at large, the cumulative implications of pleasurable acts of sexuality produce momentous problems that threaten the social order because of overpopulation. The race between producing food, clothing, and shelter, without polluting the environment from which these essential items come, in order to keep pace with the ever-expanding population may be the fundamental dilemma of our age. For a current score on who is ahead in this existential race, see the current editions of *State of the World*, edited by L. R. Brown and associates. The box score is sobering, to say the least, when about 225,000 infants are born each day—that means some 82,000,000 people join us on this planet Earth each year. Thus, we need to consider both individual and species-wide implications of the topic of love and sexuality.

As fascinating as sexuality and love are, they are also clouded in mystery and mystique. Our ignorance in these areas far exceeds our knowledge. For example, over one million American teenagers get pregnant unintentionally each year because of lack of basic knowledge of sexuality, lack of preventive skills or resources, and possibly because of lack of attitudes in caring about social outcomes of their own hedonic acts, as well as for other reasons.

Thus, the first paper in this part concerns the topic of sexuality and pregnancy, and serves as a point of departure on this vast subject. In introducing Susan E. Proctor's paper on the prevention of unwanted teenage sexuality, I want to discuss briefly the background of current sexual norms. This will put into perspective the several major theorists she discusses—Jean Piaget, Erik Erikson, and R. T. Mercer—who are her guides to preventive programming. These theorists help us to focus on how adolescents may be aided to make effective decisions in their own lives, decisions that indirectly affect us all every day of our lives as well.

By way of background, let me describe a paper by Sylvia S. Hacker that presents a provocative essay on the history and the future of sexual values (Sylvia S. Hacker. "The transition from the old norm to the new: Sexual values for the 1990s." *SIECUS Reports*, 1990. 18(5): 1–8). She notes that the old norms are changing, but that is it not clear what the new norms are to be. Before World War II, the norms may be described as anti-sexuality, pro-parenthood: "Sex [meaning intercourse only] is bad, except in marriage, and then you should not enjoy it too much especially if you are a woman . . . " (p. 1). Sexual thoughts, feelings, and fantasies are all bad, and one should try to sublimate them—turn these evil energies into socially useful products—or else take a cold shower and forget about it. A parallel norm is that marriage and parenthood are good, and thus, those people were suspect who were not married, or if married were without children. There was a sexual double standard related to these norms, that men could be sexually active with "bad" women, while women should not be sexually active. Instead, women were to be feminine, meaning submissive to male power and authority. Matrimony thus becomes a market place for the trade of sex (for the man) and love (care and support for the women).

Then came the sexual revolution, a massive change in sexual technology allowing individuals to regulate their own procreative cycles symbolized by "the pill," legalization of abortion, albeit with many strings attached, along with an equally massive change in attitudes about individual freedoms of expression—"doing your own thing," "the I-generation," the "liberation of women" to be able to do whatever men were able to do. Unfortunately, these changes were accompanied by increases in unwanted pregnancies and vast increases in poverty for one-parent households (mostly women), as well as sexually transmitted diseases, of which AIDS is the most recent devastation.

This new set of norms may be described as pro-sex, anti-family. By this I mean a favoring of sexual intercourse as the Eden of human behaviors, with a disregard for the responsibilities and the social institutions within which these activities had hitherto been regulated. The one-parent family is a fully functioning family, but realistically it does impose extra burdens on the parent who lacks surrogate services and resources. The vast majority of one-parent households are poor, thus setting limits on what their children may experience (such as in nutrition, health care, advanced education).

In addition, the sexual behavior considered appropriate was heterosexual; for an estimated ten percent of the citizens of this country who are gay (men) or lesbian (women), there was still a strong sentiment of homophobia in laws as well as in mores. A second revolution emerged, gay rights, as well as a more critical discussion of sexual behaviors. Mass communicators who urged people to the full "joys of sex" were countered by those who said that sexual behaviors had to have some linkages with responsibility, lest the social order break down.

Hacker's (1990) essay offers a beginning look at the new norms regarding sexuality that may be emerging out of the ashes of former policies, laws, mores, as well as AIDS statistics, unwanted pregnancies, and human misery. She points to an emerging consensus that "Sexuality is good, unwanted parenthood is bad." (p. 4). By this she means that sexuality includes much more than sexual intercourse, and that people are recognizing the need to care about how they express their sexuality, being attentive to both self and other during the many splendid expressions of intimacy, and being respectful of the wishes of self and other. These amount to the basic principles of becoming, in Hacher's expression, a "great lover," a sure way to attract audience attention even in these days of dazed TV viewing.

Writers are offering guidelines to modern norms for sexual activity. (See, for example, Robert A. Hatcher, et al., "Sexual etiquette 101," *SIECUS Reports*, 1990, 18(5):9.) These writers accept the facts that people are sexual beings, from childhood through old age, and that these feelings will be expressed in one form or another, including sexual intercourse, which often has serious consequences. Their guidelines, which I am adapting here, offer the following points:

1. There is a shared responsibility in a sexual relationship, both for the giving and receiv-

ing of a wide range of pleasures, but also a mutual responsibility that these acts do not cause harm to the parties or for potential offspring that might result.

2. Communicate openly about contraception and your sexual histories because these show concern for each partner's health and feelings. Incorporate contraception in your routine acts of becoming a "great lover." Be prepared in advance; give yourself credit for being a sensitive sexual being with good common sense.

3. Any kind of force in attaining your sexual pleasure at the expense of another is wrong, even when done under the influence of alcohol or drugs—this is no way to be a great lover. Respect when your partner says "no" to beginning or continuing sexual behaviors at any stage of the activity. Rape is illegal, and rapists may be imprisoned regardless of the contexts.

4. Sexual harassment is no joke, and violates the person's personal rights, and can have serious consequences for the victim as well as for the perpetrator.

5. In the words of Hatcher, et al. (1990, p.9): "Do unto others [in sexual activities] as you would have them do unto you." The golden rule applies everywhere, everytime, and with everyone. Don't leave home without it.

The second major theme of this part deals with homosexuality. The issues here concern identity and acceptance, both self-acceptance and social acceptance. (A related theme of health and homosexuality will be taken up in connection with AIDS in Part VIII.) The paper by Terrence Sullivan and Margaret Schneider focuses on developmental issues for adolescent gays and lesbians. The distinctions among sexual identity (personal assessment of which sex one is), gender role (the culturally based behaviors expressing gender, such as dress code), sexual preference (the choice of erotic partner), and biological-sexual endowments (male or female organs, etc.) are important to keep in mind. They may or may not appear in alignment in any particular individual. The authors also consider the service implications of these developmental needs—how are we to assist youths who come to recognize their homosexuality in a homophobic society?

The paper by Aaron Lipman discusses homosexual relationships among older persons, a topic that is frequently ignored by the helping professional. While there appears to be no one life-style characteristic of all gay or lesbian people, there are differences between younger and older homosexuals. Primary groups and community supports are just as important for elderly homosexuals as they are for heterosexuals, perhaps even more so, given the oppressive environment in which they live. The important of long-term loving support and nurturance is emphasized in this paper, regardless of the sexual preference and—I would add—the age, class, or cultural context of the people involved.

13

A DEVELOPMENTAL APPROACH TO PREGNANCY PREVENTION WITH EARLY ADOLESCENT FEMALES

Susan E. Proctor

Division of Nursing
California State University at Sacramento

The age of first sexual intercourse for female adolescents is decreasing[1] and the number of pregnancies among this group continues to increase.[2] Professionals from many disciplines have expressed appropriate concern and sex education and family planning programs have proliferated as approaches to curbing the increase in the number of teen mothers.[3] In reflecting on the problem of pregnancy in the young teen, the target population—the young adolescent—should be assessed in terms of developmental needs and levels. Consideration should be given to pregnancy prevention approaches tailored to developmental ages and stages. Methods and strategies should consider the unique, developmental characteristics of this age, and actively correlate with age-related stages and needs to improve the success rate in teen pregnancy prevention. Awareness of developmental levels also helps explain why traditional pregnancy prevention and family planning approaches often are unsuccessful with very young women.

LEVELS OF DEVELOPMENT

Experts differentiate between and among an early adolescence (ages 12–14), middle adolescence (ages 15–16), and late adolescence (ages 17–19 or to adulthood). Though the chronology varies, adolescence consists of stages, and more particularly, of distinct, yet progressive levels of development.

In addition to stages, "tasks" of adolescence have been postulated as milestones in the process of reaching adulthood. Mercer[4] identified six tasks which, together with consideration of specific developmental theories, provide a useful framework for selecting appropriate pregnancy interventions: acceptance and comfort with body image; determination and internalization of sexual identity and role;

development of a personal value system; preparation for productive citizenship; achievement of independence from parents; and development of an adult identity. This discussion considers young adolescents whose ages range from 11 or 12 through 14. Most young people in this age group have achieved none of these milestones. Yet, all the developmental tasks have implications for sexual activity, contraceptive behavior, and child rearing.

Early adolescent boys and girls are in Piaget's "concrete operations" phase of cognitive development.[5] Though moving toward "formal operations," most still make decisions based on experience. Time orientation is almost exclusively past or present. Little or no forthought goes into activities with which the young person is not solicitously absorbed or genuinely comfortable. The future, if considered, is perceived as uncertain or idealized. Few teens at this age look much beyond a few weeks or months into their future. Since development of adult values and a sexual value system requires abstract cognition and conceptualization, youngsters, whose thought processes are still "concrete," are unlikely to articulate clear values with regard to sexuality, sexual behavior, or to preplan for sexual intercourse.

Erikson[6] assumes youngsters acquire a sense of self and separateness from others when they enter the developmental stage of "identity vs. identity diffusion." Acquisition of adult identity as an "ego" requires development of certain cognitive concepts about the self as self. The process also demands acceptance and internalization of sexual identity and sexuality, a development rarely found in early adolescents. Part of accepting oneself as a sexual being involves reasonable comfort with body image, a feeling less likely to exist during early adolescence than at any other time of childhood.[7] Not uncom-

From *Journal of School Health*, 56 (8): 313–316. (October 1986). Copyright 1986. *American School Health Association, P.O. Box 708, Kent, Ohio 44240. Reprinted by permission.*

monly, a denial of overt sexuality exists among youngsters this age.[1] Young women in early adolescence may acknowledge coital experience but be uncomfortable with the suggestion that coitus is a regular, accepted part of their lives. When both abstract cognition and acceptance of self as a sexual being are considered, the individuation process of growing up is not complete much before ages 15–16.[6]

TRADITIONAL PREVENTION METHODS

The best pregnancy prevention method—saying "no"—would be advocated by many professionals and parents. However, a lifetime of parental admonition against early sexual activity will not necessarily result in adolescent compliance with such values. With a developmental framework for reference, other approaches to pregnancy prevention in the young teen can be examined to determine why they are or are not successful.

FAMILY PLANNING SERVICES

According to Peach,[1] when a young woman is brought to a clinic by mothers, relatives, or friends for family planning services, the young woman is more likely to keep appointments than if she comes by herself. Young women who have not internalized their sexuality will not consistently use clinic services when such participation admits to sexual activity and demands the need to future orient. Many 12–14 year old women do not have the physical mobility to attend clinics, even when reasonably accessible and affordable. Low cost and convenience are crucial elements in programs that successfully serve teens.[8]

Clinics established in high school settings seem to be successful both in reducing teen pregnancy and in providing prenatal services to teens. These clinics often provide full health services so a teen need not identify sexual concerns until in the privacy of the examining room. This "cover" is important to teens not comfortable using family planning as their presenting complaint. Established in Sweden[9] as well as in some US cities,[10] the clinics' services are available, convenient, guaranteed confidential, utilized by peers, and located in safe, familiar surroundings. These attributes seem likely to overcome the cognitive and emotional barriers to admitting sexual activity that young teens experience because of age.

SEX EDUCATION

Sex education correlates most positively with contraceptive use when the education can be individualized and related to concrete experiences in the adolescent' life such as menarche.[11] The assumption that sex or contraceptive education automatically produces appropriate behavior does not recognize the complexity of decision making with regard to sex, particularly in the early adolescent. Receiving information, frequently in large groups or classroom situations and within narrow reproductive contexts, does not necessarily translate into "adult-intended" desired behaviors.[3,12,13] such as appropriate contraceptive use by the sexually active or the potentially sexually active.

DEVELOPMENTAL APPROACHES TO PREVENTION

Using Mercer's developmental tasks and the theories described previously, approaches can be implemented by professionals, particularly school personnel who have frequent contact with the young teen (Figure 1). "Acceptance and achievement of body image" and "Determination and internalization of sexual identity and role" (Mercer tasks one and two) are vital for professionals to consider when approaching the young teen.

Awkwardness with body image and noninternalization of sexuality provide clues to approaches and interventions. Sexually active young women present a seemingly superficial or remote posture toward sex, reflecting their early developmental level.[1] Understanding of this attitude is important for the professional who works with young teen women. The timing of the intervention is a critical factor. In working with adolescents who do not comfortably acknowledge their own sexuality, suggestions or encouragement for contraceptive use might produce the desired behavior if the intervention occurs as close as possible to the time of probable intercourse. This factor acknowledges both the nonplanned nature of most 12–14 year old sexual experience and the lack of future orientation in this age group. Finally, complex interdimensional changes occurring physiologically and psychologically argue strongly for continuance and promotion of group activities such as sports, scouting, and club involvement that meet security and belonging needs and help organize a disorganized psyche.

"Development of a personal value system" (Mercer task three) promotes acquisition of a values framework for making sexual decisions. Young people should be encouraged to talk with parents about appropriate values concerning sexuality and to seek

FIGURE 1. Developmental Guide to Pregnancy Intervention

Developmental Stage	Developmental Theorist	Approaches/Interventions

Early Adolescence (12-14 yrs.)	**Piaget** Teen in concrete operations stage of development (decisions based on past or present experience)
	
	 Erikson Teen in identity vs. identity diffusion stage of development: independent identity not achieved or accomplished
		= Maximize and optimize relationship with parents
		= Utilize surrogate parent to ''link out'' to at-risk adolescents
		= Intervene to facilitate reducing family conflict
		= Reduce any social isolation experienced by at-risk adolescent
		= Promote saying ''no'' as an acceptable response to coital overtures
		= Promote involvement in clubs, activities, sports
		= Encourage communication with parents and church for acquisition of values framework
		= Employ peer counseling and teaching of sex education
		= Incorporate values framework, decision-making into sex/contraceptive education
		= Utilize developmental approaches to teaching
		  = concretize the learning whenever possible (= Role playing = Use of hypothetical scenarios for valuing and problem-solving = Multisensorial methodologies, eg. listening to others, drawing diagrams, examining contraceptive devices, etc.)
		  = conduct teaching/learning in small groups with familiar persons;
		  = provide time for private interaction with instructor
		  = avoid use of explicit audio-visual material showing insertion of speculums, IUDs, etc.
		  = concretize the sexually active adolescent's current experience by having teen write the happening, consequences, solutions
		= Target interventions as close as possible to time of probably intercourse
		= Promote appropriate clinic services as close to school setting as possible
		= Develop and offer parent education regarding adolescent growth and development, pregnancy prevention, and conflict resolution
		= Reinforce appropriate decision-making
		= Promote staying in school
		= Appeal to older male sexual partner directly for assumption of contraceptive responsibility
		= Cultivate a caring interactional style

Middle Adolescence (15-16 yrs.)	**Piaget** Concrete operations progressing to formal operations (ability to abstract, theorize, and conceptualize the not-yet experienced) **Erikson** Ego identity progressing	= Utilize all of the preceding as appropriate = Promote teen teaching of sex education = Direct appeals for sexual responsibility to teens themselves and not to parents = Implement comprehensive values-based sex education with appeal to male as well as female responsibility for pregnancy prevention
Late Adolescence 17-yrs. - adulthood)	**Piaget** Transition to formal operations now complete **Erikson** Ego identity complete	= Utilize the preceding as appropriate = Expect and promote preplanning = Anticipate that traditional and adult family planning methods and instruction will be more successful

guidance from any religious group to which they belong. Saying "no" should be presented as a plausible approach to pregnancy prevention in discussing sex and pregnancy prevention. These youngsters still are primarily in concrete operations, so professionals should tailor educational material appropriately. Also, many young girls have older boyfriends as sexual partners. It is wise and reasonable to appeal to the more abstract cognition of these young men in their likely position as primary decision makers in contraception.[3] They can be encouraged to take responsibility for planning for contraception and ensuring its use.

RELATIONSHIPS

"Achievement of independence from parents," and "Development of an adult identity" (Mercer tasks five and six) allow the professional to consider the profound impact of peers, significant others, and parents on young teen decision making with regard to sexual activity. One plausible approach to pregnancy prevention involves maximizing and optimizing the relationship with the young woman's parents. Alternatively, this approach substitutes a surrogate parent to provide the emotional base absent in homes where parent-child relationships have deteriorated or are nonexistent. These approaches are modeled on work done by Welches[14] who studied adolescent females' perceived relationships with their parents and any concurrent sexual activity.

Young women were queried as to whether their relationship with each parent was "above" or "below average," requiring a subjective response from each young woman as she evaluated her parental relationship against a perceived mental norm.

Of those young women who saw their relationship with both parents as above average, only 6.4 percent were sexually active. Some young women saw their relationship with mother as below average and with father as above average. Among this group, nearly 67 percent reported being sexually active. Of girls who saw their relationship as above average with mother, but as below average with father, 44 percent were sexually active. Among the group who saw their relationship with both parents as below average, 37.5 percent reported being sexually active. Welches cautioned against concluding that a perceived better relationship with father is indicative of sexual acting out. However, she did note that in all four groups, sexually active young women were less likely to use contraceptives if they perceived the relationship between their parents to be

less than desirable. This theme of the adolescent's response to parental discord and family conflict repeatedly is linked either to sexual activity or nonuse of contraceptives.[1,3]

Communication between teen and parent is frequently presented as a measure of the quality of the relationship with greater or more frequent communication correlating with more responsible sexual behavior.[3] There is at lease some contradictory evidence. Some studies[15,16] suggest parental knowledge of teen sexual activity and communication about the activity does not affect either continuance of sex or use of contraception. However, in neither study were qualitative dimensions placed on the communication and researchers did not determine if tacit permission giving was inherent in the parent-child communication. Certainly, cultural or emotional pressure from parents, or from parents' personal history of becoming involved sexually at an early age correlate positively with teen sexual activity.[17, 18]

Interventions based on family relationships can promote family integrity, reduce familial conflict, and enhance parent-child relationships. Peer relationships also are valuable when choosing interventions as demonstrated by the effectiveness of peer counseling and teaching.[4]

PARENT SURROGATES

A pregnancy prevention approach based upon Welches' work is the concept of the professional acting as a parent surrogate. A surrogate is particularly appropriate in schools or in other settings where development and maintenance of frequent, consistent, comfortable relationships are possible. As trusted figures in the young woman's life, adults can establish relationships with youngsters at risk for pregnancy. Figure 2 lists risk factors to aid the professional in identifying youngsters at higher risk for pregnancy. Since frequent contact is essential, the school is likely setting and adults in the school are the most likely surrogates.

Desirable personal characteristics, such as being a trusted, well-liked adult, are essential to develop and maintain close relationships with at-risk teens. Youngsters at high risk for pregnancy are assigned to surrogates who work to develop a close, caring, attentive relationship with the youngster over time. Depending upon the parental relationship needed by the young woman, the surrogate can be male or female. Surrogates' roles involve at least daily contact with the teen, combined with follow-up on absences either through home visits or telephone calls. Daily contact can be encouraged by assigning "targeted" teens as student aides or assistants for nurses, counselors, administrators, librarians, or other school staff who use students in this capacity. Teachers with sufficient time also would be appropriate surrogates. An intense campaign of one-on-one intervention requires individuals with adequate time and opportunity to assume the role effectively.

IDENTIFYING ADOLESCENTS AT RISK

Surrogates must know who need intervention. Risk factors in a young woman's life may constitute "red flags" for pregnancy risk depending upon the circumstances (Figure 2). Recent significant loss or change intensifies vulnerability, and upsets security and belonging, increasing the likelihood a young women may become sexually active.[4] If a young woman's immediate peer group is sexually active, professionals should be aware of the greater likelihood that the young teen herself is sexually active.[4] A young woman previously pregnant has a greater

likelihood of becoming pregnant again than a never-pregnant teen has of becoming pregnant a first time,[18] particularly if she was not enrolled in a school program at time of pregnancy or if she has a history of school drop-out.[19] Also, if the mother, grandmother, or sister was pregnant as a teen,[18] tacit permission may be given so pregnancy may indeed be intentional. Young women who have been sexually abused may continue sexual behavior as an acting-out phenomena.[20]

Having few if any girl friends[4] as well as having "older" boyfriends[1,3] should be recognized as possible signs a young girl already is sexually active and may seek sexual relationships to fill peer relationship voids. Older, 12–14-year-old adolescent males, are at about the same point cognitively and psychosexually as are adolescent girls. Though intensely curious about sex, few are sexually active,[2] and most have not internalized their sexuality to any greater degree than have their female peers. Therefore, most sexual partners of young adolescent females will not be young men their own age.

Conflict[13,18] at home frequently is reported among teens who are sexually active and who seek other relationships to compensate for what is missing in their home life. Substance abuse interferes with cognition and decision making, increasing the chance of unplanned sexual intercourse.[4] Other risk factors include situations that make teens feel uncomfortable, different, or unacceptable. Conditions such as poor academic performance[17] or physical deformities[4] may contribute to lower self-esteem and feelings of vulnerability.

Self-esteem must be considered cautiously. Perhaps all adolescents have inadequate self-esteem. One study[21] indicated adolescents who already were mothers had lower self-esteem than teens who never had been pregnant or had chosen abortion. However, lower self-esteem does not necessarily translate into noncontraceptive use.[13] Self-esteem should be viewed carefully by the surrogate as to its real meaning as a risk factor.

FIGURE 2. Factors Associated with Increased Likelihood of Sexual Activity in Young Female Adolescents

- recently experienced significant loss / change
- perceived poor relationship with parent(s)
- immediate peer group sexually active
- previously pregnant
- history of nonattendance at school
- mother, sister, and / or grandmother pregnant as teen
- history of sexual abuse
- few, if any, girlfriends
- "older" boyfriend
- parental / familial conflict
- substance use or abuse
- scholastically underachieving
- looking / feeling unacceptable, different, or inferior
- low self-esteem

References

1. Peach EH: Counseling sexually active very young adolescent girls. *MCN* 1980; 5(3):191–195.
2. *Teen-age Pregnancy: The problem that hasn't gone away.* New York, The Alan Guttmacher Institute, 1981, pp. 6–21.
3. Kastner L S: Ecological factors predicting adolescent contraceptive use: Implications for intervention. *J Adol Health Care* 1984; 5(2): 79–86.
4. Mercer R T: *Perspectives on Adolescent Health Care.* Philadelphia, J B Lippincott Co. 1979, pp 3–28, 402–411.
5. Piaget J. Inhelder B: *The Psychology of the Child.* New York, Basic Books, 1969.
6. Erikson E: *Identity: Youth and crisis.* New York, W W Norton & Co. 1968.

7. Simmons R G, Rosenberg F, Rosenberg M: Disturbances in the self image at adolescence. *Am Soc Rev* 1973; 38(5): 553–568.

8. Kisker EE: The effectiveness of family planning clinics in serving adolescents. *Fam Plann Perspect* 1984; 16(5): 212–218.

9. Jones E F, Forrest J D, Goldman N, et al: Teen-age pregnancy in developed countries: Determinants and policy implications. *Fam Plann Perspect* 1985; 17(2): 53–62.

10. Taylor B, Berg M, Kapp L, et al: School-based prenatal services: Can similar outcomes be attained in a non-school setting? *J Sch Health* 1983; 53(8): 480–486.

11. Saefer E, Schall T, Sobel E, et al: Menarche: Target age for reinforcing sex education for adolescents. *J Adol Health Care* 1985; 6(5): 383–386.

12. Dunn P: Reduction of teen-age pregnancy as a rationale for sex education: A position paper. *J Sch Health* 1982; 52(10): 611–618.

13. Kellinger K G: Factors in adolescent contraceptive use. *Nurs Pract* 1985; 10(9): 55–62.

14. Welches L J: Adolescent Sexuality, in Mercer R T (ed): *Perspectives on Adolescent Health Care.* Philadelphia J B Lippincott Co. 1979, pp. 29–41.

15. Furstenberg F F, Herceg-Baron R, Shea J, et al: Family communication and teen-agers' contraceptive use. *Fam Plann Perspect* 1984; 16(4) 163–169.

16. Newcomer S F, Udry J R: Parent-child communication and adolescent sexual behavior. *Fam Plann Perspect* 1985; 17(4): 169–174.

17. Cohen S J: Intentional teen-age pregnancies. *J Sch Health* 1983: 53(3): 210–211.

18. Miller S H: *Children as Parents: Final report on a study of childbearing and childrearing among 12–15 year olds.* New York, Child Welfare League of America, 1983.

19. Polit D F, Kahn J R: Early subsequent pregnancy among economically disadvantaged teen-age mothers. *Am J Public Health* 1986; 76(2): 167–171.

20. Tsai M, Feldman-Summers T, Edgar M: Childhood molestation: Variables related to differential impact on psychosexual functioning in adult women. *J Abnorm Psych* 1979; 4:407–417.

21. Freemen E W, Rickels K, Huggins G R, et al: Urban black adolescents who obtain contraceptive services before or after their first pregnancy. *J Adol Health Care* 1984; 5(3): 183–190.

14

DEVELOPMENT AND IDENTITY ISSUES IN ADOLESCENT HOMOSEXUALITY

Terrence Sullivan
*Ministry of Community
and Social Services
Toronto*

Margaret Schneider
Central Toronto Youth Services

To the doctor, you were sick; to the lawyer, you were a criminal; to the minister, you were wicked.

(Adair and Adair, 1978, p. 242)

Adults are often reluctant to listen carefully to adolescent messages regarding sexuality. When young people identify themselves as being gay or lesbian, this is often dismissed as a phase, adjustment reaction, or experimentation. While it is certainly accurate that homosexual experimentation is common in early adolescents, and that some of it is transient, our experience would indicate that taking the assertions of self-identified young homosexuals at face value is probably a more useful starting point for helping professionals and one which does not deny what they may feel they are. Joanne's poem is instructive:

> I have a problem, I feel so sad
> I'm going crazy, it's getting bad
> The friends I have that aren't like me
> Tell me I am wrong
> The ones I know who really are
> Tell me I'm too young
> How am I wrong when it's in my heart?
> Am I too young when I fit the part?
> I am gay, that I know
> But to my friends that is not so.
> How to cope with folks like these?
> Are they or I the ones I please.

> Joanne, 18 years in Heron (1983)
> *One Teenager in Ten*

The same failure to listen in the case of explicit messages regarding adolescent sexual aggression has recently brought us to an abrupt new view of offense perpetrators in adolescence (Ryan, 1986).

While there is clearly no link implied between gay youth and offenders, in both cases our polite preference often tends to be to ignore adolescent sex-

ual reality. In the case of homosexual adolescents, one of the unintended effects of this 'head in the sand' approach is a steady assault on adolescent self-esteem which is reinforced right into adulthood where outright discrimination and minority stress become part of the homosexual reality.

A DEVELOPMENTAL ORIENTATION

In 1967, Simon and Gagnon wrote a landmark article on homosexuality. Dissatisfied with the proper psychiatric focus on homosexuality, they argued for a change in focus. Rather than viewing homosexuals as a uniform group within a common etiological background, they called for the study of homosexuality as part of a general maturation process, as one aspect of sexual development, with a focus on developmental tasks and the individual and social factors affecting the lifestyle of homosexuals.

At the same time, professionals in psychology, social work, and psychiatry have begun to relinquish the view of homosexuality as pathological. Homosexuality is now officially considered to be an "alternate lifestyle", rather than a mental illness, by both the American Psychiatric Association and the American Psychological Association. However, in some professional quarters, and certainly in the public's eye, homosexuality is still considered to be sick, deviant, and/or immoral.

We will argue, as we have elsewhere (Eisner, 1982; Sullivan, 1984) that homosexuality should be depathologized and destigmatized. This argument centres around two principal axes. First, recent research, using adequate control groups and non-psychiatric populations of subjects, has failed to support the contention that homosexuality is a sign of mental illness. Secondly, the pathological per-

Reprinted by permission from *Child and Adolescent Social Work*, 4(1):13–24. Copyright © 1987. Human Sciences Press. The views expressed in this paper do not necessarily reflect those of the Ministry of Community and Social Services.

spective tends to increase stress for the homosexual individual who is thereby stigmatized. It becomes a difficult task for the homosexual to establish and maintain a sense of self-esteem and positive identity. These developmental tasks often become sources of distress for the homosexual adolescent.

In this paper, we are particularly concerned with the maturation of the homosexual adolescent. We will consider the relationship between the adolescent's developing sexual awareness and his/her psychosocial development which take place in a historic and contemporary context which largely rejects homosexuality.

There is a rich literature on the development of gender identity, object choice, and sexual behavior in childhood and adolescence (Constantine and Martinson, 1981; Diamond, 1979; Diepold and Young, 1979; Miller and Simon, 1980; Rutter, 1980). The purpose of this exploration is not to rehash once again the genesis of homosexuality, or the factors that contribute to the same-sex erotic preference, but rather to attempt an examination of the special stresses and problems associated with homosexual behavior and identification in adolescence.

Sexual preference is but one key element of sexual behavior among a number of developmentally important categories.[1] Diamond's (1979) model of sexual development accommodates nicely much of the current research on sexuality, and comprises four important categories to be studied in a complete developmental sexology:

1. sexual identity (personal assessment of which sex one is)
2. patterns or gender role (culturally-bound behaviors like dress code and hairstyle)
3. mechanisms (biologically-based behaviors such as erection, vaginal lubrication; orgasm and
4. object choice/preference (choice of erotic partner).

Diamond's model acknowledges constitutional bias toward certain sexual behaviors, and is interactive in the sense that biological programming and environment interact to produce a whole spectrum of sexual behavior and types. Our discussion will focus largely on the first, second, and fourth categories of Diamond's typology.

SEX ROLE AND GENDER ROLE IDENTITY

Children learn very early on (three to four years) what sex they are. Shortly after that time, they accurately identify other people's sexes, and most recognize the inevitability of becoming a "mommy" or a "daddy" when they grow up. Children first recognize sex differences on the basis of appearance patterns (hair, clothes), and, by about seven years of age, children reliably discriminate on the basis of genital cues. This development of sex constancy, while related to the child's cognitive level, is not apparently related to gender role preference (Rutter, 1980). While there is considerable overlap in which behaviors are generally regarded as masculine and feminine, there are important differences in both gestures and play between the sexes. By age two or three, children have a good knowledge of the prevailing gender role stereotype. Most children develop clear preferences in gestures, toys, and activities by age five or so. From age four or so, boys become increasingly more gender-typed in their behavior than girls, and other children of both sexes are less tolerant of gender-atypical behavior in boys. Consider, with these observations, some developmental data on childhood gender-related behavior in children who later develop homosexual preference.

Several studies have confirmed that many male and female homosexuals exhibit a variety of cross-gender preferences and role behavior in childhood.[2] (Bell et al., 1981; Harry, 1983; Saghir and Robins, 1973; Whitham, 1980). The degree of reported cross-gender activity for homosexuals varies from three to six times the level for heterosexuals, depending on the measures of cross-gendering used. We begin to get a picture that distinguishes a majority of "pre-homosexual" children very early on from their counterparts. Harry's study (1983) purports that cross-gender characteristics in childhood can be predictive of adult cross-gender characteristics. Few adults develop cross-gender characteristics who did not show these in childhood.

On the other hand, Bieber (1962) found that only two percent of a sample of homosexuals in therapy were rated by their analysts as "effeminate", and 95% of homosexuals in a different study rated themselves as "moderately or strongly masculine" (Evans, 1969). Silverstein (1972, cited in Davison and Neale, 1982) contends that many male homosexuals have a firm identification of themselves as male. Finally, studies of gender role comparing lesbians and heterosexual women find a higher incidence of androgyny, rather than strictly cross-typed gender role among lesbians (Eisner, 1983; McCauley & Erhardt, 1977; Van Cleave, 1978).

While there does seem to be some connection between cross-gender role behavior early on and homosexual development, the relationship is far from perfect. There seems to be a substantial proportion of homosexual adults who did not exhibit cross-gender behavior as children, nor do they as adults. Furthermore, homosexuals tend to be androgynous, rather than cross-gender typed, and generally perceive or experience themselves as appropriately masculine or feminine, male or female.

Since the late 1970's, the stereotypical image of the gay male has evolved from an effeminate to an ultra-masculine image, typified by a fashion for uniforms, leather, and sports gear. Similarly, the "butch/femme" dichotomy among lesbians (that is, the ultra-masculine woman coupled with the ultra-feminine woman) has all but disappeared. These changes in image suggest that cross-gender roles among homosexuals may be a function of social pressures and fashion, rather than an inherent element of homosexuality.

In summary, the relationship between sex role, gender role, and homosexuality is unclear. However, the fact that we assume a connection may have important consequences for the maturing adolescent, who may be erroneously labelled gay based on his/her gender role behavior, or the developing homosexual adolescent who may feel compelled to act out the stereotype of the homosexual by adopting cross-gender behavior.

DEVELOPMENT OF A HOMOSEXUAL IDENTITY

Becoming aware of one's same-sex preference is called "coming out". "Coming out" is defined as "the developmental process through which gay people recognize their sexual preferences and choose to integrate this knowledge into their personal and social lives" (De Monteflores and Schultz, 1978, p. 59).

A number of models and descriptions of the coming-out process can be found in the literature, for example, works by Cass (1979), Coleman (1982), Lee (1977), Plummer (1975), Ponse (1978), Schafer (1976), Troiden (1979), and Troiden and Goode (1980). These models, studies, and reviews of the coming-out process are disparate in scope, perspective, and emphasis. For example, Cass (1979) emphasizes the cognitive aspects of coming out, focusing on a cognitive dissonance as the motivation for movement through the process. Lee (1977) places more emphasis on the behavioral aspects of coming out, in particular self-disclosure and

involvement with the gay community. Some models, such as Schafer's (1976), end with the adoption of the homosexual label, while Cass (1979) and Troiden (1979), for example, go beyond adoption of the label and include emergence of a positive gay identity as part of the process. Furthermore, these models do not agree with regard to the relative chronology of the first homosexual experience, initial contact with the gay subculture, and labelling oneself as gay.

Differential reports on the ordering of events is, in part, a function of male/female differences in the coming-out process. Females most often become aware of their sexual orientation as a result of a particular emotional involvement (Simon and Gagnon, 1967a; 1967b), while, for males, emotional involvement, and, sometimes, physical involvement, is subsequent to recognition of their sexual orientation (Simon and Gagnon, 1967a; 1967b; Troiden and Goode, 1980). With regard to contact with the gay community, Plummer (1975) and Dank (1971) depict male homosexual identity as being formed within the context of the homosexual subculture, while Schafer (1976) found that the lesbians in her sample formed their homosexual identity prior to contact with the lesbian community.

In the development of any general model, individual differences tend to be obscured. In fact, there are vast differences in the coming-out process in terms of important events, ordering of events, time span, level of stress and distress, and ability to cope. If we are to generalize at all about the coming-out process, it appears that there is not one, but three, distinguishable patterns.

Eisner (1982) proposed and tested a model of the coming-out process which reconciles the different approaches to coming out, and accommodates individual and sex differences. She conceptualized the coming-out process as a progression of cognitions which are linked to specific events. The cognitions are divided into three developmental stages. The first stage is a pre-homosexual stage, during which the individual becomes aware of a sense of being different. The next stage involves cognitions which emerge as the individual becomes increasingly aware of the possibility that s/he might be gay. The third stage begins when the individual labels him/herself gay.

These cognitions are linked to events in four major categories: contact with the homosexual community; the development of intimate, same-sex relationships; self-disclosure; and events outside of a "homosexual context", such as moving, taking a trip, etc. The model reflects the fact that some events differ in significance across individuals. For example, some people will definitely define themselves as gay after contacting the community, while others will do so after establishing a long-term same-sex relationship or subsequent to self-disclosure. This model makes it possible to generalize about and compare various samples of homosexuals.

Emerging from Eisner's study was evidence for these patterns to the coming-out process. On one hand are individuals who describe themselves as "always" having been gay. For these people, sexual preference, which emerged during maturation from child to adult, was always homosexual. In contrast, some individuals defined themselves as exclusively heterosexual until they were well into adulthood when they rather suddenly began to define themselves as homosexual, usually as a result of falling in love with a person of the same sex. The third pattern is characterized by individuals who vascillated between homosexuality and heterosexuality until well into adulthood.[3]

Common to all three patterns are two tasks which must be accomplished before closure can be reached. First, a positive feeling about being gay must develop. This may take place either before or after the individual begins to definitely self-label as homosexual, but, until it develops, the individual is bound to be preoccupied with the issue, on a conscious or unconscious level. Negative feelings about homosexual identity will impair general self-esteem, and may lead to a variety of self-defeating behaviors. Secondly, sexual preference must be integrated into the rest of one's identity, and put in its proper perspective. Cass (1979) calls this "Identity Synthesis."

What is "proper perspective"? The question is easier to answer by focusing on what is *not* a "proper perspective". We know that the homosexual population is as varied as the rest of the population with regard to occupation, interests, socioeconomic status, age, religion, intimate relationships; in fact, any human characteristic imaginable. A person's sexual orientation tells us little about his/her identity. For most people, gay or straight, sexual orientation is not the most salient part of their identity. Rather, it exists in harmony with a full inventory of traits that comprise any individual. It is a frequent pitfall of both gay and straight people that they allow the characteristic "gay" to diminish or obscure the other attributes of a person. Thus, we

often see gay people who go through a phase of acting out their image of the archetypal gay man or woman. As one lesbian stated,

> At the beginning, the main thing in my life was 'I'm a lesbian.' So I had the flannel shirt and the jeans and the whole thing and I thought that's the way to go about it. I got through that when I got more relaxed about myself. Then being gay took its rightful place. It's a fact in my life, just like the fact that I wear glasses (Eisner, 1982, p. 174).

THE ADOLESCENT AND THE COMING-OUT PROCESS

What are the consequences of being a gay adolescent? To answer this question, we must consider the coming-out process within the larger framework of the adolescent's general development, with particular focus on self-esteem, sense of identity, and social skills. All adolescents are faced with the task of development in these three areas. However, this business is somewhat more difficult for the gay youth, who must develop self-esteem in the context of a society which largely rejects homosexuality; who must integrate his/her sexual preference into the rest of his/her identity; who must develop the necessary social skills to negotiate through a rejecting society as well as function within a gay community.

We know that many homosexuals feel different from their peers as youngsters, because of gender role or a growing awareness of their sexual preference. For example, Bell et al. report that, compared to heterosexual men, homosexual men recall feeling different from other boys their age, both in grade school and in high school. These differences were similar, but less marked, for girls. These findings were consistent with the acknowledged difference in self-perception that results in less interest in opposite-sex peers, and more interest in same-sex peers. Male and female homosexuals reported dramatically greater feelings of being sexually different from their peers than did heterosexuals. Moreover, homosexual adults report more negative self-concepts and negative feeling states while growing up than did their heterosexual counterparts.

The Bell et al. (1981) study found that homosexuals generally reported lower levels of social involvement with same-sex peers both in the grade school years and in high school. Similarly, a significant portion (about 20%) of male and female homosexuals reported more close friends of the opposite sex during grade school and high school in comparison to heterosexuals. This suggests a different pattern of adolescent socialization for many homosexual youths. Frequency of dating was about the same for heterosexual and homosexual men and women, although the homosexuals reports a lower degree of enjoyment of dating.

Emerging from this research is a portrait of a young person growing up with a general sense of being different from his/her peers. This feeling may feed into a sense of alienation the youth may experience as s/he became aware of a same-sex sexual preference, and interfere with the development of self-esteem and identity. For any young person with a sense of difference (be it due to emerging sexual preference or because s/he is the only kid at school with parents on welfare), the issue at this time may be whether or not it is all right to be different. What may distinguish those who cope well with the stress of coming out, versus those who do not, may be a sense that it is all right to be different.

Malyon (1981) has outlined a useful model for looking at how adolescents make homosexual adaptation. He outlines three possible interim solutions to resolving the sexual identity crisis that faces prehomosexual adolescents. One solution involves a *repression* of same-sex desires, and constitutes a common but less than satisfactory adaptation. He argues that repression often eventuates in panic with little opportunity to integrate these new-found desires. A second solution requires a *suppression* of same-sex desires, and often results in a developmental moratorium wherein the individual tries to accommodate expectations of the heterosexual culture. Malyon claims that identity issues then re-emerge in the third or fourth decade, and effort is made to integrate these in the course of coming out. This "biphasic adolescence" allows for the integration of this previously compartmentalized intimate material and completion of the identity formation process. In the first two solutions, part of the developmental priority becomes an elaborate set of defenses and attempts to pursue a heterosexual preference. These defenses of denial, compensation, suppression, and compartmentalization serve to diminish confict in the external world, but inhibit the socialization of erotic and intimate desires, thereby interfering with the ego resources necessary for more complete psychological integration. Solution three involves *disclosure,* or "coming out". This process as a developmental sequence has been widely commented on (Coleman, 1982). For youth who opt for disclosure of homosexual identity in adolescence, a crisis

of acceptance and identification ensues. Social and parental attitudes mitigate against self-acceptance.

The choices for a homosexual or prehomosexual adolescent who is struggling with his/her gay identity or coming out are limited. The youth has little access to gay or lesbian communities which are typically adult-oriented. In some jurisdictions, prohibitive legislation makes it difficult to get counselling or social services necessary for self-affirmation, and to support the adolescent shaken and stressed by this crisis. He/she can choose to complete this disclosure within the hostile and alienating social environment of mainstream heterosexual culture, or she/he can seek support and social opportunities in the adult gay community. Although little data exist here, one would predict that more gays leave home earlier in order to choose this latter strategy for self-disclosure: acceptance into the adult gay community.

The premature assumption of adult roles creates its own special problems. Some gay adolescents, lacking the necessary life skills, may hustle on the street as an adaptation, although not all male prostitutes are gay. Allen (1980) noted that about one-third of 98 male prostitutes interviewed in his study had been, or were runaways. For others, the newly-acquired lifestyle may revolve around bars, impersonal promiscuous sex, drugs, disco, and booze. These experiences may be exciting, alienating, or both, but are clearly far from the secure confines of family life, school, and more familiar adolescent realities.

Sex differences in the coming-out process imply that certain issues may be different for young gay males and young gay females. The visible gay subculture seems to be more important to the males than to the females. Males tend to come in contact with the subculture in search of sexual experience and a gay identity, while females tend to come in contact with it after their first sexual experiences and after they have identified themselves as gay. Adult lesbians tend to be less involved in the gay subculture than gay men (Saghir and Robins, 1973; Simon and Gagnon, 1967b), and this may be the result of the fact that lesbians are more likely to be in a monogamous relationship at any given time, and therefore, do not need to frequent the gay bars or clubs in order to find sexual partners. Gay men are generally more sexually active than gay women. They tend to have more sexual partners (Cotton, 1975), are more likely to have participated in group sex (Schafer, 1977), to have one-night stands (Albro and Tully, 1979), and engage in anonymous sex, a practice which is virtually unheard of among lesbians (Lee, 1977). Thus, young gay men are more likely to be drawn into a lifestyle which revolves around bars, bath-houses, and promiscuity, and must be made aware of the consequences.

SERVICE ISSUES

For those adolescents who do come out, the "crisis competence" that follows the coming-out sequence lends self-respect and ego integrity to those youth who can see the process through without fragmenting. This competence allows for a developmental redirection toward a reliance on the sources of social support in the gay community and affirms a positive gay identity.

The special need for services for gay adolescents is now beginning to surface in professional discourse on counselling (Chng 1980; Hart, 1982; Kremer, Zimfer, and Wiggers, 1975; Malyon, 1981; Needham, 1971; Price, 1982; Thompson and Fishburn, 1977). These range from dealing with the individual issues of confusion, family tension, peer problems, and self-contempt to the larger need of educating families, schools, and communities on homosexual preference in adolescence. Some of this will be done through conventional generic agencies, and some of this work will be delivered through services developed explicitly for gay youth, such as the Institute for the Protection of Lesbian and Gay Youth in New York City.

The challenge for the teaching and the helping professions is to begin the slow and uphill climb to depathologize adolescent homosexuality.[4] What we lack is a nonpejorative, normal variation approach which recognizes sexual preference as one dimension in the area of sexual behavior and personality development.

In responding to this challenge, the special professional classes vested with authority over childhood sexuality may begin to reverse the pattern of stigma faced by gay adolescents, and regulate the discourse on adolescent homosexuality toward developmentally meaningful, nonpejorative descriptions of the experience. In this way perhaps a new generation of gay and lesbian young people can find some measure of support from those adults who work most closely with them.

Notes

1. As Foucault (1980) comments, using the medico-psychological vernacular, we reinforce the dominance of medicine and inadvertently acknowledge the disease model of homosexuality. This irony has not escaped Plummer (1981) who makes similar comments on discussions of homophobia.
2. Homosexual, in most of the empirical studies to be cited, refers to a definition based on the Kinsey scale. This is not meant to imply any clear discontinuity between heterosexual and homosexual behaviour, but rather represents a popular convention for definition. In addition, most of the empirical studies cited here on childhood patterns are retrospective studies employing adults and subjects to the methodological and sampling biases associated with volunteers and retrospection (Bentler and Abramson, 1981).
3. Perhaps not surprisingly, these three patterns were prominently identified in Freud's very early description of "inversion" in *Three Essays On The Theory Of Sexuality,* one of his earliest works (1905).
4. The Sexual Orientation and Youth Project at Central Toronto Youth Services is involved in a three year education and research project designed to assist children's service professionals in the task of working with adolescent sexual preference issues. Film and published material are available from the authors.

References

Adair, N., and Adair, C. (1978). *Word is out.* San Francisco: New Glide.

Adelman, M. R. (1977). A comparison of professionally employed lesbians and heterosexual women on the MMPI. *Archives of Sexual Behaviour, 6,* 192–201.

Albro, J. C., and Tully, C. (1979). A study of lesbian lifestyles in the homosexual micro-culture and the heterosexual macro-culture. *Journal of Homosexuality, 4,* 331–44.

Bell, A. P., Weinberg, M. S., and Hammersmith, S. K. (1981). *Sexual preference.* Bloomington: Indiana University Press.

Bentler, P. M. and Abramson, P. (1981). The science of sex research: Some methodological considerations. *Archives of Sexual Behaviour, 10,* 225–49.

Bieber, I. (1962). *Homosexuality: A psychoanalytic study.* New York: Basic Books.

Cass, V. S. (1979). Homosexual identity formation: A theoretical model. *Journal of Homosexuality, 4,* 219–35.

Chng, C. L. (1980). Adolescent homosexual behaviour and the health educator. *The Journal of School Health,* 517–21.

Coleman, E. (1982). Developmental stages in the coming out process. *Journal of Homosexuality, 7,* 31–43.

Constantine, L., and Martinson, F. M. (Eds.). (1981). *Children and sex.* Boston: Little, Brown & Co.

Cotton, W. L. (1975). Social and sexual relationships of lesbians. *Journal of Sex Research, 11,* 138–48.

Dank, B. M., (1971). Coming out in the gay world. *Psychiatry, 34,* 180–97.

Davison, G. C., and Neale, J. M. (1982). *Abnormal psychology.* Toronto: John Wiley & Sons.

De Monteflores, C., and Schultz, S. J. (1978). Coming out: Similarities and differences for lesbians and gay men. *Journal of Social Issues, 34,* 59–72.

Diamond, M. (1979). Sexual identity and sex roles. In V. Bullough (Ed.) *The frontiers of sex research.* New York: Prometheus Books.

Diepold, J. and Young, R. D. (1979). Empirical studies of adolescent sexual behaviour: A critical review. *Adolescence, 14,* 45–64.

Eisner, M. (1982). *An investigation of the coming out process, lifestyle, and sex-role orientation of lesbians.* Unpublished doctoral dissertation. York University, Toronto.

Evans, R. B. (1969). Childhood parental relationships of homosexual men. *Journal of Consulting and Clinical Psychology, 33,* 129–35.

Foucault, M. (1980). *The history of sexuality.* New York: Vintage Books.

Harry, J. (1983). Defeminization and adult psychological well-being among male homosexuals. *Archives of Sexual Behaviour, 12,* 1–19.

Hart, J. (1982). Counselling problems arising from the social categorization of homosexuals. *Bulletin of the British Psychological Society, 35,* 198–200.

Heron, A. (1983). *One teenager in ten: Writing on gay and lesbian youth.* Boston: Alyson Publications.

Kremer, E. B., Zimpfer, D. G., and Wiggers, T. T. (1975). Homosexuality, counselling, and the adolescent male. *Personnel and Guidance Journal, 54,* 94–99.

Lee, J. A. (1977). Going public: A study in the sociology of homosexual liberation. *Journal of Homosexuality, 3,* 49–78.

Malyon, A. K. (1981). The homosexual adolescent: Developmental issues and social bias. *Child Welfare, 60,* 321–30.

McCauley, E. A., and Ehrhardt, A. A. (1977). Role expectations and definitions: A comparison of female transsexuals and lesbians. *Journal of Homosexuality, 3,* 137–47.

Miller, P. Y., and Simon, W. (1980). The development of sexuality in adolescence. In J. Adelson (Ed.), *Handbook of adolescent psychology,* New York: Wiley.

Needham, R. (July, 1977). Casework intervention with a homosexual adolescent. *Social Casework,* 387–94.

Plummer, K. (1975). *Sexual stigma.* London: Routledge and Kegan Paul.

Plummer, K. (1981). *The making of the modern homosexual.* London: Hutchinson.

Ponse, B. (1978). *Identities in the lesbian world: The social construction of the self.* Wesport, Conn.: Greenwood Press.

Price, J. H. (1982). High school students attitudes towards homosexuality. *The Journal of School Health.* October, 472.

Ryan, G. (1986). Annotated Bibliography: Adolescent Perpetrators of Sexual Molestation of Children. *Child Abuse and Neglect, 10,* 125–31.

Rutter, M. (1980). *Scientific foundations of developmental psychiatry.* London: Heinman.

Saghir, M., and Robins, E. (1973). *Male and female homosexuality: A comprehensive investigation.* Maryland: Williams and Wilkins.

Schafer, S. (1976). Sexual and social problems of lesbians. *Journal of Sex Research, 12,* 50–69.

Schafer, S. (1977). Sociosexual behaviour in male and female homosexuals. *Archives of Sexual Behaviour. 6,* 355–64.

Simon, W., and Gagnon, J. H. (1967a). The lesbians: A preliminary overview. In W. Simon and J. H. Gagnon (Eds.), *Sexual deviance.* New York: Harper & Row.

Simon, W., and Gagnon, J. H. (1967b). Femininity in the lesbian community. *Social Problems, 15,* 212–21.

Sullivan, T. (1984). Adolescent homosexuality: Social constructions and developmental realities. *Journal of Child Care,* 1(6), 12–27.

Thompson, G. H., and Fishburn, W. R. (1977). Attitudes toward homosexuality among graduate counselling students. *Counsellor Education and Supervision,* December, 121–30.

Troiden, R. R. (1979). Becoming homosexual: A model of gay identity acquisition. *Psychiatry, 42,* 362–73.

Troiden, R. R., and Goode, E. (1980). Variables related to the acquisition of a gay identity. *Journal of Homosexuality, 5,* 383–92.

Van Cleave, C. (1978). Self identification, self identification discrepancy, an environmental perspective of women with a same-sex preference. *Dissertation Abstracts International, 38* (10-A), 5932–33.

Whitham, F. (1980). The pre-homosexual male in three societies: U.S., Guatemala, and Brazil. *Archives of Sexual Behaviour. 9,* 87–99.

15

HOMOSEXUAL RELATIONSHIPS

Aaron Lipman
Department of Sociology and the Center for Social Research in Aging
University of Miami

An emergent literature on homosexuality suggests that there may be many concomitants of aging that transcend the question of sexual preference. An important empirical task is to find which factors in the aging process are different for homosexuals because of their lifestyle choices and which factors are shared by all aged individuals in analogous subcategories.

Accepted definitions of homosexuality focus mainly on erotic attraction to members of the same sex (Marmor, 1980). However, both male and female homosexuals have objected, saying that the word homosexual implies relationships based solely on sex and does not connote the important components of love, commitment, companionship, and lifestyle (Peplau, 1982–83). Furthermore, whether one is male or female affects the lifestyles of homosexuals in radically different ways. Thus, many lesbians object to being categorized as "gay," pointing out that the male lifestyle community is quite different from their own. The male is associated with patriarchy, which these lesbians claim has traditionally oppressed and victimized all women (Daly, 1978). In other words, homosexuals of both genders insist that homosexuality is a way of life encompassing the entire personality structure rather than merely the one-dimensional facet of sexual orientation.

GENDER UNIFORMITIES

The literature on elderly homosexuals suggests that gender difference exerts a greater influence on behavior than does sexual orientation. Most elderly homosexuals had their early socialization in heterosexual families and were reared in masculine or feminine roles. Thus, females were socialized to assume roles that were nurturant, supportive, noncompetitive, sensitive, and emotional, while male roles were defined in terms of instrumentality and dominance (Riddle and Sang, 1978). In adulthood, lesbians are

found to be much like other females in their views on sex, relationships, and romance (Tanner, 1978; Vetere, 1982–83). Gagnon and Simon (1967) report that patterns of overt sexual behavior on the part of lesbians tend to resemble closely those of heterosexual females and differ radically from those of both heterosexual and homosexual males. Silverstein (1981) also characterizes lesbianism as being predominantly a phenomenon of femininity, and male homosexuality as predominantly a phenomenon of masculinity.

Among homosexual males, sex may be more significant than it is among homosexual females. In comparing elderly gays and elderly lesbians, Minnigerode and Adelman (1978) found that the males frequently viewed their homosexuality in terms of sexual activities, and were more in favor of anonymous, impersonal and casual sex without love than were their female counterparts. Lesbians viewed sex in terms of interpersonal relationships (Blumstein and Schwartz, 1983). Several studies confirm that lesbians appear to place greater emphasis on emotional intimacy and equality than do gay men (Chafetz, 1974). For the females, serial monogamy had been the dominant life pattern (Raphael and Robinson, 1980, 1981). However, Bell and Weinberg (1978) report that most homosexuals, both male and female, want to have a steady love relationship and find this preferable to having only casual liaisons. According to these findings, male and female attitudes and behavior toward the sexual partner appear to be very much expressions of the sexual script learned by men as men and women as women, regardless of their sexual orientation. It is their choice of object that sets homosexuals apart.

Women are traditionally the caretakers, and since the lesbian is for all intents and purposes the unmarried daughter, it usually falls upon her to take on the responsibility of caring for an aging or ailing parent (Martin and Lyon, 1972). Generally, then, recent research suggests that these culturally defined gender roles transcend sexual preference in patterning gay and lesbian behavior.

LIFESTYLES

No uniform lifestyle characterizes all gay men or all lesbian women. Bell and Weinberg (1978) developed a typology designed to correlate homosexual lifestyles with psychological and social adjustment, and have delineated five lifestyle patterns. Of the five, two describe couple relationships. The *closed-coupled* relationship resembles heterosexual marriage and involves a strong emotional commitment to that relationship on the part of both individuals. These couples were found to be the best adjusted and happiest. They had few sexual partners, few sexual problems, and engaged in a low amount of "cruising" (the purposive search for potential sexual partners and friends). Not unexpectedly, the number of closed couples among lesbians (28 percent) was found to be almost double that among gay men (10 percent). *Open-coupled* relationships were found in almost equal numbers among lesbians and gays (18 percent of males and 17 percent of females). This relationship involved less commitment, and both members had clandestine outside affairs. While they were not as happy or adjusted as the closed couples, the open couples were comparable in adjustment to their heterosexual counterparts in dyadic relationships.

Other factors characterize the lifestyles of "single" homosexuals. Of the three groups who were not in couples, two showed high levels of sexual activity and number of partners; the differentiating factor between *functionals* (15 percent males, 10 percent females) and *dysfunctionals* (12 percent males, 5 percent females) was their sociability and adjustment. As the designations imply, the functionals were socially and psychologically adjusted compared to the dysfunctionals, who were prone to sexual, social, and psychological problems and who expressed regret over their homosexuality. Finally, the *asexuals* (16 percent of the males, 11 percent of the females), who lived alone and had infrequent sexual contacts, were characterized by their relative social isolation. Only the dysfunctionals and asexuals were found to be more poorly adjusted psychologically than their heterosexual control groups.

It was once widely believed that the homosexual couple reflected the same set of complementary gender roles as did the traditional heterosexual mar-

riage, with one partner playing the female role of wife and the other assuming the male role of husband (Peplau, 1982–83). In this view, decision making, division of household tasks, and sexual interaction are presumably modeled after heterosexual gender roles. The male role player supposedly is the dominant one in the initiation of sex and in decision making, while the female role player is left to cook and take care of household tasks.

Recent research indicates that neither male nor female homosexual relationships necessarily follow this pattern. They do not appear to rely on traditional roles to define each participant's role activities in the relationship. Various studies (McWhirter and Mattison, 1984; Saghir and Robins, 1973; Bell and Weinberg, 1978; Tanner, 1978) report very little evidence of a male-female sex-role dichotomy in the performance of household tasks, for example (Harry, 1982–83; Tanner, 1978). Generally, then, such dichotomies as active/passive, dominant/submissive, "butch"/"femme," or inserter/insertee, appear to have been derived from heterosexual relationships. Researchers claim that in reality, role differentiation is more varied; role flexibility and turn-taking are more common patterns (Larson, 1982; Marecek et al., 1982–83; Peplau and Gordon, 1982).

Homosexual relations change over time. McWhirter and Mattison (1984) studied the stages of development of relationships in gay couples. For the elderly couple, they describe four characteristics of the last stage (couples who have been together more than 20 years). The first characteristic, *achieving security* (relational as well as financial), results in strong feelings of well-being. The individuals have a sense of permanence in their relationship that provides the security of companionship. The second characteristic, *shifting perspectives,* involves the realization that there are fewer years ahead of than behind the couple. There are also concerns about health problems, growing old, and the mate's death. The third characteristic, *restoring the partnership,* involves the reaffirmation of the relationship. The final characteristic, *remembering,* involves reminiscing, or what Butler (1974) has termed "life review." This enables the individuals to achieve a sense of integration, meaning, and perspective in old age, a characteristic that we recognize from the literature dealing with the heterosexual elderly, as well.

AGE DIFFERENCES

Compared to younger gay males, older gays have fewer sexual partners, lower frequency of sex, spend less time cruising and have longer relationships (Saghir and Robins, 1973; Weinberg and Williams, 1974; Bell and Weinberg, 1978; Harry and DeValle, 1978; Berger, 1982; Silverstein, 1981). On the other hand, older homosexuals reported a greater sense of well-being than younger homosexuals (Weinberg and Williams, 1974). Older homosexuals had more stable self-concepts and were less concerned about exposure of their homosexuality. In Silverstein's study (1981), older gay couples were also found to be the most content. Silverstein rarely found a couple who had lived together for more than 20 years who regretted having continued the relationship. According to Peplau and Amaro (1982), this pattern of establishing relatively stable, enduring relationships characterizes most lesbian relationships, as well.

There is a broad range of views concerning the viability of such long-term relationships. At one extreme is the harsh condemnation expressed by the psychoanalyst Bergler (1956), who believed that the worst heterosexual marriage was a thousand times better than the best homosexual "marriage." At the other end are the more favorable views of researchers who conclude not only that homosexuals are capable of sustaining a relationship with another for long periods of time, but also that these relationships are extremely satisfying (Oliver, 1976; McWhirter and Mattison, 1984; Silverstein, 1981). However, as noted by Peplau (1982–83), a paucity of valid information about long-term relationships of older gays and lesbians still exists. Generally, it can be added that research on homosexuality in all its forms tends to lack methodological rigor. Especially neglected is the problem of sampling.

PRIMARY GROUPS

Primary groups are the basis for the traditional informal support system of the elderly. For both elderly gay men and lesbians, the literature describes a friendship support network that is assumed either to take the place of family ties or to reinforce and supplement those family ties that exist (Raphael and Robinson, 1980, 1981; Bell and Weinberg, 1978; Friend, 1980). Thus, Raphael and Robinson (1981:16) assert that "those lesbians who did not come out [declare their homosexuality] with family members or who came out and received continuing negative family responses . . . had weak or totally absent kinship ties which they replaced with friendship networks." For elderly gay men, faced by rejec-

tion and the loss of family support when they declare their homosexuality, strong friendship ties with their peers give them the support they seek. Bell and Weinberg (1978) reported that elderly homosexual men have more friends than their heterosexual counterparts. Francher and Henkin (1973) and Friend (1980) also report this phenomenon. Whether these friends replace or merely supplement the family, most recent studies have described aging homosexuals, both male and female, as having more friends on the average than do heterosexuals of similar age. For both gay men and lesbians, the reaction of family toward their homosexuality determined the existence and quality of kinship support. Where that reaction was negative, strong friendship ties appear to have filled the gap.

Both elderly lesbians and elderly gays have been found to be similar in that individuals in each group tend to associate mainly with others like themselves (McWhirter and Mattison, 1984). Older gay men associate mainly with other older gay men, and older lesbians with other older lesbians (Kelly, 1977; Raphael and Robinson, 1980; Robinson, 1979). Their closest friends are other homosexuals. Neither group was found to associate with many heterosexuals of either the same or opposite gender.

COMMUNITY SUPPORTS

Ours is an urbanized society, and in urban centers the Gay Rights movement has allowed and encouraged elderly homosexuals to form a network of supportive relations and to engage in collective action. This mutual support is important in the fight against discrimination in employment and for the recognition of many rights currently denied them. This collective action also helps the individual achieve a sense of social integration. In addition, although they are not yet national in scope, there are a number of organizations and community-center facilities for elderly homosexuals where they can meet others of their own age in a benign environment. Thus the homosexual subculture, defined as deviant by the larger society, provides support for its members in old age.

DISCUSSION

Period and cohort changes make generalizations about homosexual relationships in later life difficult. We cannot assume that homosexuals in the future will necessarily have characteristics or behavior similar to those of homosexuals today. We may, however, be able to extrapolate from heterosexual studies of relationships in later life and make use of known propositions that will also apply to the relationships of homosexuals.

In attempting to make such applications, it is immediately apparent that homosexuals show both similarities and differences in comparison with the general society. We know that in the heterosexual world, old age social supports from the kin group and community have a significant impact on allowing individuals to retain their autonomy and live independently rather than resort to institutionalization. Indeed, family members represent the older person's most significant social resource. We also know that mutual support over a long period of time can generate high marital satisfaction among older couples. Cross-sectional studies confirm a curvilinear trend in marital satisfaction, with the later postparental years defined as one of the happiest times of married life (Rollins and Cannon, 1974; Anderson, Russell and Schumm, 1983). Centrality of the spouse is substantiated by the fact that death of a spouse, divorce, and separation represent the three serially highest ranked stressors (Holmes and Rahe, 1967). For both men and women, being married is the single most important factor preventing institutionalization (Health Care Finance Administration, 1981).

We are so accustomed to viewing the world from a heterosexual orientation that such findings demonstrating the importance of a spouse are not generalized to the homosexual context. Yet almost all of the propositions set forth above characterize the homosexual world. What is crucial is not the presence of a spouse *per se;* it is that the spouse is an accurate index of integration into a dyad and of having a confidant relationship. Hoyt and Babchuck (1983) report that spouses are 30 times more likely to be selected as confidantes than are young children or extended relatives.

These findings that stress the importance of a spouse have to be interpreted within a general proposition that can apply both to homosexuals, who have no legal status of marriage, and to heterosexuals, whose statuses and roles are sanctioned by the community. The more general proposition is that satisfying primary relations, the levels of meaningful interaction with others, and the degree of integration in the group are important variables affecting the life satisfaction and even survivability of the older person.

Thus, there are parallels between the gay/lesbian situation and the general society. For homosexuals, integration into the gay or lesbian community and an exclusive dyadic relationship are analogs to the situation of heterosexuals. Although gays and lesbians have lacked the institutional support of marriage, many have lived with their mates for many years. They have developed an exchange relationship in which so much has been invested in the past that they can draw from each other in the future. For these reasons closed-coupled homosexuals who have a strong commitment to the dyadic relationship were the happiest and best adjusted.

Generally, then, companionship, commitment, intimacy, ego-enhancement, and fulfillment are human potentials and can be desired and achieved by homosexuals as well as heterosexuals. Social and community ties apply to both homosexuals and heterosexuals, playing a critical role in both the determination of health status and mortality. In sum, the characteristics and functionality of long-term relationships show many similarities between homosexuals and heterosexuals and tend to transcend the issue of sexual preference.

References

Anderson, S. A., Russell, C. S. and Schumm, W. A., 1983. "Perceived Marital Quality and Family Life-Cycle Categories: A Further Analysis." *Journal of Marriage and the Family* 45(1):127–39.
Bell, A. P. and Weinberg, M. A., 1978. *Homosexualities: A Study of Diversity Among Men and Women.* New York: Simon and Schuster.
Berger, R. M., 1982. *Gay and Gray.* Urbana, Ill.: University of Illinois Press.
Bergler, E., 1956. *Homosexuality: Disease or Way of Life?* New York: Hill and Wang.
Blumstein, P. and Schwartz, P., 1983. *American Couples.* New York: William Morrow and Co.
Butler, R. N., 1974. "Successful Aging and the Role of the Life Review." *Journal of the American Geriatric Society* 22(12):529–35.
Chafetz, J. S., 1974. *Masculine, Feminine or Human? An Overview of the Sociology of Roles.* Itasca, Ill.: Peacock.
Daly, M., 1978. *Gyn/Ecology: The Metaethics of Radical Feminism.* Boston: Beacon Press.
Francher, S. J. and Henkin, J., 1973. "The Menopausal Queen: Adjustment to Aging and the Male Homosexual." *American Journal of Orthopsychiatry* 43(4):670–74.
Friend, R. A., 1980. "GAYging: Adjustment and the Older Gay Male." *Alternative Lifestyles* 3(2):231–48.

Gagnon, J. and Simon, W., 1967. "The Lesbian, A Preliminary Overview." In J. Gagnon and W. Simon, eds., *Sexual Deviance*. New York: Harper and Row.

Harry, J., 1982–83. "Decision Making and Age Differences Among Gay Male Couples." *Journal of Homosexuality* 8(2):9–21.

Harry, J. and DeValle, W. B., 1978. *The Social Organization of Gay Males*. New York: Praeger.

Health Care Finance Administration, 1981. *Long Term Care: Background and Future Directions*. Washington, D.C.: U.S. Department of Health and Human Services.

Holmes, T. H. and Rahe, R. H., 1967. "The Social Readjustment Rating Scale." *Journal of Psychosomatic Research* 11(2):213–18.

Hoyt, D. R. and Babchuck, N., 1983. "Adult Kinship Networks: The Selective Formation of Intimate Ties with Kin." *Social Forces* 62(1):84–101.

Kelly, J., 1977. "The Aging Male Homosexual: Myth and Reality." *The Gerontologist* 17(4):328–32.

Larson, P. C., 1982. "Gay Male Relationships." In W. Paul, J. D. Weinrich and J. C. Gonsiorek, eds., *Homosexuality: Social, Psychological and Biological Issues*. Beverly Hills, Calif.: Sage.

Maracek, J., Finn, S. E. and Cardell, M., 1982–83. "Gender Roles in the Relationships of Lesbians and Gay Men." *Journal of Homosexuality* 8(2):45–50.

Marmor, J., 1980. "Overview: The Multiple Roots of Homosexual Behavior." In J. Marmor, ed., *Homosexual Behavior: A Modern Reappraisal*. New York: Basic Books.

Martin, D. and Lyon, P., 1972. *Lesbian/Woman*. San Francisco: Glide Publications.

McWhirter, D. P. and Mattison, A. M., 1984. *The Male Couple: How Relationships Develop*. Englewood Cliffs, N.J.: Prentice-Hall, Inc.

Minnigerode, F. A., and Adelman, M. A., 1978. "Elderly Homosexual Women and Men: Report on a Pilot Study." *Family Coordinator* 27(4):451–56.

Oliver, L., 1976. *Male Homosexual Dyads: A Study of Thirty Couples*. Ph.D. dissertation, George Washington University, Washington, D.C.

Peplau, L. A., 1982–83. "Research on Homosexual Couples: An Overview." *Journal of Homosexuality* 8(2):3–21.

Peplau, L. A. and Amaro, H., 1982. "Understanding Lesbian Relationships." In E. R. Allgeirer and N. B. McCormick, eds., *Gender Roles and Sexual Behavior*. Palo Alto, Calif.: Mayfield.

Peplau, L. A. and Gordon, S. L., 1982. "The Intimate Relationships of Lesbians and Gay Men." In E. R. Allgeirer and N. B. McCormick, eds., *Gender Roles and Sexual Behavior*. Palo Alto, Calif.: Mayfield.

Raphael, S. and Robinson, M., 1980. "The Older Lesbian: Love Relationships and Friendship Patterns." *Alternative Lifestyles* 3(2):207–29.

Raphael, S. and Robinson, M., 1981. Lesbians and Gay Men in Later Life. *Generations* 6(1):16–18.

Riddle, D. I. and Sang, B., 1978. "Psychotherapy with Lesbians." *Journal of Social Issues* 34(3):84–100.

Robinson, M., 1979. *The Older Lesbian*. Master's thesis, California State University, Carson.

Rollins, B. C. and Cannon, K. L., 1974. "Marital Satisfaction Over the Life Cycle: A Reevaluation." *Journal of Marriage and the Family* 36(2):271–82.

Saghir, M. and Robins, E., 1973. *Male and Female Homosexuality: A Comprehensive Investigation*. Baltimore: Williams and Wilkins.

Silverstein, C., 1981. *Man to Man: Gay Couples in America*. New York: William Morrow and Co.

Tanner, D. N., 1978. *The Lesbian Couple*. Lexington, Mass.: D. C. Heath and Company.

Vetere, V. A., 1982–83. "The Role of Friendship in the Development and Maintenance of Lesbian Love Relationships." *Journal of Homosexuality* 8(2):51–65.

Weinberg, M. S. and Williams, C. J., 1974. *Male Homosexuals: Their Problems and Adaptations*. New York: Oxford University Press.

PART IV

ADAPTATION

INTRODUCTION

From a systems perspective, each component of the society is in constant adaptation with regard to every other component. This involves responding or initiating actions vis-a-vis others so that each party obtains or maintains some desired objective. Consider a simple social event: You are on a street and someone is walking straight toward you. As soon as you are aware of this situation, you begin to make adaptive responses. If the other person is blind (as signaled by his white cane sweeping and tapping the sidewalk as he moves), then you make a wide accommodation so as to allow this person to pass without bumping into you or hitting you with his cane. (But what do you do if you see this person moving toward some dangerous object not ordinarily on city streets? You would probably do something that breaks the usual adaptive response so as to warn the blind person.)

If the other person is a stranger, indeed, a person with obvious differences to you—of size, color, dress, apparent life style, age, and so forth—you may also move to give this person a wide space in which to pass you, not wanting to provide any excuse for possible confrontations. (Is this fear response or a stereotyping response? Or is it rational behavior?)

What if that other person is well known to you? Do you continue on your collision course in anticipation that both of you will stop just at the right moment to prevent a crash? Suppose that that other person is your very best friend in the whole world. What inner sensations and outer behaviors might you be aware of as you move closer and anticipate a conversation with this best friend? Or, what if you don't like that person well known to you? How do you deal with this social situation?

In all of these instances, we are adapting. We are subtly changing inner states and outer actions to accommodate to the new information. But so is the other party. Suppose that the other person perceives you as a stranger, while you think you recognize him or her as a friend. Now that person moves aside to give you a wide berth, just as you move onto a direct collision course. You start to raise your hand (in a gesture of friendship) and the other person perceives your raised hand to be a threatening gesture. . . . And so on, you get the picture.

Adaptation is intrinsically interpersonal, or intersocial. My example involved a physical space (the street), socio-cultural conventions (gestures of friendship, gestures of threat), social roles (acquaintances or strangers), and many personal events (feelings, thoughts, and actions). All may be involved in adaptative behaviors. As will be seen in some of the following readings, people may take an active, problem-solving approach to coping, or they may take a passive, problem-avoidance approach. The active approach appears to be related to lower adverse effects of stress, although this relationship needs further documentation. (See C. H. Holahan and R. H. Moos [1987], ''Personal and contextual determinants of coping strategies,'' *Journal of Personality and Social Psychology, 52*:5, 946–955.)

Myrna B. Shure presents a paper that is part of a systematic series of studies (with her colleague, George Spivack) on an interpersonal cognitive problem-solving approach used with very young children, school-aged youngsters, and adolescents as well. By very carefully developing a skills training program, and then employing it with strong experimental designs, Shure and Spivack have been able to demonstrate effective ways to train young people in social competence. The implications of this kind of documented field studies are enormous.

Lyn Lawrence and Kenneth R. McLeroy's paper employs a key concept developed by Albert Bandura, the social learning theorist, in the context of health education. Self-efficacy—one's belief about one's ability to perform some behavior—becomes a central variable in helping people to help themselves, by changing their beliefs about being able to achieve some desired outcome. (I include as an editor's note some information from a recent paper by Lyn Lawrence, Susan R. Levy, and Laurna Rubinson, applying this theory to AIDS prevention with pregnant minority adolescents.)

A very different kind of paper, by Joe B. Hurst and John W. Shepard, examines the multitude of events that follow a group of persons after their common place of employment shuts down. Responses to the powerful stresses of plant closing varied with the individual workers depending on their age, experience, skill, self-esteem, and use of social networks and systems. Clearly, all aspects of the social configuration are involved in the adaptive response, as the model used by these authors indicates. (For a critical discussion of the concept of stress, see K. Pollack. (1988). "On the nature of social stress: Production of a modern mythology." *Social Science and Medicine, 26*:3, 381–392.)

In the second section of this part, I have selected several articles on problems in living. The first paper, by Gabrielle A. Carlson and Javad H. Kashani, involves a study of depression, the most common mental health problem, viewed from the perspective of three studies involved preschoolers, prepubertal children, adolescents, and adults. In each, there were similar symptoms of depressed mood, but some attributes of depression increased with age (such as feelings of hopelessness); others decreased with age (such as somatic complaints).

A second paper by Verona C. Gordon and Linda E. Ledray focuses in depth on depression in women. Explanations for this condition, more frequently found among women than men, include genetic, endocrinological, and learning considerations. Several theories are discussed with regard to understanding and treating or preventing depression. Particularly noteworthy are those sociocultural factors that lead to restrictions of roles women can play in the family and in society, with subsequent frustrations. These may be experienced as motivational deficits common in depression, as feminist theorists suggest. Yet, there are many explanations for depression, and no definitive answers.

A final paper in this section involves improving the mental health of black Americans using the experiences from the community mental health movement to understand the problems more fully and to design better ways to prevent them. In a paper excerpted here, Harold W. Neighbors presents a critical history of the community mental health movement, but he finds much to offer in advancing the mental health of black Americans (and presumably other minority groups). His approach involves a configural view, looking for social antecedents of psychological distress so as to take action before these produce problems in mental health. He focuses on preschool and school experiences, plus job training programs, as having particular preventive potential.

Adaptation takes many forms, from personal efforts to the collective efforts of millions. We have to adapt to, and change, both our interior environments, and also the oppressive social and cultural environments that inhibit free and fruitful development in an open and just society. Helping professionals play a large part in the full continuum of personal and social adaptations.

A. Problem Solving and Coping with Stress

16

SOCIAL COMPETENCE THROUGH PROBLEM SOLVING IN INNER-CITY FIFTH GRADERS:
IS IT TOO LATE?

Myrna B. Shure
Division of Psychology
Hahnemann University

Research in children's social skills, peer relations, and general social adjustment has been studied in a myriad of ways, some taking primarily a behavioral point of view (e.g., Hops and Greenwood, 1981), some primarily a cognitive one (e.g., Selman, 1980), and some, a systematic combination of both (e.g., Meichenbaum, 1977). My colleague George Spivack and I have gone the cognitive route, specifically looking at how people solve typical, everyday interpersonal problems, what specific skills are relevant to peer relations and mental health, and what aspects of peer relations and mental health a cognitive problem solving intervention could impact.

In young low socioeconomic status (SES) children, ages 4 and 5, we have learned that intervention to enhance what we call ICPS, or Interpersonal Cognitive Problem Solving skills, can significantly reduce observable negative impulsive and inhibited behaviors, and increase positive qualities as concern, or at least visible awareness of peers in distress, and how much the child is liked by his or her peers (Shure and Spivack, 1982; Spivack and Shure, 1974). Within a wide Binet-IQ range, gains in ICPS skills that best related to improved social adjustment were: (1) alternative solution thinking (e.g., how one child can get to play with a toy that another child has); and (2) consequential thinking (what might happen next if, for example, someone grabs that toy). We also learned that: (1) ICPS impact on behavior lasted when measured one and two years later; (2) if a child was not trained in nursery, kindergarten was not too late; and (3) one exposure to the four month program had the same behavioral impact as two. Further, well-adjusted children trained in nursery were less likely to begin showing behav-

ioral difficulties in kindergarten and first grade than were comparable controls, highlighting implications of the ICPS approach for primary prevention.

If kindergarten and first grade are critical transition points for younger children, we know that junior high is for older ones (e.g., Blyth, Simmons, and Carlton-Ford, 1983). We thought if we could intervene before that time, we might be able to prevent mental health dysfunction as youngsters make that move. Today I'm going to tell you about our first step toward the development of the ICPS model for older kids, specifically for low SES public elementary school fifth graders.

In this study, 8 teachers trained 88 boys and 114 girls. The goal was not to evaluate the practical impact of training as a program (by comparing group mean scores of trained youngsters vs. controls), but rather, to test the prior theoretical question of whether ICPS skills function as significant behavioral mediators at this age. An ICPS skill would be viewed as a mediator if increased scores on its measures correlate with changes on measures of observed behavioral adjustment (independent of IQ and other impersonal cognitive abilities). A correlation of change in the trained ICPS skill with change in observed overt behaviors would provide support for a direct link between the ICPS skill and adjustment. However, to test for possible effects of repeated ICPS testing, or natural developmental gains, 60 ICPS and behaviorally comparable youngsters, 30 boys and 30 girls from different but SES-comparable schools, were added as controls.

To test the ICPS/behavioral mediation theory for this new age group, we created a series of 55 age-appropriate lesson games for use by teachers in the classroom (Shure & Spivack, 1982). Through

Reprinted by permission of the author. This paper was originally presented at a meeting of the American Psychological Association in Toronto, Ontario, 1984.

pictures, puppets, and role-playing techniques, sequenced exercises were designed to enhance the ability to appreciate the perspectives of others (role
taking) and the problem-solving skills found to be
related to behavioral adjustment measures at this
age. These included alternative solution thinking
(Asarnow and Callan, 1984; Richard and Dodge,
1982; Shure, 1980), consequential thinking (Shure,
1980), and means-ends thinking, or the ability to
plan sequenced steps toward a stated goal, circum-
vent potential obstacles, and recognize that goal attainment may take time (March, 1981; 1982;
Pelligrini, 1985; Shure, 1980).

Throughout 15 training weeks, the concept
"There's more than one way" was stressed to develop a problem-solving style of thought. There's
more than one way: (a) to *explain* another's *behavior*
(e.g., "Maybe he didn't wave because he's mad at
me," or, "Maybe he just didn't see me."); (b) to
explain another's *motivation* (e.g., "Maybe that boy
[sitting by himself watching others play] wants to be
alone," or, "Maybe the others won't let him
play."); (c) to *find out* others' feelings and preferences (by watching, by listening, and by asking); (d)
to *solve a problem* (with different solutions and step-
by-step plans). Children are also helped to see that
there's more than one way that oneself or others
might react should a solution or plan be carried out
(potential consequences).

With the goal being to teach children *how* to
think, not what to think, they were never told solutions, consequences, or sequenced steps (plans).
Rather, children were encouraged to think of their
own ideas, and then to evaluate whether those ideas
were or were not good ones, in light of their potential consequences. In addition, teachers were trained
to incorporate a problem-solving style of communication during the day when actual problems would
arise, an extension which, if applied outside of the
formal lessons, can help children use ICPS thought
more effectively when they face real problems on
their own.

Excluding those whose behavior could not improve from the analyses because they were already
at or very near the top of the scale, the major finding was that, overall, gains in ICPS, but not multiple perspective-taking scores (as measured by Feffer
and Gourevitch, 1960) correlated with gains in behaviors, most consistently with positive, prosocial
behaviors in both boys and girls. In both sexes, it
was improvement in the number and range of solu-

tions that best related to these behavior gains, most
consistently to teacher ratings of concern for others,
peer sociability, and the degree to which the child
was liked by peers. In boys, though not girls, gains
in consequential and means-ends skills also related
to prosocial changes. ICPS linkage gains with negative, aberrant behaviors were less clear. Although all
changes were in the predicted direction, only solution skills linked significantly, in girls only, for
behaviors reflective of overemotionality and aggression. However, for both impatience and inhibition,
there were no statistical improvements correlating
with gains in ICPS. Nevertheless, the findings of solution thinking as a behavioral mediator in girls
were important. Increased prosocial behavior was
accompanied by decreased impulsive factor scores of
overemotionality plus aggression, with partial correlations showing it was the cognitive *solution* skills
which directly mediated both.

Although Feffer's multiple perspective taking
did not relate directly to behavior gains, it did accompany increased means-ends scores in boys and
number and range of solutions in girls, all of which
did link to prosocial behavior gains. Perhaps awareness of or sensitivity to another's point of view may
not be sufficient in itself to solve a problem or reduce conflict, but it could enrich the quality of
problem-solving thinking if the latter were operative
at the time. We also learned that while ICPS gains
did not link with academic gains (functional reading
and math grade book levels and California Achievement Test scores), prosocial behavior gains did. This
is theoretically logical and extremely interesting.
Nothing should suggest that training interpersonal
cognitive skills should improve impersonal cognitive
ones. But, if behavior gains can improve academic
ability, and if ICPS can improve behavior, then we
have an additional potential for the ICPS approach.
That no ICPS/behavior/achievement linkage occurred
in the controls suggests the theoretically relevant
linkages of trained youngsters cannot be attributed to
mere test-taking experience or to the four-month period which elapsed between pre- and posttesting.

The possiblity exists that in contrast to preschool and kindergarten youngsters, ICPS training of
fifth graders affects prosocial behaviors sooner and
more consistently than negative impulsive and inhibited ones. Perhaps longer and/or more intense training
is required to bring out more convincing aberrant
behavior change needed to reveal the cognitive/
aberrant behavior linkages hypothesized. This seems

reasonable in light of significant pretraining correlations of research mentioned earlier, and by the consistent predicted direction of non-significant ICPS/aberrant behavior change linkages in this study.

Perhaps intensity is an issue. Preschool and kindergarten programs involve *daily* training. Due to curriculum demands, implementation three times a week is logistically most feasible, and may account for other studies of older children, where linkages exist at all, being relatively weak or inconsistent (e.g., Weissberg, et. al., 1981). Given the more immediate ICPS gains, that ICPS and behaviors are correlated phenomena, and the possibility that aberrant behaviors are simply more habitual in older than in younger children (and therefore more resistant to change), the pursuit of more intense or extensive ICPS intervention appears logical.

It is possible that thrice-weekly training within a single school year does affect aberrant behaviors, but only surfaces at a later time. Gesten and his colleagues (Gesten, et. al., 1982) found that while trained second and third graders showed significant immediate ICPS gains (called SPS [Social Problem Solving] by this research team), both positive and negative (acting out) behavior gains showed up in ratings of teachers one year later. Whether these gains can be linked to immediate or latent ICPS (SPS) gains is not yet clear. That most immediate behavior gains of controls returned to baseline at follow up, a group whose SPS skills never significantly improved suggests promise for future research.

It appears that one cannot assume that within a three- to four-month time frame, ICPS intervention will affect all interpersonal behaviors equally at different ages, or that specific ICPS skills will always have the same impact on both boys and on girls. And, in addition to *quantity* of solutions, consequences, and means-ends components, perhaps we need to examine other dimensions of these skills as well. Ken Rubin and others have argued that the *quality* of solutions may be at least as important as the quantity (e.g., Rubin and Daniels-Beirness, 1983). We also know that other, yet to be discovered ICPS skills must exist as well. Before concluding that it is too late, or logistically too difficult for ICPS intervention to more substantially mediate behavior of school-aged children, both the consistencies and the questions raised are sufficiently inviting to probe.

We have now collected data on a new sample of youngsters, some trained twice (in grades 5 and 6),

some trained only once (in grade 5). I might add that we now call ICPS, when training kids, *I Can Problem Solve*, a name the youngsters have latched onto easily, and enthusiastically. We also had groups receiving comparable amounts of training in *impersonal* cognitive skills (e.g., logic, Piagetian conservation tasks, etc.). Not only were immediate ICPS/behavioral/academic impacts evaluated and compared, but also we followed the youngsters into junior high (grades 7 and 8). We attempted to assess the impact of differential amounts and types of intervention on how these youngsters would cope with the difficult transition to junior high. We were encouraged to learn that Elias (1984) has found that ICPS (SPS) intervention helped to reduce the intensity of stressors experienced at transition to middle school (grade 6), and that the amount of stress experienced was directly related to the length of training (the more training, the less intensity of stress). This is remarkable considering the range of stressors encountered, "from serious public and mental health problems such as becoming involved with smoking or drinking to issues of coping with peer pressure, academic requirements, and the logistics of being in a large, unfamiliar school" (ms. p. 11).

Although the data are still being analyzed, it appears that alternative solution thinking is still the single most powerful mediator to behavior, that positive prosocial behaviors improve earlier than negative, especially impulsive ones, and that a re-exposure to the ICPS intervention (in grade 6) may be necessary to reduce impulsive behaviors. Unfortunately, it does not appear that behavioral gains held up through junior high. It is possible that ICPS intervention is not powerful enough to withstand the stresses of transition to junior high. It is also possible that teachers could not get to know the children well enough (they only saw them 40 minutes per day) and/or were more concerned with teaching their subject than with the subtleties of observing how tuned in a child was to the feelings of others.

Further analysis of the data such as that of Elias, and continued assessments of overt behaviors will help us better understand which indices of mental health at this age are (and are not) mediated by ICPS abilities and therefore are (and are not) alterable by the ICPS approach. They will also begin to shed light on the efficacy of the ICPS approach for this age and SES group through questions such as these: Whom does it help? How does it help? How long does it take? How long does it last?

References

Asarnow, J. R., and Callan, J. W. Children with peer adjustment problems: Social cognitive processes. In J. R. Asarnow (Chair), *Social skills in preadolescents: Assessments and training.* Symposium presented at the meetings of the American Psychological Association, Toronto, Canada, August 1984.

Blyth, D. A., Simmons, R. G., and Carlton-Ford, S. The adjustment of early adolescents to school transitions. *Journal of Early Adolescents,* 1983, *3,* 105–120.

Elias, M. Project AWARE: Social problem solving as prevention model. Progress Report No. 36828, Washington, D.C.: National Institute of Mental Health, 1984.

Feffer, M. H., and Gourevitch, V. Cognitive aspects of role-taking in children. *Journal of Personality,* 1960, *28,* 383–396.

Gesten, E. L., Rains, M., Rapkin, B., Weissberg, R. G., Flores de Apodaca, R., Cowen, E. L., and Bowen, G. Training children in social problem-solving competencies: A first and second look. *American Journal of Community Psychology,* 1982, *10,* 95–115.

Hops, H., and Greenwood, C. R. Social skills deficits. In E. Mash & L. Terdal (Eds.), *Behavioral assessment of childhood disorders.* New York, Guilford Press, 1981.

Marsh, D. T. Interrelationships among perspective-taking, interpersonal problem solving, and interpersonal functioning. *Journal of Genetic Psychology,* 1981, *138,* 37–48.

Marsh, D. T. The development of interpersonal problem solving among elementary school children. *Journal of Genetic Psychology,* 1982, *140,* 107–118.

Meichenbaum, D. *Cognitive-behavior modification: An integrative approach.* New York: Plenum Press, 1977.

Pelligrini, D. Social cognition and competence in middle childhood. *Child Development,* 1985, *56,* 253–264.

Richard, B. A., and Dodge, K. A. Social maladjustment and problem solving in school-aged children. *Journal of Consulting and Clinical Psychology,* 1982, *50,* 226–233.

Rubin, K. H., and Daniels-Beirness, T. Concurrent and predictive correlates of sociometric status in kindergarten and Grade 1 children. *Merrill-Palmer Quarterly,* 1983, *29,* 337–351.

Selman, R. *The growth of interpersonal understanding: Developmental and clinical analyses.* New York: Academic Press, 1980.

Shure, M. B., and Spivack, G. Interpersonal problem solving in young children: A cognitive approach to prevention. *American Journal of Community Psychology,* 1982, 10, 341–356.

Shure, M. B. Problem solving and mental health in ten-year-olds. Final Report No. MH-27741, Washington, D.C.: National Institute of Mental Health, 1980.

Spivack, G., and Shure, M. B. *Social adjustment of young children.* San Francisco: Jossey-Bass, 1974.

Weissberg, R. P., Gesten, E. L., Carnrike, C. L., Toro, P. A., Rapkin, B. D., Davidson, E., and Cowen, E. L. Social problem-solving skills training: A competence-building intervention with second- to fourth-grade children. *American Journal of Community Psychology,* 1981, *9,* 411–423.

17

SELF-EFFICACY AND HEALTH EDUCATION

Lyn Lawrence
Kenneth R. McLeroy
Department of Public Health
University of North Carolina at Greensboro

Self-efficacy is an important concept in the recent health education literature. This paper interprets Bandura's ideas about self-efficacy for nonpsychologists, describes research in health education which has documented the importance of self-efficacy in behavior change programs, and suggests ways self-efficacy can be used in designing, implementing, and evaluating health education programs.

SELF-EFFICACY THEORY

"Efficacy" is an individual's objective ability to perform a specific behavior. Efficacy can be measured by observing whether or not an individual actually exhibits the behavior. "Perceived self-efficacy" is an individual's judgment of the ability to do the behavior.[1-6] Thus, efficacy is an objective measure of performance, while perceived self-efficacy is a judgment individuals make about their ability to do the behavior. Bandura and others frequently use "self-efficacy" to mean "perceived self-efficacy," since an individual's perception is implied in most contexts in which the concept is used.

Bandura[1,4-7] reports one's belief in the ability to do a behavior (self-efficacy) is an important link between knowing what to do and actually doing it. Many instances exist in health education where simply providing health information, and increasing an individual's desires to do a particular behavior, do not lead to behavior change. The surgeon general's warnings on cigarette packages have not discouraged all smokers, though most smokers indicate a desire to quit. This situation suggests many smokers lack the skills necessary to quit and subsequently believe they are unable to quit. Individuals need to feel they are capable of performing a task before they are likely to attempt it.

Self-efficacy theory[1,3,4,6,8] suggests people's beliefs in their abilities to perform specific behaviors influence: (1) their choice of behavior and the situations which will be avoided or attempted, such as attempts to reduce drug, alcohol, or cigarette use, or efforts to initiate exercise regimens or to practice relaxation; (2) the effort they will spend in attempting a specific task, more energy often is devoted to a task when it is perceived that it will be successful, such as brushing and flossing the teeth; (3) how long a person will persist with a task, even when facing difficulties such as maintaining an exercise program; and (4) emotional reactions such as anxiety, since negative emotions may be aroused when an individual is confronted with the threat of failure.

Knowing what to do and believing one can do it are not the only determinants of behavior.[1,4-7,9] A person also must know how to do it (skills) and want to do the behavior (incentives). Knowing that reducing food intake and increasing exercise can produce weight loss is not enough. People need skills, such as counting calories and energetic exercise patterns to lose weight, and incentives such as improving physical attractiveness. Thus, health education programs must include knowledge of what to do, skills to do it, and incentives for doing it.

Self-efficacy also is related to a specific behavioral task. According to Bandura[3,6] no global sense of self-efficacy exists. A global sense of self-efficacy probably involves self-esteem, self-confidence, or some other general factor. Some relationship may exist between self-efficacy perceptions and these general concepts, but these relationships have yet to be explained adequately. Self-efficacy can be generalized, but the concept of self-efficacy differs from self-esteem since self-esteem focuses on self-worth rather than on performance.[6] Self-efficacy differs

Journal of School Health, 56(8):317–321 (October 1986). Copyright © 1986, American School Health Association, P.O. Box 708, Kent, Ohio 44240. Reprinted by permission.

153

from self-confidence; self-confidence incorporates ideas about control over the outcomes of behaviors, rather than control over behavior itself.

However, one's perceptions of self-efficacy for a specific behavior can be generalized at different times, settings, and behaviors. Belief in the ability to maintain a diet may or may not influence one's perceptions of the capacity to exercise. Since little research has been conducted on the generalization of self-efficacy, it is difficult to assess the extent to which it is generalizable. Some practical measurement problems also occur in using more general measures of self-efficacy.

Another important aspect of self-efficacy for health educators involves its predictive capability. Determining how one perceives the ability to perform a behavior in a certain situation indicates the likelihood of one actually performing the behavior, given the proper incentives. If you think you can, and you want to, you probably will. This simple statement has important implications for health education, as will be discussed.

SELF-EFFICACY SOURCES

Bandura[1-4,6] lists four ways people learn about their ability to do specific tasks as performance accomplishments, vicarious experience, verbal persuasion, and emotional arousal. Educational programs use these techniques in various ways.

PERFORMANCE ACCOMPLISHMENTS

An individual's performance of a behavior usually provides the best indicator of the ability to do it. Success increases the expectation of mastery. The converse also is true. However, the importance of setting should not be neglected. Individuals often believe they can perform in one situation but not in another. Swimming a mile indoors does not mean that one believes he or she could swim a mile during a hurricane.

VICARIOUS EXPERIENCE

Seeing others perform an activity without adverse consequences can generate expectations in individuals that they also will be able to perform the activity and to improve performance with effort and persistence. Since this response is based on social comparison processes, it frequently provides a less dependable source than the direct experience of performing the behavior.

VERBAL PERSUASION

This source is common in health education programs. Individuals can be convinced of having the ability to do a behavior through others telling them they are able to do it. Efficacy expectations aroused through verbal persuasion usually are not as strong as those produced through vicarious experience or performance accomplishments.

EMOTIONAL AROUSAL

Self-efficacy perceptions can be affected by stressful or taxing circumstances that produce emotional arousal. Emotions such as anxiety or depression frequently are interpreted as indicators of the ability to do a specific task. Therefore, high levels of anxiety may affect perceptions of the ability to perform specific behaviors. One also can argue that emotional arousal can improve perceptions of the abilities to do a behavior, since high levels of arousal may be interpreted as indicating the importance of the task.

Information from any, or all, of these sources must be interpreted by the individual before the sources will affect efficacy expectations. The most important interpretive factors include the reasons an individual gives for success or failure. For instance, if success is perceived as resulting from skill, rather than by luck or chance, it is more likely to enhance self-efficacy. Failures attributed to situational circumstances, rather than to personal shortcomings, are less likely to reduce perceptions of self-efficacy. In the case of verbal persuasion, individuals' interpretations of why someone is telling them information about their ability to perform a specific task is important in determining if verbal persuasion will affect efficacy expectations. A competitor telling a person that he or she cannot win a race would be expected to have very different effects on efficacy than if a friend or spouse provided that information.

MEASUREMENT OF SELF-EFFICACY

Bandura's early work involved the clinical treatment of phobic reactions. The original self-efficacy scales he developed consisted of a list of increasingly difficult tasks (Guttman scales). Respondents estimated their ability to cope with each task by indicating the likelihood of successful performance on a scale of 0–100. Numerous modifications of this instrument have been developed for different populations and behaviors.

Figure 1 lists a sample of items from a self-efficacy scale for young adolescents[10] designed to predict their ability to resist smoking cigarettes. To simplify the distinctions for the age group, only six intervals were used on this adolescent scale. Each

FIGURE 1. An Example from a Self-efficacy Scale for Smoking Behavior of Young Adolescents

1	2	3	4	5	6
I am very sure I would smoke	I most likely would smoke	I probably would smoke	I probably would NOT smoke	I most likely would NOT smoke	I am very sure I would NOT smoke

How sure are you that you could resist smoking cigarettes:

When your friends are smoking . . . . _____

When you are by yourself . . . . _____

When you are mad at your parents or teacher . . . . _____

When your brother or sister is smoking . . . . _____

When you want to relax . . . . _____

Lawrance L: *Self-efficacy as a predictor of smoking behavior in young adolescents*, thesis, University of Illinois, Champaign, Ill, 1985.

item describes a specific coping skill related to social or emotional situations in which youngsters are likely to smoke cigarettes. The scale then measures their perceived ability to resist smoking in each setting.

RELATED CONCEPTS

Many other theories contain ideas similar to the concept of self-efficacy. Some confusion may arise as related theories can influence, or be influenced by self-efficacy perceptions. Two theories—locus of control and learned helplessness—warrant discussion since they most often are confused with self-efficacy.

LOCUS OF CONTROL

Locus of control is a generalized belief that people can control what happens to them (outcomes of interest).[1,11] Conversely, self-efficacy is not generalized, but is linked to a specific behavior. More importantly, control over outcomes includes two components: an expectation that behavior will lead to a desired outcome (outcome expectation) and a belief that one can perform the required behavior (self-efficacy expectation) (Figure 2). This distinction[1,4,9] is important since a person might believe that certain actions will produce specific results, but feel incapable of performing those actions. A person might believe they will lose weight if they do not eat ice cream, but be totally unable to walk past the ice cream parlor without indulging.

If people think specific behaviors lead to desired outcomes, and yet think they are incapable of performing the behaviors, the result may be personal helplessness, depression, anxiety, low self-esteem,

and low self-efficacy. More importantly, self-efficacy is a better predictor of behavior than locus of control because it is more specific in terms of behavior, setting, and time.

LEARNED HELPLESSNESS

Learned helplessness[12,13] refers to cognitive, emotional, and behavioral deficits that result from being exposed to uncontrollable events. Classic examples of learned helplessness include the depression, random behavior patterns, and confused thinking that may occur after exposure to natural catastrophes, concentration camps, and related events. Learned helplessness differs from self-efficacy in that learned helplessness refers to consequences from being exposed to uncontrollable events, while self-efficacy is an expectation that one can perform a behavior. Efficacy-based futility is alleviated by increasing competency and expectations of personal effectiveness. Outcome-based futility is alleviated by reducing exposure to uncontrollable events, changing one's perceptions of desired outcomes, or changing the probability relationships between behaviors and outcomes such as reward structures.

APPLICATIONS OF SELF-EFFICACY THEORY

Starting with Bandura's studies of snake phobics, numerous applications of self-efficacy have been made to preventive and rehabilitative health behaviors. Self-efficacy has been used to explain behavior changes, predict effects of different treatment methods, and improve treatment performance.

Outside of health education, self-efficacy theory has been used to explain educational achievement, racial behavior in children, career choice,

FIGURE 2. Diagrammatic Representation of the Difference between Efficacy Expectations and Outcome Expectations

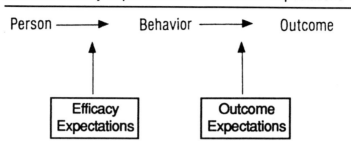

Bandura A: Self-efficacy: Toward a unifying theory of behavior change. *Psychol Rev* 1977;84(2):193.

writing performance of college students, and sales performance in business. Specific health education applications have been used in the areas of addictive behaviors such as smoking, alcohol and heroin, pain control, eating disorders, cardiac rehabilitation, and adherence to regimens.

For smoking cessation, several studies have examined the relationship between self-efficacy and smoking relapse. DiClemente[14] measured self-efficacy to resist smoking cigarettes in various social and stressful situations. His subjects recently had ceased smoking through various smoking cessation techniques. At a five-month follow-up, persons who relapsed had lower initial levels of self-efficacy than those who abstained. Self-efficacy was a stronger predictor of relapse than demographic factors, smoking history, or degree of nicotine dependence. Condiotte and Lichtenstein[15] found results consistent with those of DiClemente. Self-efficacy was a significant predictor of who would relapse, how soon, in what type of social situation, and their response to subsequent smoking.

Self-efficacy for smoking cessation is relevant to individual behavior change, as well as for health education programs, since most smokers who quit do so without professional assistance. DiClemente, Prochaska, and Gilbertini[16] divided their subjects into five levels of the behavior change process: immotive smokers (low self-efficacy); contemplators; recent quitters (within the previous six months); long-term quitters (more than six months, and showed a high self-efficacy); and relapsers. Self-efficacy ratings distinguished recent quitters from contemplators and relapsers. Prochaska et al.[17] also found self-efficacy to be a significant predictor in the natural environment of self-changers. During a

two-year period, self-efficacy ratings forecast the progression from contemplation to action and from action to maintenance of nonsmoking.

Marlatt and Gordon[18,19] studied addictive behaviors involving heroin, alcohol, and cigarettes and postulated a common relapse process based on cognitive factors. Relapse can be avoided if self-efficacy to resist use of the substance is high. Self-efficacy also increases with successful resistance to high risk situations. Results from a smoking cessation study by Barrios and Niehaus[20] were consistent with self-efficacy and Abstinence Violation Effect[18] models. Self-efficacy ratings were higher for successful quitters than for unsuccessful quitters, and lowest in negative mood situations.

The evidence indicates consistently that self-efficacy can predict smoking abstinence and relapse, regardless of treatment methods, methods of measuring self-efficacy, and populations under study. It is a better predictor of behavior than physiological dependence, coping history, motivation to quit, confidence in treatment, and expectancies concerning the rewards of smoking.

Self-efficacy also has been used in studies of pain control related to cold exposure, dental treatment, childbirth, and tension headaches. The effects of self-efficacy on laboratory-induced pain (cold pressors) were studied by Nuefield and Thomas.[21] Pain control was achieved by cognitive means, relaxation techniques, and placebos. The strength of perceived self-efficacy to tolerate pain correlated well with both pain threshold and tolerance.

Dental phobics and low fear dental patients were studied by Klepae, Dowling, and Huage.[22] The low-fear group has a significantly higher self-efficacy rating of tolerance for tooth pain than did dental phobics. Both groups also were similar in their perceived self-efficacy ratings of tolerance for pain administered to the forearm.

Manning and Wright[23] suggest that the success of prenatal preparation (relaxation and cognitive pain control techniques) to reduce medication consumption during delivery is mediated partly by changes in perceived self-efficacy. They found that successful childbirth training techniques produced an increase in perceived self-efficacy. The more efficacious women were less likely to request medication and tolerated pain for a longer time. Self-efficacy was a better predictor of pain tolerance during childbirth than ratings of the importance of having a medication-free delivery.

Holroyd et al.[24] studied pain control applied to tension headaches. They found that increased self-efficacy predicted subsequent reductions in headache activity, while EMG activity achieved during treatment did not, suggesting high self-efficacy to manage pain directly reduces stress that causes headaches. This finding could suggest some future research with those who suffer from chronic arthritis or other painful illnesses.

Some research has applied self-efficacy theory to eating disorders, mainly in obesity and weight control. Chambliss and Murray[25] manipulated self-efficacy to increase weight loss by clients in a behavioral treatment program. This result was achieved by telling half of the patients their medication was ineffective and that their own control had produced the weight loss. Self-efficacy increased the ability to reduce weight in subjects with an internal locus of control.

Much of the psychological recovery from heart attacks involves social processes. Spouses' ideas about their partner's physical capabilities can greatly influence recovery. Taylor et al[26] found that when the wife was involved actively in the treadmill test of her husband's physical stamina, she assessed the patient as having a higher physical efficacy than if she had not been present during the test. The fastest recovery occurred when both patient and spouse estimated physical efficacy as being high.

Kaplan, Atkins, and Reinsch[27] studied patients having chronic obstructive pulmonary disease and their adherence to walking programs. Perceived self-efficacy to participate in a program of exercise was a better predictor of adherence to the walking regimen than was a general health locus of control measure.

Beck and Lund[28] used persuasive communication about the seriousness of, and susceptibility to, periodontal disease to compare the level of perceived self-efficacy with fear arousal designed to affect compliance with a regimen of brushing and flossing. Perceived self-efficacy was the most important predictor of subsequent behavior, including the increased fear levels.

[Editor's Note: In a related paper, Lyn Lawrence, Susan R. Levy, and Laurna Rubinson applied the concept of self-efficacy to AIDS prevention with pregnant minority teenagers. An abstract of their paper contains the following summary:

AIDS education, the only immediate solution to containment of AIDS, encourages active risk reduction among high-risk populations. Self-efficacy is a construct that can measure the likelihood preventive behaviors will be performed, and thus could be applied to identify specific areas where AIDS education should be augmented. In this study, pregnant, mostly black, teens (N = 58) attending an alternative school in a large, midwestern city completed a self-efficacy scale to identify self-perceived areas of vulnerability to participating in preventive behaviors and avoiding high-risk behaviors concerning AIDS. The AIDS Self-efficacy Scale identified four areas of greatest vulnerability: using condoms, discussing previous homosexual activity, discussing previous bisexual activity, and telling a partner about an experience with a bisexual. The last three situations result from an inability to discuss a partner's past sexual history, indicating a need to be very specific in these areas. School health interventions should recognize and deal with issues sexually active teens have identified as most difficult, particularly specific aspects of sexual histories, and provide these adolescents with prevention skills necessary to reduce high-risk behavior. (From "Self-efficacy and AIDS Prevention for Pregnant Teens," *Journal of School Health,* January 1990, *60*:1, 19–24.)]

CONCLUSION

Despite the range of health applications in which self-efficacy theory has been applied, remarkable consistency exists in its ability to predict behavior. Self-efficacy theory has several important implications for health education. Ratings of perceived self-efficacy can help identify individuals at risk for certain unhealthful behaviors. Among those who have quit smoking, relapsers can be distinguished from abstainers.[15] Measures of self-efficacy, because they are situation-specific, can be used to identify high risk situations in which individuals may feel unable to cope. Social settings in which alcoholics are most likely to find themselves unable to resist drinking can be identified. These two applications indicate the specific target group and the types of coping skills that need to be included in a health education program.

Self-efficacy also can be used to measure outcomes of health interventions. Measures of self-efficacy can serve as indicators of relevant behaviors, and as important outcomes of health education efforts to generalize coping mechanisms to other behaviors, settings, and time frames. Since self-efficacy is linked strongly to behavioral performance, it can serve as a substitute measure of behavior change resulting from health education programs. Self-efficacy also can provide a measure of the extent to which specific skills, learned to deal with one problem, transfer to other behaviors, settings, and times. "A strong sense of efficacy for behaving in a healthy fashion is central to self-regulation of one's life,"[29] so the extent to which self-efficacy is generalized from one health problem to another is an important outcome of health education programs. The extent to which perceptions of self-efficacy actually are generalized is an important measurement issue. Little work has been conducted in health education to develop measurement strategies for assessing the generalization of self-efficacy. Assuming that measurement difficulties can be resolved, it is an important issue for health education programs.

References

1. Bandura, A.: Self-efficacy: Toward a unifying theory of behavioral change. *Psychol Rev* 1977;84(2):191–215.
2. Bandura, A.: *Social Learning Theory.* Englewood Cliffs, NJ, Prentice Hall, 1977.
3. Bandura, A.: Self-referent thought: A developmental analysis of self-efficacy, in Flavell, J. H., Ross, L. (eds): *Social Cognitive Development: Frontiers and possible futures.* Cambridge, England, Cambridge University Press, 1981, pp 200–239.
4. Bandura, A.: Self-efficacy mechanism in human agency. *Amer Psychol* 1982;37(2):122–147.
5. Bandura, A.: The self and mechanisms of agency, in Suls, J. (ed): *Social Psychological Perspectives on the Self.* Hillsdale, NJ, Erlbaum, 1982, pp 3–39.
6. Bandura, A.: *Social Foundations of Thought and Action: A social cognitive theory.* Englewood Cliffs, NJ, Prentice Hall, 1985, pp 390–453.
7. Bandura, A.: Recycling misconceptions of perceived self-efficacy. *Cog Ther Res* 1984;8(3):231–255.
8. Bandura, A., Adams, N.: Analysis of self-efficacy theory and behavioral change. *Cog Ther Res* 1977;1(4):287–308.
9. Bandura, A.: Reflections on self-efficacy. *Advances Behav Res Ther* 1978;1:237–269.
10. Lawrance, L.: *Self-efficacy as a predictor of smoking behavior in young adolescents,* thesis, University of Illinois, Champaign, Ill, 1985.
11. Rotter, J.: Generalized expectancies for internal versus external control of reinforcement. *Psychol Mono* 1966;80(1).
12. Maier, S., Seligman, M. E. P.: Learned helplessness: Theory and evidence. *J Exper Psychol* 1976;105(1):3–46.
13. Abramson, L., Garber, J., Seligman, M. E. P.: Learned helplessness in humans: An attributional analysis, in Garber, J., Seligman, M. E. P. (eds): *Human Helplessness: Theory and applications.* New York, Academic Press, 1980, pp 3–34.
14. DiClemente, C.: Self-efficacy and smoking cessation maintenance: A preliminary report. *Cog Ther Res* 1981;5(2):175–187.
15. Condiotte, M., Lichtenstein, E.: Self-efficacy and relapse in smoking cessation programs. *J Consult Clin Psychol* 1981;49(5):648–658.
16. DiClemente, C., Prochaska, J., Gilbertini, M.: Self-efficacy and the stages of self-change of smoking. *Cog Ther Res* 1985;9(2):181–200.
17. Prochaska, J., DiClemente, C., Velicer, W., Ginpil, S., et al.: Predicting smoking status for self-changers. *Addict Behav* 1985;10(4):395–406.
18. Marlatt, G., Gordon, J.: Determinants of relapse: Implications for the maintenance of behavior change, in Davidson, P., Davidson, S., (eds): *Behavioral Medicine: Changing health lifestyles.* New York, Brunner/Mazel, 1980, pp 424–452.
19. Marlatt, G., Gordon, J.: *Relapse Prevention: Maintenance strategies in the treatment of addictive behaviors.* New York, Guilford Press, 1985.
20. Barrios, F. X., Niehaus, J. C.: The influence of smoker status, smoking history, sex, and situational variables on smoker's self-efficacy. *Addict Behav* 1985;10(4):425–430.
21. Neufield, R. W. J., Thomas, P.: Effects of perceived efficacy of a prophylactic controlling mechanism on self-control under painful stimulation. *Can J Behav Sci* 1977;9(3):223–232.
22. Klepae, R. K., Dowling, L., Hauge, G.: Characteristics of clients seeking therapy for the reduction of dental avoidance reactions to pain. *J Behav Ther Exper Psychiatr* 1982;13(4):293–300.
23. Manning, M., Wright, T.: Self-efficacy expectancies, outcome expectancies, and the persistence of pain control in childbirth. *J Person Soc Psychol* 1983;45(2):426–431.

24. Holroyd, K. A., Penzien, D. B., Hersey, K. G., Tobin, D. L., et al.: Change mechanisms in EMG bio-feedback training: Cognitive changes underlying improvements in tension headache. *J Consult Clin Psychol* 1984;52(6):1039–1053.

25. Chambliss, C., Murray, E.: Efficacy attribution, locus of control, and weight loss. *Cog Ther Res* 1979;3(4):349–353.

26. Taylor, C., Bandura, A., Ewart, C., Miller, N., et al.: Raising spouse's and patient's perception of his cardiac capabilities following a myocardial infarction. *Amer J Cardiology* 1985;55:635–638.

27. Kaplan, R., Atkins, C., Reinsch, S.: Specific efficacy expectations mediate exercise compliance in patients with COPD. *Health Psychol* 1984;3(3):223–242.

28. Beck, K., Lund, A.: The effects of health threat seriousness and personal efficacy upon intentions and behavior. *J Appl Soc Psychol* 1981;11(5):401–415.

29. Schunk, D. H., Carbonari, J. P.: Self-efficacy models, in Matarazzo, J. D., Weiss, S. M., Herd, J. A., Miller, N. E., et al. (eds): *Behavioral Health: A handbook of health enhancement and disease prevention.* New York, John Wiley and Sons, 1984, pp 230–247.

18

THE DYNAMICS OF PLANT CLOSINGS:
AN EXTENDED EMOTIONAL ROLLER COASTER RIDE

Joe B. Hurst
John W. Shepard
Counselor and Human Service Education
University of Toledo

An alarming number of business and corporate failures has marked the last decade as one of job insecurity. Professional counselors and psychologists are focusing attention on the dynamics of unemployment and its implications for theorizing, model building, assessment, intervention strategies, and comprehensive programs (Amundson and Borgen, 1982; Cairo, 1983; Cianni-Surridge, 1983; Edelwich and Brodsky, 1980; Finley and Lee, 1981; Lopez, 1983; Shifron, Dye, and Shifron, 1983). For example, one important aspect of counseling unemployed workers is understanding the economics of a recessionary economy and four distinct types of unemployment—demand deficiency, structural, frictional, and seasonal and hidden unemployment (Shifron et al., 1983). Demand deficient or recessionary unemployment has unique circumstances that counselors need to consider, including (a) helping clients accept that they cannot control the economy and are not responsible for what happened to them, (b) maintaining clients' job search enthusiasm so they can avoid joining the hidden unemployed (i.e., those who have stopped looking), (c) helping clients develop coping skills for handling the humiliating status of unemployment and the resulting grief, anger, and depression, and (d) dealing with family members' feelings, self-esteem, and support skills.

In this article we depict a particular plant closing and the prolonged emotional "roller coaster ride" taken by the employees of the plant. We describe a model for understanding the plant-closing process, a comprehensive career adjustment program for over 100 employees, and implications for counselors in the field.

THE DYNAMICS OF UNEMPLOYMENT

In addition to understanding recessionary economics, counselors should also understand the dynamic process of unemployment and its effects on people and their families. The model described here is based on two others that describe and explain the dynamics of unemployment.

THE EMOTIONAL ROLLER COASTER

Amundson and Borgen (1982) developed a model of the dynamic process of job loss and job seeking by integrating theory involving the grieving process (Finley and Lee, 1981; Kubler-Ross, 1969) and job search burnout (Edelwich and Brodsky, 1980). "The model . . . to explain the dynamics of unemployment connects the job loss–job search factors into a process that may be described as an emotional 'roller coaster' " (Amundson and Borgen, 1982, p. 563). The key to understanding the unemployment process is to examine dislocated workers' self-concepts as they progress along their "ride." The components of the model include (a) job loss—denial, anger, bargaining, depression, and acceptance; and (b) job search—enthusiasm, stagnation, frustration, and apathy. The entire process is described as follows:

> If the desired end point of the continuum . . . is reemployment, then it is important to examine the forces along the continuum which may impede or facilitate reaching that goal. The initial set of forces restraining effective job search activities are found in the first valley. . . . They include the denial, anger, bargaining, and depression phases of the grieving process and may present themselves in employment counseling settings as unfinished business related to job loss. Next come facilitating forces characterized by acceptance . . . and enthusiasm related to job search. Ideally the energy made available by these forces leads to an effective job search and employment. Clients who come for counseling with these forces operating are often energetic and cooperative. . . . It is important to recognize a second set of negative or restraining forces that can occur, par-

ticularly in times of slow economic growth and high unemployment. These "burnout" factors (stagnation, frustration, and apathy) come into play following repeated ineffective job search attempts and can present themselves to employment counselors as intense passive resistance. (Amundson and Borgen, 1982, p. 563)

At one point the clients view themselves as workers, a valued position in our society. Subsequently, at another point, clients accept the roles of unemployed workers at the end of their own grieving over the loss of their jobs. It is then that energy from completion of grieving leads to an enthusiastic job search. If reemployment is not secured, clients may find themselves entering periods of stagnation, frustration, and apathy (job search burnout) and having self-concepts associated with chronic unemployment, a worthless position in society.

CORPORATE FAILURE

Lopez (1983) argued that victims of corporate failure experience a unique set of situational and emotional factors. He summarized this unique condition as follows:

It is likely that victims of corporate failure experience a different and perhaps more variable sequence of emotional reactions than that of the typical fired or laid-off worker. . . . The denial phase . . . may be quite protracted . . . Once a company fails, there is absolutely no possibility for workers to entertain bargaining notions of within-company transfer or relocation. . . . There remains no "living" target toward which to project one's anger. A sense of diffuse frustration seems to prevail. . . .
Unlike other job losers who have terminated for poor performance or low productivity, the victims . . . have

generally demonstrated good productivity, high job satisfaction, and strong corporate allegiance. Indeed, a failing company seems to provoke worker solidarity and thus indirectly delays each individual's emotional preparation for job loss. Once the company folds, job loss is immediate, irreversible, and democratic; everyone loses. (Lopez, 1983, p. 632)

According to Lopez (1983), there is a prebankruptcy period (see Table 1), characterized by "gloomy forecasts, layoffs, management changes, and wage and hiring freezes" (p. 631). Rather than preparing employees emotionally, this period tends to stimulate a survival reaction in which workers accept freezes and cutbacks and expend considerable energy to help the company stay alive. During this period, younger workers are terminated, leaving a homogeneous nucleus of workers who have (a) a common history of job satisfaction and security, (b) a high degree of camaraderie and corporate allegiance, (c) emotional and financial ties to the company (e.g., age, tenure, accrued benefits, seniority), and (d) the urge to "prevent the loss of both a future and a long-standing corporate identity" (Lopez, 1983, p. 631). Additionally, supportive contact diminishes as people search for and find jobs. With no systematic program to help workers adjust and find reemployment, the company's traditional, organized system breaks down, workers democratically experience the loss together, and the "unhealthy industry" provides diminishing opportunities for employment. Some employees suffer from dampened hopes because of their ages, specialized skill areas, and resulting limited job opportunities; others realize the need for retraining and a career change.

TABLE 1. Unique Factors in Corporate Failures

Factors	Prebankruptcy Period	Corporate Closing Period
Situational Factors	1. Management changes 2. Cost reductions 3. Reassignment and seniority bumping 4. Layoffs and terminations 5. Homogenized workforce 6. Survival reactions, renewed energy and work 7. Worker solidarity	1. Democratic loss experience 2. Daily contact diminishes or stops with supportive co-workers 3. No system to aid job search and adjustment 4. Withholding of final pay and benefits 5. Diminished industry ability to absorb unemployed workers 6. Older and more specialized affected most by outlook
Emotional Factors	1. Prolonged denial 2. Shock, disbelief 3. Relief or hope 4. Lingering hope 5. Passive acceptance 6. Company allegiance 7. Personal concerns and worries	1. No bargaining power 2. Untargeted anger 3. Diffuse frustration 4. Unique individual responses to depression 5. A new lease on life and energy to explore options 6. High distress and alienation of self 7. Dampened hopes 8. Shock over career change 9. Serious personal concern

THE EXTENDED ROLLER COASTER RIDE

In our experience in working with over 100 employees involved in a plant closing, the models developed by Amundson and Borgen (1982) and Lopez (1983) seem to be valid and can be combined and expanded into a comprehensive model depicting the dynamics of plant closings, corporate failures, and extended layoffs. The following sections contain background descriptions of the plant, its closing, and the resulting effects on its employees. Serving as career counselors, we obtained the information and statistics cited from personal interviews.

DESCRIPTION

The name of the company is not used here to ensure confidentiality. The plant was located in the Midwest and was one of two area businesses in which mechanical and electrical products were assembled. The company had a long and consistent record of success, and its products had a national reputation. After being purchased by another corporation, the company moved its administrative staff to another midwestern city, opened a southern assembly plant, and reduced its plant staff from more than 1,000 to fewer than 200 employees.

The company had unionized and nonunionized employees. The clients who were tested and counseled formed a core staff of 150 employees in the following departments: management, production, supervision, secretarial, accounting, engineering, shipping, and receiving and maintenance.

Of the 150 employees in the plant, 120 (80%) were appraised and 115 (77%) were seen individually by a counselor. The career testing included the use of three instruments: (a) the Wonderlic Personnel Test, to assess problem-solving ability and occupational and training potential (Dodrill, 1981, 1983; Wonderlic, 1981, 1983); (b) the Personal Profile System, to determine work personality, patterns of behavior, and values (Kaplan and Kaplan, 1983; Kostiuk, 1983; Performax Systems International, 1977, 1981); and (c) the Self-Directed Search, to examine occupational interests and alternatives (Holland, 1978, 1981; Prediger, 1981).

Three trained counselors examined the results of these instruments and the employees' work histories. During the session a counselor helped each employee identify skills, strengths, interests, potential, goals, alternatives, future job search needs and plans, personal concerns, and needs for follow-up support. After the session each employee received a summary of what was discussed and a letter of recommendation based on the assessment, the person's work record, and the counselor's impressions. A copy of the summary was given to the job search instructors for follow-up in developing a professional resumé and an organized plan.

The program for the employees combined the services of several local agencies and those supplied by the company and union. The program was funded by the local Private Industry Council (PIC) under the Job Training and Partnership Act (JTPA) Title III and by the company. The services were provided in the plant by the company's administration and personnel department (CAP), the union (WU), the PIC staff, the local Bureau of Employment Services (BES), a private firm for career appraisal and vocational guidance (GC), a series of classes on job search skills (JC), and a free placement referral service (JDU). The services provided by each are as follows:

CAP: General planning, support, and coordination; establishment of a "job available" corner for studying current openings and an employment message bulletin board; scheduling of group and individual sessions regarding policies, finances, benefits, and final arrangements; creation, publication, and dissemination of a company booklet consisting of employee resumés.

WU: Input into planning, sponsorship of group presentations by local agencies, and individual employment, support, and referrals.

PIC: Program organization, funding, coordination, monitoring, and support.

BES: Registration, eligibility determination, placement information, and referrals; assistance with completing work history information.

GC: Career assessment, individual sessions, summary report to job club instructors and employees, a letter of recommendation, and continued support; discussion of leisure and personal concerns with job seekers and early retirees.

JC: Five 2-hour classes on conducting a job search, including developing resumés, telephoning, completing applications, forming networks, and interviewing.

JDU: Job placement referrals, administering job training contracts and tax credit reimbursements to employers.

The overall goals of the program were to increase information, support, acceptance, self-awareness, confidence, career planning, job search options, enthusiasm, and direction for dislocated employees.

Information and formal (i.e., a questionnaire) feedback suggested that workers did feel a greater sense of competence, self-esteem, hope, and enthusiasm after the program. Comments focused on the empathy, caring, professionalism, and efficiency of all involved staff and on the uses of new techniques for job searching. A few people viewed the program as a company strategy to promote worker acceptance and cooperation and to reduce unemployment compensation.

A MODEL

Information derived from these sessions led to the construction of the model presented in Figure 1. The model illustrates the emotional ups and downs discussed by Amundson and Borgen (1982) and Lopez (1983) and depicts the extended nature of the ride for a majority of the employees. In the following discussion we describe its components and use case data to illustrate key points. Amundson and Borgen's (1982) original model is depicted in the figure by a solid line; Lopez's (1983) model of corporate failure is included in the first valley (1–6) and the third valley (13–18).

The company had a consistent record of success for more than 40 years. The extended employment period represents a vast accrual of skills, experience, benefits, and seniority by hundreds of workers. There had been personnel reductions, plant integration and relocation, and new ownership 5 years before Point 1, the time of the first concern about plant closing and relocations. As illustrated in the first valley (1–6), the prebankruptcy situational and emotional factors were present. Clients who were interviewed expressed their memory of the factors discussed in Table 1. The homogeneity factor was best illustrated by the characteristics of these employees. Their ages ranged from 35 through 63, with a mean of 48. Most of the employees had worked only for that company, except during a past strike or temporary layoff, and had not looked for other employment in more than 15 years. Approximately 30% had been with the company for more than 25 years, and several had been there between 30 and 40 years. Except for approximately 5%, they tended to loyally defend the company and were concerned about maintaining their best work until they left. Depending on role and seniority, there were three distinct ending dates (i.e., June 21, August 1, and "the last day in 1984"). Finally, based on the Personal Profile System (Performax Systems International, 1983), most employees had similar work personalities and work patterns. Most had comparable Wonderlic Personnel Test scores (Wonderlic, 1983) and similar interests identified through the Self-Directed Search (Holland, 1981).

Throughout the first valley some younger workers, as well as older ones who tended to have less seniority and skills, experienced the grieving process and moved through denial, anger, bargaining, depression, acceptance, and job search phases. At the same time, those who remained experienced the prebankruptcy factors and the solidarity and enthusiasm of maintaining corporate survival (Points 5 to 6). Some employees weathered the unemployment storm along the straight employment security line because of their seniority, positions, optimism, or denial and hope. It was as though they were going to be "working there forever."

Once the plant closing was announced (Point 6), the majority of the employees joined together behind two or three determined leaders and a new manager to prove to the national management that the plant could be made more profitable. This led to the increased enthusiasm and work productivity represented in the "bubble" from Point 6 to Point 7, a heavy emotional and energetic investment in company survival that resulted in steady increases in production over 6 months (35% in one month). Some workers remained on the employment line because of their seniority, denial, or hope. In the second valley of this line, however, the feelings of job security of most employees were shattered, although approximately 10% continued to hold a false sense of security. This false security was reflected in several employees' saying they would work until their last day without looking for other employment (a disloyal act to many). About 10% of the employees followed the employment line to early retirement and reemployment in leisure or part-time work.

The line from Points 8 and 9 to Point 11 represent a number of employees who displayed what Lopez (1983) referred to as prolonged denial and emotional postponement of loss and grief. Many workers remarked that they did not blame themselves or the company but resented decision makers in a huge corporation who did not know what they were doing. Some directed their anger toward employees in a southern plant where production facilities were being relocated. A few bargained for

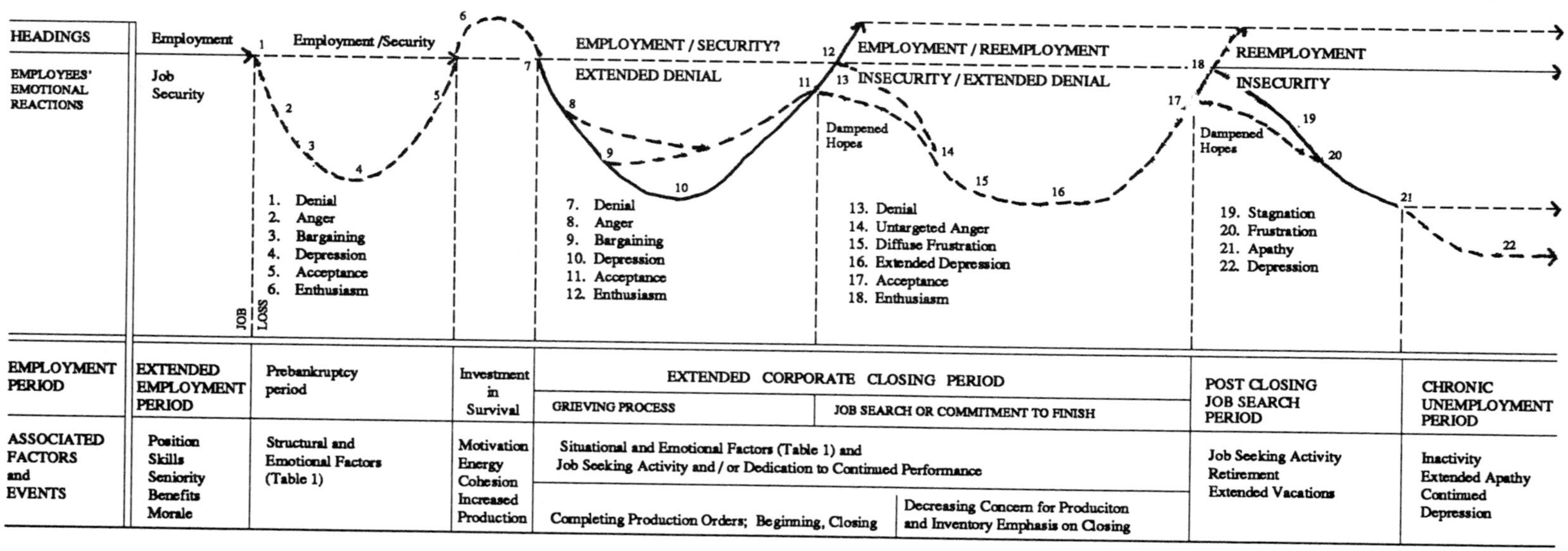

FIGURE 1. The Extended Roller Coaster Ride of a Plant Closing

relocation. Most elected to stay in their present homes because their houses were paid for, their spouses were satisfactorily employed, or they wanted to stay near family and friends. For some, bargaining manifested itself in negotiating for severance pay, health benefits, retirement income, and assistance. The few (5%) who suffered depression (Point 10) in the second valley seemed to do so because of recent layoff experiences, low self-concept and confidence, or immobilizing worry (Dyer, 1977).

Acceptance (Point 11) was generally marked by renewed energy to search for a job (40% to 50%) and to continue personal or company work standards (60% to 75%). Approximately 40% of these employees were experiencing dampened hopes because of their age, lack of job-seeking experience, anxiety about presenting themselves, perception of limited job opportunities in the area, and low self-concepts. Most of them viewed themselves as old, unskilled, and overspecialized (or not specialized enough). Also, they had not considered their functional, transferable skills and potential (Bolles, 1980), a key point of emphasis in this program.

Point 12 becomes another Point 1 (13), because it is at this position that many employees actually leave and begin the loss and grieving cycle. Uncharacteristic of those experiencing Lopez's (1983) democratic loss, employees in this situation left in waves (i.e., reemployment before termination and three different termination dates). For some, the path from Point 12 to Point 18 is the high road, so to speak, because they are the lucky, reemployed ones. Some continue on a straight, insecure, "employment" path. These include employees who are (a) retiring, (b) awaiting their termination date, (c) sure they will find something ("when I look after my vacation"), and (d) not in need of rapid reemployment (those with working spouses or financial reserves).

Some employees followed the extended acceptance or prolonged denial (and hope) path from Points 14–17. Approximately 20% of the employees passively accepted the end, whereas 1% to 2% expressed lingering hope or denial that they would ever be unemployed. In the future, most of them will continue this path; none to this point have fallen to the prolonged depression path. Those employees most likely to experience prolonged depression are the few who are handicapped by physical, skill, and age barriers and those with very low self-esteem. Regardless of the path, there tend to be feelings of loss, sadness, resentment, and anger because of the end of the company, close collegial relationships, and a way of life for most employees (Lopez, 1983).

At Point 17, there tended to be two distinct paths. Those who had enthusiasm initiated and maintained an active job search. Some have found a high road to reemployment, one that is characterized by renewed and increased self-esteem, a better or comparable job, a new career, or satisfying retirement. Their full sense of job security, however, may never return. After losing a secure job of 15 or more years, employees reported that they were aware of the distinct possibility that it could happen again. Many stated that they would never feel secure in any position in the future.

The second path can lead along dampened hopes to either extended enthusiasm (e.g., through counseling, brighter economic picture, increased job interviews, or personal referrals) or stagnation and job burnout.

> The initial stages of a job search are often characterized by high hopes, high energy, and unrealistic expectations about job possibilities. Following this initial enthusiasm, job search efforts may stagnate as the reality of the situation becomes apparent. . . . As the job search extends over time and repeated rejections are experienced, there is often a movement toward frustration and anger. In this frustration the need for a scapegoat emerges . . . increasing reliance on alcohol or drugs may begin to surface. Finally, a general feeling of apathy may develop . . . a minimum amount of time is spent in the job search, and a negative self-fulfilling prophecy begins to emerge. There is generally a low level of energy and an increasing lack of self-confidence. (Amundson and Borgen, 1982, p. 563)

As a result, at Points 21 and 22 the chronic unemployed begin to experience extended apathy and depression. In our experience in counseling the long-term unemployed (2 to 3 years), many of these people are waiting for someone to actively find them a job or are really committed to not working.

IMPLICATIONS

The dynamics of unemployment have several implications for professional counselors, especially for those in career and adjustment counseling. Assuming that a client can be anywhere along the loss and search cycle, counselors can use interview, assessment, and listening skills to identify the client's point on the roller coaster and associated situational and emotional factors. Dislocated clients will be dealing with continual job and financial insecurity.

Lopez (1983) acknowledged several practical counseling approaches for working with employees dislocated because of business failures. These included:

1. Clarifying marketable, transferable work skills, reviewing vocational assessment results, and focusing on developing short-term plans to reorient clients to the reality of their situations.
2. Providing ample opportunities for clients to express their feelings and focusing on vocational and personal concerns.
3. Assessing clients' financial, familial, marital, and other personal support.
4. Providing clients with up-to-date information on referral services, employment outlook, and local placement services.
5. Reminding clients that they are proven, skilled, mature workers whose job losses are not attributable to incompetence or negligence (Lopez, 1983).

Other intervention activities can focus on the three stages of the unemployment cycle: job loss, job search, and burnout. Loss and search interventions can include (a) understanding clients' feelings and challenging them to see other perspectives of their loss, (b) assisting in resolving conflicts related to the loss, (c) developing a realistic view of skills and strengths, (d) evaluating with clients their options and job search approaches and skills, (e) continuing to support clients, (f) developing specific action plans, and (b) practicing necessary skills for implementing the plans. Finally, burnout strategies can be focused most effectively on validating client feelings, suggesting activities that build self-concept, and identifying new approaches to job search (Amundson and Borgen, 1982).

Workers need to view realistically themselves, their occupational characteristics (e.g., skills, interests, potential, work personality), and the employment situation. A majority of the employees counseled had a limited or negative view of themselves and their skills. Some perceived their skills and experience as commonplace or even as barriers to reemployment. In counseling, many of them became aware of their tendencies to undersell themselves, limit their job searches, and succumb to dampened hopes. Assessment and intervention strategies need to be focused realistically on these tendencies.

The employees in the plant closing were characteristically loyal, cooperative, skilled, reliable, and dedicated. Several feared (or used as an excuse for inaction) initiating a job search that would result in employment before their scheduled termination date. Others postponed their search and hence their emotional reactions for various reasons. Most described their acute fear of searching for a job after years of comfortable job security. A real fear of the unknown was present. Counselors need to emphasize the reality of job search and to confront the conflicting feelings of loyalty, anxiety, allegiance, personal panic, anger, depression, denial, enthusiasm, and relief. They should also assist clients in accepting their fears as a natural and potentially motivating force. Training in and practice of job search skills should be important components of programs for dislocated employees. Other important elements are providing accurate information, personal support, and appropriate referrals. Vocational assessment and counseling can contribute significantly to the career development, personal adjustment, and active job search activities of dislocated workers (Fundle and DeBlassie, 1981; Glamser and DeJong, 1975; Goulader and Mann, 1981; Hanson, 1981; Herr, 1982).

The need for working with unemployed workers is increasing because of business failures, technological innovations, economic fluctuations, and social changes. One challenging area is in JTPA programs for the chonically unemployed and for skilled, dislocated workers. In the future counselors are more and more likely to encounter clients involved directly or indirectly with one or more points on the unemployment roller coaster. Those who understand and are sensitive to the length, peaks, and valleys of such a ride can identify and use appropriate interventions.

We are developing a follow-up questionnaire that will be administered in the near future. One weakness of the program and limitation of this article was the lack of rigorous use of data collection instruments that could have provided a documented testing of the model proposed here (Mitchell, 1982; Ofsanko, 1983; Oliver, 1979; Tittle, 1982).

Readers should note further that the proposed model was validated on only one plant closing. Because plants and their populations differ in region and purpose, additional research needs to be conducted regarding the roller coaster rides that occur as a result of other plant closings.

References

Amundson, N. E., and Borgen, W. A. (1982). The dynamics of unemployment: Job loss and job search. *Personal and Guidance Journal, 60,* 562–564.

Bolles, R. N. (1980). *The three boxes of life: And how to get out of them.* Berkeley, CA: Ten Speed Press.

Cairo, P. C. (1983). Counseling in industry: A selected review of the literature. *Personal Psychology, 36,* 1–18.

Cianni-Surridge, M. (1983). Technology and work: Future issues for career guidance. *Personal and Guidance Journal, 61,* 413–417.

Dodrill, C. B. (1981). An economical method for the evaluation of general intelligence in adults. *Journal of Consulting and Clinical Psychology, 59,* 668–673.

Dodrill, C. B. (1983). Long term reliability of the Wonderlic Personnel Test. *Journal of Consulting and Clinical Psychology, 51,* 316–317.

Dyer, W. (1977). *Your erroneous zones.* New York: Avon Books.

Edelwich, J., and Brodsky, A. (1980). *Burn-out: Stages of disillusionment in the helping professions.* New York: Human Sciences Press.

Finley, M. H., and Lee, A. T. (1981). The terminated executive: It's like dying. *Personnel and Guidance Journal, 59,* 382–384.

Fundle, J., and DeBlassie, R. R. (1981). Unemployment in the postindustrial age: Counseling the redundant worker. *Journal of Employment Counseling, 18,* 183–189.

Glamser, F. D., and DeJong, F. (1975). The efficiency of pre-retirement preparation programs for industrial workers. *Journal of Gerontology, 39,* 595–600.

Goulader, J. S., and Mann, W. H. (1981). Some new ideas on employability counseling. *Journal of Employment Counseling, 18,* 168–175.

Hanson, M. C. (1981). Career counseling in organizations. In D. H. Montross and C. J. Shinkman (Eds.), *Career development in the 80's.* Springfield, IL: Thomas.

Herr, E. L. (1982). Testing for career counseling, guidance, and education: Reactions to the symposium articles. *Measurement and Evaluations in Guidance, 15,* 159–163.

Holland, J. L. (1978). *The Self-Directed Search: A guide to educational and vocational planning.* Palo Alto, CA: Consulting Psychologists Press.

Holland, J. L. (1981). *The Self-Directed Search: A manual.* Palo Alto, CA: Consulting Psychologists Press.

Kaplan, S. J., and Kaplan, B. E. (1983). *A study of the Personal Profile System.* Minneapolis: Performax Systems International.

Kostiuk, E. S. (1983). *A study of behavioral styles of chief executive officers.* Minneapolis: Performax Systems International.

Kubler-Ross, E. (1969). *On death and dying.* New York: Macmillan.

Lopez, F. G. (1983). The victims of corporate failure: Some preliminary observations. *Personal and Guidance Journal, 61,* 631–632.

Mitchell, A. (1982). Uses of tests in programs of career guidance and education. *Measurement and Evaluation in Guidance, 15,* 153–158.

Ofsanko, F. (1983). Validity generalization—Report of conference. *Industrial-Organizational Psychologist, 20,* 34–36.

Oliver, L. W. (1979). Outcome measurement in career counseling research. *Journal of Counseling Psychology, 26,* 217–226.

Performax Systems International. (1977). *The Personal Profile System: A plan to understand yourself and others.* Minneapolis: Author.

Performax Systems International. (1983). *The Personal Profile System manual.* Minneapolis: Author.

Prediger, D. (1981). A note on Self-Directed Search validity for females. *Vocational Guidance Quarterly, 30,* 117–129.

Shifron, R., Dye, A., and Shifron, G. (1983). Implications for counseling the unemployed in a recessionary economy. *Personal and Guidance Journal, 61,* 527–529.

Tittle, C. (1982). Career guidance: Program evaluation and validity. *Measurement and Evaluation in Guidance, 15,* 22–25.

Wonderlic, E. F. (1981). *Personnel Test (Form IV).* Northfield, IL: E. F. Wonderlic and Associates.

Wonderlic, E. F. (1983). *Personnel Test: Manual* (2nd ed.). Northfield, IL: E. F. Wonderlic and Associates.

PART IV

B.   Problems in Living

19

PHENOMENOLOGY OF MAJOR DEPRESSION FROM CHILDHOOD THROUGH ADULTHOOD:
ANALYSIS OF THREE STUDIES

Gabrielle A. Carlson
Department of Psychiatry
State University of New York at Stony Brook

Javad H. Kashani
Department of Psychiatry
University of Missouri at Columbia

The clinical picture of what is currently called major depression *(DSM-III)* is derived from experience with depressed adults. Although there are differing views as to the significance of prominence of particular symptoms, there is a general consensus that the disorder is composed of a range of signs and symptoms in affective, cognitive, psychomotor, and vegetative spheres. What has not been clear is which aspects of the clinical picture are fixed, core symptoms and which are likely to be modified by variables such as age, sex, culture, and race. Moreover, clinicians and researchers interested in a developmental perspective have speculated on what impact age and development might have on depressive phenomenology (1–3) (table 1).

To our knowledge, no one has undertaken a systematic study of depressive symptoms from infancy through adulthood, and we felt some light might be shed on the validity of theoretical speculations by comparing data from studies (albeit separately done) of preschool, prepubertal, adolescent, and adult populations.

METHOD

Three studies were selected for inclusion because they systematically examined the age group in question with comprehensive interviews and specific criteria.

In the study of adults, Baker et al. (4) used the Renard Psychiatric Interview and the Feighner et al. criteria (5) (although the latter had not been published as such in 1971), both of which were models for the Research Diagnostic Criteria (RDC) (6) and the Schedule for Affective Disorders and Schizophrenia (SADS) (7). They studied 100 psychiatri-

cally hospitalized patients with unipolar depression and made diagnoses based on the structured interview of patients and review of past psychiatric records, and interviews of family members when possible.

We included the study of Ryan et al. (8) because it reported on prepubertal children and adolescents who met the RDC for major depression, had no major physical illnesses, and had IQs over 70. The subjects were interviewed with the Present Episode Version of the SADS for School-Age Children (Kiddie-SADS-P) (9) on two separate occasions, 2 weeks apart, by independent interviewers. With the Kiddie-SADS-P, parents are interviewed first to elicit the history and symptoms of the child's disorders, then the child is interviewed, and a summary rating is made on the basis of information from both. Symptom frequencies are reported for the worst period of the index episode.

To collect a sample of depressed preschool children who met unmodified *DSM-III* criteria for major depression, it was necessary to interview 1,000 preschool children over a 5-year period. These children had been referred to the only unit in mid-Missouri that evaluates and treats preschool children with serious behavioral and developmental disorders. Although there were (and still are) no comprehensive structured interviews geared for the demands of a complete psychiatric evaluation of preschool children, a semistructured interview for parents was used that encompassed *DSM-III* criteria. In addition, the child was interviewed separately by a child psychiatrist and a clinical child psychologist. Further, specific interactions between parent and child were recorded by use of an observation room with a one-way mirror. Information was obtained from the

From *American Journal of Psychiatry*, 1988, *145*(10):1222–1225. Copyright © 1988, The American Psychiatric Association. Reprinted by permission.

TABLE 1. Speculative Manifestations of Depressive Symptoms Through Childhood[a]

Adult Symptom	Childhood Symptom				
	0–36 Months	3–5 Years	6–8 Years	9–12 Years	13–18 Years
Dysphoric mood	Sad or expressionless face, gaze aversion, staring, irritability	Sad expression, somberness or labile mood, irritability	Prolonged unhappiness, somberness, irritability	Sad expression, apathy, irritability	Sad expression, apathy, irritability, increasing complaints of depression
Loss of interest or pleasure	No social play	Decreased socialization	Decreased socialization	Adult presentation	Adult presentation
Appetite or weight change	Feeding problems	Feeding problems	Adult presentation	Adult presentation	Adult presentation
Insomnia or hypersomnia	Sleep problems	Sleep problems	Sleep problems	Adult presentation	Adult presentation
Psychomotor agitation	Tantrums, irritability	Irritability, tantrums	Irritability, tantrums	Aggressive behavior	Aggressive behavior
Psychomotor retardation	Lethargy	Lethargy	Lethargy	Lethargy	Adult presentation
Loss of energy	Lethargy	Lethargy	Lethargy	Lethargy	Adult presentation
Feelings of worthlessness		Low self-esteem	Low self-esteem	Guilt, low self-esteem	Guilt
Diminished concentration			Poor school performance	Poor school performance	Poor school performance
Recurrent thoughts of death or suicide		Accident proneness	Accident proneness, morbid outlook	Adult presentation	Adult presentation
Anxiety	Separation/attachment problems	School phobia	Phobias, separation anxiety	Phobias, separation anxiety	Adult presentation
Somatic complaints		Present	Present	Present	Present

[a]From Weinberg et al. (1), Bemporad and Wilson (2), and Herzog and Rathbun (3).

preschool if the child attended one, and the diagnosis was based on all information (10, 11).

Since the preschool youngsters were likely to be severely impaired, and the adult sample was an inpatient sample, it was felt that the sample of children and adolescents selected by the higher cutoff of the Kiddie-SADS-P would be more directly comparable. A chi-square analysis was performed with the Bonferroni correction to reduce the experiment-wise error to the 0.05 level. This required use of a significance (alpha) level of 0.003 for each statistical test.

RESULTS

Preschool children (N = 9) were between ages 2½ and 6 years. The mean ages of the prepubertal (N = 95), adolescent (N = 92), and adult (N = 100) groups were 9.6, 14.7, and 45.9 years, respectively. The sex distribution followed what has come to be a recognized pattern. Males were more common in the preadolescent samples (male:female ratio = 6:3 and 59:36 in the preschool and prepubertal youngsters),

whereas females predominated in the postpubertal groups (ratio = 42:50 and 31:69 in the adolescents and adults, respectively).

The clinical phenomenology is reported in table 2.

DISCUSSION

There are a number of reasons why it is necessary to interpret these results with caution. First, these studies were carried out by different investigators, at different sites, and on different populations over a 15-year time course. Second, with the preschool and adult samples, symptoms were counted on a present/absent basis, whereas with the prepubertal and adolescent samples, symptoms were graded by severity. We felt that the severity of impairment of the preschoolers and adults was more comparable to a moderate level of symptom severity on the Kiddie-SADS-P, but there is no way to be certain that the severity of symptoms was comparable across groups. However, the use of a

TABLE 2. Depressive Signs and Symptoms in Four Age Groups With Major Depression

Sign or Symptom Present	Preschoolers (N=9)[a]		Prepubertal Children (N=95)[b]		Adolescents (N=92)[b]		Adults (N=100)[c]		χ^2	p
	N	%	N	%	N	%	N	%		
Increases with age										
Anhedonia	2	22.2	63	66.3	68	73.9	77	77	13.5	<0.003
Worse in morning	0	—	18	18.9	13	14.1	46	46	29.2	0.0000
Hopelessness	0	—	19	20.0	43	46.7	56	56	27.8	0.0000
Psychomotor retardation	3	33.3	27	28.4	33	35.9	60	60	22.2	0.000
Definite delusions	0	—	4	4.2	4	4.3	16	16	11.6	0.003
Decreases with age										
Depressed appearance	8	88.9	23	24.2	15	16.3	0	—	24.1	0.0000
Self-esteem	6	66.7	60	63.2	53	57.6	38	38	14.4	0.002
Somatic complaints	9	100.0	55	57.9	45	48.9	29	29	27.8	0.0000
Any hallucinations	0	—	28	22.0	13	14.1	9	9	15.2	0.0005
Curvilinear relationship with age										
Fatigue	8	88.9	62	65.3	66	71.7	97	97	33.4	0.0000
Agitation	7	77.8	57	60.0	38	41.3	67	67	15.2	0.001
Anorexia	9	100.0	30	31.6	33	35.9	80	80	65.0	0.0001
Nonsignificant relationship with age										
Depressed mood	9	100.0	86	90.5	81	88.0	100	100	12.9	0.004
Poor concentration	5	55.6	71	74.7	73	79.3	84	84	5.4	0.140
Insomnia	9	100.0	57	60.0	58	63.0	71	71	7.6	0.054
Suicidal ideation	6	66.7	48	50.5	45	48.9	0	—	5.2	0.156
Suicide attempts	0	0	24	25.3	31	33.7	15	15	9.1	0.010

[a]From study by Kashani and Carlson (11).
[b]From study by Ryan et al. (8).
[c]From study by Baker et al. (4).

Kiddie-SADS-P cutoff designating mild symptom severity eliminated the significance only of hopelessness ($\chi^2=9.3$, p=0.009), psychomotor retardation ($\chi^2=6.3$, p=0.09), and agitation ($\chi^2=5.2$, p=0.15). Third, the preschool sample was significantly smaller than the others, although this is because major depression was so rare in the 1,000 children studied to procure the group. Finally, assessment procedures for *DSM-III* and *DSM-III-R* diagnoses are not precisely the same across the age groups. The cognitive limitations of very young children preclude the use of verbally mediated structured interviews to make *DSM-III* diagnoses. Similarly, parent interviews are not terribly relevant in the adult samples.

On the positive side, the methodology was quite similar in that each study had accepted subjects from psychiatrically referred samples and only if they met specific criteria. In addition, ascertainment of criteria was systematic and done by state-of-the-art assessment procedures. The criteria (Feighner et al., RDC, *DSM-III*) were, for the most part, the same. Finally, while better methodology is desirable, it seems unlikely that any single institution or collaborative study will undertake the sys-

tematic examination of people from ages 2½ to more than 60 years in the foreseeable future.

Categories of significant findings included those in which the symptoms increase in frequency with age, those in which they decrease in frequency, those which have a curvilinear distribution, and those symptoms not significantly altered with increasing age.

Those symptoms which increase with age confirm some of what we know about age and depression. Anhedonia, diurnal variation, psychomotor retardation, and delusions are symptoms of psychotic depression that may become more prominent syndromically in older adults (12). The presence of delusions is difficult to establish in young children; although the kinds of delusions seen in depressed adults (i.e., guilt, poverty, disease) may occur in children, they are significantly less frequent (13). The concept of hopelessness seems to require some perspective of the future, which is more abstract than one sees in children. In fact, it was not felt that this symptom could even be reliably ascertained in preschool children. On the other hand, as Kazdin et al. (14) have reported, children experience hopelessness more frequently than heretofore suspected.

Depressive symptoms that become less prominent with increased age give us some clues about other age-related alterations in psychopathology. Depressed appearance was not reported in Baker et al.'s study of adults (4), and its prominence in early childhood had diminished by adolescence. Kashani and Carlson (11) have noted the importance of somatic complaints in preschool children. The significance of a higher frequency of hallucinations in childhood depression is less obvious. However, if one defines hallucinations stringently, such that the child is *certain* the hallucinations are a reality, the difference in frequency disappears. Hallucinatory phenomena in children are not rare and may not have the diagnostic specificity they have in adults (13, 15, 16).

Fatigue, agitation, and poor appetite occurred frequently in preschoolers and adults and less frequently in children and adolescents. It is possible that these symptoms have different meanings at different ages. Temper tantrums and irritability, rather than pacing and hand wringing, are the ways in which one customarily defines agitation in young children. Although these behaviors were clearly more common in depressed preschool children than in nondepressed psychiatric control subjects (10), such temperamental behavior is not diagnostically specific. Similarly, picky eating and unenthusiastic appetites are, as parents of preschoolers will testify, quite common. On the other hand, adults are not homogeneous developmentally. Elderly depressed subjects apparently experience more agitation, hypochondriasis, and initial insomnia than young adults

with depression, suggesting that some symptoms may increase again in old age (17).

Symptoms that did not change with age included depressed mood (by definition), diminished ability to concentrate (at least as measured by drop in school performance), sleep disturbance, and suicidal ideation. The fact that the last problem occurred in over half the patients *regardless of age* is interesting. The observation that suicide per se is infrequent in children, especially compared to the frequency of suicidal ideation and attempts, has no ready explanation. Lack of sustained interest in suicide and lack of ability to plan a successful suicide are among some of the possible reasons for this disparity (18).

In summary, data comparisons made in this paper, although not without limitations, confirm observations that have been made anecdotally. Age and development may alter some of the manifestations of depression and make certain signs and symptoms more or less prominent. There is, of course, the tautology that all samples were selected with a preconceived notion of what constitutes major depression. Hence, we cannot clarify the question of alternate forms of depression occurring at different ages, nor can we comment on whether some other signs or symptoms not regularly asked about have additional significance. Nonetheless, while there appear to be several specific developmental modifications, at least on the basis of the diverse sampling of age groups from different studies, the basic symptom picture of serious depressive disorder was relatively unchanged regardless of age.

References

1. Weinberg, W. A., Rutman, J., Sullivan, L., et al.: Depression in children referred to an educational diagnostic center: diagnosis and treatment. J Pediatr 1973; 83:1065–1072

2. Bemporad, J. R., Wilson, A.: A developmental approach to depression in childhood and adolescence. J Am Acad Psychoanal 1978; 6:325–352

3. Herzog, D. B., Rathbun, J. M.: Childhood depression: developmental considerations. Am J Dis Child 1982; 138:115–120

4. Baker, M., Dorzob, J., Winokur, G., et al.: Depressive disease: classification and clinical characteristics. Compr Psychiatry 1971; 12:354–365

5. Feighner, J. P., Robins, E., Guze, S. B., et al.: Diagnostic criteria for use in psychiatric research. Arch Gen Psychiatry 1972; 26:57–63

6. Spitzer, R. L., Endicott, J., Robins, E.: Research Diagnostic Criteria: rationale and reliability. Arch Gen Psychiatry 1978; 35:773–782

7. Spitzer, R. L., Endicott, J.: Schedule for Affective Disorders and Schizophrenia. New York, New York State Psychiatric Institute, Biometrics Research, 1978

8. Ryan, N. D., Puig-Antich, J., Ambrosini, P., et al.: The clinical picture of major depression in children and adolescents. Arch Gen Psychiatry 1987; 44:854–861

9. Chambers, W. J., Puig-Antich, J., Hirsch, M., et al.: The assessment of affective disorders in children and adolescents by semi-structured interview: test-retest reliability of the K-SADS-P. Arch Gen Psychiatry 1985; 42:696–702

10. Kashani, J. H., Ray, J. S., Carlson, G. A.: Depression and Depressive-like states in preschool-age children in a child development unit. Am J psychiatry 1984; 141:1397–1402

11. Kashani, J. H., Carlson, G. A.: Seriously depressed preschoolers. Am J Psychiatry 1987; 144:348–350
12. Gurland, B. J.: The comparative frequency of depression in various adult age groups. J Gerontol 1976; 31:283–292
13. Chambers, W. J., Puig-Antich, J., Tabrizi, M. A., et al.: Psychotic symptoms in prepubertal major depressive disorder. Arch Gen Psychiatry 1982; 39:921–927
14. Kazdin, A. E., French, N. H., Unis, A. S., et al.: Hopelessness, depression and suicidal intent among psychiatrically disturbed inpatient children. J Consult Clin Psychol 1983; 51:504–510
15. Rothstein, A.: Hallucinatory phenomena in childhood: a critique of the literature. J Am Acad Child Psychiatry 1981; 20:623–635
16. Kotsopoulos, S., Kanigsberg, J., Cote, A., et al.: Hallucinatory experiences in non-psychotic children. J Am Acad Child Psychiatry 1987; 26:375–380
17. Brown, R. P., Sweeney, J., Loutsch, E., et al.: Involuntional melancholia revisited. Am J Psychiatry 1984; 141:24–28
18. Carlson, G. A., Asarnow, J. R., Orbach, I.: Developmental aspects of suicidal behavior in children, I. J Am Acad Child Adolesc Psychiatry 1987; 26:186–192

20

DEPRESSION IN WOMEN:
THE CHALLENGE OF TREATMENT AND PREVENTION

Verona C. Gordon
School of Nursing
University of Minnesota, Minneapolis

Linda E. Ledray
Sexual Assault Resource Service
Hennepin County Medical Center, Minneapolis

Recent research reports on the incidence of depression indicate women preponderate in all age groups and in most countries. This finding appears to be more than an artifact of data collection techniques or health care utilization factors.

With such a large number of women evidencing symptoms of depression and seeking treatment, it is imperative that psychosocial nurses [and other helping professionals—Ed.] better understand the evidence available concerning the suggested mechanisms of etiology. This is important because a better understanding of the issues involved will facilitate the development and utilization of more efficacious treatment strategies to meet the needs of this ever-growing population.

ARE WOMEN REALLY MORE DEPRESSED?

Evidence suggests that the rate of depression in women is twice that of men. Is this actually the case or do these data instead reflect a higher use of mental health facilities by women? Are women more willing than men to admit they are depressed and to seek professional help? Does it indicate a tendency for mental health professionals to more frequently label women as depressed than men?

Weissman and Klerman (1977) did an extensive review of data from clinical observations, surveys of persons not under treatment; and studies of suicide and suicide attempters. The data were strikingly consistent across these various populations. The 2:1 sex ratio was upheld across studies in the United States, as well as in most foreign countries. This was true both for studies based on individuals in treatment and community surveys.

While more men are successful suicide completers, women rank first in suicide attempts with a 2:1 ratio. Based on the community survey, they con-

clude that the statistics are not an artifact of women being more willing to seek care.

When compared to men, one consistent finding throughout the literature is that while women preponderate in depressive populations, this is accounted for almost totally by higher rates for married women (Radloff and Rae, 1979; Thrunher, 1976; van Keep and Prill, 1975; Nathanson, 1975; Coleman and Miller, 1975; Weissman and Klerman).

Married women are consistently found to have higher rates of depression than single, widowed, or divorced women, and single, married, divorced, or widowed men. Marriage thus appears to have a protective effect for men and a detrimental effect on women.

Consistent with these data is the finding of the NIMH, National Institute of Aging (NIA) Workshop on the Older Women (1978) indicating that after the age of 65 men become more depressed, nearly equaling the rate seen earlier with women. They attribute this to the impact of environmental stress and changes in role which men experience after retiring.

Helgason (1979) found in a prospective epidemiological investigation of affective disorder that the female predominance decreases with increasing age. This was felt to be the result of a substantial increase in the rates of depression in both men and women 76 years of age and older, but especially in men. While the estimated expectancies through 62 years of age were 6.8%, this figure rose to 12.2% at 76 years of age.

In attempting to address the concern that women surpass men in documented evidence because they are more likely to identify and acknowledge depression, Paykel, Prusoff, and Uhlenhuth (1971) evaluated women's response to stress. The specific question was if women rate the same situations as more stressful than men. While some indi-

From *Journal of Psychosocial Nursing*, 1985, 23(1):26–34. Reprinted by permission.

vidual differences were found in ratings of how upsetting life events were, they did not find a significant difference based on sex.

GENETIC TRANSMISSION

Significantly different incidence rates have been found between males and females in genetic studies of depression. While females preponderate in unipolar depressive populations, the sex distribution in bipolar illness is nearly equal (Zerbin-Rudin, 1979). The initiation of the Danish Central Psychiatric Registry in 1920 (Bertelsen, Harvald, and Hauge, 1977) and the Danish Twin Registry has made possible an extensive and comprehensive investigation of twins with affective disorders in that country.

Numerous studies comparing rates of depression of monozygotic (MZ) and dizygotic (DZ) twins have confirmed the hypothesis that a strong genetic component exists for bipolar depressive psychosis. Bertelsen et al. found that MZ twins pairwise concordance rates for bipolar affective disorder are much higher than DZ twins across studies.

In addition, the number of discordant MZ twins observed indicated that other factors, primarily environmental, also play a significant role. While the evidence remains conflicting and inconclusive, reports of twin studies today generally support one of two theories.

Gershon, Bunney, Lockman, et al. (1976) proposed a multithreshold explanation, which included a genetic, environmental interaction. This model postulates a genetically determined susceptibility to affective illness with two or more thresholds. As environmental factors raise an individual's liability past the first threshold, a unipolar psychosis occurs. Surpassing the second threshold results in a bipolar illness.

An important point made by Gershon et al., (1979) is that the concordance rates for depression in MZ twins with exactly the same genes is not 100%, as one might expect, but rather 70%.

This demonstration allows for the premise that considerable variability may be due to other factors, including possible environmental influences. An extension of this multithreshold model to account for the higher percentage of women in unipolar depression populations would result in an additional lower unipolar threshold for women.

An alternative theory suggests that these two illnesses are genetically separate entities. Considerable difficulty has occurred in attempts to evaluate the data, however, since both illnesses will occur in the same family (Zerbin-Rudin) and agreement as to criteria for diagnostic classification has been difficult to standardize (Akiskal, Rosenthal, Rosenthal, et al. 1979).

One of the most debated hypotheses results from the substantial number of depressed females in the population and the X-linked inheritance theory. If the gene for depression is located on the X-chromosome and is a dominant trait, females who have two X-chromosomes would indeed be expected to be affected twice as often as males who have only one X-chromosome.

Studies evaluating this issue are, however, often in direct opposition. While inconclusive, initial research presented evidence suggesting an X-linked dominant genetic factor was involved in the transmission of bipolar affective disorder (Winokur, 1970). This is a curious finding in light of the large number of women in the unipolar affective populations, not bipolar populations.

In addition, more sophisticated recent studies (Lechman, Gershon, McGinniss, et al., 1979; Gershon, Targum, Matthysse, et al., 1979) have refuted the hypothesis that bipolar affective psychoses is transmitted by a single major gene of the X-chromosome.

The most crucial evidence against the X-linkage hypothesis is the occurrence of father-son transmission (Mendlewicz and Rainer, 1974; Goetzl, Green, Whybrow, et al., 1974). This finding is significant since an X-linked trait could not be transmitted from a father to his son. Only daughters receive their father's X-chromosome. The conclusions are obfuscated, however, because it is possible that the mother is also either suffering from the disorder or a latent carrier.

ENDOCRINOLOGICAL FACTORS

Another biological factor that has received considerable attention is the relationship between female hormones and affective illness. This is of interest due to the frequence of depression related to the post-partum period, menopause, the use of oral contraceptives, and the menstrual cycle.

Depression has long been recognized as the most common psychological side effect of oral contraceptive use (Raye, 1963). However, serious methodological problems are incurred in the majority of the studies that address this problem. They typically employ no control groups, are not blind, and all too often include only women who have come for medical attention.

A recent blind study by Fleming and Seager (1978) found no difference in the incidence of depression between users of oral contraceptives and matched controls. This study reported that the incidence of depression more significantly related to age, personality, and occupation. Fleming and Seager also found that older women, with higher neuroticism scores, not working outside the home, were more likely to be depressed.

A similar situation is found in studies relating depression to the menstrual cycle. Once again depression is a frequently recognized primary problem associated with premenstrual tension.

As with studies of oral contraceptives, however, reviews of research in this area have indicated considerable problems with response biases and social expectations (Sommer, 1973; Parlee, 1973). The use of patient populations to collect information, rather than community surveys of healthy adult women, is also of concern because it results in the collection of biased data (Hertz, Steiner, Zuckerman, et al., 1971).

Dalton (1980) reported three intriguing case studies in which women successfully pleaded diminished responsibility in a London Court for charges of manslaughter, arson, and assault, which they claimed was the result of premenstrual tension. The histories from police and prison reports revealed recurrence of violent offenses at monthly intervals peaking at the 29th and 30th day of their menstrual cycle.

Since then Dalton has treated about 20,000 women in England for PMS (Premenstrual Tension Syndrome) and the notion of diagnosing and treating depressed women with progesterone for PMS has gained widespread credibility in various areas of the United States.

The same biochemical etiological factors are in question regarding postpartum depression. Handley, Dunn, Baker, et al. (1977) found an increase in blood tryptophan level positively correlated with depression four days post-partum (N = 18). This finding has not been replicated, however, except by the same research team (Handley, Dunn, Waldron, et al., 1980).

In response to the Handley, et al. initial findings, Harris (1980) attempted to treat 55 bottle-feeding mothers with L-tryptophan in a double-blind study with a placebo group. While 70% of their population experienced some degree of postpartum depression, they did not find a differential response based on the L-tryptophan therapy.

Nott, Franklin, Armitage, et al. (1976) reached the same conclusion regarding the etiological impact of hormones on post-partum depression. While they did not find L-tryptophan therapy was correlated with depression, they did find that depressed mood in the six weeks before birth and a history of premenstrual tension were predictive of depressive mood post-partum.

Unfortunately, Harris did not evaluate blood levels of tryptophan. This confounds the conclusions one might draw. One possible conclusion might be that while tryptophan levels and post-partum depression are correlated they are not causally related. Therefore patients could not be expected to respond differentially to the use of tryptophan as the therapeutic intervention measure.

Depression associated with menopause is another topic of concern. Until recently involutional melancholia has been an official diagnostic classification of the American Psychiatric Association. A distinct pattern of symptoms has been identified in the Diagnostic and Statistical Manual of Mental Disorders (DSM-II) and in reported research projects (Notman, 1979; LaRocco and Polit, 1980).

Numerous studies have found, however, that while this symptom pattern is often identified in women of this age group, the only symptom consistently identified in relation to menopause are vasomotor instability manifested as hot flashes and the subsequent profuse perspiration (LaRocco and Polit).

Two primary etiological theories are suggested to account for this symptom pattern. The first is a biological theory relating the effects to hormonal imbalances resulting from a lowering of estrogen levels. The second theory suggests the syndrome is actually the result of social-cultural influences and the basic personality structure of the individual.

Researchers have attempted to establish the validity of the biological theory by showing that estrogen replacement theory can eliminate the psychological symptoms of menopause, such as depression (Kerr and Vaughn, 1975).

While an intuitively reasonable hypothesis, Campbell and Whitehead (1977) found in double-blind, randomized, cross-over placebo trials that a placebo was effective in relieving many menopausal symptoms, including vaginal dryness, memory problems, urinary frequency, and coital disinterest.

In addition, recent concern has been raised regarding the prevalence of routine estrogen therapy in menopausal women. Weinstein (1980) cautions against this practice, except in specifically identified patient populations.

The second theory suggesting the importance of psychosocial and cultural factors has recently received considerable support. A number of researchers have suggested that symptoms of the menopausal syndrome are a socially acceptable target for the expression of needs that actually have etiologies other than biological. These stem from midlife stress with personal, family, social, and cultural impact and demands on the women (Notman).

While researchers often recognize menopause as a factor, it is the environmental and psychological stress on the woman, not biological changes, that are felt to be responsible for symptoms such as depression at this period.

BEHAVIORAL THERAPY

Three theoretical models provide the central focus for the psychosocial etiological explanation of the high rates of depression in women. These include Lewinsohn's (1974) behavioral explanation, Seligman's (1975) learned helplessness model, and Beck's (1979) cognitive model. Recently, attempts have been made to integrate these theoretical models and provide a more comprehensive understanding of the issues involved (Abramson, Seligman, Teasdale, 1978; Eastman, 1976).

From a behavioral point of view, depression results when a woman is no longer in a position where she is receiving frequent positive reinforcement. This deficit of positive reinforcement is most likely to correspond with a reduction in social activity and/or social contact (Lewinsohn).

Consistent with this explanation, the sex role stereotyping in our culture has repeatedly been identified by researchers as of primary significance in the high incidence of depression with women (Weissman, 1979; Nathanson, Kilpatrick, 1975). Thus stereotyping appears to result in significant limitations of available social, vocational, and personal opportunities for women, especially married women.

Evaluating the impact of role restrictions for women from a behavioral approach, a number of factors appear significant. Brown, Bhrolchain, and Harris (1975) found an important variable separating depressive from nondepressive married women was employment outside the home. Employment helped prevent depression in women under the same level of stress as those not employed. Lack of employment outside the home was found to severely restrict a woman's social contacts and thus social support and reinforcement.

Unemployed, married women consistently reported frustration with their roles. Housewives have few alternative sources of gratification. Their work is unskilled, unstructured, relatively invisible, and of very low social prestige. Little job satisfaction is obtained from housework by most women, who expressed boredom, a lack of ego strength, and low sense of personal worth or achievement.

The absence of an intimate supportive relationship with the husband or boyfriend also greatly increased the risk of depression in women (Brown et al.).

While the unemployed housewife is less common today due to recent social change and the high economic demands on a family, women are still often expected to defer their career goals to those of their husband. Weissman, Pincus, Radding, et al. (1973) found these career disruptions frequently result in depression among women.

Often the husband's career necessitated a geographic relocation, resulting in a loss of employment for the women. They postulated that this geographic instability, coupled with a separation from traditional group and religious affiliations and support, was responsible for their high rates of depression. They also found the depression subsided when the women returned to work.

Even when women do work, however, their expected deferential position to their husbands often results in their accepting jobs that provide less satisfaction and personal rewards (Nathanson).

The Empty Nest Syndrome, in addition to role restrictions, is another precipitant of depression frequently encountered in women. Rates of depression are high for women just after their children leave home with the abrupt loss of the maternal role and its rewards (Oliver, 1977).

Powell (1977) found employment outside the home prior to this time helped assuage the impact of role disruption and loss of self-esteem precipitating the depression. In the 80 women interviewed, all in the empty nest stage, a direct inverse relationship was found between employment outside the home and rates of depression. The unemployed were the most depressed, those employed part time experienced intermediate rates, and those employed full time were doing the best.

As long as the children remained at home, employment was not found to be as significant a factor in this study. Once the children left the home, however, the homemakers found the experience quite traumatic, while the career oriented women did not.

McLean (1982) has been critical of the field of behavior research in that it has been slow to focus attention on what he describes as the "common cold" of mental health, clinical depression. Behavior therapies focus on the alteration of personal behavior in depressed individuals in the belief that this is the most effective way to change negative thoughts and ideas.

Over the last 10 years, Lewinsohn and his colleagues have conducted the most systematic research programs to develop a behavioral theory of depression. Their efforts have been focused in two areas: determination of the relationships between pleasant and unpleasant mood-related events and depression and the functional relationship between social competence and depression.

Social competence is related to depression in as much as it represents a powerful means of influencing social reinforcement. The essential component of Lewinsohn's theory is response-contingent positive reinforcement.

McLean was critical of Lewinsohn's work in stating that it is not empirically established in controlled clinical studies. He writes that although depressed clients may increase their involvement in activities by behavioral strategies of reinforcing pleasant events, many depressed individuals may have a "ho-hum" attitude toward pleasant events thinking, "these events would be fun, if I deserved to enjoy them."

Furthermore, McLean believes the standardized "pleasant events" lose their reinforcing properties because they are not seen as terribly relevant in context to the depressed client's backlog of "unresolved and nagging personal problems."

Barron (1966) believes depressed people may avoid reinforcing pleasant activities because persons who are depressed are uncomfortable at the attention they may earn while completing these events.

Padfield (1976) studied 24 rural women of low socioeconomic status. He compared the efficacy of a behavioral approach that focused on increasing the rate of pleasant activities with the efficacy of a nondirective counseling approach. The women received weekly treatment on an individual basis for three months. Results did not favor one approach over the other.

A variety of sources suggest that social factors play an important role in the causation, maintenance, and therapeutic resolution of clinical depression. Basically, the social-interaction model subscribes to the belief that individuals receive their sense of self-esteem from others through interactions by means of social reinforcement—approval, acceptance, recognition, support, etc.

Youngren and Lewinsohn (1977) found depressed people interact socially at lower rates, receive and offer less social reinforcement, report lower levels of enjoyment of those interactions in which they engage, worry more about social interactions, are less comfortable in asserting themselves, and display less skill in social interactions.

Bothwell and Weissman (1977) report social deficits in the functioning of their female subjects well beyond the acute episode of their depression, thus suggesting the presence of a learning deficit.

That family members and relatives of depressed patients are able to induce relapses by clients to further depression by means of surprisingly little verbal criticism was found by Vaughn and Leff (1976).

Coyne (1976) and Hammen and Peters (1978) write that interactions between depressed and nondepressed persons may be intentionally avoided because of the mutually aversive effect they have on each other.

Taylor and Marshall (1977) employed behavioral techniques designed to produce positive reinforcements in the depressed client's social interactions. These depressed subjects improved significantly, but not differentially, in comparison with a cognitive-treatment group.

McLean and Hakstain's (1979) research found socially active clients to be significantly less prone to depression at retesting three months later. This reinforces the idea that social interaction rates and the experience of depressed mood may be related.

While there is a critical mass of empirical data that establishes a relationship between depressed mood and social skills, there is some indication that social deficits are the result of learning rather than of performance. The potential for theory and treatment development within the social interaction model from a behavioral viewpoint is tremendous (McLean).

LEARNED HELPLESSNESS

The second theoretical model, Seligman's learned helplessness model, while concerned with environmental reinforcement similar to the behavioral model, places its primary focus on the individual's perceived control over reinforcement. According to this model, learned helplessness results when the individual believes that environmental reinforcement is not dependent upon his or her behavior.

It is not the loss of reinforcement that is central, but rather the loss of control over reinforcement. Women are in essence "helpless" in managing their environment. As a result, symptoms of depression develop. These include withdrawal, loss of motivation for any activity, and a lowered ability to learn or attempt new behaviors that could result in future environmental control. There is also a concomitant belief in a lack of competence and a loss of self-esteem.

Areas of stress for women's feelings of helplessness encompass the field of sexual harassment and exploitation that women experience, such as physical and sexual abuse. Additional areas of stress are also manifested in the process of marriage, separation, divorce and childbearing.

Belle's (1982) studies of impoverished women who headed families without spouses exemplified the realm of legal and economic helplessness women encounter. This helplessness arises from situations of too many children to support, a recent separation or divorce, and the overall daily concerns that contribute greatly to the women's feelings of powerlessness and learned helplessness.

This feeling of powerlessness is one that inhibits the women's ability to cope with the situation and to determine how to handle current problems. There is also the feeling that "nothing a person does matters in whether or not rewards are obtained" (Beck).

Divorce appears to have a devastating effect on women who have been given low status and are economically dependent on their husbands. As a result of this dependency, women also develop learned helplessness, which Seligman's experiments indicate lead to depression.

Guttentag, Salasian, and Belle (1980) contend that this depression arises when life places too many demands on the low-income single mother and when there are few resources available to help her.

The concept of helplessness with loss of motivation to change is also part of the triad of negative cognition explained by Beck's (1979) theories on depression.

Although the study by Klein, Fencil-Morse, and Seligman (1976) found that depressed subjects were more likely to attribute failure to their own abilities than were nondepressed subjects, McLean states "the theory of learned helplessness has generated no unique treatment interventions."

McLean goes on to explain that clients are subjected to a variety of sources of social influence in the time when they are not in therapy. He promotes the idea of subjecting effective treatments to a "dismantling process" to learn which forms of treatment would be most useful. He also believes that theory construction would logically follow, stating that procedures without supporting theories are limited.

COGNITIVE THERAPY

The third theory of significance is Beck's cognitive model. Beck and other cognitive psychologists theorize that depression results from a misinterpretation or exaggeration of the negative meaning of losses or other environmental events.

Individuals become depressed because they view everything in their life, past, present, and future, with a sense of failure. All difficulties are attributed to their personal failure, resulting in a complete lack of self-esteem and ego strength. They see themselves and the outside world in a totally negative sense, anticipating only the worst. This negative view of the self and the world pervades their conscious experiences.

In a study on depression currently underway in Minneapolis, Evans and Hollon (1981) found that when asked to rate their mood during the day, at the end of the day, depressives consistently rated it as rather depressed. When these same individuals were asked to keep track of their mood every hour, in only several of these hourly ratings did they report feeling depressed.

Consistent with the cognitive model, however, these were the times they rememberd and focused on when asked to do the rating retrospectively. The last two theories will be considered together in order to provide a more complete conceptualization of the etiology of depression.

When considering the high incidence of depression in women from this point of view, the role restrictions and social-cultural role expectations of women appear once again to be central factors. This would be most significant with the married, unemployed housewife—the group who do indeed experience the highest rates of depression. These women are usually economically helpless and dependent on their husbands. They may have experienced career goal frustrations due to their deferential position, and thus be experiencing motivational deficits common in depression (Seligman).

In many respects the recent social changes of the feminist movement have aggravated the problem for large numbers of women. Today there is a greater discrepancy than even between expectations of women and the reality of their fulfillment. As Beck and others have recognized, this allows for more cognitive dissonance and achievement conflict.

Traditional feminine behavior centered around passivity, compliance, and receptivity. Behavior important for a woman's social acceptance and approval has traditionally been widely divergent and potentially in conflict with the ambitious, competitive, and aggressive behavior often needed for attaining career goals.

Notman, Nadelson, and Bennett note that one result of this conflict is avoidance. Problems that arise in the business world may be denied, or the woman will often attempt to resolve the problem by being "good" and helpful, consistent with the feminine role. When this approach fails or is met with a loss of ground, feelings of helplessness, powerlessness, and depression may occur.

Amidst a plethora of possible etiological explanations the overall picture appears to indicate multiple factors contributing to a woman's vulnerability to depression. Since significantly different rates of depression occur in married and unmarried women, however, it is evident that other factors, such as role expectations, also appear to have an important contributory role in the development of depression.

Rush (1982) states:

> . . . there is no evidence to date that manic-depressive or bipolar depressions respond to behavioral, cognitive, or other psychotherapeutic maneuvers. Rather lithium or antidepressant medications provide both symptom relief and prophylaxis in majority of these disorders . . . the fact that affective disorders are differentially responsive to the psychotherapies suggests strongly that there are both specific and unique effects obtained in psychotherapy that are not obtained by other treatments.

In light of this multifactorial picture, what can be done to treat or prevent the perpetuation of this very pervasive problem?

TREATMENT AND PREVENTION

Two basic concerns remain with treatment and prevention issues. First, while there has been a proliferation of programs to treat depression, treatment usually begins after the depression has reached a more serious clinical level. Depression at the subclinical level continues to go unrecognized and thus unresolved.

Second, all too often the sex role stereotyping pervasive in society in general occurs within the mental health professional community as well. This is an especially significant issue in light of the subsequent expectations for the outcome of the therapeutic process. All too often the goal is to ease the woman's compliance with the expected feminine role.

The first primary treatment concern is the lack of early identification and resolution of depression. It is unnecessary to provide treatment only when depression has reached a more serious clinical level (Beck). Rather, symptoms of subclinical depression in women should be identified and treatment programs such as self-help growth groups established to help the women deal with their depression early.

The second treatment issue was addressed very dramatically in the widely cited study of Broverman, Broverman, Clarkson, et al. (1970). The Broverman study reported that mental health clinicians characterize a healthy female very differently from a healthy male or a healthy adult, sex unspecified.

The healthy female was seen as more passive, submissive, less dependent, easily influenced, more excitable in a minor crisis, more emotional, less logical, less self-confident, and more subjective than her male counterpart.

In contrast, healthy adult males were characterized as manifesting more socially desirable traits such as ambition, competitiveness, directness, and having an easier time making decisions.

More recent studies of this issue have found that sex role stereotyping is a more serious problem with male therapists. Female therapists tend to have more contemporary attitudes toward women patients (Brown, and Hellinger, 1975). In addition, older, more experienced female therapists tended to rate women and men the most similarly, with the least stereotyping.

While the survey's hypothesis was that social workers would be the professionals with the most contemporary attitudes towards women, this was not the case. Consistent with the findings of Kjervik and Palta (1978) psychiatric nurses were identified as a professional group adhering to the fewest traditional sex role stereotypic attitudes.

All too often traditional treatment approaches reinforce the passivity and negative self-image of women, thus perpetuating the problem, rather than resolving the depression (Weissman and Klerman). While psychiatric nurses as a professional group appear to have begun to recognize and deal with the subtleties of sexism, many individuals and other professional groups must yet do so.

References

Abramson, L. Y., Seligman, M. E., Teasdale, J. D. Learned helplessness in humans: Critique and reformulation. *Journal of Abnormal Psychology* 1978; 87(1):49–74.

Akiskal, H. S., Rosenthal, R. H., Rosenthal, T. L., Kashgarian, M., Khani, M. K., Puzantian, V. R. Differentiation of primary affective illness from situational, symptomatic, and secondary depressions. *Archives of General Psychiatry* 1979; 36:635–643.

Barron, R. M. Social reinforcement effects as a function of social reinforcement history. *Psychological Review* 1966; 73:527–539.

Beck, C. T. The occurrence of depression in women and the effect of the women's movement. *Journal of Psychiatric Nursing and Mental Health Services* 1979; 17(11):14–16.

Belle, D. *Lives in Stress: Women and Depression*. Beverly Hills, California: Sage Publications, 1982.

Bertelsen, A., Harvald, B., Hauge, M. A. Danish twin study of manic-depressive disorders. *British Journal of Psychiatry* 1977; 130:330–351.

Broverman, I. K., Broverman, D., Clarkson, F. E., Rosenkrantz, P., Vogel, S. R. Sex-role stereotypes and clinical judgments of mental health. *Journal of Counseling and Clinical Psychology* 1970; 34:1–7.

Bothwell, S., Weissman, M., Social impairment four years after an acute depressive episode. *American Journal of Orthopsychiatry* 1977; 47:231–237.

Brown, C. R., Hellinger, M. L. Therapists' attitudes towards women. *Social Work* 1975; 21:266–270.

Brown, G. W., Bhrolchain, M. N., Harris, T. Social class and psychiatric disturbance among women in an urban population. *Sociology 1975*, (9):225–254.

Campbell, S., Whitehead, M. Estrogen therapy and the menopausal syndrome. *Clinics in Obstetrics and Gynaecology* 1977; 4(1):31–47.

Coyne, J. C. Depression and the response of others. *Journal of Abnormal Psychology* 1976; 85:186–193.

Eastman, C. Behavioral formulations of depression. *Psychological Review* 1976; 83:277–291.

Evans, M. D., Hollon, S., unpublished data, 1980.

Feeley, E., Pyne, H. The menopause: Facts and misconceptions. *Nursing Forum* 1975; 14(1):75–86.

Fleming, O., Seager, C. P. Incidence of depressive symptoms in users of the oral contraceptive. *British Journal of Psychiatry* 1978; 132:431–440.

Gershon, E. S., Bunney, W. E., Leckman, J. F., et al. The inheritance of affective disorders: A review of data and of hypotheses. *Behavior Genetics* 1976; 6:227.

Gershon, E. S., Targum, S. D., Matthysse, S., et al. Color blindness not closely linked to bipolar illnesses. *Archives of General Psychiatry* 1979; 36:1423–1430.

Goetzl, U., Green, R., Whybrow, P., et al. X-linkage revisited: A further family history study of manic-depressive illness. *Archives of General Psychiatry* 1974; 31:665–672.

Guttentag, M., Salasin, S., Belle, D. *The Mental Health of Women*. New York: Academic Press, Inc., 1980.

Hammen, C. L., Peters, S. D. Interpersonal consequences of depression: Response to men and women enacting a depressed role. *Journal of Abnormal Psychology* 1978; 87:322–332.

Handley, S. L., Dunn, T. L., Baker, J. M., et al. Mood changes in puerperium and plasma tryptophan and cortisol concentration. *British Medical Journal* 1977; 2(6078):18–20.

Handley, S. L., Dunn, T. L., Waldron, G., et al. Tryptophan, cortisol and puerperal mood. *British Journal of Psychiatry* 1980; 136:498–508.

Harris, B. Prospective trial of L-tryptophan in maternity blues. *British Journal of Psychiatry* 1980; 137:233–235.

Helgason, T. Epidemiological investigations concerning affective disorders, in Schoo, M., Stromgren, E. (eds.): *Origin, Prevention, and Treatment of Affective Disorders*. New York: Academic Press, Inc., 1979.

Hertz, D. G., Steiner, J. E., Zuckerman, H., et al. Psychological and physical symptom-formation in menopause. *Psycho-therapy and Psychosomatics* 1971; 19:47–52.

Kerr, D., Vaughn, C. Psychohormonal treatment during menopause. *American Family Physician* 1975; 11(2):99–103.

Kilpatrick, D. G. Depression among women: A behavioral analysis. Presented at *The female patient: Or, impatient women as outpatients*. Southeastern Psychological Association, Atlanta, 1975.

Kjervik, D. K., Palta, M. Sex-role stereotyping in assessments of mental health. *Nursing Research* 1978; 27(3):166–171.

Klein, D. F., Fencil-Morse, E., Seligman, M. E. P. Learned helplessness, depression and the attribution of failure. *Journal of Personality and Social Psychology* 1976; 33:508–516.

LaRocco, S. A., Polit, D. F. Women's knowledge about the menopause. *Nursing Research* 1980; 29:10–13.

Leckman, J. F., Gershon, E. S., McGinniss, M. H., et al. New Data Do Not Suggest Linkage Between the Xg Blood Group and Bipolar Illness. *Archives of General Psychiatry* 1979; (36):1435–1441.

Lewinsohn, P. M. A behavioral approach to depression, in Friedman, T. M., Katz, M. M. (eds.): *The Psychology of Depression; Contemporary Theory and Research*. Washington: V.H. Winston, 1974.

Lewinsohn, P. M., Shaffer, M. Use of home observations as an integral part of the treatment of depression. *Journal of Consulting and Clinical Psychology* 1971; 37:87–94.

Maoz, B., Antonovsky, A., Apter, A., et al. The perception of menopause in five ethnic groups in Israel. *Acta Obstetrics Gynecology Scandinavia Suppl* 1977; 65:69–76.

McLean, P. Behavioral therapy: Theory and research, in Rush, A. J. (ed.): *Short-term Psychotherapies for Depression*. New York: Guilford Press, 1982, vol. 2, pp. 19–45.

McLean, P. D., Hakstain, A. R. Clinical depression: Comparative efficacy of outpatient treatments. *Journal of Consulting and Clinical Psychology* 1979; 47:818–836.

Mendlewicz, J., Rainer, J. D. Morbidity risk and genetic transmission in manic-depressive illness. *American Journal Human Genetics* 1974; 26:692–698.

Nathanson, C. A. Illness and the feminine role: A theoretical review. *Social Science and Medicine* 1975; 9(2):57–62.

Notman, M. Midlife concerns in women: Implications of the menopause. *American Journal of Psychiatry* 1979; 136:1270–1274.

Notman, M. T., Nadelson, C. C., Bennett, M. B. Achievement conflict in women. *Psychotherapy and Psychosomatics* 1978; 29:203–213.

Nott, P. N., Franklin, M., Armitage, C., et al. Hormonal Changes and Mood in the Puerperium. *British Journal of Psychiatry* 1976; (128):379–383.

Oliver, R. The "empty nest syndrome" as a focus of depression: A cognitive treatment model, based on rational emotive therapy. *Psychotherapy: Theory, Research and Practice* 1977; 14(1):87–94.

Osofsky, H. J., Seidenberg, F., Seidenberg, R. Is female menopausal depression inevitable? *Obstetrics and Gynecology* 1970; 36:611–615.

Padfield, M. The comparative effects of two counseling approaches on the intensity of depression among rural women of low social-economic status. *Journal of Consulting and Clinical Psychology* 1976; 23:209–214.

Parlee, M. The premenstrual syndrome. *Psychological Bulletin* 1973; 80:454–465.

Paykel, E. S., Prusoff, B. A., Uhlenhuth, E. H. Scaling of life events. *Archives of General Psychiatry* 1971; 25:340–347.

Powell, B. The empty nest, employment, and psychiatric symptoms in college-educated women. *Psychology of Women Quarterly* 1977; 2(1):35–43.

Radloff, L. S., Rae, D. S. Susceptibility and precipitating factors in depression: Sex differences and similarities. *Journal of Abnormal Psychology* 1979; 88:174–181.

Raye, M. B. Oral Contraceptives and Depression. *Journal of American Medical Association* 1963; 522:186.

Rush, A. J. *Short-Term Psychotherapies for Depression: Behavioral, Interpersonal, Cognitive, and Psychodynamic Approaches.* New York: Guilford Press, 1982, pp. 12–16.

Seligman, M. E. P. *Helplessness.* San Francisco: Freeman, 1975.

Sommer, B. The Effect of Menstruation on Cognitive and Perceptual Motor Behavior: A Review. *Psychosomatic Medicine* 1973; 35(6):515–534.

Taylor, F. G., Marshall, W. I. Experimental analysis of a cognitive-behavioral therapy for depression. *Cognitive Therapy and Research* 1977; 1:54–72.

Thrunher, M. Midlife marriage: Sex differences in evaluation and perspectives. *International Journal of Aging and Human Development* 1976; 7:129–135.

Tucker, S. J. The menopause: How much soma and how much psyche? *JOGN Nursing* 1977; 6(5):40–47.

Van Keep, P. A., Prill, H. J. Psycho-sociology of menopause and post menopause. *Frontiers in Hormone Research* 1975; 3:32–39.

Vaughn, C. E., Leff, J. R. The influence of family and social factors on the course of psychiatric illness. *British Journal of Psychiatry* 1977; 129:125–137.

Weinstein, M. C. Estrogen use in postmenopausal women—Costs, risks, and benefits. *New England Journal of Medicine* 1980; 303:308–316.

Weissman, M. M. Environmental factors in affective disorders. *Hospital Practice* 1979; 14(4):103–109.

Weissman, M. M., Klerman, G. L. Sex differences and the epidemiology of depression. *Archives of General Psychiatry* 1977; 34:98–111.

Weissman, M., Pincus, C., Padding, N., et al. The educated housewife: Mild depression and the search for work. *American Journal of Orthopsychiatry* 1973; 43:565–573.

Winokur, G. Genetic findings and methodological considerations in manic depressive disease. *British Journal of Psychiatry* 1970; 117:267–274.

Youngren, M. A., Lewinsohn, P. M. The functional relationship between depression and problematic interpersonal behavior. Unpublished data. University of Oregon, 1977.

Zeiss, A. M., Lewinsohn, P. M., Munoz, R. F. Nonspecific improvement effects in depression using interpersonal, cognitive, and pleasant events focused treatments. *Journal of Consulting and Clinical Psychology* 1979; 47:427–439.

Zerbin-Rubin, E. Genetics of affective psychoses, in Schau, M., Stromgren, E. (eds.): *Origin, Prevention, and Treatment of Affective Disorders.* New York: Academic Press, Inc. 1979.

21

IMPROVING THE MENTAL HEALTH OF BLACK AMERICANS: LESSONS FROM THE COMMUNITY MENTAL HEALTH MOVEMENT

Harold W. Neighbors
School of Public Health
University of Michigan

. . . In summary, powerful social forces stemming from the civil rights and community mental health movements came together to focus economic and intellectual resources on the notion that psychological problems among black Americans could be prevented if mental health policy moved away from an individual-oriented clinical delivery model to one that focused on social/structural change. This new model would use a social stress conceptualization of psychopathology as the guiding framework for action and intervention (Cannon and Locke 1977). Unfortunately, many now reject this notion, feeling that community mental health overstepped its bounds and made promises that it could not deliver (Feldman 1978). While in many respects this is true, it does not necessarily follow that we must retreat from the philosophy and goals of the community mental health movement—especially with respect to the mental health of black Americans. On the contrary, we should apply a public health approach to understanding the mental health of blacks. Furthermore, we can and must pursue the idea of prevention of psychopathology in black Americans. But we cannot afford to pursue these notions in the same manner that they were pursued by the early community mental health practitioners. The climate of the 1990s will call for a different strategy. We can arrive at the point of seriously addressing the idea of psychopathology prevention in black Americans by conducting more and better epidemiologic research. Thus, this review will begin by evaluating issues relevant to the epidemiology of black mental health.

EPIDEMIOLOGIC RESEARCH ON RACE

Stimulated by the philosophy and energy of the community mental health movement and in an effort to understand better the issues relevant to black mental health, a number of epidemiologic researchers focused their efforts specifically on black Americans (Pasamanick, 1963; Fischer, 1969; Jaco, 1960). If it were not for the work of these researchers, the epidemiologic knowledge based on black Americans, while still limited, would not be where it is today (Neighbors, 1984). As a result of these early writings, a number of epidemiologic studies were conducted during the 1970s. These studies have produced a battery of findings concerning racial differences in mental health status that have accumulated over the last 15 years. The vast majority of these community surveys focusing on race relied on the symptom-checklist method of estimating mental illness prevalence. These short screening scales measure mild, global distress rather than discrete mental disorders. Despite regional and methodological differences across these studies, the following general conclusions can be drawn. First, blacks tend to have higher mean levels of distress than whites. Second, when socioeconomic status is controlled, blacks either exhibit lower levels of psychological distress (Antunes et al., 1974; Dohrenwend and Dohrenwend, 1969; Gaitz and Scott, 1972; Yancey, Rigsby, and McCarthy, 1972) or there are no racial differences (Bell et al., 1981; Mirowsky and Ross, 1980; Warheit, Holzer, and Schwab, 1973, 1975; Neff and Husaini, 1980; Roberts, Stevenson, and Breslow,

From the *Milbank Quarterly*, 1987, *65*, Suppl. 2., 348–380. Copyright © 1987. Milbank Memorial Fund. Reprinted by permission.

[Editor's note: This chapter comprises excerpts of Professor Neighbors's article. He begins by reviewing the community mental health movement in context of civil rights movement of the 1960s. We begin with his summary of this discussion.]

1981; Eaton and Kessler, 1981; Frerichs, Aneshensel, and Clark, 1981; Neff, 1985b).

In short, these data indicated that blacks were no more likely than whites to have higher rates of distress. These findings are intriguing because blacks are known to be disproportionately exposed to social conditions generally considered to be antecedents of psychiatric disorder (Farley, 1984; U.S. Health Resources and Services Administration, 1987). Such results completely contradict the assumptions underlying the theory of social causation which was so fundamental to the thinking behind the community mental health movement. Such results also contradict the minority-status argument which predicts a direct effect of race on mental health, regardless of socioeconomic status (Mirowsky and Ross, 1980). The minority-status argument predicts higher morbidity among blacks because of the added stress of racism—that is, the stress due to blocked opportunities which whites do not experience. As a result, one would expect blacks to exhibit higher rates of distress than whites at *all* levels of socioeconomic status. In other words, the minority-status argument provides good reason to believe that socioeconomic status alone does not fully capture the unique stress to which blacks are more exposed than whites. Recent evidence suggests, however, that we may not be able to discount completely the minority-status argument. An analysis of eight different epidemiologic surveys found that there *were* race differences in psychological distress, but only among people of the lower classes, a result that is consistent with the view that racial discrimination exacerbates the damage to mental health of poverty status among blacks (Kessler and Neighbors, 1986). . . .

SOCIOLOGICAL AND SOCIAL PSYCHOLOGICAL RISK FACTORS

. . . There are three basic assumptions that underlie research in the areas of race, class, and mental illness. First, everyone in the United States shares the value of striving to be upwardly mobile (Merton, 1957). Second, lower-class individuals feel like failures because they have been unsuccessful in their attempts at upward social mobility (Wheaton, 1980). Third, being poor is stressful, not only because poverty per se exposes one to more stress but also because there is stress involved in trying to advance but not being able to do so (Silberman, 1964). Blacks especially are victims of aspirations they cannot achieve (Pettigrew, 1964). The specific men-

tal health consequences of this situation for blacks are unclear. For example, we are only at the early stages of understanding how personal histories of success and failure are related to important risk factors like locus of control, self-esteem, and a sense of fatalism. Furthermore, there is still much to be learned about how these latter constructs are related to mental health measures like psychological distress and discrete disorders (e.g., DSM-III). Some researchers argue that it is more adaptive to *reduce* mobility striving in order to bring subjective aspirations more in line with the objective realities of a racist opportunity structure (Parker and Kleiner, 1966). Others feel that the most mentally healthy response is to work collectively with other, socioeconomically similar blacks to change the system and open more opportunities for advancement (Gurin et al., 1969; Gurin, Gurin, and Morrison, 1978).

Most researchers argue that having an internal sense of control has positive mental health benefits and that being external (or "fatalistic") does not. Wheaton (1980) defines fatalism as a learned, persistent attributional tendency that emphasizes environmental rather than personal causation of behavior. It increases vulnerability to stress because it undermines coping persistence and effort (i.e., reduces motivation) via long-term personal histories of failure. Wheaton (1980, 107) also states that avoiding self-blame for failure through external attributions may be ego-protective but will inevitably undermine personal feelings of efficacy even when those external explanations are plausible (as they most certainly are for blacks). Unfortunately, psychiatric epidemiologists have not explored how these ideas relate specifically to the situations of black Americans.

Research using Rotter's internal/external locus-of-control scale has shown that blacks are more externally oriented than whites (Porter and Washington, 1979). Gurin et al. (1969) were the first to show that, for blacks, Rotter's scale consisted of two dimensions—one factor made up of items phrased in the first person (personal control) and the other referring to people in general (control ideology). Comparing blacks and whites on control ideology showed that blacks were just as likely as whites to subscribe to the typical American values of the importance of work, effort, skill, and ability in striving to get ahead. Thus, the greater externality of blacks on the locus-of-control measure was actually due to a reduced sense of *personal* control only, not an endorsement of different cultural values (Gurin,

Gurin, and Morrison, 1978). Racism, then, while reducing personal control among blacks, does not erode belief in the work ethic.

The Gurins went on to argue that the reduced sense of personal control among blacks reflected a realistic perception of restricted opportunities. Thus, while blacks were more externally oriented than whites, this was due to an accurate assessment of a racist environment and such externality among an oppressed group was not necessarily a bad thing. In other words, the Gurins would disagree (for blacks at least) with Wheaton's argument that an external orientation is detrimental, no matter how plausible the explanation. In fact, when the Gurins assessed this realistic and accurate external orientation via the concept of "system blame," they found the more external blacks to have higher aspirations and to engage in more innovative coping efforts. . . .

EXPECTANCY THEORY AS A FRAMEWORK FOR INTERVENTION

Expectancy theory is based on the notion that one's belief that actions will be rewarded enhances motivation and affective behaviors. Expectancy models emphasize conscious actions on the environment to attain positive outcomes and to avoid negative results. Expectancies are not reducible to traits nor situations but represent both characterological *and* situational forces. Because of racism, expectancy research on blacks must be particularly concerned with the implications of situational assessments (Bowman, 1987). For poor blacks, expectancy problems (low and external expectancies) result from the feeling that there is little chance of attaining a particular goal. As the research of Parker and Kleiner (1966) suggests, blacks may have lower expectations in the face of objective difficulties and discouraging odds (i.e., blocked opportunities or an unfair opportunity structure) and point to the distinct possibility that such negative expectancies operate as psychological risk factors. . . .

Thus, it appears that programs designed to facilitate upward mobility among the black poor could improve mental health status by changing expectancies. But research from "War on Poverty" programs shows that expectancies do not automatically change to conform with changes in objective conditions (Gurin and Gurin, 1970). If we argue for policy changes that emphasize the creation of structural opportunities *only*, we might be missing the point. Adequate care must be taken to prepare people for these new roles, which means training programs that focus on skills and assessment of psychological concepts such as low or external expectancies. . . .

TARGETS AND SETTINGS FOR PREVENTIVE INTERVENTIONS

From a public health perspective, the ultimate goal of epidemiologic research is the application of intervention programs designed to reduce the incidence of disease, thereby reducing prevalence. A further goal of epidemiologic research is to uncover the modifiable risk factors that can form a rational basis for preventive action. Identification of black strengths and weaknesses through careful epidemiologic risk-factor research can contribute to the design of programs aimed at upgrading those weaknesses and taking advantage of those strengths to reduce the occurrence and impact of stressful social situations. By intervening in black population subgroups known to be at risk of developing low self-esteem or low/external expectancies, prevention programs could have a positive impact on black mental health outcomes. The important factor, however, will be to develop programs for such groups *before* they begin to display evidence of the types of serious mental disabilities that can result from potentially pathogenic social circumstances. There are a number of specific areas where we should intervene. If done carefully and in the right settings, we do not need to mention explicitly mental health, mental illness, psychopathology, or any other potentially stigmatizing terms.

CHILDREN IN SCHOOLS

Whenever the topic of prevention is discussed, the issue of children inevitably arises. Because of various developmental theories, many argue that the best way to ensure competent adults is to strengthen coping skills in children. This was a fundamental premise of the "Child Guidance" movement. This idea was also an integral part of the philosophy of the Head Start program. In the last few years, results from a number of studies focusing on preschool and elementary school interventions with black children have raised the distinct possibility that this is a fruitful mental health prevention strategy. More relevant for this review are studies that have attempted to intervene with low-income black youth. Head Start had a legitimate role in helping to facilitate the normal unfolding of self-esteem and social competence, defined as "the ability to master formal concepts, to perform well in school, to stay out of trouble with the law and to relate well to adults and other children'' (Palmer and Andersen, 1979, 3). Head Start's philosophy was heavily influenced by community mental health ideology, with child mental health professionals stressing prevention, early detection, and the social determinants of emotional problems. The clinicians who worked in the Head Start classrooms estimated that 10 to 25 percent of the children were suffering from serious disturbances, although systematic epidemiologic studies were never conducted (Cohen, Solnit, and Wohlford 1979).

In the 1960s, a group of preschool intervention studies were begun and, in 1975, ten of these investigators pooled efforts, relocated the children, and compared them to matched groups. For all programs, the children were predominantly poor and black. The results of these studies indicated that preschool children were significantly less likely to be set back one grade or more in school. Four out of the five studies for which data were available showed that fewer preschool children were in special education (learning disabled) classes. Five studies reported significantly higher reading scores in the preschool group; two found higher scores but the differences were not significant and one study showed no difference. Seven studies had data on arithmetic scores. Two showed significantly higher scores for the preschool group, two showed significantly higher scores on some subtests, two showed higher scores for girls but not boys, and one showed higher but insignificant scores. Thus, while no study affected all variables associated with elementary school performance, all studies affected one or another variable and some affected several. Palmer and Andersen (1979, 447) concluded that these results ''have implications not only for the academic performance of children, but for socio-emotional and cost aspects as well.'' . . .

In the Yale-New Haven Prevention Project, an elementary school that was 99 percent black and had 50 percent of the families on AFDC received an intervention (Comer 1985). Educators and mental health personnel collaborated to create a desirable social climate in the school to effect coordinated management, curriculum and staff development, teaching, and the learning process. They did not focus on the children and their families as ''patients'' but, rather, the intervention was targeted toward the organization and management system of the school in order to provide students with adequate educa-

tional skills and support. The project had four elements: (1) a representative governance and management group; (2) a parent-participation program; (3) a mental health program and team; and (4) an academic program. As part of a larger study, 16 girls and 8 boys who had been part of this elementary school intervention were contacted 3 years later. They were randomly matched on age and sex with the same number of students who attended another elementary program. The intervention group did significantly better on achievement test scores, including doing better on 9 different subscales. They also did better in language, mathematics, and school grades. . . .

THE POOR IN JOB-TRAINING PROGRAMS

Successful interventions at the pre- and elementary school level would have positive payoffs in another area that receives much attention for black Americans—job-training programs for the black unemployed. Better school performance among the black high-risk children should result in staying in school longer, increased likelihood of obtaining a diploma, and increased employment. To the extent that the early interventions with young children are successful, there should not be as many black teens or young adults in need of job-skills training later in their lives. Inevitably, however, many black youth will wind up unskilled and unemployed. For this group, job-training programs provide an opportunity to change expectancies.

Job-training programs are relevant to the concerns of this article because they should be able to teach us something about how to have an impact upon employability and thus the upward mobility of low-income blacks. Glazer (1985), citing Taggart's (1981) review of job-training programs, concluded that the most intensive programs have done best, and cites Job Corps, the Youth Employment and Demonstration Act and the Youth Incentive Entitlement Pilot Project as examples. Two studies of Job Corps found significant program effects in terms of increased employment, earnings, reduced welfare dependence, unemployment insurance usage, criminal activity, and out-of-wedlock births. Weinberg (1985) argued that the perceived role of work experience within a welfare program should be studied. He asks the very timely question, ''Can the concept of reciprocity (establishment of a quid pro quo in exchange for welfare benefits—''workfare'') lead to increased exit from welfare by imbuing an increased sense of self-worth to the recipients?'' (Weinberg,

1985, 5). In 1985 a preliminary report by the Manpower Demonstration Research Corp., evaluating new welfare approaches in 11 states, focused on workfare in West Virginia and found that 80 percent of the participants thought that a requirement to work for checks was "satisfactory" or "very satisfactory."

It seems clear that "workfare" will be a major movement within the welfare policy area. Workfare experiments are being conducted in Michigan, Pennsylvania, California, and New York. In Ohio, workfare programs are being extended into 40 of the state's 88 counties. As another example, in March of 1987, a report from the American Enterprise Institute recommended that welfare recipients be *required* to participate in education, training, and work programs in order to reduce poverty, *increase* self-esteem, and decrease behavioral dependence. It is interesting to note that the report is reminiscent of the expectancy approach to poverty in that it advocates a two-pronged approach to helping the poor. Specifically, the report said that economic improvements must be combined with an effort to change thinking and behavior among the "underclass." This is similar to the ideas psychologists were trying to promote in the early days of the "War on Poverty." . . .

The crucial point is that low-income blacks may not be victims of poor motivation as a result of inadequate predispositions (e.g., lack of a need for achievement, or a poor work ethic) but rather, suffer from negative expectancies that have resulted from a history of poor success due to slim chances. Given that this appears to be a problem of expectancies, there is hope for change. If it were purely a problem of deep-seated dispositions, then there would be no point to social programs. The new social programs mounted under the "workfare" label are in many cases motivated by a conservative ideology that views welfare as fostering dependency and leading to a culture of poverty or a permanent underclass. Nevertheless, they could have a positive impact on black expectations to the extent that they provide opportunities for successful work experiences and career paths. The positive potential of these programs is that they are not concentrating on attitudes and motivational problems only. They are also structural in focus in that they are providing jobs. If the ambition is there (and the PSID analyses as well as preliminary results from some of the workfare programs seems to show that it is) but the expectations are low, then it makes sense to create opportunities

in order to increase expectations of success. It remains to be seen, however, whether the new round of workfare programs will be able to accomplish this goal. . . .

DISCUSSION

Another important issue that needs more discussion is the notion of victim-blaming. In this regard, we must be careful to distinguish between two important points. One is the attribution of blame for the unjust social situations that blacks have been subjected to. This, clearly, is the fault of an oppressive social system set up by whites. The second is the notion that blacks can, however, in the face of oppressive conditions, take responsibility for changing those social conditions that were not necessarily the fault of blacks or the poor (Committee on Policy for Racial Justice, 1987). Related to this second point is the notion that blacks and the poor should take personal responsibility for changing individual behaviors known to be deleterious to mental health. This is not victim blaming, although some would have us think so (Crawford, 1977). Victim blaming is a one-sided attitude, that *all* of the problems of the poor are indeed *their fault* and due to deficits "within the person," with no appreciation whatsoever of the role played by social stress and oppressive environmental conditions (Gurin and Gurin, 1970; Gurin, 1970; Ladner, 1973; Ryan, 1971); Yette, 1971). The notion of individual responsibility for health behavior is completely consistent with the current trend in public health toward health promotion. The health promotion view is based on research that shows that many of the health problems of individuals are made worse by poor health behaviors (e.g., smoking, drinking, no seat belts, poor nutrition, etc.). Thus, it follows that improvements in health can be made by targeting interventions toward changing those risky behaviors. It would be a mistake not to take advantage of this promotional approach while social-change agents are advocating environmental reform. . . .

CONCLUSIONS

In closing, the following points should be highlighted. First, it has been shown that the highest rates of psychopathology reside in the lowest socioeconomic groups, and this is especially the case for black Americans (Neighbors, 1986). Research on social mobility shows that the benefits for blacks of moving up the social ladder outweigh the costs

(Kessler and Cleary, 1980; Isaacs, 1984); and that moving down in socioeconomic standing can be detrimental to black mental health (Parker and Kleiner, 1966). As a result, policies and programs designed to influence the mobility patterns of blacks can be viewed as having implications for mental health. Two settings, in particular, should command the interest of epidemiologic researchers: (1) preschool and elementary schools; and (2) job-training programs ("workfare"). Using experimental research designs along with appropriate measures of mental health outcomes (e.g., self-esteem, psychological distress, discrete DSM-III disorders), a preventive effect can be demonstrated. Finally, even if significant reductions in psychopathology cannot be demonstrated, the risk-factor model put forth in this article contains potential for a positive impact in other important areas of black American life. . . .

REFERENCES

Antunes, G., C. Gordon, C. Gaitz, and J. Scott. 1974. Ethnicity, Socioeconomic Status and the Etiology of Psychological Distress. *Sociology and Social Research* 58:361–68.

Bell, R., J. Leroy, E. Lin, and J. Schwab. 1981. Change and Psychopathology: Epidemiologic Considerations. *Community Mental Health Journal* 17:203–13.

Bowman, P. 1987. Psychological Expectancy: Theory and Measurement in Black Populations. In *Handbook of Tests and Measurements for Black Populations,* ed. R. Jones (Forthcoming.)

Cannon, M., and B. Locke. 1977. Being Black is Detrimental to Your Mental Health: Myth or Reality? *Phylon* 38:408–28.

Cohen, D., A. Solnit, and P. Wohlford. 1979. Mental Health Services in Head Start. In *Project Head Start: A Legacy of the War on Poverty,* ed. E. Zigler and J. Valentine, 259–82. New York: Free Press.

Comer, J. 1985. The Yale-New Haven Primary Prevention Project: A Follow-up Study. *Journal of the American Academy of Child Psychiatry* 24:154–60.

Committee on Policy for Racial Justice. 1987. *Black Initiatives and Governmental Responsibility.* Washington: Joint Center for Political Studies.

Crawford, R. 1977. You Are Dangerous to Your Health: The Ideology and Politics of Victim Blaming. *International Journal of Health Services* 7:663–80.

Dohrenwend, B. S. 1973. Social Status and Stressful Life Events. *Journal of Personality and Social Psychology* 28:225–35.

Dohrenwend, B. P., and B. S. Dohrenwend. 1969. *Social Status and Psychological Disorder: A Causal Inquiry.* New York: Wiley-Interscience.

Eaton, W., and L. Kessler. 1981. Rates of Symptoms of Depression in a National Sample. *American Journal of Epidemiology* 113:528–38.

Farley, R. 1984. *Blacks and Whites: Narrowing the Gap?* Cambridge: Harvard University Press.

Feldman, S. 1978. Promises, Promises or Community Mental Health Services and Training: Ships That Pass in the Night. *Community Mental Health Journal* 14:83–91.

Fischer, J. 1969. Negroes and Whites and Rates of Mental Illness: Reconsideration of a Myth. *Psychiatry* 32:428–46.

Frerichs, R., C. Aneshensel, and V. Clark. 1981. Prevalence of Depression in Los Angeles County. *American Journal of Epidemiology* 113:691–99.

Gaitz, C., and J. Scott. 1972. Age and the Measurement of Mental Health. *Journal of Health and Social Behavior* 13:55–67.

Glazer, N. 1985. Education and Training Programs and Poverty; or, Opening the Black Box. Paper delivered at a conference, "Poverty and Policy: Retrospect and Prospects," Madison, Wis., Institute for Research on Poverty.

Gurin, G. 1970. An Expectancy Approach to Job Training Programs. In *Psychological Factors in Poverty,* ed. V. Allen, 277–99. Chicago: Markham.

Gurin, G., and P. Gurin. 1970. Expectancy Theory in the Study of Poverty. *Journal of Social Issues* 26:83–104.

Gurin, P., G. Gurin, R. Lao, and M. Beattie. 1969. Internal-External Control in the Motivational Dynamics of Negro Youth. *Journal of Social Issues* 25:29–53.

Gurin, P., G. Gurin, and B. Morrison. 1978. Personal and Ideological Aspects of Internal and External Control. *Social Psychology* 41:275–96.

Isaacs, M. 1984. The Determinants and Consequences of Intergenerational Mobility among Black American Males. University Microfilms International no. 8422728. Waltham, Mass.: Heller School for Advanced Studies in Social Welfare, Brandeis University. (Unpublished Ph.D. diss.)

Jaco, E. G. 1960. *The Social Epidemiology of Mental Disorders: A Psychiatric Survey of Texas.* New York: Russell Sage.

Kessler, R. 1979. Stress, Social Status and Psychological Distress. *Journal of Health and Social Behavior* 20:259–72.

———. 1987. The Interplay of Research Design Strategies and Data Analysis Procedures in Evaluating the Effects of Stress on Health. In *Stress and Health: Issues in Research Methodology,* ed. S. Kasl and C. Cooper, 113–40. New York: Wiley & Sons.

Kessler, R., and P. Cleary. 1980. Social Class and Psychological Distress. *American Sociological Review,* 45:463–78.

Kessler, R., and H. Neighbors. 1986. A New Perspective on the Relationships among Race, Social Class and Psychological Distress. *Journal of Health and Social Behavior* 27:107–15.

Merton, R. 1957. *Social Theory and Social Structure.* Glencoe, Ill.: Free Press.

Mitowsky, J., and C. Ross. 1980. Minority Status, Ethnic Culture and Distress: A Comparison of Blacks, Whites, Mexicans and Mexican Americans. *American Journal of Sociology* 86:479–95.

Neff, J. 1985a. Race and Vulnerability to Stress: An Examination of Differential Vulnerability. *Journal of Personality and Social Psychology* 49:481–91.

———. 1985b. Race Differences in Psychological Distress: The Effect of SES, Urbanicity and Measurement Strategy. *American Journal of Community Psychology* 12:337–51.

Neff, J., and B. Husaini. 1980. Race, Socio-economic Status and Psychiatric Impairment: A Research Note. *Journal of Community Psychology* 8:16–19.

Neighbors, H. 1984. The Distribution of Psychiatric Morbidity: A Review and Suggestions for Research. *Community Mental Health Journal* 20:5–18.

———. 1985. Comparing the Mental Health of Blacks and Whites: An Analysis of the Race Differences Tradition in Psychiatric Epidemiologic Research. Paper presented at the First Conference on Racial and Comparative Research, Institute for Urban Affairs and Research, Howard University, Washington, October 17.

———. 1986. Socioeconomic Status and Psychological Distress in Black Americans. *American Journal of Epidemiology* 124:779–93.

Palmer, F., and L. Andersen. 1979. Long-term Gains from Early Intervention: Findings from Longitudinal Studies. In *Project Head Start: A Legacy of the War on Poverty,* ed. E. Zigler and J. Valentine, 433–65. New York: Free Press.

Parker, R., and S. Kleiner. 1966. *Mental Illness in the Urban Negro Community.* New York: Free Press.

Pasamanick, B. 1963. Some Misconceptions Concerning Differences in the Racial Prevalence of Mental Disease. *American Journal of Orthopsychiatry* 33:72–86.

Pettigrew, T. 1964. *A Profile of the Negro American.* Princeton: Van Nostrand.

Porter, J., and R. Washington. 1979. Black Identity and Self-Esteem: A Review of Studies of Black Self-concept. *Annual Review of Sociology* 5:53–74.

Roberts, R., J. Stevenson, and L. Breslow. 1981. Symptoms of Depression among Blacks and Whites in an Urban Community. *Journal of Nervous and Mental Disease* 169:774–79.

Ryan, W. 1971. *Blaming the Victim.* New York: Vintage Books.

Shure, M., and G. Spivack. 1982. Interpersonal Problem-solving in Young Children: A Cognitive Approach to Prevention. *American Journal of Community Psychology* 10:341–56.

Silberman, C. 1964. *Crisis in Black and White.* New York: Random House.

Taggart, R. 1981. *A Fisherman's Guide: An Assessment of Training and Remediation Strategies.* Kalamazoo: W. E. Upjohn Institute for Employment Research.

U.S. Health Resources and Services Administration. 1987. *Health Status of the Disadvantaged Chartbook,* 1986. DHHS pub. no. (HRSA) HRS-P-DV86-2. Washington.

Warheit, G., C. Holzer, and J. Schwab. 1973. An Analysis of Social Class and Racial Differences in Depressive Symptomatology, *Journal of Health and Social Behavior* 14:291–99.

———. 1975. Race and Mental Illness: An Epidemiologic Update. *Journal of Health and Social Behavior* 16:243–56.

Weinberg, D. 1985. A Poverty Research Agenda for the Next Decade. Paper delivered at a conference, "Poverty and Policy: Retrospect and Prospects," Madison: Institute for Research on Poverty.

Wheaton, B. 1980. The Sociogenesis of Psychological Disorder: An Attributional Theory. *Journal of Health and Social Behavior* 21:100–24.

Yancey, W., L. Rigsby, and J. McCarthy. 1972. Social Position and Self-evaluation: The Relative Importance of Race. *American Journal of Sociology* 78:338–59.

Yette, S. 1971. *The Choice: The Issue of Black Survival in America.* New York: Berkely Medallion Books.

PART V

SIMILARITIES
AND DIFFERENCES

INTRODUCTION

One person is a social configuration, being simultaneously

- an individual

- a member of several primary groups (such as a family, peer groups, and the like)

- a member of several secondary groups (such as having a job in a work place, or being a student at a school—social roles that are specialized as compared to the diffuse experiences of being with family or friends)

- a participant in a given culture and subculture (the dominant culture of the larger society, and whatever special subcultures that reflect one's birth and living situations)

- a member of the animal species coexisting on a physical place at a given historical time.

In effect, each individual is five different dimensions of social being all at once. It is this multiple dimensionality that makes people complex and interesting, but it does present some problems for the helping professional. To which component should we pay attention? How do the five different aspects of the individual hang together? When we push or pull at one, what will happen to the others? Fundamentally, in what ways are people similar to one another, and in what ways are they different?

This part deals with two special types of similarities and differences that make a difference in the contemporary world. The first deals with prosocial and antisocial developments, that is, the ways people learn (or do not learn) rules for relating to one another in a socially acceptable manner. It is a basic task for any society to have its citizens internalize rules for relating which will permit the society to function effectively. People differ in the degree to which they learn effective rules of relating.

The first paper by Linda Patrick and Patricia Minish deals with altruistic behavior in young children. How is it possible to rear children in such a way as to make them helpful, sharing, and comforting of others? A review of the literature suggests that modeling similar (altruistic) behaviors, and then reinforcing similar responses can increase the likelihood of altruistic behavior in children. Parents also are likely to model different (nonaltruistic) behaviors inadvertently, and thus confound the altrustic lessons.

Edward W. Gondolf's paper addresses men who batter (that is, who are involved in spousal abuse) by asking the question, at what moral stage of development are these individuals who relate so violently to their partners? What Gondolf proposes, using Lawrence Kohlberg's model of stages of moral development, is that interventions must be at the same level as the aggressor's level of moral development so that he will comprehend the meaning of his treatment. [Kohlberg expanded Piaget's earlier formulations on moral development; see also Susan Proctor, Chapter 13 in this book.]

For example, if a man is at a preoperational or egocentric level of moral development in which moral values reside in external acts, not in the person himself, then he is likely to respond primarily to superior power that controls punishments and rewards for him. This suggests institutionalization and/or controlling therapies such as behavior modification. If that man is aided to move to a concrete operational or other-oriented level of moral development in which moral values reside in performing correctly according to conventional expectancies, then he is likely to respond to authorities who can grant approval. This suggests supervised self-help groups and family therapy so as to help this man manage his behavior and his emotions. And so on, up to the cognitive level of formal operations or abstract reasoning.

As an editorial note, I should point out that Kohlberg's model, with its highest stage of moral development being abstract universals such as "justice," has been criticized for its gender limitations. Carol Gilligan proposes that there are two "voices," two ways to speak of moral goals. She suggests that women tend to emphasize the caring and sharing levels (Kohlberg's second of three stages) as being the highest form of moral development. (See, for example, Carol Gilligan and Jane Attanucci, ''Two moral orientations: Gender differences and similarities.'' *Merrill-Palmer Quarterly,* 1988, *34*(3):223–237.) Gondolf acknowledges this other point of view but recognizes that Kohlberg's model is particularly applicable to men who batter.

Kathleen D. Noble explores the dilemma of the gifted woman in a sexist society. Highly capable women have not been given the support and recognition that can guide and nurture their talents. Today, as women enter the wide range of social, political, educational, and scientific leadership positions, they are facing a variety of obstacles about the meaning of their giftedness and thus, their prosocial contributions. Noble suggests ways to encourage these women to fulfill their potentials in the face of gender-role stereotyping and social pressures.

The second major topic in this part on similarities and differences concerns the homeless. As you will discover, in some ways the homeless are very similar to everyone else, but in other ways there are some important differences that provide points of departure for service delivery. You may be astonished to read the first article, written by a homeless person. Pia McKay has written several articles on this topic in the *Washington Post.* The one presented here gives some insights into the differences among the homeless group itself.

Norweeta G. Milburn views the homeless in a broad perspective, and notes the increasing heterogeneity within this group in recent years. There are a variety of paths by which people may enter this unloved category of ''the homeless.'' Some come from problems with alcohol and drugs; others from being discharged from mental institutions with no community facilities able and willing to sustain them in their ''freedom''; still others are simply poor and unable to afford housing, or they lack the social networks necessary to provide even minimal shelter. This diversity makes planning and work with the homeless difficult indeed.

Ellen L. Bassuk and Lynn Rosenberg present a case-control study of one type of homeless population—homeless families headed by a female. This appears to be the fastest growing homeless group, accounting by some estimates for one third of the 2.5 million homeless people. The women and children in the Bassuk and Rosenberg study were compared with a comparable group of housed families headed by females. They report some important similarities and differences in these two groups that might provide clues to more nearly effective service.

Overall, helping professionals have to sort out similarities and differences. The papers in this part have provided a variety of perspectives on how this sorting out may be done. In a more technical sense, the scientific method is simply a ruleful way of distinguishing similarities and differences. Scientific practice involves the selection and performance of efficacious actions to achieve desired goals. In both scientific work and helping practice, we are always concerned with similarities and differences.

PART V

A. Prosocial and Antisocial Developments

22

CHILD-REARING STRATEGIES FOR THE DEVELOPMENT OF ALTRUISTIC BEHAVIOR IN YOUNG CHILDREN

Linda F. Patrick
Patricia A. Minish
Institute for Behavioral Research
University of Georgia

Moral training of young children in contemporary American culture focuses more on proscriptive rules and regulations, what *not* to do, rather than on positive altruistic values of what *to* do. Rising incidences of aggression, violence, and lack of involvement in other people's problems and distress has caused concern in our society. Although parents prefer that their children behave prosocially, it is likely that parents give more attention to training suppression of antisocial activity than to developing prosocial activity (Staub, 1971b). It was for the purpose of developing one aspect of prosocial behavior, that of altruism, that the literature on child-rearing strategies was explored and a prevention plan designed. The plan, a series of three workshops for parents, is based on the assumption that young children who use altruistic behaviors will be more likely to be helpful than harmful to themselves and others. Altruism is "social behavior carried out to achieve positive outcomes for another rather than for the self" (Rushton, 1980, p. 8). The importance of parents' encouragement of altruistic behavior in their children stems from the fact that children who learn to get along with others are more likely to find success and satisfaction in learning and social situations (Honig, 1982).

Although there is a substantial body of research on prosocial behavior, only a few studies have included methods for encouraging prosocial behaviors (Finkelstein, 1982; Kobak, 1979; Shure and Spivak, 1978; Yarrow, Scott, and Waxler, 1973). Finkelstein, for example, describes how a day care program dealt with aggressive peer interactions through formal and systematic prosocial curriculum intervention. Shure and Spivak have trained mothers and teachers in inner-city programs to improve children's ability to conceptualize problems for themselves. Using their "Interpersonal Cognitive Problem Solving" techniques, children are verbally encouraged to decide for themselves what and what not to do. Most of the methods suggested for encouraging prosocial behavior in children are formal, cognitively based, and intended for use in day care or school settings. None of the methods represents a comprehensive integration of research findings. Ideally, a model program for the development of altruistic behavior would be clearly based on research findings and would include affective and behavioral as well as cognitive components. Financial investment and dependency on professionals would be minimized in such a program.

It was within this framework that practical methods were designed to help parents develop awareness and skills in altruistically oriented child-rearing strategies. The development of the workshop is occurring in a series of stages. The first stage was a comprehensive review of research findings pertaining to child-rearing practices that encourage altruistic behavior in young children. This literature review forms the basis and the focus for the content of the workshops. The next step was the design and structure of the workshops, which included research in effective communication strategies. At this point, the workshops have been designed and piloted. Based on this experience and feedback from participants, the structure was further refined. Before the series is finalized, it will be presented by the authors to parent groups and evaluated for effectiveness.

Since a unique strength of this program is its basis on an integration of research findings in cog-

From the *Journal of Primary Prevention*, 1985, 5(3): 154–168. Copyright © 1985. Human Sciences Press. Reprinted by permission.

nitive, affective, and behavioral areas, a summary of these findings will be presented and specific child-rearing strategies identified that encourage altruistic behavior in young children. Following the review of literature, the program will be discussed, emphasizing the integration of these research findings into a structure for presentation to parents. Research on altruistic behavior has flourished since the late 1960s. The types of altruism receiving the most attention have included helping another in distress, sharing, generosity, and making a donation to someone in need. In the past there has been a heavy reliance on laboratory studies involving adults and older children and investigation of a small number of variables. Increasingly, however, more attention has been devoted to processes that affect altruistic behavior, to naturalistic studies, and to studies involving younger children.

AGE OF CHILD

Although much of the research on altruistic behavior in children has been conducted at kindergarten age or older, a smaller body of researchers has focused on very young children. "Young children's potentialities for altruistic behavior are quite unknown. Concerning their propensities for understanding the feelings of others, and showing kindness, and the opportunities for learning empathy and kindness, there are only the beginnings of a body of scientific information" (Yarrow, Scott, and Waxler, 1973, p. 240).

There are, however, data that indicate that very young children exhibit altruistic behaviors. Early forms of sharing have been found to be a characteristic activity of children 18 months of age and even younger. For example, Rheingold, Hay, and West (1976) documented instances of showing, giving, and partner play within a laboratory setting and later informally confirmed the results by naturalistic observation. Others concur that the acts of sympathy and sharing are first manifested at one-and-a-half to two-and-a-half years of age (Borke, 1971; Hoffman, 1975c; Yarrow and Waxler, 1977). It seems that acts of showing and giving objects to others are displayed by children as they complete their first year of life (Hay, 1979). Incidences of helping (Church, 1966; Rheingold, 1979) and aiding others in distress (Hoffman, 1975b) have also been documented for children under three years of age. Although the relation of these early types of activities to later behavior is unclear, they do serve prosocial functions and offer opportunities for additional prosocial learning (Hay, 1979).

Age and incidence of prosocial behavior seem to be unrelated until about age 4; from age 4 to age 13, the relationship is positively correlated (Mussen and Eisenberg-Berg, 1977). Thus, in general, older children are more likely to help or share than younger children and they also show a greater variety of other-oriented behavior (Rushton, 1980).

OTHER FACTORS

Differences in prosocial behavior between boys and girls have not, in general, been found (Grusec, 1971; Masters, 1971). When sex differences are found, girls are usually more generous than are boys (Midlarsky and Bryan, 1972; Moore, Underwood, and Rosenhan, 1973). One line of study, however, suggests that girls are better at giving responses that are considered socially desirable but are no more likely to exhibit altruistic behavior (Shigetomi, Hartman, Gelfand, Cohen, and Montemayor, 1979). Socioeconomic status seems to have little relation to the development or incidence of helping behaviors of children (De Palma and Olejink, 1973; Rosenhan, 1969). However, Bryan (1975) suggests consideration of the type of occupation of the parents rather than other indicators of socioeconomic status when considering children's prosocial behavior.

CONTRIBUTIONS OF CHILD-REARING PRACTICES TO THE DEVELOPMENT OF ALTRUISM

When considering child-rearing strategies, investigators have been relatively consistent in identifying factors that have had an impact on the child's development of altruistic behaviors. Meeting basic needs, adult modeling and nurturance, use of appropriate disciplinary and communication techniques are of primary importance. Giving children an opportunity to practice and discuss sharing, helping, and comforting behaviors through verbal labeling and role imitation also guides them toward altruistic behavior. Many of these factors, as well as others, are interdependent, related, and/or must appear in combination in order to attain the desired effect.

BASIC NEEDS. Children whose basic needs are met are more apt to extend help to other people than are those whose needs are not met. Bryant and Crockenberg (1980) found that for younger children, experiencing sensitive maternal responses to expressed needs related positively to comforting and sharing. Waxler, Yarrow, and King (1979) found maternal responsiveness (e.g., empathic caregiving) to be associated with prosocial behavior in children as young as one or two years of age. Approval needs are also related to helping behaviors. Children who are popular, emotionally secure, and self-confident are more apt to help other people than are children who lack social approval (Hoffman, 1975a; Yarrow, Scott, and Waxler, 1973).

WARMTH, NURTURANCE, AND AFFECTION. The results of several child-rearing studies indicate that warm, nurturant parents tend to rear altruistic children. Rutherford and Mussen (1968), for example, found that boys who scored high on a generosity measure viewed their fathers as warm and sympathetic. Laboratory experiments indicate similar findings (Staub, 1971a; Yarrow, Scott and Waxler, 1973). Children who have been exposed to warm, nurturant models are much more willing to help than are children who are exposed to a cold, aloof, or indifferent model. Yarrow et al. (1973) make the point that parental nurturance has "a special relevance for the child's acquisition of altruistic responses when one considers that nurturance [given the child] is itself an example of model of altruism" (p. 242). Research has shown that adult support, characterized by approval, warmth, and nurturance, is a crucial variable in the development of positive self-esteem, instrumental competence, and prosocial behavior (Baumrind, 1972; Mussen and Eisenberg-Berg, 1977; Openshaw, 1978; Peterson, 1976; Yarrow et al., 1973). For example, in a study of infants, the mother who was accepting, cooperative, and sensitive to her child's signals tended to have children who obeyed her more consistently than did a mother who was rejecting, interfering, and insensitive (Stayton, Hogan, and Ainsworth, 1971). The children's behavior seemed to be independent of socialization and disciplinary tactics. The effect of early maternal responsiveness was also evident in the sharing behaviors of one-year-old infants (Best and Prothro, 1981). Mothers of former intensive care nursery infants were not as responsive nor did their infants show and give as many objects as did infants who were not placed in the intensive care nursery.

MODELING. The fact that altruistic models elicit altruistic behavior in children is well established. The association appears in experimental studies such as Staub (1971a) and Yarrow et al. (1973) and in naturalistic observations (Rosenhan, 1969; Rutherford and Mussen, 1968). The effects of altruistic modeling appear to be relatively enduring, generalizable, and exhibited even when the model is not present. In a laboratory experiment, Rosenhan and White (1967) found that children who had observed a charitable model would donate "winnings" to a charity even when the model left the room. Rushton

(1975) found the children exposed to an altruistic model were more likely to donate during a posttest two months following exposure to the model than were children exposed to a selfish model. Both Midlarsky and Bryan (1972) and White (1972) found similar results, in that children exposed to a helping model within a laboratory setting were more likely to contribute to a charity five days later than were children who were exposed to a selfish model. Rice and Grusec (1975) found that exposure to an altruistic model increased the generosity of the child observers when they were tested four months later. Some research indicates that multiple models have an increased effect on altruistic behavior if the models are consistent (Fehrenback, Miller and Thelen, 1979; Liebert and Fernandez, 1970).

INDUCTION. Investigating the relation between parents' disciplinary styles and the moral development of their children, Hoffman (1970) found that love-oriented and power-assertive techniques were not effecitive. When the effects of parental discipline on measures of the child's moral affect, moral reasoning, and moral behavior were considered, the technique that fostered development in all of these areas was that of induction; that is, "techniques in which that parent gives explanations or reasons for requiring the child to change his behavior" and "that appear to conformity-inducing agents that already exist within the child" (p 286). Additionally, induction is victim centered. An adult who uses induction informs the child of harm caused to the victim and encourages the child to imagine herself or himself in the victim's place, thereby encouraging empathy and role taking. Hoffman (1975a) tested these ideas with fifth-grade children and found that children's altruism scores were positively related to the amount of victim-centered discipline employed by their parents. Parents who use induction tend to have children who show more frequent prosocial acts in nursery school (Hoffman, 1963). Additionally, parents who use induction facilitate conscience development (Aaronfreed, 1976; Burton, Macoby and Allinsmith, 1961) and enhance the child's capacity to view events from another's perspective (Hoffman and Saltzstein, 1967; Staub, 1975).

VERBAL [INSTRUCTION]—ed. When the effect of verbal instruction on children's altruistic behavior is considered in research, it is usually compared with modeling and found to have little or no effect (Bryan and Schwartz, 1971; Bryan and Walbeck, 1970a, 1970b; Grusec and Skubiski, 1970). It has been shown, however, that in donation situations, instructions will affect compliance (Weissbrod, 1980).

Midlarsky and Bryan (1972) demonstrated that verbal exhortations were effective in increasing charitable behavior if coupled with a charitable model. It can be assumed, then, that verbal [instruction] is helpful only if coupled with appropriate modeling. In hypocritical situations, when the model's actions and verbal behavior are incongruent, older children are less likely to do as the model instructs (Bryan and Schwartz, 1971).

REINFORCEMENT. It has been shown that reinforcement can increase altruistic behavior; but other characteristics of the reinforcer must be considered. One study (Midlarsky, Bryan, and Brickman, 1973), for example, found that approval from a selfish model tended to inhibit altruism. Other studies have demonstrated that social reinforcement given often and in large doses can increase altruistic behavior (Gelfand, Hartmann, Cromer, Smith, and Page, 1975; Yarrow, Scott and Waxler, 1973).

COOPERATION. It is commonly felt that a competitive environment decreases the likelihood of altruistic behaviors. Self-concern interferes with the individual's inclination to consider the needs and feelings of others. In a cross-cultural study, Kagan and Masden (1971) found that children from a society that did not stress competition were more successful at games that required cooperative interaction than were American children. Rutherford and Mussen (1968) found that competitive nursery-school boys were less likely to share with their friends than were cooperative boys.

RESPONSIBILITY. Cross-cultural evidence of children from six cultures—Kenya, Mexico, the Philippines, Okinawa, India, and New England—suggests that children who perform more domestic chores, help more with economic tasks, and spend more time caring for their younger siblings score higher on an altruism measure (Whiting and Whiting, 1975). Laboratory research confirms these findings. One group of children was given the responsibility of teaching other children to make puzzles for hospitalized children. Another group made puzzles but was given no teaching responsibilities. The group that was given the teaching responsibility was more willing to share their prizes and made more puzzles than did the control group (Staub, 1975).

In summary, this review suggests that if a parent wants to encourage altruistic behavior in children, the adult must establish a warm, nurturant relationship with the child and be a model of altruistic behaviors. If this exists, then praise, instruction, and reinforcement will enhance the effects. Additionally, an inductive style of discipline is preferred because it encourages the child to empathize with the victim. Encouraging cooperative behavior and assigning responsibilities can also help develop altruistic behaviors.

PREVENTIVE PLAN: A COGNITIVE, AFFECTIVE, AND BEHAVIOR-ORIENTED APPROACH

The prevention plan advocated for parental use with children utilizes a synthesis of cognitive, affective, and behavioral components by integrating the research findings reported above. The preventive activities are organized into a series of three workshops using a combination of information, active thought processing, discussion of feelings, role playing, and practice of models. The parents experience through active participation the same or similar processes they in turn ask of their children. These components have been identified through research as effective methods of facilitating altruistic behavior in children. We suggest that they are also the most effective methods with adults in trying to help them learn to model and explain altruistic behavior for their children.

EFFECTIVE TRAINING AND IMPLEMENTATION TECHNIQUES: MODELING AND INDUCTION

It is quite clear from the literature that two techniques stand out as having the most potential for fostering altruism—modeling and induction. Nurturance and warmth is additionally viewed as a foundation for eliciting the desired results.

Parents receive information, practice through role playing, and are asked to use modeling techniques with their children. Focus is on setting a good example by use of a "practicing what you preach" approach, use of empathy, reassurance, support, perspective taking, responsibility taking, and positive reinforcement. Many training programs have centered on cognitive and perceptual affective role taking in the form of, for example, empathy. While our program does include this concern, it also places emphasis on a consistent environment of modeled concern for others.

Natural modeling alone is not enough. The role of cognition and perspective taking has been increasingly documented as an important component. We encourage the use of induction not only in disciplinary situations, but also in prosocial encounters as a means of helping children assess the situation and put themselves in the other's position. Thus, more attention is directed to recognition of positive actions and their consequences, which often go unnoticed. For example, a parent may say, "Look at how you made Mickey smile when you gave him the truck." As has been indicated in the literature review, parents who use induction tend to have children who show more frequent prosocial behaviors even as early as in nursery school settings. Staub (1975) suggests that use of inductive statements frequently focuses attention on others' feelings. Therefore, we assume that children will learn to be appreciative of positive consequences of their own actions as they learn to exhibit more prosocially oriented behaviors.

Explanation is utilized in conjunction with modeling in all of the focus areas mentioned earlier. In addition, emphasis is placed on suggesting positive action, giving verbal instructions, stating expectations clearly and consistently, and endorsing altruistic values. It is important to note that none of these behaviors by themselves are associated with eliciting altruistic behavior. But when, for example, verbal instructions are combined with appropriate modeling, the effects are enhanced. There is also reason to believe that when children are sure of the appropriate behavior and have standards for reference, this may orient them towards aiding others and sharing (Staub, 1975).

CREATION OF AN ENVIRONMENT CONDUCIVE TO ALTRUISTIC BEHAVIOR

Our goal is to help young children, primarily infants through six-year-olds, experience and take an active part in an immediate environment that encourages showing concern for others. Parents are encouraged to create an environment that provides both opportunity and guidance, thus allowing children to engage in altruistic behaviors. Waxler, Yarrow, and King (1979) suggest that the very young years, ages 1½ to 2½, when children first begin to show acts of sympathy and sharing, is a time when child-rearing experience has a particularly strong role in influencing the form and course of a child's response to the emotional distress of others. For this reason, the importance of the early years and the overriding influence of exemplary models in fostering altruistic behavior from the beginning stages of life is a part of the educative component of the prevention plan. It is our intention that all the "actors" in the immediate environment of the par-

ticipants are influenced by our program. Parents, peers, and siblings are affected by being involved to varying degrees. Since parents are generally the primary figures available as socialization agents for the child, they are our main target audience.

The techniques are designed to be used not just in homes, and thus perhaps associated with specific situational happenings, but everywhere as a part of everyday life. No material or set up is necessary; the adults learn techniques to make the most out of naturally occurring opportunities in the everyday setting.

IMPLEMENTATION OF THE PREVENTION PLAN

In addition to disseminating information, the more effective parent education programs include training in specific guidance techniques (Crase, 1976; Dickerschied and Vartuli, 1974; Education Commission of the States, 1975). Therefore, this prevention plan includes the following components:

1. identification of the participants' feelings and values
2. information sharing
3. observation by the participants of their home environment
4. skill definition and description
5. skill observation by parents
6. skill discussion and practice (during the workshop sessions and in the home environment)
7. sharing of experiences with constructive and correctional feedback
8. evaluation

Throughout the series of workshops, emphasis is placed on starting at the current functional level of the parent or child. Responsibility is placed on the parent to identify their current level of communication skill, to choose personal and child behaviors to increase, and to practice the techniques. Active group participation and expectations of the group facilitator are built into the format of the series. Solicitation of ideas, expression of feelings, role playing, practice, and skill assimilation are interspersed throughout the sessions. Information is transmitted, but the intent is that the participants actively respond cognitively, affectively, and behaviorally to what they are learning. A distinct effort is made to relate the acquisition of techniques and information to the level and needs of the individual. This is dependent, in part, upon how much the individual participates. The opportunity to participate is offered, expected, and supported by the format, directions, and facilitator guidelines. Realistic expectations in terms of child outcomes and differential values of parents are discussed during the workshops to help insure appropriate use of developing skills.

The sessions will be written in a "pre-packaged" manual form. The workshop activities have been field tested and the manual is being designed based on these experiences. Prior to the completion of the manual the parent workshop series will be field tested and formally evaluated by the authors. This is scheduled to occur during 1984–85. The manual is being designed for use without the assistance of trained group leaders. Each activity has its own goal, plan of action, evaluation, and suggested variations for different audiences.

In addition to the parent workshop described in this article, an early education series for child-care personnel has also been developed and field tested. These prevention plans are designed for use by parent groups, human service programs, PTA's, day care centers, and primary-grade teacher inservice. Adoption and use of a prevention plan is voluntary and based on group interest.

EVALUATION OF THE PROGRAM

Evaluation of this program is envisioned in a series of stages. A total of four types of evaluation will be conducted: assessments of workshop presentation; of participants' knowledge of appropriate techniques; of home behavior; and of behavioral responses in a laboratory setting. To assess the presentation methods, participants are asked at the end of the series very general questions about the workshop (e.g., "What parts did you find most helpful?" "Were there any parts that you didn't fully understand?")

Both observation of home behavior and assessment of participants' knowledge is included in the workshop "packages" and can serve as feedback to the group facilitators. The participants are asked during the first week to record instances of helping, sharing, and comforting behaviors of their children as well as their responses to their children's behavior. At the end of the series they are asked to repeat this assignment. This activity serves to sensitize the participants to these behaviors and gives some indication of change from the first to final week. To assess knowledge gained from the series, a short pretest-posttest written assessment of the actual information learned from the workshop series is in-

cluded. Examples of questions are: "Which of the following methods are the most effective . . . ?" "Given the following situation, what would you do . . . ?"

Further evaluation under more controlled conditions will be conducted by the authors to evaluate changes in the participants' responses to children in everyday situations. After hearing brief descriptive scenarios, participants will respond to slides of several sets of children. They will be asked to report verbatim what they would say to the child and describe verbally any nonverbal action (hugging, modeling, etc.). The parents' responses will be tape recorded and later rated on the dimensions covered in the workshop (e.g., use of induction, modeling, awareness of the child's needs and abilities). This evaluation will be done before and after participation in the workshop series. The responses will be rated following the posttest by trained observers who have reached an acceptable level of reliability on practice tapes. The raters will have no knowledge of the order (pretest or posttest) of the tapes. If feasible, this evaluation will be conducted again six months later.

The combined results of these four types of evaluation will give an indication of the short-term impact on the workshop series. Both the workshop and the evaluation procedures directly address the parent's behavior with the assumption that changes in the parent's behavior will augment the child's maturation for long-term effectiveness. At this point, an evaluation of child outcome is not planned.

DISCUSSION

As has been consistently demonstrated by numerous studies, the adults with whom a child associates exert a tremendous influence on the child's behavior. Parents, through their words and especially through their actions, model and shape their children's behavior. Perhaps one of the more important aspects of this workshop series is the focus of this phenomenon. The structure of the workshop allows parents the opportunity to examine their values and to examine the congruity of their values and their behavior. It is recognized that competitive behavior oriented to personal achievement is an integral part of the value system of our society. It is also recognized that parents value prosocial behavior and hope to rear their children in a manner that will encourage behavior that positively contributes to society and that this behavior will be intrinsically rewarding to their offspring. The activities of the workshop focus on the complexities involved in integrating these divergent values in a manner that demonstrates to the child a model for behavior that is functional not only to the individual, but to society as well.

The overriding effectiveness of this program will depend on the degree to which altruistic behavior is valued in everyday words and actions in the child's environment. We believe that we have designed a program grounded in theory and research findings that provides participants with an inviting opportunity to encourage altruistic behavior in young children. If it is true that those who help others learn also learn the content and techniques better themselves, then we will have succeeded in fostering a more altruistic environment for all concerned.

REFERENCES

Aaronfreed, J. (1976). Moral development from the standpoint of a general psychological theory. In T. Likona (ed.), *Moral development and behavior: Theory, research and social issues.* New York: Holt, Rinehart, and Winston.

Baumrind, D. (1972). Socialization and instrumental competence in young children. In W. W. Hardup (ed.), *The young child: Reviews of research* (Vol. 2). Washington, DC: National Association for the Education of Young Children.

Best, D. L., and Prothro, C. B. (1981). *The effects of early mother-infant separation upon sharing behaviors of one-year-olds.* Paper presented at the Southeastern Psychological Association Convention, Atlanta, GA.

Borke, H. (1971). Interpersonal perception of young children. *Developmental Psychology, 51,* 263–269.

Bryan, J. H. (1975). *Children's cooperation and helping behaviors.* Chicago: University of Chicago Press.

Bryan, J. H., and Schwartz, T. H. (1971). The effects of film material upon children's behavior. *Psychological Bulletin, 75,* 50–59.

Bryan, J. H., and Walbeck, N. (1970a). Preaching and practicing self-sacrifice: Children's actions and reactions. *Child Development, 41,* 329–353.

Bryan, J. H., and Walbeck, N. (1970b). The impact of words and deeds concerning altruism upon children. *Child Development, 41,* 747–757.

Bryant, B. K., and Crockenberg, J. B. (1980). Correlates and dimensions of prosocial behavior: A study of female siblings with their mothers. *Child Development, 57,* 529–544.

Burton, R. V., Maccoby, E. E., and Allinsmith, W. (1961). Antecedents of resistance to temptation in four-year-old children. *Child Development, 22,* 689–710.

Church, J. (ed.). (1966). *Three babies: Biographies of cognitive development.* New York: Random House.

Crase, S. J. (1976). Parent education: An overview. *Illinois Teacher, 20,* 90–93.

De Palma, D. J., and Olejnik, A. B. (1973). *Effects of social class, moral orientations, and severity of punishment on boys' generosity.* Unpublished manuscript, Loyola University, Chicago.

Dickerscheid, J. D. and Vartuli, S. (1974). Child-rearing information . . . What do rural Ohio parents want to know? *Ohio Report on Research and Development, 591,* 12–14.

Education Commission of the United States. (1975). *The role of the family in child development: Implications for state policies and programs.* (Report No. 15). Denver: Education Commission of the States.

Fehrenbach, P. A., Miller, D. J., and Thelen, M. H. (1979). The importance of consistency of modeling behavior upon imitation: A comparison of single and multiple models. *Journal of Personality and Social Psychology, 37,* 1412–1417.

Finkelstein, N. W. (1982). Aggression: Is it stimulated by day care? *Young Child, 37(6),* 6–9.

Gelfand, D. M., Hartmann, D. P., Cromer, C. C., Smith, C. L., and Page, R. C. (1975). The effects of instructional prompts and praise on children's donation rates. *Child Development, 46,* 980–983.

Grusec, J. E. (1971). Power and the internalization of self denial. *Child Development, 42,* 93–105.

Grusec, J. E., and Skubiski, S. L. (1970). Model nurturance, demand characteristics of the modeling experiment, and altruisms. *Journal of Personality and Social Psychology, 14,* 353–359.

Hay, D. F. (1979). Cooperative interactions and sharing between very young children and their parents. *Developmental Psychology, 15,* 647–653.

Hoffman, M. L. (1963). Parent discipline and the child's consideration of others. *Child Development, 34,* 573–588.

Hoffman, M. L. (1970). Moral development. In P. H. Mussen (ed.), *Carmichael's manual of child psychology* (Vol. 2). New York: Wiley.

Hoffman, M. L. (1975a). Altruistic behavior and the parent-child relationship. *Journal of Personality and Social Psychology, 31,* 937–943.

Hoffman, M. L. (1975b). Developmental synthesis of affect and cognition and its implications for altruistic motivation. *Developmental Psychology, 11,* 607–619.

Hoffman, M. L. (1975c). The development of altruistic motivation. In D. J. De Palma and J. M. Foley (eds.), *Moral development: Current theory and research.* New York: Wiley.

Hoffman, M. L. and Saltzstein, H. D. (1967). Parent discipline and the child's moral development. *Journal of Personality and Social Psychology, 5,* 45–57.

Honig, A. S. (1982). Research in review: Prosocial development in children. *Young Children, 37(5)* 51–62.

Kagan, S., and Madsen, M. C. (1971). Experimental analysis of cooperation and competition of Anglo-American and Mexican children. *Developmental Psychology, 6.* 49–59.

Kobak, D. (1979). Teaching children to care. *Children Today, 8*(2), 34–35.

Liebert, R. M., and Fernandez, L. E. (1970). *Effects of single and multiple modeling cues on establishing norms for sharing.* Paper presented at the meeting of the American Psychological Association, Miami Beach.

Masters, J. C. (1971). Effects of social comparison upon children's self-reinforcement and altruism toward competitors and friends. *Developmental Psychology, 5,* 64–72.

Midlarsky, E. and Bryan, J. H. (1972). Affect expressions and children's imitative altruism. *Journal of Experimental Research in Personality, 6,* 195–203.

Midlarsky, E., Bryan, J. H., and Brickman, P. (1973). Aversive approval: Interactive effects of modeling and reinforcement on altruistic behavior. *Child Development, 44,* 321–328.

Moore, B. S., Underwood, B., and Rosenhan, D. L. (1973). Affect and altruism. *Developmental Psychology, 8,* 99–104.

Mussen, P., and Eisenberg-Berg, N. (1977). *Roots of caring, sharing, and helping: The development of prosocial behavior in children.* San Francisco: Freeman.

Openshaw, D. K. (1978). *The development of self-esteem in the child: Model theory versus parent-child interaction.* Unpublished doctoral dissertation, Brigham Young University, Provo, Utah.

Peterson, G. B. (1976). *Adolescent moral development as related to family power, family support and parental moral development.* Unpublished doctoral dissertation, University of Minnesota, Minneapolis.

Rheingold, H. L. (1979). *Helping by two-year-old children.* Paper presented at the biennial meeting of the Society for Research in Child Development, San Francisco.

Rheingold, H. L., Hay, D. F., and West, M. J. (1976). Sharing in the second year of life. *Child Development, 47,* 1148–1158.

Rice, M. E., and Grusec, J. E. (1975). Saying and doing: Effects on observer performance. *Journal of Personality and Social Psychology, 32,* 584–593.

Rosenhan, D. L. (1969). *Studies in altruistic behavior: Developmental and naturalistic variables associated with charitability.* Paper presented at the meeting of Society for Research in Child Development, Santa Monica, CA.

Rosenhan, D. L., and White, G. M. (1967). Observation and rehearsal as determinants of prosocial behavior. *Journal of Personality and Social Psychology, 5,* 424–471.

Rushton, J. P. (1975). Generosity in children: Immediate and long term effects of modeling, preaching, and moral judgment. *Journal of Personality and Social Psychology, 31,* 459–466.

Rushton, J. P. (1980). *Altruism, socialization, and society.* Englewood Cliffs, NJ: Prentice-Hall.

Rutherford, E., and Mussen, P. (1968). Generosity in nursery school boys. *Child Development, 39,* 755–765.

Shigetomi, C. C., Hartman, D. P., Gelfand, D. M., Cohen, E. A., and Montemayor, R., (1979). *Children's altruism: Sex differences in behavior and reputation.* Paper presented at the Society for Research in Child Development, San Francisco.

Shure, M. B., and Spivack, G. (1978). *Problem-solving techniques in childrearing.* San Francisco: Jossey-Bass.

Staub, E. (1971a). A child in distress: The influence of nurturance and modeling on children's attempts to help. *Developmental Psychology, 5,* 124–132.

Staub, E. (1971b). Helping a person in distress: The influence of implicit and explicit "rules" of conduct on children and adults. *Journal of Personality and Social Psychology, 17,* 137–144.

Staub, E. (1975). To rear a prosocial child: Reasoning, learning by doing and learning by teaching others. In D. J. De Palma and J. M. Foley (eds.), *Moral development: Current theory and research.* Hillsdale, NJ: Erlbaum.

Stayton, D. J., Hogan, R., and Ainsworth, M. D. S. (1971). Infant obedience and maternal behavior: The origins of socialization reconsidered. *Child Development, 42,* 1057–1069.

Waxler, C., Yarrow, M., and King, R. A. (1970). Child rearing and children's prosocial initiations towards victims of distress. *Child Development, 50,* 319–330.

Weissbrod, C. S. (1980). The impact of warmth and instructions on donation. *Child Development, 51,* 279–281.

White, G. M. (1972). Immediate and deferred effects of model observation and guided and unguided rehearsal on donating and stealing. *Journal of Personality and Social Psychology, 21,* 139–148.

Whiting, B. B., and Whiting, J. W. M. (1975). *Children of six cultures: A psychological analysis:* Cambridge: Harvard University Press.

Yarrow, M. R., Scott, P. M., and Waxler, C. Z. (1973). Learning concern for others. *Developmental Psychology, 8,* 240–260.

Yarrow, M. W., and Waxler, C. Z. (1977). The emergence and functions of prosocial behavior in young children. In R. C. Smart and M. S. Smart (eds.), *Readings in child development and relationships.* New York: Macmillan.

23

CHANGING MEN WHO BATTER:
A DEVELOPMENTAL MODEL FOR INTEGRATED INTERVENTIONS

Edward W. Gondolf
Western Psychiatric Institute and Clinic
University of Pittsburgh

INTRODUCTION

Efforts to intervene in wife abuse have dramatically expanded since the founding of shelters for battered women 12 years ago. In recent years, a variety of interventions have emerged to deal with the perpetrators of wife abuse—the men who batter. These interventions cover a wide range of punitive and therapeutic modalities: jailing, mandated counseling, accountability education, supervised self-help groups, anger control treatment, and family therapy. A recent survey estimates that 89 counseling programs for batterers are in operation nationwide (Pirog-Good and Stets-Kealey, 1985). At the same time, several states are following Washington's example of enforcing criminal laws and procedures in domestic violence cases (see Crane, 1985).

This variety of interventions, however, faces three major problems: (1) The interventions are most often implemented in piecemeal fashion. (2) The interventions are generally uncoordinated and may even be in competition (Gondolf, 1985). (3) The counseling programs, in particular, experience low recruitment, high drop out and high recidivism (Gondolf, 1987).

While practical concerns have no doubt contributed to the implementation problems, the lack of a theoretical rationale for coordinating interventions also lies behind the problems. The array of interventions rests largely on cognitive psychological models for anger control (Sonkin *et al.*, 1985), family systems theories of treatment (Weidman, 1986), and deterrence theories of stopping deviance (Sherman and Berk, 1984). These tend to support one mode of intervention over another rather than suggest how various interventions might complement one another. Moreover, they focus on short-term interruption of the violent behavior, rather than a long-term reform and change of the batterer.

An alternative approach is suggested by developmental theory. As Zigler and Glick (1986) demonstrate in *A Developmental Approach to Adult Psychotherapy*, developmental theory may be applied to a variety of diagnostic groups, including schizophrenics, affective disorders, and personality disorders. They specifically discuss the implications of developmental theory for the treatment of alcoholics, a category somewhat analogous to batterers.

In the following discussion, I apply Kohlberg's (1981) developmental theory to men who batter in order to formulate a model for integrating the diversity of batterer interventions. Kohlberg's emphasis on moral development seems particularly suited for batterers given their disregard of women and control of others (Gondolf, 1985). This developmental theory is especially useful because it accounts for a process of change that addresses the batterer's cessation of verbal and psychological abuse as well as physical abuse. In other words, it offers a more complete picture of the long-term process of becoming nonabusive, rather than focus simply on extinguishing battering, as many behavior therapies tend to do.

The Kohlberg theory presents six sequential stages of change within three levels of development that are typified by denial, behavior change, and personal transformation. It may therefore be argued that men who batter are fixated at a low stage of development and need to move to higher stages. This kind of change process implies that the interventions for batterers need to be integrated into a series of interventions that corresponds to the developmental stage of the batterer and further it.

As a batterer moves toward a higher stage of development, he may become more responsive to another form of intervention which is more appropriate to that stage. Therefore, one kind of intervention is not sufficient to change batterers, and an

From the *Journal of Family Violence*, 1987, 2(4): 345–359. Copyright © Plenum Publishing Company. Reprinted by permission.

intervention that does not correspond to the batterer's stage of development is not likely to be effective. Batterers may in fact be at different stages of change. This may explain why some are responsive to jailing, as the Minneapolis Police Study (Sherman and Berk, 1984) indicates, and others more responsive to counseling.

THE PREMISES OF
DEVELOPMENTAL THEORY

Developmental theory has become an established interpretation of human growth and change. It is rooted in Piaget's (1932) notions of cognitive development which have been refined and elaborated by such contemporaries as Kohlberg (1981). Kohlberg has adopted Piaget's theories to explain the development of moral judgment and to arrange interventions to promote this development. [Moral Discussion groups, for instance, have been shown to advance the moral reasoning of delinquent boys (Niles, 1986).] More advanced stages of moral judgment are thought to have a direct influence on resolving conflicts and precipitate behavioral change. [The later proposition has not been conclusively demonstrated because of shortcomings in research design (Blasi, 1980).]

According to Kohlberg's theory, individuals move through a sequence of stages toward higher levels of reasoning and more moral action. This development is the outgrowth of one's capacity to accommodate certain social stimuli and his or her encounter with appropriate stimuli. In other words, development is not merely an outgrowth of maturation. One must be mentally equipped to engage new aspects of his or her social environment, and one's social environment must sufficiently prompt new ways of conceiving of the world. In the process, the way one makes moral choices is restructured and constitutes a different reasoning process identified as a stage. Individual behavior tends to be more consistent and humane the higher one's stage of development, according to Kohlberg.[1]

Kohlberg presents three levels of moral judgment based on Piaget's three levels of cognitive reasoning (see Table 1). Level I is an egocentric state (Piaget's preoperational level) in which other persons are relatively undifferentiated. The world beyond the individual is largely a monolithic object from which to protect against or obtain. Appropriate interactions with one's social environment begin to alter one's conceptions. Eventually, the individual

becomes aware that other individuals exist with feelings and needs like one's own. The person, as a result, attains the more "other" oriented reasoning of Level II (Piaget's concrete operational level). Ultimately at Level III, the individual adopts principles that propel him or her to engage society and serve its betterment (Piaget's formal operational level).

Six successive stages of moral development correspond to these three levels—two stages to each level. The individual may make his or her moral judgments on the basis of (1) the physical consequences of obedience and punishment, (2) the reciprocity of naive egotism, (3) conformity to a good-boy image, (4) respect for authority and social order, (5) adherence to contractual and legalistic rights, or (6) choices of conscience or principle. In response to the quality of one's experiences, reasoning is restructured from a basis of rewards and punishments, to a basis of peer pressure and empathy, and finally to a basis of principles and mutual trust—that is, from the physically inflicted constraints to abstractly conceived ideals.

The individual may, however, become arrested, impeded or accelerated at any stage (Kohlberg, 1981). That is, our mental growth may not be sufficient to accommodate new forms of interaction; our social environment may not adequately stimulate us or actually deprive us of needed interactions; or social interaction may be appropriate and sufficient to prompt the development of a new orientation. Those endeavoring to promote our development need to be at least a stage higher in order to offer the kind of interaction that is growth producing and not merely reinforcing (Kohlberg and Turiel, 1971).

DEVELOPMENTAL THEORY
AND BATTERERS

Recent clinical assessments of men who rape, molest, or abuse alcohol appear to corroborate this theory of stage development. The rapists in Groth's (1979) noted qualitative study, *Men Who Rape,* for instance, begin treatment at a stage with little concern or consciousness of anyone but themselves (Level I). Their own needs and wants almost overpower them. As they are confronted with the consequences of their behavior—how the rape hurts them, so to speak—they start to examine themselves and consider some behavior change (Level II). With appropriate and extended treatment, some of the men began to develop a modicum of empathy for their victims.

TABLE 1. Kohlberg's Levels and Stages of Moral Development

Levels	Basis of Moral Judgment	Stages of Development
I	Preoperational: egocentric Moral value resides in external, quasiphysical happenings, in bad acts, or in quasi-physical needs rather than in persons and standards.	Stage 1: Obedience and punishment orientation. Egocentric deference to superior power or prestige. Stage 2: Naively egoistic orientation. Right action is that instrumentally satisfying the self's needs and occasionally others: Naive egalitarianism and orientation to exchange and reciprocity.
II	Concrete Operational: other oriented Moral value resides in performing good or right roles, in maintaining the conventional order and the expectancies of others.	Stage 3: Good-boy orientation. Orientation to approval and to pleasing and helping others. Conformity to stereotypical images of majority of natural role behavior. Stage 4: Authority and social-order maintaining orientation. Orientation to "doing duty" and to showing respect for authority and maintaining the given social order for its own sake.
III	Formal Operational: Abstract reasoning Moral value resides in conformity by the self to shared standards, rights, or duties.	Stage 5: Contractual legalistic orientation. Recognition of starting point in rules or expectations for the sake of agreement. Duty defined in terms of contract; general avoidance of violation of the will or rights of others. Stage 6: Conscience or principle orientation. Orientation not only to actually ordained social rules but to principles of choice involving appeal to logical universality and consistency. Orientation to conscience as a directing agent and to mutual respect and trust.

Source: Kohlberg (1981).

In in-depth interviews with 15 reformed batterers, the men who had stopped their abuse described themselves moving through similar stages of change (Gondolf and Hanneken, 1987). All of the batterers referred to a process of moving from denial of their abuse toward a willingness to change as a result of some confrontation or constraint. They eventually developed some empathy for their wives. Two of the men were increasingly involved in social action, but most of the reformed batterers were still struggling with self doubts and were relatively isolated but seeking more involvement with their community.

Kohlberg's six stages of moral development (and three levels corresponding to Piaget's) might be used to explain the apparent change process in reformed batterers.[2] In adapting Kohlberg's theory to batterers, I have made a few necessary extrapolations (see Table 2). One, the levels and stages have been relabeled to emphasize the batterer's outlook toward his abuse. Two, the stages are characterized by the men's attitude toward women, as well as their behavior toward them. Three, the most appropriate

intervention for a particular stage is determined on the basis of its modality. Four, the intensified resistence to stage development caused by delayed development and prolonged stage fixation (Kohlberg and Turiel, 1971) is acknowledged in the intervention shortcomings.

The stages of change for men who batter and their implications for intervention are discussed below:

LEVEL I. DENIAL

The batterer is egocentric ("me" oriented), thinking primarily of furthering his own physical needs in a dualistic world of me-against-them. He denies that he has been abusive and fails to consider the consequences of his abuse. As a result, the man lapses into physical abuse despite his promises to the contrary and repeated treatment efforts.

STAGE 1. DEFIANCE The batterer is preoccupied with his own needs and wants, and views his wife as another "object" to control and manipulate for his own advantage. The batterer at this stage is, there-

TABLE 2. Developmental Model for Changing Men Who Batter

Level Change Stage	I. Denial		II. Behavioral change		III. Personal Transformation
	1. Defiance	2. Self-justification	3. Self-change	4. Relationship building	5. Community Service
Intervention	•Wife leave, •Divorce, •Jailing •Behavior modification	•Accountability Education, •Court-ordered counseling,	•Supervised Self-help groups	•Personal growth workshops, •Follow-up groups; •Family therapy	•Self-help co-leader; •Agency volunteer; •Service activity
Modality	Constraint	Confrontation	Behavior management	Emotive development	Self-concept restructuring
Motivating Factor	Fear/insecurity	Guilt	Pain/self-interest	Emerging empathy	Confidence/social awareness
Attitude to Women	Objectification		Acknowledgment		Intimacy
Abuse to Women	Physical Emotional		Less physical more emotional		Nonabusive
Shortcomings	Resentment	Projection	Self-congratulations	Complacency	Over-zealous/dogmatic

————————— Women-Battering culture

6. Social action

•Shelter support
•Men's collective
•Retraining Human services
•Building alliances
•Men's centers

Implications: (1) Batterers move toward change through a series of developmental stages. (2) Interventions must be appropriate to the men's change stage. (3) Supervised self-help groups are not sufficient in themselves. (4) Interventions must ultimately be directed toward dismantling women-battering culture.

fore, relatively unaware of any moral wrong or personal consequence to his abuse, and does as impulse dictates. He is most likely to minimize the abuse as inconsequential, or justify it as doing what is necessary for his survival.

The appropriate way to intervene is with constraint. That is, the batterer needs to be physically separated from his wife by having the wife leave for a shelter or divorce him, or by jailing the man. As most batterers seeking help report, they began to seek help when their wives left them or called the police. This constraint appears to motivate the batterer by generating fear for his own physical well-being.

The batterer at this stage identifies himself in relationship to external objectifications and actions. He might characteristically note: "I know I am a man when others do what I tell them." Therefore, isolating the batterer from these identifiers may also raise some motivating psychological insecurity.

The main shortcoming of constraining interventions is the batterer's possible backlash of resentmentto what he perceives as undeserved punishment.

STAGE 2. SELF-JUSTIFICATION The batterer begins to consider that his behavior may be abusive and have consequences at least for himself, if not for his wife. The abuse, however, may still be justified as a convenient way to meet one's needs. That is, the violence is perceived as instrumental.

The most appropriate intervention is to confront the batterer with the dysfunctional aspects of his behavior. This may be accomplished through accountability education programs that instruct the batterer in his responsibility for the abuse, and the legal and social consequences of his behavior. The batterer must be coerced to participate through court-mandate or threat of rejailing, because he still reasons on the basis of rewards and punishments. Ideally, this intervention will stimulate a sense of guilt for being unfair and impractical in his behavior. A batterer might begin to relent, "I only made things worse for myself by abusing her," and start his movement toward the next stage of reasoning. The major shortcoming of this intervention is that men may project the blame for his problems onto the victim.

LEVEL II. BEHAVIORAL CHANGE

The batterer becomes willing to change his behavior in order to gain the approval of others and feel better about himself. His emotional isolation begins to break down as he accepts more interaction and exchange. In sum, he becomes more "other" oriented and thus develops some concern about his wife. As a result, he is likely to diminish and even curtail his violence.

STAGE 3. SELF-CHANGE The batterer accepts that he is physically abusive and becomes aware of his "bad" image as an abuser. Consequently, he wants to stop his violence which at this point he views as "expressive"—something out of his control and largely counterproductive. He wants to gain control of himself in order to project what Kohlberg refers to as the "good-boy" image that is more functional than his previous macho bullying.

Supervised self-help groups appeal to this desire for self-change. They are useful at this stage in that they teach the man how to control his behavior through techniques like time-outs and self-talk. In the process, the batterer considers primarily his own self-interest—how being abusive affects him. A typical comment might be: "For the first time, I see that I am hurting myself as much as her. I don't have any real friends." He also becomes aware of his own deficiencies like his unexpressiveness, extreme stress, and emotional pain. This awareness may lead to severe depression as well as self-consciousness.

The main shortcoming to intervention of this kind is that the batterer may become self-congratulatory. He may expect his wife to suddenly appreciate him for "controlling" his physical abuse and even leave the program claiming he is cured. Unfortunately, the process of change—and the end of psychological abuse—is far from complete. In fact, while physical abuse may lessen, the psychological abuse may actually increase as the man verbalizes his newly discovered hurts and uses them to manipulate his wife.

STAGE 4. RELATIONSHIP BUILDING This stage is characterized by the batterer's capacity to develop relationships with some emotional dimension. His growing awareness of his own feelings enables him to recognize the feelings of others. Therefore, the man is able to develop a sense of respect for others and for authority beyond his personal will.

At this stage, the man is apt to be responsive to interventions that further his understanding of sex-roles and their contribution to abuse. He might typically note of his previous abuse, "I had simply not been able to express my feelings before and was threatened when my wife expressed hers." Personal growth workshops, which conduct role plays and further self-disclosure, help the man bond with other men. Some follow-up groups explore, as well, the batterer's relationship to his father and other relatives, and in that way prompt men to "relate" to significant others in general. This capacity for relationships is gradually transferred to the home or enables constructive family therapy.

This modality of emotive development raises in the batterer some sense of empathy. The man may therefore develop a relationship with his wife and may even become acceptable to her. However, the batterer may as a result become complacent and reluctant to change further. The possibility of relapse consequently persists.

LEVEL III. PERSONAL TRANSFORMATION

The batterer at this level begins to think abstractly about his relationships and the social world in general. He sees himself not only as a person who is affected by society, but also as a person who can in turn influence the world around him. He becomes in the process able to define principles and moral values to guide his behavior. As a result, the man becomes nonabusive—not only physically but psychologically as well.

STAGE 5. COMMUNITY SERVICE The man becomes interested in bettering himself through helping others. He actually wants to become a fuller person, free of some of the lingering self-doubts about his potential abusiveness. He therefore strives to end his inadvertent psychological abuse and becomes capable of intimacy without feeling threatened.

The appropriate intervention in this case is some sort of outreach to the community. The man may give to others through assisting as a co-leader of a self-help group, as Alcoholics Anonymous has required for years and some batterer programs now encourage. He may be expected to "give" of himself to the community at large, as well. Some criminal courts and drug programs, in fact, have experimented with community service as a mode of rehabilitation. Offenders have worked as truck drivers for a Good Will Store or recreation leaders for handicapped children. In the process, a new self-concept is being formed or reinforced. The man's confidence is furthered and social awareness heightened.

The primary shortcoming of this intervention is that men in this position sometimes become over-zealous and dogmatic in their "conversion." They may be harder on reforming batterers in a self-help group than the other batterers can bear. Or they may push beyond their own capacities in an effort to prove themselves.

STAGE 6. SOCIAL ACTION The man begins to adopt ethical principles with regard to human dignity and a just society. He can grasp how these abstract concepts have meaning and function. He is concerned not only about his own wife but also about women in general; consequently he becomes supportive of the women's movement and what it stands for.

This outlook is reinforced in social action that addresses the women-battering culture which gave rise to the man's abuse. The now "reformed" batterer may work to raise funds for a shelter or campaign for other women's issues like comparable worth, as some men in batterers programs like RAVEN, Second Step, and Men for Nonviolence have done. He may gain needed social support through a men's consciousness-raising organization that works on men's issues like fathering and competition. Or he may help in retraining human service workers, like alcohol counselors, to recognize and address abuse. There may be a place, as well, for establishing men's centers that provide temporary shelter and social support for other men in change.

ACCOUNTING FOR OTHER THEORIES

Kohlberg's notion of stage development can account for many of the prevailing explanations for battering. The most prominent explanation for battering is intergenerational transmission which asserts that batterers learn abuse from their families of origin (Kalmuss, 1984). In light of Kohlberg's theory, a dysfunctional family of origin not only "teaches" violent behavior, but also impedes the development of the young male—and female. A lack of suitable interaction fixates development at Stage 1 or 2 which is more prone to abuse.

According to a feminist analysis, batterers are oversocialized into a male sex role within a patriarchal social structure that supports violence against women (Bograd, 1984). In fact, most men may be slowed in the sequence of what Kohlberg terms moral development, because of the gender differences promoted by society. Men are predisposed to a self-serving, competitive, and even oppressive out-

look. They are therefore more likely to accept a "me-against-the-world" attitude of Stage 1.

The institutions of American society, according to Kohlberg, function predominantly at Stage 1 and 2, making them prone to conflict and oppression. Since men take a primary role in those institutions, men's development is more likely than women's to be impeded by the institutional environment.

But why are "underdeveloped" men attacking women? In line with the developmental theory, the feminine attributes of empathy, cooperation, and inclusiveness are antithetical to the mental constructs of the egocentric level of Stages 1 and 2. As men who batter frequently report, their wives' emotional capacities greatly threaten them. The batterers respond to the perceived threat with instrumental violence that attempts to remove the threat to their emotional underdevelopment.

Moreover, the presence of a battering culture has been well established by researchers ranging from Straus et al. (1980) to Dobash and Dobash (1979). The norms that support the degradation of women, control of wives, and non-intervention into "family affairs" constitute a culture that promotes wife battering. Ultimately, men who batter must come to terms with this culture, as well as their own behavior. In fact, enabling a man to address this culture may be the ingredient that brings healing. In striving to "treat" the culture, the former batterer moves to the more ethical Stage 6.

The radical feminist charge that "all men are potential batterers" may also be explained by this developmental theory (Adams, 1982). All men are at various stages of change, impeded more or less by a sexist culture that largely operates at Stage 2. It takes a conscious effort to assure development to Stage 5 or 6 considering that society at large does not offer men the interaction required to promote such advancement.[3]

PROGRAMMATIC ISSUES

Kohlberg's developmental theory also helps to interpret some of the current programmatic issues. It suggests, for example, that the reasons for the ineffectiveness of self-help groups—the limited recruiting, high drop out, and significant recidivism—may be related to the inappropriateness of the intervention, rather than to the design of the intervention itself. That is, the unresponsive men may simply be at a change stage which is insufficient to accommodate the assumptions of self-change. Those that drop out of self-help groups may be at the denial level needing more constraint or confrontation, or at the relationship building stage warranting more personal growth emphasis.

Some supervised self-help programs have expanded to accommodate men at a change stage prior to and following the self-change stage (Stage 3). RAVEN in St. Louis and Men for Non-Violence in Fort Wayne, for instance, have established a 6-week accountability education program (Stage 2) that precedes the 12 weeks of self-help group sessions. Participation in the self-help group is succeeded by enrollment in a follow-up support group that deals more with relationship issues and personal growth (Stage 4).

The thrust of this analysis is that a match between the batterer's development and mode of intervention is essential in order to change men who batter. The theory therefore implies some preliminary means of diagnosis: the man's motivating factor, attitude toward women, and kind of abuse may indicate the stage level of the batterer.[4] For example, a man may report that he is seeking help because he is fearful of what the police might do to him, and primarily minimizes the abuse "as no big deal." He claims that he did not hurt his wife whom he views as an object and whom he physically attacks with little remorse. If this is the case, the batterer is a poor candidate for self-help groups (Stage 3) and would most likely be more responsive to some sort of constraint, like jailing (Stage 1).

Also, Kohlberg has devised "moral dilemmas" for assessing similar stage development. Nevertheless, a practical diagnostic tool designed especially for assessing the change stage of batterers would be useful in furthering integrated interventions. This developmental theory, in sum, shifts the basic research question for program evaluation. Instead of the preoccupation with "what works?" the question becomes: "Are the prescribed interventions effective for batterers at a particular stage of development?"

IMPLICATIONS

There are other implications of this developmental model for integrated interventions. One, the model suggests that it is not enough to simply stop men's violence through constraint or confrontation (Stages 1 and 2). Intervention needs to continue to direct the batterer toward further development where psychological abuse is also likely to stop (Stage 5). In fact, the theory implies that intervention should be continued until men are prepared to take social action against the woman-battering culture in order to insure their recovery (Stage 6).

Two, different types of batterers may merely be men at different change stages. Even the so-called nonbatterers may be men who have moved to at least the relationship-building stage without fixating at a prior stage more prone to violence. They may, in this light, be unwitting accomplices to abuse, tolerating and often promoting the wife-battering culture. They have yet to pass the threshold into Level 3 of personal transformation where social action takes place.

Three, the model also implies a means for prevention, as well as intervention. If men are prompted to move through the sequence of developmental stages "normally," then abuse will be less likely. Reforming batterers through integrated interventions will lead some men toward dismantling the battering culture and preventing abuse. Ultimately, we as a society must make a commitment to assuring the moral development in all men that precludes abuse of women and violence in general.

ACKNOWLEDGMENT

This paper was developed under a faculty research grant from the Graduate School of Indiana University of Pennsylvania (IUP), Indiana, Pennsylvania.

NOTES

1. Stage slippage may occur in which we exhibit a higher stage in one domain, like our business, and a lower stage in our family. This would explain why there are frequent reports that batterers have a "Dr. Jekyll and Mr. Hyde" personality. It may also be that batterers at Stage 2 are merely "putting on" the higher Stage 4. Kohlberg has suggested that because of some superficial similarities in his Stage 2 and Stage 4, individuals occasionally may appear to be at Stage 4 when they are really at Stage 2. They mouth lofty "law and order" principles of Stage 4 but maintain a dualistic "good guy-bad guy" reasoning process of Stage 2.

2. Gilligan's (1982) stages for women may be useful in interpreting the behavior of battered women and the most appropriate service for them. Many battered women may have their development impeded because of the isolation and deprivation, not to mention the violence, inflicted by their spouse. This would account in part for the observations that some women manifest "learned helplessness" (Walker, 1979; Shainess,

1977) while others, who are at a higher stage, appear more as creative survivors (Bowker, 1983). Similarly, developmental theory might explain why certain women respond to shelter care, empowerment education, or consciousness-raising and others do not.

3. On the other hand, women, according to Gilligan's (1982) revision of Kohlberg's masculine stages, develop differently. In part perhaps because of the more nurturing situations that women have maintained within their own feminine "counter culture" to the larger patriarchy of society. Gilligan's (1982) noted conception of women's "different voice" suggests that women may in fact be in a developmental sequence that is "better" than men's. Gilligan's stages show women to be more nurturing, global, and cooperative in their reasoning. This is a capacity, according to Gilligan, that our postindustrial society desperately needs in order to survive. Gilligan's theory implies, therefore, that the men's course of development is not sufficient in itself. The male course of development should optimally be turned toward the female's or at least some androgyny should be sought.

4. The "Attitude Toward Women" Scale (Spence and Helmreich, 1972) may also be a useful device in assessing a man's development and the appropriate intervention. However, it has not as yet been shown to correlate directly to abuse.

REFERENCES

Adams, D. (1982). Women batterers: The sins of our brothers. *Sojourner* (May).

Blasi, A. (1980). Bridging moral cognition and moral action: A critical review of the literature. *Psych. Bull.* 88: 1–45.

Bograd, M. (1984). Family systems approaches to wife battering: A feminist critique. *Am. J. Orthopsychiat.* 54: 558–568.

Bowker, L. (1983). *Beating Wife-Beating,* Lexington Books, Lexington, Mass.

Crane, S. W. (1985). The Washington State Domestic Violence Act: An evaluation project. *Response* 8: 13–16.

Dobash, E. R., and Dobash, R. (1979). *Violence Against Wives: The Case Against Patriarchy,* Free Press, New York.

Gilligan, C. (1982). *In a Different Voice: Psychological Theory and Women's Development,* Harvard University Press, Cambridge, Mass.

Gondolf, E. (1984). Anger and oppression in men who batter: Empiricist and feminist perspectives and their implications for research. *Victimology* 10: 311–324.

Gondolf, E. (1985). Fighting for control: A clinical assessment of men who batter. *Social Casework* 61: 48–54.

Gondolf, E. (1987). Evaluating programs for men who batter: Problems and prospects. *J. Fam. Violence* 2: 95–108.

Gondolf, E., and Hanneken, J. (1987). The Gender Warrior: Reformed batterers on abuse, treatment and change. *J. Fam. Violence* 2: 177–191.

Groth, N. (1979). *Men Who Rape: The Psychology of the Offender,* Plenum, New York.

Kalmuss, D. (1984). The intergenerational transmission of marital aggression. *J. Marriage Family* 46: 11–19.

Kohlberg, L. (1981). *The Philosophy of Moral Development,* Harper and Row, San Francisco.

Kohlberg, L. and Turiel, E. (1971). Moral development and moral education. In Lesser, G. (ed.), *Psychology and Educational Practice,* Scott, Foresman, Chicago.

Niles, W. (1986). Effects of a moral development discussion group on delinquent boys. *J. Counseling Psych.* 33: 45–51.

Piaget, J. (1932, 1965). *The Moral Development of the Child,* Free Press, New York.

Pirog-Good, M., and Stets-Kealey, J. (1985). Male batterers and battering prevention programs: A national survey. *Response* 8: 8–12.

Shainess, N. (1979). Vulnerability to violence: Masochism as a process. *Am. J. Orthopsychiat.* 33: 174–189.

Sherman, L., and Berk, R. (1984). The specific deterrent effects of arrest for domestic assault. *Am. Sociol. Rev.* 49: 261–272.

Sonkin, D., Martin, D., and Walker, L. (1985). *The Male Batterer: A Treatment Approach,* Springer, New York.

Spence, J., and Helmreich, W. (1972). The attitudes toward women's scale: An objective instrument to measure attitudes toward the rights and roles of women in contemporary society. *J. Suppl. Abst. Service: Cat. Select. Doc. Psychol.* 2(66): Ms. No. 153.

Straus, M., Gelles, R., and Steinmetz, S. (1980). *Behind Closed Doors: Violence and the American Family,* Anchor/Doubleday, Garden City, New York.

Walker, L. (1979). *The Battered Woman,* Harper and Row, New York.

Zigler, E., and Glick (1986). *A Developmental Approach to Adult Psychotherapy,* Wiley, New York.

24

THE DILEMMA OF GIFTED WOMEN

Kathleen D. Noble
University of Washington

Many issues are relevant to human growth and development, but the study of the gifted has special significance. From this population our cultural, political, educational, and spiritual leadership has historically arisen. But to date very little attention has been paid to the emotional and social development of the gifted, in general, and of gifted women in particular. We know little about gifted women's psychological development and needs, the unique problems they encounter in their personal and professional lives, and the costs to themselves and society of not having their marked abilities recognized and nurtured.

What little data exist suggest that at the elementary school level, at least one-half of all children *identified* as gifted/talented/highly capable are girls; by junior high school, less than one-fourth are still so identified (Clark, 1983; Silverman, 1986). By adulthood, it is likely that the majority of gifted women will settle for far less than their full potential, while most of their male peers will go on to positions of leadership in education, science, industry, the arts, and other sectors of society (Kerr, 1985).

The role of sexism in obscuring the recognition and expression of giftedness in women is irrefutable. Our society has a long-standing history of ambivalence toward highly capable women, and over time many women internalize that ambivalence. As Christ (1980) observed,

> Being female means that even if she gets A's, her career will not be as important as that of a boy who gets B's. Being female means that *she* is not important, except in her relationship to boys and men. Being female also means being given ambivalent messages. Parents and teachers rarely will tell a girl that she is less important than her brothers and other boys . . . The message of her inferiority will be communicated in more subtle ways: a lack of concern, by failure to fully nurture her potential for growth and development, by not expecting her to succeed at difficult tasks. And because

the messages are mixed, a woman may feel that her mother's, father's, or teacher's lack of attention to her stems from some specific failing of her own. Internalizing the voices of her oppressors, the currents of her feelings of inferiority and self-hatred run strong and deep. (p. 15)

Even when women do succeed in taking themselves seriously, many find that they have only a limited range of options through which to express their abilities. As a culture, we acknowledge and reward only those talents and abilities that have direct, marketable value, and what has value has largely been determined by and for men. We tend, therefore, to dismiss "gifts" that aren't rewarded materially or that aren't technologically oriented, and we discount those that are stereotypically "female" (e.g., the ability to love, to understand, to empathize, to be compassionate, to be altruistic, to cope, to survive, to live life with grace, integrity, and authenticity). Yet, by failing to appreciate the value of these abilities in ourselves and others, we perpetuate a misogynistic and constricting conception of giftedness. This is an important and complex issue, but beyond the scope of this paper. (See Getzels and Dillon [1973] and Gilligan [1982] for further elaboration.)

Clark (1983) questions whether the "secure, self-sufficient, successful, self-actualizing gifted woman is commonly found in and supported by our society" (p. 356). Certainly social support is generally lacking, but I don't believe the gifted woman is not "commonly found." Rather, I will argue that a significant part of the problem lies in our reluctance or inability to recognize giftedness in women, and that part of the solution lies in teaching women to recognize, accept and nurture giftedness in themselves and each other. I will also suggest the kinds of psychological and educational interventions which would enable us to maximize the development and achievement of highly capable women, and research directions that would add substantially to our knowledge base.

WHAT IS GIFTEDNESS?

According to Getzels and Dillon (1973), the term "gifted" became the standard designation for persons of superior ability during the early twentieth century. It is, however, not a definition because the term specifies neither the type of ability nor the degree of superiority demonstrated.

Although there are many different kinds of giftedness, our conception has largely been molded by standardized tests of intelligence and studies of scientific talent. The result is that most of the emphasis in gifted education, research, and selection criteria for specialized programs is placed on intellectual and academic skills as measured by available standardized intelligence and achievement tests. Very little attention is paid to the more imaginative, feeling, affective and creative components of giftedness.

For the purposes of this discussion, the term "gifted" will encompass superior ability in one or more of the following areas: (a) intelligence (e.g., high scores on various intelligence tests); (b) academic aptitude (potential or demonstrated); (c) creativity (e.g., performing and visual arts, scientific discoveries, literature, etc.); (d) rate of growth or development of a socially desirable variable which is significantly higher than found in the general population (e.g., moral judgment, ethical or compassionate awareness, leadership, psychomotor ability); and (e) talent (e.g., a special ability or aptitude, performance or achievement, capability or acquired behavior).

WHO ARE THE GIFTED?

The gifted are not a homogeneous group; in fact, the more gifted a person becomes, the more unique she or he is likely to appear. There are however, salient characteristics which consistently appear in groups of gifted individuals, both female and male. Several models are useful in approaching the phenomena of giftedness (e.g., Clark, 1983; Gardner, 1983; Getzels and Dillon, 1973); of these, Clark's framework is especially helpful in establishing the context for this discussion.

Clark (1983) organized the differentiating characteristics of the gifted into five domains (cognitive, affective, physical, intuitive, and societal), and offered a comprehensive description of each domain, as well as examples of related educational, psychological, and programmatic needs. According to Clark, some of the discriminating characteristics of gifted individuals in each domain are the following.

COGNITIVE

The gifted demonstrate an intensified and accelerated activity of mind which includes the ability to retain, comprehend and process large amounts of information, as well as a heightened capacity for perceiving unusual and diverse relationships among people, concepts and situations. They possess a high level of language development, unusually varied interests, curiosity, persistence, and goal-directedness. They also demonstrate an ability not only for problem solving, but for raising new questions.

> [T]he signal mark of the truly gifted, or for that matter, the fully functioning person, is not only the possession of the technical skills and information for solving problems but also the curiosity and imagination for finding problems. (Getzels and Dillon, 1973, p. 720)

AFFECTIVE

Gifted individuals possess intense, rich and extremely differentiated interpersonal feelings. They tend to be very sensitive to the expectations and feelings of others, and to hold high expectations of themselves and others. This unusual emotional depth is often accompanied by a keen sense of humor, long-standing feelings of being different, heightened self-awareness, idealism, and an acute sense of justice.

PHYSICAL

The gifted frequently show a discrepency between their physical and intellectual development. They appear to possess an unusual amount of energy, which can manifest as rapid speech and/or hyperactive behavior.

INTUITIVE

Fascination with the unknown, and an early concern for intuitive knowing and spiritual/philosophical ideas are characteristic of the gifted. They tend to be unusually open to experience, to show heightened moral and ethical awareness, and to have a strong need for consistency between abstract values and personal actions.

SOCIETAL

The gifted are strongly motivated by a need for self-actualization, for challenge, and for opportunities to use their many and varied talents. They frequently search for ways in which to be meaningfully involved with social problems and with the "meta-needs" of society. They often show a capacity for leadership which is recognized by themselves and others, and often at an early age.

ISSUES CONFRONTING GIFTED WOMEN

It is evident that men have been more prominent and more numerous than women in areas of high achievement, but they have been so by reason of differing opportunities rather than differing abilities. In any case, the issue is not the relative superiority of men or women, but the neglect of talent among those of the female population who are in fact gifted or may be found to be so. (Getzels and Dillon, 1973, p. 712)

Although there is a dearth of literature related to giftedness in women, some patterns and trends have been identified and will be discussed in this section.

PERSONALITY CORRELATES

Several researchers have found that gifted women score more like men than women not identified as gifted on measures of self-concept, interests, values and personality (Callahan, 1980; Mills, 1980; Solano, 1983; Wells, Peltier, and Glickauf-Hughes, 1982). From an early age, they appear to be more achievement-oriented, more interested in nontraditional professions, more rebellious against sex-role stereotyping, and more rejecting of outside influences that hinder their development than are their female peers of lesser ability. They also appear to be more androgynous, to have higher self-esteem, and to show a great deal of persistence in the face of adversity (Blaubergs, 1978; Hollinger, 1983).

This is not to say that gifted women are more "masculine" than other women; rather, they seem to combine the characteristics, values, attitudes, feelings, goals and expectations of both sexes. For example, like other women, they feel strongly compelled to nurture, care deeply about relationships and family life, and experience difficulties placing their own needs above those of others (Rodenstein and Glickauf-Hughes, 1977; Silverman, 1986).

SOCIAL PRESSURES

Many studies suggest that, unlike gifted males and females not identified as gifted, almost all gifted women have found it necessary at some time in their lives to hide their abilities in order to survive socially. Several factors contribute to this.

First, cultural ambivalence toward female independence takes its toll on the ranks of gifted women. The majority of these women are gradually conditioned by the educational system and by parents to view themselves as less capable than males, and are socialized to be passive, to avoid taking risks, to hold lower expectations for success and to eventually discount their own skills and accomplishments

(Blaubergs, 1980; Fox, 1981; Hollinger and Fleming, 1984; Whitmore, 1980). Further, male and female teachers appear to like gifted males better, consider them more capable, and negatively perceive qualities in gifted females that they positively perceive in males (e.g., analytical skills, originality, nontraditional approaches to learning and problem solving) (Blaubergs, 1980; Cooley, Chauvin, and Karnes, 1984; Fox, 1981).

Second, the pre-adolescent peer group tends to reject a girl who appears to be too smart or too successful, and this trend does not appear to reverse itself over time except in certain highly selective environments such as all-female high schools or colleges (Tidball and Kistiakowsky, 1976). Consequently, gifted females often feel they must choose between developing their abilities and being rejected socially or considered "unfeminine" (Callahan, 1980; Fox and Richmond, 1979; Kirschenbaum, 1980; Schwartz, 1980). Third, gifted females frequently encounter hostility toward their abilities, not only in communities that devalue intellectual gifts in women, but also in settings that tacitly support both traditional and nontraditional aspirations in women (Fox, 1981; Kirschenbaum, 1980; Silverman, 1986). Unfortunately, we do not know how often this hostility takes the form of violence against women. To my knowledge, no investigation has yet explored the representation of gifted females among populations of sexually, physically, and/or emotionally abused women and girls. Yet, as Whitmore (1980) observed, there is a definite tendency among children and adults to punish and reject the person who is different. Such treatment will undoubtedly obscure the expression of giftedness in some women, and compromise others' ability to take their gifts seriously and cultivate them assiduously.

CULTURAL EXPECTATIONS

Roeper (1978) observed that the real milestone in the history of the gifted female was the advent of the women's movement, because doors were finally opened to women that had previously been closed. It is true that women have made progress over the past twenty years, and that more women have access to more educational and employment opportunities than ever before. But mainstream culture changes more slowly than many of us would wish, and despite these new opportunities, gender-role stereotyping and the strength of traditional value systems frequently burden gifted women with what has been described by Rodenstein, Pfleger and Colangelo (1977) as a classic double bind. That is, the traditional behavioral expectations for gifted individuals and women are often inconsistent and mutually exclusive.

For example, gifted students are usually expected to succeed in traditionally male-dominated fields such as science, math, law, medicine and business. Yet gifted females are generally not encouraged and are frequently discouraged from studying science and math, and gender-role stereotyping still affects the number of options females perceive as acceptable and attainable. When women do enter nontraditional fields, as did Barbara McClintock, a brilliant scientist whose life work in cytogenetics is revolutionizing the field of molecular biology (Keller, 1983), many have no role models, mentors, support systems or traditions for dealing with these new opportunities. Further, women are still expected to be less intelligent, to earn less and be less educated than their male partners, and to interrupt their careers when demands of their mates and/or children interfere (Blaubergs, 1980; Cox and Daniel, 1983; Fox, 1983; Higham and Navarre, 1984; Schwartz, 1980).

For some gifted women, the consequences of dealing with this double bind can be fatal. Russo, Miller, and Vitaliano (1985) estimate that the rate of suicide and morbidity among female physicians and medical students, for example, although similar to that of male physicians, medical students and males in the general population, is *three times* that of females in the general population. This may be because

> they have greater accessibility to lethal means of suicide . . . ; females have difficulty integrating their traditional roles with those of the physician; they encounter hostility in a traditionally male-oriented environment; and they lack mentors and support (p. 118).

COGNITIVE STYLES

Another factor contributing to the psychological discouragement experienced by many gifted women is their tendency to view mediocrity in any area as a loss of self-esteem and the turning down of an opportunity as a loss of potential and consequently a personal failure (Silverman, 1986). Others experience a profound sense of inadequacy, and attribute their successes when they occur to luck or chance rather than to ability (Covington and Omelich, 1979; Dweck and Licht, 1980). This can manifest as an "imposter" mentality, characterized by a pervasive anxiety that one's facade of competence will eventually be discovered, resulting in failure and humilia-

tion. Eventually these perceptions will lead to a crippling or paralysis of exceptional ability. The result of struggling with cultural confusion about what is and is not appropriate for gifted women can be underachievement, underemployment, chronic dissatisfaction with one's life, depression, anxiety, illness, eating disorders, perfectionism, isolation, and the exhaustion of the superwoman syndrome.

These issues are certainly alive for most women, but gifted women are affected much more powerfully and deleteriously because of their "enormous awareness of the complexities and dangers of the world" (Roeper, 1978, p. 7). Although Garmezy and Tellegen (1984) have argued that intelligence serves as a major protective factor for individuals in coping with adversity and life stressors of varying intensity, gender-role socialization mitigates much of this protection for gifted women. Exceptional cognitive ability, as previously noted, is frequently accompanied by increased capacities for empathy, differentiated feelings, and relatedness, leading to an enhanced identification with and responsivity to the expectations of others. When these latter include (as they usually do) the need for women to be dependent, to place attachment to others above attachment to self, to avoid entering a challenging world and competing with men, and to substitute protection from others for realization of potential, it is no wonder that so few women reach maturity with their giftedness intact.

DIRECTIONS FOR PREVENTION, INTERVENTION, AND FUTURE RESEARCH

Higham and Navarre (1984) and Fox (1981) suggest several factors that are productive of a high level of adult achievement in all people. These include: (a) a secure emotional base; (b) warm, nurturing parents who encourage exploration; (c) parent and teacher encouragement of independent thinking, independent behavior and tolerance for change; and (d) role-model identification, self-acceptance, early success experiences and self-confidence. Certainly many gifted women do not grow up in such ideal environments. But feminist psychologists and educators can help to create a climate conducive to the development of superior ability in women by implementing some of the following suggestions.

Psychological education must be available to gifted females from a very early age to help them make lifestyle choices, specifically in regard to career and family. Young gifted women particularly need help in dispelling three self-defeating myths: (a) that a choice between having a career and a family is always necessary; (b) that career and lifestyle planning is irreversible; and (c) that choosing a single lifestyle will inevitably lead to discontent and dissatisfaction with one's life (Rodenstein and Glickauf-Hughes, 1977). Further, gifted women need to learn that it may not be possible or desirable to live up to the "superwoman" ethos, and that choosing a lifestyle may involve making some difficult compromises and trade-offs.

Feminist-oriented psychotherapy to assist gifted women of all ages to develop autonomy, independence, psychological stability, assertiveness, self-confidence, positive self-image, self-esteem and a sense of social competence is vitally important. Gifted women frequently need help in unlearning a fear of creativity, building confidence, and gaining acceptance for their creative abilities (Schwartz, 1977). Further, gifted women must understand that their perception of their own ability is an essential dimension to explore in therapy as their self-perception is usually much lower than their actual ability (Hollinger, 1983). We must also keep abreast of research in sex differences in order to assist our clients to understand the prevalence of attitudes and stereotyping that are detrimental to the fullest expression of their abilities. As Navarre (1980) discovered, awareness can greatly reduce the negative impact of sexism on women's willingness to develop and display their gifts.

Career counseling assists gifted women in planning a lifestyle that allows for the achievement of leadership status within a career, as well as developing the ability to understand and work with multipotentiality (Rodenstein et al., 1977). Gifted women frequently have the ability to be successful in so many areas and activities that they have difficulty choosing a direction or focus for their lives. Secondary school counselors should also make a special effort to alert adolescent women to college scholarship and grant information. For many gifted women, money is a barrier to higher education, and "the effects of socioeconomic status on educational attainment are greater for girls than for boys" (Jensen and Hovey, 1982, p. 153).

Specific math/science course and career counseling should be available throughout a woman's elementary and secondary school career. Gifted females, like their less able peers, are still largely socialized into traditionally female, low-paying occupations. Without adequate preparation in math

and science, many will not be able to participate in a socioeconomic system that increasingly demands those skills (Higham and Navarre, 1984). Access to such coursework, however, may not be enough. As many investigators have discovered (e.g., Blaubergs, 1980; Cooley, et al., 1984; Fox, 1981; Rodenstein, et al., 1977), many gifted girls are unlikely to receive sufficient academic preparation or counseling at the K–12 level, because many teachers believe male students are inherently better at those subjects, and many counselors do not perceive careers in scientific or technological fields as appropriate for females. A concerted effort must be made by concerned teachers, counselors, and psychologists to encourage gifted girls not to jeopardize their future options by neglecting adequate preparation in these areas.

Role models and mentors are crucial, if for no other reason than that "no child will choose a career that she does not know about or cannot identify with" (Higham and Navarre, 1984, p. 52). Gifted women are exposed to fewer same-sex role models than are their male counterparts in daily life, literature, the arts, and the media, and sex-role stereotyping is still the rule rather than the exception in educational materials. Opportunities to interact with role models and mentors can significantly enhance a gifted woman's acceptance of her own abilities and career possibilities (Fox and Richmond, 1979; Navarre, 1980; Schwartz, 1980).

Psychologists and counselors must be aware of their own expectations, attitudes, and behaviors toward gifted girls and women. We must remember that we are products of a culture that has a history of ambivalence toward recognizing or addressing the special needs of the gifted. Some of this ambivalence stems from a fear of creating a caste system, an intellectual elite who will denigrate others who are less able. Another part arises from a fear that recognizing high potential or ability will place an individual, especially a child, in a high pressure situation which might compromise her or his personal development. But an even stronger component is the belief that special attention need not be paid the gifted because they will develop satisfactorily and self-sufficiently without it. This belief is false. The gifted person will not succeed against all odds, especially if this person is female. In fact, without counseling and educational interventions aimed specifically at the challenge of being both gifted and female, the majority of gifted women will continue to disappear (Shakeshaft and Palmieri, 1978).

Women psychologists must become more aware of their own abilities so that they can better nurture the high abilities of their clients (Silverman, in press). Silverman observed that "many feminist therapists are gifted women who do not recognize their giftedness, and their clientele is frequently composed of unrecognized gifted women" (L. K. Silverman, personal communication, February 1987). If we fail to see ourselves in the fullness of our abilities, we cannot see the gifts in others nor empower them to reach their potential.

Psychology training programs must incorporate specialized coursework and training opportunities in gifted psychology. As Silverman (1983) observed, "few teachers, counselors, psychologists or even specialists working with the gifted recognize that the gifted have a unique set of affective needs" (p. 2). Counseling the gifted is a complex activity for which few are or will be adequately prepared unless a body of knowledge based on research is introduced into psychology preparation programs.

Support groups' popularity and availability for dealing with a vast array of issues and challenges attest to their efficacy in helping people to manage their lives more effectively. For school-aged and adult gifted women, a supportive peer network can provide a means of exploring changing life roles, values, methods of conflict resolution, and strategies for dealing with situations that arise from sex-role stereotyping (Navarre, 1980). According to Blaubergs (1980),

> many parents, teachers, and counselors of the gifted continue to reflect attitudes and sex-stereotypes that are detrimental to the expression of the abilities of gifted girls. An understanding of the prevalence of such attitudes, and an awareness that they do not reflect a necessary reality, or often any reality at all, can help to remove this barrier to the gifted girls' achievement (p. 15).

Family counseling and parent education programs are necessary, since families tend to underestimate or ignore the abilities of gifted daughters. Families especially need to learn ways to support the autonomy and emotional development of gifted daughters, to help them learn to contend with opposition, and to understand the meaning and impact of giftedness in an individual's life (Callahan, 1980; Ehrlich, 1982; Schwartz, 1980).

In-service training programs must be developed for K–12 school district personnel (e.g., teachers, counselors, school psychologists, and administrators) to raise their awareness of the many forces inhibiting gifted female students from developing their potential. Such programs should specifically address the ways in which the educational system contributes to women's systematic devaluation of their own abilities, and undermines their access to opportunities for maximum growth.

Comprehensive research programs must be created to expand existing knowledge about the nature of the psychological development of highly capable women; internal and external forces (e.g., family/work/education) that negatively affect gifted women's mental and physical health and inhibit them from taking advantage of opportunities for achievement; and the special issues affecting gifted minority women, gifted disabled women, and women who are culturally or economically disadvantaged. It is also important to ascertain the frequency with which gifted females are victims of sexual, physical, and/or emotional abuse, as well as the incidence and prevalence of various forms of self-sabotage among this population (e.g., eating disorders, depression, learned helplessness, and substance abuse). Ultimately, we must explore ways in which research findings from all these programs can be translated into effective programs for individual and social change.

References

Blaubergs, M. (1978). Personal studies of gifted females: An overview and commentary. *Gifted Child Quarterly, 22*, 539–547.

Blaubergs, M. (1980). The gifted female: Sex-role stereotyping and gifted girls' experience and education. *Roeper Review, 2*, 13–15.

Callahan, C. M. (1980). The gifted girl: An anomaly? *Roeper Review, 2*, 16–20.

Christ, C. P. (1980). *Diving deep and surfacing: Women writers on spiritual quest.* Boston: Beacon Press.

Clark, B. (1983). *Growing up gifted: Developing the potential of children at home and at school.* Columbus: Merrill.

Cooley, D., Chauvin, J. C., and Karnes, F. A. (1984). Gifted females: A comparison of attitudes by male and female teachers. *Roeper Review, 6*, 164–167.

Covington, M. V., and Omelich, C. L. (1979). Effort: The double-edged sword in school achievement. *Journal of Educational Psychology, 71*, 169–182.

Cox, J., and Daniel, N. (1983). Special problems and special populations: Identification. *G/C/T, 30,* 54–61.

Dweck, C. S., and Licht, B. G. (1980). Learned helplessness and intellectual achievement. In J. Garber and M. E. P. Seligman (eds.). *Human Helplessness.* New York: Academic.

Ehrlich, V. Z. (1982). *Gifted children: A guide for parents and teachers.* Englewood Cliffs, NJ: Prentice-Hall.

Fox, L. H., and Richmond, L. J. (1979). Gifted females: Are we meeting their counseling needs? *Personnel and Guidance Journal, 57,* 256–259.

Fox, L. H. (1981). Preparing gifted girls for future leadership roles. *G/T/C, 17,* 7–11.

Fox, L. H. (1983). Mathematically able girls: A special challenge. *Chronicle of Academic and Artistic Precocity, 2,* 1–2.

Gardner, H. (1983). *Frames of mind: The theory of multiple intelligences.* New York: Basic.

Garmezy, N., and Tellegen, A. (1984). Studies of stress-resistant children: Methods, variables, and preliminary findings. In F. J. Morrison, C. Lord, and D. P. Keating (eds.), *Applied Developmental Psychology* (pp. 231–283). Orlando: Academic.

Getzels, J. W., and Dillon, J. T. (1973). The nature of giftedness and the education of the gifted. In R. M. W. Travers (ed.), *Second handbook of research on teaching* (pp. 689–731). Chicago: Rand McNally.

Gilligan, C. (1982). *In a different voice.* Cambridge, MA; Harvard University Press.

Hall, E. G. (1980). Sex differences in IQ development for intellectually gifted students. *Roeper Review, 2,* 25–28.

Hall, E. G. (1982). Accelerating gifted girls. *G/C/T, 25,* 48–50.

Higham, S. J., and Navarre, J. (1984). Gifted adolescent females require differential treatment. *Journal for the Education of the Gifted, 8,* 43–58.

Hollinger, C. L. (1983). Counseling the gifted and talented female adolescent: The relationship between social self-esteem and traits of instrumentality and expressiveness. *Gifted Child Quarterly, 27,* 157–161.

Hollinger, C. L. (1985). The stability of self-perceptions of instrumental and expressive traits and social self-esteem among gifted and talented female adolescents. *Journal for the Education of the Gifted, 8,* 107–126.

Hollinger, C. L., and Fleming, E. S. (1984). Internal barriers to the realization of potential: Correlates and interrelationships among gifted and talented female adolescents. *Gifted Child Quarterly, 28,* 135–139.

Jensen, E. L., and Hovey, S. Y. (1982). Bridging the gap from high school to college for talented females. *Peabody Journal of Education, 59,* 153–159.

Keller, E. F. (1983). *A feeling for the organism: The life and work of Barbara McClintock.* New York: W. H. Freeman.

Kerr, B. A. (1985). *Smart girls, gifted women.* Columbus: Ohio Psychology.

Kirschenbaum, R. (1980). Combating sexism in the preschool environment. *Roeper Review, 2,* 31–33.

Mills, C. (1980). Sex-role-related personality correlates of intellectual abilities in adolescents. *Roeper Review, 2,* 29–31.

Navarre, J. (1980). Is what is good for the gander, good for the goose: Should gifted girls receive differential treatment? *Roeper Review, 2,* 21–25.

Rodenstein, J. M., and Glickauf-Hughes, C. (1977). Career and lifestyle determinants of gifted women. Madison, WI: University of Wisconsin, Research and Guidance Laboratory for Superior Students. (ERIC Document Reproduction Service No. ED 194–689).

Rodenstein, J. M., Pfleger, L. R., and Colangelo, N. (1977). Career development of gifted women. *Gifted Child Quarterly, 21,* 383–390.

Roeper, A. (1978). The young gifted girl: A contemporary view. *Roeper Review, 1,* 6–8.

Russo, J., Miller, D., and Vitaliano, P. P. (1985). The relationship of gender to perceived stress and distress in medical school. *Journal of Psychosomatic Obstetrics and Gynecology, 4,* 117–124.

Schwartz, L. L. (1977). Can we stimulate creativity in women? *Journal of Creative Behavior, 11,* 264–267.

Schwartz, L. L. (1980). Advocacy for the neglected gifted: Females. *Gifted Child Quarterly, 24,* 113–117.

Shakeshaft, C., and Palmieri, P. (1978). A divine discontent: Perspective on gifted women. *Gifted Child Quarterly, 22,* 468–477.

Silverman, L. K. (1982, March). *Emotional development of gifted children.* Presentation at the Workshop on Counseling, Area I-South Service Center for Gifted Education. Chicago, IL.

Silverman, L. K. (1983). Issues in affective development of the gifted. In J. Van Tassel-Baska (ed.). *A practical guide to counseling the gifted in a school setting* (pp. 6–21). Reston, VA: Council for Exceptional Children.

Silverman, L. K. (1986). What happens to the gifted girl? In C. J. Maker (ed.). *Defensible programs for the gifted* (pp. 43–89). Rockville, MD: Aspen.

Silverman, L. K. (in press). Feminine development through the life cycle. In M. A. Douglas, and L. E. Walker (eds.). *Feminine psychotherapies: Integration of therapeutic and feminist systems.* Norwood: Ablex.

Solano, C. H. (1983). Self-concept in mathematically gifted adolescents. *Journal of General Psychology, 108,* 33–42.

Tidball, M. E., and Kistiakowsky, V. (1976). Baccalaureate origins of American scientists and scholars. *Science, 193,* 646–652.

Tomlinson-Keasey, C., and Smith-Winberry, C. (1983). Educational strategies and personality outcomes of gifted and nongifted college students. *Gifted Child Quarterly, 27,* 35–41.

Wells, M. A., Peltier, S., and Glickauf-Hughes, C. (1982). The analysis of the sex role orientation of gifted male and female adolescents. *Roeper Review, 4,* 46–48.

Whitmore, J. R. (1980). The etiology of underachievement in highly gifted young children. *Journal for the Education of the Gifted, 3,* 38–51.

PART V

B. Homelessness

25

WE BAG LADIES AREN'T ALL ALIKE

Pia McKay

Pia McKay is a former English teacher in the Washington, D.C., public schools with a master's degree from Columbia University. She became a homeless person in 1981 after she began having psychotic episodes relating to her foster childhood. She has lived in shelters since then and has been unable to sustain a steady job. She described her experiences in a 1986 Outlook *article entitled "My Home is a Lonely Bed in a Dreary D.C. Shelter."—Editorial note from the* Washington Post *where this article appeared.*

Back in the '60s when the first strange ladies with bulging bags began appearing on the streets and foraging in garbage bins, I was as astonished as everyone else. A new word—"bag ladies"—was born as we, feeling superior, discussed these strange people, their strange behavior and the whole strange phenomenon we now call homelessness.

Two decades later, I am homeless myself, and our cities and towns teem with others like me. Most of you are no longer surprised by the homeless. But you are understandably offended, and deeply disturbed by our presence—by this refugee population whose numbers are growing alarmingly. So now Washington—like cities all over America and Europe—is struggling to deal with its homeless hundreds. Yet so far no one has gotten very far. Nothing is working satisfactorily.

In my view, the big mistake people make in trying to help the homeless is that they expect, or hope, that one single solution will solve the problems of all us. Generally we, the homeless, are viewed as strands on the same gray mop. Some people say that we are all crazy; some that we are all lazy; some that we are all poor; some that we are all drunks or drug addicts; some that we are all ordinary people fallen on hard times.

My view from the park bench, from the narrow cot in crowded shelters, from the shuffling lines at feeding stations is that we are not all alike by any means and that, in fact, the solution for one of us can spell disaster for another. Low-cost housing, for example, is a wonderful idea for many of us. Yet that "solution" would be no more than a sentimental gesture for women who throw rolls of toilet paper

down the toilet or, forgetting to take their tranquilizers, tear off refrigerator doors. Similarly, many women seem to need cheap shelter only until an emergency is over; many, many others remain in the shelter system for years.

How else are we different from one another? Here are some of the homeless ladies I have known in the past six years:

• The Child, in her sixties, had had a stroke. She babbled and seemed to have regressed to childhood. She regularly got money from her grown children, and her daughter desperately wanted her mother to live with her—with plenty of room for private accommodations. But she refused repeatedly until, finding herself too often hit over the head and robbed (shelters frequently are located in high-crime neighborhoods), she finally gave in and went home. It took years.

• The Tippler is a vigorous, bright and often charming woman in her fifties who worked for the government for over 20 years. She is an alcoholic and a shoplifter, and not above stealing from her friends. Every evening she staggers into a shelter—if she can make it. Sometimes she falls flat on her back and lies sprawled on the sidewalk all night in a drunken stupor.

"You can't cure an alcoholic, if he doesn't want to be cured," she chirps. "And I don't want to be cured."

Without any remorse, she tells me (our cots are adjacent) that just about every day she slips into a liquor store at noon when it is very busy and filches a half gallon and a fifth of vodka, which she consumes largely herself or with a buddy. She has been seriously injured in car accidents and in falls; she has been raped and sodomized while drunk; she has been thrown out of numerous shelters and long ago was disowned by her family.

• The Broken Heart, a handsome woman in her thirties, immigrated to this country to follow an American man who had been her lover in eastern Europe. She was an immensely likable, hardworking, humorous woman until, suddenly, she would fall into a crying jag. She would become depressed for months at a time and, in a mixture of languages, declare that nothing, really, was worthwhile. One day, following a doomed love affair (he was married), she announced to a number of people that she was going to commit suicide. True to her word, she jumped off the 14th Street Bridge.

• The Gourmand, plump and in her early thirties, can chat about life in Europe and Asia. Growing up, she traveled from school to school following her divorced mother, who worked for the U.S. government. She gorges so much that at times she gags at the table as she forces the food down. She plaits her long blond hair in girlish pigtails and wears short, tight dresses; she looks like an enormously fat baby. Although she is articulate and clearly capable, she refuses to work (or see a psychiatrist). She keeps talking about looking for a job and engages others to help her in what seems like a sincere search when, in fact, she spends her days idling, seeking enjoyment, passing the time until the next meal.

• The Tigress, in her thirties, is easy-going unless someone insists she follows directions or finish what she started; then she yells and curses, demanding her rights. She often indulges cheerfully in petty prostitution, ducking off into the bushes in exchange for a cup of coffee and a pack of cigarets. Sometimes she talks loud and long, whether anyone is listening or not. In one of these monologues, she spoke in shock, in outrage, about the day she discovered her mother in bed with the mother's niece. "My mother! In bed! With her NIECE!"

• The Queen—now that it is getting cold—will be coming off the streets and into a shelter. She moves like a little wounded doe when anyone approaches her. All day long she stations herself in one or two places, perhaps facing the wall, perhaps near a garbage pail. She eats and sleeps on the floor. Once her jaw was hideously swollen from bad teeth. I urged her to see a dentist. That was one of the few times the Queen was grateful for any show of kindness. Usually, for all her seeming vulnerability, her

piteousness, she is shockingly imperious and disdainful, queen of her domain, despising the world, scornful of those who reach out to her.

• The Lazybody, 25, from an Asian country, is an exchange student. Or is she? She wants to go to school so that she can teach English as a second language, she says. Or she wants to find domestic work. But always something interferes; always there is some impediment. She lies around in bed day after day, quietly going over notes, reading books, sleeping.

• The Lonelyheart, in her sixties, worked as a waitress for some 20 years, she says. She has children. They never come to see her. She had two husbands. One was an alcoholic, whom she felt compelled to leave; the other, an oddly religious man with whom she would spend all Sunday in church. He died, she says in her wispy voice, from overeating.

• The Collector, in her twenties, has a face like a brown silk rose. In the shelter a few days, she gathered bags and bags and bags of clothing she got from donations, plus a few stolen things, for a bright and independent future. She has two children whose whereabouts remained vague. She was full of energy and told us that she had landed herself a cleaning job. Then one day she was gone. Where? What happened?

Aside from homelessness itself, these women and their hundreds of sisters and brothers have little in common. No single plan will be of much use to them. I know that many sincere public officials and sensitive private citizens are working hard to help. But things obviously are not going right. Though I certainly am far from being an expert in curing the problems of homelessness, my unique experience convinces me that several steps not yet tried might put us on a more productive path.

First, the homeless should be diagnosed and then special shelters should be set up for each group—for the elderly, for alcoholics, for drug addicts, for those with a manageable mental illness, and so forth—as we already have for homeless pregnant women.

As things stand now, we have a hodgepodge of people in a hodgepodge of shelters. The system is awkward and it can be oddly cruel, as when alcoholics receive a government check and use it to stay drunk all the time. They sober up only for a few days near the end of the month when the money runs out.

Because of the boat-bailing way the shelter system has sprung up, it has no benevolent bureaucratization. Each shelter works as a separate suzerainty—with a young staff that is often too inexperienced to deal efficiently with the tides of people who wash up on their doorsteps. Now that we know that homelessness is not going to go away of itself, it is time to take a long and broad view. Instead of a shelter-by-shelter approach directed by shifting personnel and volunteers, we need a permanent, coordinated system that deals not just with the city but with the suburbs as well. If that were done, for example, an alcoholic woman could be placed in a home with other alcoholics and receive specific and tough treatment. Instead, she now wanders from one shelter to another, where the social workers don't know her history and aren't wise to her.

In short, we must get homeless people into appropriate programs. Otherwise, efforts are wasted or, in some cases, a would-be beneficiary instead becomes a victim of good intentions. Though I applaud Mayor Koch's efforts in New York to help the hard-core street persons by hospitalizing them—as my experience tells me they will often endanger themselves—my experience also tells me they are not necessarily going to a better existence.

In this regard, I believe fervently that one popular method of helping the homeless—the use of psychotropic drugs—has gotten out of hand. I realize, of course, that for some people, drugs along with psychotherapy are the readiest, if not the best, remedies we have. But they should not be used indiscriminately. Consider these different experiences:

• The Pursued takes drugs. When she does not, she charges about wildly striking defensive poses against invisible enemies; once she stabbed another woman. With drugs she is placid and pleasant.

• The Beauty refuses to take drugs. Once, she says, she was Miss California. Her father and mother are buried in the Arctic Circle. She has killed 800 people. The FBI forced her to take cocaine. She is going to run for the Senate. When social workers suggest she take drugs, she replies, "I'm not crazy." She walks around all day with her arms over her head whispering. One thing I believe: She could have been Miss California. She is indeed very beautiful.

• The Backslider takes drugs. A school teacher, she lived in shelters for about two years. Every time she thought she was fine and went back to work, she suffered a breakdown. But now, after getting accustomed to drugs, she says she feels absolutely normal. She has a job she likes.

• Miss Tripwire takes drugs. When she stopped taking them, she landed in a psychiatric ward; for days she held up her leg, fearing that if she lowered it to the floor, she would start World War III. Now she has a job and a social life.

• The Hippie took drugs and landed in a psychotic episode. A flower child of the '60s, she had abused drugs for years. "I was the last person who should have taken drugs," she says. Her brother helped her pull herself together, and now she has a very good job.

Then there was my own experience—a nightmare. After a year of homelessness—which I spent in stunned disbelief that I was living among people whose sentences I could not parse, that I was being rolled out of the shelter in the morning seven days a week including Christmas and herded in at night to sleep (maybe) among a hostile and often stinking tribe, that I was weeping in self-pity while gratefully accepting yet another glob of macaroni on a soggy paper plate—I betook myself to a clinic and was given a prescription with few questions asked.

At first I took drugs willingly, even eagerly. The immediate effect was startling and ghastly. The first drug seemed to knock out my automatic nervous system; I had to think through consciously the process of walking, step by step. Other drugs made me feel that my soul had left and that my body alone remained, and I stumbled about on the streets just keeping that shell from injury. On still another drug, I grew frantic and raced around the streets all day, arriving at one place and then jumping up to rush to another.

The trouble is that a patient is expected to find the right drug by trial and error, wading through the pharmacopeia and monitoring the effects, one drug after another, without much professional guidance. A homeless person is, of course, wandering around the streets while he goes through this. Eventually I became convinced that drugs would not cure me and managed to get off them even though the shelter providers angrily insisted that the symptoms I described were merely side effects.

Wedged down as I am among the homeless, I might have become their unblinking advocate. But I have not. While we, the homeless, need a zealot like Mitch Snyder to fight for us, surely society at large has rights, too. The public has a right not to be offended, harrassed and embarrassed.

Even in the laid-back atmosphere of Snyder's Community for Creative Non-Violence, we felt the insult of people who defecated on the stairs, who urinated wherever the urge took them. When caught, such people were summarily thrown out.

People who refused to cooperate—in quieting the incessant blast of rock music, for example—eventually exhausted other people's patience, which led to fury and violence. Those people, too, were thrown out—as were those who refused to bathe.

Everyone has rights, after all; and if some people spin too far outside the social sphere, surely some of their rights are forfeit. The suffering of the weak and wandering arouses pity rightly; but in pitying them, one should not be tempted into sentimentality.

The great weakness of the shelter system as it stands now is this human reality: We homeless people sometimes do crazy things, and eventually we are thrown out. Or something goes wrong and out we go. Maybe someone doesn't like what we've done or said or who we are, and we're gone. Nobody has a clear idea of what to do with us, so we drift from shelter to shelter for years until, one day, we die.

26

A DESCRIPTIVE PERSPECTIVE ON HOMELESSNESS

Norweeta G. Milburn
Institute for Urban Affairs and Research
Howard University

Homelessness in the United States has been identified as a pressing social problem within the last few years, and has received considerable attention in numerous media accounts (e.g., Cordes, 1984), gubernatorial investigations (e.g., Cuomo, 1983) and congressional hearings (e.g., U.S. House of Representatives, 1982). Nonetheless, it is difficult to accurately describe the national prevalence of homelessness, because the size of the total homeless population is not known (Fisher and Breakey, 1985). Estimates of the number of homeless people nationwide have varied from as high as two million (Hombs and Snyder, 1982) to a more conservative range of 250,000 to 350,000 (Bobo, 1984). These estimates depend, in part, upon who is reporting them. They tend to be higher when reported by advocates for homeless people and lower when reported by government agencies.

Homelessness is not a new phenomenon. The initiation of homelessness as a social phenomenon has been linked to the movement of work from agricultural to commercial activities and the increased urbanization of society (See Cohen and Sokolovsky, 1989, for a historical perspective on the development of homelessness). As a social problem in the United States, it initially received attention in the late 1800's and early 1900's (Anderson, 1923; Mohl, 1971). Yet, the nature of the population has seemingly changed over the years. During the Great Depression, homeless individuals included hobos, tramps, vagrants and migrant laborers as well as those who were economically deprived (Caplow, 1940; Cross and Cross, 1937; Gary, 1931; Locke, 1935). This population shifted somewhat from the 1950's to 1970's, to occupants of urban skid row areas, who at that time primarily represented male, chronic alcoholics (Bahr, 1969a, 1969b, Levinson, 1957; Spradley, 1970; Wiseman, 1970).

In the 1970's, after the widespread deinstitutionalization of the mentally ill, the homeless population was expanded to include the seriously mentally ill, both individuals who were released from mental institutions and individuals who had never received mental health treatment because of changes in committment laws (Lazare, Cohen and Jacobson, 1972; Priest, 1976; Segal, Baumohl and Johnson, 1977). More recently, the population has again expanded to include the economically deprived, including women and their children as well as single men and runaway youth (Snow, Baker, Anderson, and Martin, 1986; Hope and Young, 1986). The number of families in shelters for homeless people has increased significantly. Most of these families are single parents with children (U.S. Department of Housing and Urban Development, 1989).

The homeless population has become increasingly more heterogeneous over the years (Morrissey and Dennis, 1986). Migrant laborers, tramps, those who are intermittantly employed, chronic alcoholics as well as other substance abusers, and the seriously mentally ill can still be found among the homeless population. Yet recent data suggest that while demographic characteristics of the homeless population vary across the country, the current American homeless population is predominately male, mostly single, usually under age 40, and slightly more likely to be ethnic minority in areas where ethnic minorities are well represented in the overall population—with Blacks the overwhelming majority in this group (Arce, Tadlock, Vergare and Shapiro, 1983; Levine and Stockdill, 1986; Martin, 1986; Morse and Calysyn, 1985; Roth, Bean, Lust and Saveanu, 1985; U.S. Department of Housing and Urban Development, 1989).

Despite these demographics trends, it is important to note that the homeless population consists of individuals with diverse needs (Hope and Young, 1986; Morrissey and Dennis, 1986). Some homeless individuals are seriously mentally ill and in need of

Reprinted with permission as a 1989 revision of a paper that appeared in the *Urban Research Review,* 1987, *11*: 9–11.

mental health treatment as well as related social services. This subgroup includes individuals who have been deinstitutionalized as well as a number of individuals who have never received mental health treatment (Roth, Bean and Hyde, 1986; Lamb, 1982, 1984; Bachrach, 1984). Other homeless individuals are substance abusers in need of drug and alcohol treatment. Recent studies suggest that 40 to 50 percent of the homeless population are alcohol abusers and 10 to 15 percent abuse other drugs such as barbituates, minor tranquilizers and marijuana (Levine, 1984; Mulkern and Spence, 1984). Some are poly-drug users (Arce, et al., 1983). In addition, comorbidity of mental disorders can occur among homeless individuals. For example, in a Los Angeles study of homeless people in skid row areas, 12 percent had a dual diagnosis of substance abuse and a serious mental illness (Koegel and Burnam, 1987). There are homeless individuals who do not have mental health problems but lack the income needed to secure adequate housing (Baxter and Hopper, 1982). And there are homeless individuals who lack instrumental social support from family and friends to carry them through situational crises such as a fire or job loss that leaves them without adequate housing.

With all of this diversity within the homeless population, what do these individuals have in common? What is central to homelessness? The obvious answer is that homelessness is not being adequately housed. However, homelessness is more than the lack of adequate housing. Homelessness is a period during an individual's lifetime when he/she does not have adequate housing *and* the resources such as money, family and friends to acquire this housing (Milburn and Watts, 1985; Levine, 1984). Consequently, homeless people are individuals who are at a point during their life cycles when they are not able, due to situational and/or personal factors, to secure and maintain adequate housing (Watts and Milburn, 1987).

Some researchers and advocates argue that homelessness is simply not having housing, because, to argue otherwise, places the blame for homelessness upon the individual rather than looking at the role societal forces play in contributing to homelessness (Baxter and Hopper, 1982; Morse, 1986). From this point of view, homelessness represents a lack of

fit between individuals and American society; in particular, American society's failure to provide an opportunity structure that meets the needs and characteristics of all its citizens, including those individuals who are not able to successfully meet basic needs such as food, housing and clothing. Consequently, changes must occur at both the societal and individual levels to alleviate homelessness.

The lack of resources clearly implicated in homelessness and the potential causal relationship should be taken into account when homelessness is defined. This lack of resources is also linked to societal structures. To acquire and maintain housing, individuals must have (1) *personal resources* such as stable mental and physical health, independent living skills, job skills, and a functional educational level (literacy and math skills); (2) *environmental resources* such as access to a caring and service-oriented health and mental health system (e.g., one that provides outreach services and engages in case management), as well as affordable,* appropriate and available housing; (3) *economic resources* such as employment, financial assistance from family and friends, access to Supplemental Security Income (SSI) and other public assistance; and (4) *social resources* such as family and friends (Baxter and Hooper, 1982; Brickner, Scanlan, Conanan and Elvy, 1986; Fischer and Breakey, 1985; Laufer, 1981; Levine, 1984; Morse and Calsyn, 1986; Ridgeway, Spaniol and Zipple, 1986; Segal, et al., 1977; Watts and Milburn, 1987).

It is important to recognize that homelessness has a temporal component that modifies its impact upon individuals. The period of time that individuals are homeless can be temporary or prolonged (Arce, et al., 1983; Hoffman, Wenger, Nigro and Rosenfield, 1982; Rooney, 1980). In addition, this period can be cyclical with an individual moving in and out of being homeless (Piliavan, Sosin and Westerfelt, 1987; Farr, Koegel and Burnam, 1986). Recent research has attempted to operationalize the temporal quality of an individual's homeless state by defining it in terms of the length of time an individual is homeless and the number of times he/she has been homeless (Farr, Koegel and Burnam, 1986). This operational definition attempts to tap the recency of homelessness as well as its cyclical nature. Using it, several temporal categories of homelessness can be

---

*Affordable housing, as defined by the federal government, is housing that costs no more than 30 percent of a family's income (Clay, 1987).

derived. Individuals who are recently homeless, usually for 6 months or less, and are experiencing their first episode of homelessness are viewed as the *newly* homeless. Those who have been homeless for any length of time and are experiencing their second or more episode of homelessness are viewed as the *intermittently* homeless. Individuals who are not recently homeless and are experiencing their first episode of homelessness are defined as the *chronic* homeless.

The temporal quality of an individual's homeless state is related to his/her personal, environmental, economic and social resources. Individuals with more resources will be less likely to become homeless, and if they do become homeless, less likely to become the chronic homeless. Viewing homelessness from this perspective allows one to better understand the common thread that links diverse subgroups within the homeless population.

How homelessness should be defined has been a major concern of researchers and policymakers (Dennis, 1987). Considerable discussion has focused on whether the definition of homelessness should be inclusive or exclusive. The most inclusive is to define homelessness as a continuum ranging from not housed to housed (Dennis, 1987). Such a definition allows for more empathy and identification with homeless people among those who are not homeless since it implies that being housed is a temporary state that can easily change for any housed person. While this is theoretically true, it may over simplify the plight of people who are homeless and continue to be homeless. The most exclusive is to define homelessness as the condition of those people who sleep in shelters or on city streets (Rossi, Wright, Fisher and Willis, 1987).

There are several issues pertaining to homelessness and its perpetuation that will have to be addressed in the future to help alleviate this social problem. First, the multifaceted nature of homelessness must be acknowledged. Homelessness is not a mental health problem, nor is it a housing problem, nor is it an economic problem. Homelessness is precipitated by underemployment and unemployment, inadequate benefits from government assistance programs such as Aid to Families with Dependent Children (AFDC) and SSI, inadequate services for those with mental health problems including the serious mentally ill and substance abusers, and the shortage of low and moderate income housing (Hope and Young, 1986).

Homeless people often have multiple needs. Service systems, including health, mental health, housing, job training and vocational rehabilitation among others, must collaborate to address these needs (Roth, et al., 1986). Second, the low and moderate income housing stock is declining dramatically in the United States. Given trends in population growth, increases in the number of poor Americans, and the continuing decline in low-rent housing, it is projected that by the year 2003 affordable housing will be unavailable for 18.7 million Americans (Clay, 1987). Innovative techniques for providing appropriate and affordable housing will have to be developed, supported and widely disseminated. Third, homeless people are often reluctant to seek mental health services and often need assistance working through the bureaucratic structure when seeking other social services. Aggressive outreach efforts have been the most successful at providing mental health and health services to homeless people (Struening, 1983; Wright, Knight, Weber-Burton and Lam, 1987). More thought must also be given to the ethnic diversity of the homeless population and how cultural norms and beliefs may influence health and mental health practices, especially when planning and implementing health and mental health services (Martin, 1986). The underutilization of formal, clinic-based mental health services by Blacks, for example, has been documented (see Neighbors and Taylor, 1985, for a review). Lastly, the increasing role that the criminal justice system is playing in providing "care" for some homeless people is alarming. It is not uncommon for homeless people to have spent time in jail or had contact with the police (Fischer and Breakey, 1985; Farr, et al., 1986; Ladner, 1986).

With the growing concern about homelessness, there has been an increase in activities to address this problem at local, state and national levels. On the local and state level, in addition to efforts by community and church groups, advocacy organizations, and local government programs to provide food, shelter and other human services for homeless individuals, many jurisdictions (cities, counties and states) have begun to document the prevalence of homelessness and the demographics of the homeless population in their locales (e.g., Caulk, 1983; National Coalition for the Homeless, 1983; Simpson and Kilduff, 1984; Torrey, Bargmann and Wolfe, 1985). Some states, primarily in the eastern and central sections of the country as well as California, through funds from the National Institute of Mental Health (NIMH), have also been able to develop a database on the "demographics, mental states and service needs" of the homeless who are seriously mentally ill (Morrisey and Dennis, 1986).

On the national level, NIMH and other units of the Alcohol, Drug Abuse and Mental Health Administration (ADAMHA) have continued their activities by supporting the establishment of and providing funding for clearinghouses and resource centers to provide information on homelessness and mental illness and various meetings on the needs of homeless subgroups, including homeless women and homeless alcoholics, among other activities. Other federal agencies such as the Department of Housing and Urban Development (HUD) and the Department of Defense (DOD) have also been involved in initiatives pertaining to the homeless. For example, HUD recently presented non-monetary awards to various projects in locations nationwide that were providing "shelter and services for low-income people" as part of the United Nations 1987 International Year of Shelter for the Homeless (U.S. Department of Housing and Urban Development, 1986). Congressional concerns have lead to the passage of legislation pertaining to homelessness, such as the Steward B. McKinney Homeless Relief Act which authorized $442.7 million in fiscal year 1987 and $616 million in fiscal year 1988 for a number of human service programs for the homeless population. Some of these programs are stopgap activities to deal with the immediate crisis of homelessness; however, others are targeted at the systemic precipitators of homelessness.

This legislation included funding for: (1) *housing programs* such as emergency shelter, transitional housing for families with children and the mentally disabled (e.g., serious mentally ill), permanent housing for the handicapped, and the rehabilitation of single-room occupancy (SRO) dwellings; (2) *health programs* such as outpatient services for physical health, mental health, drug and alcohol abuse problems, as well as case management services; community mental health demonstration programs targeted for the serious mentally ill who are homeless or at risk for being homeless; emergency services in residential settings for the serious men-

tally ill homeless including outreach, outpatient treatment/rehabilitation, staff training, case management and other supportive services; and the development and implementation of alcohol and drug abuse treatment services; (3) *community service and education programs* such as grants for community action agencies to provide comprehensive emergency services for homeless people including follow-up services; demonstration projects to provide basic skills, remedial education, job-seeking skills, and job counseling grants to develop and implement literacy and basic skill programs for homeless adults; grants for programs that are successfully addressing the needs of homeless children in schools; and grants for the establishment of state offices of Coordinator of Education of Homeless Children and Youth to ensure that homeless children have access to the full range of educational services that they are entitled to; and *nutrition programs* such as funds for the emergency distribution of surplus foods to the poor including homeless people through community-based food programs as well as modifications in the eligibility requirements for food stamp recipients and provisions for the increased distribution of surplus food (e.g., flour, cornmeal and cheese).

In addition, the legislation provided for the establishment of an Interagency Council on Homelessness to facilitate the federal government's response to homelessness. The secretaries/administrators of 15 federal agencies comprised this council and HUD served as the lead agency for this activity. Two private foundations, the Pew Memorial Trust and the Robert Wood Johnson Foundation, have also responded to the need for programs to address homelessness and have provided over $25 million to fund health care programs for homeless individuals in 18 cities (Levine and Stockdill, 1986).

These efforts serve several purposes which will, one hopes, prevent the problem of homelessness in the United States from continuing to grow. The research activities have and will continue to help accurately delineate the needs of the homeless population and ways to adequately address those needs. In addition, funds have been provided by the federal government and private sector to develop and implement programs and other activities designed to alleviate homelessness.

References

Anderson, N. (1923). *The hobo: The sociology of the homeless man*. Chicago: University of Chicago Press.

Arce, A. A., Tadlock, M., Vergare, M. J., & Shapiro, S. H. (1983). A psychiatric profile of street people admitted to an emergency shelter. *Hospital and Community Psychiatry, 34* (9), 812–816.

Bachrach, L. L. (1984). Interpreting research on the homeless mentally ill: Some caveats. *Hospital and Community Psychiatry, 35* (9), 914–917.

Bahr, H. M. (1969a). Family size and stability as antecedents of homeless and excessive drinking. *Journal of Marriage and the Family, 31* (3), 477–483.

Bahr, H. M. (1969b). Lifetime affiliation patterns of early and late onset heavy drinkers on skid row. *Quarterly Journal of Studies on Alcohol, 30* (3), 645–656.

Baxter, E., and Hopper, K. (1982). The new mendicancy: Homelessness in New York City. *American Journal of Orthopsychiatry, 52*, 398–408.

Bobo, B. F. (1984). *A report to the Secretary on the homeless and emergency shelters*. Washington, DC: U.S. Department of Housing and Urban Development.

Brickner, P., Scanlan, B., Conanan, B., and Elvy, A. (1986). Homeless persons and medical care. *Annals of Internal Medicine, 104*, 405–409.

Caplow, T. (1940). Transiency as a cultural pattern. *American Sociological Review, 5*, 731–739.

Clauk, R. S. (1983). *The homeless poor: 1984*. Portland, OR: Department of Human Services, Social Services Division.

Clay, P. L. (1987). *At risk of loss: The endangered future of low-income rental housing resources*. (Report prepared for the Neighborhood Reinvestment Corporation, Washington, DC), Cambridge, MA: Massachusetts Institute of Technology.

Cohen, C. I., & Sokolovsky, J. (1989). *Old man of the bowery: Strategies for survival among the homeless*. New York: Guilford Press.

Cordes, C. (1984, February). The plight of homeless mentally ill. *APA Monitor, 13*, pp. 1.

Cross, W. T., and Cross, D. E. (1937). *Newcomers and nomads in California*. Stanford: Stanford University Press.

Cuomo, M. (1983). *1933–1983—Never again. A report to the National Governors Association Task Force on the Homeless*. Portland, NGA.

Dennis, D. L. (1987). *Research methodologies concerning homeless persons with serious mental illness and/or substance abuse disorders*. Rockville, MD: National Institute of Mental Health.

Farr, R., Koegel, P., and Burnam, A. (1986). *A study of homelessness and mental illness in the skid row areas of Los Angeles*. (Report prepared for the National Institute of Mental Health). Los Angeles, CA: Los Angeles County Department of Mental Health.

Fischer, P. J., & Breakey, W. R. (1985). Homelessness and mental health: An overview. *International Journal of Mental Health, 14* (4), 6–41.

Gary, F. (1931). *The Tramp-His Meaning and Being*. London: Dent.

Hoffman, S. P., Wenger, D., Nigro, J., and Rosenfeld, R. (1982). *Who are the homeless? A study of Randomly Selected Men Who Use the New York City Shelters*. New York: New York State Office of Mental Health.

Hombs, M. E., and Snyder, M. (1982). *Homelessness in America: A Forced March to Nowhere*. Washington, DC: Community for Creative Non-Violence.

Hope, M., and Young, J. (1986). *The Faces of Homelessness*. Lexington, MA: Lexington Books.

Koegel, P., and Burnam, M. A. (1987). Traditional and nontraditional homeless alcoholics. *Alcohol Health and Research World, 11* (3), 28–34.

Ladner, S., Crystal, S., Towber, R., Callendar, B., and Calhoun, J. (1986). *Project Future: Focusing, understanding, targeting and utilizing resources for the homeless mentally ill, elderly, youth substance abusers and employable*. (Report prepared for the National Institute of Mental Health.) New York: City of New York, Human Resource Administration.

Lamb, R. H. (1982). Young adult chronic patients: The new drifters. *Hospital and Community Psychiatry, 33* (6), 465–468.

Lamb, R. H. (1984). Deinstitutionalization and the homeless mentally ill. *Hospital and Community Psychiatry, 35* (9), 899–907.

Lazare, A., Cohen, F., and Jacobson, F. (1972). The walk-in patient as customer. *American Journal of Orthopsychiatry, 42* (5), 872–883.

Laufer, W. S. (1981). The vocational interests of homeless, unemployed men. *Journal of Vocational Behavior, 18* (2), 196–201.

Levine, I. S., and Stockdill, J. W. (1986). Mentally ill and homeless. A national problem. In B. Jones (eds.)., *Treating the homeless: Urban psychiatry's challenge* (pp. 1–17). Washington, DC: American Psychiatric Association Press.

Levine, I. S. (1984). Homelessness: Its implications for mental health policy and practice. *Psychosocial Rehabilitation Journal, 13* (1), 6–16.

Levinson, B. M. (1957). The socioeconomic status, intelligence and psychometric pattern of native-born white homeless men. *Journal of Genetic Psychology, 91*, 205–211.

Locke, H. J. (1935). Unemployed men in Chicago shelters. *Sociology and Social Research, 19*, 420–428.

Martin, M. (1986). *The Implications of NIMH-Supported research for homeless mentally ill racial and ethnic minority persons*. Rockville, MD: National Institute of Mental Health.

Milburn, N. G., and Watts, R. J. (1985). Methodological issues in research on the homeless and homeless mentally ill. *International Journal of Mental Health, 14* (4), 42–60.

Mohl, R. A. (1971). *Poverty in New York: 1783–1825*. New York: Oxford University Press.

Morrissey, J. P., and Dennis, D. L. (1986). *NIMH funded research concerning homeless mentally ill persons: implications for policy and practice*. Rockville, MD: National Institute of Mental Health.

Morse, G. (1986). *A contemporary assessment of urban homelessness: Implications for social change.* (Report #1986-2). St. Louis, MD: University of Missouri, Center for Metropolitan Studies.

Morse, G., and Calsyn, R. J. (1986). Mentally disturbed homeless people in St. Louis: Needy, willing, but underserved. *International Journal of Mental Health, 14,* 74–94.

Mulkern, V., and Spence, R. (1984). *Illicit drug use among homeless persons: A review of the literature.* (Report prepared for National Institute on Drug Abuse). Boston, MA: Human Service Research Institute.

National Coalition for the Homeless. (1983). *Downward spiral: The homeless in New Jersey.* New York: Author.

Neighbors, H. W. and Taylor, R. J. (1985, June). The use of social service agencies by Black Americans. *Social Service Review,* 259–268.

Priest, R. G. (1976). The homeless person and psychiatric services: An Edinburgh survey. *British Journal of Psychiatry,* 128–163.

Ridgeway, P., Spaniol, L., and Zipple, A. (1986). *Case management services for persons who are homeless and mentally ill: Report from an NIMH workshop.* (Report prepared for the National Institute on Mental Health) Boston, MA: Boston University, The Center of Psychiatric Rehabilitation, Sargent College of Allied Health Professions.

Rooney, J. (1980). Organizational success through program failures: Skid row missions. *Social Forces, 58,* 904–923.

Rossi, P. H., Wright, J. D., Fisher, G. A., and Willis, G. (1987). The urban homeless: Estimating composition and size. *Science, 285* (3), 1336–1341.

Roth, D., Bean, Jr., G. J., and Hyde, P. S. (1986). Homelessness and mental health policy: Developing an appropriate role for the 1980's. *Community Mental Health Journal, 22* (3), 203–214.

Roth, D., Bean, J., Lust, N., and Saveanu, T. (1985). *Homelessness in Ohio: A study of people in need.* Columbus, OH: Ohio Department of Mental Health.

Segal, S. P., Baumohl, J., and Johnson, E. (1977). Falling through the cracks: Mental disorder and social margin in a young vagrant population. *Social Problem, 24* (3), 387–401.

Simpson, J., and Kilduff, M. (1984). *Homelessness in Newark: A report on the trailer people.* Newark, NJ: Newark Committee on the Homeless.

Snow, D. A., Baker, S. G., Anderson, L., and Martin, M. (1986). The myth of prevasive mental illness among the homeless. *Social Problems, 33* (5), 408–423.

Spradley, J. P. (1970). *You owe yourself a drunk: An ethnography of urban nomads.* Boston, MA: Little, Brown, and Company.

Struening, E. (1983). *Community support systems evaluation program preliminary report.* New York: Psychiatric Institute.

Torrey, E. F., Bargmann, E., & Wolfe, S. M. (1985). *Washington's grate society: Schizophrenics in the shelters and on the street.* (Available from Public Citizen Health Research Group, 2000 P Street, NW, Washington, DC 20036).

U.S. Department of Housing and Urban Development. (1986, November). *Recent research results: Special IYSH Issue.* Washington, DC: Author.

U.S. Department of Housing and Urban Development (1988, March). *A Report on the 1989 National Survey of Shelters for the Homeless.* Washington, DC: Author.

U.S. House of Representatives. (1982). *Homelessness in America.* (Serial No. 97–100). Washington, DC: U.S. Government Printing Office.

Watts, R. J., & Milburn, N. G. (1987). A framework for research and action on homelessness. Unpublished manuscript.

Wiseman, J. P. (1970). *Stations of the lost: The treatment of skid row alcoholics.* Chicago: University of Chicago Press.

Wright, J. D., Knight, J. W., Weber-Burton, E., & Lam, J. (1987). Ailments and alcohol: Health status among the drinking homeless. *Alcohol Health and Research World, 11* (3), 22–27.

27

WHY DOES FAMILY HOMELESSNESS OCCUR?
A CASE-CONTROL STUDY

Ellen L. Bassuk

*Department of Psychiatry, Harvard Medical School;
Center for Health and Human Resources Policy,
John F. Kennedy School of Government, Harvard University*

Lynn Rosenberg

Boston University School of Medicine

INTRODUCTION

In the last several years, homelessness has become part of the life experience of growing numbers of American women and children. Homeless families, generally headed by women, may account for one-third of the estimated homeless population of 2.5 million people, and are the fastest growing subgroup.[1,2]

Despite the magnitude and seriousness of the problem of family homelessness, little is known about its antecedents, course, and consequences. Researchers have described serious unmet medical needs[3-6] and emotional problems[7-9] of homeless families, but no systematic comparison of homeless and housed families has been carried out. This report describes a sample of homeless and housed families from Boston, Massachusetts; the major purpose was to identify some of the unique correlates of family homelessness.

METHODS

SUBJECTS

HOMELESS FAMILIES. Eligible subjects were all members of homeless families (at least one parent with at least one minor child, or a pregnant woman) residing in family shelters in Boston from April to July 1985. Families in shelters for battered women, in facilities serving specialized populations (e.g., teenage mothers), and in facilities housing fewer than three families were not eligible.

We were able to arrange access to six of eight family shelters. Members of 50 homeless families with 90 children out of a possible 64 families with 105 children were interviewed. One family, headed by a married couple, was excluded, leaving 49 female-headed families with 86 children. Nonpartic-

ipating families were similar to participants in terms of age, gender, and ethnicity of the parent, the length of stay at the shelter, family size, and the children's ages and gender.

The sample most likely underrepresented Hispanics since we were unable to arrange access to one shelter that houses Hispanic families primarily. Homeless families with serious behavioral or emotional problems also may have been underrepresented since the larger shelters turn away approximately 10 to 15 families each week, usually excluding first those exhibiting behavioral problems.

HOUSED FAMILIES. Since the homeless families were headed by females, we decided that an appropriate comparison group would consist of Boston families headed by women who were poor (i.e., likely to be on welfare) but who were housed. Families sharing apartments as well as primary tenants were included.

To locate eligible housed families, we used 1980 census information to identify blocks in Boston with a high prevalence of poor families headed by women. These were blocks with at least 33 per cent of the residents living below the poverty level and at least 50 per cent of the households headed by women, and in which there were at least 10 such households. Twenty-eight such blocks were identified, in 12 census tracts, primarily in Dorchester and Roxbury.

We had planned to frequency-match the ethnic distribution of the housed families to that of the homeless families (of which about one-third were white). Once in the field, it became necessary to modify the study design. The ethnic distribution of some neighborhoods had changed since the 1980 census and the number of white families was less than anticipated. Therefore, we identified additional

From the *American Journal of Public Health*, 1988, 78(7): 783–788. Copyright © 1988 by the American Public Health Association. Reprinted by permission of the publisher and the authors.

blocks in which at least 90 per cent of the households were white, at least 33 percent of the residents were living below the poverty level, at least 43 per cent of households were headed by females, and where there were at least 10 such households. There were eight such blocks, primarily in South Boston and East Boston.

We had planned to sample the selected blocks randomly and to obtain participating families from each block in proportion to the numbers of families on that block. Once in the field, we found this to be infeasible since in many instances no one was home. Once it became known that we were carrying money to pay participating families, safety considerations prevented us from returning if a family was not home. We therefore knocked on consecutive doors in each block until the projected numbers of participants had been enrolled. Among the 820 households approached, there was no one home at 464, and 238 did not meet the definition of a female-headed family. Of 118 eligible female-headed families, 37 refused to participate and the remaining 81 were interviewed on weekdays during daylight hours from April to July 1986, the same months during which data on homeless families were obtained one year before.

DATA COLLECTION

The data were collected by personal interview of the mothers and children by a psychiatrist (ELB) or psychologist. A bodyguard accompanied the interviewers during the data collection from the housed families. We obtained written informed consent from the mother to interview all members of the family. Housed families were offered monetary incentives to participate. Most questions were the same for the housed and homeless mothers, although some were modified to account for differences in housing.

MOTHERS. A semi-structured interview consisting of approximately 260 questions was administered to each mother to obtain information on demographic factors; developmental background including early relationships with caretakers; family disruptions and patterns of violence; housing, income, and work histories; nature of relationships; parenting; medical and psychiatric histories; and use of services. In addition, a structured questionnaire, the Social Support Network Inventory,[10] was modified and administered. Psychiatric diagnoses were made by a psychiatrist (ELB) using DSM-III inclusion and exclusion criteria.[11] These diagnoses were made on the basis of responses to the semi-structured interview and probes. Although some controversy exists about the reliability and validity of various DSM-III diagnoses,[11] the use of such criteria has been reported to enhance agreement among clinicians and investigators.

CHILDREN. The interviewer played with or talked to each child before administering standardized instruments. The Denver Developmental Screening Test[12,13] was used to assess children five years of age or younger, and the Children's Depression Inventory[14] and the Children's Manifest Anxiety Scale[15] were administered to older children.

DATA ANALYSIS

Univariate analyses were carried out in which the proportion of homeless mothers with a particular characteristic was compared with the corresponding proportion among housed mothers. These comparisons were based on those with known values of a particular factor. Multiple logistic regression analysis was used to assess the relation of several factors at once to homelessness.[16]

In the results described below, the differences cited were generally present in the two major ethnic groups in the study, Whites and Blacks.

RESULTS

THE MOTHERS

GENERAL CHARACTERISTICS. As shown in Table 1, the homeless and housed mothers were similar in terms of age and ethnic group. Almost all the mothers were currently single, but a greater proportion of homeless than housed mothers had been married. The homeless and housed women became mothers for the first time at similar ages and had similar numbers of children. Almost all the families were receiving welfare, and about half of each group had been receiving aid for dependent children (AFDC) longer than four years.

Half of the homeless mothers and one-third of the housed mothers grew up outside the Boston area, and 24 per cent and 11 per cent, respectively, grew up outside the United States.

The homeless women reported a higher level of educational attainment than the housed. Employment histories of the two groups were similar, with more than half having worked only occasionally or not at all.

The homeless mothers had moved much more frequently than the housed mothers. In the previous five years, none of the homeless mothers had moved less than twice, two-thirds had moved at least four times, and one-fourth had moved at least 10 times;

TABLE 1. Selected Characteristics of 49 Homeless and 81 Housed
Families

Characteristics	Homeless	Housed
Age of Mother (years)		
Mean	28	29
Range	18 to 49	18 to 58
Mean Age at Birth of First Child	20	19
Mean Number of Children	2.4	2.5
Ethnic Group	No. (%)	No. (%)
White	16 (33)	26 (32)
Non-White	33 (67)	55 (68)
Marital Status		
Single	28 (57)	61 (75)
Divorced/Separated/Widowed	20 (41)	19 (24)
Married	1 (2)	1 (1)
Education*		
Less than 12 years	17 (36)	52 (64)
High school graduate	18 (38)	24 (30)
Some college	12 (26)	5 (6)
Employment History		
Some work experience	18 (37)	30 (37)
Worked occasionally	12 (24)	13 (16)
Minimal or never worked	19 (39)	38 (47)
Currently Receiving Welfare	47 (96)	81 (100)
Length of Time on Welfare*		
<2 years	16 (35)	26 (32)
2–4 years	12 (26)	14 (17)
>4 years	18 (39)	41 (51)

*% of those with known values

in contrast, two-thirds of the housed mothers had moved once or not at all, 5 per cent had moved at least four times, and none had moved 10 or more times. In the previous year alone, the homeless mothers had moved an average of four times.

The homeless mothers had more frequently lived with a man or doubled up with friends or relatives and had less frequently lived independently. Sixty-seven per cent of the homeless compared to 12 per cent of the housed families had previously stayed in an emergency shelter or welfare hotel. Just before the current shelter stay, only 14 per cent of the homeless were living independently (8 per cent in non-subsidized apartments and 6 per cent in subsidized housing), and 85 per cent were doubled up. By contrast, at the time of the interview, 72 per cent of housed mothers were living in public housing of subsidized apartments (of which two-thirds were in housing projects), 5 per cent in non-subsidized apartments, and 23 per cent were doubled up.

THE MOTHER'S CHILDHOOD. The homeless mothers had less frequently been born into households headed by women than the housed mothers (29 per cent vs. 48 per cent), but by the time of adolescence about two-thirds of each group were living in female-headed households.

The fathers of the homeless women were more available to them in childhood; those men were more frequently the fathers of the siblings of the now homeless mothers and were more likely to keep in contact with their daughters than were the fathers of the housed women. They also were less likely (45 per cent vs. 69 per cent) to have such problems as alcoholism, physical illness, mental illness, and poverty.

The mothers of the homeless women had less commonly received AFDC than mothers of the housed women (30 per cent vs. 58 per cent) while a greater proportion of the mothers of the homeless women than housed women had worked (70 per cent vs. 35 per cent).

Similar proportions of homeless (69 per cent) and housed mothers (57 per cent) reported a major family disruption (e.g., divorce, death) during childhood; the age at the time of the first disruption and the nature of the disruption were also similar.

Having been abused as a child was much more frequently reported by homeless (17 of 41 who were willing to answer) than by housed mothers (5 per cent).

CURRENT RELATIONSHIPS. When the mothers were asked to name up to three supports (i.e., people on whom they could count during times of stress), housed mothers reported many more supports than the homeless (Table 2); 22 per cent of the homeless compared with only 2 per cent of the housed mothers were unable to name *any* adult supports, while 26 per cent and 74 per cent, respectively, named three adult supports. The homeless women less frequently named their mothers or other family members as supports and more frequently named a minor child. The housed mothers more commonly named females among their supports than did the homeless. In addition, two-thirds of the adult supports of housed mothers were seen daily compared to one-third of the homeless supports. These patterns held for women who had grown up in the Boston area and for those who had not.

Twenty-eight per cent of the housed mothers reported that one or more family members outside the nuclear family were living with them, and about half had members of their extended family living in the same housing project or within walking distance.

RELATIONSHIPS WITH MEN. The homeless mothers tended to have had fewer major relationships with men than the housed women, and this was so within each age group. Overall, 14 per cent of the homeless reported no relationships and 30 per cent described two or more; in contrast, 5 per cent of the housed women had none and 64 per cent two or more. About two-thirds of the men with whom the homeless women had their most recent relationships had poor work histories, substance abuse problems, battering tendencies, or other problems, in contrast to one-third of the most recent boyfriends of the housed mothers.

Forty-one per cent of the homeless mothers willing to respond described a relationship in which they had been battered, compared with 20 per cent of the housed mothers. The homeless mothers tended to escape the relationship by going to battered women shelters, while most housed mothers turned to close friends for help.

HEALTH/MENTAL HEALTH STATUS. About one-fourth of the housed and homeless mothers reported medical problems (Table 3). A total of 16 (33 per cent) homeless and 10 (12 per cent) housed mothers had substance abuse or psychiatric problems; eight (16 per cent) homeless and five (6 per cent) housed mothers reported alcohol or drug problems; 13 (27

TABLE 2. Supports of 49 Homeless and 81 Housed Mothers

Support Named	Homeless No.	Homeless (%)	Housed No.	Housed (%)
Number of Adult Supports				
None	11	(22)	2	(2)
1	13	(26)	6	(7)
2	12	(24)	13	(16)
3	13	(26)	60	(74)
Minor Child Named as Support	15	(31)	3	(4)
Type of Adult Support Named (not mutually exclusive)				
Mother	12	(24)	49	(60)
Father	5	(10)	8	(10)
Other Family Member*	14	(29)	63	(78)
Spouse/Boyfriend	13	(27)	14	(17)
Friend	15	(31)	28	(35)
Professional	4	(8)	1	(1)
Gender of Adult Supports*†				
Male	27	(46)	42	(27)
Female	32	(54)	113	(73)
Frequency of Contact with Adult Supports				
Monthly or less	26	(34)	15	(7)
Weekly	24	(32)	57	(27)
Daily	26	(34)	140	(66)

*Members of mother's family excluding mother, father, and spouse/boyfriend
†Other than mother and father

TABLE 3. Medical and Psychiatric Problems of 49 Homeless and 81 Housed Mothers

Problems Identified	Homeless		Housed	
	No.	(%)	No.	(%)
Medical Problems	13	(27)	17	(21)
Substance Abuse	8	(16)	5	(6)
Alcohol	6		4	
Drug	5		2	
Psychiatric Hospitalization or Diagnosis	13	(27)	8	(10)
Psychiatric hospitalization	4		3	
DSM-III, Axis I Diagnoses	11		5	
Schizophrenia	3		0	
Major affective disorder	1		2	
Substance abuse	4		1	
Mental retardation	3		2	

per cent) and eight (10 per cent), respectively, were judged to have psychiatric disability. With regard to the latter, four homeless and three housed mothers had been hospitalized for psychiatric reasons; after the interview, 11 homeless and five housed mothers were assigned DSM-III Axis I diagnoses indicating the presence of major psychiatric clinical syndromes. These diagnoses did not cluster into any one category in either group.

Seven homeless (14 per cent) and seven housed (9 per cent) mothers had been in jail.

SERVICE UTILIZATION. Overall, the homeless less frequently reported current involvement with a housing or human service agency (50 per cent vs. 75 per cent). Smaller proportions of homeless mothers than housed mothers were receiving food stamps (55 per cent vs. 83 per cent), WIC (Women, Infants, and Children Supplemental Food Program) (33 per cent vs. 54 per cent), or housing subsidies (Section 8 or Certificate 707) (28 per cent vs. 61 per cent).

THE CHILDREN

GENERAL CHARACTERISTICS. The mean age of the children, both the 86 homeless and 134 housed, was 6.4 years. Slightly more than half of each sample were preschoolers, aged 5 years or less. Fifty-four per cent of the homeless children and 39 per cent of the housed children were male.

Three-fourths of the homeless mothers indicated that the child's father had no relationship at any time with the child or that the relationship had ended, compared with 44 per cent of the housed mothers; fewer homeless than housed mothers (11 per cent vs. 34 per cent) reported that the fathers took some financial responsibility for the child.

Thirteen (27 per cent) of the 48 homeless mothers willing to respond on this question were currently under investigation for neglect or abuse of their children compared to 12 (15 per cent) of 80 housed mothers.

PRESCHOOLERS. On the Denver Developmental Screening Test, 54 per cent of the 48 homeless preschoolers tested manifested at least one major developmental lag compared to 16 per cent of 75 housed preschoolers.

SCHOOL-AGE CHILDREN. On the Children's Depression Inventory, the mean total score of the 31 homeless children who completed the test was 10.3 compared to 8.3 for 33 housed children. A cutoff point of 9 indicates the need for psychiatric evaluation. On the Children's Manifest Anxiety Scale, 31 per cent of the 29 homeless children tested compared to 9 per cent of 34 housed children had a T-score of 60 or higher, indicating the need for psychiatric referral and evaluation. According to the mothers, 41 per cent of the homeless compared to 23 per cent of the housed children were currently failing or doing below average work in school.

MULTIVARIATE ANALYSIS. To assess whether differences observed in the univariate analyses would persist when several factors were considered simultaneously, we carried out multiple logistic regression analyses. On univariate analysis, history of having been abused as a child or adult and history of substance abuse or psychiatric difficulties were positively correlated with homelessness (that is, more prevalent among homeless mothers). Having grown up in a family on welfare and having three adult supports were inversely correlated with homelessness (that is, more prevalent among housed mothers). We included terms for these factors in the logistic regressions, and also included terms for the mother's age and race and for having grown up in the greater

Boston area. All of the relationships observed on univariate analysis persisted in the multivariate analysis. When the analysis was repeated, this time comparing the homeless to those housed mothers who had shared apartments or had been homeless, the results were similar.

DISCUSSION

The present study—the first systematic comparison of homeless and housed families—has several limitations that should be borne in mind when interpreting the results. The interview setting was different for the homeless and housed mothers, and this may have contributed to differences in reporting. The sample was small, multiple comparisons were made, and differences may have arisen by chance. There were problems reaching the target populations of both homeless and housed families. Not all shelters allowed access to their homeless clients. In addition, when they were full, the shelters tended to turn away problem families first; thus, the sample may underrepresent the most seriously troubled families. The housed families lived in dangerous crime-ridden areas. For safety reasons, attempts to contact them were made only during daylight hours, when many were not home. As a result, the sample of housed mothers probably overrepresents those who do not have jobs, and these women may have been more likely to be on welfare for long periods. If future studies are to overcome problems of selection of homeless and housed families, they will require a large investment of money, time, and personnel.

Nationwide most AFDC families stay on welfare for less than two years.[17] Although only 30 per cent of Massachusetts families remain on AFDC for more than two years, almost 70 per cent of the housed families in the present study had received welfare for that long.[18] Possibly the housed group was weighted with long-term welfare recipients because the sampling scheme required at least 10 eligible housed families to reside in a sampled block: this might have resulted in selection of women from housing projects, a group that tends to be on welfare for long periods. Although the sample may not be representative of all poor housed families, it does not appear to overrepresent those who are best off. Rather, it contains a higher proportion of those persistently poor families who have difficulty getting off welfare.

Comparisons of other features of the housed women with published data are problematic. For ex-

ample, studies from the 1960s and 1970s indicate that families receiving AFDC tended to move repeatedly.[19,20] In the present study, the housed mothers moved infrequently. We are not aware of any published data on the characteristics of long-term AFDC recipients. It is plausible, however, that the low frequency of moves by housed mothers in the present study is explained by the severity of the current housing crisis which has made it necessary for those in public housing and subsidized apartments to stay there.[21] As another example, recent data indicate that in Massachusetts some 70 per cent of AFDC families must find housing in the private housing market.[22] In the present study, half of the housed families lived in housing projects. As noted, whether this is so for long-term AFDC recipients is not known.

The comparison of homeless and housed mothers revealed some important similarities and striking differences:

- In both groups the mothers were poor, currently single, had little work experience, and had been on welfare for long periods.
- Many of their children had serious developmental and emotional problems.
- A greater proportion of homeless than housed mothers had been born into female-headed families, but by adolescence the proportions were similar.
- A smaller proportion of homeless mothers had been on welfare as children and a greater proportion had had contact with their fathers.
- Similar proportions of homeless and housed mothers had suffered major family disruptions during childhood.
- The homeless mothers had much more frequently been abused as children, and also had been more frequently battered as adults.
- The support networks of the homeless women were fragmented and included proportionately more men, while the housed mothers had frequent contact with their mothers, other female relatives, and extended family living nearby.
- A greater proportion of homeless than housed mothers had substance abuse or psychiatric problems.
- Despite the scarcity of low-income housing and of housing subsidies, as well as long waiting lists for public housing in Boston,[22] most housed families were living or had lived in public housing or in private subsidized housing while almost none of the homeless had managed this.

• Few housed mothers had histories of homelessness. By contrast, the homeless families moved often and two-thirds had previously resided in shelters or welfare hotels.

What differences might explain why the housed mothers were able to find and retain housing while the homeless were not? Although luck may contribute to a poor family's ability to find secure housing, the nature and extent of a family's support network play an important role in determining whether it will need emergency shelter. It has been reported that poor families headed by women tend to have interconnected kin and non-kin domestic networks comprised predominantly of women.[19,20] With the current housing crisis, it is difficult to imagine how poor families can survive in the community unless they have supports to act as a safety net during stressful times. For example, a recently evicted poor mother will generally have the opportunity to double up if she has a large extended family living nearby or if she has many close friends. In the present study, the housed families had such supports. The homeless mothers did not, but we cannot exclude the possibility that homelessness stressed and weakened their support networks.

What accounts for the fragmented supports of the homeless women? Certain aspects of the mothers' childhoods are unlikely explanations; although more housed than homeless mothers were born into female-headed families, by adolescence two-thirds of the families of both groups were female-headed; major family disruptions during childhood affected similar proportions, more than half, in each group and at similar ages. In some ways the homeless mothers had backgrounds that might be considered more favorable than those of the housed: during childhood their fathers had more contact with them and their families were less frequently on welfare. However, the homeless mothers experienced more family violence than the housed. In particular, 42 per cent of homeless mothers willing to respond reported having been abused as children. This pattern of violence continued into adult life: about the same proportion of homeless mothers reported having been abused by their boyfriends or husbands. More homeless than housed mothers were also being investigated for abuse or neglect of their own children. The greater frequency of family violence suffered by the homeless mothers may explain, in part, their difficulty as adults in forming and maintaining adequate supportive relationships.

The presence of chronic mental illness has been invoked to explain homelessness.[23,24] In the present study, serious psychopathology may have affected the ability of homeless women to find and retain housing or to maintain the support networks that would assist them. Psychiatric disability can explain only a small part of family homelessness in this study, however, since it affects only a minority of the homeless women. There might even have been an overestimation of the proportion with severe psychopathology since the investigator who made the psychiatric diagnoses was not blind to whether the mother was homeless or housed.

Although chronic mental illness was absent in a majority of the homeless mothers, this is not to say that they and their families did not have significant emotional difficulties. In several respects—such as difficulties in relationships with family, family violence, the severity of the problems of the children, and use of services and agencies—they are similar to the "multi-problem" families first described several decades ago.[9,25,26]

It has been further suggested that homeless families are part of a "culture of poverty," with the implication that the economic and social problems of these families will persist and become intergenerational.[27,28] To the contrary, in the present study the homeless were less likely to have grown up on welfare than the housed mothers, and the latter were the ones who were knowledgeable enough to maintain housing for themselves and their families and to obtain other benefits, such as food stamps. Furthermore, the types of emotional difficulties which affected the homeless mothers may well be amenable to intervention (e.g., supportive environments such as transitional housing).[29]

The present findings must be considered in the context of the current housing crisis.[30] In Massachusetts and other areas of the country, the supply of low income housing has been greatly reduced while rents have skyrocketed. Given these circumstances, the additional problems faced by homeless mothers of small children make even more difficult the already daunting task of finding and keeping a place to live that is affordable on current AFDC benefits. Any solution to this problem requires a commitment to increasing the supply of decent, affordable housing and providing adequate income maintenance. However, without practical help from social welfare agencies that is focused on rebuilding supportive relationships, the quality of life will continue to be severely compromised.

ACKNOWLEDGMENTS

Supported by the Robert Wood Johnson Foundation. Boston Safe Deposit and Trust Company. Godfrey B. Hyams Trust, and the Boston Foundation.

References

 1. US Conference of Mayors: A Status Report on Homeless Families in America's Cities: A 29-City Survey, Washington DC: The Conference, May 1987.
 2. Bassuk EL: The homelessness problem. Sci Am 1984; 251:40–45.
 3. Acker PJ, Fierman AH, Dreyer BP: An assessment of parameters of health care and nutrition in homeless children. Am J Dis Childr 1987; 141:388.
 4. Wright J: Effects of homelessness on the physical well-being of children, families, and youth. National evaluation of the Johnson-Pew "Health Care of the Homeless" Program, Feb. 24, 1987.
 5. Chavkin W, Kristal A, Seabron C, Guigli P: The reproductive experience of women living in hotels for the homeless in New York City. NY State J Med 1987; 87:10–13.
 6. Columbia University: Homeless families living in hotels: The provision of publicly supported emergency temporary housing services. Prepared for the Human Resources Administration, City of New York, May 1985.
 7. Bassuk EL, Rubin L, Lauriat A: Characteristics of sheltered homeless families. Am J Public Health 1986; 76:1097–1101.
 8. Bassuk EL, Rubin L: Homeless children: A neglected population. Am J Orthopsychiatry 1987; 57:279–286.
 9. Kronenfeld D, Phillips M, Middleton-Jeter V: The Forgotten Ones: Treatment of Single Parent Multi-Problem Families in a Residential Setting. Washington, DC: US Dept Health and Human Services, Grant Number 18-P-90705/03, 1978–1980.
10. Flaherty J, Gaviria FM, Pathak D: The measurement of social support. The social support network inventory. Compr Psychiatry 1983; 24:521–529.
11. Diagnostic and Statistical Manual of Mental Disorders, 3rd Edition-Revised (DSM-III-R). Washington DC: American Psychiatric Association, 1987.
12. Frankenburg WK, Goldstein A, Camp B: The revised Denver Developmental Screening Test. Its accuracy as a screening instrument. J Pediatr 1971; 79:988–955.
13. Frankenburg WK, Fandal AW, Thornton SM: Revision of Denver Prescreening Developmental Questionnaire. J Pediatr 1987; 110:653–657.
14. Kovacs M: The Children's Depression Inventory. A self-rated depression scale for school-aged youngsters. Pittsburgh: University of Pittsburgh School of Medicine, April 1983.
15. Reynolds CR, Richmond BO: Revised Children's Manifest Anxiety Scale Manual. Los Angeles: Western Psychological Services, 1985.
16. Armitage P: Statistical Methods in Medical Research. New York: John Wiley, 1971.
17. Bane MJ, Ellwood D: The Dynamics of Dependence: The Routes to Self-Sufficiency. Washington DC: US Dept of Health and Human Services, June 1983 (Contract No. HHS-100-82-0038).
18. The Facts about Welfare: Being Poor in Massachusetts. Boston: Department of Public Welfare, 1985.
19. Stack CB: All Our Kin: Strategies for Survival in a Black Community. New York: Harper & Row, 1974.
20. Susser I: Norman Street. New York: Oxford University Press, 1982.
21. Dumpson JR: A Shelter Is Not a Home: Report of the Manhattan Borough President's Task Force on Housing for Homeless Families. March 1987.
22. Gallagher E: No Place Like Home: A Report on the Tragedy of Homeless Children and Their Families in Massachusetts. Boston: Massachusetts Committee for Children and Youth. 1986.
23. Arce A, Vergare M: Identifying and characterizing the mentally ill among the homeless. *In:* Lamb HR (ed): The Homeless Mentally Ill. Washington DC: American Psychiatric Association. 1984; 75–89.
24. Snow D, Baker S, Anderson L, Martin M: The myth of pervasive mental illness among the homeless. Soc Problems 1986; 33:407–423.
25. Pavenstedt E (ed): The Drifters: Children of Disorganized Lower Class Families. Boston: Little Brown & Co, 1967.
26. Geismer L, LaSorte M: Understanding the Multi-Problem Family. New York: Associated Press, 1964.
27. Lewis O: The Children of Sanchez. New York: Random House. 1961.
28. Banfield E: The Unheavenly City: The Nature and Future of Our Urban Crisis. Boston: Little Brown, 1968.
29. Wilson J: The Truly Disadvantaged: The Inner City, the Underclass and Public Policy. Chicago: Univ of Chicago Press, 1987.
30. Hartman C: The housing part of the homelessness problem. *In:* Bassuk EL (ed): The Mental Health Needs of Homeless Persons. New Directions for Mental Health Services. San Francisco: Jossey-Bass, 1986; Vol 30.

CONFLICT
AND COOPERATION

INTRODUCTION

In this part, we will deal with several major problem areas. First, we will look at the range of abusive situations. Then we will consider family conflicts and resolutions. Third, we will explore the question of intergenerational relations, and finally we will examine substance abuse and delinquency. Each of these involves conflict and cooperation among the participants.

First, abuse. Arlene Rubin Stiffman begins this section with an overview of physical and sexual abuse of children. What is the meaning of abuse? Who is involved? Where does abuse take place? She also presents some information about her own research on abused runaways.

Then Edward M. Levine and Eugene J. Kanin review the literature on sexual violence among dates and acquaintances, or, in the vernacular, date rape. The authors claim that increases in date rape may be due to changing sexual morality (the equalization of sexual freedom for females vis-à-vis males), the role of mass media in treating human sexuality, and the widespread use of alcohol among adolescents and college students.

There is no paper in this section specifically on spousal abuse, but I remind you of the paper by Edward W. Gondolf, "Changing Men Who Batter" (pages 207–214 of this anthology), that deals with this topic.

Finally, there is an excerpt from a paper by Sharon Powell and Robert C. Berg on elder abuse. This is a topic on which there is as yet very little public information, but the problem may be of significant scale to be put on the national agenda for social action.

Altogether, violence within the family and between friends and acquaintances is a distressing fact of contemporary life in America. These papers are points of departure for thinking and action to prevent and to ameliorate such violence.

The second section of this part deals with family conflicts and resolutions. A paper by Dorothy Field and Sylvia Weishaus reports on a study of marriages that have lasted over fifty years. What changes over time do marital partners experience by the time of their golden wedding anniversary? Field and Weishaus report interesting differences between husbands and wives on these experiences.

Arnold L. Stolberg and Martin Bloom consider the effects of the divorce adjustment process on child development and functioning. Stages in parental adjustment to divorce mean different kinds of nurturing for the children. The authors point to important information for helping professionals that may be used to prevent some predictable problems for children occurring as a result of divorce.

Patsy Skeen, Robert B. Covi, and Bryan E. Robinson review the literature on stepfamilies. What do we know about stepfamilies and how do they differ from primary families? What are the special problems associated with stepfamilies and how can practitioners help to resolve these problems?

The third section of this part involves intergenerational relations. Martha N. Ozawa introduces some startling facts on the relationship between the education of minority youths today and the kind of retirement support system majority elderly can expect when they retire. It appears that if we do not provide minority youth today with a solid education to enable them to participate fully in our complex society, then they are not going to be available to pay the level of taxes that will be needed to underwrite the expectable costs of social security in the future.

Jane E. Myers considers the relationship patterns between adult children and their aging parents. There are important developmental experiences occurring to both at these tandem stages in their lives. For example, mid-life women have been the traditional helpers of older parents, but today, large proportions of these women are in the labor force and are not available for this traditional help role. This is but one of many factors creating stress in the extended family. With understanding and occasional aid from friends, relatives, or helping professionals, it is possible to resolve many of these stresses.

Edward F. Lawlor discusses the intergenerational equity debate that is raising the question of whether or not the distribution of the nation's resources between young and old is fair. From some perspectives, it appears as if the elderly are getting far more than their fair proportion; from other points of view, it may be that both youth and the old need more assistance: it should not be an either/or question when both are needful. This developmental policy issue is likely to reappear in new forms over time.

The final section of this part concerns substance abuse and delinquency, increasingly difficult problems facing society. Lloyd D. Johnston, Patrick M. O'Malley, and Jerald G. Bachman present an overview of their longitudinal findings on Monitoring the Future, a project involving on-going surveys of succeeding generations of high school seniors since 1975. With this powerful set of data, they can describe the trends in illicit drug use (generally downward), trends in alcohol use (extremely high usage is recorded; although there has been some decrease among high school students, use among college students has not changed appreciably), and trends in cigarette smoking (little decrease since 1981; female high school students are now more likely than males to start smoking). The variations in gender, education, and class are important for preventive programming.

Mario A. Orlandi offers a planning model for the community level regarding the prevention of substance abuse. The model is sensitive to subcultural variations. He discusses the culture-specific factors in substance abuse prevention for black Americans, Hispanic Americans, Asian Americans, and Native Americans.

J. David Hawkins and Joseph G. Weis present a social development model that integrates the family, school, peer groups, and community agencies as socialization agents for preventing delinquency. This important example of model construction interrelates many facets of the social configuration; it suggests ways of involving youths in skills training and for providing consistent reinforcement for pro-social behavior in these settings. This type of conceptualizing may be applied to many other social concerns as well.

Overall, we as individuals and as a society must deal with conflict and cooperation in nearly every aspect of life. What we can learn about ways of dealing with problems in one sphere may be transferred as hypotheses for dealing with concerns in other spheres.

PART VI

A. Abuse

28

PHYSICAL AND SEXUAL ABUSE OF CHILDREN:
WHAT, WHO, AND WHERE?

Arlene Rubin Stiffman
School of Social Work
Washington University

Child abuse: these are words that we repeatedly see in the news and hear in the media. What is it? Where do we find it? and What happens to the victims? Reported abuse cases have escalated in recent years. Yet, we still cannot predict which families and which children are most at risk, and we still persist in ignoring the possible presence of abuse in treatment situations where current knowledge indicates a history of abuse. This chapter presents basic background information about child abuse and discusses one study that illumines the difficulties in applying that knowledge to particular situations.

THE BACKGROUND

WHAT IS CHILD ABUSE?

While early definitions defined child abuse in terms of acts which *impaired* a child's physical or emotional health and development, recent definitions add the condition of simple *endangerment* to that of impairment (Study of National Incidence and Prevalence, 1988). Child maltreatment, although frequently equated with child abuse, is usually subdivided into "abuse" and "neglect," with "abuse" an act of commission, and "neglect" an act of omission. Child maltreatment/abuse includes physical abuse, emotional abuse, physical neglect, inadequate supervision, and sexual abuse. Some observers believe that the use of the word endangerment in the definition forces abuse to include both those acts that are clearly dangerous and observable as well as those which are sometimes questionable. Anyone who has ever parented a child must admit, in moments of honesty, that there were times when his or her lack of supervision "endangered" the child.

In the 1960's, the first state laws were passed that required public agencies to report suspected cases of child abuse or neglect. Since 1974, when

The Child Abuse Prevention and Treatment Act was signed into law, the number of reported child abuse and neglect cases reported to child protection service agencies has increased annually (Study of National Incidence, 1988). Yet, despite this increase, child abuse is still thought to be highly underreported. The U.S. Department of Health and Human Services estimates that one to two percent of all children are involved in child abuse or neglect in any given year (Study of National Incidence, 1988) and other researchers conclude that approximately 14 of every 100 children between the ages of three and seventeen experience violence each year (Straus, Gelles, & Steinmetz, 1980).

In 1986, a nationwide study of reported cases of abuse found that an estimated 16.3 children per 1,000, or a total of more than one million children nationwide, experienced demonstrable harm from abuse or neglect (Study of National Incidence, 1988). Endangerment raises that number by half again, to an estimated 25.2 children per 1,000, or a total of more than one and one-half million children.

Over half of all abuse reports were for physical abuse (53 percent), one third were for emotional abuse (30 percent), and one quarter were for sexual abuse (24 percent). Some studies, which were based on interviews of adults rather than on reported abuse cases, estimate that 20 percent of all youths experience incestuous sexual abuse (Russell, 1984); while other estimates of sexual abuse range from 20 percent (Kercher and McShane, 1984) to 38 percent (Finklehor, 1979). Sexual abuse in these estimates is defined as including intimate touch as well as intercourse.

The rate of abuse in 1986 was 74 percent greater than it had been in a similar 1980 study (Study of National Incidence, 1988). The rates of physical abuse increased by 58 percent, and those of sexual abuse tripled. However, rather than in-

This paper was written for this anthology, 1990.

creases in the actual occurrence of physical harm, increases in reporting and changes in the definition of abuse might have caused the change of rates (Powers and Eckenrode, 1988). When researchers examined the type of reported injuries, only the category of moderate injuries increased (by 89 percent), therefore the change of definition to include endangerment rather than only demonstrable harm may have caused the increase in reports (Study of National Incidence, 1988). Nevertheless, the rates of abuse and the absolute numbers of abused children warrant a closer look at the individuals involved in order to see how they might be helped.

WHO IS INVOLVED?

Who are these children who are abused? And who are the parents that abuse? There are many myths surrounding abuse. One myth states that young children, who can't defend themselves, are the most frequent victims of abuse. Other myths say that abusers are usually from poor families or are most often Black. However, a close look at the research presents a somewhat different picture.

AGE. Although the rates of maltreatment confirm the supposition that young children experience the most abuse (Wolfe, 1987), when neglect is excluded, the picture changes. The myth indicates that physical abuse is concentrated in the youngest age groups, and the number of such reports decreases with age (Powers and Eckenrode, 1988). In contrast, research indicates that the incidence of physical abuse increases with age. Abuse among 0–2 year olds is less frequent than abuse to children of other ages (Study of National Incidence, 1988). Adolescents account for 47 percent of all child abuse reports, a figure greater than the proportion of teens in the general population of children and youth (American Humane Association, 1984). In addition, many authors suggest that the true prevalence may be greater, since abuse and neglect are often unrecognized and/or not reported in the older age group (Garbarino, Schellenbach, Sebes et al., 1986). When abused, however, very young children are more likely to experience severe or fatal injury, reflecting their greater vulnerability to physical harm. Moderate injuries/impairments, in contrast, are more prevalent in the older age brackets.

The pattern of reported abuse in adolescents is different than that in children: adolescents experience more physical injury and emotional maltreatment, three times as much sexual abuse, and less neglect (American Humane Association, 1984). Substantiation rates decrease with age for physical abuse and neglect reports, but increase with age for sexual abuse reports (Study of National Incidence, 1988). These changes in the rates of different types of abuse may be related to the developmental levels of the children involved. In the case of sexual abuse, language skills are particularly critical for substantiation. Thus, the younger the child, the less able he/she is to effectively communicate information about the abuse. Physical abuse, however, has observable outcomes which may lead to higher substantiation rates for younger children.

SEX: The child's sex affects both the rates and types of maltreatment. Adolescent maltreatment appears to be mainly a female phenomenon (13.1 per 1,000 females vs. 8.4 per 1,000 males) (Olson and Holmes, 1986; Powers and Eckenrode, 1988; Study of National Incidence, 1988). Nevertheless, it is important to recognize that these data are based on reports which may not accurately reflect gender differences in maltreatment among adolescents. For example, males may be perceived to be less vulnerable, in less need of protection, and more capable of taking care of themselves than are adolescent females (Powers and Eckenrode 1988). Therefore individuals may choose to report fewer incidences of abuse of male adolescents than female adolescents.

RACE AND SOCIOECONOMIC STATUS: Race and socioeconomic status are often confounded in our society, and thus must be discussed together. Although recent national studies have shown race/ethnicity to have no association with maltreatment (Study of National Incidence, 1988), individual studies of reported abuse have stated that young black children may be at increased risk for maltreatment (American Association for Protecting Children, 1987: Hampton and Newberger, 1985). This effect may be due to the effects of social class, or other variables associated with minority group status (e.g., poverty, unemployment). It may also reflect increased surveillance of this population because of its increased chances of coming in contact with other service providers (e.g., public welfare).

Interestingly, in contrast with studies of abuse of young children, studies of adolescent abuse have shown a predominance of white youths (Olsen and Holmes, 1986; Powers and Eckenrode, 1988; Stiffman, 1989).

THE ABUSERS: Abuse has been analyzed from a sociocultural perspective (White, Benedict, Wulff, and Kelley, 1987; Gelles, 1973), which assumes that frustration and stress are important causal factors. Marital disputes, unemployment, family stress, or a "problem child" could create stress, and factors such as norms sanctioning violence could intensify it. Steele (1987) points out that four conditions must be in place for abuse to occur: the predisposition for abuse from personality or from earlier life history, a stressor or crisis, lack of sources of help, and a child who is perceived as unsatisfactory in some way.

The predisposition to abuse may be due to intrapersonal factors or to personal history. There is some controversy about personality flaws and minor mental health problems in abusers. The most recent consensus indicates that they are no more prevalent than in other sectors of society (Steele, 1987). However, there is good evidence that child abusers have higher rates of major mental illness (e.g., Taitz, 1980), and, notably, substance abuse (e.g., Blumberg, 1979). The child abusers may have learned the behavior in childhood through being victims of abuse (e.g., Steele, 1987), or having poor parental models (Altemeier, O'Connor, Vietze, Sandler and Sherrod, 1984). They may have unrealistic expectations for their children's behavior and development (e.g., Steele, 1987).

In addition to those individual factors, abusers may live in an environment that predisposes them toward abuse, or, at least, does not mitigate against abuse. The abusers may be isolated from the community, have little support from family or friends (e.g., Egeland, 1979; Garbarino et al., 1986), and have a pattern of violent relationships (e.g., Egeland, 1979; Friedman, Sandler, Hernandez and Wolfe, 1981; Straus et al., 1980).

Stressors and crises may be interconnected with the low socioeconomic level of abusers (e.g., Egeland, 1979); Straus et al., 1980). This may lead to frequent moves, unemployment, crowding, large families (e.g., Altemeier, et al., 1984), and teenage or unwed parenthood (e.g., Egeland, 1979; Taitz, 1980).

The victim of abuse may also be a trigger in a system predisposed to abuse. The child may have been unplanned or unwanted (Altemier et al., 1984), difficult to parent due to low birthweight or prematurity, handicapped in some manner (White et al., 1987), or deliberately provoking (Steele, 1987).

WHAT ARE THE EFFECTS?

EFFECTS OF ABUSE. Regardless of the rates of abuse or the causes of abuse, the focus of legislation is on the life and health of the child. However, the behavioral and emotional consequences of abuse merit equally strong concern. In an excellent and classic article, Ray Helfer (1987) points out that the

events that occur during childhood have a critical effect on later functioning. This is especially true of events that influence the learning of interpersonal skills. For the abused child, the senses (touching, smelling, hearing, and seeing) all become associated with fear, so abused children learn to not listen, not look, not be touched, etc. (Wilson, 1987). Helfer also points out that early childhood is the time for learning how to get one's needs met in an acceptable manner, how to take responsibility for one's own actions, how to make decisions, how to trust, and how to control one's actions. In each of these areas, the learning and experiences of abused children mitigate against such skills: many abused children have their needs for attention and contact met only through violence. Abused youngsters appear either to not be required to accept any responsibility or to have to accept the responsibilities for their parents (Slade, Steward, Morrison, and Abramowitz, 1984). Abused children are rarely given choices, or are punished for wrong decisions, so they can never experience learning to make decisions. Abused children often have never been able to trust, to feel safe. They also often never learn that feelings and actions are not always the same: one can be angry and not necessarily act upon that anger.

Helfer's description of the developmental effects of abuse make it clear that, despite the fact that fatalities are more prevalent for the very young, the effects may be equally profound for the adolescent. While for young children the risks are primarily that of bodily harm, for older children the risks include failure to learn the skills needed for successful functioning. These skill deficits may be cognitive or academic (Friedrich and Einbender, 1983), and may be accompanied by low self-esteem (Reidy, Anderegg, Tracy and Colter, 1980). The effect of abuse may manifest itself during adolescence in drug abuse (Cavaiola and Schiff, 1988), delinquency or aggression (Kinard, 1982; Tong, Oates, and McDowell, 1987), pregnancy, running away (Stiffman, 1989), depression (Allen and Tarnowski, 1989), and suicide (Stiffman, 1989). These behaviors may obscure a history of abuse as the primary causal agent, because intervention focuses on the child's behavior rather than the precipitating maltreatment situation (Powers and Eckenrode, 1988).

ILLUSTRATIVE EXAMPLE OF ABUSE IN RUNAWAYS

LISA: A CASE HISTORY

This chapter will now introduce a young lady who is a composite illustration of many of the issues concerning abuse, its effects, and the need to consider it in treatment.

'Lisa' is a 15 year old girl with a pale face and nondescript brown hair. She is wearing jeans with a torn knee, a tight off-the-shoulder jersey top open at the midriff, and three colors of eyeshadow. At our first interview, she saunters into the room, still snickering from a just-ended conversation loaded with sexual innuendos. She is very excited because her boyfriend has promised her that he will take care of her forever. "He's really neat! He has a great car! He doesn't care what I do. He just likes me." (at this remark, she rotates her pelvis and grins knowingly) "He's older," she guesses, "—19."

During the interview our research team questions her about her family. Her Dad is no longer with the family, but comes around and bothers them from time to time. He drinks and often beat her when drinking. Her mother and siblings live in a two bedroom apartment. They fight constantly. There is never enough money, privacy, or peace. She ran away when she and her Mom fought about her skipping school to be with her boyfriend.

Later, in the same tone of voice that she uses to tell about skipping school, she relates that her uncle had sex with her when she was seven. She never told anyone because "no one would care" and it was "no big deal." She has had boyfriends since age 12 and says she had two abortions.

Despite her snickering and sauntering, her scores on the depression scale show she is feeling very depressed, and she reports a former suicide attempt. Her long-term plan is to get married, buy a car and a house and have babies and "raise them right." She hasn't attended school in a month, uses drugs occasionally, and shoplifts. She says that she is a "together person." Only our probing and testing reveals her underlying sadness. Her surface appearance is one of control and defiance.

The shelter's goal, as written in her case record, is to return her to her home and help them develop better control of her acting out behaviors. There is no note about her history of abuse or her suicide attempts, as she did not volunteer the information to the shelter intake worker: no one asked her, and protective services had never been involved with her family. The research team found out about the abuse and suicide attempts only by direct questioning.

The study that led us to meet Lisa has been described elsewhere (Stiffman, 1989), so this chapter will not go into detail on the methods of the research (the interested reader can pursue those in the original report). However, it is interesting to see how Lisa illustrates the findings from that research study and the above-cited literature review. It is also interesting to see how her need for help illustrates some real pitfalls in working with abused adolescents.

Lisa's family is very typical. The most frequent reason cited for running away is usually a family disturbance centering around parental control issues (Blood and D'Angelo, 1974; Gullota, 1978; Roberts, 1982; Spillane-Grieco, 1984). Runaways experience high levels of parent/child conflict (Sommer, 1984; Adams and Munro, 1979; Justice and Duncan, 1976; Novy and Donohue, 1985; Wolk and Brandon, 1977), low levels of parental emotional support (Wolk and Brandon, 1977; Englander, 1984; Young, Godfrey, Matthews, and Adams, 1983), and low parent-child empathy or positive regard (Spillane-Grieco, 1984).

Lisa's experience of physical and sexual abuse is not unusual for runaways. Two studies of runaways report that approximately three-quarters of the youths had experienced physical violence directed toward themselves by a parent in the year prior to running away (Farber, Kinast, McCoard, and Falkner, 1984). Various other studies report that 14 percent to 27 percent of runaways cite physical violence as a reason for running (Gullota, 1978; Roberts, 1982; Shaffer and Caton, 1984).

Information regarding sexual abuse of children who run is sparse and inconsistent. Some studies report that 2 percent to 7 percent of female runaways have been molested by a family member (Gullota, 1978; Shaffer and Caton, 1984). However, when the definition of sexual abuse is widened to include intimate touch as well as intercourse, some authors state that up to 73 percent of female runaways may have experienced some form of sexual abuse (McCormack, Janus, and Burgess, 1986; Gullota, 1978). Nevertheless, sexual abuse does not appear to be the primary reason for leaving home. Only one of 30 runaways that Spillane-Grieco (1984) interviewed gave sexual abuse as a reason for leaving.

Lisa's sexual acting out, school behavior, and drug use are also common problems of abused youths. Abused children have a greater than average risk for developing emotional and/or behavioral problems (Wolfe, 1987; Altemeier, O'Connor, Sherrod, and Tucker, 1986). These are likely to include aggression (e.g., Garbarino et. al., 1986; Tarter, Hegedus, Winsten, and Alterman, 1984), delinquency (e.g., Wolfe and Mosk, 1983; McCormack, Janus, and Burgess, 1986), depression, alcohol and drug use, and distrust (e.g., Shaffer and Caton, 1984), low social competence (e.g., Kazdin, Moser, Coldus, and Bell, 1985), low self-control (e.g., Wolfe, 1987), and depression (e.g., Salzinger, Kaplan, Pelcovitz, Samit, and Kreiger, 1984). Nevertheless, not all abused youths are like Lisa. Some do not develop such problems (Wolfe, 1987), and sometimes running away is thought to constitute a 'healthy and adaptive response to an impossible situation' by youths who are maltreated (Gilbert and Pines, 1981, as quoted in Tarter et al., 1984).

Lisa's father fits a typical pattern for abusers. It is well documented that parental alcoholism or drug abuse may contribute to physical or sexual abuse of children (e.g., Straus, Gelles, and Steinmetz, 1980). This also appears to be a factor in running away. Approximately half of runaway subjects interviewed in two separate studies report that a family member actively abuses alcohol or drugs or is a criminal (Novy and Donohue, 1976; Shaffer and Caton, 1984). However, seldom do the youths say that a parent's alcohol or drug use was the reason for running (Gullota, 1978).

Last of all, let's discuss the recommendations for helping Lisa. Her experience is not unusual. Reconstituting the family is often the focus of services for the estimated quarter of a million youths (almost 2 percent of all youths aged 10 to 17) who run away each year (Brennan, Huizinga and Elliot, 1978; Sommer, 1984). However, this service orientation may not take into consideration that some families of runaways are abusive. Thus, service providers may be making some potentially dangerous recommendations.

THE FINDINGS OF THE STUDY OF RUNAWAYS.

The study that Lisa took part in specifically examined the extent of physical and sexual abuse among runaway youths, the association of that abuse with parental mental health problems, and the youths' own behavior and mental health. To do this, we interviewed 291 youths aged 12 to 18 from runaway shelters in St. Louis, Missouri. We asked the youths detailed questions about their family situations, their behaviors, and their feelings. We asked them to complete the Child Behavior Checklist Self-Report (Achenbach and Edelbrock, 1981), the Beck Depression Inventory (Albert and Beck, 1975), a modified version of the Adolescent Life Change Event Questionnaire (Carlson, Kaiser, Yeaworth, and Carlson, 1984), and the Rosenberg Self-Esteem Scale (Rosenberg, 1965). We also asked them a lot of questions about suicidal thoughts and behaviors, types and amounts of drug and alcohol use, experi-

ence with police, family relationships, mental health of family members, previous runaway behaviors, school performance, social activities, friendships and behaviors of friends, and treatment history. Of particular importance were two questions: "Have you ever had sex with or been sexually abused by a family member?" and, "Have you ever been so severely physically punished that you were bruised or injured?"

Our interviews revealed that abuse is widespread in runaways. Almost half of the 291 runaways report having been physically (n = 128) or sexually abused by a family member (n = 28). Interestingly, the pattern of abuse by race and sex in the runaways paralleled that which is known about adolescent abuse in general. Adolescent abuse is largely a female phenomenon, and more common among white youths than black youths. Only slightly more than one third of the abused youths are black, whereas over half are white. Only one in five abused youths are male, while three of every four are female. Note that, if abuse were distributed equally, one abused youth would be male for every two and half abused youths that are female.

The family situations of the abused and nonabused runaways were remarkably similar. There were no significant differences between the abused and nonabused youths in family stability (the number of families or institutions that the youth has lived in), in their current relationships with their parents, or in parental alcoholism, depression, or suicide attempts. However, there were striking differences in the mental health of the parents. Abused youths were twice as likely to report that a parent was a drug abuser and fifty percent more likely to report that a parent fit a profile of antisocial personality disorder.

The history of many of the youths reinforced Steele's (1987) statement that stress was a necessary condition for abuse. The abused youths, and thus their families, were significantly more likely to experience higher numbers of negative life events (excluding incidents of physical and sexual abuse). Over their lifetime, abused youths experienced an average of 26.4 negative life events, whereas nonabused youths experienced only 2/3 as many, at 19.1. A breakdown of the percentage of abused and nonabused runaways who experience each type of event yielded interesting results for those who might be tempted to 'blame the victim' by saying that the abused youths' behavior may have caused those events. Significantly higher percentages of the abused experienced events which can be classified as 'things outside of their control.' Specifically, these events include the death of a friend, having a sick parent, being beaten (not by parents), moving to a new school, moving to a new home, getting a new family member, and seeing a killing. These events were distinct from events such as being fired or failing in school, which might be partially the consequence of the youths' own behavior. Breaking up with a boy or girl friend is the only event that varied significantly between abused and nonabused runaways and that was potentially within the adolescent's own control.

Helfer stated that abused youths have missed many opportunities for learning and thus have problems functioning (1987). This was certainly true of Lisa, and true of the abused runaways as a group. Abused youths had more behavioral problems and depressive symptoms that nonabused youths. The abused youths had significantly higher scores on Achenbach's Behavior Problem Checklist and on Beck's Depression Inventory. It is interesting to note that, for both behavior problems and depression, the mean score for nonabused runaways was at the borderline cutoff point between a clinically significant and a normal problem level. In contrast, the mean score for abused runaways was clearly in the clinical problem range. Therefore, both groups of youths had problems, but the level of those problems were clinically significant (i.e., warranted treatment) for the abused youths.

Lisa told us that she used drugs, but, as a whole, drug use was not more prevalent among abused runaways than nonabused runaways. Abused and nonabused youths did not differ in extent or type of alcohol or drug use. Lisa also presented herself socially much the way the other runaways did, and that manner did not distinguish dramatically between abused and nonabused runaways. The abused and nonabused youths did not differ very much in their self-esteem scores. The self-esteem of both abused and nonabused runaways was low, reflecting the many problems of both groups of youths relative to nonrunaways.

CONCLUSIONS

The review of abuse and the illustrative study reinforce the importance of dealing with abuse and its consequences. One and a half million youngsters are reported each year for abuse, yet that may be just the tip of the iceberg. When a broad definition

of abuse including endangerment is used, it is likely that many families are not brought to the attention of protective services. It is also likely that the lack of attention is especially true for adolescents who are presumed to be able to take care of themselves. Yet we know that the strict narrow definition of abuse which focuses on physical condition does not accurately reflect the painful situation of many youth growing up today. Their wounds may not be visible, but the effects of the abuse are apparent in their behavior, interpersonal skills, and mental health.

The illustrative study points out some important facts about the consequences of abuse in adolescents even when life and limb have not been harmed. The abuse history of these adolescents who have run away also illuminates the need for recognizing abuse and incorporating it in treatment plans.

The study showed that almost half of runaway youths had been either physically or sexually abused, a proportion dramatically larger than that of the population at large. Nevertheless this proportion for runaways was lower than some estimates (Farber et al., 1984; James, McCormack, Burgess, and Hartman, 1987), but much higher than others that were discussed in studies of abuse as the precipitate for running away (Gullota, 1978; Spillane-Grieco, 1984; Shaffer and Caton, 1984; Roberts, 1982). The study also shows that approximately 10 percent of the youths reported experiencing incest, a figure almost double that of some estimates for incestual sexual abuse of youths in shelters (Gullota, 1978; Shaffer and Caton, 1984), and less than half that of estimates for incestuous abuse in the general population (Kercher and McShane, 1984). It may be less than that reported in the general population because those estimates are derived from retrospective reports by adults and have been defined to include intimate touch. Our question dealt only with 'having sex.' Also, many runaway teens are still young. They may have yet to experience such abuse, or they may be afraid to report it for fear that then they will not be able to return home if they reveal incest.

The findings about parental mental health from both the study (that 1 in 3 abused youths report that their parents have antisocial personality and/or drug problems) and from the literature review focus attention on the need for family-oriented intervention, and strengthen the notion that some major mental illnesses play a strong role in abuse.

The behavioral consequences of abuse are highlighted in this study. It is apparent from reviewing the literature and from the study of runaways that abused youths need mental health services. In the runaway study, the mean behavior problem scores and mean depression scores of the abused youths fell into the clinically significant area. These mental health consequences are also frightening when the behavioral profiles of these abused youths are compared with those behaviors and experiences that precipitate an individual to become an abuser. The signs of preparation for intergenerational transmission are clear. The youths are already programmed with several correlates of abuse: a history of abuse or mental health problems, and stressors.

The demographic results point up the particular vulnerability of females to such abuse, and their need for shelter. While the general literature shows that greater numbers of adolescent females than males are reported as abused (Powers and Eckenrode, 1988; Study of National Incidence, 1988), the discrepancy is not nearly as great as it is among runaway youths. The study of runaways also points up the lesser vulnerability of black youths to abuse and running away, a fact consistent with the literature on sexual and physical abuse of adolescents (McCormack, Janus, Burgess, 1986; Powers and Eckenrode, 1988). The race differences may indicate that black families have particular strengths that limit such abuses, or that black families have resources that keep the youths from having to seek public shelter. Extended family networks that serve to provide shelter in crises, or keep the abuse from occurring, may be one such protective device.

This study, in combination with the review of abuse, focuses attention on several important areas that should be incorporated into service delivery programs. We must begin to think of the effects of abuse as including the engendering of maladaptive behavioral as well as physical problems. Then those individuals involved in providing services for behav-ioral problems must become as alert as emergency room physicians to indicators of abuse. Only they must look for behavioral problems that are the results of abuse rather than for bruises, burns or other obvious physical trauma. Unless we do this, we may make some very serious errors in trying to help these youngsters.

The runaway study particularly showed that individuals involved in providing services for runaway youths should certainly include systematic investigations of the possibility of a history of abuse. This is probably equally true for those who provide services for delinquent youths, drug abusing youths, suicidal youths, etc. The existence of behavior problems on the part of the youth, particularly when the behavior problems are characteristic of thought disorder and depression, may be an additional indicator for carefully examining the home environment. Further, when treatment aims to reunite the child with his or her parents, service providers must be watchful for any indications of abuse, particularly in the presence of parental drug or alcohol abuse or antisocial personality.

Unfortunately, at the present time, there are few alternative placements available for youths, yet our findings point up the possibility that return to their family may mean entrapment in a situation fraught with mental illness, stressful events, and the possibility of abuse. This may doom the youths to perpetuating in the next generation the very damage that was wrought upon them. Society must provide these youths with protection: and this may mean temporary or interim shelter for the few years that remain until they are able to assume responsibility for themselves. We must also find ways to ameliorate the behavioral effects of the abuse so that we can prevent further generations from suffering in the same way.

References

Achenbach, T. M. and Edelbrock, C. T. (1981). Behavioral problems and competencies reported by parents of normal and disturbed children aged 4 through 16. *Monographs of the Society for Research in Child Development* 46, Serial No. 188.

Adams, G. R. and Munro, G. (1979). Portrait of the North American runaway: A critical review. *Journal of Youth and Adolescence* 8: 359–373.

Albert, N. and Beck, A. (1975). Incidence of depression in early adolescence: A preliminary study. *Journal of Youth and Adolescence* 4: 301–306.

Allen, D. M. and Tarnowski, K. J. (1989) Depressive characteristics of physically abused children. *Journal of Abnormal Child Psychology,* 17: 1–11.

Altemeier, W. A., O'Connor, S., Vietze, P., Sandler, H. and Sherrod, K. B. (1984). Prediction of child abuse: A prospective study of feasibility. *Child Abuse and Neglect* 8: 393–400.

Altemeier, W. A., O'Connor, S., Sherrod, K. B., and Tucker, D. (1986). Outcome of abuse during childhood among pregnant low income women. *Child Abuse and Neglect* 10: 319–330.

American Association for Protecting Children (1987). *Highlights of Official Child Neglect and Abuse Reporting* 1986. American Humane Association, Denver.

American Humane Association. (1984). *Trends in Child Abuse and Neglect: A National Perspective*. The American Humane Association, Denver, CO.

Beck, A. T., Ward, C. H., Mendelsohn, M., Mock, J., and Erbaugh, J. (1961). An invention for measuring depression. *Archives of General Psychiatry* 4: 561–571.

Blood, L. and D'Angelo, R. (1974). A progress report on value issues in conflict between runaways and their parents. *Journal of Marriage and the Family* 3: 486–491.

Blumberg, M. L. (1979). Collateral Therapy for the abused child and the problem parent. *American Journal of Psychotherapy* 33: 339–353.

Brennan, T., Huizinga, D. and Elliot, D. S. (1978). *The Social Psychology of Runaways*. Lexington: Lexington, MA.

Carlson, M. L., Kaiser, K. L., Yeaworth, R. C., and Carlson, R. E. (1984). An exploratory study of life-change events, social support & pregnancy decisions in adolescents. *Adolescence* 19: 765–780.

Cavaiola, A. A. and Schiff, M. (1988). Behavioral sequelae of physical and/or sexual abuse in adolescents. *Child Abuse and Neglect* 12: 181–188.

Egeland, B. (1979). An at risk approach to the study of child abuse. *American Journal of Orthopsychiatry* 4: 48–50.

Englander, S. W. (1984). Some self-reported correlates of runaway behavior in adolescent females. *Journal of Consulting and Clinical Psychology* 52: 484–485.

Farber, E. D., Kinast, C., McCoard, W. D. and Falkner, D. (1984). Violence in families of adolescent runaways. *Child Abuse and Neglect* 8: 295–299.

Finklehor, D. (1979). *Sexually Victimized Children*. The Free Press, New York.

Friedman, R., Sandler, J., Hernandez, M., and Wolfe, D. (1981). Behavioral assessment of child abuse. In E. Mash and L. Terdal (eds.) *Behavioral Assessment of Childhood Disorders*. New York: Guilford Press.

Friedrich, W. A. and Einbender, A. J. (1983). The abused child: A psychological review. *Journal of Clinical Child Psychology* 12: 244–256.

Garbarino, J., Schellenbach, C. J., Sebes, J. M. and Associates. (1986). *Troubled youth, troubled families: Understanding families at-risk for adolescent maltreatment*. Aldine, New York.

Gelles, R. (1973). Child abuse as psychopathology: A sociological critique and reformulation. *American Journal of Orthopsychiatry* 43: 611–621.

Gullota, T. P. (1978). Runaway: Reality or myth. *Adolescence* 13: 543–550.

Hampton, R. L. and Newberger, E. H. (1985). Child abuse incidence and reporting by hospitals: Significance of severity, class, and race. *American Journal of Public Health* 75: 56–60.

Helfer, R. E. (1987). The developmental basis of child abuse and neglect: An epidemiological approach. In Helfer, R. E. and Kempe, R. S. (eds.) *The Battered Child, 4th edition*. Chicago: The University of Chicago Press, 60–80.

James, D., McCormack, A., Burgess, A. W. and Hartman, C. (1987). *Adolescent Runaways: Causes and Consequences*. Lexington Books, Lexington, MA.

Justice, B. and Duncan, D. F. (1976). Running away: An epidemic problem of adolescence. *Adolescence* 11: 365–371.

Kazdin, A. E., Moser, J., Coldus, D, and Bell, R. (1985). Depressive symptoms among physically abused and psychiatrically disturbed children. *Journal of Abnormal Psychology* 94: 298–307.

Kercher, G. A. and McShane, M. (1984). The prevalence of child sexual victimization in an adult sample of Texas residents. *Child Abuse and Neglect* 8: 495–501.

Kinard, E. M. (1982). Experiencing child abuse: Effects of emotional adjustment. *American Journal of Orthopsychiatry* 52: 82–91.

McCormack, A., Janus, M. D., and Burgess, A. W. (1986). Runaway youths and sexual victimization: gender differences in an adolescent runaway population. *Child Abuse and Neglect* 10: 387–395.

Novy, D. B. and Donohue, S. (1985). The relationship between adolescent life stress events and delinquent conduct. *Adolescence* 20: 313–321.

Olsen, L. J. and Holmes, W. M. (1986) Youth at risk: Adolescents and maltreatment. *Children and Youth Services Review* 8: 13–35.

Powers, J. L. and Eckenrode, J. (1988). The maltreatment of adolescents. *Child Abuse and Neglect*, 12: 189–199.

Reidy, T. J., Anderegg, T. R., Tracy, R. J. and Colter, S. (1980). Abused and neglected children: The cognitive, social and behavioral correlates. In G. J. Williams and J. Money (eds.) *Traumatic Abuse and Neglect of Children at Home*. Baltimore: John Hopkins University Press, 284–290.

Roberts, A. R. (1982). Stress and coping patterns among adolescent runaways. *Journal of Social Service Research* 5: 15–27.

Rosenberg, M. (1968). *Society and the Adolescent Self-Image*. Princeton University Press, Princeton, NJ.

Russell, D. E. H. (1984). The prevalence and seriousness of incestuous abuse: Stepfathers vs. Biological Fathers. *Child Abuse and Neglect* 8:15–22.

Salzinger, S., Kaplan, S., Pelcovitz, D., Samit, C., and Kreiger, R. (1984). Parent and teacher assessment of children's behavior in child maltreating families. *Journal of the American Academy of Child Psychiatry* 23: 458–464.

Shaffer, D. and Caton, C. L. M. (1984). *Runaway and homeless youth in New York City: A report to the Ittleson Foundation*. New York State Psychiatric Institute and Columbia University, NY.

Slade, M. S., Steward, M. S., Morrison, T. L. and Abramowitz, S. I. (1984). Locus of control, persistence, and use of contingency information in physically abused children. *Child Abuse and Neglect* 8: 447–457.

Sommer, B. (1984). The troubled teen: Suicide, drug use, and running away. *Women and Health* 9: 117–141.

Spillane-Grieco, E. (1984). Characteristics of a helpful relationship: A study of empathic understanding and positive regard between runaways and their parents. *Adolescence* 19: 63–75.

Steele, B. (1987). Psychodynamic factors in child abuse. In Helfer, R. E. and Kempe, R. S. (eds.) *The Battered Child, 4th edition.* Chicago: The University of Chicago Press, 81–114.

Stiffman, A. R. (1989). Suicide attempts in runaway youths. *Suicide and Life-Threatening Behavior* 19: 147–159.

Stiffman, A. R. (1989). Physical and sexual abuse in runaway youths. *Child Abuse and Neglect* 13: 417–426.

Straus, M. A., Gelles, R. J., and Steinmetz, S. (1980). *Behind Closed Doors: Violence in the American Family.* Doubleday/Anchor: Garden City, NY.

Study of National Incidence and Prevalence of Child Abuse and Neglect: 1988. US DHHS, Office of Human Development Services. Administration for Children, Youth and Families, Children's Bureau, National Center on Child Abuse and Neglect.

Taitz, L. S. (1980). Effects on growth and development of social, psychological, and environmental factors. *Child Abuse and Neglect* 4: 55–65.

Tarter, R. E., Hegedus, A. E., Winsten, N. E. and Alterman, A. I. (1984). Neuropsychological, personality, and familial characteristics of physically abused delinquents. *Journal of the American Academy of Child Psychiatry* 23: 668–674.

Tong, L., Oates, K., and McDowell, M. (1987). Personality development following sexual abuse. *Child Abuse and Neglect* 11: 371–383.

White, R., Benedict, M. I., Wulff, L., and Kelley, M. (1987). Physical disabilities as risk factors for child maltreatment: A selected review. *American Journal of Orthopsychiatry* 57: 93–101.

Wilson, A. L. (1987). Promoting a positive parent-infant relationship. In Steele, B. Psychodynamic factors in child abuse. In Helfer, R. E. and Kempe, R. S. (eds.) *The Battered Child, 4th edition.* Chicago: The University of Chicago Press, 434–443.

Wolfe, D. A. and Mosk, M. D. (1983). Behavioral comparisons of children from abusive and distressed families. *Journal of Consulting and Clinical Psychology* 51: 702–708.

Wolfe, D. A. (1987). *Child Abuse: Implications for Child Development and Psychopathology.* Sage, Newbury Park.

Wolk, S. and Brandon, J. (1977). Runaway adolescents' perception of parents and self. *Adolescence* 12: 175–187.

Young, R. L., Godfrey W., Matthews, B. and Adams, G. R. (1983). Runaways: A review of negative consequences. *Family Relations* 32: 275–281.

29

SEXUAL VIOLENCE AMONG DATES AND ACQUAINTANCES:

TRENDS AND THEIR IMPLICATIONS FOR MARRIAGE AND FAMILY

Edward M. Levine
Center for Teaching Professions
Northwestern University

Eugene J. Kanin
Department of Sociology/Anthropology
Purdue University

INTRODUCTION

In recent years the crime of rape has received unprecedented attention and, as with other serious offenses, keen interest has developed regarding this trend. However, the rise in incidence that has been reported in the *Uniform Crime Reports* and in select cities in recent years has been largely discredited as real, largely because the increase in the rates of reported rape reflects a greater willingness of victims to report their having been victimized. And this has been variously attributed to the influence of the women's movement, the modification of rape statutes, and to the increase in the general level of education regarding the rights of rape victims (Sheley, 1985).

While it would be difficult to make a definitive case for a real increase in the rate of official forcible rape, rape among intimates—date and acquaintance rape—is another matter. Evidence can now be gathered to show that serious sexual violence (termed date rape) has increased dramatically during the last 30 years. Although the questionnaire studies of the late 1950s dealing with sexual aggression did not focus on rape, per se, case material collected at the time from the sample populations show rape to have been an exceptional occurrence.

For example, from one study in which 82 cases were collected, only three cases of rape were identified, all of them date rapes (Kirkpatrick and Kanin, 1957). Another study of the experiences of high school seniors examined 91 case studies among whom only four date rape victims were found (Kanin, 1957). From 1957 to 1961, Kanin requested his female undergraduate students anonymously to report on their victimization experiences, and of the 372 reports of female victimization, 13 cases of forcible rape were found (3.5 percent), 11 of which

were readily identified as date rape, the remaining two being acquaintance rape victims. Thus, investigations revealed a date rape incidence of only 3.8 percent.

In contrast, recent studies of female college students revealed strikingly higher figures. Koss and Oros (1982) found that 8.2 percent of their sample of female college students reported having had forced sex; Wilson and Durrenberger (1982) reported 15 percent in their study; Parcell (1973) found 14.6 percent; and Rapaport (1984) reported 14 percent. And more recent data from a study of 727 college females found that slightly more than 15 percent of them had been victims of date rape (Kanin, 1985). In addition, Korman and Leslie's (1982) research found that there was a higher rate of sex aggression at the genital level experienced by college females, a trend that had been detected somewhat earlier by Kanin and Parcell (1977), who found that the incidence of sex aggression experienced by college females was shifting dramatically from stranger to date and acquaintance rape.

Other evidence pertinent to our case that serious sexual aggression had become more commonplace for university women in their dating-courtship relations can be culled from the sex aggression studies from the mid-1950s to the late 1970s. This has increased from 13 percent in the early 1970s to 20 percent in the late 1970s (Kirkpatrick and Kanin, 1957; Kanin and Parcell, 1977; Korman and Leslie, 1982). Korman and Leslie (1982) also noted that "sexually exploitative attempts are becoming more coitally direct and that more women are experiencing these attempts."

Data about college women collected since the 1970s consistently show much higher instances of date rape. In an unpublished study of a random sam-

From *Journal of Family Violence*, 1987, 2(1): 55–65. Copyright © 1987. Plenum Publishing Corporation. Reprinted by permission.

ple of senior college women at a large midwestern state university, Parcell found that 14.7 percent reported having been victims of forced intercourse. Koos and Oros (1982), reporting on an investigation at a comparable kind of university, found that 8.2 percent of the college women had intercourse ("when you didn't want to because he used some degree of physical force," "twisting your arm," "holding you down," etc.). Furthermore, 3.1 percent had intercourse against their will because of threats to subject them to physical force, and 6 percent affirmed that they had been raped. Since these response categories are not mutually exclusive and can all be legally subsumed under rape, it is not possible to arrive at a sample figure of incidence of forced intercourse/rape. Nonetheless, the data are compelling and the problems are not far from the incidences obtained by other studies. Indeed, there are other investigations showing that 15 percent of college women have reported rape victimization (Wilson and Durrenberger, 1982; Rapaport, 1984; Kanin, 1985).

Although this survey of evidence should be viewed with a degree of caution, since the studies from which they are drawn represent certain problems in sampling and contrasting populations from different institutions, there is nevertheless a preponderance of and a consistency in the evidence from the past 30 years indicating that the college female is increasingly finding herself a target of sexual victimization and violence. This is now also true for female high school seniors (and perhaps even younger teenagers). In addition, males much more frequently resort to sexual aggression with no preliminary erotic intimacies than they did three decades ago.

Because such fear-inducing experiences may engender profoundly troubling emotional problems among sexually victimized females with regard to their attitudes toward marriage and family, the purpose of this study is to describe certain of the sociocultural changes that have occurred during the past generation and that appear to be largely responsible for the emergence of these trends in aggressive sexual behavior among younger males.

TRADITIONAL SEX STANDARDS

The human desire for sexual gratification is not governed by an instinct, an autonomous force that compels men and women to seek sexual gratification irrespective of their wishes. Instead, human sexual feelings and behavior are stimulated by the sex drive or impulse which becomes most intense and powerful during adolescence and young adulthood, after which its influence over human behavior gradually diminishes. Furthermore, its expression is greatly limited by the constraining influence of the moral values of tradition and religion, norms, and individual preferences that are inculcated in children by their parents, as well as emphasized by society through social institutions such as the schools. Historically, these standards have generally served to protect females against the predatory sexual propensities of males.

These values were part of the same tradition that upheld a double standard of sexual rights and responsibilities for postpubertal males and females. That is, adolescent and young adult males were generally free to enjoy such sexual pleasures as they found or that were offered them by sexually congenial women. Once married, they were expected to observe marital fidelity, although their extramarital affairs were not exceptional.

By contrast, females were expected to remain chaste until marriage and be completely faithful to their husbands thereafter. Economically dependent on their husbands, who regarded them as the weaker sex, women were also envisaged as the guardians of sexual and other moral standards that were considered as being centrally important for the stability of the family and for human well-being. Thus, modesty was a cardinal virtue of unmarried females, while the sexual posturing and dalliances of bachelors were taken for granted and commonly overlooked.

After that point in history when parents arranged their children's marriages, single, young (and even older) women who worked were obliged to live at home until they married, while their male counterparts were free to come and go as they pleased. Teenage girls were expected to introduce their dates to their parents at home so the latter could learn something about their character and their families. Parents also knew where their daughters were going, and when their dates would bring them home. The most difficult choice then confronting most adolescent girls was whether or not to give a boy a goodnight kiss on the first date, for to do so might lead him to consider her forward and improperly interested in his amorous advances which might undermine her defenses against them. While these standards still hold for some adolescent females, they have weakened considerably during the past generation, and have been rejected or abandoned by numbers of them.

WOMEN'S INDEPENDENCE AND THE NEW SEXUAL FREEDOM

The use of the contraceptive pill and the concomitant erosion of traditional values related to marriage and family and sexual behavior by the cultural revolution of the late 1960s (Levine, 1981, 1985) were major factors leading to the fundamental changes in intersexual relationships that are so prevalent today. These changes gained considerable momentum from the successes of the women's movement in breaking down the barriers to women's social and economic inequality, with the result that the double sexual standard collapsed for ever-growing number of females. Many assertive young women contend that it relegated them to a subordinate status in their relationships with men and was, therefore, a completely out-moded standard that had lost its relevance.

Armed with college and professional degrees and enjoying the satisfaction of having jobs and careers and the financial independence this provided them, increasing numbers of young women went on to claim much the same social rights and options that men have traditionally enjoyed. For example, it is no longer unconventional for working women to pay for their luncheons and dinners when dating, to invite men to be their guests for an evening date, and to engage in premarital sex almost as freely and unperturbedly as do men. In brief, women's occupational and social independence has been translated into a sexual freedom that begins to approximate that which men have had throughout the ages.

These transforming changes in women's occupational and social roles, as well as in their values and attitudes concerning their social and sexual relationships with men, have led to corresponding changes in the lives of adolescent females. That is, once women attained equality with men, the new logical step was for them (and their husbands) to raise their daughters to become fully independent, with the schools and the mass media affirming and exemplifying female equality in all important spheres of life. Consequently, steadily growing numbers of young women have been attending college for a generation and more, but especially since the early 1970s. And adolescent girls, more than ever before, anticipate working several years before they marry, are much freer in deciding when and whom to date, and are generally much less limited by their parents' regulations. Furthermore, numbers of adolescent girls are unhesitant about calling boys for dates or merely to talk with them, and are also sex-

ually active—alarmingly so for those who become pregnant in their early teens, which is no longer uncommon among white, middle class high school girls.

Today, adolescents are well aware that even if their parents understandingly and helpfully counsel them to remain sexually abstinent, they are also resigned, however ruefully, to their children being sexually active during their teen years. Adolescent boys guiltlessly ignore parental pieties about their behaving responsibly toward girls, and easily find girls as willing as they are to engage in sexual intercourse. The confluence of the equalized social relationships between the sexes, the sexual freedom so widely enjoyed today by adolescents and young adults, and females' greater willingness to engage in coitus make them more vulnerable to being raped.

The changing context within which the sexual victimization of females occurs is illustrated by earlier studies that provide substantial data indicating that aggressive sexual behavior followed after consensual sexual activity, such as kissing, petting, and more intensely erotic behavior (Kirkpatrick and Kanin, 1957; Kanin, 1957). However, female college students today report a surprisingly large percentage of both sexual aggression and rape that were spontaneously initiated by their male companions without any antecedent consensual, erotic activity. Approximately 44% of these sexual aggressions were not preceded by any form of consensual sex play (Kanin and Parcell, 1977). More explicitly, this phenomenon involved the males attempting to engage in sexual intercourse at once, rather than their engaging in a sequential seductive order involving kissing, fondling, and the like in order sexually to arouse the female.

The apparently growing tendency of males to dispense with such sexual preliminaries prior to seeking coercively to gain sexual gratification from their female companions may be partly due to the influence of the entertainment media. That is, these media often portray sexual settings in which males and females are intimately involved, but with the amorous or courtship sequences that might properly lead to this, being seldom, if ever, depicted. Thus, the trend in contemporary sexual behavior of date and acquaintance rapists suggests an equivalence of male and female sexuality in the sense that such males are heedless of females' rights when the former are highly sexually aroused, behavior that is partly legitimized by the entertainment media.

It may also be the case that adolescent and college males now have far higher expectations of gaining sexual gratification from casual dates because of the changes in the roles and attitudes of their female counterparts, and are, therefore, much less willing to allow them to frustrate their sexual desires. To the extent that young women are viewed as being uninhibited by traditional standards governing female sexual behavior, and are regarded as being equally knowledgeable about and interested in sex as are their dates, then males holding these views may expect females to treat coitus as casually as they do in thought and fantasy. Consequently, the unwillingness of females to comply with their dates' demands for sexual intercourse may lead to sexual aggression or rape—which males may increasingly consider acceptable because they no long find clear-cut, generally respected standards ruling out such reactions. What they deem to be wholly unjustifiable is the refusal of their dates to accede to their demand for sexual gratification, since this is seen as a completely arbitrary response. In their eyes, sexual freedom for females does not countenance sexually frustrating their dates. Sex on demand on one night stands has become normative among many young males for whom a kiss good night or even mild petting are hopelessly juvenile responses.

A study that tends to affirm this interpretation found that numbers of adolescents of both sexes now believe that extenuating circumstances limit females' right to preserve their sexual integrity. In a sample of 432 adolescents, 54 percent of the males and 42 percent of the females agreed that forced sexual intercourse *is* permissible if the girls led the boy on, sexually excited him, or agreed to have sex with him and then changed her mind (Ehrhart and Sandler, 1985). Attesting to how greatly dating norms and environments have changed are data from another study reporting that 75 percent of the female college students in its sample said that they had experienced sexual aggression, that these incidents most often occurred during their senior year of high school or their first year of college—and that they had taken place on the *first* date in either their rooms or the room of their dates (Burkhardt, 1983). Other research mentioned in the *Chronicle of Higher Education* (1983) involving United States and Canadian male college students stated that 35 percent of the sample said that they might commit rape if they could be certain that they would not be apprehended. Although this probably reflects their fantasy life more than their inclination, it is nonetheless symptomatic of negative changes in young men's attitude toward young women, and a worrisome sign of the times.

THE CULTURE OF SEX AND THE EQUALIZATION OF WOMEN

The attenuation of the traditions and norms that protected adolescent and adult females against male sexual aggression and violence has been paralleled by the popularity of magazines that feature nude females in sexually explicit poses. Paradoxically, while these magazines have prospered by exploiting young women who are deliberately portrayed as sex objects, numbers of college women regard them as unobjectionable, partly because sex has become a common subject for social and public discussion, as well as because exposing oneself to the public, if not condoned, is considered by them to be a matter of individual choice, and its legitimacy a matter of personal opinion.

Insofar as opinions are based on personal choice and right, then they tend to be equalized, for all have rights to their opinions, however dubious or slanted others may judge them to be (Levine and Ross, 1977). This relativistic standard, in tandem with the growing educational, familial, and occupational equalization of females, has modified younger men's image of women. That is, inasmuch as adolescent and older females generally want to be regarded and dealt with primarily as individuals who are on an equal footing with males, and since the media flood the public with both suggestive and explicit sexual themes, images, and fantasies that demean and degrade female sexuality, males increasingly seem to view females primarily as asexual competitors, and secondarily in terms of their gender. Consequently, males may increasingly believe that bargaining, pressuring, and threatening are acceptable, if not truly legitimate, means to employ in attempting to induce women to be sexually compliant. Thus, male aggressiveness in intersexual relationships appears to become more prevalent the more closely the females' way of life and degree of sexual freedom approximate those of males. Indeed, while Janet Chafetz (1985) found that equality in marriages had a positive effect on spouses' intimacy, her insightful comment that intersexual equality also generated more marital disputes and conflict and increased the difficulty of resolving them is also pertinent here.

DRINKING AND RAPE

Throughout history, drinking immoderately or to excess has led men and women to act in careless, thoughtless, and wanton ways, including their seeking hasty sexual gratification regardless of the sentiments of their spouses or companions. Today, drinking is so commonplace among adolescents and young adults (Levine and Kanin, 1986) that there is some cause for concern that the incidence of rape will increase. The consumption of alcoholic beverages at fraternity parties, often a major reason for holding and attending them, appears to be an influential factor in the growing incidents of date and acquaintance rape (*Time*, 1983; Myers *et al.*, 1984; Erhart and Sandler, 1985).

One of the primary effects of over-drinking is the weakening and even the loss, however momentary, of self-control. With considerable leisure time and few restrictions to limit their use of it, teenagers and college students easily find the opportunity to become erotically involved. And males who otherwise would refrain from or hesitate about compelling their female companions to provide them with sexual gratification are, under the influence of alcohol, much less inhibited about using force in order to obtain their compliance when it is withheld. In such circumstances, rape-prone males are even more likely to yield to their impulses, and are also least likely to worry about the adverse consequences that they and/or their female companions may suffer.

As for young women, over-drinking is often directly responsible for numbers of them becoming involved in, as well as their being unable to extricate themselves from, awkward or compromising situations that facilitate their being sexually abused or raped. And some have drunk so heavily as to have forgotten if they agreed or were forced to have sex with their dates or companions. Those who assume, incorrectly, that they willingly did so may fail to guard themselves against immoderate drinking in similar situations in the future, thereby again placing themselves in jeopardy.

THE CONSEQUENCES OF RAPE VICTIMIZATION FOR MARRIAGE AND PARENTING

There is growing evidence indicating that adolescent and adult females who were victims of rape during their childhood years were troubled by learning and behavioral problems in school, become involved in drug use and sexual promiscuity in adolescence, and run away from home in order to escape further sexual molestation or an unrelieved atmosphere of tension. In adulthood, such women often suffer sexual dysfunctions, guilt, and distrust of men, as well as other kinds of emotionally hin-

dering problems (Santiago *et al.*, 1985). For those who do not resolve these problems with counseling and/or therapy, there can no longer be any doubt that such unfortunate individuals continue to sustain seriously impairing psychopathologies that greatly interfere with their enjoying, or completely deny them, a reasonably fulfilled life.

For example, studies reported by the *Chicago Tribune* (1984) noted that there is an unusually high percentage of adult female rape victims who were sexually assaulted as children. Such evidence strongly suggests that the trauma resulting from rape has not only remained, but also apparently inhibited their developing sufficient self-esteem and self-confidence in order to establish mutually gratifying relationships with men whom they like, and are somehow drawn to or sought out by those who manipulate and abuse them. The men who rape them, themselves very likely lacking in self-esteem and self-confidence as well, apparently detect the weakness and vulnerability of such women and ruthlessly vent their anger on them.

Data from a study by Petrovich and Templer (1984) tend to confirm this curious parallel between such women and a group of convicted rapists. They found that of 86 convicted rapists in a California prison, 59 percent reported having been heterosexually molested before age sixteen. This finding, of course, does not permit the conclusion that their having been heterosexually molested as children caused them to become rapists. However, it is noteworthy that the authors mentioned that some of these rapists said that they wanted to punish their victims because of some real or imagined suffering they believed that women inflicted on them.

While this is limited evidence, it serves to widen the scope of research focusing on the sexual molestation of children of both sexes, since the traumatic repercussions afflicting some subjected to sexual abuse as children go on to affect their adult lives very detrimentally. And it prompts the suggestion that additional research is needed to determine to what extent, if any, being raped by dates and acquaintances adversely affects young women's attitudes about marrying and rearing children. That is, do these women tend to remain apprehensive about trusting men and overly cautious about marrying? If this tends to be the case, are they attracted to men who prove to be abusive to them emotionally and sexually?

As for those who marry and have children, it is eminently worth knowing if they transmit their residual doubts and fear of men to their daughters, thereby leading them to become excessively apprehensive about men and marriage. As prospective parents, the scarred emotions of the victims of date and acquaintance rape are likely to color the attitudes about human sexuality that they impart to their children, and may warp their daughters' attitudes toward men and marriage. As for the perpetrators of date and acquaintance rape, they may be utterly indifferent to teaching their sons to respect the integrity of females and equally delinquent in instructing their daughters to demand that they are entitled as a matter of right to be respected by all males, and especially by those with whom they socialize.

CONCLUSION

An accumulating body of evidence indicates that the last 30 years have witnessed a disturbingly high increase in the sexual victimization of teenage and college females by dates and acquaintances. This trend seems to be partly the result of young females having much the same degree of freedom in their social and sexual relationships that their male counterparts enjoy. It is also attributable to the largely unrestrained ways in which human sexuality is featured in the mass media and popular culture, and which have diminished young people's inhibitions about seeking and gaining sexual gratification, increasingly during their adolescent years. This is very likely facilitated by their widespread and growing use of alcoholic beverages.

Given this set of conditions and the declining influence of the standards that once protected unmarried females against male sexual predations, there is a strong likelihood that younger females, and perhaps older ones as well, will increasingly constitute an at-risk population with regard to being raped by dates and acquaintances, a trend that is all the more disconcerting in view of its ramifications for the well-being of marriage and family.

References

Burkhart, B. (1983, December.) Presentation at Acquaintance Rape and Rape Prevention on Campus Workshop, Louisville, Ky.

Chafetz, J. (1985), Marital intimacy and conflict: Irony of spousal equality. *Free Inq. Creative Sociol,* 2: 191–199.

Chicago Tribune (1984, September 25), pp. 1, 8.

Chronicle of Higher Education (1983, August 31), p. 9.

Ehrhart, J., and Sandler, B. (1985, November). *Campus Gang Rape: Party Games.* Paper presented at the Project on the Status and Education of Women, Washington, D.C., Association of American Colleges.

Kanin, E. (1957). Male aggression in dating-courtship relations. *Am. J. Sociol.* 63: 197–204.

Kanin, E. (1985). *Rape among Intimates.* Paper presented at the Annual Meeting of the American Society of Criminology.

Kanin, E., and Parcell, S. (1977). Sexual aggression: A second look at the offended females. *Arch. Sexual Behav.* 6: 67–76.

Kirkpatrick, C., and Kanin, E. (1957). Male sex aggression on a university campus. *Am. Sociological Rev.* 22: 52–58.

Kornman, S., and Leslie, G. (1982). The relationship of feminist ideology and date expense sharing to perceptions of sexual aggression in dating. *J. Sex Res.* 18: 114–129.

Koss, M., and Oros, C. (1982). Sexual experiences survey: A research instrument investigating sexual aggression and victimization. *J. Consult. Clin. Psychol.* 50: 455–457.

Levine, E. (1981). Middle class family decline. *Society* 1: 72–78.

Levine, E. (1985). The plight of the middle class family. *J. Fam. Cult.* 1: 29–41.

Levine, E., and Kanin, E. (1986). Adolescent drug use: Its prospects for the future. *J. Fam. Cult.* 1: 4.

Levine, E., and Ross, N. (1977). Sexual dysfunctions and psychoanalysis. *Ame. J. Psychiatr.* 234: 646–651.

Myers, M. B., Templer, D., and Brown, R. (1984). Coping ability of women who become rape victims. *J. Consult. Clin. Psychol.* 52: 73–78.

Petrovich, M., and Templer, D. (1984). Heterosexual molestation of children who later became rapists. *Psychological Rep.* 54: 810.

Rapaport, K. (1984). Quoted in: A disturbing look at rape. *National on-Campus Report.*

Santiago, J., Perez, F., Gorcey, M., and Beigel, A. (1985). Long-term psychological effects of rape in 35 rape victims. *Am. J. Psychiat.* 142: 1338–1340.

Rape: The sexual weapon. (1985, September 5). *Time,* p. 27–28.

Wilson, W., and Durrenberger, R. (1982). Comparison of rape and attempted rape victims. *Psychological Rep.* 50: 198.

30

WHEN THE ELDERLY ARE ABUSED:
CHARACTERISTICS AND INTERVENTION

Sharon Powell
The Counseling Center
Arlington, Texas

Robert C. Berg
Department of Counselor Education
North Texas State University

. . . Our definition of elder abuse is multifaceted and includes the following dimensions. Elder abuse is the willful infliction by a caretaker or other of physical pain, injury or mental anguish, unreasonable confinement or deprivation of services essential to the maintenance of mental and physical health (O'Malley, Segars, Perez, Mitchell, and Kneupfel, 1979). This definition encompasses the following forms of abuse.

Physical abuse refers to instances where the "elderly person has been hit, slapped, bruised, sexually molested, cut, burned, or physically restrained" (Gray Panthers of Austin, 1983, p. 2).

Financial abuse refers to the illegal or improper act of using resources belonging to an elderly person for monetary or personal benefit (Lau and Kosbert, 1979).

Verbal/emotional abuse refers to situations in which "the elderly person is insulted, treated as a child, frightened, humiliated, or threatened" (Gray Panthers of Austin, 1983, p. 2).

Active neglect is defined as situations in which "the abuser withholds items necessary for daily living, such as food, medicine, money, or bathroom assistance" (Gray Panthers of Austin, 1983, p. 2).

Passive neglect refers to instances which generally involve harm resulting from inadequate knowledge about caring for the elderly. It is characterized by situations in which the elderly person is left alone, isolated, or forgotten" (Gray Panthers of Austin, 1983, p. 3).

A review of research on elder abuse by Pedrick-Cornell and Gelles (1982) paints a bleak picture regarding our state of knowledge. Lack of quality data has led to statements presented as facts that have no scientific foundation but are used to frame both policy and programs to treat and prevent the abuse of older persons. Particularly lacking are examinations of documented cases that focus on attempts to provide assistance to elderly victims once they have been identified.

This investigation provides information that can be obtained only through systematic study and description of actual cases of elder abuse. The major areas of focus involve: information concerning the types of abuse that are occurring; descriptions of abusive situations; descriptions of case management strategies used and their related consequences, and characteristics of both abuser and abused that may be related to the final closure of the case. . . .

DISCUSSION

The results of this study point to the probability that the elderly abuse victim is 75 years of age or older, female, white, and widowed. There does appear to be some connection between race and type of abuse, with some indication that, if the victim is white, there is a strong likelihood that the abuse experienced will be physical and financial. This study also indicates that approximately half of the elderly abuse victims have several limitations in physical and/or mental functioning and have some degree of dependence upon their abusers.

[Editor's Note: The paper by Sharon Powell and Robert C. Berg describes the phenomenom of elder abuse and reports the demographic findings of a pilot study. Their study examined 60 cases from an Adult Protective Services agency in the North Central Texas area. In the following excerpt, we begin with their definition of terms, and continue with the section discussing the implications of their research. While these 60 cases are but a tiny fraction of the estimated half million to two and one-half million cases of elder abuse a year (Pedrick-Cornell and Gelles, 1982), they represent a carefully documented sample.]

One of the important findings of this study is that it should caution against making the assumption that when an elderly person is living independently, abuse does not occur. This study indicates that as many as 80 percent of elder abuse victims may reside in their own homes, and at least 50 percent of these individuals may be functionally independent. In cases where a relative suddenly moves in with an elderly individual, it should not be assumed that the relative does so in order to care for the "dependent" older person. It may also be that the individual is moving in against the older person's wishes and taking advantage of the elderly person's resources and possibly subjecting him or her to additional forms of abuse.

Some case management strategies, such as home visits by the caseworker and enlisting the aid of friends and relatives are less likely to be refused by the elderly person than are others. "Protective" services seem to work best when viewed more in terms of "supportive" services. Perhaps the role of caseworker is not so much that of crisis intervention as it is that of coordinating existing services to enable and promote independent living.

IMPLICATIONS

One of the most pressing issues is that too many cases of elderly abuse go unreported. One of the most important steps to be taken is to increase the level of awareness of elder abuse. Education about the nature and causes of elder abuse is imperative for both the general public and those professional workers caring for the elderly. In particular, the public needs to be made more aware of the stress related to caring for an elderly person and of the services helpful in dealing with that stress (Gray Panthers of Austin, 1983).

It is important to answer the question of who is at greatest risk of maltreatment, in order to develop appropriate screening procedures and alert helping professions to the need for intervention. Sensitizing medical personnel, social service workers, and the general public may lead to a higher degree of suspicion for elder abuse, which may assist in prevention as well as more timely interventions (Rathbone-McCuan, 1980; Salend et al., 1984).

Unfortunately, the identification of victims is made more difficult because the elderly are not tied to many social networks. Isolation of the elderly from community resources increases the probability that abusive situations will go unreported. Perhaps

one answer to this problem would be to increase transportation services for the elderly, which could promote both community involvement and independent functioning.

This study discovered that one-fifth of abuse victims reside in the home of the abuser, and those victims are likely to be experiencing physical and/or emotional impairment. Since it is impractical to expect each family to have the resources to handle this burden (Gelles & Cornell, 1985), one means of alleviating the abusive situation and preventing its repetition or initial occurrence might be to provide family counseling at the time that an aged person moves into a relative's home. Such counseling would emphasize the physical and psychological processes of aging and would include special instructions on care of a sick and elderly person (Gray Panthers of Austin, 1983). Programs that offer respite care can provide support to families and allow them time away from the work and responsibility involved in the care of an aging person. Respite care can provide a convenient, socially sanctioned "breather" (Johnson and Bursk, 1977).

Studies suggest that good health for elderly people can be an important variable in how elderly parents and their adult children regard their relationship. Poor health may exacerbate poor family relationships (Johnson and Bursk, 1977). Poor health appears to increase the elderly person's vulnerability to abuse by increasing dependency. Improved health care services for the elderly may decrease the probability that they will find themselves in a dependent and potentially abusive relationship.

One cannot ignore the responsibility of some victims in cases of elder abuse. It may be that many abusive situations could be eliminated if the elderly were encouraged to be more assertive in demanding that their wishes be respected. Society currently does little to encourage the autonomy of elderly individuals. Often the elderly victim sees no alternative but to remain in an abusive situation; therefore it is important to eliminate feelings of helplessness in older individuals if they are going to resist the attempts of others to abuse them.

It is recognized that many families are unwilling or incapable of being caretakers of highly dependent older members, and a continuing need exists for adequate formal care systems and protective services. However, moving the elderly person from the home should generally be the last alternative chosen. Deterioration, dependency, and excess disability may result from premature institutionalization

(Tobin and Leiberman, 1976). Custodial care can hardly be considered treatment since there are no active steps for solution to the problem, and, in reality, the person may be no better off than the original condition (Levy, Derogatis, Gallagher, and Gatz, 1980).

Caseworkers may find it particularly frustrating when the victim wishes to abandon prosecution or assistance and return to the abusing situation. It is important to cultivate in caseworkers the ability to understand the situation and withhold judgment. It is important that the caseworker not convey disappointment if the person elects to remain in the abusing situation. However, it is essential that caseworkers honestly explain their fears and let elderly individuals know that they can always return for assistance.

Elderly victims often want information, reassurance, and someone to talk with about the abuse; thus, establishing rapport during the initial contact is essential. Those who work with elderly abuse victims should have knowledge in the area of gerontology and training to work with multigenerational family issues. Caseworkers also need to remember that too much of an effort to "rescue" may under-mine elderly individuals' confidence in their ability to help themselves. It is important that the elderly be involved to the greatest extent possible in locating resources for assistance.

Even in states with specific legal sanctions against elder abuse, little court-related activity takes place. This study found no evidence that those who abuse the elderly are being prosecuted. Clearer laws need to be established that define the areas of responsibility that relatives and caretakers have for elderly individuals who are in need of assistance.

In conclusion, elder abuse will probably continue until the elderly can be offered viable alternatives to remaining in an abusing situation and until society begins to address some of the issues surrounding our nation's elderly. Should society continue in the assumption that children know what is best for their parents and are entitled to rights of control? Who is responsible for providing support systems to aid families who have the responsibility of elderly kin? Where is the economic motive for providing help for the aged who are at the end of economic productivity? Perhaps the answers can be found when society begins to recognize the importance of *valuing* human life as well as extending it.

References

Block, M. R., and Sinnott, J. (1979) *The battered elder syndrome: An exploratory study.* Unpublished manuscript, University of Maryland.

Costa, J. J. (1984). *Abuse of the elderly.* Lexington, MA: D.C. Heath.

Gelles, R. J., and Cornell, C. P. (1985). *Intimate violence in families.* Beverly Hills, CA: Sage.

Gray Panthers of Austin, (1983). *A survey of abuse of the elderly in Texas.* Austin, TX: Gray Panthers of Austin.

Johnson, E. S., and Bursk, B. J. (1977). Relationships between the elderly and their adult children. *The Gerontologist*, 17, 90–96.

Lau, E. E., and Kosberg, J. I. (1979). Abuse of the elderly by informal care providers. *Aging*, 299, 10–15.

Levy, S. M., Derogatis, L. R., Gallagher, D., and Gatz, M. (1980). Interventions with older adults and evaluation of outcome. In L. W. Poon (ed.), *Aging in the 1980's* (pp. 41–61). Washington, DC: American Psychological Association.

O'Malley, H., Segars, H., Perez, R., Mitchell, V., and Kneupfel, G. M. (1979). *Elder abuse in Massachusetts: A survey of professionals and paraprofessionals.* Boston, MA: Legal Research and Services for the Elderly.

Pedrick-Cornell, C., and Gelles, R. J. (1982). Elder abuse: The status of current knowledge. *Family Relations*, 31, 457–465.

Rathbone-McCuan, E. (1980). Elderly victims of family violence and neglect. *Social Casework*, 61, 296–304.

Salend, E., Kane, A., Staz, M., and Pynoos, J. (1984). Elder abuse reporting: Limitations of statutes. *The Gerontologist*, 24, 61–69.

Tobin, S., and Leiberman, M. (1976). *Last home for the aged: Critical implications.* San Francisco, CA: Jossey-Bass.

B. Family Conflict and Resolution

31

MARRIAGE OVER HALF A CENTURY:
A LONGITUDINAL STUDY

Dorothy Field
Sylvia Weishaus
Institute of Human Development
University of California, Berkeley

Until recently marriages that endured 20 years or longer have been considered "long-term." Yet it is very likely that a marriage of 40 years differs considerably from the same marriage at 20 years, and the relationship will probably evolve further by the time the marriage is 50 or 60 years old. Factors such as retirement, relationship with adult children, mobility, health, and time availability are very different at each of these stages. And only in recent years have marriages of 50 or more years duration been plentiful enough to be studied.

In the 1960s studies reported an inevitable linear decline in marital satisfaction (Blood and Wolfe, 1960; Luckey, 1966). But during the 1970s researchers noted a curvilinear trend in satisfaction, often with a precipitous drop during the child-rearing stage, but moving up again in the post-parental period, although not attaining the original level (Anderson, Russell, and Schumm, 1983; Glenn, 1975; Rollins and Cameron, 1974).

Current studies of long-term marriages have had mixed results, finding that marital satisfaction or quality ranges from quiet desperation through resignation to great fulfillment. Todd (1984), studying 48 couples married 50 years or more, found strong dissatisfaction in about half; usually the wives expressed less happiness. Other studies found a high level of both conflict and satisfaction in marriage (Argyl and Furnham, 1981) and a decrease in marital problems after the children left (Argyl and Furnham, 1981), as well as a "remarkably close" relationship after 50 years (Parron, 1982).

All of these studies, however, are cross-sectional, assessing marriages at one time only. It would be valuable to examine the course taken by the *same marriages* over many years. Are the results to date cohort-specific, or do they describe changes

that are likely to take place in most long-term marriages? Would the effects noted in the cross-sectional studies appear over time in individual marriages as well?

We cannot depend on retrospective reports from the couples themselves, for their perceptions of the marriage have been shown to change with time and circumstances (Field, 1981a, 1981b). Only a longitudinal study, in which the same husbands and wives have been interviewed over many years, can assess stability or change in marital adjustment and marital satisfactions.

We are fortunate that longitudinal data exist in the Berkeley Older Generation Study. This is a group of people, now old-old, who are the survivors of a representative group of young adults first seen in Berkeley, California, 55 years ago. Seventeen couples survived and were interviewed in old-old age, and these are the subjects of this study.

METHOD

SUBJECTS

Members of the Berkeley Older Generation Study were part of a sample drawn from parents of every third baby born in Berkeley in 1928–1929, and they still are representative of surviving people of their ages in the United States at this time. They were intensively interviewed in young adulthood (1928–1929), when their babies became part of the Guidance Study (Macfarlane, 1938) or the Berkeley Growth Study (Bayley, 1956) at the Institute of Human Development, University of California, Berkeley; again in middle age, 1945–1947; in young-old age, 1968–69 (Maas and Kuypers, 1974); and in old-old age, 1982–1983. The 17 couples have been married 55 to 69 years, with an average of 59 years.

From a paper presented at the Gerontological Society Meeting in November, 1984. An abstract appeared in *The Gerontologist*, 24: 290, Special Issue October 1984. Reprinted by permission of the authors.

Ages at the final interview range from 73 to 93 for the men and 73 to 88 for the women; the modal birth year is 1900. Only 14 of the couples were interviewed in young-old age, and some of the variables have been coded to date on only a sub-sample of this group. In old-old age Ns are reduced for some of the variables: two of the wives are suffering from Alzheimer's disease, and fewer variables can be scored for them.

Although the subjects of study at most number only 34 people and in many analyses the N is smaller than this, it is the *only* known group of married couples about whom there is information gathered over more than 50 years.

ANALYSIS

DATA GATHERING. In all the interviews husband and wife were interviewed separately by two different interviewers. These were wide-ranging, semi-structured, open-ended interviews covering many topics. Because the participants were so familiar with the Institute and its aims and were so certain of the confidentiality of their disclosures, we believe that our subjects revealed far more about themselves than would otherwise have been the case. In old-old age all but three of the couples were interviewed by the two authors; one of us was a member of the interview team for the others.

CODING. Each interview was read and coded by two trained psychologists. The final codes were based either on complete independent agreement between the raters or were made only after a thorough discussion between the raters had eliminated any disagreements. All raters were "naive": no rater read the transcript of the other member of a couple, nor did a rater read a transcript from another period of a person she had already coded.

The marital adjustment rating was designed in the early years of the Guidance Study of Macfarlane (1938) and her coworkers: the same scale was used for each time period:

1. exceptionally happy adjustment, frankness, affection, agreement, interests
2. above average, many satisfactions, no disruptions
3. normal adjustment, occasional upsets, real satisfactions
4. working arrangement difficult, more or less chronic tension
5. extreme conflict, separation, disrupting

The marital adjustment ratings described above were based exclusively on a reading of one interview. In addition, the two authors made a clinical rating of the marital adjustment of each couple in old-old age based on all the impressions we gathered during the interviews, including the interactions between the members of the couple before and after the interviews and during breaks for tea and cookies. Only after the interviews were read and coded did we begin the case studies of each couple that we have reported at other meetings (Weishaus and Field, 1984a, 1984b).

ANALYSIS. It is obvious that we can report here only a fraction of the rich data we have been able to gather. We will examine the perceptions of the spouses about their mutual affairs, particularly, of course, the marriage itself, and how these perceptions change over time. Through correlational analysis we will examine associations between many attributes and situations and marital satisfactions, and we will compare the men with the women on the strength of these associations. We will focus on the transition between young-old (YO), when the couples had been married more than 40 years, and old-old (OO), nearly 15 years later.

RESULTS

AGREEMENT ABOUT THE MARRIAGE

It is clear from our results that husbands and wives view their marriage differently: the correlations for the rating of marital adjustment are only .40 in YO and .20 in OO. At both periods the men view their marriages more favorably than do the women, although this difference reaches significance only in OO, $t(15) = 2.18$, $p = .014$. On the 5-point scale given above the mean was 2.4 for the women and 2.0 for the men in YO and 2.0 and 1.6 in OO.

The clinical rating made by the authors (mean = 2.38) was compared with the ratings made on the basis of reading one spouse's interview. The clinical ratings are very similar to the women's ratings, but the men's ratings indicate greater marital adjustment than the independent clinical judgment shows. The wives seem to be more realistic assessors of their marriages. The correlations with the clinical ratings are high for both: $r = .59$ for women and .62 for men. The members of the couple agree with the interviewers' assessments of their marriage more strongly than they agree with each other's assessments.

Not only do the men take a more favorable view of their marriages in general, they also report fewer disagreements than do the women, both in

YO, $t(7) = 3.06$, $p = .018$, and in OO, $t(14) = 2.75$, $p = .016$. Not surprisingly, the number of disagreements correlates with marital adjustment at both life stages: rs = .55 and .45 for the women and .39 and .75 for the men at YO and OO, respectively.

Predictably, the men rate more highly the importance of sex to the relationship than do the women in OO, $t(8) = 2.08$, $p = .074$. The correlation between spouses cannot be computed, for *every* man reported that sex was always an important part of the relationship for both of them. (Only four women made this report!) The importance of sex is only marginally associated with marital adjustment for the wives, r = .23, but it is strongly so for the husbands, r = .75. (This question was not asked in YO.)

The husbands take a rosier view of the earlier years, as well, for their retrospective reports of their marriages in the past are higher than those of their wives in YO, $t(4) = 2.45$, $p = .07$, and in OO, $t(13) = 2.13$, $p = .054$. The spouses' views of marital adjustment color their recollections of their marriages in the past, r = .33 and .47 for the women and .85 and .54 for the men, at YO and OO respectively.

Although both members of the couple are likely to agree in OO about how much they do together, r = .58, only for the men does this affect marital satisfaction: the more activities are shared by the couple the greater the husband's satisfaction, r = 70. (For women, r = 13.) In YO, however, both wives, r = .60, and husbands, r = .78, who report that they do many things together are high in marital satisfaction.

When asked in YO if they felt they had grown apart over the years, only one woman and none of the men felt that the relationship had grown more distant. Instead, 29% of the women and 25% of the men reported that they had grown *closer*. In OO this proportion increased to 47% and 37%, reflecting the increasing satisfactions that we observed in the case studies. The feeling of growing closer is correlated with marital adjustment for women, r = .26 and .51, and for men, r = .65 and .49, in YO and OO. However, the two members of each couple are much more likely to agree that they have grown closer in OO, r = .45, than they were in YO, r = .05.

Marital adjustment is stable across time as well. The correlations between YO and OO are .62 and .63 for women and men. It is interesting that there is more consistency in wives' and husbands' views of their marriages over time than there is between husbands' and wives' assessments of the marriage at the same time.

SOCIO-ECONOMIC FACTORS

The men report that their families are financially better off than do the women, but this diference is significant only in OO, $t(14) = 2.26$, $p = .041$. The financial status of the family has little effect on the quality of the marriage either for women, r = -.34 and .27, or men, r = -.20 and .34, in YO and OO, respectively.

Amount of education plays no role in marital satisfaction, r = .20 and -.12 for women and -.27 and -.12 for men, in YO and OO. The occupation of the husband is not a factor in marital satisfaction at either life stage, r = .14 and .20 for women and .35 and .24 for men in YO and OO.

FAMILY CIRCUMSTANCES

These couples have an average of 2.2 children; only one couple has as many as four. The number of children has little effect on the marital adjustment of the parents, r = .10 and .38 for women and -.32 and .08 for men, in YO and OO. For the most part, there is considerable agreement within the couples about their children: Their reports agree about relationships, r = .43, contact with, r = .46, and bond with children, r = .69 in OO. Yet the parents are not in agreement about how close are their feelings with their children, r = -.21, nor about how well satisfied they are with the adult children at age 50+, r = .09.

The amount of satisfaction they feel toward their children is not associated with marital satisfaction in OO, r = .20 for women and -.04 for men. By and large, they are quite well satisfied with the way their children have turned out (means of 1.6 on a 5-point scale). (Too little information is available from YO to report.)

The amount of contact the couples have with their children has little effect on their marital satisfaction YO, r = .01 and .38, but more in OO, r = .20 and .52, for women and men. Those whose marital satisfaction is high have more contact with their children.

Marital satisfaction is strongly associated with bond with child at both times for both members of the couple: r = .41 and .58 for women and .53 and .49 for men, in YO and OO. The entire family seems to be tied up in the feelings of satisfaction; even at this late stage of life the children play an important role in the family dynamic.

FRIENDSHIP AND CLUB ACTIVITIES

Most of this group are less involved beyond the family in OO then they were in YO, $t(12) = 3.86$, $p = .002$ for women and $t(13) = 1.79$, $p = .09$ for men. But this involvement is not related to marital adjustment: $r = .23$ and $-.09$ for women and $r = -.21$ and $.09$ for men in YO and OO. Although the sexes do not differ in the amount of such activity, they apparently are not involved as couples, for the relationship between spouses' amount of activity is nonexistent: $r = .10$ in YO and $.06$ in OO.

The women are more involved with friends than the men in OO, $t(11) = 1.93$, $p = .08$, and more women feel that they still want and need friendships, $t(12) = 3.12$, $p = .009$. These differences, while evident, were not significant in YO. The desire for friendship is not related to marital satisfaction at either life stage for the men, $r = .09$ and $-.25$, and only somewhat more for the women in OO, $r = .14$ and $-.40$. Women with high marital satisfaction do not feel as great a need for friendships.

Both men and women feel they still want friendships, for the over-time correlations are .68 for women and .47 for men. However, the actual contact with friends has dropped for the men, $t(7) = 2.36$, $p = .05$, from once or twice a week in YO to twice a month on average in OO. The women have maintained their contacts unchanged. Of course, it is likely that more of the men's friends have been lost to death.

The frequency of club activities, including church attendance, is related to marital satisfaction in OO both for women, $r = -.51$, and men, $r = -.41$. The greater the frequency of activity the *less* likely it is that marital satisfaction will be great. There was no such association in YO, $r = .18$ and .10. Men and women are about equally active at each life stage. Both men and women are somewhat less active in clubs in OO than they were in YO, but this longitudinal difference is too slight to be significant.

PERSONAL CHARACTERISTICS

Intelligence is not associated with marital satisfactions either for women, $r = .13$ and .12, or for men, $r = .33$ and .22, in YO and OO.

There is little association between self-reported health and marital adjustment in YO, $r = -.25$ and $-.18$, or OO, $r = -.40$ and .06. Men are significantly less healthy in OO than they were in YO, $t(13) = 2.35$, $p = .035$; the women are unchanged.

Both men and women still report themselves as better than average in health, also noted by Cockerham, et al. (1983). It appears that health affects marital quality only in that illness in one partner is constructive to the relationship, increasing the bond between partners.

The degree of anomie has some association with marital satisfaction in YO for husbands, $r = .38$ and wives, $r = .66$, and for husbands in OO, $r = .47$ (wives $r = .06$). In OO the men were less likely to report feelings of alienation and lack of purpose than were the women, $t(10) = 2.29$, $p = .045$, but there was no difference in YO. As a group, these old people are low in anomie, with mean scores of 17.7 and 16.1 for the women and 19.0 and 18.2 for the men in YO and OO, on a scale running from 5 to 25.

In view of their generally more optimistic responses, it is not surprising that the men are rated higher than the women in life satisfaction in YO, $t(12) = 3.00$, $p = .041$, and in OO, $t(14) = 3.17$, $p = .007$. Life satisfaction is more closely related to marital adjustment in YO, $r = .50$ and .53, than in OO, $r = .13$ and .36 for women and men, respectively. There is virtually no drop in life satisfaction over the years from YO to OO, either for men or for women.

CONCLUSION

In sum, it appears that the men are generally more satisfied with their lives: more marital satisfaction, more feelings of agreement with their wives, more pleasure in the way their relationships have been over time, more pleasure in shared activities and in closer affectional ties. These feelings of well-being about the marital relationships are echoed in their life satisfaction, lack of anomie, satisfaction with financial circumstances, and their apparent contentment in pulling back a little from their former level of outside activities.

Yet we must note that two of the men are primary caregivers for the two Alzheimer's patients, one of whom is maintained at home; one man is the sole caretaker for a cancer-ridden wife (who died within six weeks after the interview), two are coping with wives who have moderately troublesome memory losses, one is cancer-ridden himself (and died three months after his interview). In fact, only seven of the 17 couples are free of serious health problems. In spite of all this, the men are generally satisfied.

We come away with a strong impression of buoyancy in these old men. They have coped with adversity and still are coping, and for the most part they are doing it very well. They are survivors, they know it, and they are proud of it.

And what about the women? They are just as involved with clubs, and church as they were and they continue to affirm the importance of friendship. They are just as involved with family as ever. They have not declined in health (according to their own assessments of it). However, they do acknowledge that they are counting on others more than they did.

This generation of women was socialized to be helpmeets. It was never as important for them to put the best face on things. Although the women, too, are caring for sick partners, and have seen their circles constrict, our longitudinal material shows that they are remarkable in their adaptability to changing circumstances. Yet they are modest and unassuming about their accomplishments. We suggested above that the women may be more realistic about their marriages, and we suspect that this is the case in other aspects of their lives, as well. Fewer of the variables are associated with marital adjustment; fewer have changed over time. The women seem somehow less affected by their experiences.

Clearly, we plan to pursue these findings further. We will look for situations and characteristics from earlier life stages that predict marital satisfactions in old age. We will compare these married couples with other members of the study who are widowed or remarried. We will compare them with people who were seen in YO but did not survive. Our hunch is that these long-term marital survivors have capacities that have enabled them to get the most out of their relationships. We do know that as couples they think of themselves as survivors, and they express pride in this fact.

References

Anderson, S. A., Russell, C. S., and Schummn, W. A. (1983) Perceived marital quality and family life-cycle categories: A further analysis. *Journal of Marriage and the Family, 45*, 127–139.

Argyle, M., and Furnham, A. (1983) Sources of satisfaction and conflict in long-term relationships. *Journal of Marriage and the Family, 45*, 481–492.

Bayley, N. (1956) Individual patterns of development. *Child Development, 27*, 45–74.

Blood, R. O., and Wolfe, D. M. (1960) *Husbands and wives: The dynamics of married living.* Glencoe, Ill.: Free Press.

Burr, W. R. (1970) Satisfaction with various aspects of marriage over the life cycle. *Journal of Marriage and the Family, 32*, 29–37.

Cockerham, W. C., Sharp, K., and Wilcox, J. (1983) Aging and perceived health status. *Journal of Gerontology, 38*, 349–355.

Cuber, J. F., and Haroff, P. B. (1966) *Sex and the significant Americans.* Baltimore: Pelican.

Field, D. (1981) Retrospective reports by healthy intelligent people of personal events of their adult lives. *International Journal of Behavioral Development, 4*, 77–97.(a)

Field, D. (1981) Retrospective reports of aging spouses of past events in their lives together. Paper presented at meetings of the International Society for the Study of Behavioural Development, Toronto, August, 1981.(b)

Glenn. N. D. (1975) Psychological well-being in the postparental stage: Some evidence from national surveys. *Journal of Marriage and the Family, 37*, 105–110.

Luckey, E. B. (1966) Number of years married as related to personality perception and marital satisfaction. *Journal of Marriage and the Family, 28*, 44–48.

Maas, H. S., and Kuypers, J. A. (1974) *From thirty to seventy.* San Francisco: Jossey-Bass.

Macfarlane, J. W. (1938) Studies in child guidance: 1. Methodology of data collection and organization. *Monographs of the Society for Research in Child Development, 3* (whole No. 19).

Rollins, B. C., and Cameron, K. L. (1974) Marital satisfaction over the family life cycle: A reevaluation. *Journal of Marriage and the Family, 36*, 271–282.

Todd, J. (1984) Personal communication. November 13, 1984.

Weishaus, S., and Field, D. (1984) Continuity and change in half-century marriages: A longitudinal study. Paper presented at meetings of the American Orthopsychiatric Association, Toronto, April, 1984.(a)

Weishaus, S., and Field, D. (1984) Half century of marriage: Continuity or change? Paper presented at meetings of the National Council on Family Relations, San Francisco, October, 1984.(b)

32

CHILD DEVELOPMENT AND FUNCTIONING DURING THE DIVORCE ADJUSTMENT PROCESS:
BASES OF PREVENTIVE HELPING

Arnold L. Stolberg
Department of Psychology
Virginia Commonwealth University

Martin Bloom
School of Social Work
Rutgers, The State University of New Jersey

Divorce breaks up the most significant system of social influences in the lives of its members, particularly the children. Given the fact that divorce is to occur in a given family, then a brief check of relevant systems identifies numerous relationships that will likely be modified. There will be major changes between a child and his or her noncustodial as well as the custodial parent. There may be changes between siblings (who also may be separated); possible additions in stepparents, stepsiblings, steprelatives, or other adult relationships (i.e., parents' dates); changes in living place with consequent changes in neighbors, friends, school peers, commercial establishments, church, recreational centers, etc.; and possible changes in geographical location and cultural life style. Each of these changes may have marked influences on ordinary life developments of children, such as self-identity and self-esteem emerging through interactions with parents, family, and significant others. Thus, on conceptual grounds, we should expect many factors to influence children's adjustment to divorce.

Until recently, only a small number of personal variables have been considered central to a child's adjustment to divorce, such as the age and sex (Hetherington, 1979; Hetherington, Cox, and Cox, 1977; Berg-Cross and Shiller, 1985). Stolberg and his colleagues (Stolberg, Ellwood, and Draper, 1989; Stolberg and Anker, 1983; Stolberg, Camplair, Currier, and Wells, 1987) and others (Emery 1982; Flynn, Hurst, and Breckinridge, 1984) have presented a programmatic series of studies about the multidimensional factors affecting the adjustment to divorce, particularly parental and environmental determinants of children's cognitive, affective, and behavioral responses to the family breakup. The Stolberg group has also presented a model of the

divorce adjustment process that provides the foundation for this present paper.

We will review briefly the empirical evidence regarding the configuration of factors (intrapersonal, interpersonal, and sociocultural) that affect the child's adjustment process. These data provide the basis for constructing a model of the divorce adjustment process, and offer some practice principles for social workers and other helping professionals who might become involved in these events.

These facts are particularly important for those helping professionals who may be involved in giving advice and support before, during, and after the divorce proceedings because conventional wisdom, such as expressed in the "tender years doctrine" that assumes that mothers are the best custodians of young children, has influenced custody proceedings even though the validity of this doctrine remains untested. Another instance of conventional wisdom that lacks empirical clarity is the assumption that single-parent custody is preferable to joint custody. However, recent research suggests that the more time children spend with the noncustodial parent, the fewer the stressful events they report (Stolberg, Camplair, Currier, and Wells, 1987). These data raise the question of whether or not joint custody may offer more emotional supports for children than single-parent custody. This is an empirical question, not merely a value position from conventional wisdom.

THE CONFIGURATION OF FACTORS AFFECTING CHILDREN'S ADJUSTMENT TO DIVORCE

Intrapersonal factors. Gender and age have traditionally been viewed as central to children's adjustment to the divorce process. With some con-

---

This paper was written for this anthology, 1990.

sistency, more boys have been identified as having-trouble in the adjustment process than girls. Longitudinal studies of up to 10 years duration have identified some observable problems that appear to be reactions to their parents' divorce (Hetherington, Cox, and Cox, 1977; Wallerstein, 1983; Hetherington, Cox and Cox, 1981; Guidubaldi, et al. 1983.) Boys continue to display more impulse control problems, and have conduct disorders as well as more problems in developing and maintaining friendships than do girls two years after the divorce (Hetherington, Cox, and Cox, 1977). By the fifth year, boys and girls have roughly equivalent adjustments, although boys continue to be rejected by their peers more than are girls. Follow-up studies ten years after divorce continue to show a residue of impulse control disorders and problems in academic settings.

Children show a variety of intrapersonal reactions to divorce. Cognitive reactions, such as self-blame, feeling different from peers, and heightened sensitivity to interpersonal incompatibility have been noted (Kelly and Berg, 1978; Kurdek and Siesky, 1980a, 1980b). Affective reactions include feelings of anger and sadness, and worry about the future, depending on the ages of the children (Berg-Cross and Shiller, 1985). Behavioral responses include deficits in prosocial behavior and high frequencies of acting out and aggressive behavior (Stolberg, Camplair, Currier, and Wells, 1987).

Interpersonal factors. Recent studies have demonstrated that life-change events are more significant determinants of children's postdivorce adjustment than are gender and age (Stolberg, Camplair, Currier, and Wells, 1987). Hostility between parents, changes in peer groups and schools, and decreased time spent with both parents are among the significant adjustment influences at the interpersonal level (Emery, 1982; Stolberg and Anker, 1983; Stolberg, Camplair, Currier, and Wells, 1987).

Socio-Cultural factors. Changes in the social environment brought about by the divorce, such as moving to a new home, changing schools, etc., are also significant influences in children's adjustment to divorce (Stolberg, et al., 1987). Nine out of ten children in one-parent families live with their mothers rather than their fathers (Moles, 1988), a fact which has strong socioeconomic implications on the lives of children. This is especially true of black and Hispanic children who are more likely than white children (54 percent and 29 percent compared to 18 percent respectively) to be living in one-parent families (Moles, 1988).

MODEL OF THE DIVORCE ADJUSTMENT PROCESS

The model of the divorce adjustment process presented here is adapted from Stolberg, Ellwood, and Draper (1989) to illustrate the several roles social workers might play in these events. Four time-linked stages are proposed, each with its own demands, and each moderated or intensified by the presence of one or more configural conditions—intrapersonal (or internal cognitive or affective events), interpersonal (behaviors or communications), familial, social structural and/or physical environmental (all events external to the person involved). The four stages of the divorce adjustment process are (1) the predecision period; (2) the final separation period; (3) the period of adjustment to the separation; and (4) the recovery-redefinition period. We hypothesize that optimal divorce adjustment results from the presence of economic and social supports, minimal environmental change, maintenance of appropriate parenting skills, positive self-perceptions and mastery-oriented coping.

(1) *Predecision period.* Major characteristics of this first phase of the divorce process are the build up of conflict to a "marital point of no return," when the emotional investment in the marriage begins to be withdrawn, along with the concomitant consideration of possible marital separation. These considerations may include new jobs or training, relocations and resettlements. Such considerations themselves generate considerble stress, especially in connection with competing demands of regular life tasks. Marital partners may cycle in and out of this predecision phase several times before they complete it and go on to the next divorce adjustment phase. (An undetermined number of marital partners may enter this first phase and eventually leave it to stay married.) The major change of this stage is the lack of emotional availability even with the continued presence of the parents. There is much anger, poor modeling of interpersonal relations and conflict resolution, with a consequence of insecurity felt by the child regarding the future of his or her family.

(2) *Final separation period.* A sustained physical separation of the marital partners marks the beginning of the final separation period, which generally lasts 9 months to a year. While the spouses are separated, there may be more conflict between parents because the separation of the family may take away whatever moderating effect its presence may have had on the adults. Children may clearly hear their parents arguing on the telephone, or see

examples of their conflicts when the children change homes. Thus, children risk losing all the essential elements of their life—parents, school, peers, neighborhood—all those elements that they use to help define their identity and development.

Divorcing adults have four major tasks of adjustment in this period: First, the marital partners have to resolve emerging legal conflict, a stage on which many of the other interpersonal conflicts are played out. Second, the children still have to be cared for, even though the emotional demands of separation and impending divorce are draining on the parents. This is a time when children's problems stemming from the divorce proceedings become readily apparent (Stolberg and Anker, 1983; Stolberg, Camplair, Currier, and Wells, 1987; Wallerstein, 1983), particularly when they are relocated at a new home, with a new neighborhood, school, and new friends. Third, partners must each rebuild their own social networks to provide the needed social support for them as separated persons, which replaces the intimate supports the spouse had formerly provided. Fourth, the partners must work to achieve emotional adjustment with regard to all of these major events.

Overall, this period is thought to be as stressful as the predecision period, and more so than the next two stages. The character of the stress has shifted from interpersonal hostility of the first period, to separating and readjusting to the changing marital and family situation in the second.

(3) *The period of adjustment to separation.* In this period the separated adult directs attention to the matters of renewed stability and regained equilibrium. All aspects of the social configuration are involved in these efforts: the separated adult's psychological equilibrium, the interpersonal efforts related to child care and family life, the social sphere of work and education, and the physical realm involving such things as renewed maintenance of the house. The major issues of this phase are the success of the custodial parent, and the meaningfulness of the noncustodial parent.

Stolberg and Bush (1985) suggest that if optimal child adjustment is to occur, there must be related improvements in parenting behavior at the same time. Changes in one area affect changes in other areas. A new stability is reportedly reached in many families about two years after separation, marking the end of this third adjustment period. This stability involves a new life style incorporating

the new elements of the changed social configuration-which the separated adult and his or her children now occupy. Those who are able to construct this new life style are more likely to deal with the difficulties related to the breakup than those who are not able to make a new life style for themselves (Spanier and Casto, 1979).

(4) *Recovery-redefinition period.* The major demands of this fourth and final period in the divorce adjustment process involve reaching permanent stability within the family (or families, if either partner should get remarried). Also, redefinitions of family relationships among the family members (including new stepfamily members, if any) must occur. Time and experience lead to modus operandi that are acceptable to all concerned; hostility and anger between parents generally decreases, and there is increased cooperation or compliance around parenting issues. Most family members come to understand and to accept the facts of the divorce as facts, and come to term with these facts.

However, there may be chronic maladjustment stemming from the divorce among some children. Anger may continue for several years after the marital dissolution. Primary-grade boys who were of preschool age at the time of the divorce have been found to experience more enduring problems than girls at two to five years after the divorce (Hetherington, Cox, and Cox, 1977, 1981).

CHILDREN'S ADJUSTMENT TO DIVORCE

With the above information as background, we want to highlight some of the evidence regarding children's adjustment to divorce for purposes of suggesting preventive and interventive strategies at relevant points in the divorce adjustment process. We are suggesting that different strategies are more nearly appropriate at one rather than another of these adjustment periods.

We also suggest that children's needs vary by age, and interventions or preventions must reflect these differential needs. For example, Kalter (1987) offers a developmental vulnerability model that focuses on long-term problems for children of divorce. Three major concerns are described in detail: handling anger and aggression, the issue of separation-individuation, and gender identity. Regarding anger and aggression, he points out that divorce situations stimulate intense angry feelings at the same time that family processes are supposed to help youngsters develop internalized modes of coping with these feelings. Children at different stages in their development may react differently, and some may externalize these feelings into aggressive behaviors (Kalter, p. 591).

Likewise, with the separation issue, the absence of another emotionally involved adult at the time children are both trying to separate from a powerful caretaking parent-child relationship to a more independent status presents different kinds of problems depending on the age of the child (Kalter, p. 594).

Gender identity is the third developmental concern for children of divorcing families, and differs by the sex of the child. After a divorce, a son may find himself in a complicated relationship with his mother—he tries to withdraw from anxiety-raising closeness to the mother, just as she tries to get closer to the son for her own emotional needs (Kalter, p. 596). A daughter, in a father-absent household, may lack the "continuous sense of being valued and loved as a female," a vital element in feminine development (Kalter, p. 597). Thus, it appears necessary in this process-oriented view of divorce to consider the long-term effects of divorce on children, particularly the differential effects at different stages of divorce and at different ages and the different genders of the children involved.

(1) *Predecision period factors related to children's adjustment.* This period is perhaps the most stressful of all for children (Luepnitz, 1979) who may be acutely aware of their parents' marital problems and conflicts, even if parents take some effort to keep this knowledge from them (Cantor, 1979). Several factors are important to note. First, children view the apparent reasons for their parents' conflicts as stressful and incomprehensible (or trivial). Second, children often blame themselves for much of the marital conflict. Third, awareness of and coping with the family problems depends on the developmental age of the affected children (Berg-Cross and Shiller, 1985).

Infants and toddlers are highly dependent on parents, and may be greatly affected by the diverted attention of the custodial parent as by the absence of the noncustodial parent. Preschool children are more aware of the loss of a parent, but do not have the coping skills to address this loss, and so may lose recently acquired skills.

Young school-aged children at least have the diversion of other people in their lives, but a divorce

tends to refocus attention within the family, thus possibly restricting normal development and the mastery of developmental tasks. Indeed, sometimes tasks are learned out of the typical order, as when a child tries to master complex problem solving skills so as to "solve" the family's problems or become a "parent" to the family. Divorce has been shown to disrupt the important developmental process of positive self-esteem and accurate self-evaluation (Stolberg, Hayes, Zacharias, Nuzzo, and Updegrove, 1989). Coping skills are only partly developed, so that these children may feel sad, but may not have the skills to resolve this sadness. Children may inaccurately blame themselves for the family's problems (Kurdek, 1981). The development of impulse control may be disrupted as parents and other external control sources become less available during the divorce period. Self-concerned parents may exhibit a variety of poor modeling during this time period.

Adolescents of divorcing parents are already seeking some independence, and may deal with the difficulties of the family dissolution by involvement in other social groups. Sometimes precocious sexual activity or involvements with drugs are untoward forms of reaction to the parental divorce.

(2) *Final separation period related to children's adjustment.* This is another kind of difficult and stressful period for children. Although the location of parental hostilities may be changed, a whole new set of stresses emerge. Some preadolescent children view these new events as unjustified, and consequently feel great anger in the stressful situation they see caused by their parents' actions (Wallerstein and Kelly, 1980). Children who had thought of their homes as happy found this period of final separation more difficult than did children who had recognized conflicts existing within the family (Landis, 1960). When the separation required that children move to new locations, with the severing of old friendships and the formation of new ones, these new stresses added to the anger of children.

Separated parents facing their own varied challenges of independent living have less time and energy to devote to their children just at a time when the new stresses demand more parental attention. This adds to the guilt of attentive parents (and not all separated parents are attuned to the shifts in their attention away from their children). But the result of this diverted attention sometimes means children develop problems in self-control (Stolberg and Anker, 1983; Stolberg, Camplair, Currier, and Wells, 1987;

Wallerstein, 1983). Shifting role models sometimes add difficulty to children's forming self-concept (Stolberg, Camplair, Currier, and Wells, 1987).

(3) *The period of adjustment to separation as related to children's adjustment to divorce.* The common finding of this period, that things get worse before they get better, has implications for children's reactions during this period. Stresses are still high on children until routines are established, such as putting the visitation schedule into stable operation. As parents become more stable in their separated living pattern, so they become more stable in their physical and emotional availability to the children. Even though the economic situation of women with children deteriorates ordinarily after divorce, there is some virtue in predictability as new economic roles are established. Resettlement in new locations now becomes part of the new routines, thus reducing another stressor in children's lives.

(4) *Recovery-redefinition period in the adjustment of children to divorce.* The routines of life are now relatively stable, perhaps without the rancor that used to accompany such routines during the pre-decision period. Some children have been maturing over these several years, and may have more personal skills and experiences by which to cope with persisting problems and new life challenges. It is likely that some of their friends have also experienced divorce, so that they need not feel so different from their peers. However, children ordinarily do not share these feelings with peers, and so continue to carry the burdens of their distress. It is also important to note that some children do not make good progress, even though the adults in their lives may recover. Such children may be considered the permanent victims of the divorce.

Cutting across all of these periods are the idiosyncratic responses some children may have to the events surrounding their parents' divorce that lead to persisting feelings of anger or sadness, and restricted or diverted development. Serious psychological difficulties may be manifested. Some children have increased internalized problems and may exhibit social isolation, physiologic symptoms, and anxiety or depression. If these problems do not get resolved within six months of the divorce, this would be the basis for serious concern about the child's development.

With regard to the acting out child who may reflect a chronic family instability, the concern is about increasing failure to achieve expectable socialized roles. In addition, there are related early warning signs of major behavioral problems to come, such as anger, social rejection (rather than self-imposed isolation), failure to do homework orordinary household chores, and experimentation with socially unsanctioned activities such as drugs, sex, and alcohol.

POINTS OF PREVENTIVE HELPING: ROLES FOR SOCIAL WORKERS AND OTHER HELPING PROFESSIONALS

Social workers frequently encounter members of divorcing families in a variety of contexts, from schools where children of divorcing parents may be having behavior problems or declines in academic or social performance, to family service agencies where parents seek help with direct issues. There may be divorce counseling, which seeks to prevent the divorce if possible, or mediation, which seeks to prepare for the realities of the divorce. Parents may also seek help with indirect issues, such as children's problems; of these, practitioners should be observant to note whether or not parental problems are the underlying issue.

There also may be referrals from clergy, pediatricians/physicians, attorneys, or other helping professionals or relatives of the divorcing parties. The common question involves what can be done to help the children and the separated adults through this stressful period in the lives of the family members. Let's look at this question from three perspectives: first, how to do preventive work with the divorcing parents; second, how to do preventive work with the children; and three, how to integrate preventive work with parents, children, and the larger social system.

1. *Parents.* One beginning point regarding prevention is to note the obvious though neglected fact that when parents get divorced, children are still members of the original family (and whatever other families are formed). Children still have two parents, and sometimes additional ones or perhaps temporary surrogate parents. This provides the basis for a general helping orientation to assist parents in parenting—or more precisely, coparenting—skills throughout the divorce phases (Ellwood and Stolberg, manuscript). That is to say, both parents are to be encouraged to continue parenting, albeit in a modified way.

Because divorcing parents always remain parents to their children, they have to face the issues of this long-term demand even in the face of immediate conflict between spouses. Social workers and other helping professionals can articulate options facing divorcing parents regarding their parenting duties. One option involves permitting the present conflict to engulf their child's development with its probable untoward effects on the child, and the future need of remediation. (Marital hostility has been found to have immediate and long-term effects on the adjustment of children from divorced families (Emery, 1982; Jacobson, 1978).) This adversarial position is most likely to be present during the beginning stages of divorce, when the adult conflicts tend to overwhelm the other parent-child considerations. Interparent hostility needs to be minimized and parenting skills enhanced.

The other option involves forms of cooperation with regard to their mutual responsibilities to the children. There are various degrees of such cooperation, from minimal legal support, to more extensive psychological and physical involvements with the child throughout his or her time of being a dependent. How much coparenting occurs after divorce may be predicted by how much coparenting occurred before divorce; the greater the earlier coparenting, the more like the postdivorce coparenting.

Clearly, the helping professional should promote the cooperative option, to the extent that this is feasible, given the trend of the data favoring coparenting on the healthy development of children of divorce. The custodial parent usually experiences greater stresses during the separation period (with more responsibilities for the day-to-day rearing of the children) while at the same time having fewer social supports. The custodial parent therefore should be aided to reestablish social and emotional support systems, either through existing natural helping networks or by joining self-help groups of persons undergoing like stresses.

The custodial parent may also need help in developing the skills for one-parent child-rearing procedures, and daily family life functioning. One or both of the parents may need assistance in job training and economic functioning. Economic stability has been noted as a contributor to adjustment in divorcing families, particularly on women (Albrecht, 1980; Kressel, 1980; Smith, 1980; Stolberg and Anker, 1983).

2. *Children.* With their different capacities to understand and to adapt to their parents' divorce, children of different ages require different kinds of assistance. In general, all children need assistance to continue their growth and development, even in the face of the dissolution of the family as they have known it. This includes aid in continuing development of their positive self-esteem, their impulse control and anger control, and their problem-solving abilities. The specific content of aid directed toward these objectives will differ according to the age and cognitive-affective maturity of the individual child.

There are three general types of programs in primary prevention: the first involves prevention of predictable problems; the second deals with the protection of existing strengths; and the third seeks to promote desired states of functioning. With regard to prevention programs for children, we will sketch briefly those that may be based on the predictable problems following divorce as discussed above. For example, it is likely that there will be occasions when the child is angry at one or both parents, and learning effective anger control (not suppression) may be a valuable skill. We can also consider prevention programs that protect the health and mental health that currently exist for the child of a divorcing family. An example of this might be a program that supports the child's self-esteem (assuming that it is currently at an appropriate level) and helps to continue its appropriate growth. We can consider promoting skills and attributes that the child does not currently possess but which seem desirable to all concerned, especially in context of the divorce. For instance, problem-solving skills will likely be needed to enhance the child's development in general, but with the special needs that are likely in a divorce situation (which gives these skills a preventive flavor as well as a promotive one).

These four cognitive-behavioral skills—anger control, problem-solving skills, development in self-esteem, and communication skills—are in fact taught in a school-based prevention program for children of divorce (Stolberg, 1989). In this and similar programs, there is some encouraging empirical evidence that self-concept is improved; that reductions in behavior problems and anxiety occur; and that social skills are enhanced (Stolberg and Garrison, 1985). (Also see Pedro-Carroll and Cowen, 1985.)

3. *Parents, Children, and the Community.* The most common sources of help for the adults in divorcing families are their own family and close friends, along with lawyers and possible personal physicians or pediatricians. It is therefore of greatest importance to recognize that in some cases, what is "best advice" from these various sources may be at odds with what research suggests may be in the best interests of the children.

Consider this case example: Mr. and Mrs. X moved recently to a midwestern city from their home in the south. Mr. X stayed several weeks longer in the south to complete business, and when he arrived in the new city, his wife announced that she wanted an immediate separation. While they had been arguing for some months before the move, he thought that was simply tension reflecting the relocation. The three children, a girl of 6, and two sons, 8 and 11, were confused at the turn of events. The wife tried to get the husband to leave the home, but he refused, so she left, leaving the children with him. In fact, she soon moved in with a male friend of their mutual acquaintance. This combination of events was very problematic for the husband. Advice from his family was that "she was no good, and he should get out while the getting was good." This advice was perhaps well-intentioned, but it was likely to have been made on the basis of limited information, and favored short-term solutions (satisfactions of immediate anger) rather than recognizing the long-term needs of coparenting.

Mr. X went to a lawyer, and received similar advice. Because adultery was present, the lawyers saw this case as an "easy win" on legal grounds. The "easy win," however, might increase interparental hostility and may therefore reduce the possibility of effective coparenting, which research has shown to reduce problems in the children while encouraging the meeting of normal developmental needs.

The children were being seen by a new pediatrician for routine matters—the children were in good health—and while she was told of the separation, she did not notice any psychological problems beyond some expressions of sadness by the children, nor did she anticipate problems in meeting ordinary developmental tasks.

Thus, the best of familial and professional intentions may have led to unfruitful results in the long run. The implications of this case are that greater efforts must be made to help clients and their regular and natural support systems to be open to the full range of information, and to consider the values and outcomes of all persons involved in the short and the long run. This includes both the avoiding of destructive suggestions, and also the engaging in constructive planning.

Professionals in primary prevention have to learn how to communicate with these natural support systems in the community. For example, the Dallas Association of Young Lawyers recently won the American Bar Endowment Outstanding Public Service Award (1989) for a film being shown to all adults who are seeking divorce in Dallas—*Child Custody Battles: Don't Forget the Children*. A poignant moment in the film comes when the judge addresses one set of parents to the effect that he (the judge) cannot undo what has gone on before in the family; he cannot know a child or the parents as well as they all know each other. But what he can say with assurance is that the effects of divorce litigation will be far worse than anything that has gone on in the home, except for child or spousal or drug abuse. This is the type of message that helping professionals have to get across to parents and friends of divorcing people, as well as to the various professionals who might be consulted in the course of thinking about divorce. These messages can be summarized as follows (Stolberg, Ellwood, and Draper, 1989):

(1) Educate people as to the realities of divorce, especially with the potential harmful effects on children immediately, and over the short and long run.
(2) Set the ground rules for behaviors within the divorce context so that parents can work together for the sake of the children.
(3) Win the support of both parties and talk with them together so that they hear the same thing at the same time.
(4) Refer the divorcing persons to professionals trained in appropriate counseling and mediation, as needed.

SUMMARY

Attempting to minimize the untoward effects of divorce on the children is like steadying a merry-go-round with its many simultaneous circular, up-and-down, and sideways motions. However, the more nearly we are prepared to observe and to correct for these often contradictory motions, the more likely we are to be able to prevent predictable problems and promote desired forms of development.

This paper has summarized briefly the empirical evidence describing children's adjustment to divorce, particularly as it is affected by personal, familial, and environmental factors. Four phases of the divorce adjustment process have been described, and suggestions have been offered for preventive efforts to minimize children's untoward responses to divorce.

References

Albrecht, S. L. Reactions and adjustments to divorce: Differences in the experiences of males and females. *Family Relations*, 1980, *1*, 59–68.

Berg-Cross, L. and Shiller, V. Divorce and subsequent custody arrangements: Implications for child development and opportunities for preventive and interventive helping. In: Bloom, M. (ed.) *Life Span Development: Bases for Preventive and Interventive Helping*. New York: Macmillan, 1985.

Cantor, D. Divorce: A view from the children. *Journal of Divorce*, 1979, *2*, 357–362.

Emery, R. E. Interpersonal conflict and the children of discord and divorce. *Psychological Bulletin*, 1982, *92*, 310–330.

Flynn, E. J., Hurse, E. F., and Breckinridge, E. Symposium on Preventive Strategies for Children of Divorce. Bethesda, Maryland: National Institute of Mental Health, 1984.

Guidubaldi, J., Perry, J. D., and Cleminshaw, H. K. The legacy of parental divorce: A nationwide study of family status and selected mediating variables on children's academic and social competencies. *School Psychology Review*, 1983, *12*, 300–323.

Hetherington, E. M. Divorce: A child's perspective. *American Psychologist*, 1979, *34*:10, 851–858.

Hetherington, E. M., Cox, M., and Cox, R. Effects of divorce on parents and children. In: Lamb, M. (ed.) *Nontraditional Families*. Hillsdale, N.J.: Lawrence Erlbaum Associates, 1981.

Jacobson, D. The impact of marital separation/divorce on children: I. Parent-child separation and child adjustment. *Journal of Divorce*, 1978, *1*, 341–360.

Kelly, R. and Berg, S. Measuring children's relations to divorce. *Journal of Clinical Psychology*, 1978, 34, 215–221.

Kressel, K. Patterns of coping in divorce and some implications for clinical practice. *Family Relations*, 1980, *2*, 234–240.

Kurdek, L. A. An integrative perspective on children's divorce adjustment. *American Psychologist*, 1981, *35*, 856–866.

Kurdek, L. A. and Siesky, A. E. Children's perceptions of their parents' divorce. *Journal of Divorce*, 1980a, *3*, 339–378.

Kurdek, L. A. and Siesky, A. E. The effects of divorce on children: The relationship between parent and child perspectives. *Journal of Divorce*, 1980b, 4, 85–99.

Landis, J. The trauma of children when parents divorce. *Marriage and Family Living*, 1960, 22, 7–13.

Luepnitz, D. A. Which aspects of divorce affect children? *Family Coordinator*, 1979, *1*, 79–85.

Moles, O. School performance of children from one-parent families: Findings and implications. Paper presented at the National Association of Social Workers Annual Conference, 1988.

Pedro-Carroll, J. A. L. and Cowen, E. L. The Divorce Intervention Project: An investigation of the efficacy of a school-based prevention program. *Journal of Consulting and Clinical Psychology*, 1985, *53*, 603–611.

Spanier, G. and Casto, R. Adjustment to separation and divorce: An analysis of fifty cases. *Journal of Divorce*, 1979, *2*, 241–253.

Stolberg, A. L. and Anker, M. M. Cognitive and behavioral changes in children resulting from parental divorce and environmental change. *Journal of Divorce*, 1983, 7:2, 23–41.

Stolberg, A. L. and Bush, J. P. A path analysis of factors predicting children's divorce adjustment. *Journal of Clinical Child Psychology*, 1985, *14*, 49–54.

Stolberg, A. L., Camplair, C., Currier, K., and Wells, M. Individual, familial and environmental determinants of children's post-divorce adjustment and maladjustment. *Journal of Divorce*, 1987, *11*:1, 51–70.

Stolberg, A., Ellwood, E., and Draper, D. A. (1989). The pediatrician's role in children's adjustment to divorce. *The Journal of Pediatrics*, 1989 (February), 187–192.

Stolberg, A. L., Hayes, M., Zacharias, M., and Nuzzo, C. L. Divorce as a disrupter of the normal development of children's self-evaluation skills. Paper presented at the Southeast Psychological Association Conference, 1989.

Wallerstein, J. S. Children of divorce: The psychological tasks of the child. *American Journal of Orthopsychiatry*, 1983, *53*, 530–543.

Wallerstein, J. S. and Kelly, J. B. *Surviving the Breakup: How Children and Parents Cope with Divorce*. New York: Basic Books, 1980.

33

STEPFAMILIES: A REVIEW OF THE LITERATURE WITH SUGGESTIONS FOR PRACTITIONERS

Patsy Skeen
Robert B. Covi
Department of Child and Family Development
University of Georgia

Bryan E. Robinson
Department of Human Services
University of North Carolina at Charlotte

Everyone has heard the story of the wicked stepmother who gave Cinderella the vilest household tasks and tried to prevent her from receiving the attention of a young prince. The Cinderella story adversely affects popular views about stepfamilies. Actually, the relationships portrayed in that fairy tale misrepresent the kinds of relationships that exist among many stepfamilies today. Although stepfamily relationships are different from primary family relationships, the chances for success are not as bleak as they were in Cinderella's case.

In this article we briefly summarize the research concerning stepfamilies, discuss the uniqueness of stepfamily relationships, note issues particularly troublesome to stepfamilies, and provide some guidelines for individuals interested in helping stepfamilies.

WHAT DO WE KNOW ABOUT STEPFAMILIES?

The analogy of Cinderella exaggerates the problems of stepfamily relations, but it is no exaggeration to say that the number of stepfamilies, also known as *reconstituted* or *blended* families, will continue to increase rapidly (Duberman, 1977). Currently, 6.5 million children, or 10.2 percent of children under 18, live in stepfamilies (Francke and Reese, 1980; Jacobson, 1980). Stepfamilies are here to stay as prevalent forms of American family life (Kompara, 1980). The level of complexity in these families ranges from a widow with one child who marries a bachelor to four divorced individuals, all with joint custody of their children, trying to form two new households. In some cases children visit rather than live with stepparents (Visher and Visher, 1978b).

Research findings concerning the problems of children in stepfamilies are mixed. Some indicate more difficulties for children living in stepfamilies than for children living with both biological parents. Bowerman and Irish's (1962) data, based on questionnaires completed by stepchildren, revealed that households involving steprelations were characterized by more stress, more ambivalence, and lower cohesiveness than were non-stepfamily households. Nye (1957) also found more adjustment problems in stepfamilies than in unbroken families, but he noted that the greatest adjustment difficulties existed in unbroken families in which unhappy environments prevailed.

Touliatos and Lindholm (1980) asked teachers to rate the behavior of children in kindergarten through eighth grade. Compared with children in intact homes, children in homes with a mother and stepfather were rated as having more conduct problems (e.g., negativism, aggression) and socialized delinquency (e.g., bad companions, cooperative stealing), and those in homes with a stepmother and father were rated as having more conduct problems.

Other studies have seemed to indicate fewer problems for children in stepfamilies. One investigation (Bohannan and Erickson, 1978) showed that stepchildren are just as happy and just as socially and academically successful as are children in unbroken families. Perhaps the best-known study on stepfamilies was conducted by Lucile Duberman (1973). She surveyed husbands and wives involved in stepfamilies and asked them to evaluate their own children's relationshps with their stepparents. She found that 64 percent of the stepfamilies had excellent relationships and that stepparent-child relationships were better among those of higher than those

From the *Journal of Counseling and Development*, 1985, *64*(2):121–125. Copyright © American Association of Counseling and Development. Reprinted by permission.

of lower social classes and better among Protestant than among Catholic stepfamilies.

Lending additional support to these findings, two national surveys found no social or psychological differences between high school students brought up in stepfather families and those raised in natural parent families (Wilson, Zurcher, McAdams, and Curtis, 1975). Burchinal (1964) assessed the questionnaire responses of adolescents and parents from unbroken, broken, and reconstituted families. He found no significant differences in the personality and social relationships among the three groups. Santrock, Warshak, Lindbergh, and Meadows (1982) also observed unbroken, broken, and blended families. They concluded that the social behavior of children in stepfamilies is not necessarily less competent than that of children in intact or broken families. Other reports indicate that stepfamilies have no more difficulty than do unbroken families (Bernard, 1956; Bohannan, 1970; Bohannan and Erickson, 1978; Goode, 1956; Landis, 1962; Stinnett and Walters, 1977).

These conflicting reports are partly due to the differences in research methodology (Robinson, in press). For example, as mentioned above, Duberman surveyed only the husbands and wives involved in stepfamilies and asked spouses to evaluate their own children's relationships with their stepparents. In contrast, Bowerman and Irish's data were based on questionnaires completed by stepchildren, who might have evaluated relationships differently from their parents. Changing social attitudes about divorce may also account for some differences. In summary, children from stepfamilies can have mostly positive, mostly negative, or mixed experiences—the same as children from unbroken families (Wilson et al., 1975).

WHAT IS IT LIKE TO BE A MEMBER OF A STEPFAMILY?

More than one-half of the stepfamilies formed after divorce include stepfathers (Rallings, 1976). Stepfathers tend to be either inattentive and disengaged, giving the mother little child-rearing support, or very actively involved, often with a tendency to be restrictive, especially toward sons. But if the stepfather is able to set consistent limits and communicate warmly and well with the children, and if the mother welcomes the stepfather's support, the stepchildren (especially boys) generally function better than do children in single-parent families or con-

flicted, nondivorced families (Hetherington, Cox, and Cox, 1982; Robinson, in press).

The presence of stepfathers in homes in which the natural parents divorced before the child reached 5 years of age had a positive effect on 6- to 11-year-old boys (Santrock, 1972). Oshman and Manosevitz (1976) also found that stepfathers have a positive effect on stepsons. Children ages 9 to 15, however, are less likely to accept a good stepparent than are younger or older children (Hetherington et al., 1982). Wallerstein and Kelly (1980) found that younger children, particularly girls, are more accepting of stepfathers. Older children and adolescents felt resentment with a stepfather present. Most children compared the new stepfather with the natural father. In most cases the stepfather did not replace the natural father, except when children and fathers rejected each other. Stern (1978) suggested that fathers are likely to be more successful disciplinarians when they adopt a slow, gentle, flexible approach and develop a friendship to foster the child's participation, instead of trying to control the child through authoritarian means.

Some stepfathers whose biological children lived with their mothers felt pain and regretted the time spent with stepchildren when they could spend so little time with their own (Brooks, 1981). Although stepfathers tend to be self-critical and unsure of themselves in the stepparenting role, they get equally high ratings from their spouses and stepchildren as biological fathers (Bohannan and Erickson, 1978). In fact, there is evidence suggesting that stepfathers have better relationships with stepchildren (Duberman, 1973) and adjust easier to the stepparenting role (Bowerman and Irish, 1962) than do stepmothers.

Younger stepmothers were found by Duberman (1973) to have better relationships with stepchildren than did older stepmothers. Wallerstein and Kelly (1980) found, however, that younger stepmothers had more difficulty, especially with teenage girls. Adolescent girls tended to compete more with stepmothers than boys did with stepfathers. Moreover, stepmothers had better relationships with children under 13 than with teenage children. Draughon (1975) suggested that stepmothers can expect better success by being the child's friend than by trying to become a second mother.

Duberman (1973) found that stepsibling relationships are crucial to the success of stepfamilies. In most cases the presence of stepsiblings makes the remarriage much more complex (Wallerstein and

Kelly, 1980). The better the relationships between stepsiblings, the better the total family integration. Generally, there is an acceptance among stepsiblings; however, children who are less assertive, who are physically unattractive to the parents when compared to other siblings, and who are younger and unable to care for themselves have more problems. Furthermore, when there is still unresolved anger toward the separation and divorce, there is more of a likelihood of friction between the stepsiblings (Wallerstein and Kelly, 1980). When remarried couples have a child together, their children from former marriages are more likely to have harmonious relationships. Sometimes, however, children from the former marriages feel left out or not as important as the new child who belongs to both the natural parent and the stepparent (Brooks, 1981). According to adolescents, divided loyalties and discipline are the most stressful part of stepfamily living, whereas being a member of two households is less stressful (Lutz, 1983).

Children who lose a parent by death and children who lose a parent by desertion or divorce are affected in different ways. Children who lose a parent by death are ready to accept a new parent before the parent is ready to remarry, especially if the child is young (Furman, 1974). In all cases reported by Furman (1974), the remarriage of the parent rekindled old memories of the deceased parent. Children who never knew or could not remember the lost parent questioned whether they were lovable.

Children of divorced parents have more difficulty accepting the loss of a parent, are disappointed when the fantasy of parental reconciliation is not realized (Furman, 1974), and seem to be more frustrated and angry than those who lose a parent by death. Children whose identification with the absent parent is very strong, who cling to a fantasy of reuniting with the absent parent, or who have greater anxiety about being abandoned by the remaining parent are especially likely to have difficulties when parents remarry (Tessman, 1978).

PRIMARY FAMILY VERSUS STEPFAMILY

Life in a stepfamily is different from life in a primary family. There are clear structural differences in how intact, nuclear families and stepfamilies interact (Capaldi and McRae, 1979; Draughon, 1975; Jones, 1978; Kompara, 1980; Nelson and Nelson, 1982; Perkins and Kahn, 1979; Roosevelt and Lofas, 1976; Sager, Walker, Brown, Crohn, and Rodstein, 1983; Schulman, 1972; Visher and Visher, 1978a).

Negative feelings and thoughts are common in all families; however, parents and children are bound in a way that stepparents and stepchildren are not. What can be acceptable from a natural parent or child is often totally unacceptable from a "stranger" who has now become a family member. These difficulties may be intensified if there are unresolved conflicts between a stepfather and a biological father with the child caught in the middle. Furthermore, conflicts between stepparents and biological parents escalate when the unmarried couples are in conflict with each other (Duberman, 1975). For these reasons and because of the special challenges of the stepfamily discussed above, open and effective communication seems to be essential in stepfamilies.

In the stepfamily, solidarity must be reestablished. Status, duties, and privileges also must be redefined in the context of the new family system (Duberman, 1973). Such tasks are difficult because stepfamily members have separate histories, memories, and habits. Learning to be an effective stepparent is an especially unique and difficult challenge (Fast and Cain, 1966; Komara, 1980). Not only must stepparents become instant parents, but, as Kompara (1980) pointed out "in a remarriage the partners have received their training from two different parental family settings and the children have been partially socialized by the first parents" (p. 69). In contrast, primary family members have had a lifetime to establish their relationship patterns.

Another special challenge of the new stepfamily is dealing with the past. Stepfamily members must mourn the loss of the primary family (Thies, 1977), and parents must resolve their relationships with their former spouses and help their children deal successfully with the divorce (Kleinman, Rosenberg, and Whiteside, 1979). Also, former spouses and their relatives continue to be part of the new stepfamily's interactions. Former spouses use the children to continue the battle that was not ended with divorce, and they enlarge their combat arena to include the stepparent (Brooks, 1981).

Children in stepfamilies must adjust to a complex family interaction:

> The child has to adjust to one and sometimes two stepparents (one of whom is visited) and still retain relationships with the biological parent out of the home, biological siblings in and/or out of the home and develop a relationship with stepsiblings who may be in and/or out of the home. (Jacobson, 1980, p. 2)

As a result of this complex interaction, children may experience divided loyalties (Visher and Visher,

1979). Sometimes stepchildren feel twice defeated—first for not preventing the divorce and second for not preventing the remarriage. Belief in the myth that members of new stepfamilies should instantly love each other sets these families up for failure (Kompara, 1980; Visher and Visher, 1978a), and their failure rate is high. Over 44 percent of newly blended families fail within the first 5 years (*Stepfamily Bulletin*, 1980).

According to Cherlin (1978), the instability of blended families can be attributed to the absence of institutionalized roles and patterns of behavior pertaining to remarried families. There are no clear role prescriptions to help clarify the nature of interactions between former spouses and between noncustodial, biological parents and stepparents. The lack of defined role expectations or guidelines for acceptable stepfamily behavior causes role uncertainty and stress in stepfamily relationships (Fast and Cain, 1966; Johnson, 1980; Messinger, 1976; Rallings, 1976) and increases the probability of a second (or a third) marital disruption (Cherlin, 1978).

Another contributor to the instability of stepfamilies is the increased complexity of relationships that were called *quasi-kin* by Bohannon (1970). This term refers to former spouses and the relatives of former spouses. With this complex of quasi-kin relationships there is an increase in the ambiguity of roles that may result in role strain in the stepfamily (Cherlin, 1978).

The idea that there is greater instability in stepfamilies because of the absence of societal norms to regulate the interactions between stepfamily members and quasi-kin was examined by Clingempeel (1981). He found that people from simple stepfamilies (in which only the wife had children from the previous marriage) showed higher marital quality than did people from complex families. Furthermore people who maintained only moderate contact with quasi-kin showed better marital quality than did people who maintained either high or low contact with quasi-kin.

SPECIAL PROBLEMS ASSOCIATED WITH STEPFAMILIES

Stepfamilies have complex psychological and structural characteristics that have not been fully recognized and accepted by many public institutions, including the legal system and the school system. Visher and Visher (1979) pointed out how the school system, a major force in a child's socialization,

reinforces the conflicts and hurt feelings in stepfamilies. The making of Mother's Day and Father's Day cards can be confusing for pre-school and primary school children. Usually school notices, report cards, and invitations to open school days are sent to only one set of parents, which increases stress and miscommunication between parents. Graduation ceremonies often specify that only one set of parents may attend, forcing the child to choose between parents and stepparents. The inability of society (in this case, schools) to respond to the stepfamily's needs contributes to its members' feeling different.

Another of the challenges facing stepfamily members is the potentially negative connotation of *step*. The concepts stepmother and stepfather have more negative connotations than do other family positions. The prefix still seems to suggest a negative stereotype (Ganong and Coleman, 1983).

The legal system has also contributed to the difficulties faced by stepfamilies. Although there is no overriding body of federal family law, each state specifies the reciprocal rights and duties of family members. Notably absent from all state statutes is the specification of rights and duties of stepparents regarding stepchildren (Wald, 1981). A stepparent is not obligated to take the children of a spouse's former marriage into the home, yet many stepparents help rear and support children who belong to someone else and assume the status and obligations of a parent without formal adoption. Under these circumstances the stepparent is considered to be in loco parentis. A person in loco parentis takes the place of the parent and has all the rights, duties, and obligations of a natural parent. But voluntary stepchild support can be terminated at will. The support rights of stepchildren in stepfamilies or in divorced stepfamilies are highly uncertain. At present, the laws are in transition. For instance, a stepfather who assumes the responsibility of supporting a stepchild may or may not have any legal rights toward that child even though he may be in loco parentis. It is up to individual state courts to decide (Kargman, 1983). These rulings are sometimes unclear and vary from one court jurisdiction to another.

Financial matters often are a source of conflict in stepfamilies. One or both parents may have financial obligations to "another" family. In younger stepfamilies, conflict about money generally revolves around child support and alimony. Older couples may have conflicts over wills and distribution of property among stepchildren and biological children (Sager et al., 1983). Furthermore, the issue of money may or may not have been settled at the time of the divorce, and some problems may still remain at the time of the remarriage. For example, a former wife may feel deprived, or a new husband may find that the expense of another family strains his budget to the point that he may resent what he believes is an unfair financial burden. Also, a new spouse may resent the idea that his or her income may go to meet obligations to another household (Sager et al., 1983).

Money has a symbolic and emotional impact on the stepfamily. According to Fishman (1983), the manner in which finances are handled may reflect the commitment expressed by remarried couples to each other and to each other's children. Fishman (1983) found two kinds of economic behavior in stepfamilies. Some stepfamilies adopt the "common pot" approach to family economics pooling all their resources, and tend to value interpersonal harmony and closeness. Other stepfamilies adopt the "two pot" economy, valuing autonomy and independent control of money. In these families, each spouse contributes a specific amount to the ongoing maintenance of the household. In either case, the task of the stepfamily is to develop economic values that attend to the needs of both the family and the individual. The task of the therapist is to help stepfamily members develop the "common good" approach and to encourage personal autonomy (Fishman, 1983).

One of the most difficult issues for stepfamily members to deal with is sexuality. It has been suggested that in stepfamilies there is a loosening of sexual boundaries (Perlmutter, Engel, and Sager, 1982). This loosening is related to the structural nature of the stepfamily, which is nonbiological and nonlegal and has not had the advantage of a long developmental period to form intimate parent-child ties. Indeed, the only tie that stepfamily members share is a close social tie; there is, however, the potential for emotional attachments to grow over time (Wald, 1981).

The increase in the affectionate and sexual atmosphere in the home during the time that new couples are more romantically involved may also contribute to the loosening of sexual boundaries. Young adolescents with stepsiblings of the opposite sex can further intensify the sexual climate in the stepfamily household (Sager et al., 1983, p. 293). It is not unusual for stepfamily members to experience sexual fantasies, increased anxiety, distancing behavior, or even anger in response to and in trying to

cope with these sexual issues. In more extreme circumstances, a sexual relationship can develop between a stepparent and a stepchild. Sexual abuse is much more prevalent between fathers and daughters than between other family members. Berliner's (1977) data on sexual abuse of children revealed that 75 percent of assailants were fathers or stepfathers of the children abused and 7 percent were the mothers' live-in boyfriends. Incest between stepfathers and stepdaughters is reported to be more prevalent than between biologically related fathers and daughters, although there are no clear data to support such a contention (Meiselman, 1978).

The loosening of sexual boundaries in stepfamilies does not lead automatically to sexual abuse. Remarried families are capable of coping with this added stress, as they are with other stresses in their lives.

HOW CAN PRACTITIONERS HELP?

It would be helpful for practitioners, no matter what their particular focus, to keep in mind several research findings. Schulman (1972) identified two important characteristics that distinguish stepfamilies from intact families. First, fantasies and hopes play a much larger role in family interactions in stepfamilies than they do in intact families. Second, stepparents expect more gratitude and acknowledgment from stepchildren than natural parents expect from their children. According to Visher and Visher (1979), stepparents' expectations of themselves are unrealistically high. What is important in being a stepparent is understanding the children's needs. Also, it is important that a stepparent not force loyalty issues or attempts to replace a lost or absent parent (Tessman, 1978).

Stepfamily members need to relinquish the myth that it will be easy to form a new stepfamily (Duberman, 1973; Jacobson, 1980; Visher and Visher, 1978a, 1978b). Counselors can be an important resource to stepparents and stepchildren, especially in the development of effective communication skills both before and after the formation of the new blended family. Different families have developed different communication patterns and styles. When two different families join to become one, the potential for communication problems is great.

Counselors can help prospective "new" families prevent or reduce stress by encouraging them to participate in remarriage preparation courses (Messinger, 1976) or pre-stepfamily workshops. Jacobson (1980) recommended a rehearsal for reality in which soon-to-be blended family members express their feelings and anticipate potential problems that might arise after the marriage. Through the use of preparation courses or workshops and with the help of a trained counselor, couples can work out their inevitable differences in values, establish family boundaries, clarify roles, develop faith in their parent-child relationships, and accept the initial rejection of stepchildren (Visher and Visher, 1978b).

Counselors can help family members, especially children, mourn the loss of the initial family and help in the formation of the new one. Counselors can also be of assistance in helping stepparents work out their relationships with noncustodial parents. It is also important to aid parents in developing satisfying couple relationships separate from their parenting roles.

Programs have been designed to enhance communication between husbands and wives. One of the more well-known programs, Couples Communication (Miller, Nunnally, and Wackman, 1975), has a nationwide network of instructors. It is possible for any couple in almost every major city to join a group. For counselors working in the school setting, the establishment of a parent education program for stepfamilies can be very effective. Structured programs such as Parent Effectiveness Training (Gordon, 1970) and Systematic Training for Effective Parenting (STEP) (Dinkmeyer and McKay, 1976) can be modified for stepfamilies. In addition to these prepackaged programs, there are literally dozens of books on parenting that can be used as instructional manuals in stepfamily educational programs.

Counselors can use books, puppets, drama, and other techniques in working with individual children and groups of children in the school setting. Some groups can be limited to stepchildren; others can include all children. Stepchildren and nonstepchildren can be valuable supports to each other. Counselors should also encourage teachers to work with children in the classroom (see Skeen, Robinson, and Flake-Hobson [1984] for a discussion of the role of the classroom teacher in helping young stepchildren and their families).

There are many tasks that are important for the stepfamily to accomplish (Kleinman et al., 1979). Stepfamily members must become aware of the shifting of alliances both within and outside the stepfamily. They must determine what the role of discipline should be and clarify the boundaries within each stepfamily subsystem.

The issue of guilt seems to be important in newly formed stepfamilies. There is guilt left over from the earlier separation and divorce and guilt associated with the rivalry between a stepparent and a natural parent. Roman and Haddad (1978) suggested that stepparents be thought of as additional parents rather than as substitute parents. This helps clarify the roles between biological parents and stepparents and between biological children and stepchildren. Another approach is to consider the stepparent a special friend.

There is a need for more understanding of the problems faced by stepfamilies and for the provison of support and encouragement to stepparents. Turnbull and Turnbull (1983) suggested that the most critical element for success in counseling the stepparent is the development of a relationship of warmth and understanding. To this end, they have developed the "Ten Commandments of Stepparenting," designed to help stepparents deal with the conflicts and stresses they have to face. These are simple guidelines for survival and include the following advice for stepparents:

1. Provide neutral territory so that each family member can feel that he or she has a special place that belongs to him or her.
2. Avoid trying to fit a preconceived role, but try to be kind, intelligent, and a good sport.
3. Set limits and enforce them, work out the rules ahead of time, and support each other when the rules have to be enforced.
4. Allow an outlet for the children's feelings for the natural parent. Children need to express these feelings.
5. Expect ambivalence; it's normal.
6. Avoid mealtime misery.
7. Avoid expecting instant love; it takes time to establish bonds.
8. Avoid taking all the responsibility; the child has some too.
9. Be patient; it takes time to work through problems.
10. Maintain the primacy of the marital relationship. Some stepparents spend too much time and energy trying to work out their stepparent roles and neglect their own relationships (Hetherington et al., 1982).

CONCLUSION

Research findings concerning children growing up in stepfamilies are mixed. Some studies indicate that children in stepfamilies have more difficulties than do children living with both biological parents; others suggest no major differences in either family type. We can conclude, however, that the nature of the stepfamily network is markedly different from the unbroken family network. As a result, stepfamilies may experience unique problems. Although the transition from unbroken families to stepfamilies is not an easy one, it is possible for most blended families to manage their lives with reasonable success (Schulman, 1972).

If the stepfamily is accepted as a real and viable type of family, the same characteristics that create its challenges can also produce its rewards. Dealing with losses and transitions can equip people to cope with the shifts and losses that occur throughout life, and knowing that interpersonal relationships take work can lead to rewarding and close personal relationships. A good relationship between spouses can provide children with a realistic model for their own future adult relationships (Visher and Visher, 1982).

References

Berliner, L. (1977). Child abuse: What happens next? *Victimatology, 2,* 2.

Bernard, J. (1956). *Remarriage: A study of marriage.* New York: Dryden.

Bohannan, P. (ed.). (1970). *Divorce and after.* New York: Doubleday.

Bohannan, P., and Erickson, R. (1978). Stepping in. *Psychology Today, 11,* 53–59.

Bowerman, C. E., and Irish, D. P. (1962). Some relationships of stepchildren to their parents. *Marriage and Family Living, 24,* 113–121.

Brooks, J. B. (1981). *The process of parenting.* Palo Alto, CA: Mayfield.

Burchinal, G. (1964). Characteristics of adolescents from unbroken, broken, and reconstituted families. *Journal of Marriage and the Family, 26,* 44–50.

Capaldi, F., and McRae, B. (1979). *Stepfamilies: A cooperative responsibility.* New York: New Viewpoints/ Vision Books.

Cherlin, A. (1978). Remarriage as an incomplete institution. *American Journal of Sociology, 84,* 634-650.

Clingempeel, W. G. (1981). Quasi-kin relationships and marital quality in stepfather families. *Journal of Personality and Social Psychology, 41,* 890–901.

Dinkmeyer, D., and McKay, G. D. (1976). *Systematic training for effective parenting.* Circle Pines, NM: American Guidance Service.

Draughon, M. (1975). Step-mother's model of identification in relation to mourning in the child. *Psychological Reports, 36,* 183–189.

Duberman, L. (1973). Step-kin relationships. *Journal of Marriage and the Family, 35,* 283–292.

Duberman, L. (1975). *The reconstituted family: A study of remarried couples and their children.* Chicago: Nelson-Hall.

Duberman, L. (1977). *Marriage and other alternatives* (2nd ed.). New York: Praeger.

Fast, I., and Cain, A. C. (1966). The stepparent role: Potential for disturbances in family functioning. *American Journal of Orthopsychiatry, 36,* 485–491.

Fishman, B. (1983). The economic behavior of stepfamilies. *Family Relations, 32,* 359–366.

Framo, J. L. (1979). Family theory and therapy. *American Psychologist, 34,* 988–992.

Francke, L. B., and Reese, M. (1980, February 11). After remarriage. *Newsweek,* p. 66.

Furman, E. (1974). *A child's parent dies: Studies in childhood bereavement.* New Haven, CT: Yale University Press.

Ganong, L. H., and Coleman, M. (1983). Stepparent: A pejorative term? *Psychological Reports, 52,* 919–922.

Goode, W. J. (1956). *Women in divorce.* Glencoe, IL: Free Press.

Gordon, T. (1970). Parent effectiveness training. New York: Wyden.

Hetherington, M. E., Cox, M., and Cox, R. (1982). Effects of divorce on parents and children. In M. E. Lamb (ed.), *Non-traditional families.* Hillsdale, NJ: Erlbaum.

Jacobson, D. S. (1980). Stepfamilies. *Children Today, 9,* 2–6.

Johnson, H. C. (1980). Working with stepfamilies: Principles of practice. *Social Work, 25,* 304–308.

Jones, S. M. (1978). Divorce and remarriage: A new beginning, a new set of problems. *Journal of Divorce, 2,* 217–227.

Kargman, M. W. (1983). Stepchild support obligations of stepparents. *Family Relations, 32,* 321–238.

Kleinman, J., Rosenberg, E., and Whiteside, M. (1979). Common developmental tasks in forming reconstituted families. *Journal of Marriage and Family Therapy, 5,* 79–86.

Kompara, D. R. (1980). Difficulties in the socialization process of stepparenting. *Family Relations, 29,* 69–73.

Landis, J. T. (1962). A comparison of children from divorced and nondivorced unhappy marriages. *Family Life Coordinator, 11,* 61–65.

Lutz, P. (1983). The stepfamily: An adolescent perspective. *Family Relations, 32,* 367–375.

Meiselman, K. (1978). *Incest.* San Francisco: Jossey-Bass.

Messinger, L. (1976). Remarriage between divorced people with children from previous marriages: A proposal for preparation for remarriage. *Journal of Marriage and Family Counseling, 2,* 193–200.

Miller, S., Nunnally, E. W., and Wackman, D. B. (1975). *Alive and aware*. Minneapolis: Interpersonal Communication Programs.

Nelson, M., and Nelson, G. (1982). Problems of equity in a reconstituted family. A social exchange analysis. *Family Relations, 31*, 223–231.

Nye, F. I. (1957). Child adjustment in broken and in unhappy unbroken homes. *Marriage and Family Living, 19*, 356–361.

Oshman, H. P., and Manosevitz, M. (1976). Father absence: Effects of stepfathers on psychosocial development in males. *Developmental Psychology, 12*, 479–480.

Perkins, T. F., and Kahn, J. P. (1979). An empirical comparison of natural-father and stepfather family systems. *Family Process, 18*, 175–183.

Perlmutter, L. H., Engel, T., and Sager, C. J. The incest taboo: Loosened sexual boundaries in remarried families. *Journal of Sex and Marital Therapy, 8*, 83–96.

Rallings, E. M. (1976). The special role of stepfather. *Family Coordinator, 25*, 445–449.

Robinson, B. E. (in press). The contemporary American stepfather. *Family Relations*.

Roman, M., and Haddad, W. (1979). *The disposable parent: The case for joint custody*. New York: Penguin Books.

Roosevelt, R., and Lofas, J. (1976). *Living in step*. New York: Stein & Day.

Sager, C. J., Brown, H. S., Crohn, H., Engel, T., Rodstein, E., and Walker, L. (1983). *Treating the remarried family*. New York: Brunner/Mazel.

Sager, C. J., Walker, E., Brown, H. S., Crohn, H. M., and Rodstein, E. (1981). Improving functioning of the remarried family system. *Journal of Marital and Family Therapy, 1*, 3–13.

Santrock, J. W. (1972). The relations of type and onset of father absence to cognitive development. *Child Development, 43*, 455–469.

Santrock, J. W., Warshak, R., Lindbergh, C., and Meadows, L. (1982). Children's and parents' observed social behavior in stepfather families. *Child Development, 53*, 472–480.

Schulman, G. L. (1972). Myths that intrude on the adaptation of the stepfamily. *Social Casework, 53*, 131–139.

Skeen, P., Robinson, B. E., and Flake-Hobson, C. (1984). Blended families: Overcoming the Cinderella myth. *Young Children, 39*, 64–73.

Stepfamily Bulletin. (1980, Fall). New York: Human Sciences Press.

Stern, P. N. (1978). Stepfather families: Integration around child discipline. *Issues in Mental Health Nursing, 1*, 326–332.

Stinnett, N., and Walters, J. (1977). *Relationships in marriage and family*. New York: Macmillan.

Tessman, L. (1978). *Children of parting parents*. New York: Jason Aronson.

Thies, J. M. (1977, Summer). Beyond divorce: The impact of remarriage on children. *Journal of Clinical Child Psychology*, pp. 59–61.

Touliatos, J., and Lindholm, B. W. (1980). Teachers' perceptions of behavior problems in children from intact, single-parent and stepparent families. *Psychology in the Schools, 17*, 264–269.

Turnbull, S. K., and Turnbull, J. M. (1983). To dream the impossible dream: An agenda for discussion with stepparents. *Family Relations, 32*, 227–230.

Visher, E. B., and Visher, J. S. (1978a) Common problems of stepparents and their spouses. *American Journal of Orthopsychiatry, 48*, 252–262.

Visher, E. B., and Visher, J. S. (1978b). Major areas of difficulty for stepparent couples. *International Journal of Family Counseling, 6*, 70–80.

Visher, E. B., and Visher, J. S. (1979). *Stepfamilies: A guide to working with stepparents and stepchildren*. New York: Brunner/Mazel.

Visher, E. B., and Visher, J. S. (1982). Stepfamilies in the 80's. *Conciliation Courts Review, 20(1)*, 15–23.

Wald, E. (1981). *The remarried family: Challenge and promise*. New York: Family Service Association of America.

Wallerstein, J. S., and Kelly J. B. (1980). *Surviving the break-up: How children actually cope with divorce*. New York: Basic Books.

Wilson, K. L., Zurcher, L. A., McAdams, D. C., and Curtis, R. L. (1975). Stepfathers and stepchildren: An exploratory analysis from two national surveys. *Journal of marriage and the Family, 37*, 526–536.

PART VI

C. Intergenerational Relations

34

THE NATION'S CHILDREN:
KEY TO A SECURE RETIREMENT

Martha N. Ozawa
School of Social Work
Washington University

During the past decade, the United States has turned conservative in its commitment to social welfare spending, in part because of the public's disillusionment over many programs that started in the Great Society era of the 1960s and in part because of the public's sense of urgency in fostering economic growth. The recent ideological shift notwithstanding, this article argues that demographic shifts will force the United States to spend more—not fewer—tax dollars, not only for the growing elderly population but for the shrinking child population.

Indeed, public interest in developing the human capital in the nation's children should increase in coming years. As fewer and fewer babies relative to the total population are born in coming decades, and because social security benefits are financed essentially on a pay-as-you-go basis, the public will find it to its own interest to ensure that each child will become a more productive worker than his or her earlier counterpart so that future generations of retirees will be adequately provided for.

This article deals with such intergenerational issues. What are the demographic trends? What are the types of children being born who eventually will be called upon to support the baby-boom generation? Is there a case for a more focused public interest in children? What might be the strategies for developing the nation's children? What types of programs might be appropriate?

DEMOGRAPHIC TRENDS

Like many other industrialized nations, the United States will face profound demographic changes in coming decades. On all counts, the nation is aging rapidly. The median age, which was 30.6 years in 1982, is expected to reach 36.3 in the year 2000 and 41.6 in 2050. The proportion of persons age 65 and over will increase from the 1982 level of 11.6 percent to 13.0 percent in 2000 and to 21.8 percent in 2050.[1] Furthermore, the elderly themselves are aging. The segment 85 years of age and over is growing the fastest. By the year 2050, over 16 million people—or 5.2 percent of the projected population—will be 85 and over.[2]

The nation's ability to support the elderly would not be adversely affected if other age groups were growing equally in proportion. Unfortunately, this is not the case. Throughout this century, except for the two decades after World War II when the now famous baby-boom generation was born, the birthrate in the United States has been steadily declining.[3] As a result, children under 18 years of age constitute a decreasing proportion of the total population. In 1960, they consituted 35.7 percent but only 27.0 percent in 1982.[4] Projections indicate that they will be only 25.0 percent in the year 2000, 21.6 percent in 2030, and 20.9 percent in 2050.[5]

Some might argue that as long as the dependency ratio (the combined number of children and elderly persons per one hundred working-age persons) does not drastically increase, the growth in the aged population does not create a financial problem for the nation.[6] This argument holds only in part, however. In the future, per capita public expenditures for the elderly will have to increase because of the growing number of the old-old (those age 75 and over). Also, as argued later, per capita public expenditures for education and other related programs will have to increase to nurture each child to be an ever more productive worker. Thus, the problem is the changing composition of the dependent population: the aged will increasingly become a larger segment of it, while children will increasingly become a smaller segment.

With the declining birthrate, increasing life expectancy, and the increasing rate of early retirement, the ratio of workers to beneficiaries will decline.

From *New England Journal of Human Services*, 1986, 6(3): 12–19. Copyright © 1986 Osiris Press, Inc. Reprinted with permission.

The federal government, through the social security amendments of 1983, has set the stage for encouraging later retirement as well as for gradually raising the normal retirement age. However, private corporations and state and local governments that provide retirement pensions have yet to follow the federal government's lead in these regards. In the absence of a measurable change in employment practices, it is projected that when the baby-boom generation retires, each beneficiary (including those who receive disability or survivors' benefits) will have to be supported by only two workers compared with the current three. Put another way, by that time there will be thirty-eight elderly persons per one hundred working-age individuals compared with the current nineteen.[7] With such demographic changes, the tax burden of future workers will have to increase drastically or benefit levels will have to be lowered— unless children become more productive workers when they grow up than their counterparts were in previous generations.[8] Such a prediction will hold because social security benefits are, and undoubtedly will continue to be, financed essentially on a pay-as-you-go basis: that is, taxes on the earnings of workers in any given year will continue to be the main source of funds for retirees receiving benefits that year.

The financing of social security retirement benefits will be only part of the problem facing future generations of workers. The financing of medical care for the elderly is another important element. Expenditures for Medicare, for example, grew at an average annual rate of 17.7 percent between 1970 and 1982 and are projected to continue growing at an annual rate of 14.4 percent. The expenditures, $70 billion in 1982, are expected to reach $112 billion in 1988.[9]

Will future generations of workers be more productive and thus more able than the present one to bear the increasing financial burden of supporting the elderly? This question is hard to answer because the response depends on many uncertain factors, including future global economic changes. However, it can be answered in part by looking at the demographic shifts that are taking place within the population—the child population in particular—and also looking at the economic and familial living conditions under which children are being raised.

An increasing proportion of future generations of children will be nonwhite. In 1984, 18.4 percent of all children were nonwhite. The U.S. Bureau of the Census projects that 20.6 percent of children will be nonwhite by the year 2000, 24.0 percent by 2030,

and 25.2 percent by 2050. This disproportionate increase in nonwhite children reflects higher birthrates among nonwhite segments of the population and also anticipated future declines in infant mortality rates among nonwhites.[10] These data indicate that future retirees will increasingly depend on the earning capabilities of nonwhite workers. And because whites still will be expected to live longer, these nonwhites will be asked to support the predominantly white elderly.[11]

The problem is clear. As nonwhite children rapidly become more prominent in the child population—which is shrinking in relation to the total population—these nonwhite children will have to be just as productive as white children in earning capabilities, or even more so, in order to ensure that the average earnings of future generations of workers will be greater than those of previous generations. In this regard, the role of nonwhite children will indeed become crucial in ensuring old-age income security for the nation's elderly, and the nation's white elderly in particular.

No doubt, some nonwhite children will do as well as white children do in developing their human capital. For example, it is widely known that, in general, Chinese-American and Japanese-American children tend to perform better than white children in school. But in number, they will constitute only a small minority. With even lower birthrates than that of whites, these two groups will not significantly change projected average figures for nonwhites.[12] As long as blacks constitute a large proportion of the nonwhite propulation (82.0 percent in 1984 and projected to be 75.3 percent in 2030 and 73.4 percent in 2050), the focal point of interest should be placed on black children.[13]

Will black children be able to respond to the national call for boosting the average earnings of future workers by becoming productive adults? Past data and current trends indicate they probably will not. At the dawn of life, they are already handicapped. Black children are more likely than others to be born prematurely—the result primarily of lack of proper prenatal care—and this often leads to the development of major handicaps such as low IQ, hearing loss, and spastic disorders.[14] Also, the probability is high that they will be born out of wedlock. In 1982, 566 per 1,000 black infants were born out of wedlock compared with 120 per 1,000 for white infants.[15]

Whether born out of wedlock or not, many black children grow up with only a mother at home. In 1982, 41 percent of all black families were headed by females, compared with 13 percent of all white families.[16] If black mothers do not work, black children are probably destined to be "kids on welfare" with inadequate provison for food, shelter, and clothing. If black mothers work, black children probably are left to fend for themselves since many black unmarried mothers cannot earn enough to provide proper child care.

The unfortunate early childhood of many black children often leads to inadequate or poor performance at school. As a result, the high school dropout rate among black youths is much higher than among white youths.[17] Being a high school dropout and on welfare is a sure ticket to joining the ranks of unemployed youths. If black youths in such a predicament do find jobs, they may face job discrimination. A study shows that, other things being equal, youths from welfare families do much worse in the job market.[18]

Young black women face a double jeopardy. First, their job prospects are just as poor as those of young black men as a result of their childhood development at home and at school. Second, if they decide to try to develop a socially acceptable adult life through marriage, they find that there are not enough marriageable males to go around. Marriageable males are defined as males with employment. Within each age group, the number of employed males per one hundred females is much smaller for black women than for white women, and the difference between the two has been widening.[19] An alternative for these young black women would be to have children out of wedlock and establish an independent household, an option in part facilitated by Aid to Families with Dependent Children (AFDC). As shown by a study by Bane, it seems that this is exactly what many black women do, start a new life cycle with the same problems as the old one.[20]

The job market for uneducated blacks is expected to become tougher in the future. While blatant job discrimination against blacks no longer occurs, thanks to civil rights laws enacted since the 1960s, blacks will still suffer from the consequences of structural changes taking place in the world's economy. Here in the United States, service sectors employing both skilled and unskilled workers are expanding, but employment opportunities in manufacturing industries are shrinking.[21] This implies that having a well-paid blue-collar job—which has been one important avenue to becoming a middle-class family—is rapidly closing for many blacks.[22]

The foregoing discussion indicates that future cohorts of the elderly—that is, today's and tomorrow's working generations—should have reason to worry. Unlike conditions in the past when social security contributions guaranteed old-age income and health security because more than an adequate number of workers were contributing to support the beneficiaries, in the future the degree to which retirees will obtain such security will decline. Under pay-as-you-go financing, the degree to which they obtain such security is a function of the ratio of workers to beneficiaries—and this ratio will continue to decline. One way to make up for such a predicament is to make sure that each future generation of workers is more productive than the one that preceded it. For that to occur, the nation needs to develop greater human capital in each of its children, especially black and other nonwhite children.

THE CASE FOR CHILDREN

Socialization of children through nurturing and education has been considered mainly as a private responsibility and prerogative. However, when the people of a country express their desire for an outcome different from what private efforts have produced in this regard, then public interest in the development of children emerges. When positive externalities are anticipated from public intervention, then the public considers it appropriate to justify public spending for programs deemed necessary to accomplish the objective. Thus, the idea of developing human capital in children through public subsidies begins to emerge.[23]

There are two reasons why the public may come to accept such an idea. One reason is the intergenerational linkage in financing social security programs for the elderly, which we already have discussed. The other reason is the declining private interest in having children; some couples prefer to have none at all, while others prefer to have only a few. In the aggregate, American women currently are not giving birth to enough children to sustain a stable population.

A few observations suggest sources of the declining private interest in having children. First, industrialization has reduced parents' economic benefits from having children. Before the United States became highly industrialized, children worked side by side with their parents in farming and in cottage industries. Furthermore, having children was a kind of insurance against old-age misery and income insecurity. No longer. Like other industrialized societies, the United States institutionalized—that is, socialized—the way one ensures old-age income and

health security by developing social security programs. This means that individuals no longer necessarily need their own children for such purposes. All
they need are someone's children. In short, since the
private financial linkage between elderly parents and
adult children has been broken through establishing
social security and related programs, private economic incentives for having children have diminished. However, educational and health care costs
for raising children are increasing. Of course, all
this does not negate the fact that many people desire
to have children for noneconomic reasons. The point
is, however, that there seems to be a diminishing
economic return for the increasing costs incurred in
raising one's own children.

One can also observe that women are increasingly placing the primary locus of life satisfaction
and aspiration not in raising children but in competing and succeeding in the labor market. Work gives
them opportunities to test their marketable skills,
measure the economic value of what they can offer,
develop social relationships at the workplace, and
establish economic independence. In a paid-
work-oriented society, the workplace is ultimately
where women find their identity as individuals. As
women become more successful in earning higher
wages, their preference for work outside of the home
over raising children at home further increases because the implicit price of (or forgone earnings due
to) raising children increases accordingly.

This view is supported, in part, by research
findings: the number of children born to women is
inversely related to women's education; the desired
number of children is inversely related to education;
and highly educated women are more likely to succeed in having the desired number of children than
are less educated women.[24] All these indicators
seem intertwined with the fact that birthrates are
lower among white women than among black
women. Currently, only 1,700 children are born to
each 1,000 white women, while 2,300 children are
born to each 1,000 black women. Among all races
together, only 1,800 children are born to each 1,000
women, 300 children fewer than necessary to sustain
a stable population in the long run. Even with the
immigrants projected to come to the United States,
the nation will barely be able to maintain its population after the year 2030.[25]

Women who decide to have children are finding
it increasingly difficult to raise them. Working
mothers—the fastest growing segment in the female
labor force—have to divide their attention between

paid work and housework. Indications are that their
husbands are not sharing household chores commen-
surate with mothers' time lost at home because of
work outside of the home.[26] To many mothers, the
responsibilties of both motherhood and paid work
are too much to carry. Children suffer accordingly.

Children of divorced, separated, or never married parents do worse. In addition to the fact that
they do not receive the parental care and guidance
that two parents might be able to provide, many of
them suffer from a growing new phenomenon: the
feminization of poverty. In 1982, 47.8 percent of
female-headed families with children were poor. All
this becomes part of the grim experience of the nation's children. The incidence of poverty among
children has been steadily on the rise since 1970,
from 13.8 percent to 21.3 percent in 1982. This increase is in stark contrast to the enormous improvement in the poverty rate for the nation's elderly:
24.5 percent in 1970 down to 14.6 percent in 1982.[27]

Such facts lead us to believe that there is a case
for establishing public interest in developing the nation's children. For its perpetuation, the macro system requires a birthrate at a certain level. The
number of children that women desire, however,
clearly seems to be smaller than what the macro system requires. Also, the financial and other burdens
placed on individual families to raise children do not
seem in balance with the private benefits they derive
from having children. These conditions seem to justify the consideration of public subsidies for people
to bear and raise children.

During the past fifty years, the government had
taken over a great deal of the financial responsibility
for the nation's elderly by enacting social security
and other related programs. A study by Lampman
and Smeeding shows that the level of transfers
through government programs increased from 2.8
percent of the nation's personal income in 1935 to
11.2 percent of such income in 1979, while the level
of transfers through interfamily giving declined from
6.5 percent in 1935 to 5.0 percent in 1979.[28] Out of
these increasing public social welfare expenditures,
an ever larger portion is devoted to supporting the
elderly. This is indicated by the increasing percentage of federal outlays that goes to the elderly—from
21 percent of total federal outlays in 1971 to 27 percent in 1983, and it is expected to reach 35 percent
by the year 2000 and 65 percent by 2020.[29]

These data indicate that the public accepts the
idea that the government has a major responsibility
for ensuring income and health security for the el-

derly. To the extent that the public has accepted this idea, it will inevitably have to accept the corollary concept that financial responsibility for raising the nation's children rests, in part, with the government. As the demographic distribution becomes even more skewed, with an increasingly larger proportion of elderly and an increasingly smaller proportion of children, public interest in taking such a policy stance is expected to grow.

FUTURE STRATEGIES

If the public realizes that the development of children is, in part, a public responsibility, then what strategies should the government take? It is hard to suggest a monolithic approach. What one can do is clearly state the objectives of government in subsidizing the costs of raising children, determine from the experiences of the past two decades which aspects of social welfare spending are acceptable to the public, and develop programs—incorporating public preferences—to accomplish the objectives set forth.

On the basis of the foregoing discussion, one can set forth the following two objectives: (1) encourage all families to have more children, regardless of their financial backgrounds, and (2) develop to the fullest potential the human capital of nonwhite children. These two objectives are not mutually exclusive.

LESSONS FROM THE PAST

In developing subsidy programs for the nation's children, it is important to make sure that the government does not repeat past mistakes. That is, if policymakers develop programs in a way that goes against the dominant sentiment of the public, they cannot gain public acceptance for initiating such programs, let alone support for continuing them. Thus, policymakers should understand those aspects of social welfare spending the public supports and those aspects it does not support. What aspects does it like? What aspects does it object to? Past experiences give us a clue to the answers to these questions.

One phenomenon that has been reaffirmed through the Great Society experiences of the 1960s and their aftermath is that the public upholds the merit of political equality and legal equality. It supports government intervention, if necessary, to make sure that all citizens have an equal opportunity to participate in political processes and to make sure

that people are treated equally under the law. This underscores the importance the public attaches to equality of opportunity to pursue one's happiness. In other words, the public wishes every person to have a fair shot at developing his or her own life.

On the other hand, the American public is opposed, in principle, to government intervention that aims to achieve economic equality. Upholding the principle of economic equality necessitates income redistribution through government programs and, more important, connotes equality of results—which goes against the traditional belief in equal opportunity. The public believes that the fairest and most efficient way to distribute income is through the mechanism of the free market. Government intervention in redistributing income results in a distortion of income distribution based on merit. The market as a mechanism of income distribution enjoys higher prestige in this country than in any other industrialized country.[30] Many programs developed through the War on Poverty underscored the importance of equal opportunity as their program goals. Head Start, Upward Bound, Follow Through, the Teacher Corps and Title I of the Aid to Education Act, the Job Corps, the Neighborhood Youth Corps, the Manpower Development and Training Act, and the Work Incentive Program are examples of such programs. Also, the public's consistent support for financing education in public schools and state colleges and universities reflects its willingness to provide the nation's children with a fair chance to develop their human capital.

Past experiences also indicate that the public supports programs that pool resources from contributors and enable them to face life's contingencies such as retirement, disability, unemployment, and death. Thus, social insurance programs of all types—Old-Age, Survivors, and Disability Insurance (OASDI) in particular—have expanded despite the resurgence in recent years of conservative political ideology. Social insurance expenditures as a percentage of the gross national product (GNP) increased from 3.3 percent in 1966 to 8.0 percent in 1983.[31] Public perception notwithstanding, these contributory programs are powerful vehicles both for equalizing income distribution and for preventing many families—especially the elderly—from becoming poor.[32] No matter. Most people consider these programs as insurance programs for drawing benefits when they meet with a crisis identified under the law rather than as programs for redistributing income.

Past experiences suggest that public support is relatively strong for welfare programs if they are meant for specific purposes, such as providing food and housing. The American public seems to have little tolerance for chronic conditions of starvation, homelessness, and lack of needed medical care. Thus, it seems willing to compensate needy families temporarily for these deficiencies so they will "have a second chance."[33] However, pure income poverty is largely tolerated.[34] The public's positive attitude toward in-kind welfare programs and its negative attitude toward means-tested cash assistance programs are clearly reflected in the differential trends in expenditures for these two types of programs. Expressed as a percentage of the GNP, outlays for Medicaid, aid for food and nutrition, housing aid, and energy assistance have steadily expanded. The expansion of Medicaid has been phenomenal. In contrast, outlays for means-tested cash assistance programs have been steadily declining since 1976.[35]

Looking back over the past two decades, some now say that the public was not behind President Johnson's attempt to eradicate poverty. They argue that lack of sufficient income is one's own making and thus is a just desert.[36] In that sense, the War on Poverty was a presidential war, not a national war.

A clear set of public attitudes toward social welfare spending emerges from this brief review of past experiences. The public believes in the idea of equal opportunity as a goal for government spending; it emphasizes the idea of contributing to a system before receiving benefits—that is, the concept that people have to invest their money if they wish to receive benefits later; and it believes that social welfare programs should have specific purposes other than eradicating poverty. It seems constructive to have these ideas in mind in developing subsidy programs for children.

SUBSIDY PROGRAMS FOR CHILDREN

Given prevailing public attitudes toward social welfare spending, how should the government approach the development of programs aiming to accomplish the two objectives set forth? First, it seems obvious that the traditional welfare approach would not only be inappropriate but also counterproductive toward accomplishing the objectives. The issue at hand is how the government should (1) facilitate the development of human capital to the fullest potential in nonwhite children and, at the same time, (2) encourage all families to have more children by subsidizing the costs of raising children. The target of the subsidies would not be just poor children but also nonpoor children. Also, since these two objectives are associated with different, although not mutually exclusive, segments of the child population, a single program would not be able to bring about the desired outcomes. In short, several programs with specific purposes, all taking a universal orientation, would be required.

With these factors in mind, one can explore a few basic programs. For the purpose of developing human capital in nonwhite children, social provisions for pre- and postnatal care, basic medical services in childhood, and quality education might be appropriate. To make pre- and postnatal care available, the government might contract with private physicians to provide needed services. Or it might hire physicians for this specific purpose.

Basic medical care might also be provided as an integral part of the system of public education. The provision of quality education might require the restructuring of funding mechanisms for public education. It might mean that state governments should take a major role in financing public education so that per pupil expenditures would be more uniform within states. The federal government might then provide funds to minimize interstate variations because of differences in states' capabilities to finance public education. (Of course, more funds alone would not guarantee quality education for nonwhite children. However, since the inner-city schools many nonwhite children attend are now poorly financed, more adequate funding would at least be a partial answer to developing human capital among nonwhite children.) A nutritional program for preschool children and school children might be an appropriate supplement to these programs. It is expected that such programs would help nonwhite children, especially those in low-income families, to develop their capabilities more fully than they do at present because these children are now suffering from a lack of the services these programs would provide if implemented.

However, the benefits from these programs by themselves would not seem to offer much of an incentive for middle-class families to have more children. Since a major concern of parents in deciding the number of children they desire seems closely related to the anticipated high costs of college education, policymakers might consider the provision of tax deductibility for the tuition and fees parents pay for their children's college education. The higher the income bracket, the higher the value of such a provision as long as the federal tax law maintains progressive marginal tax rates.

To meet the ongoing costs of raising children, policymakers might also consider the provisions of a refundable tax credit and exemption for children. The value of a refundable tax credit in relation to family income would be greater for low-income families than for high-income families.[37] The value of an exemption in relation to family income would be greater for high-income families than for low-income families, again assuming the federal income tax law retains progressive marginal tax rates. The combination of tax credits and exemptions would facilitate a simultaneous, vertical and horizontal redistribution of income to families with children. In a sense, it would take a double-decker approach to income redistribution through taxation: a refundable tax credit would ensure a minimum floor of income for all children regardless of the level of family income; an exemption would result in tax savings on account of children, the value of which would go up as family income goes up. Tax expenditures for both credits and exemptions for children would be paid for by childless individuals and childless families. These monetary measures might well influence the decision of parents—including middle-class parents—who, for economic reasons, desire only a small number of children.

How does this suggested package of programs stand up against the public attitudes toward social welfare spending that have been evident in the past? Would it appeal to the public? Let's recall the key concepts involving public attitudes. They are equality of opportunity, investment, and functional specificity. The provisions for pre- and postnatal care, basic medical care, nutritional benefits, and quality education all strike as programs for ensuring equal opportunity for nonwhite children to grow to their fullest potential. They are programs for equalizing opportunities—not equalizing results. At the same time, they are all related to specific purposes. Even the monetary provisions for tax deductibility of tuition and fees, for a refundable tax credit, and for an exemption should appeal to the public, especially to parents. Men and women in today's labor force should look at these monetary provisions, as well as human-capital development provisions, as an investment for their own old-age security. In contrast, working people—and other taxpayers too—should consider public spending for means-tested cash assistance programs, such as AFDC, as money spent

with no return. They should understand that the public spending for the programs suggested here would help bring about their own well-being in old age.

IMPLICATIONS

What might be the implications of adopting subsidy programs for children? Can the nation afford them? What about current welfare programs? Would they be eliminated? To what extent would poor families benefit from such subsidy programs for children? What might be the effects on the private sector? Even in an affluent country like the United States, money does not grow on trees. If the government decided to adopt programs such as those explored in this article, many current welfare programs targeted to nonaged segments of the population obviously would have to be either curtailed or eliminated. Furthermore, laws, rules, and regulations governing social security and public and private pensions would have to be continuously changed so that the elderly past age 65 whose physical and health conditions have vastly improved over the years are given incentives to keep working.

More important, before public consensus for subsidy programs for children could be built up, the government—through public debate and hearings—would need to shift the philosophical foundation for social welfare spending for nonaged segments from an antipoverty-oriented welfare mentality to an investment-oriented growth mentality. When the government has succeeded in transforming the philosophical base, then public support for funding subsidy programs might involve more than the zero-sum game. That is, the public might assess the social benefits from these subsidy programs more highly than it assesses the social benefits from current welfare programs. If this occurred, then the public would not necessarily consider children's subsidy programs merely as replacements for current welfare programs. Consequently, it is entirely possible that the public would be willing to commit more public funds to children's subsidy programs than what is spent on current programs.

Moreover, poor families with children might benefit more from these suggested programs than from the current programs. Past experience shows that the poor have benefited more from programs that are not specifically targeted to them than from means-tested programs. This has occurred because the scope of nonmeans-tested programs is much greater than the scope of means-tested programs.[38]

Thus, the argument follows that the universal-type programs discussed here, if widely supported by the public, might ultimately be more effective both as antipoverty instruments and as income-equalization measures. Past experience indicates that it would be prudent for policymakers to develop and expand nonmeans-tested (universal-type) programs if they really intend to increase the living standards of the poor.[39] Beyond the short-term forecast, the long-term benefits from these programs that would accrue to beneficiary families and the public could be substantial. However, measuring such benefits would require a long-range study involving behavioral changes; this would take considerable time to carry out. Therefore, for the moment, we can only hypothesize about the net long-range effect of children's subsidy programs such as those explored in this article and wait to see whether future developments substantiate our hypothesis.

Finally, as public interest in children is firmly established through implementing governmental programs such as those we have discussed, the private sector might take a more progressive stance in employment practices. For example, corporations and nonprofit organizations employing women with children might decide to provide flexible hours for these women and absorb the cost of day care for the children. Some employers might make such a move for economic reasons, others for projecting a socially responsible image to the public. In short, as public interest in children increases, employers might consider it in their own long-term interest to move in this direction.

CONCLUSIONS

One important consequence of adopting subsidy programs for children is that the target of social welfare spending for the nonaged shifts from poor families to children. Such a transformation in target

population is not inconceivable. Many European countries have been consolidating their programs so that social welfare programs and tax policies create a horizontal redistribution of income from childless families to families with children.[40] Japan, a late-comer in social welfare spending, has accelerated its spending since the 1970s, not for welfare programs but for programs that deal with the development of children—those who are physically handicapped, mentally retarded, or fatherless.[41] Japan and the European countries that are switching the emphasis of their social welfare programs to children are going through profound demographic shifts. It seems they have already recognized the demographic imperative—that is, the mandatory force of population changes—in social welfare spending. In the main, the demographic imperative presents to all these countries one major change to cope with: the increasing proportion of the elderly in relation to the total population.

The United States, however, will have to face two major population changes, both accelerating in the coming decades: (1) the increasing proportion of the elderly—with the concomitant shrinking of the number of workers in relation to the number of elderly—that most other industrialized nations are encountering; and (2) the increasing number of nonwhite children in proportion to the number of white children. This means that we in the United States will have to do more than switch our focus to our children. We will also have to give extra-special attention to nonwhite children who, up to now in many instances, have not had a chance to develop to their fullest potential.

Today and in the coming years, can we be motivated to invest the time, know-how, and physical and financial resources in all our children so they can have a fuller opportunity to become healthy, productive citizens? Our future, as well as theirs, depends on how we meet this challenge.

Notes

1. U.S. Bureau of the Census, Current Population Reports, Series P-25, No. 952, *Projections of the Population of the United States, by Age, Sex, and Race: 1983 to 2080* (Washington, D.C.: U.S. Government Printing Office, 1984), Tables C and F, pp. 6 and 8.
2. Ibid., Table 6, p. 92.
3. In 1910, the birth rate expressed as the number of live births per 1,000 population was 30.1; it was down to 16.0 in 1982. See U.S. Bureau of the Census, *Statistical Abstract of the United States: 1984,* 104th edition (Washington, D.C.: U.S. Government Printing Office, 1983), Table 83, p. 63.
4. Ibid., Table 30, p. 31.
5. U.S. Bureau of the Census, Current Population Reports, Series P-25, op. cit., Table F, p. 8.
6. See, for example, William Crown, "The Prospective Burden of an Aging Population," *Of Current Interest,* 4:1 (October 1984): pp. 1–3.

7. U.S. Bureau of the Census, Current Population Reports, Series P-25, op. cit., Table D, p. 6.
8. This can be clearly argued on the basis of mathematical relationships between demographic composition, tax rate, and benefit level. The mathematics of average benefits for each cohort can be expressed as follows:

$$t \cdot Nw \cdot W = Nb \cdot B; \text{ therefore, } B = t \cdot \frac{Nw}{Nb} \cdot W,$$

in which total tax receipts = total benefits; tax receipts = payroll tax rate (t) times number of workers (Nw) times average covered earnings (W); total benefits = the number of beneficiaries (Nb) times average benefits (B). See Sylvester J. Schieber, *Social Security: Perspectives on Preserving the System* (Washington, D.C.: Employee Benefit Research Institute, 1982), p. 136.
9. U.S. Congress, Congressional Budget Office, *Changing the Structure of Medical Benefits: Issues and Options* (Washington, D.C.: Congressional Budget Office, 1983), pp. 1–2.
10. U.S. Bureau of the Census, *Statistical Abstract of the United States: 1984*, op cit., Table 84, p. 63; and U.S. Bureau of the Census, Current Population Reports, Series P-25, op. cit., Tables B-2A, B-2B, and B-2C, pp. 141–44.
11. The elderly will be overrepresented by white elderly persons for the foreseeable future. In 1984, 90.5 percent of all elderly persons were white, although only 85.5 percent of all persons were white; in 2030, the respective proportions are projected to be 84.5 percent and 79.3 percent, and in 2050, 80.9 percent and 77.0 percent. See U.S. Bureau of the Census, Current Population Reports, Series P-25, op. cit., Table 6, pp. 39–106.
12. The rank-order of fertility rates, from high to low, by ethnicity is as follows: Hispanic; black; white, excluding Hispanic; Chinese-American; Japanese-American. See Victor R. Fuchs, *How We Live: An Economic Perspective on Americans from Birth to Death* (Cambridge, Mass.: Harvard University Press, 1983), p. 63.
13. U.S. Bureau of the Census, Current Population Reports, Series P-25, op. cit., Table 6, pp. 39–106.
14. For instance, in 1982, among blacks 12.4 percent of infants at birth weighed less than 2,500 grams (5 pounds 8 ounces) compared with 5.6 percent among whites. See *Monthly Vital Statistics Report*, 33:6, Supplement (September 1984), Table 6, p. 29. Also see S. P. Kumar, E. K. Anday, L. M. Sacks, R. Y. Ting, and M. Delivoria-Papadopoulos, "Follow-up Studies of Very Low Birth Weight Infants (1,250 grams or less) Born and Treated within a Perinatal Center," *Pediatrics 66* (September 1980): 438–44; Ronald S. Cohen et al., "Favorable Results of Neonatal Intensive Care for Very Low-Birth-Weight Infants," *Pediatrics 67* (1982): 621–25; and U.S. House of Representatives, Select Committee on Children, Youth, and Families, *Children, Youth, and Families, 1983: A Year-End Report*, 98th Cong., 2nd sess. (Washington, D.C.: U.S. Government Printing Office, 1984), Tables 1 and 2, pp. 131–32.
15. *Monthly Vital Statistics Report*, op. cit., Table 17, p. 30.
16. U.S. Bureau of the Census, *Statistical Abstract of the United States: 1984*, op cit., Table 56, p. 46.
17. "State Education Statistics," *Education Week*, (January 18, 1984), pp. 12–13.
18. Richard B. Freeman and H. J. Holzer, "The Crisis of Black Youth Joblessness," *The Public Interest*, forthcoming, cited by Nathan Glazer, "Education and Training Programs and Poverty: Or, Opening the Black Box" (Paper delivered at the Conference on Poverty and Policy: Retrospect and Prospects, sponsored by the Institute for Research on Poverty and the U.S. Department of Health and Human Services, Williamsburg, Va., December 6–8, 1984), 35.
19. For instance, within the age group of 20–24 years, the number of employed males available for 100 females was identical for white and black groups, but the numbers started to diverge in the late 1970s. In 1980, there were only 51 black employed males per 100 black females compared with 70 white employed males per 100 white females. See William Julius Wilson and Katherine M. Neckerman, "Poverty and Family Structure: The Widening Gap between Evidence and Public Policy Issues" (Paper delivered at the Conference on Poverty and Policy: Retrospect and Prospects, sponsored by the Institute for Research on Poverty and the U.S. Department of Health and Human Services, Williamsburg, Va., December 6–8, 1984) Figure 4, 68.
20. Mary Jo Bane, "Household Composition and Poverty" (Paper deliverd at the Conference on Poverty and Policy: Retrospect and Prospects, sponsored by the Institute for Research on Poverty and the U.S. Department of Health and Human Services, Williamsburg, Va., December 6–8, 1984). Also see Mary Jo Bane and David T. Ellwood, "Single Mothers and Their Living Arrangements," working paper supported by a U.S. Department of Health and Human Services grant, Contract No. HHS-100-82-0038.
21. For further discussion, see Robert Z. Lawrence, "Sectorial Shifts and the Size of the Middle Class," *The Brookings Review* (Fall 1984): 3-11; and Robert Z. Lawrence, *Can American Compete?* (Washington, D.C.: The Brookings Institution, 1984).
22. Barry Bluestone, "Whither the Middle Class? Labor Market Prospects for the Decade Ahead" (Paper presented at Annual Program Meeting, Council of Social Work Education, Washington, D.C., February 21, 1985).
23. For theoretical discussion on this, see Harvey S. Rosen, *Public Finance*, Chapters 6 and 7 (Homewood, Ill.: Richard D. Irwin, 1985), pp. 98–149.
24. Robert T. Michael, "Education and the Derived Demand for Children," *Journal of Political Economy 81*, (March-April 1972: S128-64; Robert J. Willis, "A New Approach to the Economic Theory of Fertility Behavior," *Journal of Political Economy 81* (March-April 1973): S14-64.
25. U.S. Bureau of the Census, Current Population Reports, Series P-25, op. cit., Tables A-4, A-5, and A-6, pp. 130–32.

26. C. Russell Hill and Frank P. Stafford, "Parental Care of Children: Time Diary Estimate of Quantity, Predictability, and Variety," *Journal of Human Services 15* (Spring 1980): 219–39.

27. U.S. Bureau of the Census, Current Population Reports, Series P-60, No. 144, *Characteristics of the Population Below the Poverty Level: 1982* (Washington, D.C.: U.S. Government Printing Office, 1984), Tables 1 and 18, pp. 7 and 18.

28. Robert J. Lampman and Timothy Smeeding, "Interfamily Transfers as Alternatives to Government Transfers to Persons," *Review of Income and Wealth,* Series 29, No. 1 (March 1983): 45–66.

29. U.S. Bureau of the Census, *Statistical Abstract of the United States: 1984,* op. cit. Tables 604 and 616, pp. 367 and 376; and Alan Pifer, "Final Thoughts," *Annual Report 1982* (New York: Carnegie Corporation of New York, 1982), p. 7.

30. Gary Burtless, "Public Spending for the Poor: Trends, Prospects, and Economic Limits" (Paper delivered at the Conference on Poverty and Policy: Retrospect and Prospects, sponsored by the Institute for Research on Poverty and the U.S. Department of Health and Human Services, Williamsburg, Va., December 6–8, 1984), 55.

31. Ibid., 27.

32. Ibid., 21; Martha N. Ozawa, "Income Redistribution and Social Security," *Social Service Review,* 50:2 (June 1976): 209–23; Martha N. Ozawa, "Distributive Effects of Survivors Insurance Benefits and Public Assistance," *Social Service Review,* 58:4 (December 1984): 604–21; and Sheldon Danziger and Robert Plotnick, "Demographic Change, Government Transfers, and Income Distribution," *Monthly Labor Review 100* (April 1977): 7–11.

33. Hugh Heclo, "The Political Foundations of Anti-Poverty Policy (Paper delivered at the Conference on Poverty and Policy: Retrospect and Prospects, sponsored by the Institute for Research on Poverty and the U.S. Department of Health and Human Services, Williamsburg, Va., December 6–8, 1984), 38.

34. Burtless, op. cit., 13.

35. Ibid., Figures 2 and 3, pp. 11 and 14.

36. See, for example, ibid.

37. For more detailed discussion on this, see Martha N. Ozawa, "Income Security: The Case of Nonwhite Children," *Social Work,* 28:5 (September-October 1983): 347–53.

38. Ozawa, "Income Redistribution and Social Security," op. cit.

39. Heclo, op. cit., p. 26.

40. See Alfred J. Kahn and Sheila B. Kamerman, *Income Transfers for Families with Children: An Eight-Country Study* (Philadelphia, Pa.: Temple University Press, 1983); and Sheila B. Kamerman and Alfred J. Kahn, eds., *Essays on Income Transfers and Related Programs in Eight Countries* (New York: Cross-National Studies, Columbia University School of Social Work, 1983).

41. See *Shakai Hosho Nenpo, 1984* (Tokyo: Sorifu, Shakai Hosho Seido Shingikai Jimukyoku, 1984); Shakai Hosho Kenkyujo, ed., *Shakai Hukushi Kaikakuron, I, Shakai Hukushi Seisaku no Tenboo* (Tokyo: Tokyo Daigaku Shippankai, 1984); and Shakai Hosho Kenkyujo, ed., *Shakai Hukushi Kaikakuron, II, Shakai Hukushi Jissen no Kadai* (Tokyo: Tokyo Daigaku Shippankai, 1984).

35

THE MID/LATE LIFE GENERATION GAP:
ADULT CHILDREN WITH AGING PARENTS

Jane E. Myers
Department of Counselor Education
University of Florida

The changing demography of America's population has received increasing attention in both the popular and professional literature. Increases in life spans have created tremendous potential for intergenerational and multigenerational relationships. Industrialization, rapid technological change, mobility, and a host of other factors have combined to create new relationship patterns in U.S. society. At the same time that there are more people with potentially more types of interactions, there are fewer role models for successful relationships, especially multigenerational family relationships. The resulting ambiguity and fear is reflected in the popular media, particularly when there is an attempt to help prepare adults for "The Hardest Decision" (Badgwell, 1986–1987) with respect to their aging parents. Most adults simply have not been adequately prepared for assuming greater responsibility for their parents (Johnson and Spence, 1982).

For most older persons, aging occurs in a family context (Morgan, 1981). Only 4 percent to 5 percent of the people 60 and above reside in long-term care institutions, 10 percent to 15 percent are largely homebound because of physical or emotional conditions, and 80 percent or more are able to function independently. Yet, between 80 percent and 90 percent die in institutional settings, including hospitals (Butler and Lewis, 1983).

Thus, the fears reflected in the media and discussed among adults are not totally unfounded—at some point, most adults are or will be faced with infirmity, disability, and decisions with respect to the aging and eventual death of their parents. Most are unprepared for the emotional trauma that ensues (Johnson and Spence, 1982). Many are seeking counseling assistance, but few counselors are trained to provide the help needed. This article is an initial step toward filling the gap in the information available to help counselors deal with adults and their aging parents, both personally and professionally.

A LOOK AT AGING PARENTS

Older people are sometimes viewed as the most heterogeneous of any population subgroup. Attempts to describe them reflect demographic analyses of characteristics of older persons as a whole. In this section some of the psychosocial concerns of older persons are reviewed, including normative developmental issues and tasks of the later stages of life.

About two-thirds of America's 25.5 million older persons are female. More than one-half (51 percent) of these older women are widows, whereas only 22 percent of older men are widowers. Only 17 percent of older men live alone or with nonrelatives, compared to 43 percent of older women. More than one-sixth of the elderly population are poor by federal standards, with female and minority elderly persons overrepresented in the total. The median income of older families in 1980 was less than $12,881, compared to $22,548 for families with household heads under the age of 65 (Brotman, 1982).

The average life expectancy at birth for women is now 77.2 years, compared to 69.5 years for men. Older men who endure physical declines usually are cared for by their wives. Older women depend on the support of children and other family members or institutional care.

It has been well established that the needs of older persons are the same *type* as the needs of persons of any age, but there is a substantial difference in *degree* (Myers, 1984). The needs of older persons tend to increase with advancing age; at the same time, financial, personal, and interpersonal resources decrease. A primary need of older persons is to maintain their independence (Butler and Lewis,

From the *Journal of Counseling and Development*, 1988, 66:331–335. Copyright © American Association of Counseling and Development. Reprinted by permission.

303

1983). Life satisfaction—a feeling of general well-being—correlates highly with this variable and also with perceived health, income, education, marital status, and interactions with family members (Lohman, 1977). Moreover, those older persons having a purpose in life, who report feeling useful, experience greater life satisfaction.

Harris and Associates (1974), reporting on an extensive national survey, noted that only 12 percent of older persons report feeling very lonely. Most older persons both depend on and are largely satisfied with family relationships. Approximately 83 percent of older men and 57 percent of older women live with their families.

Life span developmental theorists have viewed the major life tasks of aging largely outside the context of multigenerational family relationships. Havighurst (1972), for example, listed the developmental tasks of aging as follows: adjusting to decreased physical strength and health, adjusting to retirement and reduced income, adjusting to death of a spouse, establishing an explicit affiliation with one's age group, meeting social and civic obligations, and establishing satisfactory physical living arrangements.

Erikson (1950) discussed the central psychosocial crisis as one of integrity versus despair, concentrating on the older person's inner life. In his opinion, individuals need to achieve a lifetime view of relative congruence between (a) their real and ideal selves and (b) their goals and strivings and their accomplishments. Little is said about relationships with adult children and other family members, yet these persons are a major source of support and interaction for older persons.

A LOOK AT ADULT CHILDREN

Adult children of aging parents can be young, middle aged, or, increasingly, even old themselves. Because most are in "mid-life," this section focuses on persons in the middle-age range of 35 to 55. Middle-aged persons have been called the "command generation," because they occupy most societal positions of leadership and authority. They also have been called the "sandwich generation," with their needs sandwiched between those of their adolescent children, who seek increasing independence, and those of their aging parents, who are faced with a loss of independence. "Middlescence" is seen as a transition time comparable to that of adolescence, but with a major difference: Adolescents move toward increased status, whereas middle-aged persons move toward decreased status (Fried, cited in Dobson and Dobson, 1985).

Demographically, middle-aged person constitute approximately 20 percent of the U.S. population, compared to almost 12 percent of those over 65 (Van Hoose and Worth, 1982). The ratio of women to men varies with each age group, beginning in the mid-20s with 101 women to 100 men and increasing to 258 women per 100 men by the age of 80 (Butler and Lewis, 1983). Most middle-aged persons are married, living with families, and experiencing the peak income of their lives.

Middle age also is a peak time for independence and career mobility. It is the time when personal mortality becomes apparent, prompted by normative signs of physical changes and declines. A shift in time perspective occurs (Neugarten, 1968), and people begin to see their lives less as the time since birth and more in terms of time remaining until death. The realization that life is finite prompts what Buehler (1967) referred to as the self-assessment phase of life. It is a time for evaluation, reevaluation, stock taking, and planning for the future. The recognition of personal aging and declining reserves of energy creates a need to examine lifelong goals and the extent to which they have been reached. For some, the transitions of mid-life lead to now-or-never decisions affecting family, career, spiritual, and personal aspects of life.

Once children leave the home, couples can again relate as individuals. Intimacy surfaces as an issue, and numerous challenges to mid-life marriages result (Van Hoose and Worth, 1982). Women in particular may enjoy new-found freedoms from child care and housekeeping responsibilities and may begin to pursue independent educational, career, and leisure pursuits.

Havighurst (1972) described middle age in terms of seven challenging developmental tasks: (a) achieving social and civic responsibilities, (b) establishing and maintaining an economic standard of living, (c) assisting teenage children to become responsible adults, (d) developing adult leisure time activities, (e) relating oneself to one's spouse as a person, (f) accepting the physiological changes of middle age, and (g) adjusting to aging parents. Erikson (1950) echoed many of these tasks, describing the central psychosocial crisis as generativity versus self-absorption, leaving something of value to the next generation versus becoming invested in purely personal goals.

The focus of development for people in the middle generation is on their relationships with those who are younger. Middle-aged persons also must look ahead, relate to older family members, and assist them in meeting the transitions of later life successfully. Central issues for both generations revolve around independence—achieving, maintaining, or losing it—and around family relationships and supports.

ADULT CHILDREN AND AGING PARENTS

American families are experiencing rapid changes, which Morgan (1981) summarized in two categories: demographic changes and social role changes. These changes are explored below, including a discussion of myths and realities of mid-life and late-life family relationships, family stress situations and responses, and family relationship patterns.

DEMOGRAPHIC CHANGES IN THE FAMILY

Treas (1983) cited research in which questions are raised as to whether multigenerational households have ever been the norm in U.S. society, simply because most persons have not lived long enough to become dependent on their children. Several factors suggest that such households are destined *not* to become the norm.

A consequence of today's increasing residential mobility is that there are frequently long distances between adults and their aging parents. Hence, primary day-to-day support networks for older persons are increasingly likely to include neighbors, friends, and social service agencies (Cantor, 1985). Divorce may add to the numbers of older persons not having a spouse to care for them; others, because of custody decisions, will have decreased contact with their children (Morgan, 1981). Long-term declines in fertility and numbers of offspring will decrease the available family support network for aging individuals (Cherlin, 1983). The women's liberation movement and increasing proportions of women in the labor market leave fewer adult children to care for aging parents (Horowitz, 1985).

Contrary to popular belief, most older persons would like only to live near their children, not with them (Harris and Associates, 1974). In 1970, fewer than 5 percent of households included a parent or parent-in-law. Fewer than 8 percent of households today include three generations (Miller, 1982). In general, most older persons maintain their own homes and develop a kinship pattern described as "intimacy at a distance" (Treas, 1983). Almost 90 percent of older persons report having seen one of their children in the last month, and 75 percent have a child who lives less than 30 minutes away (Treas, 1983).

MID-LIFE AND LATE-LIFE FAMILY RELATIONSHIPS

Family relationships and roles provide a sense of continuity, personalized interaction, and affection during the life span (Morgan, 1981). Because of the decline of other roles for older persons, family ties are increasingly important sources of affirmation and meaning (Cherlin, 1983). Treas (1983) noted that people rely on family bonds of affection or obligation to alleviate societal shortcomings in care for older people. Most people turn to kin with their troubles. Aging parents most often turn to adult children.

Mid-life women, the traditional "kin-keepers" who arrange for and maintain contact with family members, are increasingly entering the labor market and achieving economic, social, and personal independence (Treas, 1983). Although employment may significantly decrease the hours of assistance to parents provided by sons, it has no effect on assistance from daughters (Stoller, 1983). Overall, married children of both sexes provide less help. Older parents are more likely to live with an unmarried child and twice as likely to live with a daughter as they are with a son (Miller, 1982).

Shanas (cited in Morgan, 1981) noted that one of the most pervasive beliefs in U.S. society is that older persons are neglected and alienated from their families. Research consistently shows that both siblings and children maintain contact with older family members. Although most frail and sick older persons are cared for by family members, some families value the independence of generations to such an extent that institutional care is preferable to "kin care" that involves sharing households (Morgan, 1981).

Parent-child relationships are affected, often adversely, by prevalent negative stereotypes and misconceptions about the needs of aging parents. The "abandonment" stereotype (i.e., "children neglect their parents") was mentioned above. Common, inaccurate stereotypes indicate that most old persons are likely to be institutionalized, that they will move in with their children if they are not institutionalized, and that they believe their children are responsible for their care. Attempts to treat a multifaceted problem by focusing only on the needs of one generation lead to misunderstandings and conflicts (e.g., "What am I to do about Mother?") (Miller, 1982).

Research indicates that the typical pattern of relationships between adult children and older parents is one of mutual aid. Studies have repeatedly shown that older persons give more help, both material and financial, to their children than they receive from these children. Their primary need for support from children is emotional rather than financial (Brody, Johnsen, and Fulcomer, 1984). A greater sense of commitment from children seems to foster mutual affection (Quinn, 1983).

The quality of intergenerational relationships is determined by affection and communication, with filial responsibility being significant to adult children (Quinn and Keller, 1983). Cicirelli (1981) reported that adult children expressed a greater degree of filial obligation than their parents expected from them. This finding may be related to what Morgan (1981) described as the "crisis of filial maturity" (p. 99), a common response of adult children to the increasing dependency of their aging parents. It reflects a recognition that the parent, viewed from childhood as a source of strength and support, is vulnerable, potentially weak, and eventually mortal. Resolution of this crisis is important for the future development of the adult.

Unfortunately, achieving "filial maturity" can be difficult, because there is a lack of appropriate role models, education, and information. Role expectations for adult children can be confusing and may change according to the day-to-day circumstances of the aging parent (Johnson and Spence, 1982). The consequences of this ambiguity are discussed below.

FAMILY STRESS SITUATIONS AND RESPONSES

Adult children lack role models for relating to an older generation while in mid-life; aging parents lack role models for being old. Some adults have difficulty acting in ways they recall their own parents as having done, once they are faced with the need to care for an aging parent and perhaps alter their own unique life-styles. Others fear a future time when care might be needed. All share the question of how to continue their lives, now in midstream, while relating to loved ones whose needs are

changing in unprecedented ways. The question is often one of how to maintain the quality of one's own life while helping to ensure the quality of life for a parent in the later years. Major sources of stress include the aging process itself, roles and role changes, care giving, decision making, dependency, and death. Numerous emotional responses are possible.

Adult children may find their roles with aging parents changing in undetermined and unforeseen ways. Often, both sides fail to realize that traditional roles must be altered (Dobson and Dobson, 1985). Children may deny or reject role changes because they expect parents to be perfect, especially mothers (Oberleder, 1982). Role reversals, prompted by extremely frail or dependent older parents, are the most extreme situation. Role changes and role strains are more common. Lack of preparation for caring for aging parents, competition for time and care of adolescent children, interference with personal freedom achieved during mid-life, and sibling rivalry over care for aging parents are sources of strain.

In addition to the various role strains, there is the challenge of coping with parents' sensitivity to their increasing dependency (Miller, 1981). Aging parents may perceive themselves as having fewer assets with which to balance the resources of their children. They may need assistance in such diverse areas as socialization and personal development; daily living needs, including housecleaning, laundry, shopping, and cooking; transportation and escort service to medical appointments; and the sharing of leisure time. Also, they may need personal assistance during times of illness or crisis (Cantor, 1985; Miller, 1981). Virtually all of the tasks that confront adult children in giving assistance to aging parents have been described as "sources of stress, burden, or similar upset—even to the point of placing the caregiver at risk of ill health" (Radowski and Clark, 1985, p. 618).

Care for aging parents is now viewed as a normative family stress (Brody, 1985). Brody et al. (1984) found that adult children perceive as appropriate adjustment of family schedules and help with costs of health care. Adjustment of work schedules and sharing of households are not appropriate. Many interacting factors affect the levels of stress experienced by families, including ages of parents and adult children, health, finances, socioeconomic status, number and spacing of children in each generation, and sex, financial condition, location, and retirement status of children (Miller, 1981). The most extreme levels of stress are experienced when physically or mentally impaired older parents are cared for by family members (Poulshock and Deimling, 1984), especially when parents exhibit disruptive behavior and impaired social functioning (Deimling and Bass, 1986).

Older persons may experience increasing indecisiveness in response to feelings of helplessness and loss of control over their physical and environmental resources (Bumagin and Hirn, 1985). Adult children find themselves in an ambiguous and confusing situation, responding to seemingly daily or even more frequent fluctuations in the decision-making skills of their parents. A major issue relates to how much responsibility for their parents they actually should assume. The most stressful and painful conflict occurs when a decision regarding where to live, especially a decision possibly involving institutionalization, seems inevitable (Miller, 1981).

Different aspects of these issues surface for adult children who live in close proximity to their aging parents (Cohen, 1983). When the aging parents are nearby, caretaking responsibilities, shared households, and anger toward other, more distant and less involved relatives are predominant issues. The potential friction in intergenerational living described by Treas (1983) involves not only life-style differences and conflicts over household authority but also issues related to dependency. Adult children living at a distance may experience guilt, emotional distancing, resentment, and the anger of other relatives.

In general, relationships between adult children and aging parents raise a plethora of sometimes conflicting emotional responses. The decision to institutionalize a parent, although often the last resort, may be accompanied by feelings of guilt, sadness, grief, or relief (Mines, Rockwell, and Hull, 1980). Other issues that may be faced by adult children include (a) being unprepared for the burdens imposed by aging parents, (b) coming to terms with the indignities of aging, (c) dealing with dependency issues, (d) coping with the increased self-centeredness of their parents, and (e) overcoming communication difficulties with both parents and siblings (Cohen, 1983). They may need to learn to say no to the unreasonable demands of parents (Dobson and Dobson, 1985).

Setting limits and recognizing that not all wishes can be fulfilled can arouse feelings of anxiety and guilt for adult children (Bumagin and Hirn,

1985). At the same time, aging parents may feel hurt and rejected, experiencing a position of increasing powerlessness within which it is impossible for any person to be "happy" (Oberleder, 1982). They may react by decreasing communications, often perceived by adult children as withholding information. Both adult children and aging parents tend to avoid discussions of problems and illnesses so as not to worry one another. Interactions may reflect reactions to changing circumstances or long-standing patterns of relating.

FAMILY RELATIONSHIP PATTERNS

Lifelong difficulties in interactional patterns in families may be exacerbated as parents age (Johnson and Spence, 1982). Unresolved conflicts can be reactivated by crises such as changing dependencies, institutionalization, or death (Morgan, 1981). "Middle-aged children may have difficulty in handling the reversal of roles with an aging parent whom they previously experienced as rejecting, unloving, and uncaring" (Miller, 1981, p. 421). They may resent the dependency needs of parents when their own needs for dependency on their parents have not been met. Unresolved sibling rivalries also may surface, with hostile feelings contributing to confusion over roles and care-providing needs.

Aging parents and their adult children may exist for years or even decades in patterns of mutual independence that promote emotionally satisfying relationships (Cherlin, 1983). These relationships can be disrupted by the loss of power experienced by older persons, who consistently report being terrified of being dependent and unable to care for themselves (Oberleder, 1982). Communication patterns can become disrupted, so that parents and children fail to recognize the similarity of their concerns. Bumagin and Hirn (1985) listed some of the parallel concerns for children and their parents:

1. How can I get my children/parents to listen to me? vs. Who listens to old people?
2. How can I have a life of my own? vs. How can I stay independent?
3. How can I balance all of my responsibilities? vs. Who will take care of me?

For both sides, the future may look increasingly bleak. Both may be unaware of possible interventions and resources, especially those that can be provided by counselors.

STRATEGIES FOR INTERVENTION

Strategies for intervention to meet the needs of adult children and their aging parents are discussed below. These include individual and group counseling, education and workshops, and use of resource materials.

Individual counseling with adult children or their aging parents is not unlike individual counseling with anyone. Counselors should be aware of the issues faced by clients and of their own biases with regard to these issues, especially the aging process itself. Lack of such awareness by counselors can encourage "taking sides" and can eliminate the objectivity needed to help clients deal with their relatives. Individual counseling with aging parents may focus on helping them achieve and maintain feelings of independence and ego integrity, and be more accepting of their adult children. Counseling with adult children can help them clarify their values and priorities with regard to their families and themselves, work through emotions such as anger, and be more understanding and accepting of their parents.

The effectiveness of individual counseling is limited. Counselors can expect to have the most success when the family becomes the unit of treatment (Kuypers and Trute, 1978). Group counseling involving one or more families can be oriented to therapy or education. Often, the focus of groups is on adult children only, especially those caring for dependent parents. These groups have been shown to be successful in modifying attitudes and approaches of adult children to older relatives (Hartford and Parsons, 1982; Miller, 1981). Johnson and Spence (1982) found that adult children having poor relationships with parents reported in groups that the responsibility belonged to the relative, not to them. In general they wanted better relationships, and group strategies were useful in helping to achieve them.

Dobson and Dobson (1985) described a series of structured workshops for adult children designed to provide information about the aging of parents and opportunities for processing the resulting attitudes and emotions. The success of such approaches seems to be related to the widespread lack of preparation for "parenting" older parents (Miller, 1982). There are few instances of workshops or groups designed to bring adult children and their aging parents together for education or therapy. Mulvaney, Gray, and Carroll (1982) suggested that such groups may be effective in improving intergenerational communication. These authors developed a two-part questionnaire in which children and parents were asked to describe how well the other knows or understands them. This questionnaire forms the basis for discussion.

Whatever approaches are used, counselors will need to know about referral agencies and persons to help meet the needs of adults and aging persons in their community. Innovative strategies, such as bibliotherapy, may be helpful. For example, adult children and their parents could be asked to read *The Giving Tree* (Silverstein, 1964). Reactions to the book could be discussed at home or in a subsequent counseling session.

CONSIDERATIONS FOR COUNSELORS

Counselors working with adult children and their aging parents will encounter extremes of involvement ranging from elder abuse to mutual respect and love. They may expect to witness complex and long-standing patterns of interaction and a host of negative and hostile emotions that need to be expressed and resolved. As the family or individual dynamics unfold, the counselor may need to examine the issue of *who* is the client. The question of whose needs and values are preeminent is important, as the counselor may unwittingly provide support for one side or another. Often, the adult child will summarize the issue as follows: "Either my parent or me—either I take care of my parent or I live my own life. I can't do both." To help resolve these feelings, counselors first must deal with their perspectives on the issue, including relationships with their own parents.

An important goal of counseling is to help both adult children and aging parents achieve a balance between their needs. Both should be aware of the positive impact of family ties and should be encouraged to build and to maintain such ties. Setting limits on what each can and will do in terms of interactions, support, care giving, and services is an important step in developing awareness and mutual respect for one another's needs. Assertiveness training for both groups may help to improve positive communications.

Often, both adult children and their aging parents are so overwhelmed by the circumstances at hand that they can see no solutions and no future. Counselors can help them to achieve a future orientation that includes the potential for life satisfaction and rewarding relationships. One approach is to have each step back and examine the nature of friendships outside of the family. Such relationships usually are characterized by active listening and caring behaviors (McGinnis, 1979). A logical question to ask is whether friendly relationships are desirable between adult children and their aging parents. If so, counselors can begin to make clients aware of the potential for treating relatives with the respect accorded to friends and can encourage some time out from old patterns of relating while new roles are rehearsed.

Most adults and their aging parents experience satisfying emotional relationships. Family crises such as institutionalization and death may create disruption in these relationships; however, most families manage to adjust. For those families in which hostile and negative feelings threaten the happiness of adult children as well as their aging parents, there are a variety of strategies that counselors may employ to promote positive intergenerational communication and support.

References

Badgwell, N. (December 1986–January 1987). The hardest decision. *Modern Maturity*, pp. 82–84.

Brody, E. M. (1985). Parent care as a normative family stress. *The Gerontologist, 25*, 19–24.

Brody, E. M., Johnsen, P. T., and Fulcomer, M. C. (1984). What should adult children do for elderly parents? Opinions and preferences of three generations of women. *Journal of Gerontology, 39*, 736–746.

Brotman, H. (1982). *Every ninth American* (Committee Publication No. 97-332). Washington, DC: U.S. Government Printing Office.

Buehler, C. (1967). Human life as a central subject of humanistic psychology. In J. Bugental (Ed.), *Challenges in humanistic psychology* (pp. 83–91). New York: McGraw-Hill.

Bumagin, V. E., and Hirn, K. F. (1985). *Aging is a family affair.* New York: Thomas Y. Crowell.

Butler, R. M., and Lewis, M. I. (1983). *Aging and mental health: Positive psychosocial approaches.* St. Louis: C. V. Mosby.

Cantor, M. H. (1985). Families: A basic source of long-term care for the elderly. *Aging, 34*, 8–13.

Cherlin, A. (1983). A sense of history: Recent research on aging and the family. In M. Riley, B. Hess, and K. Bond (Eds.), *Aging in society: Selected reviews of recent research.* Hillsdale, NJ: Erlbaum.

Cicirelli, V. G. (1981). *Helping elderly parents: The role of adult children.* Boston: Auburn House.

Cohen, P. (1983). A group approach for working with families of the elderly. *The Gerontologist, 23*, 248–250.

Deimling, G. T., and Bass, D. M. (1986). Symptoms of mental impairment among elderly adults and their effects on family caregivers. *Journal of Gerontology, 41*, 778–784.

Dobson, J. E., and Dobson, R. L. (1985). The sandwich generation: Dealing with aging parents. *Journal of Counseling and Development, 63*, 572–574.

Erikson, E. (1950). *Childhood and society.* New York: Norton.

Harris, L., and Associates. (1974). *The myth and reality of aging in America.* Washington, DC: National Council on the Aging.

Hartford, M. E., and Parsons, R. (1982). Groups with relatives of dependent older adults. *The Gerontologist, 22*, 394–398.

Havighurst, R. J. (1972). *Developmental tasks and education.* New York: David McKay.

Horowitz, A. (1985). Sons and daughters as caregivers to older parents: Differences in role performance and consequences. *The Gerontologist, 26*, 612–618.

Johnson, E. S., and Spence, D. L. (1982). Adult children and their aging parents: An intervention program. *Family Relations, 31*, 115–121.

Kuypers, J. A., and Trute, B. (1978). The older family as the locus of crisis intervention. *Family Coordinator, 27*, 405–411.

Lohman, N. (1977). Correlations of life satisfaction, morale, and adjustment measures. *Journal of Gerontology, 32*, 73–75.

McGinnis, A. L. (1979). *The friendship factor.* Minneapolis, MN: Augsburg.

Miller, S. J. (1981). The 'sandwich' generation: Adult children of the aging. *Social Work, 26*, 419–423.

Miller, S. J. (1982). Aging parents and their middle-aged children. *Educational Horizons, 50*, 179–183.

Mines, R. A., Rockwell, L., and Hull, S. B. (1980). Plans and attitudes of family members caring for aged parents: Implications for counseling. *Counseling and Values, 24*, 175–180.

Morgan, L. A. (1981). Aging in a family context. In R. H. Davis (Ed.), *Aging: Prospects and issues* (pp. 98–112). Los Angeles: University of Southern California Press.

Mulvaney, P., Gray, K., and Carroll, K. (1982). An exercise in understanding: A way of improving communication between aging parents and their adult children. *Human Development, 3*, 23–27.

Myers, J. E. (1984). *Counseling older persons: An information analysis paper.* Ann Arbor, MI: ERIC/CAPS.

Neugarten, B. (1968). *Middle age and aging.* Chicago: University of Chicago Press.

Oberleder, M. (1982). *Avoid the aging trap.* Washington, DC: Acropolis Books.

Poulshock, S. W., and Deimling, G. T. (1984). Families caring for elders in residence: Issues in the measurement of burden. *Journal of Gerontology, 39*, 230–239.

Quinn, W. H. (1983). Personal and family adjustment in later life. *Journal of Marriage and the Family, 45*, 57–73.

Quinn, W. H., and Keller, J. F. (1983). Older generations of the family: Relational dimensions and quality. *American Journal of Family Therapy, 11,* 23–30.

Radowski, W., and Clark, N. M. (1985). Future outlook, caregiving, and care-receiving in the family context. *The Gerontologist, 25,* 618–622.

Silverstein, S. (1964). *The giving tree.* New York: Warner Books.

Stoller, E. P. (1983). Parental caregiving by adult children. *Journal of Marriage and the Family, 45,* 851–858.

Treas, J. (1983). Aging and the family. In D. S. Woodruff & J. E. Birren (Eds.), *Aging: Scientific perspectives and social issues* (pp. 92–108). Los Angeles: University of Southern California.

Van Hoose, W. H., and Worth, M. R. (1982). *Adult in the life cycle.* Dubuque, IA: Wm. C. Brown.

36

THE INTERGENERATIONAL EQUITY DEBATE

Edward F. Lawlor

School of Social Service Administration
University of Chicago

A growing controversy about the "fairness" of public resource allocation to the young and the old is evident in the popular press, in the appearance of a new literature about generational justice, and in Congressional debate about domestic entitlements. The proponents of a reassessment of our public policy along generational lines are gaining strength in visibility, if not in numbers. As it is currently constructed, the intergenerational equity debate is built upon several simple and compelling ideas:

• Raw demographics will create undeniable economic and social pressures if labor market behavior, health care utilization, and the structure of social security remain unchanged. In the long term these forces will undermine productivity and economic growth.

• The tightened fiscal environment, a product of poor economic performance, creates zero sum games of resource allocation between the older population and other "deserving" groups, especially children.

• In order to address this coming crisis of public resource allocation and avoid generational warfare, a significant reduction in the public commitment of resources to the aged is required.

Until recently, most supporters of the current structure of social insurance and public policy for the aged dismissed the intergenerational equity critique as simple "granny-bashing," the scapegoating and blaming of the aged and age-based programs for a variety of larger economic and social problems. The recent vigor and visibility of the intergenerational equity movement suggest, however, that a larger and more substantive response is required from proponents of public policy for the aged.

A PROFILE OF THE INTERGENERATIONAL EQUITY MOVEMENT

In a 1984 article in the *Scientific American,* Samuel Preston sparked this new debate with a controversial and widely discussed analysis of the fairness of public taxing and spending policies for programs serving children and the elderly.

Preston's observations about the relative standing of children and the aged clearly resonated with an emerging public concern. Preston claimed that (1) federal expenditures for children are only one-sixth the outlays for programs for the aged, even though children in poverty vastly outnumber the population of older persons in poverty; (2) indicators of the well-being of children (e.g., educational standards, child suicide rates) suggest that recently the status of children has been declining in contrast to trends in the well-being of the elderly; (3) improvements in health, as indicated by mortality data, have been disproportionately concentrated in the aged population; and (4) the politics of public resource allocation almost guarantee that this apparent distortion in generational equity will continue.

In the three years since the Preston article, the call for intergenerational equity has served as a convenient rallying cry for a number of diverse interest groups, from those whose primary concern is the plight of children in our society to those who are displeased with the performance and prospects of the economy. In order to understand the political significance of the generational equity movement, it is necessary to step back and examine the positions of these constituents. The force of the attack on resources devoted to the support of the aged will ultimately be a direct reflection of the strength of the constituents' complaints.

From *The Public Policy and Aging Report,* 1987, *1*(2): 1–3, 8–10. Copyright © 1987. Policy Research Associates, Inc. Reprinted by permission.

ADVOCATES FOR CHILDREN

News of the declining status of children has been coming in waves during the middle part of the 1980s. The most cited piece of evidence, the national poverty statistics, indicates that the number of poor families with children has increased by 35 percent since 1979. Currently, about 22 percent of all children fall below the federal poverty line, the poverty rate for black children being more than 40 percent. The current poverty status of children relative to the aged represents a virtual reversal of their positions in late 1960s (see Figure 1). Moreover the news carries weekly reminders that such indicators as educational test scores, physical fitness standards, school dropout rates, and levels of violence among children demand increasing public attention and resources.

The call for generational equity coming from child advocates, however, is not simply based on the observation that children are doing worse. The intergenerational argument is fueled by some evidence that cost effective interventions are available for children, if only the government would make resources available. The House Select Committee on Children, Youth, and Families, for example, claims that:

$1 spent on the Food for Women, Infants, and Children Program (WIC) saves $3 in short run hospital costs.

$1 spent on immunization programs saves $10 in later medical expenses.

$1 spent on preschool educational programs saves $4.75 in later social costs.

These claims, while arguable on technical grounds, make for compelling politics. Many in the intergenerational movement claim that social spending on programs for children is inadequate because children have no standing in the political process. Children do not vote, and despite the existence of advocacy groups such as The Children's Defense Fund, there is a perception that the interests of children are not vigorously represented in the legislative arena.

Finally, the advocates for children make a qualitative distinction between the "product" of public expenditures for children and spending for the aged. Spending on children has the character of prevention and investment, while spending on the aged has the aura of maintenance and consumption. The intergenerational equity movement has not failed to make use of this imagery and language.

FIGURE 1. Poverty Rates for Children and the Aged

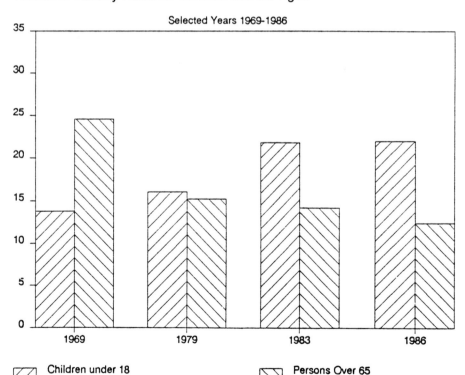

SOURCE: U.S. Bureau of the Census

THE FISCAL RESPONSIBILITY CAMP

Another dimension of the intergenerational equity movement is made up of those observers of the economy who worry about effects of ballooning trade and budget deficits and low levels of personal saving and investment on the long term performance of the economy. Support of income security and health care programs for the aged looms large in the diagnosis of economic disease by these critics: by their estimates social insurance spending for the aged accounts for much of the increase in federal debt over the long term and crowds out productivity gains that would result from increased investment.

Typical of the fiscal responsibility camp is Peter G. Peterson, a former Secretary of Commerce, who has waged a vigorous and strident campaign against social security and Medicare spending increases. Peterson sees over half of all federal benefits going to the aged, making them the obvious target for deficit reduction measures. He goes further than Preston, estimating that federal spending for the aged is ten times the spending for children on a per capita basis. Federal spending on infrastructure and non-defense R and D, which Peterson sees as primarily oriented toward future generations, amounted to $357 per child in 1986, roughly equal to his estimate of the increase in federal benefits for each older person occurring every six months.

Peterson concludes that "[i]f in the medium term the Baby Boom has channeled a sufficient share of its income into education, training, tools, and infrastructure to permit a quantum leap in productivity by the next generation of workers, it may enjoy a prosperous and contented old age. But if the flow of invested endowments from each generation to the next has ceased—and if each generation instead insists on its 'right' to consume all its own product and part of the next generation's as well—then we can count on a meager and strife-torn future."

To be sure, underlying the fiscal responsibility camp is a large measure of conservative ideology, a belief that a large public sector is counterproductive and that a relatively unbridled (and untaxed) private sector is necessary for healthy and sustained economic growth. By any measure, the large social insurance structure that has been built up around income security and health programs for the aged represents the most significant target for anyone interested in limiting the size of the public sector.

Although this is not the place to offer a point by point rebuttal to the champions of fiscal responsibility, it is important to reflect on the purpose and performance of social security as well as its fiscal implications over the medium term. Social security retirement income operates as a large scale transfer program, lifting a large number of aged persons out of poverty and effectively supplementing other sources of retirement income for the nonpoor elderly, such as savings and private pension benefits.

As even the most adamant fiscal critics would admit, evidence that social security suppresses national savings and depresses investment is inconclusive at best. Over the medium term before the baby boom generation reaches retirement age, social security will be generating quite large surpluses which will function as additions to savings and reduce federal debt in the national economy.

ADVOCATES FOR MEANS-TESTING OF GOVERNMENTAL PROGRAMS

Still a third dimension of the intergenerational movement consists of advocates of means-testing, those who believe in making the eligibility and size of governmental assistance dependent on a recipient's income and assets. These critics are not simply concerned with the size of the budget devoted to programs for the aged but rather are concerned that benefits are not targeted on the poor elderly and nonelderly. Thus, much of the critique and policy emphasis of this group is devoted to attacking the universal entitlement features of many age-based programs and substituting means-testing provisions. (To illustrate that not all proponents of intergenerational equity are necessarily proponents of means-testing, one needs only to look at the argument being put forward by Daniel Callahan in his new book *Setting Limits* which calls for increased use of age testing as a method for allocating health care resources.)

The means-testing perspective has even entered into the Presidential campaign, with candidate Bruce Babbitt advocating new taxes on social security benefits and new income-based taxes and premiums for Medicare beneficiaries. Babbitt would like to raise $3 billion from taxing social security benefits, diverting those revenues to SSI.

GENERATIONAL EQUITY AND PUBLIC POLICYMAKING

Much of the discussion of intergenerational equity takes place far from the day-to-day policymaking arena. Where the intergenerational perspective is strongest is in its articulation of the large scale social and economic dilemmas that will attend the retirement of the baby boom generation. Despite the enormity of the issues facing the country in 2010, there are few insights in this movement about how to deal with this demographic transition prospectively. The proponents of intergenerational equity have few answers for the undeniable political imperative to distribute short run benefits and respond to immediate crises.

There are few examples of our political system responding to anticipated problems 30 years out into the future. To put this political dilemma in some context, this response would be equivalent to enacting public policy to address societal conditions in 1965 from the perspective of 1935, when social security was enacted.

Nevertheless, there are a number of signs indicating that the intergenerational perspective will be an increasing force in the discussion of the overall social budget, economic policymaking, and the shape and scale of public policy for the aged. First, the "personnel" who make up the new intergenerational equity movement are an intellectually potent, articulate, and highly visible group. Although there are differences of opinion among this group, Samuel Preston, Phillip Longman, Norman Daniels, Rick Moody, Governor Richard Lamm, Daniel Callahan, Peter Peterson, Michael Boskin, Senator David Durenberger, and Representative James R. Jones collectively have generated intense interest in generational justice in a brief period of time.

Second, there is now an institutional home for this perspective, the Americans for Generational Equity (AGE), devoted to keeping both intellectual and political attention on these issues. Its stated mission is "to promote greater public understanding of problems arising from the aging of the U.S. population and to foster increased public support for policies that will serve the economic interests of the next century's elderly."

Third, present and anticipated economic instability will intensify the search for fiscal measures to limit the size of the federal deficit. The size and growth of the social insurance component of the budget will bring about continuing scrutiny and criticism of the federal commitment to these programs. There are already several shifts in the design of policymaking for the aged that are at least consistent with and have possibly been influenced by the ideas of the intergenerational movement.

For example, the 1983 social security amendments made two major changes which affect the rel-

ative burdens and benefits of the program across generations. Higher income beneficiaries (individuals with more than $25,000 and couples with more than $32,000) are now subject to taxation on one-half of their social security benefits. More importantly, these standards are not indexed for inflation, meaning that an increasing number of social security beneficiaries will be subject to a form of implicit means-testing over time.

In that same legislation, the age of eligibility for full benefits was gradually increased over the next several decades. The "intent" of this latter change is to improve the fiscal condition of the trust fund over time and also to signal to younger workers that future social security coverage, especially for early retirement, is constrained.

New requirements for cost-sharing in Medicare, especially as they are reflected in the current catastrophic legislation, place increased responsibility for health care expenses on the aged themselves and limit the responsibilities of current workers.

In the current public policy debate, intergenerational equity is narrowly at issue in the financing and distribution of Medicaid benefits. For example, a 1983 change in interpretation by the Health Care Financing Administration permits states to begin taxing children of individuals receiving Medicaid nursing home reimbursement. This change represents a small, but perhaps philosophically important, attempt to change the generational and familial boundaries of responsibility for long term care.

More broadly, Medicaid coverage and benefits (where spending for health care of low income children and nursing home care of the aged is allocated out of the same budget, and where long term care expenses are claiming an increasing share of resources) are an area of ongoing policy debate where generational interests are clearly visible, if not contested.

Elements of the intergenerational equity perspective also make their way into the ongoing discussion of some tax provisions, such as the treatment of estates and bequests. Changes in the 1986 Tax Reforms Act eliminated the extra personal exemption for the aged as a group yet at the same time provided new tax protections for the very low income elderly. Finally, marginal changes in the social security program, such as the current debate over reducing cost of living adjustments (COLA's), are part of the ongoing discussion of the politics and consequences of intergenerational equity.

THE FUTURE OF THE INTERGENERATIONAL EQUITY MOVEMENT

A larger and more sophisticated discussion of intergenerational equity will require a clearer articulation of what is meant by "fairness" among generations. Implicit in many of the comparisons of spending on children and the aged is a notion that resource flows from the federal government should be more equal. Deeper consideration of specific sources of support and needs of these different groups is called for. The starting assumption of the intergenerational equity movement seems to be that spending for children and the elderly should be equal, or at least more nearly equal than it is now.

However, the financing of care and education for children may ultimately be less costly and certainly is distributed over families, state and local governments, and federal sources in very different ways than the financing of income security and health care for the aged. Simple comparisons of federal spending on children and the aged are very deceptive in this respect.

In order to move the intergenerational equity debate beyond theatrics, a number of changes in the terms of debate will be required.

First, consideration of equity should be built around a contemporary notion of dependency and appropriate public response. Alternative conceptions of dependency will produce very different pictures of the problem, yet much of the debate has been driven by crude and virtually meaningless demographic "dependency ratios." These ratios treat people such as our President as dependents and incapacitated individuals at younger ages as nondependents. New research that employs more sophisticated economic concepts of dependency radically changes the intergenerational equity picture.

Second, serious and direct attention needs to be paid to the requirements of sustained long term economic growth and international competitiveness. This requires a change of perspective on both sides of the intergenerational equity debate: partisans of programs for the aged can no longer afford to be agnostic about macroeconomic policymaking, and proponents of intergenerational equity need to examine the performance of the economy more rigorously. As it stands, the intergenerational analysis of economic distress sees the aged population as an albatross weighing on the economy, depressing savings and long-term investment behavior, independent of all the other more complicated economic factors. This is a simple and appealing "bogeyman" explanation of economic distress, but it is unsupported by evidence and is certainly an inadequate explanation of the complex set of macroeconomic adjustments that are taking place.

Third, the demographic transformation in the next century calls for a recognition that all does not stay the same, and that work needs to begin on the development of appropriate nonhysterical approaches, such as labor market interventions, that will dampen the potential impact of the aging baby boomers. It is remarkable, for example, how little attention immigration policy has received in the context of the intergenerational equity debate.

Many observers, particularly advocates for the aged, believe that the intergenerational equity movement is dangerous and counterproductive to the long term consideration of federal policymaking for the aged. The analysis and debate of differential impacts across age categories are believed to be very socially devisive. Indeed, many of the proponents of generational equity warn that if nothing is done in the medium term to contain the resource demands of an aging population, "generational warfare" will erupt. Although this threat is commonly asserted, the content and consequences of generational warfare are still mysterious. The politics of social welfare spending are obviously richer and more complicated than the zero sum game portrayal offered by the intergenerational perspective. One of the seminal insights of early students of the politics of aging was that social policy (and other) issues are contested along a number of dimensions—regional, moral, ideological—with age-affiliations playing a small part in most participant's political orientation. There is an interesting question about how age-affiliation is changing in importance as age-based advocacy groups (such as AARP) grow in stature and saavy, and intergenerational equity groups (such as AGE) attempt to recast social policy issues along age lines.

However, public opinion data continues to show widespread consensus and support for social insurance programs even across age groups. Recent data from The Gallup Organization, roughly paralleling the period of time since publication of the Preston article, show remarkably stable support for social security and Medicare relative to other spending choices:

The federal budget deficit is now about $175 billion per year. There are only a few ways to reduce it. Do you approve or disapprove of the following ways? (The Gallup Organization)

Approval rating on	4/85	1/86	7/87
Cut defense spending	66%	59%	58%
Cut social programs such as health and education	39%	42%	21%
Raise income taxes	18%	22%	16%
Cut entitlements such as social security and Medicare	9%	9%	9%

CONCLUSION

For the foreseeable future, it is these attitudes toward the current structure of social insurance that are the frontier for the intergenerational equity movement. Without significant changes in public attitudes toward reform of social insurance, no large scale restructuring of public policy across generational lines is possible.

Suggested Readings _____

June Axinn and Mark J. Stern, "Age and Dependency: Children and the Aged in American Social Policy," *The Milbank Memorial Fund Quarterly,* Fall 1985, pp. 648–670.

Norman Daniels, "Justice Between Age Groups: Am I My Parent's Keeper?," *Milbank Memorial Fund Quarterly,* Summer 1983, pp. 489–522.

John L. Palmer and Stephanie G. Gould, "Economic Consequences of Population Aging" in Alan Pifer and Lydia Bronte, *Our Aging Society: Paradox and Promise.* New York: W. W. Norton, 1986, pp. 367–390.

Peter G. Peterson, "The Morning After," *The Atlantic,* October 1987, pp. 43–69.

Samuel H. Preston, "Children and the Elderly in the U.S.," *Scientific American,* December 1984, pp. 44–49.

D. Substance Abuse and Delinquency

37

ILLICIT DRUG USE, SMOKING, AND DRINKING BY AMERICA'S HIGH SCHOOL STUDENTS, COLLEGE STUDENTS, AND YOUNG ADULTS, 1975–1987:

OVERVIEW OF KEY FINDINGS

Lloyd D. Johnston
Patrick M. O'Malley
Jerald G. Bachman
Institute for Social Research
University of Michigan

This monograph reports findings from the on-going research and reporting project entitled Monitoring the Future: A Continuing Study of the Lifestyles and Values of Youth. Each year since 1975, in-school surveys of nationally representative samples of high school seniors have been conducted. In addition, in each year since 1976, representative subsamples of the participants from each previously graduating class have been surveyed by mail. (Note that the high school dropout segment of the population—about 15 percent of an age group—is of necessity omitted from the coverage of all three populations.)

Findings on the prevalence and trends in drug use and related factors are reported in this volume for high school seniors and also for young adult high school graduates 19–29 years old. Trend data are presented for varying time intervals, ranging up to twelve years. Results are given separately for college students, a particularly important subset of this young adult population, for which there currently exist no other nationally representative data.

A number of important findings emerge from these three national populations—high school seniors, young adults through age 29, and college students. They have been summarized and integrated in this chapter so that the reader may quickly get an overview of the key results.

TRENDS IN ILLICIT DRUG USE

• Without question the most important development in 1987 was a sharp downturn for the first time in the use of **cocaine** in all three population groups. Annual prevalence of use fell by about one-fifth in each group, and 30-day prevalence fell by an even larger proportion.* Since cocaine use had become so widespread, and has been demonstrated to be so hazardous, the fact that it is finally showing signs of a decline is particularly encouraging. As we predicted earlier, the decline occurred when young people began to see experimental and occasional use as more dangerous; and this happened in 1987, probably partly because the hazards of cocaine use received extensive media coverage in the preceding year, but almost surely in part because of the cocaine-related deaths in 1986 of sports stars Len Bias and Don Rogers.

As with all the illicit drugs, lifetime cocaine prevalence climbs with age, actually reaching 40 percent by age 27 to 28. Unlike all of the other illicit drugs, active use—i.e., annual prevalence or monthly prevalence—also climbs substantially after high school.

• Also encouraging was the fact that the use of **crack cocaine** appeared to level in 1987 at relatively low prevalence rates, at least within these populations. This occurred despite the fact that the crack

---

Reprinted from *Illicit Drug Use, Smoking, and Drinking by America's High School Students, College Students, and Young Adults, 1975–1987*. National Institute on Drug Abuse. U.S. Department of Health and Human Services, Publication No. (ADM) 89-1602. 1988.

*Annual prevalence is the percent reporting any use in the prior twelve months, while 30-day prevalence is the percent reporting any use in the prior 30 days.

phenomenon continued a process of diffusion to new communities that year. In the 1986 survey about half (52 percent) of the schools in the national sample showed some positive prevalence of crack, but by 1987 this statistic had risen by half to 77 percent. Clearly the diffusion of this drug form to most of the nation's communities and schools has occurred—despite the widespread perception that crack is primarily an inner city problem. In 1987, lifetime prevalence for seniors stands at 5.6 percent, and annual prevalence stands at 4.0 percent—almost exactly where it was in 1986 (4.1 percent) despite the further diffusion of the drug. Among young adults one to ten years past high school, lifetime prevalence is slightly higher (6.3 percent) and annual prevalence slightly lower (3.1 percent) than among seniors. Again, the annual prevalence among young adults is almost identical to what it was in 1986 (3.2 percent), providing further evidence that use has leveled.

College students one to four years past high school showed an increase in annual prevalence (from 1.3 percent to 2.0 percent) between 1986 and 1987, but it is not statistically significant. However, they still have an annual rate less than half that observed among their age-mates not in college (4.4 percent). (In high school annual crack prevalence among the college-bound is also about half of what it is for those not bound for college (2.8 percent vs. 5.5 percent).)

Regional differences in crack use among seniors are similar to what they are for cocaine in general: highest in the West (6.3 percent annual prevalence), followed by the Northeast (4.1 percent), the North Central (3.6 percent) and the South (2.9 percent). Use is highest in the large cities (4.8 percent), followed by nonmetropolitan areas (4.1 percent), and the smaller cities (3.5 percent).

We believe that the particularly intense media coverage of the hazards of crack cocaine, which took place quite early in what could have been a considerably more serious epidemic, likely had the effect of "capping" that epidemic early by deterring many would-be users and by motivating many experimenters to desist use. (While 5.6 percent of seniors report having tried crack, only 1.5 percent indicate use in the past month.)

• The decline in **cocaine** use in 1987 was accompanied by a further decline for a number of other drugs as well. The annual prevalence of **marijuana** use among seniors fell to the lowest level since the study began (36 percent, down 2.5 percent

from 1986). A similar decrease occurred among college students (37 percent, down 3.9 percent) and among all young adults one to ten years past high school (down 1.7 percent to 35 percent). **Daily marijuana use** fell significantly for seniors (down 0.7 percent to 3.3 percent) but showed no further decline among young adults (4.2 percent) or college students (2.3 percent). For seniors this represents a two-thirds overall drop in daily use from the peak level of 10.7 percent, observed in 1978. College students have also dropped by two-thirds from our first reading of 7.2 percent in 1980.

• Another widely used class of illicit drugs showing an important shift in 1987 is **stimulants** (or more specifically, amphetamines). There continued to be significant declines in use among all three populations in 1987 as part of a longer-term trend that began in 1982. Since 1982, annual prevalence has fallen from 20 percent to 12 percent among seniors and from 21 percent to 7 percent among college students. In general, the decline has been sharper among young adults, including college students, than among high school seniors. (This sharper decline among young adults also appears to be true for **marijuana, LSD,** and **methaqualone.**)

• Concurrent with this drop in illicit amphetamine use is a significant increase in the use of over-the-counter **stay-awake pills,** which usually contain caffeine as their active ingredient. Their annual prevalence among seniors doubled in five years, from 12 percent in 1982 to 25 percent in 1987.

The other two classes of nonprescription stimulants—the **"look alikes"** and the over-the-counter **diet pills**—have actually shown some fall-off in recent years. Still, 38 percent of young women have tried diet pills by the end of senior year, 21 percent have used them in the past year, and 9 percent in just the past month.

• **LSD** use has been fairly constant over the last several years in all three populations, following a period of some decline.

• **PCP** use also had been constant for several years among high school seniors at quite a low level (annual prevalence of 2.4 percent in 1986). It fell further in 1987 to 1.3 percent, far below its peak level of 7.0 percent in 1979. (PCP is not reported for the follow-up surveys, because it is included in only one questionnaire form, yielding too few cases.)

• The annual prevalence of **heroin** use has been very steady since 1979 among seniors at 0.5 percent to 0.6 percent. (It had earlier fallen from 1.0 percent in 1975.) The heroin statistics for young adults and college students have also remained quite stable in recent years at low rates (about 0.2 percent). However, it appears that among the young adult population one to four years past high school, including college students, there was some drop in heroin use between 1980 and 1982. The use of **opiates other than heroin** has been quite level over the life of the study. Seniors have had an annual prevalence rate of 5 percent or 6 percent since 1975. Young adults in their twenties have generally shown a similar cross-time pattern.

• After a long and substantial decline which began in 1977, **tranquilizer** use among high school seniors appears to have stabilized in the last several years at around 6 percent annual prevalence (compared to 11 percent in 1977), at about 5 percent for the young adult sample, and at about 4 percent for the college student sample.

• The long-term gradual decline in **barbiturate** use, which began at least as early as 1975, when the study began, continued in 1987; the annual prevalence among seniors fell to 3.6 percent (compared to 10.7 percent in 1975). Annual prevalence of this class of sedative drugs is even lower among the young adult sample (2.1 percent), and among college students specifically (1.2 percent). All three groups showed declines in 1987, but they were too small to be statistically significant.

• **Methaqualone,** another sedative drug, has shown quite a different trend pattern. Its use rose steadily among seniors from 1975 to 1981, when annual prevalence reached 8 percent. It then fell rather sharply to 1.5 percent by 1987, including a significant drop in 1987 of 0.6 percent. Use also fell among all young adults and among college students, both of which now have an annual prevalence of use of just 0.8 percent. In recent years, shrinking availability may well have played a role in this drop, as legal manufacture and distribution of the drug ceased.

• In sum, the three classes of illicitly used drugs which now impact on appreciable proportions of young Americans in their late teens and twenties are **marijuana, cocaine,** and **stimulants.** Among high school seniors they show annual prevalence rates in 1987 of 36 percent, 10 percent, and 12 percent respectively. Among college students the comparable annual prevalence rates in 1986 are 37 percent, 14 percent, and 7 percent; and for all high school graduates one to ten years past high school (the "young adult" sample) they are 35 percent, 16 percent, and 9 percent.

AGE-RELATED DIFFERENCES

• A number of additional interesting findings emerge from the sections in this report dealing with age-related changes in use. One is that the already high proportion of young people who by senior year have at least tried **any illicit drug** (57 percent in 1987) grows substantially larger up through the mid-twenties (where it reaches nearly 80 percent in 1987). There is a similar rise in the proportion using **any illicit drug other than marijuana** (36 percent among seniors in 1987 vs. about 60 percent among those in their mid-twenties). Lifetime prevalence for **marijuana** reaches about 75 percent by the mid-twenties (vs. 50 percent among 1987 seniors) and for **cocaine** about 40 percent (vs. 15 percent among 1987 seniors).

• On the other hand, *active* illicit drug use among the older age groups has tended to approximate the levels observed among seniors. This has been true for the annual prevalence of **any illicit drug, marijuana,** and **tranquilizers.** It has also been true for **daily marijuana use.** In fact, the young adult sample actually has lower rates of annual prevalence than high school seniors on five drugs—**LSD, methaqualone, barbiturates, stimulants,** and **opiates other than heroin. Cocaine,** of course, is the exception in that active use rises until about age 25, where it reaches a plateau (and thereafter may decline).

COLLEGE-NONCOLLEGE DIFFERENCES

• **American college students** (one to four years past high school) show annual usage rates for a number of drugs which are about average for their age, including **any illicit drug, marijuana** specifically (although their rate of **daily marijuana use** is half what it is for the rest of their age group, i.e., 2.3 percent vs. 4.6 percent), **inhalants, LSD, heroin,** and **opiates other than heroin.** For several categories of drugs, however, college students have rates of use which are below those of their age peers, including **any illicit drug other than marijuana, cocaine, crack** cocaine specifically, **stimulants, barbiturates,** and **tranquilizers.**

Since college-bound seniors in high school had below average rates of use on all of these illicit drugs, their eventually attaining parity on some of them reflects a "catching up" to some degree. As results from the study published elsewhere have shown, the "catching up" may be explainable more in terms of differential rates of leaving the parental home and of getting married than in terms of any direct effects of college *per se*. (College students are more likely to have left the parental home and less likely to have gotten married than their age peers.)

• In general, the trends since 1980 in illicit substance use among American college students are found to parallel those of their age peers not in college. That means that for most drugs there has been a decline in use over the interval. Further, all young adult high school graduates through age 28, as well as college students taken separately, show trends which are highly parallel for the most part to the trends among high school seniors, although declines in the active use of many of the drugs over the past half decade have been proportionately larger in these two older populations than among high school seniors (particularly the declines in **LSD** and **stimulant** use).

MALE-FEMALE DIFFERENCES

• Regarding sex differences in the three populations, males are more likely to use **most illicit drugs,** and the differences tend to be largest at the higher frequency levels. **Daily marijuana use** among high school seniors in 1987, for example, is reported by 4.3 percent of males vs. 2.1 percent of females; among all young adults by 6.5 percent of males vs. 2.3 percent of females; and among college students, specifically, by 3.1 percent of males vs. 1.7 percent of females. The only exceptions to the rule that males are more frequently users of illicit drugs than females occur for **stimulant** and **tranquilizer** use in high school, where females are slightly higher. The sexes attain near parity on **stimulant** and **tranquilizer** use among the college and young adult populations.

• Insofar as there have been differential trends for the two sexes among any of these populations, they have been in the direction of a diminution of differences between the sexes. For college students, previous differences in the usage rates for **methaqualone, LSD** and **daily marijuana use** are disappearing as the prevalence rates for both sexes converge toward zero (which means that use by males has fallen more). The same is happening for daily marijuana use among young adults generally, as well as high school seniors. There is also some convergence between the sexes in **stimulant** use among all three subpopulations. The convergence is again due to a greater drop in use among males.

TRENDS IN ALCOHOL USE

• Regarding **alcohol** use in these age groups, several findings are noteworthy. First, despite the

fact that it is illegal for virtually all high school students and most college students to purchase alcoholic beverages, experience with alcohol is almost universal among them (92 percent of seniors have tried it) and active use is widespread. Most important, perhaps, is the widespread occurrence of **occasions of heavy drinking**—here measured by the percent reporting five or more drinks in a row at least once in the prior two-week period. Among seniors this statistic stands at 38 percent and among college students it stands at 43 percent.

• Regarding trends in alcohol use, during the period of recent decline in the use of marijuana and other drugs there appears not to have been any "displacement effect" in terms of any increase in alcohol use among seniors. (It was not uncommon to hear such a displacement hypothesis asserted.) If anything, the opposite seems to be true. Since 1980, the monthly prevalence of alcohol use among seniors has gradually declined, from 72 percent in 1980 to 66 percent in 1985, where it remains in 1987. **Daily use** declined from a peak of 6.9 percent in 1979 to 4.8 percent in 1984 (with no further decline through 1987); and the prevalence of drinking **five or more drinks in a row** during the prior two-week interval fell from 41 percent in 1983 to 37 percent in 1985 (with no further drop since then).

COLLEGE-NONCOLLEGE DIFFERENCES

• The data from college students show a somewhat different pattern in relation to alcohol use. They show very little drop off in monthly prevalence since 1980 (about 3 percent), no clearly discernible change in **daily use** or in **occasions of heavy drinking,** which is at 43 percent in 1987—higher than the 38 percent among high school seniors.

• The 43 percent figure in **occasions of heavy drinking** is also higher than the rate observed among their age peers (i.e., those one to four years past high school) not in college (36 percent), which means that college students are well above average on occasions of heavy drinking. Since the college-bound seniors *in* high school are consistently less likely to report occasions of heavy drinking than the noncollege-bound, this reflects "catching up and passing" their peers after high school.

• In most surveys from 1980 onward, college students have had a **daily drinking** rate (6.0 percent in 1987) which is slightly lower than that of their age peers (6.6 percent in 1987), suggesting that they are somewhat more likely to confine their drinking to weekends, on which occasions they tend to drink a lot. (Again, college men have much higher rates of daily drinking than college women: 8.8 percent vs. 3.9 percent.) The rate of daily drinking has fallen among the noncollege group from 8.7 percent in 1981 to 6.6 percent in 1987.

MALE-FEMALE DIFFERENCES

• There remains a quite substantial sex difference among high school seniors in the prevalence of **occasions of heavy drinking** (29 percent for females vs. 46 percent for males in 1987), but this difference has been diminishing very gradually since the study began over a decade ago.

A more detailed analysis shows that the divergent trends between high school students and college students in occasions of heavy drinking is due to some increase (since about 1982) among male college students specifically. (The proportion of them reporting five or more drinks in a row rose from around 53 percent in the early eighties to around 56 percent or 57 percent in the middle eighties.) Female college students showed little change during the eighties, with a constant prevalence of about 35 percent. Thus an already large sex difference at the college level has become even larger. (There has not been an increase among noncollege males comparable to that observed among college males. If anything, their prevalence may have declined a little.)

• In sum, heavy party drinking among males in college is common and appears to have become more common in recent years. Among high school students, however, there was some decline in such behaviors (which ended in 1985). Sex differences in occasions of heavy drinking appear to have been diminishing somewhat at the high school level at the same time that they were enlarging at the college level.

TRENDS IN CIGARETTE SMOKING

• A number of important findings have emerged from the study concerning **cigarette smoking** among American adolescents and young adults. Of greatest importance is the fact that by late adolescence sizable proportions of young people still are establishing regular cigarette habits, despite the demonstrated health risks associated with smoking. In fact, since the study began in 1975, cigarettes have comprised the class of substance most frequently used on a daily basis by high school students.

• While their **daily smoking** rate did drop considerably between 1977 and 1981 (from 29 percent to 20 percent), it has dropped very little in the six years since (by another 1.6 percent), despite the appreciable downturn which has occurred in most other forms of drug use (including alcohol) during this period. And, despite all the adverse publicity and restrictive legislation addressed to the subject during the eighties, the proportion of seniors who perceive "great risk" to the user of suffering physical (or other) harm from pack-a-day smoking has risen only 5 percent since 1980 (to 69 percent in 1987). That means that nearly a third of seniors still do not feel there is a great risk associated with smoking.

AGE AND COHORT-RELATED DIFFERENCES

• Initiation of daily smoking most often occurs in grades 6 through 9 (i.e., at modal ages 11 to 14), with rather little further initiation after high school (although a number of light smokers make the transition to heavy smoking in the first two years after high school). Analyses presented in this volume and elsewhere have shown that cigarette smoking shows a clear "cohort effect." That is, if a class (or birth) cohort establishes an unusually high rate of smoking at an early age relative to other cohorts, it is likely to remain high throughout the life cycle.

• As we reported in the 1986 volume, in the section on "Other Findings from the Study," some 53 percent of the half-pack-a-day (or more) smokers in senior year said that they had tried to quit smoking and found they could not. Of those who were daily smokers in high school, nearly three-quarters were daily smokers seven to nine years later (based on the 1985 survey), despite the fact that in high school only 5 percent of them thought they would "definitely" be smoking five years hence. Clearly, the smoking habit is established at an early age and is difficult to break for those young people who have it.

COLLEGE-NONCOLLEGE DIFFERENCES

• There exists a striking difference between the college-bound in high school and those not college-bound in terms of smoking rates. For example, smoking half-a-pack a day is nearly three times as prevalent among the noncollege-bound (20 percent vs. 7 percent).

• Among those one to four years past high school, those not in college show the same dramatically higher rate of smoking compared to that found among those in college, with half-pack-a-day smoking standing at 24 percent and 8 percent, respectively.

MALE-FEMALE DIFFERENCES

• Females are a little more likely to smoke than their male counterparts in high school, as well as in young adulthood for those not in college.

• Females in college have been shown in recent years to be considerably more likely than males in college to be smokers.

RELATIONSHIPS WITH OTHER FACTORS

• In the prior volume in this series we showed that smoking bears a strong negative relationship with academic performance in high school.

• It also bears a strong positive relationship with the use of all of the **illicit drugs—marijuana,** in particular—and with **alcohol** use. For example, in 1985 among the pack-a-day smokers, 98 percent had used an illicit drug, 81 percent had used an illicit drug other than marijuana, and 26 percent were current daily users of illicit drugs (mostly marijuana).

SUMMARY AND CONCLUSIONS

• To summarize these findings in trends, over the last seven years there has been an appreciable decline in the use of a number of the **illicit drugs** among seniors, and even larger declines in their use among American college students and young adults more generally. The stall in these favorable trends in all three populations in 1985, as well as an increase in active **cocaine** use that year, should serve as a reminder that these improvements cannot be taken for granted. Fortunately, in 1986 we saw the general decline resume and the prevalence of cocaine level off, albeit at peak levels; and in 1987 the general decline continued, while cocaine use took a sharp downturn for the first time in more than a decade.

• While the overall picture has improved considerably in the past seven years, the amount of illicit as well as licit drug use among America's younger age groups is still striking when one takes into account the following facts:

By their mid-twenties, nearly 80 percent of today's young adults have tried an **illicit drug,** including some 60 percent who have tried some **illicit drug other than** (usually in addition to) **marijuana.** Even for high school seniors these proportions still stand at 57 percent and 36 percent, respectively.

By age 27, roughly 40 percent have tried **cocaine.** As early as the senior year of high school, some 17 percent have done so. Roughly one in eighteen seniors (5.6 percent) have tried the particularly dangerous form of cocaine called **crack.**

One in thirty (3.3 percent) high school seniors in 1987 smokes **marijuana daily,** and roughly the same proportion (4.2 percent) of young adults aged 19 to 28 do, as well. Among all seniors in 1987, 15 percent had been daily marijuana smokers at some time, and among young adults the comparable figure is 20 percent.

About one in twenty seniors drinks **alcohol daily** (4.8 percent). Some 38 percent have had **five or more drinks in a row** at least once in the prior two weeks, and such behavior tends to increase among young adults one to four years past high school. The prevalence of such behavior among male college students reaches 54 percent.

Some 29 percent of seniors have smoked **cigarettes** in the month prior to the survey and 19 percent already are daily smokers. In addition, many of the lighter smokers will convert to heavy smoking after high school. For example, one in every four young adults aged 19 to 28 are daily smokers (25 percent), and one in five (20 percent) smoke a half-pack-a-day or more.

• Despite the improvements in recent years, it is still true that this nation's high school students and other young adults show a level of involvement with illicit drugs which is greater than can be found in any other industrialized nation in the world. Even by historical standards in this country, these rates remain extremely high. Heavy drinking also is widespread and of public health concern; and certainly the continuing initiation of large proportions of young people to cigarette smoking is a matter of great public health concern.

38

COMMUNITY-BASED SUBSTANCE ABUSE PREVENTION: A MULTICULTURAL PERSPECTIVE

Mario A. Orlandi
Division of Health Promotion Research
American Health Foundation
New York City

The goal of community-based health promotion is to enhance the quality of life of each community member by facilitating health-enhancing behaviors and by reducing health-compromising behaviors. Specific objectives of substance abuse prevention programs are to minimize involvement with abusable substances and the lifestyle patterns that such use entails, while maximizing the adoption of alternative healthy lifestyles.

Campaigns organized to achieve these objectives traditionally have involved two distinct interest groups—one includes the developers and providers of preventive interventions, the other includes decision makers and end users within the community. The two groups and their various activities can be considered as two separate but related systems. The logical sequence of events that connects these two systems begins with the basic design of intervention strategies and continues through application of the strategies in community settings. However, communities are complex collections of individuals representing various racial, ethnic, and sociocultural subgroups. This diversity typically found throughout the U.S. presents a significant challenge to the community-based substance abuse prevention efforts. Because the culturally defined lifestyle patterns exhibited by the subgroups vary considerably, designers of health promotion campaigns for heterogeneous communities must attempt to address widely varying target behaviors cohesively. This paper addresses the problems related to achieving the goals of community-based substance abuse prevention that can result from failing to recognize socioculturally defined subgroups in the community. The barriers will be defined within the theoretical context of communication-behavior change theory;[1] various strategies for overcoming these barriers will be

pursued within the frameworks of linkage theory,[2] and social marketing.[3]

MULTICULTURAL ISSUES AND GENERAL CONCERNS

Since the 1960s, significant change has occurred in the way various sociocultural subgroups are perceived in the U.S. Two relevant shifts are noted. First, a deeply rooted and undeniable need for cultural identification surfaced, and with it a sense of pride in one's heritage has become commonplace among ethnic and racial minority groups. As demands for social and racial justice were expressed, the nation began to acknowledge its ethnocentrism and take initial steps toward eliminating discrimination. Second, minority group members began to alter their roles from the traditional ones of clients and target groups to those of advocates and change agents for their causes. These trends resulted in an increased awareness of the need for effective health promotion interventions that are culturally relevant and that address specific sociocultural barriers to effective cross-cultural program dissemination.

A description of the barriers confronted when interventions are disseminated to a population subgroup outside the majority is presented in this paper, specifically focusing on drug abuse prevention efforts that target minority populations. Many relevant substance abuse prevention issues are general and pertain to most subcultures. Important implications to consider when designing prevention interventions include any of the following:

• **Language**—failure to appreciate health promotion messages when language or symbols are

From the *Journal of School Health, 56:9,* November 1986, 394–401. Copyright © American School Health Association, P.O. Box 708, Kent, Ohio 44240.

used that are not understandable or are misunderstood by the subgroup;

- **Reading level**—using printed materials that are too sophisticated or beyond the reading level of subgroup members;

- **Models**—using endorsements for the health promotion campaign from prominent individuals or organizations that are not well known to the subgroup members;

- **Inappropriate messages**—using motivational messages that are not salient to subgroup members;

- **Motivational issues**—the fear that the primary motivation for the health promotion campaign is the desire to control the subculture, robbing from it the specific practices that historically have defined it;

- **Inappropriate target**—the belief that the health promotion campaign is worthwhile, but that program designers never really intended the subculture to participate or benefit;

- **Welfare stigma**—the tendency to view the health promotion campaign as a ''handout'' and avoid it as a matter of pride;

- **Perceived responsibility**—the attitude that the campaign deals with subject areas and life choices that concern the family and the individual, not the public health establishment;

- **Relevance of health promotion**—the belief that more pressing concerns such as poverty, crime, unemployment, and hunger should be addressed prior to the health promotion campaign;

- **Entropy**—the tendency for subgroup members to perceive themselves as powerless or helpless when confronted with enormous economic and sociocultural barriers and to express a lack of motivation to engage in self-improvement activities.

Various culture-specific factors, in addition to these general issues, need to be considered when developing culturally-relevant interventions.

CULTURE-SPECIFIC FACTORS

Ethnic and minority groups in the U.S. grow up and live within unique social, cultural, and psychological contexts that shape their knowledge, attitudes, and beliefs, as well as their self-image, system of values, and lifestyle. Such environments have the potential to profoundly influence substance use and abuse behaviors. Though interest is growing, relatively few basic research or intervention development research projects have been conducted. What is known tends to be grouped into four major ethnic groups: black American, Hispanic American, Native American, and Asian American.

It is beyond the scope of this article to review all the available literature about substance abuse among these four diverse groups. That type of review will be provided in a forthcoming paper.[4] Rather, issues that have specific relevance for prevention planning and intervention development will be reviewed for each group.

BLACK AMERICAN SUBSTANCE ABUSE ISSUES

The study of drug and alcohol abuse among blacks during the past decade has employed primarily descriptive epidemiological approaches and has focused on cross-sectional measures of prevalence. In recent years, a disproportionately large number of research studies of substance abuse among ethnic or minority groups has concerned blacks as compared to other groups.[5,6] Reviews of the literature noted several factors that correlated with substance abuse in black communities. These include economic factors such as poverty, unemployment, and lack of job opportunities, attitudinal factors such as feelings of hopelessness associated with ghetto life, frustration from continuing discrimination and perceived rejection, and sociocultural factors such as peer pressure, class conflicts, breakdown of family structure, lack of social support, and inadequate educational preparation.[7-9]

Despite this accumulated body of research, the relevant understanding of black substance abuse is lacking. Specifically missing is the appropriate information and insight necessary to design effective preventive interventions for this population. Several factors are worth noting.

First, an ingrained assumption permeating most studies is that black behavior is best understood by comparisons to white norms. The most serious implication of this assumption is that potentially relevant factors related to the symbolic meaning and cultural indices of substance use among blacks is obscured. Understanding such factors is critical to the development of culturally relevant interventions.

Second, there is a serious lack of agreement regarding a clear definition of substance abuse in general or of specific substance abuse behaviors. As described by King,[10] this lack of consensus not only has implications for intervention design, but it also effects the nature of the feedback that individuals receive from their peer group and community about what is or is not "acceptable behavior."

Third, while research has been devoted to individual differences among black substance abusers, little is known about the personality variables and intrapsychic factors that contribute to understanding the heterogeneity of the population group. The emphasis has been on attempts to identify common underlying etiological factors. This approach obscures relevant idiosyncrasies.

Fourth, insignificant attention has been devoted to studying members of the black community who are not substance abusers. More studies that attempt to identify factors which are relevant to the subjective norms imposed by this particular subculture, with respect to both health-promoting and health-compromising behaviors, are needed.

Fifth, various culturally specific social forces such as the predominance of matriarchic family structures and the central organizing role of the church among black communities, have not been utilized fully in developing preventive strategies.[8,9]

Sixth, the factors responsible for the high prevalence of substance use among black children and adolescents are poorly understood.[7]

Finally, the lack of systematic, longitudinal multivariate studies and the failure to employ ethnographic and other culturally sensitive data collection procedures also have impeded progress.

HISPANIC AMERICAN SUBSTANCE ABUSE ISSUES

The second largest ethnic group in the U.S. is the Hispanic American population, estimated at 23 million.[11] This group is highly heterogenous and comprised of many different subgroups. The four main subgroups are Mexican American, Puerto-Rican, Cuban, and Central/South American (including Caribbean Islander). True, across-the-board analyses of the entire population are unavailable because most research has focused predominantly on Mexican Americans.

It is difficult to compare findings across the four subgroups because they differ considerably with respect to education, income, occupation, health status, and degree of acculturation. Further, there is considerable confusion and a lack of consensus about the terms used to describe the various Hispanic subgroups, further complicating data analysis.[10,11] Nonetheless, several findings relevant to prevention planning efforts have been reported.

A major factor in determining whether Hispanics tend to become substance abusers or not seems to be their response to the stress of acculturation, and the struggle for mobility into the mainstream culture and upward socioeconomic success.

Second, the temporal sequence of use observed among Mexican Americans who use more than one substance tends to be marijuana followed by heroin.[13] It has been suggested that marijuana use among this group may be considered only as serious as tobacco use is among Anglos. If true, this would indicate the first substance use viewed as "serious" by this group may be heroin—a pattern not typically observed among other ethnic subgroups.

Third, many studies have reported that inhalant use is a particularly prevalent problem among Mexican-American adolescents and more so than in the general population.[14]

Fourth, of the various Hispanic subgroups, heroin addiction is prevalent particularly among Puerto Ricans. Drug dependence was reported to rank second among causes of death for Puerto Ricans ages 14–44 in New York City where one of every 14 "persons of Spanish origin" was described as an opiate abuser.

Fifth, cocaine abuse is a particular problem among the Cuban-American Hispanics of southern Florida.

Sixth, the Hispanic culture, due to the concept of machismo, places positive value on males drinking alcohol, while disapproving of the same behavior among females.[15] This results in a tendency for Hispanic American males to be heavier drinkers than the general population, while Hispanic American females abstain from drinking more often than their general population counterparts.[16]

Seventh, machismo also influences the effectiveness of prevention or treatment initiatives. This trait can keep males from seeking help and from heeding warnings about the dangers of substance use.[17]

Eighth, the concept of the *barrio* or neighborhood is a particularly salient and positive social force within Hispanic American communities. This factor and other potential aids to prevention planning often are overlooked.

ASIAN AMERICAN SUBSTANCE ABUSE ISSUES

More than 32 nationalities are covered by the term Asian American, yet this ethnic subgroup remains proportionally a small one, totaling about 3.5 million in 1980. Substance use variations have been reported among the different nationalities, a factor making generalizations about this group problematic. Burmese and Indonesian immigrants come from a Moslem background where drinking is prohibited; the Chinese come from a Confucian/Taoist tradition in which moderate drinking is the norm; and the majority of Japanese come from a society which has adopted a more liberal, western-oriented drinking style.

Other important differences exist among the subgroups that make comparative studies difficult. Subgroups vary with respect to geographic location within the U.S., generational status in this country (the number of generations removed they are from their home countries), degree of acculturation into the mainstream of American society, degree of identification with their home country, family structure and the degree to which the family is relied upon as an organizing force and social support system, their sociopolitical identification, their religious identification, their competence in the English language, and their perception of having had a choice in relocating in the U.S.[18] Little substance abuse research has been conducted in this highly diverse ethnic group, due partially to the diversity and geographic dispersion of this group, but also to a culturally defined reluctance to being researched which stems from the routine use of negative stereotyping and a lack of culturally sensitive data collection instruments.[19] Culturally determined sensitivity and shame related to problems such as substance abuse and the belief that the responsibility for dealing with them lies with the family have serious implications for prevention and treatment efforts. One generally accepted finding is that Asian Americans consume significantly less alcohol than Anglo Americans. This is likely to be related to the well-documented facial "flushing reflex," a physiological response that causes considerable discomfort when alcohol is consumed by Asians.[20,21]

Research efforts among this ethnic group could be improved substantially by using culturally acceptable survey items and instruments, commonly accepted definitions of substance use and abuse

behavioral criteria, ethnographic approaches to identifying cultural norms, the use of longitudinal designs and control groups, and the study of Asian Americans who are not substance abusers.

NATIVE AMERICAN SUBSTANCE ABUSE ISSUES

The Native American population in the U.S., including Alaskan Natives, is estimated at 1.5 million. As with the other ethnic groups, Native Americans comprise a highly heterogeneous collection of people; one-half live on rural reservations, the other half in urban sections of the West and Midwest. The most extensive study of adolescent Native American substance use and abuse was conducted by a Colorado-based research team.[22] Though a variety of substances were experimented with by this group, the study reported that alcohol was the substance of choice. Nearly 100 percent used alcohol by the 11th grade and, by the 12th grade, significantly more Native Americans had experienced a high from alcohol than non-Native Americans. Heavy drinking is also the reason most often given for Native Americans not finishing high school.[23] It also was reported that Native American youth are exposed to other substances such as stimulants, depressants, cocaine, and heroin at an earlier age than Anglo youth.

Despite the available research findings, many gaps in the understanding of Native American substance abuse have been noted. First, most of the reported research has focused on rural Native Americans, therefore, less is known about the urban half of the population group. This is of special concern due to the steadily increasing migration patterns of Native Americans into cities such as Los Angeles, Chicago, Seattle, and Minneapolis.[24] Second, as reviewed by Leland,[25] studies of Native American substance use have focused almost exclusively on males; little relevant data is available on females. This is unfortunate because at least one study has shown that Native American women, for reasons that remain unclear, do nearly twice as well as men in alcoholism treatment programs.[26] Third, most of the available basic research data focuses exclusively on adults and contributes little to understanding adolescent prevention issues.[27] The effectiveness of promising prevention approaches that are being developed could be improved if more basic adolescent data were available.[28]

IMPLICATIONS FOR PREVENTIVE INTERVENTIONS

Ethnic variability presents a dilemma to health planners who are responsible for developing culturally relevant substance abuse prevention initiatives. The typical question is, "For the ethnic group that we are interested in, which prevention approaches work?" The problem is not that preventive innovations are not available. The problem is that programs are not available that fulfill both criteria: demonstrated efficacy and cultural relevance for particular minority or ethnic groups. Two factors contribute to this situation.

First, the extensively evaluated prevention approaches have focused primarily upon white majority target groups. These programs, many of which have been comprehensively reviewed in two recent NIDA monographs,[29,30] are the result of more than a decade of research that began with basic studies of cigarette smoking among adolescents.[31] This pioneering work helped to identify the importance of social influences and cultural norms in the initiation of substance use behaviors and set the stage for developing strategies to counter the influences. These strategies, especially those relying on social influences[32] and life skills training[33] are based on a thorough understanding of the cultural context within which substance use is initiated. However, as noted previously, the culture from which these approaches were derived was not ethnic or minority specific, but from the white majority culture. While the intent of most of these efforts was to be nonspecific with respect to ethnicity, the result typically has been programs that are more culturally relevant to the white majority than to ethnic subgroups.

Second, when prevention programs were focused at specific ethnic groups, primary importance typically was placed on service delivery, with little or no attention on pilot testing or evaluation. This has resulted in programs that are promising but of questionable efficacy. These interventions, several examples of which are reviewed in Table 1, represent various approaches that tend to have a common theme. In contrast to the extensively evaluated programs, the culture-specific interventions are not designed to be delivered in school settings. The approaches may have school-based components, but they are primarily family-based and community-based. There are several reasons for this departure that relate to some critical differences between minority and majority populations that should be considered when planning preventive interventions.

First, majority youth at highest risk for initiating substance use behaviors are the least likely to receive adequate exposure to school-based and teacher-delivered programs due to higher absenteeism and dropout rates.

Second, a classroom-based intervention occupies a small portion of any youth's time; most of his or her day is spent outside the classroom. Even in the classroom, only a small segment of curriculum time is likely to be devoted to substance abuse pre

TABLE 1. Examples of Intervention Programs that Target Specific Ethnic or Minority Groups and that Include Substance Abuse Prevention as a Focus

PROGRAM NAME	LOCATION	TARGET GROUPS	INTERVENTION APPROACHES
REMCA	Durham, NC	BA	modified Parent Effectiveness Training
Navajo Youth Enrichment Program	Fort Defiance, AZ	NA: Navajo	values clarification
Six Sandoval Indian Pueblos	Bernalillo, NM	NA: Pueblo	peer counseling
Central Valley Indian Health	Fresno, CA	NA	alternatives, counseling, tribal medicine men
Early Childhood Affective Education	Las Vegas, NV	NA: Blackfoot; HA	affective education
Minnesota Inst. on Black Chemical Abuse	Minneapolis	BA	mass media, social skills training
Dr. Salsa's Medicine Show	Boston	HA; BA	music-oriented radio program
Hui O'Imi Hale	Honolulu	AA: Hawaiian	traditional family-oriented therapies
Youth Essential Service (Y.E.S.)	Boston	AA: Chinese	counseling, social services, employment
Families United Network (F.U.N.)	Denver	MC	family communication, problem solving
TICADA	Tulsa, OK	NA	social skills training, role models
West Dallas Community Centers	Dallas	HA; BA	education, alternatives, urban youth team
BHACA Boxing Team	Casa Grande, AZ	MC	alternatives decision-making, exercise
Barrio Nuevo Prevention Program	Casa Grande, AZ	HA: Mexican	alternatives, peer counseling
Channel One: Alethia House	Birmingham, AL	MC	communication skills, parental involvement
Channel One: Fort Defiance	Window Rock, AZ	NA: Navajo	alternatives, counseling
Channel One: Del Norte	Del Norte, CO	HA	alternatives, recreation
Free D.C.	Washington, DC	MC	alternatives, employment

BA = black American
NA = Native American
HA = Hispanic American
AA = Asian American
MC = multicultural

Where specific subgroups are targeted this is indicated. Multicultural programs have more than one ethnic or minority focus. Further details as well as contacts for these programs are provided in references 38 and 39.

vention. This time-related exposure factor increases the need for school-based interventions to utilize highly salient, culturally relevant, and targeted approaches.

Third, integrated approaches that emphasize the involvement of the family, church, and other organizations capitalize on the growing sense of pride and ownership.

Fourth, interventions that have a broader focus and which target various elements of a community are more likely to influence the sources of illicit substances and the community's general attitude toward substance use—factors that increase the probability the program will be maintained.

Needs identified by different ethnic and minority subcultures in the substance abuse prevention area are significant and extremely complex. Program planners acting on behalf of these groups typically have not utilized existing intervention approaches and materials that are the product of intervention development research programs. Rather, they have opted to develop new approaches based upon principles of cultural relevance. Intervention development research has targeted white majority populations in efforts to establish program efficacy. Each approach can create both positive and negative consequences.

PREVENTIVE INTERVENTIONS: TWO APPROACHES

Two basic but contrasting approaches to developing substance abuse prevention innovations can be described. The first approach assumes that most existing materials and programs are developed for members of the majority population by individuals who are insensitive to, or unaware of, the needs of specific minority subcultures. Therefore, health advocates who are members of a particular subculture, or change agents acting in their behalf, opt to develop programs from their personal knowledge of the target group rather than to rely on existing interventions. This approach can maximize relevancy to the subculture in question and can result in programs that are acceptable to the target subgroup. However, the approach may fail to utilize existing knowledge and expertise about the efficacy of various health promotion strategies, which could be relevant to crosscultural applications.

Contrary to the first method, the second approach relies on existing resources. It assumes that existing materials and programs, especially those demonstrated to be efficacious for majority populations, can and should be used with little modifica-

tion. The advantage is that the interventions in question have received some formative evaluation and subsequent redesign. In addition, this process, which is often made possible through grants and other funding sources, typically results in fairly sophisticated and appealing programs. To its disadvantage, the degree of cross-cultural reformulation and redesign required, both qualitatively and quantitatively, can easily be underestimated. It generally is understood that considerably more than literal translations from the original into other languages is required. However, the issue of whether, and to what degree, strategies designed for majority populations are relevant to multicultural populations is complex and not completely resolved.

The two approaches represent different and somewhat idiosyncratic orientations toward formulating culturally relevant intervention messages. To understand the significant differences and similarities between the two approaches, it is useful to compare them within the same theoretical framework, in this case a communication-behavior change framework.

PREVENTIVE INTERVENTIONS: A COMMUNICATION-BEHAVIOR CHANGE PERSPECTIVE

Farquhar et al[1] described a planning process, referred to as the communication-behavior change (CBC) framework, that is useful in developing effective community-based health promotion interventions. The approach is based on the work of many researchers, but draws most heavily on the social learning model of Bandura,[34] the hierarchy of learning model of Ray,[35] and the communication-persuasion model of McGuire.[36] In addition to providing a comprehensive model for developing and evaluating new interventions, this framework also can serve as a rubric for comparing different interventions and for analyzing the factors most likely to be responsible for an intervention's success or failure. A basic premise of the CBC framework is that health promotion interventions should be conceptualized as a series of communicated messages that have several highly specific characteristics.

The characteristics include, among others:

• **message factors:** the context, form, and structure of the health promotion message; messages should be structured in the language and style that is appropriate and culturally relevant to the target group;

- **channel factors:** the characteristics of the media used to convey the message; channels selected for transmitting the messages should be able to consistently reach a high percentage of the specific target group;

- **source factors:** the attributes of the individual, group, or organization perceived to be the source of the message; the message sources should be highly respected individuals or organizations and perceived as credible by the target population members;

- **destination factors:** the characteristics of the targeted change that the message seeks to cause; the target population must perceive the targeted change as feasible and salient; and

- **receiver factors:** the attributes of the target audience; the messages should be relevant to the cognitive ability, belief structure, and the value system of the intended receivers.

A second premise of the CBC framework is that optimally designed health promotion interventions, which have considered these communication factors, can be evaluated in terms of the process and outcome characteristics or objectives of the communicated message. The characteristics, which relate to different components of a hierarchical behavior change model, include process and outcome characteristics. Process characteristics are the tasks to be conducted by program providers: gain attention, provide information, provide incentives, provide models, provide training, provide cues to action, and provide support for continued self-management. Outcome characteristics include the changes to be induced from program recipients: increase awareness, increase knowledge, increase motivation, learn and practice skills, participate in trial behaviors, experience environmental support, take action, practice self-management and maintenance, and develop social support and practice health advocacy.

A considerable body of research has demonstrated the success of community-based health promotion campaigns based either directly or indirectly upon the CBC framework. Since the model also can be used to identify factors that should be considered when developing and evaluating interventions for specific subcultures, it helps to define the challenge to the developer of culturally sensitive health promotion interventions. In addition to requiring communications with highly specific message characteristics such as channel, source, and receiver, different members of a culturally distinct population group are likely to need emphasis placed on different variables and at different points along the hierarchical behavior change continuum. Some members may require more basic information, others more incentive to participate, and still others may be ready for specialized training.

From this perspective, each intervention development approach fails to utilize information that could considerably improve the likelihood of success. The first approach, which attempts to develop entirely new intervention strategies, is likely to be successful in identifying appropriate message, channel, destination, source, and receiver characteristics. However, this approach may not achieve meaningful behavior changes because of the difficulty involved in formulating interventions that move individuals from their respective levels of awareness, knowledge, belief, attitude, and intention through to action. The second approach would attempt to rely on existing health promotion strategies, making use of interventions that have considered the behavior change theoretical continuum. However, this approach also is likely to be unsuccessful unless culturally relevant and accurate information is utilized in the development of communications for specific target subgroups. Figure 1 contains a description of the relationship between these two approaches and a

FIGURE 1. Three Different Approaches to Innovation Planning and Development for Specific Applications

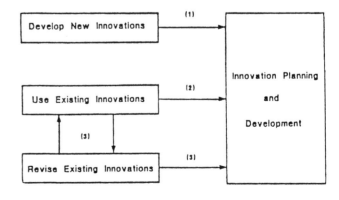

Approach 1 involves developing new innovations for specific applications that make little or no use of existing approaches.
Approach 2 makes use of existing approaches with the assumption that little or no modification will be necessary.
Approach 3 involves revising and modifying existing innovations to match the needs of a new application.

third approach, which is essentially a synthesis of these two and a resolution.

LINKAGE: A THIRD APPROACH

The two approaches to intervention development reviewed in this article were described in their most exaggerated forms to highlight weaknesses. Another approach that directly addresses the weaknesses was described by Havelock[2] and expanded by Kolbe and Iverson.[37] This approach, utilizing a framework called a linkage model, involves integrating three separate but interactive subsystems into a single general systems model (Figure 2).

The first subsystem is the resource system, comprised of the available health promotion programs and materials; the developers and researchers who have designed and tested these interventions; and the agencies, institutions, and individuals who facilitate the effective dissemination and adoption of the interventions. Some, but not all, individuals and agencies who design and test interventions also disseminate them. Further, evaluations of interventions vary considerably: some receive extensive field testing for efficacy, others are not evaluated. The

FIGURE 2. An Overview of the Linkage Approach to Innovation Dissemination

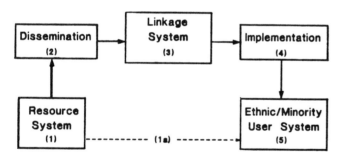

1) The Resource System consists of researchers, developers, trainers, consultants, services, products, and materials.
1a) The Non-Linkage Approach to Dissemination is when the resource system and user system interact directly, without the benefit of an intervening linkage step; tailoring of available innovation approaches to the specific needs of an individual target group is unlikely.
2) The Dissemination Process is the range of activities carried out specifically to result in the spread of an innovation to specific target groups.
3) The Linkage System consists of representatives of the resource system, representatives of the user system, change agents and, strategic planning activities.
4) The Implementation Process may be carried out either by members of the user system who have received training or by members of the resource system in systems where a linkage approach is utilized. The important point is that the implementation process, as well as the innovation itself, have been developed through collaboration thus increasing the likelihood that efficacious approaches will be used in a culturally-sensitive manner whenever possible.
5) The User System consists of the individuals, organizations, agencies, groups, and networks representing a specific ethnic or minority cultural group.

resource system also includes a repertoire of protocols, strategies, instruments, consultants, and trainers that represent specific experiences and skills.

The second subsystem, the user system, is comprised of the institutions, organizations, and individuals interested in committing human, financial, or environmental resources to adopting an intervention. The particular user system that this paper focuses on is a collective of interest groups representing socioculturally defined subcultures within the general community.

The two subsystems, representing users and potential resources, highlight the distinction between the two approaches to intervention development previously described. Attempts to develop new interventions that make little or no use of existing resources often are initiated by individuals who are members of the user subsystem. Their reluctance to use existing resources may stem from misinformation about resource availability or from concerns about the applicability of the resources for their specific interest groups. Similarly, the developers of programs and materials included in the resource system have targeted the interventions for majority population groups. Developers who also have evaluated these interventions typically have used majority test populations that are more accessible. The lack of specific attention devoted to minority populations or socioculturally defined subgroups is not likely to be an indication that the needs of these groups are misperceived. It is more likely due to the commonly accepted logic of intervention development research that calls for demonstrating that a health promotion strategy is feasible and efficacious for the majority, before attempting to demonstrate its generalizability to specific minority populations.

Improved communication and collaboration between the resource system and the user system is a solution to the deficiencies presented by the two approaches. As presented in Figure 2, a third subsystem, the collaborative exchange system or linkage system, can be defined. This system consists of the individuals and the actions required to collaboratively develop culturally sensitive interventions and dissemination strategies. The individuals interacting within the linkage system include representatives of the user and resource groups, plus "change agents" who objectively facilitate the collaboration. The role of the change agent can be filled by members of the user or resource system, or an independent third party. However, the critical aspect of the linkage model involves the actions that are conducted as a function of this collaborative exchange system. The actions can better be understood in the context of a specific approach to information exchange: the social marketing approach.

SOCIAL MARKETING PERSPECTIVE

Social marketing was defined by Kotler[3] as "the design, implementation, and control of programs seeking to increase the acceptability of a social idea or cause in a target group." This approach is relevant to the issues addressed in this paper because of its orientation toward the concept of "optimal fit" between interventions and designated target groups. Social marketing is a communication perspective that defines the relationship between providers and consumers of social change interventions as well as a protocol for collecting data required for program planning. According to this perspective, members of the resource system do not enter into the linkage process with the intention or goal of "selling" users a predetermined intervention strategy. Instead, they should determine the limitations, needs, and expectations of the user group.

Further, because optimally effective intervention messages must consider several culturally relevant communication factors, they also gather information about message, channel, destination, source, and receiver characteristics that is likely to increase the efficacy of the intervention message. This information is used to determine which available intervention strategies can be applied without modification, which are potentially applicable if modified, and which are unlikely to be effective in a particular community application, even with modification.

Similarly, when this approach is utilized, users do not enter into this linkage process with the expectation that they will need to adopt an existing intervention model or develop an entirely new program. The emphasis instead is on flexibility, strategy planning, and optimal use of resources. Certain conditions must exist for this approach to work effectively. First, representatives of the resource and user systems must be knowledgeable of their respective areas of expertise. Second, each group must re-

late to the other group as experts in their field, without whose input the intervention planning process would be less effective. Third, the user group should feel a sense of ownership toward the intervention plan as it evolves, rather than have a perception that the plan was developed for them or that it was handed down to them; they are active participants, rather than passive receivers. Social marketing can be perceived as a combination of data collection activities and subsequent strategic planning activities.

The goal of the process is for the linked resource and user subsystems to effectively conduct health promotion activities among culturally defined subgroups.

SUMMARY

Despite the World Health Organization's goal of "Health for All by the year 2000," a variety of economic and logistic constraints render the literal attainment of this goal unrealistic. A significant factor that will influence the effectiveness of worldwide health promotion efforts in the 1980s and the 1990s, is the dissemination of viable intervention strategies across cultural boundaries.

Given an understanding of the problem, who should initiate a collaborative process like the linkage process? Who should function as change agent? Should all minority or subcultural populations be given the opportunity to engage in a linkage or collaborative exchange process? How should decisions about involvement be made if participation is limited by fiscal or other reasons? How can quality control be maintained after crosscultural program dissemination? How can individuals knowledgeable and sensitive to crosscultural issues become more integrally involved in the resource development and intervention research process? These questions must be answered.

Several principles that must be considered to effectively disseminate health promotion innovations crossculturally have been identified. Effective drug abuse prevention efforts must consider these factors while striving to improve collaborative communications across various cultures. This paper has suggested a model for achieving this goal.

References

1. Farquhar J. W., Maccoby N., Solomon D. S.: Community applications of behavioral medicine, in Gentry WD (ed): *Handbook of Behavioral Medicine.* New York, The Guilford Press, 1984, pp 437–478.

2. Havelock R.: *Planning for Innovation Through Dissemination and Utilization of Knowledge.* Ann Arbor, Mich, Institute for Social Research, The University of Michigan, 1971.

3. Fox K. Kotler, P.: The marketing of social causes: the first 10 years. *J Marketing* 1980;44:24–33.

4. US Dept of Health and Human Services: *Drug Abuse Among Ethnic and Minority Populations.* Washington, DC, National Institute on Drug Abuse, Prevention Research Monograph, to be published.

5. Liyama P., Nishi S. M., Johnson B. D.: *Drug Abuse Among US Minorities: An annotated bibliography.* New York, Praeger Publishers, 1976.

6. Korchin S. J.: Clinical psychology and minority problems. *Am Psychol* 1980;35:262–269.

7. Brunswich A. F.: Black youths and drug-use behavior, in Beschner G. M., Friedman A. S. (eds): *Youth Drug Abuse.* Lexington, Mass, Lexington Press, 1979, pp 443–490.

8. Halikas J. A., Darvish H. S., Rimmer J. D.: The black addict: I. Methodology, chronology of addiction, and overview of the population. *Am J Drug Alcohol Abuse* 1976;3(4):529–543.

9. Harper F. D.: Alcohol use among North American blacks, in Israel Y, Glaser R. B., Kalant H, Popham R. E., et al (eds): *Research Advances in Alcohol and Drug Problems.* New York, Plenum Press, 1978, pp 349–366.

10. King L. M.: Social and cultural influences in psychopathology. *Ann Rev Psychol* 1978;29:231–262.

11. Szapocznik J. (ed): *Mental Health, Drug and Alcohol Abuse: An Hispanic assessment of present and future challenges.* Washington, DC, US Government Printing Office, NCOSSMHO, 1979.

12. Nobel E. P. (ed): *Third Special Report to the US Congress on Alcohol and Health from the Secretary of Health, Education, and Welfare.* Washington, DC, National Institute on Alcohol Abuse and Alcoholism, US Dept of Health, Education, and Welfare publication no (ADM) 78–569, 1978.

13. Crowthers B.: Patterns of drug use among Mexican Americans. *Int J Addict* 1972;(4).

14. Padilla E. R., Ramirez A. M., Morales R., Olmedo E. L.: Inhalent, marijuana, and alcohol abuse among barrio children and adolescents. *Int J Addict* 1979;14:943–964.

15. Maril R. E., Zavaleta A. N.: Drinking patterns of low-income Mexican American women. *J Stud Alcohol* 1979; 40(5):480–484.

16. Engmann D. *Alcoholism and Alcohol Abuse Among the Spanish Speaking Population in California: A needs and services assessment.* San Francisco, Engmann and Associates, 1976.

17. Abad V.: *Machismo and Alcoholism Among Puerto Ricans.* Read before the Fourth Annual Alcoholism Conference of the National Institute on Alcohol Abuse and Alcoholism, Washington, DC, 1974.

18. Nakagawa B., Watanabe R.: *A study of the use of drugs among the Asian-American youth of Seattle.* Seattle Demonstration Project for the Asian-Americans, 1973.

19. Sue D. W., Sue S.: Ethnic minorities: Resistance to being researched. *Professional Psychol* 1972;3(3):11–17(b).

20. Ewing J. A., Rouse B. A., Pellizzari E. D.: Alcohol sensitivity and ethnic background. *Am J Psychiatr* 1974;131(2):206–210.

21. Wolf, P. H.: Ethnic differences in alcohol sensitivity. *Science* 1972;175:449–450.

22. Oetting E. R., Beauvais F., Edwards R., Velarde J., et al: *Drug Use Among American Indian Youth.* Fort Collins, Colo, Western Behavioral Studies, Colorado State University, 1983.

23. Royce J. E.: *Alcohol Problems and Alcoholism.* New York, Free Press 1981.

24. Officer: The American Indian and federal policy, in Waddell J., Watsom M. (eds): *The American Indian in Urban Society.* Boston, Little, Brown, and Co, 1971, pp 8–65.

25. Leland J.: Women and alcohol in an Indian settlement. *Med Anthropol* 1978;2:85–120.

26. Shore J. H., von Fumetti B.: Three alcohol programs for American Indians. *Am J Psychiatr* 1972;128:1450–1454.

27. Wiebel-Orlando J.: Substance abuse among American Indian youth: A continuing crisis. *J Drug Issues* 1984;14:331–358.

28. Schinke P., Gilchrist L., Shilling R., Walker R., et al: Strategies for preventing substance abuse with American Indian youth. *White Cloud Journal of American Indian Mental Health* 1985;3(4):12–18.

29. US Dept. of Health and Human Services: *Preventing Adolescent Drug Abuse: Intervention Strategies.* Washington, DC, National Institute on Drug Abuse. Research Monograph no 47, US Dept of Health and Human Services publication no (ADM) 83–1280, 1983.

30. US Dept of Public Health: *Prevention Research: Deterring drug abuse among adolescents.* Washington DC, National Institute on Drug Abuse, Research Monograph no 63, US Dept of Health and Human Services publication no (ADM) 85–1334, 1985.

31. Evans R. I.: Smoking in children: Developing a social psychological strategy of deterrence. *Prev Med* 1976–5:122–127.

32. Flay B. R.: What we know about the social influences approach to smoking prevention: Review and recommendations, in *Drug Abuse Among Children and Adolescents.* Washington, DC, US Dept of Health and Human Services, NIDA Research Monograph no 63, US Dept of Health and Human Services publication no (ADM) 85–1334, 1985.

33. Botvin G. J., Wills T. A.: Personal and social skills training: Cognitive-behavioral approaches to substance abuse prevention, in *Drug Abuse Among Children and Adolescents.* Washington, DC, US Dept of Health and Human Services, NIDA Research Monograph no 63, US Dept of Health and Human Services publication no (ADM) 85–1334, 1985.

34. Bandura A.: *Social Learning Theory.* Englewood Cliffs, NJ, Prentice Hall, 1977.

35. Ray M. L., Sawyer A. G., Rothschild M. L., Heeler R. M., et al: Marketing communication and the hierarchy of effects, in Clarke P (ed): *New Models For Mass Communication Research.* Beverly Hills, Calif, Sage, 1973.

36. McGuire W. J.: The nature of attitudes and attitude change, in Lindsey G., Aronson E. (eds), *The Hand-book of Social Psychology.* Reading, Mass, Addison-Wesley, 1969.
37. Kolbe L. J., Iverson D. C.: Implementing comprehensive health education: Educational innovations and social change. *Health Educ Q* 1981;8(1):57–80.
38. US Dept of Health Education and Welfare: Multicultural *Perspectives on Drug Abuse and its Prevention: A resource book.* Washington, DC, National Institute on Drug Abuse, US Dept of Health, Education, and Welfare publication no (ADM) 78–671, 1979.
39. US Dept of Health and Human Services: Multicultural perspective in drug abuse prevention, in *Prevention Networks.* Washington, DC, National Institute on Drug Abuse, US Dept of Health and Human Services publication no (ADM) 85–1373, 1984.

39

THE SOCIAL DEVELOPMENT MODEL:

AN INTEGRATED APPROACH TO DELINQUENCY PREVENTION

J. David Hawkins

Center for Social Welfare Research
School of Social Work
University of Washington

Joseph G. Weis

Center for Law and Justice
Department of Sociology
University of Washington

THE PROBLEM

Juvenile delinquency is a persistent social problem (Stark, 1975). Over 40 percent of the total arrests for the eight major FBI "index" crimes—murder, forcible rape, robbery, aggravated assault, burglary, larceny, arson, and motor vehicle theft—are of youths under 18 years old. By far the largest number of juvenile arrests are for larceny and burglary (Galvin and Polk, 1983). The social and economic costs of juvenile delinquency are high (National Advisory Committee on Criminal Justice Standards and Goals, 1976) and public fear of victimization is pervasive, with more than two-thirds of adults in the U.S. worrying about the prospect of becoming the victim of a typical juvenile offense—residential burglary (Weis and Henney, 1979)—and 87 percent perceiving a "steady and alarming increase in the rate of serious juvenile crime" (Galvin and Polk, 1983).

THE HISTORY OF PREVENTION AND CONTROL

Historically, there have been two ways to deal with juvenile crime: prevention and control. Prevention is an *action* taken to preclude illegal behavior before it occurs. Control is a *reaction* to an infraction after it has been committed (Lejins, 1967). Prevention can be differentiated further into two broad categories: early intervention and primary prevention. Early intervention seeks to identify predelinquents or youths who are high risks for delinquency and to correct their behavioral tendencies or criminogenic circumstances before delinquency results. In contrast, primary prevention does not seek to "correct" individuals who are identified as on the path to delinquency. Rather, it attempts to preclude the initial occurrence of delinquency, primarily at organizational, institutional, social structural, and cultural levels. Thus, it also has been called preclusive prevention (Weis and Hawkins, 1981).

From the passage of the first juvenile court statute in Illinois in 1899 to the signing of the Juvenile Justice and Delinquency Prevention Act of 1974, the juvenile justice system had almost total responsibility for dealing with juvenile crime. This system is largely reactive, seeking to *control* juvenile crime by responding to illegal acts by juveniles brought to its attention. It also practices early intervention by responding to individuals whose behavior, environment, or other attributes are thought to be predictive of delinquency. These youngsters are often brought to the attention of the juvenile court for "status offenses"—noncriminal misbehavior which is viewed as indicative that the child is headed for more serious trouble (Gough, 1977). Although ostensibly a paternalistic institution of control *and* prevention, the juvenile justice system primarily engages in the control of juvenile offenders and presumed predelinquents (Weis, Sakumoto, Sederstrom and Zeiss, 1980).

In the 1960s and 1970s, collective criticisms mounted against the juvenile justice system resulted in a new juvenile justice philosophy embodied in the Juvenile Justice and Delinquency Prevention Act of 1974 and its subsequent amendments. The new *dual functions* philosophy of juvenile justice separates formal legal control from prevention.

The dual functions philosophy restricts the responsibility of the juvenile court to the control of juvenile criminals, a responsibility consonant with its status as a criminal justice institution with the power to deprive law violators of liberty. At the same time, the juvenile court's mandate to intervene before

From the *Journal of Primary Prevention*, 1985, 6(2): 73–97. Copyright © 1985. Human Services Press. Reprinted by permission.

young people commit delinquent acts is severely restricted under this new philosophy. Mandatory deinstitutionalization of youths accused only of status offenses, diversion of youths who engage in both minor crimes and noncriminal misbehavior, and the removal of certain status offenses from the jurisdiction of the juvenile court in some states, have limited the court's authority to engage in the corrective prevention of youth crime. The court's major responsibility now is to control identified juvenile criminals through rehabilitation and punishment. The task of *preventing* youth crime has been removed from the court and given back to communities.

The limitation of the juvenile court's authority does not signal a preference for control over prevention. On the contrary, the change embodies the belief that informal socialization units such as families, schools, and communities are both more appropriate and more likely to succeed in preventing juvenile crime than is the juvenile justice system (e.g., Woodson, 1981). In a major exposition of this philosophy of juvenile justice, the President's Commission on Law Enforcement and Administration of Justice and its Task Force on Juvenile Delinquency emphasized the importance of the primary prevention of juvenile crime outside the juvenile justice system.

> In the last analysis, the most promising and so the most important method of dealing with crime is by preventing it—by ameliorating the conditions of life that drive people to commit crimes and that undermine the restraining rules and restrictions erected by society against antisocial conduct. (1967, p. vi)
>
> Clearly it is with young people that prevention efforts are most needed and hold the most promise. It is simply more critical that young people be kept from crime. . . . They are not yet set in their ways; they are still developing, still subject to the influence of the socializing institutions that structure—however skeletally—their environment. . . . But the influence to do the most good must come *before* the youth has become involved in the formal criminal justice system. (1967, p. 41)

Prevention of juvenile crime is an essential element in the current philosophy of juvenile justice. Reforms such as diversion and deinstitutionalization are not likely to decrease the initial rates of criminal acts by juveniles. At best, they can prevent further penetration into the juvenile justice system. Without effective means for decreasing the number of youths who initially engage in delinquent acts—that is,

without effective delinquency prevention at the family, school, and community levels—the costs of youth crime, the fear of victimization, and the number of youths processed through the juvenile courts will remain high.

In summary, under the dual functions philosophy of juvenile justice, the juvenile court has been limited to the control of juvenile offenders. While prevention has been legislatively mandated as essential to the success of the philosophy, the juvenile court's power to engage in either primary prevention or early intervention has been severely limited. Instead, families, schools, and communities have been given back the task of preventing youth crime. For this philosophy to succeed, a pressing task is to find effective means in these units for preventing youth crime.

PAST EXPERIENCE AND PROSPECTS

The history of juvenile crime prevention provides little cause for optimism about this task. Given the control orientation of the juvenile justice system during its first 75 years of operation, there have been only a small number of early intervention efforts and even fewer primary prevention programs. The knowledge and techniques of delinquency prevention have not been well developed. Most efforts at delinquency prevention that have been evaluated rigorously show ambiguous, mixed, or negative results (see, e.g., National Council on Crime and Delinquency, 1981; Lundman and Scarpitti, 1978; Newton, 1978; Powers and Witmer, 1951; Wright and Dixon, 1977). Of 10 delinquency prevention programs with experimental designs which were carried out prior to 1970, nine failed to reduce rates of official delinquency among experimental subjects as compared with controls (Berleman, 1980). It should be noted that most of these projects were early intervention efforts, focused on high-risk youths, rather than primary prevention programs.

Unfortunately, even some of the recent federal program initiatives in delinquency prevention have provided little information about effective approaches. The *Preliminary Report of the National Evaluation of Prevention* funded in 1978 by the Office of Juvenile Justice and Delinquency Prevention reported that "few of the projects actually attempted to prevent delinquency" (Krisberg, 1978, p. 28). These federally funded prevention efforts appeared to lack the conceptual foundation, clear focus, and commitment to rigorous research necessary to generate the knowledge required for effective delinquency prevention (Krisberg, 1978).

Two general implications for delinquency prevention can be drawn from past attempts. First, a major goal of future efforts should be the development of a tested body of knowledge about effective prevention programs. Since past efforts in delinquency prevention have been largely ineffective, it is not sensible to replicate and generalize existing exemplary programs as the preferred approach. New delinquency prevention efforts should be created and tested within a research and development framework. Both their efforts and effects must be documented using rigorous research designs if techniques of effective delinquency prevention are to be developed.

Second, the best empirical evidence available on correlates, causes, and theories of delinquent behavior as well as on delinquency prevention programs should be used as a basis for selecting promising prevention approaches. This position was stated directly by the National Task Force to Develop Standards and Goals for Juvenile Justice and Delinquency Prevention in its volume *Preventing Delinquency* (1977, p. 8):

> . . . it is necessary to clarify assumptions about what causes delinquency before deciding what to do about it. . . . Since theory sets forth assumptions about what causes crime, the theories, by implication, should also suggest appropriate action to reduce delinquency.

Additionally, the best available evidence regarding delinquency prevention programs should be used (Task Force on Juvenile Justice and Delinquency Prevention of the National Advisory Committee on Criminal Justice Standards and Goals, 1977).

TOWARD A MODEL OF DELINQUENCY PREVENTION

At the National Center for the Assessment of Delinquent Behavior and its Prevention we have conducted a comprehensive review of theories and research on delinquency, secondary analyses of self-reported delinquency data sets, and a national survey of prevention programs, to identify promising approaches to delinquency prevention. Our work suggests three general principles for delinquency prevention:

1. Prevention approaches should focus on the causes of delinquency if they are to be effective (Hawkins, Pastor, Bell, and Morrison, 1980).

2. There are multiple correlates and causes of delinquency. They operate within the institutional domains of family, school, peers, and community (Henney, 1976; Sakumoto, 1978; Sederstrom, 1978; Weis et al., 1980a, 1980b; Worsley, 1979; Zeiss, 1978). Effective prevention should address these multiple causes in all of these settings.

3. Delinquency results from experiences during the process of social development. Different causal elements are more salient at different stages in the developmental process. Therefore, different prevention techniques are required at different stages in the socialization of youths (Weis and Hawkins, 1981).

Delinquency prevention should not only be responsive to the "causes" of delinquency, but also to the manner in which etiological factors interact in the process of social development. If prevention efforts are to address the apparent complexities of causal relations, they should be targeted at factors as they emerge and interact during the different stages in youngsters' lives. In short, a dynamic, multifaceted model of delinquency prevention is required.

An integration of *control theory* (Briar and Piliavin, 1965; Hirschi, 1969; Matza, 1964; Nettler, 1974; Nye, 1958; Reckless, 1961; Reiss, 1951; Toby, 1957) and *social learning theory* (Akers, 1977; Akers et al., 1979; Burgess and Akers, 1966) promises to meet these requirements by specifying the empirically supported elements, units, and processes necessary in a comprehensive model of delinquency prevention.

Empirical tests of control theory (Hindelang, 1973; Hirschi, 1969; Kornhauser, 1978) have shown that "attachment" to family, school, and conventional others, "commitment" to conventional lines of action, and "belief" in the validity and legitimacy of the legal order are elements of a social bond to conventional society which prevents delinquent behavior. Control theory specifies that family and school are important *units* of socialization which should be the foci of prevention efforts. The goal of these efforts should be to strengthen the *elements* of the social bond (attachment, commitment, and belief) between youths and society. But control theory does not specify how such a bond develops within the units of socialization.

In contrast, social learning theory (Akers, 1977; Akers et al., 1979; Burgess and Akers, 1966) specifies the *processes* by which behavior—whether conforming or criminal—is learned and maintained. According to social learning theory, behavior is learned when it results in a reward (positive reinforcement) and it is not learned or is extinguished when not rewarded or punished. Within the social context of interaction, reinforcement contingencies determine whether an individual learns conforming or criminal behavior. Thus, according to social learning theory, differential involvement with those who reinforce criminal or conforming behavior will determine whether or not a youth adopts criminal behavior patterns.

In addition to specifying the processes by which conforming and delinquent behaviors are learned, social learning theory's emphasis on social influence fills a void in control theory. It suggests that association with delinquent peers can contribute to delinquent behavior. Control theory fails to account for the empirical evidence which shows that peer influence is directly and strongly related to delinquent behavior (Elliott et al., 1982; Hindelang, 1973; Hirschi, 1969; Jessor and Jessor, 1977). However, an integration of control and social learning theories allows for the incorporation of peers as an important unit of socialization.

The social development model of delinquency prevention derived from integrating control and social learning theories is presented in Figure 1. As shown in the figure, social development is a process in which the most important units of socialization—families, schools, and peers—influence behavior sequentially, both directly and indirectly.

In each unit of socialization, three types of process variables (opportunities for involvement, skills, and reinforcements) determine whether a youth's participation in that unit will contribute to the development of a bond of attachment and commitment to and belief in conventional society.

In the social development model, opportunities for involvement are viewed as necessary, but not sufficient, for the development of a social bond. We hypothesize that youths must have opportunities to interact with conventional others and to be involved

in conventional activities in order to develop attachment and commitment to conventional others and lines of action. However, we hypothesize that such interactions and involvements will lead to social bonding only if they are positively experienced and evaluated by youths. Two factors appear to affect the extent to which youths are likely to perceive their involvements as rewarding: the level of skill applied by youths during involvement or interaction and the availability of reinforcements from the environment for desired behavior. Therefore, we hypothesize youths' possession of the skills for involvement and interaction is a second necessary condition for the development of a social bond. Finally, we hypothesize that the availability of consistent rewards for skillfully handled involvements and interactions is the third prerequisite necessary for the development of a social bond.

Research by Elliott et al., 1982, supports the hypothesis that the development of a social bond of attachment, commitment, and belief between a youth and conventional society will decrease the likelihood that the youth will associate with delinquent peers. We hypothesize that a social bond to conventional society also will prevent delinquent behavior, both directly and indirectly, by decreasing the likelihood of association with delinquent peers.

The bonding process begins in the family. When youths experience opportunities for involvement in the family, when they develop the requisite social, cognitive, and behavioral skills to perform as expected in family activities and interactions and when they are rewarded consistently for adequate performance in the family, they will develop a bond of attachment, commitment, and belief in the family. When these three conditions are not present in the family, a bond to family is not likely to develop.

Bonding to school is conditioned by the extent to which social bonds to the family have developed by the time the child enters school as well as by the extent to which the child experiences opportunities for involvement, develops skills, and is rewarded for skillful performance at school. Similarly, social

FIGURE 1. The Social Development Model

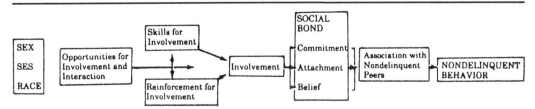

bonds to peers, whether prosocial or delinquent, will develop to the extent that youths have opportunities for involvement with those peers, the skills to perform as expected by those peers and the rewards that are forthcoming from interaction with those peers. We do not suggest that strong bonds of attachment to family and school will preclude the development of strong bonds of attachment to peers so long as the norms of family members, school personnel, and peers regarding appropriate performance or behavior do not conflict. However, we suggest that the formation of social bonds to family and school will decrease the likelihood that youths will develop attachments to *delinquent* peers in adolescence, since the behaviors rewarded in family and school and those likely to be rewarded by delinquent youths are not compatible.

However, if the process of developing a social bond to conforming others has been interrupted by uncaring or inconsistent parents, by poor school performance, by inconsistent teachers, or by circumstances which make conventional involvement unrewarding, youths are more free to engage in delinquent behavior *and* more likely to come under the influence of peers who are in the same situation. Such youths may then provide each other with the social and psychological supports, rewards, and reinforcements which are not forthcoming in more conventional contexts (e.g., Cohen and Short, 1961). Consequently, such youths are more susceptible to those who reinforce deviant actions, as well as to the direct reinforcement offered by delinquent involvement.

As a foundation for delinquency prevention, the social development model implies that families, schools, and peer groups are appropriate objects for intervention, depending on the developmental stage of the child. Interventions which seek to increase the likelihood of social bonding to the family are appropriate from early childhood through early adolescence. Interventions which seek to increase the likelihood of social bonding to school are appropriate from early childhood through early adolescence. Interventions which seek to increase the likelihood of social bonding to school are appropriate throughout the years of school attendance. Interventions which seek to increase social bonding prosocial peers are appropriate as youths approach and enter adolescence. It should be noted that interventions consistent with the model do not directly treat individual youths in hopes of changing their attitudes or behavior. Rather, the model suggests that prevention approaches should seek changes in the units of so-

cialization to increase opportunities for rewarding involvement in conventional activities, the development of skills for successful participation and interaction, and clear and consistent systems of reinforcement for conforming behavior.

PROMISING PROGRAMS

The social development model provides an empirically grounded theoretical base for designing, implementing, and assessing delinquency prevention programs. In the remainder of this paper, we review some interventions which appear consistent with the model.

This list is by no means exhaustive. It includes approaches currently in operation across the country, although a number of these programs do not hold an explicit goal of delinquency prevention and few have been evaluated rigorously. Thus, except where otherwise noted, their selection is based on their fidelity with the model of social development, rather than on their proven effectiveness in delinquent prevention. It is clear that identifying and developing proven prevention approaches will require a long-term commitment to systematic research and evaluation.

FAMILY INTERVENTIONS

The social development model assumes both direct (Bahr, 1979; Jensen, 1972; Stanfield, 1966), and indirect (Elliott et al., 1982; Krohn, 1974) influences of the family on delinquent behavior. The indirect effects are through school experiences, belief in the moral order, and peer group associations. There is sufficient evidence to conclude that strong attachments between youths and their parents inhibit delinquency (Hirschi, 1969; Nye, 1958; Reckless et al., 1956). Family structure appears to be less important as a predictor of delinquency than is attachment to parents (Nye, 158; Sederstrom, 1979; Weis et al., 1980; Wilkinson, 1974). Family focused interventions seek to increase parent-child attachment.

1. PARENTING TRAINING

Parenting training for delinquency prevention is one vehicle for achieving this goal. Parenting training should seek to teach parents effective family management and child rearing skills (Fraser and Hawkins, in press). Parents should have the skills to:

a. Provide developmentally appropriate opportunities for their children to be involved with other family members and in family tasks. It is hypothesized that when parents provide children with developmentally adjusted participatory roles in the family as contributors to family functioning and when they reward children for performance in these roles, attachment to the family will be enhanced and delinquency prevented. Additionally, the greater the affection, nurture, and support shown children by parents, the greater the likelihood of attachment between parents and children and the less the likelihood of delinquency (Hirschi, 1969; Jensen, 1972).

b. Communicate effectively with their children—parenting skills rely in good part on effective communication between parent and child. The more parents and children communicate with one another regarding thoughts, feelings, and values, the stronger the attachment between children and parents (Hirschi, 1969; Krohn, 1974). Parents can be assisted through parenting training in opening and maintaining lines of communication with their children, in empathetic listening, and in basic interaction skills (Alexander and Parsons, 1973; Patterson and Reid, 1973).

c. Define clear and consistent expectations and sanctions for family members—fairness and impartiality of discipline appear related to family attachment and family control (Bahr, 1979; Hirschi, 1969; Nye, 1958; Stanfield, 1966). Sanctions used to punish should be moderate and inclusionary and imply no rejection or ostracism of the child. Consistent parental discipline also appears to increase the likelihood of belief in the moral order (Bahr, 1979). Parenting training can assist parents in developing consistent discipline practices and can also provide parents with the skills to utilize positive reinforcement to shape the life of the child (Alexander and Parsons, 1973). Finally, parents should be consistent in modeling law-abiding behavior for their children if children are to develop belief in the legal order. Parenting training can emphasize the importance of this modeling by parents.

By including parenting training as a school- or workplace-based program and by recruiting parents intensively through schools, work place, and community organizations, broad cross sections of the parent population may be involved in parenting training. Parenting training may be beneficial at several stages during the child's social development.

The content of training can be altered to suit the developmental level of children whose parents are included. For example, for parents of fourth graders, emphasis might be placed on involving children in contributory roles in the family and rewarding satisfactory performance of those roles. Content for parents of seventh graders might emphasize behavioral contracting and negotiation of rights and responsibilities during the process of adolescent individuation. Parenting training for delinquency prevention seeks to improve parenting skills, thereby increasing attachment between children and parents and improving the control effectiveness of the family. (See Wall et al., 1981, and Fraser and Hawkins, in press, for examples and reviews of parenting training programs.)

2. FAMILY CRISIS INTERVENTION SERVICES

A promising early intervention approach focused on the family is crisis intervention for families of children aged 12 to 16. Family crisis intervention services which use an educational approach to families as systems have been shown effective for both early intervention and primary prevention (Alexander and Parsons, 1973; Klein et al., 1977). Experimental evidence indicates that when both parents and children are trained in communication, contingency contracting, and negotiation skills, delinquency referrals are reduced among "status offenders" and minor delinquents. This approach also appears to reduce the likelihood of delinquency referrals of younger siblings (Klein et al., 1977).

As runaways and children in conflict with their parents have been deinstitutionalized, diverted, or removed entirely from jurisdiction of the juvenile court, greater responsibility for controlling children has been returned to families. The systems-oriented, skills-training approach to family crisis intervention services seeks to increase effective parental supervision and family communication in families in conflict, to increase attachment between parents and children where these attachments have become weak or broken, and thereby to prevent delinquent behavior. (See Wall et al., 1981, pp. 46, 127 for examples.)

SCHOOL-FOCUSED INTERVENTIONS

Research has linked academic failure, as measured by grades and achievement test scores, to delinquent behavior (Elliott and Voss, 1974; Hirschi, 1969; Jensen, 1976; Linden, 1974; Polk and Schafer,

1972). At the individual level, academic achievement appears to be a predictor of delinquent behavior that transcends social class and ethnicity (Call, 1965; Jensen, 1976; Polk and Halferty, 1966; Stinchcombe, 1964), suggesting that providing a greater proportion of students with opportunities to experience success in school should hold promise for preventing delinquency.

A second school factor related to delinquency is commitment to academic or educational pursuits. When students are not committed to educational pursuits, they are more likely to engage in delinquent behavior (Elliott and Voss, 1974; Hirschi, 1969). Similarly, attachment to school is related to delinquency. Students who do not like school are more likely to engage in delinquent acts than those who do (Hirschi, 1969). These data suggest that educational innovations which encourage students to feel part of the school community and to become committed to educational goals hold promise for preventing delinquency.

1. SCHOOLS-WITHIN-A-SCHOOL

The size of a school and the number of students taught per teacher may help determine the availability of opportunities for active participation in school. In large schools where teachers see a number of different students each day, teachers are generally less able to establish interpersonal relationships with students and to utilize a broad range of rewards for student participation (Garbarino, 1980). In the absence of warm interpersonal relationships between students and teachers, delinquency is more likely (Gold, 1978). Consistently, research has shown correlations between rates of school crime and both school size and average number of students taught by teachers. Smaller schools are characterized by lower levels of student offenses when ability level, racial composition, and economic status of students are controlled (McPartland and McDill, 1977; National Institute of Education, 1978; Smith et al., 1976). Similarly, where fewer students are seen each day by a teacher, rates of school crime are lower. Given the fiscal pressures facing school districts, it is not usually feasible to alter school size, though the number of different students seen by teachers can be affected by organizational change such as the creation of schools-within-a-school.

The schools-within-a-school concept refers to the division of a larger school into smaller units called houses. This subdivision of schools can provide the benefits of a small school setting while al-

lowing for the diversity of resources and course offerings afforded by a large school. Schools-within-a-school may be subdivisions of educational structure (subdividing students, teachers, guidance counselors, and administrators) or may be distinct social entities in which academic and extracurricular activities such as student government and sports are decentralized.

The schools-within-a-school plan is designed to promote the development of interpersonal relationships (Yaglou, 1968), to provide for "increased attention to the individual pupil" (Barrett, 1971), and to increase "opportunities to take the initiative, to enjoy recognition, to exercise leadership" (Kleinert, 1969). It is hypothesized that this restructuring of schools will produce increases in the quantity and quality of opportunities for active participation in school roles and in the contacts between students and teachers, which in turn will lead to greater commitments to school and attachments between students and teachers. These attachments and commitments should enhance a belief in the value and legitimacy of the educational process.

2. RESTRUCTURED METHODS OF INSTRUCTION

Traditional teaching methods and grading practices do not guarantee the success of all students (McPartland and McDill, 1977; Silberman, 1970). A promising approach to the development of social bonding to school is to train teachers in instructional methods which will enable a broader range of students to experience academic success without compromising academic standards. Systematic changes in classroom instructional practices should increase the proportion of students who experience academic success, increase students' attachments to teachers and nondelinquent peers, and increase students' beliefs in the fairness of school. Promising instructional methods for achieving these goals are interactive teaching, proactive classroom management, and student team learning.

• *Interactive Teaching*—Interactive teaching is a method based on the supported assertion that under appropriate instructional conditions, virtually all students can learn most of what they are taught (Bloom, 1976). The approach requires the specification of clear and specific instructional objectives that students must master in order to proceed to additional coursework. Each student is required to demonstrate a certain cognitive level of mastery of these instructional objectives. Students' grades are determined by demonstration of this mastery rather than by comparison of their ability to that of other students. The student is supported as necessary in repeated trials on a task and is assisted by "formative evaluations" that measure progress toward mastery and identify areas of difficulty. The student receives small incremental rewards that are clearly tied to performance in the attainment of the established instructional objectives (Block, 1971; Brophy, 1979).

• *Proactive Classroom Management*—Proactive classroom management trains teachers to prevent behavioral problems in the classroom before they occur. Strategies include the establishment of clear rules, the teaching of management systems that give students responsibilities, the effective use of praise, clear direction giving, and the systematic use of the least disruptive intervention in the classroom needed to maintain order. Proactive classroom management strategies have been shown to relieve teacher stress and to create a positive climate for learning (Brophy, 1979; Emmer and Evertson, 1980).

• *Student Team Learning*—Successful mastery of learning tasks, student motivation, positive student attitudes toward teachers and school, and student self-esteem are greater when students learn in cooperative classroom situations rather than in competitive or individualistic ones (Johnson and Johnson, 1980; Slavin, 1979). Student team learning is an instructional technique which groups students together to perform tasks in the classroom. In student team learning, the attainment of individual student goals depends simultaneously on the success of other students. This encourages students to influence one another to do their best academically. In short, student team learning creates a general classroom norm favoring learning and academic performance (Slavin, 1978).

3. STUDENT INVOLVEMENT IN SCHOOL CLASSROOM POLICY FORMULATION AND DISCIPLINE PROCEDURES

While adolescents are not usually in a position to take on major work roles, commitments to conventional lines of action can be enhanced by providing them opportunities to find meaningful roles in shaping the institution in which they are most directly involved—their school and its classrooms (Coleman, 1961).

Students can be provided opportunities to be involved in formulating certain school policies and discipline procedures. Attention should be given to recruitment of a broad range of "natural leaders" for participation in policy making and disciplinary bodies to insure that participatory roles are created for students not typically involved in traditional student leadership groups. (See Open Road Student Involvement and Positive Peer Culture in Wall et al., 1981, pp. 75, 90 for examples of programs which provide opportunities for mixed student groups.)

It is hypothesized that increasing opportunities for student involvement in school policy and discipline will increase student attachment to school, commitment to conventional lines of action, and belief in the moral order.

4. LIFE SKILLS TRAINING

Developing youths' cognitive and social skills is the major function of schools. Thus, many promising school-based prevention components focus on student skill development. For example, the methods of instruction discussed earlier seek to increase cognitive skills. Life skills training is a specific addition to the school curriculum.

Life skills training assumes that young people need to learn basic communication, decision making, negotiation, and conflict resolution skills in order to perform effectively in interpersonal situations with family members, teachers, or peers. The premise is that schools should teach these skills for interpersonal functioning just as they teach cognitive skills. If young people have these skills, they are more likely to find their interactions with conventional others rewarding and to develop attachments to these others. These skills may also contribute to academic success and to attachment and commitment to schools. On the other hand, when these skills are absent, young people may become frustrated in interaction with others, may be more susceptible to delinquent influences, and may turn to unacceptable behaviors to meet their needs.

A number of effective curricula are available. (See Schaps and Slimmon, 1975; Wall, et al., 1981, pp. 40, 97 for examples.)

5. LAW-RELATED EDUCATION IN CIVIL, CRIMINAL, CONSUMER RIGHTS, AND RESPONSIBILITIES

A second curriculum addition seeks ultimately to increase belief in the law by educating students about the functions of the law and their rights and responsibilities under it. By including attention to civil and consumer law as well as to criminal law, students can learn how to use the law for their own protection and how to use legal means to achieve their goals. By exploring the use of the law to achieve personally desired ends, this intervention seeks to develop belief in the law. (See National Street Law Institute in Wall et al., 1981, p. 68.)

6. EXPERIENTIAL PREVOCATIONAL TRAINING AND EXPLORATION

A final change in curriculum focuses on preparing students for the world of work while still in school. Young people's expectations and aspirations are related to their commitments to conventional lines of action (Hirschi, 1969). Schools can provide young people with information and experiences which will help them develop aspirations and expectations for attaining legitimate employment which they view as worthy of a personal commitment. If schools can help students make commitments to legitimate careers, delinquency should be reduced.

One mechanism for achieving this goal is experiential prevocational training and exploration, in which students are exposed to a wide range of possible career options and informed of the skills and training required to attain these. First hand exposure to career options can increase students' understanding of actual career opportunities while providing opportunities to contribute to placement sites, thus making participation more immediately rewarding. This should, in turn, increase the development of aspirations and commitments to legitimate career roles.

Experiential prevocational training can begin in classrooms in middle and junior high and continue through high school. During the early years, the program should be based largely in the classroom, with field trips to work sites. In subsequent years, opportunities for work experiences in the community can be included and articulated with traditional course work necessary for high school graduation. (See Experience-Based Career Education in Wall et al., 1981, p. 43.)

7. CROSS-AGE TUTORING

Cross-age tutoring is an early intervention strategy aimed at insuring satisfactory skill development for students in primary grades who are evidencing special difficulties in school. An additional function is to provide older students with opportunities to perform a productive role (as tutors), which may increase commitment to education and attachment to school. To maximize the preventive power of this in-

tervention, selection of tutors should be based on teacher recommendations. Students whose cognitive skills are adequate for the tutoring role but whose commitments to school appear marginal should be included in the tutor pool along with students traditionally selected for leadership roles.

8. SCHOOL CLIMATE ASSESSMENT AND IMPROVEMENT

Research has shown that cooperation between teachers and the school administrator characterizes schools with low rates of teacher victimization (Gottfredson and Daiger, 1979). An approach which has shown promise for enhancing administrator and teacher cooperation is school climate assessment and improvement (see Fox et al., n.d.). This is a process in which the administrator and staff commit themselves to realistic appraisal of program, process, and material determinants of the school's social and educational milieu. These determinants include variables such as "opportunities for active learning," "varied reward systems," "continuous improvement of school goals," "effective communications," and "a supportive and efficient logistical system." Faculty and administration collaboratively identify school variables in need of improvement and implement activities to address these problems. Where improvement activities focus on developing consistent expectations for student behaviors and a clear, common set of policies and procedures for dealing with infractions of rules, the school environment is more likely to be perceived by students as equitable. Students are more likely to develop belief in the fairness of the school in this situation. As a result, delinquent behavior should be inhibited.

9. CHILD DEVELOPMENT SPECIALIST AS PARENT CONSULTANT

We have noted that consistent expectations are likely to facilitate belief in the moral order. Students are probably more likely to develop attachments to school when their parents and the school staff are in agreement regarding expectations for behavior and performance. One method for enhancing consistency of expectations and sanctions in the child's environment is to insure ongoing communication between schools and parents. Child development specialists in schools can insure that parents are routinely contacted regarding special achievements of their children in the classroom and emerging needs for assistance to insure skill development. They can train parents in home-based reinforcement of student learning (Barth, 1979) and coordinate recruitment of parents for classroom involvement and assistance in school decision making. (See Child Development Specialist and Regional Intervention Program in Wall et al., 1981, pp. 26, 103.)

PEER-FOCUSED INTERVENTIONS

1. PEER LEADERSHIP GROUPS

Peer leadership groups have been instituted in a number of middle, junior, and senior high schools across the country. One model of peer leadership which appears promising involves informal leaders of a number of major student cliques and groups, not just traditional student body leaders or students in trouble. Generally, members are nominated by teachers and students and a peer program coordinator is responsible for final selection of members. Student members of the peer leadership groups meet daily for an hour as part of their regular school activities. An explicit goal of these peer leadership groups is to identify school problems perceived by students and to work with the school administration to develop reasonable and enforceable school policies regarding these problems. Peer leadership groups can also serve as recruitment pools for student judicial bodies to handle student grievance and disciplinary referrals for violations of school rules. Designed this way, peer leadership groups can avoid the problems of peer-oriented approaches which focus wholly on delinquent groups (Hawkins and Fraser, 1983; Klein, 1969).

Peer leadership groups seek to encourage leaders of delinquency-prone groups to establish ties to more conventional peers. The approach suggested here presumes that ties will be developed as group members work together. It is also hypothesized that attachment to school will be enhanced by performance of these functions. Finally, to the extent that informal peer group leaders are identified and selected for participation, it is hypothesized that these leaders may, in turn, influence members of their own cliques toward more positive attitudes to school as school policies are altered in response to their participation. In this way delinquency prone groups may be coopted. (See Open Road Student Involvement Project and Positive Peer Culture in Wall et al., 1981, pp. 75, 90; Hawkins and Fraser, 1983.)

COMMUNITY INTERVENTIONS

The community provides a broad context for youth development. While families, schools, and peers have the most immediate effects on individual youths, community characteristics influence these socializing groups. Furthermore, aggregate level data show that crime rates are associated with characteristics of community areas (Shaw and McKay, 1942). Community areas offer general norms and expectations for deviant or conforming behavior which may indirectly influence youths. Two community-focused interventions appear promising for delinquency prevention.

1. COMMUNITY CRIME PREVENTION PROGRAM

This is the community block-watch model which has been successful in reducing residential burglaries where implemented. (See Community Crime Prevention Program in Wall et al., 1981, p. 30; Greenberg et al., 1982; Fowler et al., 1979.) This approach is included not only for its obvious deterrent potential, but perhaps, more important, for its use of social networks of neighborhood members engaged in shared activities around the common goal of crime prevention. This involvement can generate a sense of shared concern and power in a community and a set of community norms against crime. It is hypothesized that these norms can contribute to a climate in which criminal actions are viewed by community youths as both risky and unacceptable rather than as an accepted part of growing up.

2. COMMUNITY YOUTH DEVELOPMENT PROJECT

Community-focused youth participation and advocacy projects may also hold promise for delinquency prevention. In these projects community members, including youths, are organized into committees to mobilize resources to develop a community environment conducive to nondelinquent youth development. The major goal here, which is clearly problematic, is the involvement of community youths who are not typically involved in leadership roles in schools. If these youths are involved in planning and organizing activities to improve opportunities for youths in the community, they may develop stakes in conformity. A range of projects may be initiated. Regardless of the specific activity, the major goal is to involve youths who may not have established commitments to education or attachments to school with ties to a legitimate group which can lead to conventional commitments and attachments outside the school. (See Youth Community Development Project in Wall et al., 1981. p. 135.)

CONCLUSION

The discovery of effective methods for preventing youth crime before juvenile justice system involvement is the key to the ultimate success of this country's "dual functions" philosophy of juvenile justice. Extensive research on the etiology of juvenile crime over the past two decades has provided clues for that discovery. The social development model and its cause-focused primary prevention and early intervention strategies provide an organizing framework for designing and selecting promising prevention strategies. Primary prevention and early-intervention strategies should be assessed and selected for their potential to create opportunities for involvement, skills for participation, and a consistent system of reinforcement for youths' involvement in family, school, and nondelinquent peer groups and the legitimate community. Using these criteria, the initiatives reviewed above appear promising, although few have yet been subjected to rigorous empirical testing. Systematic, rigorous tests of these interventions are now required to determine which ones ultimately can be included among proven delinquency prevention approaches.

References

Akers, R. L. (1977). *Deviant behavior: A social learning approach*. Belmont, CA: Wadsworth.

Akers, R. L., Krohn, M., Lanza-Kaduce, L., & Radosevich, M. (1979). Social learning and deviant behavior: A specific test of a general theory. *American Sociological Review, 44*, 636–655.

Alexander, J. F., and Parsons, B. (1979). Short-term behavioral intervention with delinquent families: Impact on family process and recidivisim. *Journal of Abnormal Psychology, 81*, 219–225.

Alexander, P. S., Rooney, T., and Smith, C. (1980). Background paper for the *Serious Juvenile Offender Initiative of the U.S. Office of Juvenile Justice and Delinquency Prevention*, U.S. Department of Justice. Washington, DC.

Bachman, J. G., Green, S., & Wirtanen, I. (1971). *Youth in transition. Vol. III: Dropping out–Problem or symptom*. Ann Arbor, MI: University of Michigan. Institute for Social Research.

Bahr, S. J. (1979). Family determinants and effects of deviance. In W. Burr, R. Hill, I. Nye, & I. Reiss (eds.), *Contemporary theories about the family*. New York: The Free Press.

Barth, R. (1979). Home-based reinforcement of school behavior: A review and analysis. *Review of Educational Research*, 436–458.

Bednar, R. L., Zelhart, P., Greathouse, L., and Weinberg, S. (1970). Operant conditioning principles in the treatment of learning and behavior problems with delinquent boys. *Journal of Counseling Psychology, 17*, 492–497.

Berleman, W. (1980). *Juvenile delinquency prevention programs: A review and analysis*. National Institute for Juvenile Justice and Delinquency Prevention. Office of Juvenile Justice and Delinquency Prevention, U.S. Department of Justice. Washington DC: U.S. Government Printing Office.

Block, J. H. (1971). *Mastery learning: Theory and practice*. New York: Holt, Rinehart and Winston.

Bloom, B. S. (1976). *Human characteristics and school learning*. New York: McGraw-Hill.

Briar, S., and Piliavin, I. (1965). Delinquency, situational inducements and commitment to conformity. *Social Problems, 13*, 25–45.

Brophy, J. (1979). Advances in teacher research. *Journal of Classroom Interaction, 15* (1), 1–7.

Burgess, R. L., and Akers, R. (1966). A differential association-reinforcement theory of criminal behavior. *Social Problems, 4*, 128–147.

Call, D. J. (1965). *Delinquency, frustration and non-commitment*. Eugene, OR: University of Oregon.

Cohen, A. K., and Short, J. Jr. (1961). Juvenile delinquency. In R. Merton and R. Nisbet (eds.), *Contemporary social problems*. New York: Harcourt, Brace and World.

Coleman, J. C. (1961). *The adolescent society*. New York: The Free Press.

Cressey, D. R. (1955). Changing criminals: The application of the theory of differential association. *American Journal of Sociology, 61*, 116–120.

Cressey, D. R., and Ward, D. (1969). *Delinquency, crime and social process*. New York: Harper and Row.

Elliott, D. S., Huizinga, D., and Ageton, S. S. (1982). *Explaining delinquency and drug use*. Boulder, CO: Behavioral Research Institute, Report No. 21, 1982.

Elliott, D. S., and Voss, H. (1974). *Delinquency and dropout*. Lexington, MA: D.C. Heath and Company.

Emmer, E. T., and Evertson, C. M. (1980). *Effective management at the beginning of the school year in junior high classes*. Austin, TX: Research and Development Center for Teacher Education. University of Texas at Austin. R. & D. Report #6107, 1980.

Fox, R. S., Boies, H. E., Brainard, E., Fletcher, E., Huge, J. S., Martin, C. L., Maynard, W., Monasmith, J., Olivero, J., Schmuck, R., Shaheen, T. A., Stegeman, W. H. (n.d.). *School climate improvement: A challenge to the school administration*. Bloomington, IN: Phi Delta Kappa Education Foundation.

Fraser, M. W., and Hawkins, J. D. (in press). Parent training for delinquency prevention: A review. *Child and Youth Services*.

Galvin, J., and Polk, K. (1983). Juvenile justice: Time for new direction? *Crime and Delinquency, 29* (3), 325–332.

Garbarino, J. (1977). Child abuse and juvenile delinquency: The developmental impact of social isolation. Paper delivered at Symposium on Child Abuse and Juvenile Delinquency; Seattle, WA.

Garbarino, J. (1980). Some thoughts on school size and its effects on adolescent development. *Journal of Youth and Adolescence, 9*, 1.

Glaser, D. (1978). *Coping with sociocultural causes of youth unemployment and crime.* American University Law School, Institute for Advanced Studies in Justice. (Prepared for the Office of Research and Development, Employment and Training Administration, U.S. Department of Labor.)

Gold, M. (1978). Scholastic experiences, self-esteem, and delinquent behavior: A theory for alternative schools. *Crime and Delinquency, 1978, 24*(3), 290–308.

Gordon, T. (1970). *P.E.T.: Parent effectiveness training.* New York: Wyden, Peter H.

Gottfredson, G. D. and Daiger, D. (1979). *Disruption in six hundred schools: The social ecology of personal victimization in the nation's public schools.* Baltimore, MD: Johns Hopkins University, Center for Social Organization of schools.

Gough, A. R. (1977). *Standards relative to noncriminal misbehavior* (tentative draft). Cambridge, MA: Ballinger.

Greenberger, E., and Steinberg, L. (1979). *Part-time employment of in-school youth: A preliminary assessment of costs and benefits.* Irvine, CA: University of California. Duplicated manuscript, 1979.

Hawkins, J. D., Pastor, P., Bell, M., and Morrison, S. (1980). *A typology of cause-focused strategies of delinquency prevention.* National Institute for Juvenile Justice and Delinquency Prevention, Office of Juvenile Justice and Delinquency Prevention. U.S. Department of Justice. Washington, DC: U.S. Government Printing Office.

Hawkins, J. D., and Wall, J. (1980). *Alternative education: Exploring the delinquency prevention potential.* National Institute for Juvenile Justice and Delinquency Prevention, Office of Juvenile justice and Delinquency Prevention, U.S. Department of Justice. Washington, DC: U.S. Government Printing Office.

Henney, J. S. (1976). *Middle class adolescents, social delinquency and social control theory.* Unpublished masters thesis. Seattle, WA: University of Washington.

Hindelang, M. J. (1973). Causes of delinquency: A partial replication and extension. *Social Problems, 20*, 471–487.

Hirschi, T. (1969). *Causes of delinquency.* Berkeley, CA: University of California Press.

Janvier, R. L., Guthmann, D. & Catalano, R., Jr. (1979). *An assessment of evaluations of drug abuse prevention programs.* National Institute for Juvenile Justice and Delinquency Prevention, Office of Juvenile Justice and Delinquency Prevention, U.S. Department of Justice. Washington, DC: U.S. Government Printing Office.

Jensen, G. F. (1972). Parents, peers, and delinquent action: A test of the differential association perspective. *American Journal of Sociology, 78*, 562–575.

Jensen, G. F. (1976). Race, achievement, and delinquency: A further look at delinquency in a birth cohort. *American Journal of Sociology, 82*, 379–387.

Jessor, R. and Jessor, S. L. (1977). *Problem behavior and psychosocial development: A longitudinal study of youth.* New York: Academic Press.

Johnson, D. W., and Johnson, R. W. (1980). Cooperative learning: The power of positive goal interdependence. In V. M. Lyons (ed.), *Structuring cooperative experiences in the classroom: The 1980 handbook.* Minneapolis, MN: A Cooperation Network Publication.

Klein, M. (1969). Gang cohesiveness, delinquency and a street-work program. *Journal of Research in Crime and Delinquency, 6*, 135:166.

Klein, N., Alexander, J., and Parsons, B. (1977). Impact of family systems intervention on recidivism and sibling delinquency: A model of primary prevention and program evaluation. *Journal of Consulting and Clinical Psychology, 45*, 469–474.

Kornhauser, R. R. (1978). *Social sources of delinquency: An appraisal of analytic methods.* Chicago, IL: The University of Chicago Press.

Krisberg, B. (1978). *Preliminary report of the national evaluation of prevention.* San Francisco, CA: National Council on Crime and Delinquency, 1978.

Krohn, M. D. (1974). An investigation of the effect of parental and peer associations on marijuana use: An empirical test of differential association theory. In M. Riedel & T. Thornberry (eds.), *Crime and delinquency: Dimensions of deviance.* New York: Praeger, 75–89.

Lejins, P. (1967). The field of prevention. W. Amos & S. Wellford (eds.) *Delinquency prevention: Theory and practice.* Englewood Cliffs, NJ: Prentice Hall.

Linden, E. W. (1974). *Interpersonal ties and delinquent behavior.* Seattle, WA: University of Washington, Department of Sociology.

Lundman, R. J., and Scarpitti, F. (April, 1978). Delinquency prevention: Recommendations for future projects. *Crime and Delinquency,* 207–220.

Matza, D. (1964). *Delinquency and drift.* New York: Wiley.

McPartland, J. M., and McDill, E. (eds.) (1977). *Violence in schools: Perspectives, programs, and positions.* Lexington, MA: D.C. Heath and Company.

National Advisory Committee on Criminal Justice Standards and Goals. *Juvenile justice and delinquency prevention* (1976). Report of the Task Force on Juvenile Justice and Delinquency Prevention, Washington, DC.

National Council on Crime and Delinquency (1981). *The national evaluation of delinquency prevention.* San Francisco: National Council on Crime and Delinquency Research Center.

National Task Force to Develop Standards and Goals for Juvenile Justice and Delinquency Prevention (1977). *Preventing delinquency,* Vol. 1. Washington, DC: U.S. Government Printing Office.

Nettler, G. (1974). *Explaining crime.* New York: McGraw-Hill.

Newton, A. M. (June 1978). Prevention of crime and delinquency. *Criminal Justice Abstracts,* 245–266.

Nye, F. (1958). *Family relationships and delinquent behavior.* New York: Wiley.

Patterson, G. R., and Reid, J. B. (1973). Intervention for families of aggressive boys: A replication study. *Behavior Research and Therapy, 11,* 383–394.

Polk, K., and Halferty, D. (July, 1966). Adolescence, commitment and delinquency. *Journal of Research on Crime and Delinquency,* 4.

Polk, K., and Schafer, W. (1972). *Schools and delinquency.* Englewood Cliffs, NJ: Prentice-Hall.

Powers, E., and Witmer, H. (1951). *An experiment in the prevention of delinquency.* New York: Columbia University Press.

President's Commission on Law Enforcement and Administration of Justice (1967). *The challenge of crime in a free society.* Washington, DC: U.S. Government Printing Office, 1967.

Reckless, W. (1961). *The crime problem.* New York: Appleton-Century-Crofts.

Reckless, W., Dinitz, C. S., and Murray, E. (1956). Self-concept as an insulator against delinquency. *American Sociological Review, 21,* 744–746.

Reiss, A. J. (1951). Delinquency as the failure of personal and social controls. *American Sociological Review, 16,* 196–207.

Rollins, H. H., McCandless, B., Thompson, M., and Brassell, W. (1974). Project success environment: An extended application of contingency management in inner city schools. *Journal of Educational Psychology, 66* (2), 167–178.

Romig, D. A. (1978). *Justice for our children: An examination of juvenile delinquent rehabilitation programs.* Lexington, MA: D.C. Heath and Company.

Sakumoto, K. N. (1978). *Attachment to delinquent friends: Peer influences and delinquent involvement.* Unpublished masters thesis. Seattle, WA: University of Washington.

Schaps, E., Dibartolo, R., Palley, C., and Churgin, S. (1978). *Primary prevention evaluation research: A review of 127 program evaluations.* Walnut Creek, CA: Pyramid Project, Pacific Institute for Research and Evaluation.

Schaps, E., and Slimmon, L. (1975). *Balancing head and heart: Sensible ideas for the prevention of drug and alcohol abuse. Book 2: Eleven strategies.* Lafayette, CA: Prevention Material Institute Press.

Sederstrom, J. D. (1978). *Family structure and juvenile delinquency.* Unpublished masters thesis, Seattle, WA: University of Washington.

Shaw, C., and McKay, H. D. (1942). *Juvenile delinquency in urban areas.* Chicago, IL: University of Chicago Press.

Silberman, C. (1970). *Crisis in the classroom.* New York: Vintage Book.

Slavin, R. E. (1978). *Cooperative learning.* Baltimore, MD: The Johns Hopkins University, Center for Social Organization of Schools.

Slavin, R. E. (1979). *Using student team learning.* Baltimore, MD: The Johns Hopkins University, Center for Social Organization of Schools.

Smith, C. P., Alexander, P., Halatyn, T., and Roberts C. (1979). *A national assessment of serious juvenile crime and the juvenile justice system: The need for a rational response: Volume II, definition; characteristics of incidents and individuals; and relationship to substance abuse.* Sacramento, CA: American Justice Institute.

Smith, V., Barr, R., and Burke, D. (1976). *Alternatives in education: Freedom to choose.* Bloomington, IN: Phi Delta Kappa Educational Foundation.

Stanfield, R. E. (1966). The interaction of family variables and gang variables in the etiology of delinquency. *Social Problems, 1966, 13,* 411–417.

Stark, R. (1975). *Social problems.* New York: Random House.

Stinchcombe, A. C. (1964). *Rebellion in a high school.* Chicago, IL: Quadrangle Books.

Task Force on Juvenile Delinquency (1967). *Juvenile delinquency and youth crime.* Washington, DC: U.S. Government Printing Office, 1967.

Task Force on Juvenile Delinquency Prevention of the National Advisory Committee on Criminal Justice Standards and Goals (1977). *Juvenile justice and delinquency prevention.* Washington, DC: National Advisory Committee on Criminal Justice Standards and Goals. U.S. Government Printing Office, 1977.

Toby, J. (1957). Social disorganization and stake in conformity: Complementary factors in the predatory behavior of hoodlums. *Journal of Criminal Law, Criminology and Police Science, 48,* 12–17.

Tyler, V., and Brown, G. (1968). Token reinforcement of academic performance with institutionalized delinquent boys. *Journal of Educational Psychology, 59,* 164–168.

U.S. National Criminal Justice Information and Statistics Service (1979). *Children in custody: Advance report on the 1977 census of public juvenile facilities. No.* SD-JD-SA. Washington, DC: U.S. Government Printing Office, 1979.

Wall, J. S., Hawkins, J. D., Lishner, D. and Fraser, M. (1981). *Juvenile delinquency prevention: A compendium of thirty-six program models.* National Institute for Juvenile Justice and Delinquency Prevention. Office of Juvenile Justice and Delinquency Prevention. U.S. Department of Justice. Washington, DC: U.S. Government Printing Office.

Weis, J. G., and Hawkins, J. D. (1981). *Preventing delinquency: The social development approach.* National Institute for Juvenile Justice and Delinquency Prevention, Office of Juvenile Justice and Delinquency Prevention. U.S. Department of Justice, Washington, DC: U.S. Government Printing Office.

Weis, J. G., Hall, J., Henney, J., Sederstrom, J., Worsley, K., and Zeiss, C. (1980). *Peer influence and delinquency: An evaluation of theory and practice, Part I and Part II.* Seattle, WA: Center for Law and Justice, University of Washington.

Weis, J. G., Sakumoto, K. Sederstrom, J. and Zeiss, C. (1980). *Jurisdication and the elusive status offender: A comparison of involvement in delinquent behavior and status offenses.* National Institute for Juvenile Justice and Delinquency Prevention. Office of Juvenile Justice and Delinquency Prevention, U.S. Department of Justice. Washington DC: U.S. Government Printing Office.

Weis, J. G., and Henney, J. (1979). Crime and Criminals in the United States in the 1970's: Statistical Appendix. In S. Messinger & E. Bittner (eds.). *Criminology review yearbook.* Beverly Hills, CA: Sage Publications.

Weis, J. G., Sederstrom, J., Worsley, K., and Zeiss, C. (1980). *Family and delinquency.* Seattle, WA: Center for Law and Justice. University of Washington.

Wilkinson, K. (1974). The broken family and juvenile delinquency: Scientific explanation or ideology. In R. Giallombardo (ed.), *Juvenile Delinquency* (3rd ed.). New York: Wiley.

Woodson, R. L. (ed.) (1981). *Youth crime and urban policy: A view from the inner city.* Washington, DC: American Enterprise Institute for Public Policy Research.

Worsley, K. C. (1979). *Sex differences in delinquency: Explaining the gap.* Unpublished masters thesis. Seattle, WA: University of Washington.

Wright, W. E., and Dixon, M. (January, 1977). Community prevention and treatment of juvenile delinquency: A review and evaluation. *Journal of Research in Crime and Delinquency.*

Zeiss, C. A. (1978). *Sex differences in self-reported delinquent behavior.* Unpublished masters thesis. Seattle, WA: University of Washington.

PART VII

WORK AND PLAY

INTRODUCTION

Children (and adults) "play" with things and ideas—which is the stuff from which creativity flows. (Creativity is a topic related to work and play, but space limitations prevent further consideration of it. See, for example, J. G. Nicholls (1972). "Creativity in the person who will never produce anything original and useful: The concept of creativity as a normally distributed trait." *American Psychologist 27* (8): 717–727; A. Rothenberg (1979). "Einstein's creative thinking and the general theory of relativity: A documented report." *American Journal of Psychiatry 136* (1): 38–43; N. McMann and R. Oliver (1988). "Problems in families with gifted children: Implications for counselors." *Journal of Counseling and Development 66*: 275–278.)

Many theorists (such as Piaget and Erikson) have seen play as an essential ingredient in children's development, in the practice at becoming adults and working with adult tools, as well as in the learning of social rules of relating with others. Other theorists (from Aristotle to the current issues of family magazines) see play as a catharsis of pent-up emotions and as sheer pleasure that should not be interrupted too soon for the purposes of beginning formal education in nursery school. From one point of view or the other, play is serious business in the life development of the individual.

Gary Alan Fine discusses a paradox in one aspect of play, where "good" children engage in "dirty" play, such as aggressive pranks, vandalism, sexual play, and racist invective. He explores what functions these actions may play in the development of preadolescent males, and then discusses how moral adults eventually emerge from nasty boys. Fine quotes as epigraph a line from Plutarch capturing his theme: "Though the boys throw stones at frogs in sport, yet the frogs do not die in sport but in earnest." (Also see B. J. Bredemeier and D. L. Shields, "Moral growth among athletes and non-athletes: A comparative analysis," *The Journal of Genetic Psychology*, 1985, *147* (1): 7–18.)

The next readings in this part focus on work. Barbara Levy Simon reviews the discouraging evidence regarding the feminization of poverty, wherein three-quarters of all poverty in the United States is located among women and children. She describes five dimensions of the basic structures of society that have created these untoward conditions: (1) the stereotype that women work only to supplement male earnings; (2) the sexual division of labor that continues to make women primarily responsible for the care of children, the household, and care of aged family members; (3) the pervasive racism facing minority men and women as they seek schooling, training, and jobs; (4) the dual labor market that concentrates women in poorly paying jobs, combined with the dual welfare system (reflected in the differences in support from the means-tested AFDC for the poor, and the entitlements from Social Security largely benefiting the middle-class worker); and (5) the systematic discrimination women face in the work place, the housing market, and the educational system. Simon then offers some proposals to reduce the incidence of poverty among women and children.

Stephen Joel Gill, Larry C. Coppard, and Malcolm A. Lowther describe a multidimensional theory that characterizes mid-life career development, using some of the work of Erik Erikson's life cycle model, Daniel Levinson's concept of life transitions and conflicts, as well as the ideas of other theorists. However, they point out the limitations of current knowledge supporting these conflict theories of career development. Gill, Coppard, and Lowther conclude by disputing theories that offer neat time tables of conflict-driven development during midlife. Instead, they view career development as a complex process influenced by a configuration of forces in which the individual may choose growth, maintenance, stagnation or decline. (For a discussion of retirement trends, see R. L. Clark (1988). "The future of work and retirement." *Research on Aging, 10* (2): 169–193. Clark notes the trend toward earlier retirement of men, in contrast to the trends in which women are entering the labor force in increasing proportions at all ages under 65.)

Overall, play and work represent a great cycle in life. Freud characterized the mature person as one who is able to balance his or her work and play. We learn much about work through our play. We now recognize that we must relearn how to play, during the work years as well as in retirement, in order to have a balance to life. However, some forces of discrimination and oppression prevent this balance from occurring for large numbers of people even in this affluent society.

40

GOOD CHILDREN AND DIRTY PLAY

Gary Alan Fine
University of Minnesota
Minneapolis

Though the boys throw stones at frogs in sport, yet the frogs do not die in sport but in earnest.

(Plutarch)

Everett Hughes (1971, pp. 87–97), that most incisive of sociologists, once asked how it is that some in our society become involved and then become satisfied with what the rest of us consider to be "dirty work"—those activities in which no "decent" person would engage. Hughes addressed the vagaries of the occupation order: I wish to borrow his concept and apply it to the world of play. What is the character of "dirty play?"

Play research, like other intellectual avenues, has its fashions. Early in the century, as social historians are now emphasizing (e.g., Cavallo, 1981; Kett, 1977; Macleod, 1983), children's play was an activity that adults felt the need to control and direct. Children, if left to their own devices, might play in disturbingly "immoral" ways. It was in many ways an optimistic and progressive age. Play could make the difference; it could serve as a crucible of moral socialization. In the American context, the targets of this benevolent paternalism were often the children of immigrants who were to be melted into Americans whether they wished to be or not and, it must be admitted, many so wished. In Great Britain, socialization through play was more explicitly based on class (e.g., Rosenthal, 1986).

By the postwar era the American model of play had changed (e.g., Wolfenstein, 1955). Intellectually this is reflected in the classic work by the Dutch philosopher Johan Huizinga (1955), *Homo Ludens*, subtitled *A Study of the Play Element in Culture*. Written prior to the Second World War, *Homo Ludens* had a profound influence on play research in America and throughout the world. The title and subtitle together suggest Huizinga's essential thrust—that humans are fundamentally players, and that play is an integral component of social order. This work helped to usher in the golden age of the Romanticism of Play. The childhood urge to play was considered a beneficial, innate urge, implicitly set apart from the corrupting effects of adult direction. Thus, adult-run leisure activities such as Little League baseball or the Boy Scouts were described as bureaucratic efforts to depress the naturally healthful components of children's informal activities (e.g., DeKoven, 1978; Devereaux, 1976; Yablonsky and Brower, 1979). The child was, by this view, a noble savage. This perspective too was optimistic, although the optimism was of a different character, based on the innocence of the child rather than the experience of the adult.

Recently there has been a revisionist movement in play research. This is most clearly reflected in the recent writings of Brian Sutton-Smith, and particularly in his *A History of Children's Play* (1984). Although his earlier writing fit within the romantic view of children's play, Sutton-Smith now contends that children's play is far from a Panglossian "best of all possible worlds." Children's play is not pastoral, and cruelty is as much a constitutive feature as is friendship. Indeed, one might suggest that the dystopia of play has been overlooked by some with ideological reasons for making contrasting claims about the adult world of work.

Each of these perspectives on children's play reflects an ideological view of the world, as of course is true of all theories (e.g., Gusfield, 1981). After all, social scientists do not trade in facts as much as they trade in metaphors (e.g., Gusfield, 1976; Lakoff and Johnson, 1980; Manning, 1979; Nisbet, 1976). There is no single reality of play, only techniques for ordering the way in which we choose to view it.

By addressing this issue I confront what is essentially a philosophical question: What is human nature? It is evident that all people (and all children) perform both good and bad deeds. What then does

From *Play and Culture*, 1: 43–56 (excerpt). Copyright © 1988 by Human Kinetics. Reprinted by permission.

this make them? What is natural to human beings? Because we cannot know if angels or devils reside in infants' craniums, the issue is fated never to be resolved. One response, and one with a certain appeal, is that the child's nature does not present itself until sometime later in life. Whenever it makes its appearance, this nature shapes what it is that the child can learn. If human nature is implacably black, then the child will easily acquire disruptive skills, being good only to gain rewards and avoid punishment. In contrast, it might be that the high wages of sin tempt the child from the straight and narrow path on which he or she naturally treads. Play research has a particularly central role in this debate. One might expect true nature to emerge most clearly when the child is engaging in voluntary activities, activities of which play is a quintessential example. Thus the debate over the nature of play is in part a battle for the child's soul.

In this analysis I wish to discuss a paradox that seems to be central in play research: that children can be personally wonderful, kind, and good (as the romantics would have it), but engage in play activities that moralistic adults find disagreeable (as the revisionists insist). Sato (in press) in proposing a "Play Theory of Delinquency" makes a similar point in arguing against the stigma, cultural or personal, of delinquency. He argues that these delinquents are out for a good time in particular situations (see Riemer, 1981). These young men typically realize their activities are transitory and are not something they define as central to their identities.

The lack of attention to the disagreeable side of play is perhaps surprising in that the researchers seem to have forgotten their own childhood experiences. This dirty play may aid in effective socialization, at least in our imperfect society. Yet one of the most common reactions is the horror of "good" adults when they learn their "good" children engage in such activities. This paradox seems crucial to our unraveling of the structure of children's play. I bracket the question of the nature of play near birth, focusing on that period on which I have conducted research: preadolescence.

Preadolescence has been defined as the period in which "the nicest children begin to behave in the most awful way" (Redl, 1966, p. 395). Among the tribe of preadolescents, I focus on those who are white, male, and American—basing my analysis on my 3-year study of five Little League baseball leagues and the children who participate in them

(Fine, 1987). These children, both in and outside the game, regularly engage in activities I have labeled dirty play. They are sexual and aggressive, and yet these boys are not evil satyrs. They are just boys, and boys will be boys.

DIRTY WORK

In his original treatment of good people and dirty work a quarter of a century ago, Hughes was specifically concerned with the occupational hierarchy in which some people had to engage in unpleasant activities that other people did not wish to know about in order to keep their hands clean. As Hughes wrote, "people can and do keep a silence about things whose open discussion would threaten the group's conception of itself, and hence its solidarity" (Hughes, 1971, p. 91).

In some of Hughes' formulations these dirty activities were behaviors that no decent person should agree to, such as the actions of Nazi SS officers. Hughes suggested that the citizens of Nazi Germany kept their eyes closed to this dirty work and did not attempt to stop it. The dirty workers were a closed society, and this was how the larger society wished it to be. However, Hughes extends this argument to recognize that some dirty workers (e.g., prison guards, grave diggers, janitors) are necessary for a functioning social system. Still, a membrane protects the rest of the society from contamination by these dirty workers.

The same membrane may be necessary in the world of children's play. If we accept that children's play is a rough and thorny patch, there may be a sense in which adults don't want to know what their children are doing. Children's play is to remain in the closet. The dirty play of children is likely to be a natural outpouring of some development imperatives of growing up, but how it is handled depends very much on the settings in which children and their adult guardians find themselves. . . .

[Editor's note: Professor Fine goes on to discuss four types of dirty play. The first category involves aggressive pranks, such as "mooning" passing cars (i.e., exposing one's bare bottom), "egging" houses (i.e., throwing raw eggs), and making funny phone calls or ringing doorbells and running away. These are almost always done when with a group of good friends as a kind of daring or risk taking against adults.

The second category is termed vandalism, defined roughly as a prank that gets out of control.

Examples might include breaking of a window, or tearing down a fence—in general, some daring act that violates property rights, but presumably not with malicious intent, only the amusement of the participants. Professor Fine's epigraph (from Plutarch) on boys stoning frogs captures the spirit of vandalism, and its irony.

The third category involves sexual talk, which at the preadolescent stage is concerned with establishing an identity with peers as a sexually mature and knowledgeable. Boys of this age have to balance enough interest in sex, but not too much, to keep up their social image. Sexual talk also includes deprecations of gays.

The last category Professor Fine considers is racist invective. His research dealt with white, suburban boys who had little contact with blacks. Their racist invectives generally occurred in play situations, functioned to distinguish themselves from others, and probably reflected the racist attitudes in society at large. He then continues his analysis of these forms of dirty play.]

DIRTY PLAY THEORY

The prevalence of dirty play in the lives of children, and their evident enjoyment of it, should give pause to all adults. Dirty play is hardly a phenomenon of contemporary America, as eloquently evidenced in the anthropological and historical literature (e.g., Chandos, 1984; Thrasher, 1927; Whiting and Whiting, 1975). Is there a society in which children always behave in accord with adult standards? Undoubtedly not. However, this division is particularly salient in societies such as our own that have a deeply ingrained view of the natural innocence of children (the romantic view of childhood). The existence of dirty play poses a challenge to those concerned with moral socialization. It seems to demonstrate either that children are not innocent, a profoundly troubling charge in view of the natural Rousseauean order or, equally troubling, that children are being corrupted by adults. Thus, a preadolescent who behaves in a way that is culturally condemned as sexist is either inherently flawed or has been socialized by a sexist society. The forms of cultural relativism extended to exotic cultures are not applied to our children.

But why should our children choose or need to behave in this way? I suggest four rationales: control, status, social differentiation, and socialization to perceived adult norms. These four rationales do not apply equally well to all examples of preadolescent dirty play, and they are difficult to prove in that these explanations—in the form I present them—are not in preadolescents' vocabulary. If asked, most preadolescents would admit to engaging in these activities simply because they are fun. "Fun" is the ostensible justification for playing, but it sidesteps the underlying question of why these sorts of things are seen as fun. So we must transcend the autotelic quality of play if we hope to understand the content of these activities.

CONTROL

Dirty play can be seen as a claim-making behavior. Each instance implicitly attempts to make a statement about the rights of preadolescents to engage in a set of activities and have a set of opinions in the face of pressures that prevent these claims. When children behave in accord with adult prescriptions, and they do frequently, their play causes little comment. But when a preadolescent chooses to play so as to set himself apart from adult authority, the content of play becomes an issue. Preadolescents recognize this problem and are sufficiently sophisticated to engage in their dirty play out of sight and hearing of their adult guardians. They demand for themselves the right to talk about race, sex, or authority. This play is remarkably sophisticated in that it deals with those areas of adult social structure that adults wish to preserve for themselves (see Stinchcombe, 1964). While the content of this dirty play is troubling to many adults, it is equally troubling that children should feel competent to make judgments and act on them. Children present a judgment on adult social order, typically one that differs from what adults officially put forth, although it is one that, especially in the case of sexual and racist remarks, they may privately believe.

The adult emphasis on decorum and politeness is significant in terms of the age-graded power structure. Politeness is a tactic used by those in power to keep those without power subservient. Politeness and decorum structure collective action so as to preserve order and process. If all that children can do to get their way is to request things politely from adults, then adults have full power to make decisions without consequence from those who are asking. Once a request has been rejected by the authorities, there is nothing the requester can do under this model other than accept this decision gracefully. The implicit benefit for those without power is that on the next polite request the authority might be more willing to accede. Yet there is no certainty of this and, even so, authority still remains omnipotent.

Perhaps it is appropriate to speak of these examples of dirty play that question the adult authority structure as instances of "playful terrorism." Ultimately, such terrorism is politically impotent because of the lack of organization of the "terrorist group," their lack of commitment and uniformity of their beliefs, the tight control that adults have over them, and the rewards that can be offered to those who conform. Still, it is hard to miss the potential threat to the authority structure inherent in some of this play. It is a testing of boundaries and legitimacy, and so may provoke harsh retribution.

STATUS

Dirty play is important in shaping relationships within the group as well as outside. The doing of dirty play can be a means of gaining status within a peer group. Preadolescent interaction can be seen in part as a status contest at an age at which status really matters. Status matters at all ages to some degree but, during preadolescence with its change in orientation toward adult status symbols and a social world away from the view of adults, the evaluation of peer position is particularly important.

As I discussed when referring to pranks, boys gain position from participating in these actions. There is a premium on being willing to do those things that other boys want to do but are afraid to. If there is consensus that the prank is desirable, the boy who performs it or leads the group gains status for breaking through the barrier of fear in which others are enveloped. There is risk involved in throwing eggs at houses or cars: one could be caught, beaten, grounded, or even arrested.

The costs, coupled with the lack of status rewards, suggest why it is apparently so rare for preadolescents to engage in these behaviors alone. It is not that they have a personal destructive impulse, but rather that they want to show off in the presence of friends. To think of these children as bad in a psychological sense misses the point. They are more or less amoral, in that enforcing the dictates of morality is not one of their primary goals; rather, their aim is to get by with as much interpersonal smoothness as possible. Their concern with those wonderful Goffmanian images of presentation of self, teamwork, and impression management is omnipresent.

SOCIAL DIFFERENTIATION

As I described when considering racial epithets, one collective task of preadolescents is for them to define themselves in contrast to other groups that share some characteristics. In discussing dirty play among white middle-class boys, I focused on racial and sexual differentiation. Whites are not blacks, boys are not girls. Further there is the belief, harbored fiercely by most of these boys, that whites are better than blacks and that boys are better than girls. Given the stance of today's tolerant, egalitarian society, and particularly those social scientists who choose to write about it, such beliefs are heresy, morally repugnant, and represent a social problem. Yet, from the standpoint of the preadolescent white boy, these beliefs seem perfectly natural. Ethnocentrism always does. In the lengthy landscape of human history, social differentiation has been more the rule than the exception. People regularly attempt to make their own group special and distinct. This basic need of humanity is sometimes partially overcome, but surely the desire for differentiation is not a mark of Cain.

When boys torment girls or jeer at blacks, we may see this as a kind of dirty play that does not necessarily adhere to the moral selves of these social actors. The positive side of such group actions is that the preadolescents are acquiring some measure of community spirit, even though it is at the expense of another group. Even disagreeable play that is internally directed is typically directed toward someone who is differentiated from the group on some significant dimension, such as because of a physical or social handicap, or the belief that the victim can be morally differentiated in some way (e.g., as gay). Just as it is felt that humor, to be successful, must have a "butt" and must permit the tellers to feel superior (Gruner, 1979), so it is with play that is designed to be fun.

SOCIALIZATION TO PERCEIVED ADULT NORMS

The forms of preadolescent dirty play do not simply appear out of nowhere. They are transformations of dramas that boys see enacted by older boys or adults, or learn about through television and movies. The content does matter. Yet this is content that many adults sincerely wish they had not communicated. Unfortunately, it is impossible to shield preadolescents from what we do not want them to learn. They are information vacuum cleaners and selectively use that information that fits their purposes.

Clearly the themes of preadolescent dirty play are not unrecognizable. Aggression, sexism, and racism are found in many adult activities. These themes are also indicated in movies and television dramas, even when the themes are ostensibly being disparaged. Still, audiences can select whatever information they wish from a media production, even if this material is incompatible with the official morality of the society. The best example of this during my research project was the reaction to the film, *The Bad News Bears*. Although the film ostensibly warned against the dangers of overcompetition and excessive adult involvement in youth sports, the images that preadolescents took from the film were techniques of talking dirty and acting grossly.

Frequently a moral message may be but the sugar coating for sexual or aggressive behavior that the producers use to capture an audience. This technique applies to media productions aimed at adults as well as children. For preadolescents this may be compounded in that they are often attempting to act maturely. Maturity doesn't have a clearly defined empirical meaning, but as a concept it implies a change in behavior. To prove one is acting maturely, one must act differently from before. This typically takes the form of doing those things one hadn't known about or hadn't been allowed to do under the watchful eyes of adults. As a result, many of these markers of maturity will be precisely those things that adults define as dirty play. This form of play is a consequence of the conflict between the primary reality of the situation as defined by adults and the playful definitions of children that mirror that reality in a transformed way (Sato, in press). It is not that children are being childish or immature in their play, quite the contrary. They are attempting to live up to adult standards of behavior and relate to adult issues from which they had previously been excluded.

Socialization to society's expectations has been firmly established as an important feature of children's play; yet diverse messages are learned through play, some of which may be offensive to those who have the task of guiding children's development. The agenda for children's development is not always controlled by adults, although it typically is based on a reflection of what they say and do.

CONCLUSION

Each of these four components that help to produce dirty play should underline that playing dirty is not identical to being morally culpable. The issue, as Everett Hughes raised it in light of adult dirty work, is the extent to which a person can get away with doing dirty work without that moral stigma adhering to his or her public self. Surely in practice this adhesion of blame is a variable (see Fine, 1986); a child who burns another at the stake is not likely

to receive the same evaluation as one who gives another a hot foot. The nature of the act, the past record of the child and his or her companions, and his or her location in the social (class) structure (Chambliss, 1973) affect the meanings given to the act. A single act (e.g., a rape) may tar a child and lead to reform school or jail, whereas other acts (some with deadly consequences) may be defined as unfortunate outcomes of the child's urge to explore his or her world.

The connection of dirty play with children's moral selves is a matter of negotiation, with different ideologies prevailing at different times and places among different groups, and depending on the relationship of the judge to the person being judged. The likely intention of the actor, the presence of others supporting the action, the social supports for the action, and the expected outcome influence how children's dirty play will be evaluated.

As I have implied, children's dirty play is virtually inevitable. There are so many needs and traditions connected with the doing of these actions that one is hard pressed to visualize a serious program that could eradicate these behaviors. These are play forms that respond to the developmental imperatives that we must live with (Fine, 1987). Yet adults do have one weapon, a long-term weapon to be sure, but a dramatically effective one: guilt. By planting a seed that this type of behavior is morally objectionable, we recognize that these teachings may not work immediately when given. Moral socialization in childhood often seems to be a long-term process; the messages are there for whenever the child is able or willing to accept them. Messages that denigrate dirty play eventually become effective when reward structures change and when social needs are altered.

As children grow older, and their needs for presentation of self change, they come to believe that behaviors they used to delight in are morally offensive. Although we might object to children playing concentration camp guard, holding mock lynchings, or simply torturing their peers in the name of fun, we should recognize that this too will pass. Most children recognize that their behaviors are not the same ones they will display as adults. Although sometimes morality does not change, if the new "improved" morality is supported by the structures of adult society, we can assume that dirty players emerge into saintly adults—at least *adequately* saintly adults. Children in dealing with a transformed version of raw, emotional issues may cause distress to adults, but they need not permanently smudge the very core of their angelic souls.

References _____

Best, J., and Horuchi, G. T. (1985). The razor blade in the apple: The social construction of urban legends. *Social Problems*, 32, 488–499.

Cavallo, D. (1981). *Muscles and morals: Organized playgrounds and urban reform, 1880–1920*. Philadelphia: University of Pennsylvania Press.

Chambliss, W. (1973, November). The saints and the roughnecks. *Society*, 11, 24–31.

Chandos, J. (1984). *Boys together: English public schools 1800–1864*. New Haven: Yale University Press.

Corsaro, W. (1985). *Friendship and peer culture in the early years*. Norwood, NJ: Ablex.

DeKoven, B. (1978). *The well-played game*. Garden City, NY: Anchor.

Devereaux, E. C. (1976). Backyard versus Little League baseball: The impoverishment of children's games. In D. M. Landers (Ed.), *Social problems in athletics*. Urbana: University of Illinois Press.

Dresser, N. (1973). Telephone pranks. *New York Folklore Quarterly*, 29, 121–130.

Fine, G. A. (1981a). Friends, impression management, and preadolescent behavior. In S. R. Asher and J. M. Gottman (eds.), *The development of children's friendships*, Cambridge: Cambridge University Press.

Fine, G. A. (1981b). Rude words: Insults and narration in preadolescent obscene talk *Maledicta*, 5, 51–68.

Fine, G. A. (1986). The social organization of adolescent gossip: The rhetoric of moral evaluation. In J. C. Gumperz, W. Corsaro, & J. Streeck (eds.), *Children's world and children's language*. Berlin: Mouton de Gruyter.

Fine, G. A. (1987). *With the boys: Little League baseball and preadolescent culture* Chicago: University of Chicago Press.

Garfinkel, H. (1967). *Studies in ethnomethodology*, Englewood Cliffs, NJ: Prentice-Hall

Gruner, C. R. (1979). *Understanding laughter*. Chicago: Nelson-Hall.

Gusfield, J. (1976). The literary rhetoric of science: Comedy and pathos in drinking driver research. *American Sociological Review*, 41, 16–33.

Gusfield, J. (1981). *The culture of public problems*. Chicago: University of Chicago Press.

Harris, T. (1978). Telephone pranks: A thriving pastime, *Journal of Popular Culture*, 12, 138–145.

Hughes, E. C. (1971). *The sociological eye*. Chicago: Aldine.

Huizinga, J. (1955). *Homo ludens*. Boston: Beacon press.

Kett, J. F. (1977). *Rites of passage: Adolescence in America 1790 to the present*. New York: Basic.

Knapp, M., and Knapp, H. (1976). *One potato, two potato. . . . :The secret education of American children*. New York: W. W. Norton.

Lakoff, G., and Johnson, M. (1980). *Metaphors we live by*. Chicago: University of Chicago Press.

Macleod, D. I. (1983). *Building character in the American boy*, Madison: University of Wisconsin Press.

Manning, P. K. (1979). Metaphors of the field: Varieties of organizational discourse *Administrative Science Quarterly*, 24, 660–671.

Nisbet, R. (1976). *Sociology as an art form*. Oxford: Oxford University Press.

Opie, P., & Opie, I. (1959). *The lore and language of schoolchildren*. New York: Oxford University Press.

Posen, I. S. (1974). Pranks and practical jokes at children's summer camps *Southern Folklore Quarterly*, 38, 299–309.

Redl, F. (1966). *When we deal with children*. New York: Free Press.

Riemer, J. (1981). Deviance as fun. *Adolescence*, 16, 39–43.

Rosenthal, M. (1986). *The character factory: Baden-Powell and the origins of the boy scout movement*. New York: Pantheon.

Sato, I. (in press). Play theory of delinquency: Toward a general theory of "action." *Symbolic Interaction*.

Stinchcombe, A. (1964). *Rebellion in a high school*. Chicago: Quadrangle.

Stone, G. (1959). Halloween and the mass child. *American Quarterly*, 11, 372–379.

Sutton-Smith, B. (1984). *A history of children's play*. Philadelphia: University of Pennsylvania Press.

Thrasher, F. (1927). *The gang*. Chicago: University of Chicago Press.

Whiting, B. B., and Whiting, J. W. M. (1975). *Children of six cultures*. Cambridge: Harvard University Press.

Wolfenstein, M. (1955). Some variants in moral training of children. In M. Mead and M. Wolfenstein (eds.). *Childhood in contemporary cultures*. Chicago: University of Chicago Press.

Yablonsky, L., and Brower, J. (1979). *The Little League game*. New York: Times Books.

Yobe, C. (1950). Observations on an adolescent folkway. *Psychoanalytic Review*, 37, 79–81.

41

THE FEMINIZATION OF POVERTY:
A CALL FOR PRIMARY PREVENTION

Barbara Levy Simon
School of Social Work
Columbia University

The feminization of poverty is now an all-too-familiar societal process that currently concentrates three-fourths of all poverty in the United States among women and children (Pearce, 1983, p. 70). This impoverishment of women and their children has proceeded at an alarming rate, especially among those who are not married—single parents, widowed or never-married women over age 65, and displaced homemakers (U.S. Bureau of the Census, 1985, pp. 430, 457–459, 461).

Between 1959 and 1979, the proportion of all U.S. families in poverty that were maintained by women rose sharply from 23 to 48 percent (Erie, Rein, and Wiget, 1983, p. 100). Among black families in poverty, the number maintained by women increased by 62 percent during the 1970s (Pearce, 1983, p. 70). Indeed, by 1982, two-thirds of all black children who lived in families headed by women lived in poverty (Sarri, 1985, p. 235). The proportion of the elderly poor who are women also increased markedly, from 60 to 71 percent between 1959 and 1982 (Ferree and Hess, 1985, p. 155). Women in the U.S. in 1982 were more than twice as likely as men to be poor in old age (Minkler and Stone, 1985, p. 352).

Despite the rapidly increasing participation of U.S. women in the work force, from 18.4 million in 1950 to 44.6 million in 1980, the economic status of women across the lifespan has eroded dramatically during the past two decades (Sarri, 1985, p. 237). Such patterns of women's poverty, established long before the Reagan years, have accelerated noticeably since 1981 (Hatcher, 1984, pp. 3–5).

To decelerate the feminization of poverty and then to supplant it with economic equality and opportunity, we must first identify and then change the structural foundation of this major social problem. This foundation has five sides: (1) the vitality of the cultural preconception that women are dependents of

men; (2) the sexual division of labor that continues to make women either primarily or solely responsible for children, household management, and the care of aged family members; (3) the pervasive racism encountered daily by minority men and women as they seek schooling, training, and jobs; (4) the dual labor market and its poor cousin, the dual welfare system; and (5) the systematic discrimination that women and girls face in the work force, housing market, and educational system.

THE STRUCTURAL FOUNDATION

The hoary presumption that a man must earn a "family wage" ample enough to support a wife and children has a correlative underside that proves devastating to working women—the notion that women enter the labor force only to supplement male earnings (Ehrenreich and Piven, 1984, p. 163). The consequent low wages paid to most women, together with the scant public aid available to them if they are without a male breadwinner, deliver the clear cultural message that they belong in a traditional family with a man at the helm and will suffer accordingly if they stray from that course (Abramowitz, 1985, pp. 16–17).

Women, in short, are still treated as wards of men. Many employers, many husbands, and many women themselves continue to perceive women as temporary workers whose primary commitment is to their families (Pearce, 1978, pp. 29–30). As a result, young girls are not taught to become primary breadwinners; women are pigeonholed into a few, ill-paid occupations in the work force; and employers continue to take advantage of an enormous pool of cheap labor (Pearce, 1983, p. 70).

Without widespread acceptance by both men and women of the belief that a woman is primarily a wife and mother and only secondarily a worker, private and public employers would find it impossible

From the *Journal of Primary Prevention*, 1988, 9 (1 and 2): 6–17. Copyright © 1988. Human Sciences Press. Reprinted by permission.

to sustain a wage structure that continues to pay women the proverbial 59 cents that they earn overall for every $1 men make, a ratio that has *not* improved in thirty years (Ehrenreich and Piven, 1984, p. 163). Woman as helpmeet is a conception that lives on despite widely recognized transformations in family patterns and work force demographics since 1950. This idée fixe provides ongoing cultural endorsement for a system of inadequate wages and welfare payments that leaves more and more working women and retired women poor.

The everyday enactment of the notion that women are men's dependents, the sexual division of labor between women and men, constitutes the second side of the foundation that undergirds the feminization of poverty. Women in the United States continue to be the only social actors who take primary responsibility for children, the home, and aging or sick family members. Though, as we have seen, women's rate of participation in the labor force has increased exponentially since the 1950s, researchers still find that " . . . wives do most of the household work and most of the child care" (Berk and Berk, 1979, p. 231). Media hoopla notwithstanding, wives who work full time remain responsible for 68–70 percent of all household and childraising tasks (Spitze, 1986, p. 697). The economic costs to women workers of this dual load are as severe and multiple as the physical and emotional ones (Walker, 1983, pp. 106–128). For teenage working mothers, the consequences of this double toll are extreme and lifelong.

Women, not men, interrupt jobs and careers to raise children, manage households, and care for aging relatives. The consequent gap between the continuity of men's work histories and those of women is dramatic: *73 percent* of women age 30 and over had at some point experienced a work interruption of six months or longer due to family or home care responsibilities in 1979, compared with *1.6 percent* of men (U.S. Dept. of Labor, 1985, p. 51). The disproportionate disruption in women's work patterns is one major cause of the meagerness of their wages in comparison to men's.

This disparity in earnings has, of course, obvious consequences for women in retirement. Since the Social Security payroll tax is regressive, one that takes proportionately more from the pay of low than high wage earners, women pay disproportionately high taxes into the Social Security Retirement Program and yet reap significantly less than men in old age (Abramowitz, 1985, p. 21). In 1982, for example, the average monthly benefit to retired men in the United States was $470; for retired women, $362 (Abramowitz, 1985, p. 21). Compounding this disparity in treatment of low and high wage earners is the Social Security system's penalization of workers who go in and out of the work force (Abramowitz, 1985, pp. 21–23). Benefit formulas reward continuity in work histories and inflict penalties on those who have periods of low or no earnings due to part-time work or leaves of absence taken for child-raising or caregiving. In addition, women who interrupt their work lives to take care of families and homes face reduced opportunities for vesting rights in the pension programs their employers offer (Minkler and Stone, 1985, pp. 354–355).

The sexual division of labor exacts a severe economic toll from women in another way, as well. Despite earning far less than men, women—when separated, divorced, or abandoned—become the sole or primary economic provider for their children. In 1976, 40 percent of all absent fathers in the U.S. contributed nothing to the raising of their children. The other 60 percent who did contribute made an average child support payment of less than $2,000 in a year in which the median income for all U.S. families was $13,800 (Pearce, 1985, p. 30). Whether in young adulthood, middle age, or retirement, women bear the brunt of a sexual division of labor that assures them markedly more responsibility and far less income than that accorded men.

Racial discrimination in education and employment is a third, essential side of the foundation that sustains women's impoverishment. Despite significant increases in the 1960s and 1970s in the proportions of black teenagers graduating from high school, the educational gap between black Americans and whites remains conspicuous: 41.5 percent of blacks, 25 years old and older, had not graduated from high school in 1984, a year in which only 26.7 percent of all persons in the U.S., 25 and older, had no high school diploma (Billingsley, 1987, p. 102; U.S. Bureau of the Census, 1985, p. 133). Since 1980, more than 50 percent of black teenagers drop out of high school in many cities, a statistic with grim implications for the earning power of black youth and adults (Billingsley, 1987, p. 102).

Meanwhile, teenage parenting, a rapidly increasing phenomenon among white girls, remains at exceedingly high levels in black communities. If current trends continue, more than half of all black teenage girls will become pregnant before they reach 20, the majority of whom will be unmarried (Billingsley, 1987, p. 100). Their chances for escaping poverty are slim, indeed, in a country in which the unemployment rate in March 1986 of black women between the ages of 16 and 19 who were not enrolled in school was 43.4 percent, more than three times the rate of unemployment of white women in that age group (U.S. Department of Labor, 1986, p. 73). High school drop-out rates, teenage pregnancy, and inordinately high levels of unemployment among black teens and adults are compounded by the comparatively low wages earned by blacks in general, and by black women in particular. The median family income of blacks in 1985 was 57.6 percent of that for whites (Swinton, 1987, p. 52). In 1984, the median weekly wage for full-time wage and salary workers in the U.S. was $326; for black men, $304; for black women, *$242* (U.S. Bureau of the Census, 1985, p. 419). In the words of Andrew Billingsley: ''Among the black population, poverty has come to rest most heavily on black women and children in the major cities of the nation'' (Billingsley, 1987, p. 99).

A fourth side of the structural foundation of the feminization of poverty is the dual labor market and its public parallel, the dual welfare system. As capitalism was transformed from a competitive system into a generally monopolistic one, a segmented private labor market emerged that is made up of a primary and secondary sector (Gordon, 1972). The primary sector is composed of jobs and careers which offer relatively high salaries, job security, good benefits, and excellent lateral and vertical job mobility. The secondary sector, by contrast, is a zone of low wages, few benefits, undesirable work conditions, poor job security, and little job mobility. Those adults who work in the secondary sector rarely move up into primary sector jobs. In the 1980s, 80 percent of women's jobs were clustered in just 20 of the 420 occupations catalogued by the U.S. Department of Labor, mostly in retail sales, clerical, service, and light assembly work that constitute the backbone of the secondary job sector (Ehrenreich and Piven, 1984, p. 163). This ghettoization of women into a few job categories ensures an oversupply of labor available for those jobs, thereby driving down and keeping down women's wages in accordance with supply and demand relationships.

The segmentation of the private labor market is mirrored in the public welfare system (Pearce, 1983, pp. 71–72). The primary welfare sector, made up of such programs as Social Security benefits, unemployment insurance, and workers' compensation, offers far more generous benefits than the secondary. The benefits of the primary welfare sector are viewed as entitlements for worthy recipients who do not have to take means tests or spend all their resources before qualifying. Welfare programs of the secondary sector, like Aid to Families with Dependent Children (A.F.D.C.) and Medicaid, do require means tests and the exhaustion of all economic resources before the recipient may receive benefits.

Part-time and seasonal workers, a significant block of the secondary labor force, have been excluded historically from most primary welfare protections. Women and minority workers of both genders make up a disproportionate segment of the part-time and seasonal ranks. As a consequence, such employees have only the paltry assistance of the secondary welfare sector available to them when unemployed or disabled. For example, in 1983, the average disposable income of A.F.D.C. families was less than three-quarters of the official poverty level. In that year, all fifty states left families who combined A.F.D.C. benefits, food stamps, and energy assistance *below* the poverty level (U.S. Commission on Civil Rights, 1983, p. 33 and Table 3.9).

A final side in the pentagonal foundation of the feminization of poverty is the systematic sexism that continues to pervade the family, educational system, media, work place, and housing market. Women and girls are actively discouraged from breaking out of low-paid ''women's work'' in a variety of ways. At home, on television, on movie screens, and in public schools and vocational training programs, traditional conceptions of men's and women's roles still shape socialization processes and the funneling of students and trainees into courses of study and apprenticeships. At school or on the job, women and girls who attempt to enter historically male domains continue to face risks of ostracism, sabotage of their work, sexual harassment, and physical harm. Furthermore, seniority provisions of management and labor unions, occupational segregation by gender, and the absence of affordable child care ensure the ghettoization of women in realms of low-paying work. Moreover, housing discrimination in effect forces many women who head families to live far from job opportunities in suburban industrial parks (Pearce, 1978, p. 34).

PREVENTION OF THE FEMINIZATION OF POVERTY

What can be done to crumble the five-sided base of the feminization of poverty? What measures of primary prevention can be taken in the present and future to reduce the incidence of poverty among women and their children in the United States?

Successful change strategies hinge on ongoing and realistic assessments of the forces and actors that resist the changes in question. To reduce the feminization of poverty, we must first understand who benefits from that poverty. Occupational segregation and discrimination by gender keep employers' labor costs down. The assignment of housekeeping, child care, and the care of sick and aging relatives to women, a social division of labor that excludes many women from holding primary sector jobs, benefits men in the United States in at least three ways: (1) this allocation of work reinforces men's domination of the primary labor market; (2) it ensures that they continue to enjoy more leisure time each week between paid work shifts than women do; and (3) tax rates are kept far lower than in European countries in which the public provides child care and caretaking of the sick, disabled, and the elderly. The reduction and elimination of the feminization of poverty, in short, will disrupt profit margins, transform the demography of the primary job sector, require men to yield more of their free time for domestic labor, and exact higher taxes from all workers and property owners, male and female alike. Consequently, we would be wise to expect *much* resistance as we move ahead with primary prevention efforts.

Resistance notwithstanding, preventive strategies that address both the material and cultural constraints that keep women poor are called for. In the light of the above analysis, four broad categories of action emerge as candidates for our short and long-term commitment. They include: (1) public policies that assure women of wages and income supports that will place them above, rather than below, the poverty level; (2) grassroots organizing that will put pressure on judges, administrators, and legislators to remove those obstacles that keep women out of many sorts of jobs, obstacles such as sexual harassment and the discrimination of employers and unions in assigning jobs, apprenticeships, training opportunities, and promotions; (3) the redistribution of responsibility for caring for young, sick, or old family members; and (4) the reconstruction of gender roles to make economic independence a gender-neutral attribute and to eliminate forever the stereotypes of woman as dependent and man as provider.

ON WAGES AND INCOME SUPPORTS

To abolish the feminization of poverty, women must be paid more money. Campaigns under way to enact comparable worth legislation and regulations, policies that would provide equal pay for work of comparable value, are one key route to redressing the imbalance between men and women's salaries amidst pervasive occupational segregation by gender (Remick, 1984). Full employment strategies, combining the expansion of public sector employment with incentives to private employers for hiring and training unemployed and underemployed people on a long-term basis, are equally salient in preventing more women and their children from falling into poverty.

A guaranteed national income plan designed to keep all citizens above the poverty line would also erode dramatically the feminization of poverty. Family allowances, universal income maintenance programs already in place in much of western Europe, would spread out throughout the entire taxpaying population the responsibility for providing economic security to children in the United States (Kahn, 1979, pp. 76–81). As a result, the poverty rates of female-headed families would decline.

Universal comprehensive maternity care, including health education and family planning services for teenagers and adults, might be an achievable first step toward a national health program, a broader objective that would assist women substantially in meeting the preventive and curative medical expenses that they and their children incur. Low-cost public housing, now of poor quality and in short supply in the U.S., must be dramatically expanded and improved if women-headed families are to stay out of poverty. Moreover, local passage and enforcement of anti-discrimination laws in housing and of rent controls would enable women-headed families to secure adequate accommodations at reasonable cost near suburban and urban job sites.

Reforms in Social Security are central to the reduction in poverty among older women. Benefit formulae must be changed to abolish penalties for part-time workers, seasonal workers, low-wage earners, and those who move in and out of the work force for childbearing and caregiving purposes. The Social Security benefit system should be revised to enable workers who have paid payroll taxes on low earnings throughout their lives to collect a livable income after retirement. The Employment Retirement Security Act of 1974, which did *not* require employers to provide pensions plans for employees working fewer than one thousand hours a year, needs amending to cover such part-time workers, many of whom are women (Minkler and Stone, 1985, p. 355).

Meanwhile, as these more dramatic transformations are afoot, A.F.D.C. payments must be quickly increased, indexed annually to inflation rates, and standardized nationally to insure that all recipients, regardless of geographic location, have incomes sufficient to enable them to feed, clothe, and house themselves and their families with decency and dignity. We should also reverse the multiple cutbacks in domestic programs brought by the 1981 Omnibus Budget Reconciliation Act, by subsequent Reagan budgets of 1982–1986, and by Gramm-Rudman-Hollings' legislation, that requires arbitrary, across-the-board spending cuts for 1987–1989 (Statewide Emergency Network for Social and Economic Security, 1986). These policies of the Reagan era have deepened and broadened the feminization of poverty by slashing income supports, food stamps, energy assistance, public child care funding, community and public health and mental health programs, student loans, job training and placement projects, small business loans, nutrition programs, adult literacy training, subsidies for the construction and renovation of low-cost housing, and mass transportation projects.

ON OCCUPATIONAL INTEGRATION

A second line of advance in reducing and preventing the feminization of poverty requires women workers to organize in the face of barriers that keep them segregated in a relatively tiny number of job types. Pressure should be placed on public officials, employers, and union leaders to end sex-typed patterns of assigning jobs, apprenticeships, and training opportunities. Eviscerated affirmative action laws and monitoring systems need reconstruction and rejuvenation.

Years of feminist mobilization began to reap results in 1986 from the U.S. Supreme Court on the issue of sexual harassment on the job. Much more work is required at federal, state, and local governmental levels, in unions, and in the work place itself to put a stop to this particular form of harassment, as well as to the more general types that prevent many women from even considering entering "nontraditional" jobs.

ON REDISTRIBUTING RESPONSIBILITY FOR CAREGIVING

Women are the caretakers of children, the dependent elderly, and sick people. They dominate this domain of activity generation after generation by default, since most men and the state refuse to participate in any significant way (Walker, 1983). The preponderance of the direct and indirect costs of such caregiving is therefore shouldered by those

adults in American society least able to afford them. In wages, Social Security benefits, pensions, seniority, and promotions, women pay dearly for their commitment to others.

Many women, of course, cherish this caregiving role, despite the costs to them in income, marketability, and security in old age. Many men and public policy makers, both contemporarily and historically, also claim to treasure such caregiving (Grubb and Lazerson, 1982). Yet such claims have not been backed up by husbands, sons, and fathers stepping forward to take their fair share of responsibility for caregiving. Nor has the government created the range of programs needed to provide dependents in our society with quality care. Instead of assuring adequate and accessible child care, after-school programs, respite care facilities, in-home care services and insurance, and long-term care programs for the chronically ill and dependent elderly, public officials reduce the meager budgets of such programs in one breath while hailing the sanctity of children, of the family, and of the elderly in the next. Even public funds for ensuring that child support payments are made were reduced significantly between 1981 and 1983, during a presidential administration that has given strong rhetorical support to the moral and economic salience of such enforcement (Statewide Emergency Network for Social and Economic Security, 1986).

The reduction and prevention of the feminization of poverty, in sum, hinge on the equitable redistribution of caregiving responsibilities for our young, sick, disabled, and old. This redistribution must proceed on two planes at once—between men and women within nuclear and extended families, and between the public realm and the private family. Only when men and the state become as fully involved in childraising and caregiving as women are, will the economic burden of such an important function be spread in a manner that does not impoverish women.

ON RECONSTRUCTING GENDER ROLES

As long as girls grow up in families and a culture that do not expect them to become independent actors, workers, and breadwinners, the feminization of poverty will continue. So long as boys grow up in families and a culture that teach them to take care of women when they are adults, the feminization of poverty will continue. Conceptions of female dependence on men on both conscious and unconscious levels yield female poverty and infantilization, not economic security and dignity for women. Indeed, a root cause of women's impoverishment is their perceived and actual dependence on men. Therefore, an essential remedy for the feminization of poverty is the replacement of norms of female dependence and of male protectiveness with expectations of independence and interdependence for all adults, regardless of gender. Gender role socialization that falls short of dignifying the autonomy of all women and men will only perpetuate the growing poverty of women; gender role socialization that creates expectations of gender-neutral autonomy will help reverse this troubling tide.

References

Abramowitz, M. (1985). The Family Ethic and the Female Pauper: A New Perspective on Public Aid and Social Security Programs. *Journal of Social Work Education, 21*, (2), 15–26.

Bane, M. J., and Ellwood, D. (1983). *Slipping Into and Out of Poverty: The Dynamics of Spells*. Cambridge, Mass.: Urban Systems Research and Engineering.

Berk, R. A., and Berk. S. J. (1979). *Labor and Leisure at Home: Content and Organization of the Household Day*. Beverly Hills: Sage.

Billingsley, A. (1987). Black Families in a Changing Society. In J. Dewart (ed.), *The State of Black America 1987* (pp. 97–111). New York: National Urban League.

Burnham, L. (1985). Has Poverty Been Feminized in Black America? *The Black Scholar, 16*, (2), 14–24.

Center on Budget and Policy Priorities. (1986, Feb. 5). *Administration Budget Contains Large Cuts in Programs for Poor*. Unpublished report, Washington, D.C.

Ehrenreich, B., and Piven, F. F. (1984). The Feminization of Poverty: When the "Family-Wage System" Breaks Down. *Dissent, 31*, 162–170.

Erie, S. P., Rein, M. and Wiget, B. (1983). Women and the Reagan Revolution: Thermidor for the Social Welfare Economy. In I. Diamond (ed.), *Families, Politics, and Public Policy: A Feminist Dialogue on Women and the State* (pp. 94–119). New York: Longman.

Ferree, M., and Hess. B. (1985). *Controversy and Coalition: The New Feminist Movement*. Boston: Twayne.

Gordon, D. M. (1972). *Theories of Poverty and Underdevelopment*. Boston: D. C. Heath.

Grubb, W. N., and Lazerson, M. (1982). *Broken Promises: How Americans Fail Their Children*. New York: Basic Books.

Hatcher, K. J. (1984). The Feminization of Poverty: An Analysis of Poor Women in New York City. Unpublished manuscript, prepared for Council Member Ruth W. Messinger of The Council of the City of New York.

Kahn, A. J. (1979). *Social Policy and Social Services* (2nd ed.). New York: Random House.

Keyserling, M. D. (1984, June). The Status and Contribution of American Women to the Economy: 1950–1983. *Research Papers*. National Conference on Women, the Economy, and Public Policy, Washington, D.C.

Malveaux, J. (1984). The Status and Contributions of Women of Color in the Economy: 1950–1983. *Research Papers*. National Conference on Women, the Economy, and Public Policy, Washington, D.C.

Minkler, M., and Stone, R. (1985). The Feminization of Poverty and Older Women. *The Gerontologist, 25*, 351–357.

Pearce, D. M. (1983). The Feminization of Ghetto Poverty. *Society, 21*, (1), 70–74.

Pearce, D. M. (1978). The Feminization of Poverty: Women, Work and Welfare. *The Urban and Social Change Review, 11*, 28–36.

Pearce, D. M. (1982). *The Poverty of Our Future: The Impact of Reagan Budget Cuts on Women, Minorities, and Children*. Washington, D.C.: Center for National Policy Review.

Pearce, D. M., and McAdoo, H. (1981). *Women and Children: Alone and In Poverty*. Washington, D.C.: Center for National Policy Review.

Remick, H. (ed.). (1984). *Comparable Worth and Wage Discrimination: Technical Possibilities and Political Realities*. Philadelphia: Temple University Press.

Sarri, R.C. (1985). Federal Policy Changes and the Feminization of Poverty. *Child Welfare, 44*, 235–247.

Scott, H. (1984). *Working Your Way to the Bottom: The Feminization of Poverty*. London: Pandora Press.

Spitze, G. (1986). The Division of Task Responsibility in U.S. Households: Longitudinal Adjustments to Change. *Social Forces, 64*, 689–701.

Stallard, K., Ehrenreich, B., and Sklar, H. (1983). *Poverty in the American: Women and Children First*. Boston: South End Press.

Statewide Emergency Network for Social and Economic Security. (1986, Feb.). *Left Behind: A White Paper on Poverty and Federal Budget Priorities*. Unpublished report, Albany, N.Y.

Swinton, D. (1987). Economic Status of Blacks 1986. In J. Dewart (ed.), *The State of Black America 1987* (pp. 49–73). New York: National Urban League.

United States Bureau of the Census. (1985). *Statistical Abstract of the United States: 1986* (106th ed.). Washington, D.C.: U.S. Government Printing Office.

United States Commission on Civil Rights. (1983). *A Growing Crisis: Disadvantaged Women and Their Children*. Washington, D.C.: U.S. Government Printing Office.

United States Department of Labor, Bureau of Labor Statistics. (1986). Current Labor Statistics: Employment Data. *Monthly Labor Review, 109*, (5), 73.

United States Department of Labor, Bureau of Labor Statistics. (1985). Work Interruptions and the Female-Male Earnings Gap. *Monthly Labor Review, 108*, (2), 50–51.

Walker, A. (1983). Care for Elderly People: A conflict Between Women and the State. In J. Finch and D. Groves (eds.), *A Labour of Love: Women, Work and Caring* (pp. 106–128). London: Routledge and Kegan Paul.

42

MID-LIFE CAREER DEVELOPMENT THEORY AND RESEARCH: IMPLICATIONS FOR WORK AND EDUCATION

Stephen Joel Gill
Larry C. Coppard
Malcolm A. Lowther
Department of Education and Institute of Gerontology
University of Michigan

The most popular definition of career is "a sequence of positions occupied by a person during the course of a lifetime" (Super, 1980). If middle age refers to the years ranging between ages 35 and 55, then mid-career means a sequence of positions that a person occupies during this age bracket. One is immediately struck by the difficulty of studying a span of 20-plus years as a single period in an individual's adult life, when compared with such fields as childhood and adolescent psychology that study human behavior over relatively short periods.

Traditionally, the mid-life period of workers has meant the time between the end of career exploration and the beginning of retirement. Generally, this period is considered a time when workers continue to perform the same job and adapt to any change in the work environment. Though many adults spend most of their adult lives working, employers are only beginning to recognize that workers' needs may change as they age (Root, 1981). Walz and Benjamin (1980) describe popular beliefs that prevent understanding the dynamic aspects of this period more fully:

> The prevailing view of "being an adult" means that one has come to terms with life, copes successfully with crisis and change and is generally in command of his/her world. Some theorists, examining developmental phases in career behavior, have called this life period the time of "crystallization" (Ginzberg, *et al.,* 1951), "establishment and maintenance" (Super, 1953) and "stability" (Miller and Form, 1951).

The difficulty in developing a comprehensive theory about a life period that represents almost a third of normal life span is one of several issues discussed here. The article aims to critique mid-life development theory and research and to discuss an environmental interpretation of mid-career behavior. An exhaustive review is beyond the scope of this paper. The selected works are representative of the field and offer a unique perspective.

Human resource policies and programs have been based primarily on the needs, interests and skills of younger members of the work force (Hall, 1976), and are less sensitive to middle-age employees who comprise a majority of workers. Because of this age bias, the potential contribution of 35- to 55-year-old workers is not fully utilized and problems that hinder the performance of many older workers are neither fully recognized nor often addressed (Root, 1981).

RISING EMPHASIS ON MID-LIFE WORK

Finding ways to utilize the resources of middle-age workers better is important for many reasons. As the American population ages, the work force also will age. Declining birth rates and increased longevity mean that employers in the future will depend increasingly on older employees. As people live longer and try to cope with the effects of inflation, more workers are likely to decide to stay in the labor force longer. New age discrimination laws and the raising and, in some cases, elimination of a mandatory retirement age have placed the middle years farther from retirement for many workers, giving these years new meaning within one's life span.

Moreover, the growing number of women who have entered the work force in recent years has resulted in large numbers of middle-age people employed for the first time or after many years' absence. Because of insecurities about their own ability to perform and about the expectations at the

---

work place, middle-age people often need help adjusting to the entry or re-entry process.

In addition, technological changes are rapidly making the training of many workers obsolete, creating new jobs unknown just a few years ago and eliminating others. Such changes have a disproportionate effect on the middle-age worker who invested years learning one occupation only to find that he/she must change to survive.

Education could also benefit from a better understanding of mid-life. Typically, educational systems concentrate on preparing the young to enter careers and give short shrift to adult education, which is frequently a marginal activity lacking the seriousness of career preparation programs. Weathersby and Tarule (1980) have identified two major reasons for considering seriously peoples' educational needs throughout adulthood. First, because of the decreasing pool of traditional college students, ages 18–22, it is in an institution's "enlightened self-interest" to attract and educate adult students. Secondly, educational programs offer adults an opportunity for career advancement, renewal or change. A fully articulated adult education system could help create a "learning society" where people of all ages are continually enhancing their careers through continuing education. Because educational programs are most effective when they are responsive to the needs, goals and learning styles of their students, only a clear understanding of adulthood, particularly middle age, will provide reliable guidelines for developing an adult education policy.

LITTLE KNOWN ABOUT MID-LIFE YEARS

What is known about the mid-life years? Though much has been written about the stages of life span development (Ginzberg, et al., 1951; Holland, 1973; Knefelkamp and Slepitza, 1976; Lofquist and Dawes, 1969; Roe, 1956; Schein, 1978, and Super, et al., 1957; and about middle age (Gould, 1978; Grant, 1969; Levinson, et al., 1974; Lowenthal, et al., 1974; Sheehy, 1976, and Vaillant, 1977), our understanding of the dynamics of mid-life development is limited. To date, theory and research have not adequately described this life period in terms of its impact on individuals nor provided the knowledge needed to create programs to facilitate individual development (Super and Hall, 1978).

Adult development research has characterized middle age as a period of transitions and conflict (Grant, 1969; Levinson, 1976; Lowenthal, et al.,

1975, and Vaillant, 1977). Such research purports that many experiences of middle-age people are linked to predictable life events (Weathersby and Tarule, 1980). Additionally, related literature on such topics as the "mid-life crisis" (Sheehy, 1976) and career change (Thomas, 1979) call attention to the special role that one's occupation plays in personal development during the middle years. It is obvious from this body of developmental literature that many important changes take place in the middle years and that the implications for one's career are likely to be significant.

A typical example of this developmental research is Levinson's work. He proposes an elaborate theory of male adult psychosocial development based on nine years of research, using a sample of 40 men ages 35–45. Through an analysis of life histories, Levinson developed a set of concepts that emphasize what he calls the "mid-life transition." He found that around age 22, men move into an early adulthood period, followed by a mid-life transition between ages 40 and 45, then another period of middle adulthood and a final late adult transition between ages 60 and 65. Levinson says all transition periods involve crisis, but he contends that the mid-life transition (similar to the concept of "mid-life crisis") evokes "tumultuous struggles within the self and the external world." Mid-life transition, according to Levinson, may be a "time of severe crisis" brought on by the tension between what has been achieved and what is wanted. He has observed that transitions are a normal part of life, which some people move through easily while others experience many difficulties.

Research by Levinson and others gives the basis for a development perspective that says age-related changes in the emotional, social and physical aspects of one's life are predictable. Their findings suggest that there are regular stages of adult development, and life is a "continuous process of change, sequential development and continuity from birth to death" (Kimmel, 1974).

WORK/NONWORK LIFE STAGES ADVANCED

While Levinson and others have examined adult development from an individual-centered perspective, some investigators have analyzed the individual's interaction with the environment. Schein (1978) and Hall (1976) have postulated some beliefs about mid-life career development within organizations. Schein believes understanding how one changes throughout work and nonwork life will help organizations match individual needs to organizational needs. This match, he believes, is the essence of human resource planning and development. Schein has identified what he considers to be major career and life problems that people face during mid-life:

Career Problems

- the decision to specialize or to generalize
- establishing an identity that gains recognition within the organization
- internal conflict caused by a clash between career expectations and reality
- becoming an effective mentor to younger and less-experienced employees
- balancing one's involvement among work, family and self-oriented activities
- creating an awareness that leads to a positive re-examination of self

Life Problems

- realization of one's mortality
- restimulation of feelings and conflicts that were experienced as an adolescent

- changing roles and relationships within a changing family
- realization that aging may limit opportunities

In his view, developmental tasks during mid-life involve the resolution of these problems.

Hall, influenced by Levinson, *et al.*, (1974), Erikson (1963), and Super (1957), has proposed his own model of career development (Hall, 1976). This "composite model of adult career stages" is presented in Figure 1. Hall's model represents selective integration of Erikson's life cycle stages, Levinson's periods of transition and Super's vocational life stages. But Hall's model deviates significantly from Super's vocational theory on the "maintenance" (mid-life) stage of development. Whereas Super defines this period as a time when " . . . little new ground is broken" (Super, Table 1, March 1978), Hall includes the alternate possibilities of either "stagnation" with a decrease in performance or "growth" with an increase in performance.

Hall concludes that the concerns of employees when they reach mid-career are:

- an awareness of advancing age and of death
- an awareness of physical aging

FIGURE 1. **STAGES IN CAREER DEVELOPMENT**

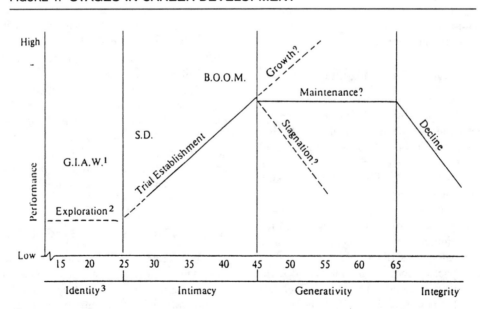

1. G.I.A.W. = Getting Into the Adult World; S.D. = Settling Down; and B.O.O.M. = Becoming One's Own Man (Levinson, et al., 1974).

2. Super (1957).

3. Erikson (1963).

• knowledge that not all career goals will be attained
  • search for new life goals
  • changes in family relationships
  • changes in work relationships
  • a growing sense of obsolescence
  • a growing sense of decreased job mobility
  • an increased concern for job security

These concerns, plus other problems, appear in Schein's description of mid-life.

Thomas (1979) tested three explanations of mid-life career change, a behavior considered characteristic of mid-life: (1) the counterculture explanation—change is spurred by a dissatisfaction with "mainstream society"; (2) the macrosocial explanation—change is an adaptation to social and economic conditions, and (3) the developmental explanation—change is a natural response to a particular life stage. Thomas' study of " . . . 73 men who had changed from higher-status careers between ages 34 and 54" partially supports the developmental hypothesis. He interviewed professionals who changed to careers for which their previous training was neither needed nor enough for the new career. A third of the sample made career changes between ages 40 and 45. When asked why they decided to start a new career, 76 percent said they wanted "to find more meaningful work," and 69 percent said that they wanted "to bring about a better fit between values and work" (Thomas, 1979). Thomas also reported that "many" of his respondents chose careers "less traditionally masculine." Each finding lends credence to Levinson's notions about a "crisis" brought on by an internal values conflict.

DEVELOPMENTAL STAGES INCONCLUSIVE

Thomas argues that the developmental position does not adequately explain career change. Not many men, he claims, either today or historically, have sought a career change when they reached mid-life, and no single theory seems to explain why some people do and others do not change careers during mid-life. The change, direction in the sense of upward or downward mobility, confuses the issue even further. Thomas posits a macrodevelopmental explanation that considers the interaction of the life cycle with the social environment.

Adult career development theory and research have contributed to knowledge in two key ways. First, they have fortified a rising awareness that adults frequently have certain needs and concerns

that motivate them toward making certain life changes. That these needs and concerns appear to be age related gives a more complete perspective on development across an individual's total life span. Secondly, a new awareness about the needs of many middle age workers, and how such needs relate to adult education and work organizations, has arisen. Much evidence exists suggesting that both adult education and work organizations could become more productive by being more responsive to changing adult needs. (Weathersby and Tarule, 1980; Hall, 1976, and Schein, 1978).

But while the life stage perspective provides conceptual order to factors that appear to influence work experience, drawing conclusions about mid-life from what is known about developmental stages is premature. An empirical base for adult career development intervention does not yet exist (Super and Hall, 1978). As Brim notes (1976), life stage theories are primarily wishful thinking:

> . . . there is as yet no evidence either for developmental periods or stages in the mid-life period, in which one event must come after another, or one personality change brings another in its wake. The existence of "stages," if proved true, would be a powerful concept in studying mid-life; meanwhile there is a danger of using this facile scheme as a cover for loose thinking about human development, without carrying forward the necessary hard-headed analyses of the evidence.

LIFE STAGE RESEARCH LIMITED

Mid-life career development research is limited in three major ways: Nonrepresentative samples; unfounded conclusions about cause and effect relationships; and monolithic explanations of multi-faceted processes. Each limitation is discussed below.

NONREPRESENTATIVE SAMPLES.

With few exceptions, most adult development research is based on nonrepresentative samples. For example, Vaillant's work is based on a longitudinal study of Harvard men (Vaillant, et al., 1977). Levinson and his associates (1974) interviewed 40 men, between ages 35 and 45, living between Boston and New York, and working in one of four occupations in 1969. Lowenthal and her associates (1974) studied four groups of male and female "transition facers," including high school seniors, newlyweds, middle-age parents and pre-retirees. Though some of Neugarten's findings stem from a large data base representing all social classes, some of her major conclusions, such as the shift in time perspective during middle age, are drawn from interviews of "100 highly placed men and women" (Neugarten, 1976). Sheehy (1976) interviewed people she calls the "pacesetter group"—healthy, motivated and middle class. Gould (1978) studied psychiatric outpatients and white middle-class men and women.

Two influential theorists on life stage development, Erikson (1963) and Super (1977), have based their beliefs about mid-life on observations of non-representative groups. Erikson, who probably has had the most influence on the construction of a life stage framework within the field of developmental psychology, based his theoretical formulations on longitudinal studies of children, observations from his psychotherapy practice and biographies of highly creative individuals (Erikson, 1968). Though each of the data sources is without doubt rich in theoretical implications, one should not view Erikson's model as anything more than a highly tentative theory. His proposition that the primary mid-life task is generativity has not been demonstrated conclusively for a representative sample of the adult population. In fact, Erikson's entire theory has yet to be tested empirically (Hall, 1976).

Super, who has probably had the most influence on a life span approach to career development, has found support for many of his ideas from a longitudinal study of males (Super, 1957). The study, begun in 1951 with ninth grade boys from Middletown, New York, has enabled him to observe his subjects in early adulthood but not yet middle age. His belief that middle age is a time of establishment and maintenance, though compelling in logic, cannot be tested until his subjects are older, and, then, only with his male population.

MOST STUDIES FOCUS ON WHITE, MALE MANAGERS

Schein's (1978) and Hall's (1976) studies of adult behavior in organizations generally have focused on elite groups. Schein's beliefs about career development are based primarily on a 12-year panel study of 44 graduates from the Sloan School of Management at the Massachusetts Institute of Technology. He has also been influenced by his 20 years of consulting with large corporations. Not surprisingly, the people he has studied are primarily white, male, upwardly mobile and business management oriented.

Hall studied new management recruits at AT&T (Berlew and Hall, 1966; Hall and Mougaim, 1968), Roman Catholic priests (Hall and Schneider, 1973),

business students (Hall and Foster, 1977), female college graduates in relation to their families (Hall, 1975) and research and development professionals (Hall and Mansfield, 1975). Though Hall's work is more diverse than possibly any other adult career development investigator, the basis of his conclusions are findings from studies of highly educated, upwardly mobile, primarily male subgroups of the general population.

Thomas's (1979) research on mid-life career change has a similar limitation. His sample is male and exclusively middle or upper middle class and college educated. Respondents were selected from managerial, professional and technical professional occupations through a referral system.

It is in the interest of scientific inquiry to develop theoretical descriptions of the life course and characteristics of the mid-life years. But, as the research indicates, most of what is now postulated about mid-life is based on subgroups that do not represent all American workers. Weathersby's and Tarule's (1980) review of adult development research leads them to conclude that most " . . . generalizations about all of human development have been made from research samples of middle-class, white males."

The research has concentrated on male managers and administrators who make up less than 10 percent of the labor force (Issacson, 1977). Because about 45 percent of all women 16 years old and older are in the labor force (Issacson, 1977), an important segment of the working population has been overlooked. Women are concentrated in a small number of occupations (elementary teaching, secondary teaching, nursing, service work, clerical work and blue collar machine operation) that have not been adequately investigated in terms of career development.

In addition, research has concentrated on workers who are projected to have continuous, ascending career paths within one occupational field. In reality, there are many exceptions to this "traditional" picture of work: Factory workers in unstable industries (i.e., automotive), noncareer military personnel, homemakers who plan a career change to coincide with family changes and all workers whose occupations do not play a central role in their career identity.

UNFOUNDED CONCLUSIONS.

The accumulated evidence does not support a causal relationship between age and life crises. Brim (1976) argues this point in his discussion of adult development as a field of study:

. . . it is in real danger from pop culture renderings of "life stages" from the public seizing on the idea of age-linked stages of development, such as the "male mid-life crisis," just as it seizes on astrology and tea leaf reading. Certainly, the evidence does not justify linkage of crises either to stages, or to specific ages, during the mid-life period.

ENVIRONMENTAL FACTORS AFFECT MID-LIFE

Brim does not deny that some men do undergo important personality changes during mid-life, but he argues that the causes are complex and varied and there is no evidence that predictable, sequential stages of development exist (Brim, 1976). Other explanations, such as social environment, historical time and an individual's life history, may offer better predictors of crisis and change than one's age (Lowenthal, 1981). Zimbardo (1978) concludes that what is known about mid-life is ambiguous; it is not yet clear whether this period is "the best of times" or "the worst of times."

The causes of crisis and change during mid-life, and the degree of satisfaction with change, may have more to do with one's response to environment than with response to age. Fozard and Popkin (1978) argue that an individual's work and home environments can have a profound effect on that person's adjustment to aging. Hall (1976) has suggested that the degree of challenge provided by the work environment in a job is related to the quality of performance during later years.

In addition, values that may stimulate important life decisions at various times during one's career vary greatly within any single age cohort (Perry, 1968), Lawrence's (1980) recent study of mid-life career changes did not find a common experience of crisis. She attributes this finding in part to the historical time in which her subjects live. It is the interaction of the individual with a rapidly changing society that provides the opportunity for either positive or negative consequences. Some people are able to adapt and develop intellectually and emotionally while others experience such great conflict that growth is blocked. Weathersby and Tarule (1980) conclude from their review of developmental stage theory: "Environment is a powerful factor in facilitating development; poverty, hostility, or serious deprivation can place ceilings on growth."

MONOLITHIC EXPLANATIONS.

Shaped by their desire to formulate simple (and possibly original) descriptions for an emerging area, investigators have seized on monolithic explanations for mid-life career development. They have created one dimensional theories to explain highly complex behavior. One behavior, considered unique to mid-life, is "mid-career change." This behavior has been studied from the perspective of those who change careers and those who do not. Hall (1979) challenges this view by presenting mid-career change on a continuum of intensity depending on the specific nature of the shift. One must examine the kind of change to understand the event fully. Taking a new job in the same organization may be a quite different experience from taking a new job in a different organization or a new job in a new organization that is also a different type of institution (such as change from government agency to business). Hall adds that any occupational career change is affected by other, concurrent changes in the person's life, such as changes involving family, location or spouse's career.

Not only is the event itself highly complex but factors causing "mid-career change" also appear highly complex. Thomas's (1979) conclusion that career change in mid-life is best explained by a "macrodevelopmental hypothesis" emphasizes the complexity of the change. Developmental (life stage) explanations alone, without consideration of the interaction of intrapersonal and environmental factors, do not adequately account for what is happening.

CAREER CHANGE NOT ALWAYS A CRISIS

When a career change does occur, it may not necessarily have crisis proportions in a person's life. In fact, the change may be a move toward greater stability rather than a radical departure from one's life course (Hall, 1979). The person may be seeking a better match of career interests, personality characteristics, skills and realities of that person's life situation with the qualities of a particular job. It may be a match that was never fulfilled during earlier career exploration processes, suggesting that any career change is part of a process that occurs over time. An individual's specific action to find a new job or to modify an old job plays a relatively minor part in a process of preparation and decision making that has occurred throughout the person's life and is affected by his/her environment.

So, to consider "mid-career change" as a one-dimensional event of a particular life stage is an oversimplification of adult development. To attempt to explain the causes of the change in monolithic terms ignores many important dimensions of a theoretically complex process.

Education plays an important role in the career development of middle-age adults. First, educators must accept that learning is different for each individual; changes in learning take place that parallel the changes occurring throughout life in situations, attitudes, expectations and needs. Once this value is accepted, educational institutions can take steps to facilitate development (Weathersby and Tarule, 1980):

> (1) identify the groups and variety of students to be served; (2) become sensitive to their goals and learning needs viewed from the broad and specific perspectives of human development; (3) define educational aims at least partially as promoting individual development, and (4) then reexamine the areas of program development and strategy, curriculum and teaching methods, faculty development and evaluation plus counseling and support services.

Lowther (1980) has argued that higher education institutions should be more responsive to the needs of middle-age adults seeking a career change. He suggests that adult students could be better assisted by changing policies in admissions, counseling, curriculum development, instructional delivery, placement and research activities to address their special needs.

IMPORTANT TO AID INDIVIDUAL NEEDS

Though life stage theory is conceptually useful to understanding adult behavior, adults must be treated as individuals. A program targeted at the stability and security needs of some middle-age adults will miss the mark for adults in need of challenge and risk taking. A program targeted at matching middle-age adults with extrinsically rewarding careers will miss the mark for adults seeking intrinsically rewarding careers. Higher education, as well as adult and continuing education, must recognize the diversity among adults of all ages.

Adult development is really a life span problem. Values and beliefs formed during childhood shape the attitudes that one has toward middle age. Also, the skills learned early in life will be useful throughout one's career. The person who learns career exploration skills (self-assessment, job search, interviewing, etc.) during adolescence will have relatively little trouble applying such skills as they are needed during adulthood. It is their absence, rather than age itself, that may bring on conflict and trauma during middle age. If a child is taught, either overtly or covertly, that being 40 is "over the hill"

and that youth is valued more highly than age, that child will likely have a difficult time making the transition into mid-life. So, the career development of adults begins with the career education of children. Ways must be found to prepare youth for the aging process. Both curriculum and counseling could help us realize this goal.

"I'm too old!" is the refrain heard again and again by middle-age individuals presented with new challenges. People are biased against learning new skills or making risky life changes at a time in their lives when they feel they should be preparing for decline and retirement. Quite often children are grown and out of the house; some financial stability in the family exists; a social support system has been formed, and the individual has developed the ability and maturity to adapt to new situations. Opportunity for change may never be greater. Middle age may be the best time to finish an undergraduate college degree or to attend a graduate or professional school. Unfortunately, misconceptions and fear often prevent this process from occurring.

On the other side, age bias exists among educators, too, which can keep motivated adults from attending college. Some graduate and professional programs continue to reject applications from older adults, particularly those who achieved a below standard grade point average 10 to 20 years ago. There is reason to believe many of these adults have experiences and motivation that would give them a higher probability of success than the much younger, career student (Weathersby and Tarule, 1980). Students and faculty need to be informed about the nature of the myths about aging that are generally believed.

AGE BIAS MUST BE CONFRONTED

Employers must also be confronted on their age bias. A 50-year-old worker may have 20 productive years left in his/her occupation (Rosow and Zager, 1980), while the traditionally more attractive, mobile, 22-year-old will probably leave his/her job after just a few years. It may be more beneficial to an employer to keep the older worker than to hire the younger one. Rosow and Zager (1980) recommend "age neutrality" in the work place, which does not mean ignoring age-related needs of workers. But it does mean not attributing qualities to a particular individual solely because of his/her age.

Our discussion of mid-life career development has implications for the work environment itself.

Hall (1976) and Schein (1978) recommend that organizations be involved in ongoing career development with their employees. They argue that the organization will benefit from being responsive to the kinds of needs that may emerge during mid-life. A worker who has an increasing need for job security and a growing fear of obsolescence might be helped by the updating of old skills and learning new ones or by giving that person a role in "mentoring" younger employees. But any organizational response to the needs of mid-life should occur with an awareness of the great diversity among individuals, some who need change and others who need stability.

This analysis disputes the belief that mid-life is a predictable time of crises, conflicts, transitions or even stability and maintenance. The theory and research reviewed here does not support a cause and effect relationship between age and certain personality and career changes. There is no doubt that middle age is a time of some trauma and change for some people, but based on the evidence, it is not reasonable to depict mid-life as a sequence of developmental stages distinguished as a problematic period of adulthood. Just as great differences exist among children and adolescents, adults can choose growth, maintenance, stagnation or decline.

Career development is a complex process influenced by many factors. Individual characteristics interact with social-environmental characteristics to shape the decisions of the person. "Career change," a behavior thought to be highly characteristic of people's needs during mid-life, must be considered in all of its various facets if its relationship to mid-life is to be fully understood. In addition, career change should not be considered unique to mid-life. The process seems to be characteristic of most age periods of the life span. Career change during youth is labeled "exploration"; if it occurs for new professionals, it is often considered a mechanism for coping with "burn-out"; career change among older workers is considered preretirement or retirement planning. Shifts in one's work at each of these states are significant and potentially as traumatic or growth enhancing as in any other stage.

Adult career development has not been studied as extensively as have other periods of life. It is a young field of study and the research lacks the needed rigor and comprehensiveness to build illuminating theory. Mid-life should be studied within the context of the years that precede and follow the mid-life span. Studies focused on previously neglected groups, such as women, and longitudinal studies of samples stratified by sex, job characteristics, work environment, career opportunities, geographic region and the socio-economic situation of the individual also are needed. In addition, the field would benefit from intensive case-studies that describe the career experiences of people with a wide range of socioeconomic and employment backgrounds.

"Mid-life crisis," and other changes proposed as part of middle age, may be part of a self-fulfilling prophecy. Society considers ages 35, 40, 45, and 50 times of transition.

> The individual passes through a socially regulated cycle from birth to death as inexorably as he passes through the biological cycle: A succession of socially delineated age-statuses, each with its recognized rights, duties, and obligations.
>
> (Neugarten, 1976)

Special birthdays and age-related humor serve to reinforce the social traditions. Literature, such as *Passages* (Sheehy, 1976) and *The Seasons of a Man's Life* (Levinson, *et al.*, 1978), which have had popular appeal, lend scientific credibility to the folk wisdom about mid-life. Expectations for the conflict and trauma attributed to middle age are created and maintained.

Questions about mid-life and the needs of middle-age students and workers remain unanswered. The interaction of important factors during this portion of a person's life are unclear. We believe that an environmental explanation that considers intrapersonal and interpersonal characteristics, attitudes toward work and life in general and in the characteristics of the person's environment, including family and work, has the greatest potential for helping us understand the complexities of mid-life career development.

REFERENCES

Berlew, D. E. and D. T. Hall. "The Socialization of Managers: Effects of Expectations on Performance," *Administrative Science Quarterly, II,* 1966, 207–223, 1966.

Brim, O. G. Jr. "Theories of the Male Mid-life Crisis," *The Counseling Psychologist, 6,* 2–9, 1976.

Erikson, E. H. *Childhood and Society.* New York: Norton, 2nd ed., 1963.

Fozard, J. L. and S. J. Popkin. "Optimizing Adult Development: Ends and Means of an Applied Psychology of Aging," *American Psychologist, 33,* 975–989, 1978.

Ginzberg, E., Axelrad, S., Ginsbur, S. W., and J. L. Herman, *Occupational Choice*. New York: Columbia University Press, 1951.

Gould, R. L. *Transformations: Growth and Change in Adult Life*. New York: Simon and Schuster, 1978.

Grant, C. H. "Age Differences in Self-concept from Early Adulthood Through Old Age," *Proceedings of the 77th Annual Convention of the American Psychological Association, 4*, 717–718, 1969.

Hall, D. T. "Midcareer change: There's Less There Than Meets the Eye." Contribution to Symposium, "Staffing Management Positions," M. London and S. Stumf, chairs, Academy of Management, Atlanta, Georgia, 1979.

Hall, D. T. *Careers in Organizations*, Santa Monica, California: Goodyear, 1976.

Hall, D. T. "Pressures from Work, Self, and Home in the Life Stages of Married Women," *Journal of Vocational Behavior, 6*, 121–132, 1975.

Hall, D. T. and F. L. Foster. "A Psychological Success Cycle and Goal Setting: Goals, Performance, and Attitudes," *Academy of Management Journal, 20*, 282–290, 1977.

Hall, D. T. and R. Mansfield. Relationships of Age and Seniority with Career Variables of Engineers and Scientists. *Journal of Applied Psychology, 60*, 201–210, 1975.

Hall, D. T. and K. Nougaim. An Examination of Maslow's Need Hierarchy in An Organizational Setting," *Organizational Behavior and Human Performance, 3*, 12–35, 1968.

Hall, D. T. and B. Schneider. *Organizational Climates and Careers: The Work Lives of Priests*. New York: Academic, 1973.

Holland, J. L. *Making Vocational Choices: A Theory of Careers*. Englewood Cliffs, New Jersey: Prentice Hall, 1972.

Isaacson, L. E. *Career Information in Counseling and Teaching*. Boston: Allyn and Bacon, 1977.

Kimmel, D. *Adulthood and Aging*. New York: John Wiley and Sons, 1974.

Knefelkamp, L. L. and R. Slepitza. "A Cognitive Developmental Model of Career Development—An Adaptation of the Perry Scheme," *Counseling Psychologist, 6*, 53–58, 1976.

Lawrence, B. S. "The Myth of the Mid-life Crisis." In E. Miller, R. Hill, and M. A. Lowther, *Adult Career Transitions: Current Research Perspectives*. Division of Research, Graduate School of Business Administration, The University of Michigan, 75–97, 1981.

Levinson, D. J. "The Mid-life Transition: A Period in Adult Psychosocial Development," *Psychiatry, 40*, 99–122, 1977.

Levinson, D. J., C. Darrow, E. Klein, M. Levinson and B. McKee. "The Psychological Development of Men in Early Adulthood and the Mid-life Transition." In D. T. Ricks, A. Thomas and M. Ross (eds.), *Life History Research in Psychopathology* (Vol. 3). Minneapolis: University of Minnesota Press, 1974.

Lofquist, L. H. and R. N. Dawes. *Adjustment to Work*. Englewood Cliffs, N.J.: Prentice Hall, 1969.

Lowenthal, M. F., M. Thurber, D. Chiriboga and Associates. *Four Stages of Life*. San Francisco: Jossey Bass, 1974.

Lowther, M. A. "Career Changes in Mid-life: Some Educational Implications," *Resources in Education* (ERIC Document Reproduction Service No. ED 176–034), 1980.

Miller, D. C. and W. H. Form. *Industrial Sociology*. New York: Harper, 1951.

Neugarten, B. L. "Adaptation and the Life Cycle." *The Counseling Psychologist, 6*, 16–20, 1976.

Roe, A. *The Psychology of Occupations*. New York: Wiley, 1956.

Root, L. *Older Workers: Problems and Potentials*. Unpublished manuscript, 1981.

Rosow, M. and R. Zager. *Work in America: The Future of Older Workers in America*. Jerome Institute, 1980.

Schein, E. H. *Career Dynamics: Matching Individual and Organizational Needs*. Reading, Massachusetts: Addison-Wesley, 1978.

Sheehy, Gail. *Passages: Predictable Crises of Adult Life*. New York: E. P. Dutton, 1976.

Super, D. E. "A Life-span, Life-space Approach to Career Development," *Journal of Vocational Behavior, 16*, 282–299, 1980.

Super, D. E. "Vocational Life Stages" (Table 1). Unpublished manuscript, 1978.

Super, D. E. "Vocational Maturity in mid-career," *Vocational Guidance Quarterly*, June, 1977.

Super, D. E. *The Psychology of Careers*. New York: Harper and Row, 1957.

Super, D. E. "A Theory of Vocational Development," *American Psychologist, 8*, 185–190, 1953.

Super, D. E. and D. T. Hall. "Career Development: Exploration and Planning," *Annual Review of Psychology, 29*, 333–372, 1978.

Thomas, L. E. Causes of Mid-life Change from High-status Careers. *The Vocational Guidance Quarterly*, 202–208, March, 1979.

Vaillant, G. E. *Adaptation to Life*. Boston: Little Brown, 1977.

Walz, G. R. and L. Benjamin. *Counseling Adults for Life Transitions*. ERIC Counseling and Personnel Services Clearinghouse, 1980.

Weathersby, R. P. and J. M. Tarule. *Adult Development: Implications for Higher Education*. Washington, D.C.: American Association for Higher Education—ERIC/Higher Education Research Report No. 4, 1980.

Zimbardo, P. G. *Psychology and Life*. Glenview, Illinois: Scott Foresman, 1978.

PART VIII

LIFE AND DEATH

INTRODUCTION

American society has been described as death denying. We tend to hide the dying from the living, and to disguise the dead as if they were alive. It is not just ordinary citizens who are death-deniers; helping professionals have been uneasy about dealing with the dying and the surviving. Our many state laws reflect our divergence of opinions about how—or whether—the dying should be cared for at all costs. These laws tap into deep-lying values that are at the base of our civilization, for it is society's fundamental purpose to survive. Questions begin when we consider survival for what purpose, with what quality of life, at what cost to the health and welfare of others?

This part of the anthology will consider the general question of death and dying, with special reference to those who are survivors. The paper by Vickie M. Mays and Susan D. Cochran describes the special psychosocial and cultural issues related to black Americans and AIDS. Blacks and Hispanics are disproportionately represented among AIDS victims, but differences exist in their patterns of transmission (more drug-related than homosexual modes), and how they respond to public health messages. (See also A. Baum and S. E. A. Nesselhof. [1988]. "Psychological research and the prevention, etiology, and treatment of AIDS." *American Psychologist, 43:* 11, 900–904, as well as other articles in this special issue on AIDS. Another useful resource is Coping with AIDS: Psychological and So-

cial Considerations in Helping People with HTLV-III Infection. [1986]. National Institute of Mental Health. DHHS Publication No. [ADM] 85-1432).

The paper by Pamela S. Moore provides an overview of information on the history, nature, and demographics of suicide. In this excerpt, Moore indicates the range of signs that may be indicative of suicidal intentions. This kind of information can be readily shared with lay people who are usually the first line of defense in observing these signs.

The last paper in this section by Marian Osterweis and Jessica Townsend deals with bereavement. Contrary to popular opinion, they note that bereavement does not necessarily follow an orderly development. Indeed, the crisis of bereavement may provide an opportunity for personal growth for some people. For others, there may be risks of premature death, about which helping professionals should be informed.

Overall, we see that life itself, as well as death, is a social affair. We are born of the union of two persons, and our life is a spiraling mass of patterned interactions. In most cases, we die within the family setting or in a social institution. It is our death, but it is shared during and afterward by our survivors, just as it is our life, which is also shared at every step of the way. The values of self-determination should operate at every step over the life course, but in fact are prevented from doing so by many social customs and institutions.

43

ACQUIRED IMMUNODEFICIENCY SYNDROME AND
BLACK AMERICANS: SPECIAL PSYCHOSOCIAL ISSUES

Vickie M. Mays
Department of Psychology
University of California, Los Angeles

Susan D. Cochran
Department of Psychology
California State University, Northridge

Acquired immunodeficiency syndrome (AIDS) is a disease that profoundly affects not only the physical health of the person afflicted but also, potentially, every facet of his or her psychosocial functioning (*1*). At present, there is no curative medical treatment available for AIDS (*2, 3*), greatly increasing the importance of psychosocial factors for preventing infection and for coping and adaptation once infection occurs. To black Americans, the impact of AIDS presents several unique considerations. These include differences from whites in patterns of infection, effectiveness of preventive health education efforts, and psychosocial issues affecting the health and mental health care of black AIDS patients.

PATTERNS OF INFECTION

Despite the general perception that AIDS is nearly exclusively a "gay disease" (*4*), and a specific perception by some members of the black community that AIDS is a "gay white disease" (*5*), AIDS has disproportionately affected blacks (*6–8*). As of December 29, 1986, 28,593 cases of AIDS in adults have been reported in the United States (*9*). Of these, approximately 25 percent have occurred among black persons, although blacks represent only 12 percent of the population. At this point, the Public Health Service (PHS) has estimated that approximately 1 to 1.5 million persons have been infected with the AIDS virus—HTLV-III/LAV (human T-cell lymphotropic virus type III/lymphadenopathy-associated virus. The International Committee on the Taxonomy of Viruses proposed the name "human immunodeficiency virus" for these viruses (*10*). If rates of infection parallel AIDS incidence ratios, then 1 to 1.4 percent of the black population is possibly infected with the virus (figures are based on the 1980 U.S. Census (*11*). In contrast, 60.2 percent of diagnosed AIDS patients have been whites,

suggesting that 0.3 to 0.5 percent of the white population may be infected. Clearly, AIDS has the potential to have a much more profound impact on the black community than among whites.

The Public Health Service estimates that by the year 1991 the cumulative number of cases of AIDS will reach 196,000 (155,000–220,000 range) (*10*). This estimate indicates an approximate tenfold increase in the cumulative number of cases at the start of 1986. Multiplying the number of cases among blacks at the start of 1986 by 10 yields approximately 49,000 cases by 1991 (table 1), if one follows the PHS model and uses the current relative incidence by ethic group. Cumulative deaths would reach 31,500. Yet the Public Health Service speculates that the empirical model used to derive these overall estimates may *underestimate* by at least 20 percent the serious morbidity and mortality attributable to AIDS because of under-reporting or under-identification of cases (*10, 12*). Racial differences in the use of health care resources and risk behaviors

TABLE 1. Projected Cases of AIDS for Black Americans[1]

Category	Total AIDS cases		Black Americans	
	1986	1991	1986	1991
Cumulative cases diagnosed at start of year.	19,000	196,000	4,750	49,000
Cumulative deaths at start of year.	9,000	125,000	2,250	31,250
Estimated number of persons infected with HIV virus.	1,000,000 to 1,500,000	...	250,000 to 375,000	...

[1] Total AIDS cases based on Coolfont planning conference, 1986 estimates. Estimates for black Americans assume that blacks will continue to constitute approximately 25 percent of all AIDS cases.

Reprinted from *Public Health Reports*, 1987 (March–April), *102* (2): 224–231.

may differentially affect the accuracy of the reporting of AIDS cases in black Americans.

In addition, the epidemiologic pattern for AIDS transmission among adult blacks differs from that of the white population, which suggests greater levels of risk to the heterosexual population (6–8) (table 2). Black homosexual and bisexual men account for 46.3 percent of all cases in blacks, and heterosexual IV drug users account for 35.4 percent. In contrast, among whites, 88.9 percent of cases are in homosexual or bisexual men, and 5.2 percent are heterosexual IV drug users. This difference in patterns of infection is most pronounced in New York City, which has the highest cumulative incidence of AIDS cases among intravenous drug users in the United States (13, 14). A second factor in the distribution among blacks is that the category of individuals with AIDS from foreign countries comprises primarily blacks from Haiti and Central Africa (15). Many of them are economically disadvantaged immigrants residing in New York or Miami who either lack private health insurance or financial resources or are ineligible for government-subsidized medical services due to their undocumented status (15, 16). Early symptoms of AIDS may be ignored and, due to cultural differences in sexual norms among Haitians, rates of nonmonogamous sexual behavior may be high (15–17). AIDS testing of military recruits reveals a higher percentage of seropositive testing in black recruits, supporting concerns about the possibility of higher rates of heterosexual transmission in blacks (18). Researchers who studied rates of seropositivity among U.S. military recruit applicants tested for antibodies to the AIDS virus found a 0.9 per 1,000 seropositive rate among white recruits but a rate of 3.9 per 1,000 among blacks (18).

The importance of accurate predictions is critical. Often, these are used as the basis for allocating Federal, State, city, and county resources. As an example, it has been suggested that intravenous drug users with AIDS suffer a higher rate of acute opportunistic diseases than do gay and bisexual men, thus requiring more extensive medical care (14). Blacks who develop AIDS are more likely to be IV drug users but, for the most part, they have lower incomes and less education than whites who are similarly afflicted. In New York City, approximately 50 percent of IV drug users are on public assistance and depend on Medicaid for health insurance (14). The average cost of hospital care for an AIDS patient is $147,000 (13, 19). However, more recent data indicate that hospital costs may vary widely according to geographic location (20). Nevertheless, hospitals in the black community are more likely to have to care for these patients and may suffer a severe drain of resources without adequate compensation.

REDUCING INFECTION RATES

Slowing the transmission rate of the AIDS virus within the black community is critical. Several specific concerns are particularly relevant when focusing on blacks who are especially at risk for HTLV-III/LAV exposure. For all black Americans in potential risk groups, health educators need to be especially sensitive to differences in the vernacular used by blacks to describe sexual behaviors and methods of intravenous drug use.

TABLE 2. Distribution of AIDS Cases in Adults, by Race and Risk Factors, December 29, 1986[1]

Risk factor	Total		White		Black	
	Cases	Percent	Cases	Percent	Cases	Percent
Homosexual or bisexual male	18,750	65.6	13,849	80.4	2,738	39.2
Homosexual or bisexual male and IV drug user	2,230	7.8	1,436	8.4	494	7.1
Heterosexual IV drug user	4,846	17.0	891	5.2	2,464	35.3
Immigrant from country where heterosexual transmission is thought to play a major role	584	2.1	3	0.0	578	8.3
Heterosexual contact with AIDS-infected or at-risk person	508	1.8	126	0.8	241	3.5
Transfusion	524	1.9	407	2.4	78	1.1
Hemophiliac	246	0.9	208	1.2	14	0.2
None of the above	905	3.2	321	1.9	383	5.5
Total cases	28,593	100.0	17,241	100.0	6,990	100.0

[1] AIDS surveillance data from the Centers for Disease Control.

BLACK HOMOSEXUAL AND BISEXUAL MEN

Public Health Service projections anticipate that information and interventions currently employed in the broader gay community will successfully lower the rate of transmission among homosexual men (10). However, assumptions that outreach efforts have reached and are effective with black gay and bisexual men are unproven. The black gay community continues to insist that the methods of educational outreach and intervention spearheaded by the white gay community have been ineffective in reaching black gay and bisexual men (21). Therefore, risk reduction behaviors within this population may actually be developing at a slower rate than among white gay men.

There is evidence that black gay and bisexual men may have somewhat different patterns of sexual behaviors from white gay men (22.) These include higher rates of both active and passive anal intercourse and bisexual involvement. Health education efforts critical to curtailing the spread of this infection may be hampered by a lack of sensitivity to ethnic and cultural differences.

INTRAVENOUS DRUG USERS

For intravenous drug users, most of whom identify themselves as heterosexual, less educational outreach has been organized. Substance abuse programs are in a precarious position. It is difficult to discuss how to sterilize drug works or paraphernalia without appearing to advocate drug use rather than abstinence. Interventions that highlight the deadly effects of AIDS or advocate abstinence to avoid infection are not likely to be effective. Drug users already face the threat of death with each injection. In contrast to the homosexual-bisexual population, many addicts tolerate poor health along with their addiction and therefore may resist AIDS messages with this focus.

INCARCERATED PERSONS

Another potential risk group are prisoners (23). Currently, blacks make up a higher proportion of the prison population than is warranted by their numbers in the general population. During periods of incarceration, prisoners may engage in homosexual behaviors but not view themselves as either homosexual or bisexual. While drug use is illegal, it does occur in prison. Drug paraphernalia, such as needles, are scarce in prisons and consequently are likely to be reused. Interventions that advocate the use of condoms or cleaning of drug works are often unacceptable to prison authorities since these facilitate illegal activities.

ISSUES IN THE CARE OF BLACK AIDS PATIENTS

Little information published to date has addressed the specific psychosocial needs of black AIDS patients. The vast majority of articles on the psychosocial impact of AIDS address the emotional and behavioral responses of white gay men with AIDS (24). Nevertheless, it could be expected that one would find a common human element in reactions to a life-threatening illness. Thus, we would expect that AIDS patients, regardless of ethnicity, experience profound psychosocial disruptions including affective distress, loss of or severe strain on existing social support systems, and financial distress (25–27). Black Americans differ in respect to the resources available and the cultural norms at work in coping with their illness. These differences may be manifested in such areas as help-seeking behavior (28), perceptions of the severity of medical or psychological problems (references 29, 30 and unpublished manuscript by V. M. Mays and C. S. Howard: "Symptom and Service Utilization Problems in a National Sample of Black Women: Implications for Psychotherapy Research"), perceived barriers to the use of health care facilities (31, 32), or the use of informal help systems (28, 33).

In thinking about adaptation to any life-threatening illness, there are three major areas of focus: psychological resources (personality, coping resources, support); sociocultural factors (social stigma, external resources); and aspects of medical care (symptoms, patient-physician relationships, treatment decisions) (34, 35). For AIDS, the adaptation is a particularly complex process, regardless of the patient's ethnicity (26, 27, 36). Some special issues are important in thinking about the black AIDS patient.

PSYCHOLOGICAL ISSUES

Psychological factors are extremely important in enduring the stress of AIDS (26). AIDS patients who demonstrate a "fighting spirit" may have a longer survival period and do better psychologically (36). This fighting stance in the face of adversity is consistent with the Southern tradition of "I can do" instilled in many American blacks (37, 38), and it may serve black AIDS patients well in coping with their disease. On the other hand, this sense of independence may also make it difficult to accept and develop appropriately dependent relationships with caretakers when those persons are outside family or community networks. This attitude is especially true for the black male for whom a sense of independence is strongly associated with maleness (37).

The role of informal social networks and family systems as alternatives or supplements to professional help has been well documented (28, 39–41). Structural characteristics of social networks may also determine use of professional help (42). For many ethnic minorities with limited access to health care information, the family and friendship networks are the dominant influence on health behavior and a trusted source of health information (43, 44). Although blacks may consider physicians as the most credible source of information, they may refrain from asking questions because they do not wish to appear ignorant, or they perceive that physicians are too busy to talk to them (44, 45).

The implications of this behavior are threefold. First, inclusion of family and friends, with permission of the patient, when information is being dispensed may enhance medical compliance by raising the level of knowledge of the informal advice network. Second, creation of an atmosphere that encourages questioning by the patient can assist in overcoming problems of reticence. Again, this may help ultimately to improve medical compliance. Third, AIDS educational interventions may be most effective if basic information is targeted to the general black population.

SOCIOCULTURAL ISSUES

Several sociocultural factors may complicate the adaptation of black AIDS patients. First, an AIDS diagnosis may result in identification of socially stigmatized behaviors that were previously hidden, such as drug abuse, sexual preference, or nonmonogamous sexual relations. As a community black Americans, for the most part, exhibit particularly negative attitudes toward homosexuality, perhaps due in part to strong religious beliefs (unpublished manuscript by V. M. Mays: "Perceived Discrimination and Black Women's Relationships").

Second, black Americans tend to maintain fairly frequent contacts with kin, receiving much support in return (46). Black AIDS patients, like other groups, have experienced rejection by family members. Yet, the impact of rejection for blacks may be more severe, given existing cultural norms emphasizing the kinship network as the provider of

both tangible and emotional social support. Elsewhere, it has been noted that persons with AIDS are in particular need of emotional and illness-related support (36). Many AIDS programs offering support services, such as buddy programs, housecleaning, and others, are found in predominantly white gay organizations, groups which generally lie outside the neighborhoods and support networks of many black gay men. There are very few full-service minority AIDS programs providing culturally specific services to black AIDS patients.

Third, past difficulties with the health care system, including long waiting periods in low cost clinics, cultural barriers in communication, and lack of financial resources, complicate the willingness of blacks from the lower socioeconomic segment to seek medical care at the first signs of AIDS-related symptoms or to seek treatment for nonemergency AIDS-related health problems, even after they are diagnosed. Time of survival after diagnosis is shorter for blacks, as they tend to seek treatment long after the appearance of early symptoms (47). This observation includes cases in black children.

ISSUES IN MEDICAL CARE

The medical care of black AIDS patients raises additional issues precipitated by possible sociocultural differences between patients and health care providers.

SYMPTOMS AND DIAGNOSIS. Three areas of disease and diagnosis are of special concern in the care of black AIDS patients. First, blacks are less likely to present with Kaposi's sarcoma, a clinical manifestation of AIDS that has a better short-term prognosis than acute opportunistic infections (48). Thus, blacks may enter treatment more severely ill and in need of greater levels of medical and psychosocial care.

Second, ethnic differences previously demonstrated in non-AIDS-related psychiatric diagnosis and in the expression of psychological distress may have implications for the treatment of black AIDS patients. Thus far, the primary psychiatric diagnoses of AIDS patients have been atypical affective disorders. In general, studies have indicated that the mental health profession tends to underdiagnose affective disorders and overdiagnose schizophrenia in blacks, particularly black males (49). Mental health professionals tend to believe that blacks rarely suffer from bipolar disorders, perhaps because they view hyperactive behavior as normal black male aggressive behavior (49). Also, as Jones and Grey (49) pointed out, blacks with affective disorders exhibit delusions and hallucinations more frequently than whites and hence are at risk for misdiagnosis of thought disorder.

The major problem seems to be cultural differences in the presentation of symptoms. For example, the tendency for black males to be somewhat remote, withdrawn, and formal in the presence of white professionals may be misinterpreted as the patient's attempt to cope with an underlying thought disorder or schizophrenic psychotic process rather than a culturally relevant stance when dealing with a nearly foreign white world. The patient may, in fact, be quite depressed but deem it culturally inappropriate to reveal this emotional distress. It is equally possible that unwillingness to talk to white physicians may be viewed as depression rather than resistance (49). Language, mannerisms, and style of behavior that are culturally determined may, if not understood, result in misdiagnosis.

Third, in the evaluation of neurological impairments seen in a significant percentage of AIDS patients (35, 50), diagnosis of impairment may be complicated in persons whose educational background and interest in current and past political affairs differ from those of the examiners. The following incident may illuminate possible pitfalls in such situations.

One of the authors, Dr. Cochran, witnessed an examination of the mental status of a hospital inpatient, an uneducated elderly black man with advanced heart disease, by several young white health professionals. Cognitive impairment was a distinct possibility. Questions assessing knowledge (for example, names of presidents and politicians) revealed a marked deficit. Yet when she asked the patient about the current baseball pennant race, the patient proved remarkably lucid, brightened considerably, and lost his withdrawn demeanor. One can only imagine the patient's thoughts during the early stages of the examination. However, when questions relevant to him were used to evaluate his cognitive abilities, no significant deficits were observed. This example underscores the importance of translating frequently used assessment procedures into the "language" of the patient.

PATIENT-PHYSICIAN COMMUNICATION. To the extent that cultural, ethnic, or racial barriers create communication difficulties for AIDS patients and their physicians, the effectiveness of the patient-physician relationship will be undermined (51). In the treatment of AIDS, the patient-physician relationship is critical to the quality of care received. A

myriad of physical ailments can occur, necessitating accurate and prompt treatment. Collaborative patient-physician relationships can facilitate this response. AIDS patients need adequate medical information about their disease in order to know what symptoms to monitor and report to their physicians, when to call their physician for unexpected assistance, and how to comply with the treatment process. If the patient and physician cannot effectively communicate, survivability of the patient is potentially compromised.

For example, in dispensing medical advice, white physicians may be unaware of differences in dietary practices, of lack of priorities given to future orientation or long-range planning, and of the influential role of kin, particularly for black women, in health behaviors. Quite often intravenous drug users function within a present-time orientation that mitigates against taking medical advice that involves planning for the future. It is best to work with, rather than against, this orientation in giving medical advice to the person with AIDS.

Neurological complications increase the risk that there will be impaired mental competence that prevents full participation in medical treatment decisions. In such instances, the standard protocol in the medical community is to turn to the family of origin for shared medical decisions. However, some black families may also be unfamiliar with medical procedures or have difficulty understanding or communicating with the physician. Hospital personnel use interpreters when there is an obvious language barrier, and it may be useful to use "interpreters," such as knowledgeable friends of the patient or culturally sensitive hospital personnel, who can assist the physician in communicating with the family.

ETHICAL ISSUES. Ethical dilemmas can readily occur in the medical care of AIDS patients (52). After repeated hospitalizations for acute opportunistic infections, AIDS patients and physicians eventually confront questions of supportive care versus life-sustaining treatments. Current ethical and legal guidelines recommend that these decisions be shared by the physician and informed, competent patients (52). Such decisions, particularly by the patient, often require some understanding of technical information. However, lower levels of education and lack of familiarity with hospital procedures in some segments of the black population may make this educational process more difficult.

Other issues may arise in the care of the black AIDS patient. For example, in deciding when heroic medical treatment is futile, physicians must be sensitive to possible biases in their own decision-making if resources available to the patient for continued inpatient or outpatient treatment appear scarce, or if the patient is likely to return to intravenous drug usage.

And, finally, cultural and religious influences in the black community may complicate decision-making about continuing treatment. Many of the major black churches, including fundamentalist Christian denominations and some Baptist traditions, view homosexuality as especially sinful (53). A recent poll found that almost 40 percent of fundamentalist Christians believed that AIDS is a punishment from God for the way homosexuals live (54). Persons who hold these beliefs may view resuscitation efforts as interfering with God's plans. In coping with these situations, health professionals can be helpful if they dispense culturally relevant advice. For example, black Americans, particularly women, frequently cope with psychological difficulties through prayer (33). Often this prayer is for God's will to be done or for a miracle. In assisting the black family confronted with difficult decisions, it may help to encourage the family to pray for guidance and support in their decisions as a way of making a miracle happen, rather than to adopt a passive or antagonistic stance.

SUMMARY AND RECOMMENDATIONS

In this review, we have sought to highlight psychosocial issues that are of particular concern when the impact of AIDS in the black community is considered. As we have noted, differences in sociocultural influences between blacks and whites necessitate a sensitivity to possible differences in patterns of infection, the impact of preventive health education efforts, and the coping process of black AIDS patients. These differences have broad implications for education, prevention, and allocation of resources within the black population. In thinking about the AIDS crisis in the black community, we recommend the following measures as a means of ameliorating the impact of AIDS on the entire black population and to help reduce the incidence of HTLV-III/LAV infection in the black community.

1. Research. Recommendations for needed research can be categorized in three broad areas:

- an examination of the role that the black family structure, community supports, cultural values, patterns of help-seeking, and perceptions of severity of medical and psychological problems play in the inhibition or facilitation of the transmission and incidence of the HTLV-III/LAV virus.
- epidemiologic studies that include large numbers of black gay and bisexual men, intravenous drug abusers (including recreational intravenous drug abusers), and heterosexuals at high risk.
- an exploration of the most effective methods for the delivery of clinical services, intervention, and prevention efforts that are consistent with the cultural, class, geographic region, and the sexual preference diversity that exists among high-risk groups of black Americans.

2. Information and education. Research for needed information and education can be categorized into three broad areas with four recommendations:

- establishment of a national clearinghouse on AIDS in the black population to provide health care professionals, community organizations, and self-help groups with accurate up-to-date information the medical, psychological, and political aspects of AIDS.
- development of prevention strategies and materials that are culturally sensitive and meaningful, as well as gender-, lifestyle-, and age-appropriate in order to inform effectively and reduce the transmission and incidence of the HTLV-III/LAV virus within the diverse population of black Americans.
- information reported by Federal agencies that includes breakdowns by both gender and ethnic group.
- collection of data by Federal agencies in a manner that allows for differences in the patterns of ethnic groups to be clearly documented to provide accurate information for health care planning and public policy use.

References

1. Hirsch, D. A., and Enlow, R. W.: The effects of the acquired immune deficiency syndrome on gay lifestyle and the gay individual. Ann NY Acad Sci 437:273–282 (1984).
2. Curran, J. W., et al.: Epidemiological trends of AIDS in the United States. Cancer Res 45:4602s–4604s (1985).

3. Marwick, C.: AIDS-associated virus yields data to intensifying scientific study. JAMA 254:2865–2879 (1985).

4. Goodman, E.: AIDS: It's no longer 'us' and 'them.' Los Angeles Times, Pt. II, p. 3, Aug. 1, 1986.

5. Martin, T.: AIDS: Is it a major threat to blacks? Ebony: 91–96, October 1985.

6. Bakeman, R., Lumb, J. R., Jackson, R. E., and Smith, D. W.: AIDS risk-group profiles in whites and members of minority groups. N Engl J Med 315:192, July 7, 1986.

7. Hardy, A. M., Allen, J. R., Morgan, W. M., and Curran, J. W.: The incidence of acquired immunodeficiency syndrome in selected populations. JAMA 253:215–220, Jan. 11, 1985.

8. Acquired immune deficiency syndrome among blacks and hispanics—United States. MMWR 35:655–666, Oct. 24, 1986.

9. Acquired immunodeficiency syndrome (AIDS): weekly surveillance report. Centers for Disease Control, Atlanta, GA, Dec. 29, 1986.

10. Macdonald, D. I.: Coolfont report: a PHS plan for the prevention and control of AIDS and the AIDS virus. Public Health Rep 101:341–348 July–August 1986.

11. Bureau of the Census: General population characteristics, Pt 1, United States summary, 1980. U.S. Department of Commerce, May 1983.

12. Morgan, W. M., and Curran, J. W.: Acquired immunodeficiency syndrome: current and future trends. Public Health Rep 101:459–465, September–October 1986.

13. Drucker, E.: AIDS and addiction in New York City. Am J Drug Alcohol Abuse 12:165–181 (1986).

14. New York City Department of Health: AIDS surveillance: the AIDS epidemic in New York City, 1981–1984. Am J Epidem 123:1013–1025 (1986).

15. Confronting AIDS: directions for public health, health care and research. Institute of Medicine, National Academy of Sciences, National Academy Press, Washington, DC, 1986.

16. Moore, A., and Le Baron, R. D.: The case for a Haitian origin of the AIDS epidemic. In The social dimensions of AIDS, edited by D. A. Feldman and T. M. Johnson. Praeger Publishers, New York, 1986, pp. 77–93.

17. Laguerre, M. S.: Haitian Americans. In Ethnicity and medical care, edited by A. Harwood. Harvard University Press, Cambridge, MA., 1981, pp. 172–210.

18. Human T-lymphotropic virus type III/lymphadenopathy-associated virus antibody prevalence in U.S. military recruit applicants. MMWR 35:421–424, July 4, 1986.

19. Hardy, A. M., et al.: The economic impact of the first 10,000 cases of acquired immunodeficiency syndrome in the United States. JAMA 255:209–215, Jan. 10, 1986.

20. Scitovsky, A. A., and Rice, D. P.: Estimates of the direct and indirect costs of acquired immunodeficiency syndrome in the United States, 1985, 1986, and 1991. Public Health Rep 102:5–17, January–February 1987.

21. National Minority AIDS Council: Minorities and AIDS: a position paper. Presented at the meeting of the National Institute of Mental Health Special Population Units and the Gay Health Foundation, Washington, DC, June 10, 1986.

22. Bell, A., and Weinberg, M.: Homosexualities: a study of diversity among men and women. Simon and Schuster, Inc., New York, 1978.

23. Acquired immunodeficiency syndrome in correctional facilities: a report of the National Institute of Justice and the American Correctional Association. MMWR 35:195–199, Mar. 28, 1986.

24. Gattozzi, A.: Psychological and social aspects of the acquired immune deficiency syndrome: Early findings of research supported by the National Institute of Mental Health. Science Communications, Rockville, MD. Apr. 15, 1986. Mimeographed.

25. Coates, T. J., Temoshok, L., and Mandel, J.: Psychosocial research is essential to understanding and treating AIDS. Am Psychol 39:1309–1314 (1984).

26. Macks, J., and Turner, D.: Mental health issues of persons with AIDS. Presented at AIDS and Mental Health Policy, Administration, and Treatment Conference, University of California, San Francisco, Sept. 13–14, 1985.

27. Morin, S. F., Charles, K. A., and Malyon, A. K.: The psychological impact of AIDS on gay men. Am Psych 39:1288–1293 (1984).

28. Neighbors, H. W., and Jackson, J. S.: The use of informal and formal help: Four patterns of illness behavior in the black community. Am J Comm Psych 12:629–644 (1984).

29. Neighbors, H. W.: Professional help use among black Americans: implications for unmet needs. Am J Comm Psych 12:551–566 (1984).

30. Wolinski, F. D.: Racial differences in illness behavior. J Community Health 8:87–101 (1982).

31. Jackson, J. J.: Urban black Americans. In Ethnicity and medical care, edited by A. Harwood. Harvard University Press, Cambridge, MA, 1981, pp. 37–129.

32. Shannon, G. W., Bashur, R. L., and Spurlock, C. W.: The search for medical care: an exploration of urban black behavior. Int J Med Care 8:519–530 (1978).

33. Neighbors, H. W., Jackson, J., Bowman, P. and Gurin, G.: Stress, coping and black mental health: preliminary findings from a national study. Prev Human Serv 2:4–29 (1983).

34. Holland, J. C.: Psychological aspect of cancer. In Cancer medicine, edited by J. C. Holland and E. Frei. Ed. 2. Lea and Febiger Publishers, Philadelphia, 1982, pp. 991–1021.

35. Holland, J. C., and Tross, S.: The psychosocial and neuropsychiatric sequelae of the acquired immunodeficiency syndrome and related disorders. Ann Int Med 103:760–764 (1985).

36. Mandel, J., and Namir, S.: Overview of treatment issues. Presented at AIDS and Mental Health Policy, Administration, and Treatment Conference, University of California, San Francisco, Sept. 13–14, 1985.

37. Mays, V. M., and Comas-Diaz, L.: Feminist therapy with ethnic minority populations: A closer look at blacks and hispanics. *In* Feminist psychotherapies, edited by M. A. Douglas and L. Walker. Ablex Publishers, New York. In press.

38. Mays, V. M.: The black American and psychotherapy: the dilemma. Psych Theor Res Prac 2:379–388 (1985).

39. Hayes, W., and Mindel, C.: Extended kinship relations in black and white families. J Marriage Fam 35:51–57 (1973).

40. Martineau, W.: Informal social ties among urban black Americans. J Black Stud 8:83–104 (1977).

41. Stack, C.: All our kin: strategies for survival in the black community. Harper and Row, New York, 1974.

42. McKinlay, J.: Social networks, lay consultation and help seeking behavior. Soc Forces 51:275–292 (1973).

43. American Hospital Association: Culture-bound and sensory barriers to communication with patients: strategies and resources for health education. PB No. 84-193028 National Technical Information Service, Springfield, VA, 1982.

44. Juarez, N.: "Healthy mothers" market research: how to reach black and Mexican-American women. Office of Public Affairs, Public Health Service, Washington, DC, 1982.

45. Crandall, L., and Duncan, R.: Attitudinal and situational factors in the use of physician services by low-income persons. J Health Soc Behav 22:64–77 (1981).

46. Hatchett, S. J., and Jackson, J. S.: Black extended kin systems: correlates of perceived family solidarity, geographical propinquity of kin, interaction with kin and aid received from kin. Presented at the Groves Conferences on Marriage and the Family, Freeport, Bahamas, 1983.

47. Greaves, W.: The epidemiology of AIDS in the black community. Presented at the AIDS in the Black Community Conference, Washington, DC, July 18, 1986.

48. Safai, B., et al.: The natural history of Kaposi's sarcoma in the acquired immunodeficiency syndrome. Ann Intern Med 103:744–750 (1985).

49. Jones, B. E., and Grey, B. A.: Problems in diagnosing schizophrenia and affective disorders among blacks. Hosp Community Psychiatry 37:61–65 (1986).

50. Perry, S., and Jacobson, P.: Neuropsychiatric manifestations of AIDS-spectrum disorders. Hosp Community Psychiatry 37:135–142 (1986).

51. Stone, G. C.: Patient compliance and the role of the expert. J Soc Issues 35:34–59 (1979).

52. Steinbrook, R., et al.: Ethical dilemmas in caring for patients with the acquired immunodeficiency syndrome. Ann Intern Med 103:787–790 (1985).

53. Chinn, H.: A day of salvation. Bay Windows, Dec 19, 1985, pp. 4–5.

54. Chandler, R.: Believers' views differ on doctrine, sex, afterlife, public policy. L. A. Times, Pt II, July 26, 1986, pp. 4–5.

44

USEFUL INFORMATION ON SUICIDE

Pamela S. Moore

SUICIDE IN HISTORY

Suicide is as old as it is universal. People have been killing themselves since the beginning of recorded time. Suicide has meant different things among various cultures through the ages. It hasn't always evoked horror. It is mentioned matter-of-factly in the Bible. It was tolerated, even honored, as a particularly decent death in ancient Greece and Rome. Suicide continues to be so honored in Asian and Middle Eastern societies today. It was the ticket to salvation for early Christian martyrs and is now believed by Islamic martyrs to be their ticket to salvation. Suicide has meant delivery from military defeat and escape from enslavement.

Suicide survived religious and secular transformation in the sixth century, as a sin against God and a crime against the community, to become a major theme for Renaissance writers. It was a cause for enlightenment philosophers and a fashion among melancholy nineteenth century romantics. In the last century, suicide captured the interest of mental health scientists, and the modern study of suicide got under way. What had been defended as an intellectual choice by enlightenment thinkers came to be seen as, if not a sign of mental illness, a means of relief from psychic pain and sorrow.

Today, in industrialized countries where suicide statistics are available, suicide ranks among the 10 most common causes of death. Such countries include Finland, Austria, Denmark, Sweden, Hungary, and Japan. In the United States, suicide is the 10th leading cause of death. Approximately 30,000 people killed themselves in 1982. More than 10 times that number attempted suicide. Worldwide, more than 1,000 people kill themselves every day. In the United States, the toll is 73 people a day. Suicide has become the focus of serious scientific inquiry and public health attention in most industrialized countries.

Until recently, suicide was a topic that few people would discuss in this country. It was considered shameful and evoked feelings of guilt in those whose lives were touched. Today, with the increasing rate of suicide among the young, many instances of suicide among two or more youngsters in the same school or community, and heavy media attention, more people are concerned and talking about it.

WHO COMMITS SUICIDE?

Almost everyone in this country has been touched by suicide, either through knowing someone who committed suicide, hearing about someone who did, or thinking about it personally. Suicide cuts across all age, racial, occupational, religious, and social groups. But the greater frequency with which it occurs in some groups suggests that social and cultural factors play a significant and complex role. The most conspicuous and consistent demographic patterns of suicide are according to age, sex, and race. The most pronounced shifts in rates are showing up in age groups, however. Suicide rates are known to increase steadily with age, but current rates for young people, age 25–34, are rivaling those in older groups. While the overall rate of suicide has remained the same, the rate has soared for adolescents and young adults (who historically have had the lowest rates) and has declined somewhat among the elderly (who historically have had the highest rates).

Elderly: People over age 60 made up only 16 percent of the U.S. population in 1980, but accounted for 23 percent of those who committed suicide. Almost 3,500 white males over age 65 killed themselves in 1982.

Adolescents and Young Adults: Among adolescents in the United States, suicide is the third most common cause of death, after accidents and homi-

[Editor's note: This material was written under contract with the Science Reports Section, Science Communications Branch, National Institute of Mental Health, 1986.]

U.S. Department of Health and Human Services. Public Health Service. Alcohol, Drug Abuse, and Mental Health Administration. Publication No. (ADM) 86–1489, 1986 (excerpt).

cide. For college students, it is the second most common cause of death. The rate has tripled in the last 30 years. In 1968, the total suicide rate for 15- to 24-year-olds was was 7.1 per 100,000. This accounted for 11.6 of the total number of suicides nationwide. By 1982, the rate had jumped to 12.2. Since 1977, over 5,000 youths, age 15–25, have killed themselves each year—about 20 percent of the total number of deaths by suicide. While suicide attempts generally out-number suicide completions by 8–10 to 1, the ratio for youth is 25–50 suicide attempts for every one suicide completion. In addition to suicide attempts and suicide completions, there is a third area of consideration: the "suicide crisis." This refers to those moments or situations when individuals struggle with the idea of suicide, become obsessed with it, and even plan a suicide in detail, but who come to grips with the intense pain and agony that accompanies a crisis of this sort, and stop short of an actual attempt. While figures on the number of suicide crises are hard to come by, it is believed that approximately one million or more young people in this country experience suicide crises of varying degrees each year.

Children: Reports of suicide among very young children are rare, but suicidal behavior is not. As many as 12,000 children, age 5–14, may be hospitalized in this country every year for deliberate self-destructive acts, such as stabbing, cutting, scalding, burning, overdosing, and jumping from high places.

Males: The overwhelming majority of completed suicides are males. They comprise approximately three-fourths of the total who commit suicide, and white males account for about 70 percent of that total. Males tend to use the deadliest weapons. Well over half shoot themselves, and the use of guns (mainly handguns) is increasing rapidly.

Females: Four times more women than men attempt suicide, usually using potentially less lethal means such as drugs and wrist-slashing. However, one-third of the women and over half of the 15- to 24-year-old females who completed suicide used guns. Recent reports indicate their growing use. The suicide rate for women, relative to men, rises steadily until about age 50. Although the suicidal rate for women has tended to stay well below the national average, its pace has accelerated over time.

Blacks: Sharp increases in suicides among young black males have in some urban areas outdistanced rates for white males in the same age group. This is a startling increase, since the overall suicide rate for blacks traditionally is about half that of whites. Rates among blacks, as well as for other non-Anglo groups, peak among males in their 20s, and those rates have been getting higher.

Married or Single: Because more adults are married, more adult suicides are married. But the greatest risk for suicide is among the widowed, separated, divorced, and those who live alone.

WHY DO PEOPLE COMMIT SUICIDE?

There are as many reasons people commit suicide as there are people who commit suicide. Among those commonly cited are: to find relief from feelings of hopelessness; to escape from an intolerable situation; to punish loved ones; to gain attention; to change other people's behavior or change one's circumstances; to join a deceased loved one; to avoid punishment; to avoid becoming a burden; to escape the effects of a dreaded disease; to seek martyrdom; to express love; and even to pursue an irrational, impulsive whim. Notes left by people who have killed themselves usually tell of irresolvable life crises. Many eloquently describe what it's like to endure chronic pain, to lose loved ones, or to lack the money to pay bills or the ability to perform the simplest tasks. "No one ever lacks a good reason for suicide," noted Cesare Pavese, an Italian writer, who himself committed suicide. The question is why they give up when most people in similar circumstances somehow manage to cling to life through the worst of times.

Mental health investigators from varied disciplines have been trying to answer that question for decades. In recent years, a whole new field of study—suicidology—has grown out of that effort. It has given rise to a research model in which disease and genetic factors are incorporated with social, psychological, and environmental factors. Psychologists have observed that some people conduct their lives in a way that predisposes them to failure and self-destruction. Social scientists point to the social and economic dislocations that drive some people to suicide. Increasingly, biological investigators are studying how irregularities in brain chemistry affect impulsive and aggressive behavior which often goes along with suicide. They all emphasize that suicide is the result of an everchanging interplay of many different factors.

SUICIDE ATTEMPTERS/SUICIDE COMPLETERS

Research findings have led investigators to view those who attempt and those who complete suicide as representing two different but overlapping groups. Other investigators view the behavior of those who attempt and those who actually kill themselves as representing a continuum of suicidal behavior. Attempters tend to be younger and are more often women, and their attempts tend to be more impulsive and ambivalent. Completers are more often older and male and choose more clearly lethal techniques for self-destruction. But researchers stress that even among the most determined, suicidal individuals don't want to die as much as they don't want to live the lives they are leading. Whatever their type, many are desperately crying for help.

Those who have made attempts, but survived, talk about having been poised between life and death, living half in this world and half in the next. They describe an inability to make plans, even to set lunch dates, because they expected to be dead. Most of all, they describe their feeling that a suicide attempt was inevitable. However, followup studies of similar individuals reveal their intense ambivalence about dying. Not only are they glad to be alive, but, for many, a suicide attempt marked a turning point—it was a dramatic signal that their problems demanded serious and immediate attention. Most of those who survived their suicide attempts indicated that what they really wanted was a change in their lives.

Recent work—comparing the lives of those who killed themselves, those who attempted, and those who died of natural causes—reveals that, in the main, the lives of those who kill themselves are often no worse than those of others who carry on. To the objective outsider, their situations are far from hopeless, and there are ways other than suicide to solve their problems. But because of stressful life situations and/or psychiatric illness, those who kill themselves don't see it that way.

Research has suggested that different disorders are linked to different suicidal behaviors. Nonfatal attempters are more likely to be characterized by neuroses, personality disorders, chemical dependence, and situational disorders. Personality disorders are frequently associated with suicidal behavior among young people, and young people tend to be attempters. Those who actually kill themselves have shown a predominance of major affective disorders including depression, alcoholism (or other chemical addiction), and schizophrenia.

SUICIDE AND DEPRESSION

It is obvious that most people who commit suicide are desperately unhappy. Moreover, scientists and mental health professionals believe the majority are suffering from a medically identifiable depression. A reported 40–70 percent or more of those who killed themselves had a history of serious depression. Depression is also a repeating factor among those who attempt suicide. Studies involving psychiatric patients indicate the average suicide rate is 30 times greater in those with serious depression than it is in the general population. Only one-fourth of the estimated 25–35 million people suffering from serious depression are getting help.

The most common depressive illness—and the one most often associated with suicide—is "unipolar" depression. This is a frequently recurring condition characterized by behavior change, dejection, and even suicidal thoughts, but without the extreme impulsivity and elation of "bipolar" depression, or manic-depressive illness. Bipolar disturbance represents an estimated 25 percent of those with serious depressive illness. Much of the work on depression and suicide over the past decade has been devoted to finding a factor or group of factors which may help to determine who is most at risk. Considerable research has pointed to hopelessness as a key factor.

SUICIDE AND HOPELESSNESS

Recent studies tend to confirm earlier work showing that suicidal thoughts and behavior are more closely related to hopelessness than to depression per se. Reseachers studying the attitudes of some severely depressed people have concluded that many *think* themselves into suicide. They misperceive the world and act accordingly. They are pessimistic, lack confidence in their abiliy to handle their problems, blame themselves, and set unobtainable goals on which they pin whatever hope they have. This finding has some treatment value, since it suggests that patients who feel hopeless need to learn how to think differently about the world. There are treatments that can help in encouraging such learning.

SUICIDE AND ALCOHOLISM

Alcoholics have extremely high rates of depression and suicide. An estimated 7–21 percent of alcoholics kill themselves, compared to about 1 percent of the general population. A recent study concerning alcoholics indicated that hopelessness is a stronger indicator of suicidal intent than depression or a previous attempt. Alcoholism is significantly involved with nonfatal suicide attempts as well as completed suicides.

SUICIDE AND SCHIZOPHRENIA

Investigators have found that those suffering from schizophrenia and other serious thought disorders, particularly if delusional or hallucinating, have a high incidence of suicide attempts. Depression is also common in a large percentage of chronic, relapsing schizophrenic patients. Patients suffering from schizophrenia often have a long history of hospitalization and figure significantly in the group of patients who commit suicide while hospitalized or shortly after discharge.

SUICIDE'S WARNING SIGNS

Researchers believe that most suicidal individuals convey their intentions to someone in their network of friends, family, or coworkers, either openly or covertly. These people represent those who are most intimately and extensively in contact with a particular suicidal individual. They are probably in the best position to recognize the signs and render help.

There is no profile or checklist for identifying a suicidal person. Suicide, like much of human behavior, is difficult to predict. Despite their best efforts even experts cannot say whether or when a person will try to commit suicide. But there are several danger signals which, particularly in combination, demand immediate concern and attention.

Previous Suicide Attempts: People who have made serious suicide attempts are at highest risk for actually killing themselves. The suicide rate for repeat attempters is up to 643 times higher than the overall rate in the general population. Between 20–50 percent of the people who commit suicide had previously made attempts.

Suicide Talk: People who commit suicide often talk about it first. Statements like, ''They'd be better off without me,'' or ''No one will have to worry about me much longer,'' can be give-aways, but a more off hand, ''I've had it,'' may also be a clue.

Making Arrangements: Some suicidal individuals take steps to put their affairs in order. They draw up or alter their wills, give away prized possessions, make arrangements for pets, and otherwise act as if they are preparing for a trip. They talk vaguely about going away. Such behavior is particularly alarming when other danger signals are also present.

Personality or Behavior Change: Often the tip-off is a change in personality or behavior. A normally buoyant person may seem increasingly down for no good reason. A regular churchgoer may stop attending services. An avid jogger may quit running. Such behavioral change, especially if accompanied by expressions of worthlessness or hopelessness, can be a sign that a person is suffering from a clinical depression, often a forerunner of suicide.

Clinical Depression: While 85 percent of depressed people are not suicidal, most of the suicide-prone are depressed. Thus, identifying and treating depression can prevent suicide. Depression is sometimes hard to detect, even for the sufferer, since its symptoms superficially resemble ordinary feelings and occurrences. But there is a pattern that can help to distinguish clinical depression from less serious mood problems. A person is likely to have a clinical depression if, in addition to depressed mood, at least four of the following symptoms continue nearly every day for at least two weeks:

- change in appetite or weight

- change in sleeping patterns

- speaking and/or moving with unusual speed or slowness

- loss of interest or pleasure in usual activities

- decrease in sexual drive

- fatigue or loss of energy

- feelings of worthlessness, self-reproach, or guilt

- diminished ability to think or concentrate, slowed thinking, or indecisiveness

- thoughts of death, suicide, wishes to be dead, or suicide attempt

A person who is depressed, uncommunicative, and withdrawn may be flashing a danger signal. And when suicide clues and depression appear against a backdrop of stressful events in a person's life, such as the loss of a spouse, relative, or job, a serious illness, or a major move, there is reason for even greater concern.

Individuals who are generally isolated, have few or poor social ties, abuse alcohol or other drugs, or have a history of physical and emotional difficulties are at even higher suicide risk when in the throes of depression. They can't think straight. While they may normally exhibit a rigid thinking style, they view life even more narrowly when in turmoil. Every issue is polarized—yes or no, black or white, life or death.

Researchers have pointed to an organiclike deficit in the thinking of severely depressed people which is similar to some neurological conditions known to cause thought and memory problems. Just when people need most to be clear-headed, they are not.

WHAT CAN YOU DO?

Listen: If a friend or family member appears depressed and exhibits any of the signals above, talk about those feelings. A troubled person needs someone who will listen. It may not be easy to discuss a friend's or relative's suicidal thoughts, but it is critical for the suicidal person to be able to talk about why he or she wants to die. Every effort should be made to understand the problems behind the statements. Although you should show interest, refrain from making moral judgments or trying to talk the person out of it. Listening is the best action.

Access: Ask specific questions about the person's suicidal thoughts: Does he or she have a plan? Bought a gun? Where is it? Stockpiled pills? Contrary to popular belief, such candor will not give a person dangerous ideas or encourage a suicidal act.

Evaluate: It is possible that a person may be extremely upset but not suicidal. Often, if a person has been depressed, and then becomes agitated and moves about restlessly, it can be cause for alarm. If the person has made clear suicide plans, the problem is more acute than if their thinking was less definite.

Be supportive: Let the person know you care. Most important, break through the suicidal person's sense of isolation, stay close, and make the person understand that he or she is not alone. Assure the person that suicidal impulses are temporary, that depression can be treated, and that problems can be solved.

Take charge: Stress that help is at hand, and waste no time finding it. Don't worry about invading someone's privacy or taking charge. Since suicidal people don't believe they can be helped, you will probably have to do more than urge them to seek professional help. You may wish to enlist the support of other family members or friends. DO NOT WAIT.

Make the environment safe: If you live with or are closely related or associated with someone who may be suicide-prone, remove any weapons and ammunition, medication or other drugs, and household items such as knives, razors, or scissors which could be used as aids to suicide. They should not be hidden on the premises but removed completely.

Do not keep suicide secret: Suicide is not a secret to be kept. Suicide talk, threats, or plans are signals for help. Sometimes distraught individuals will confide in a friend about their suicidal thoughts or plans by swearing the friend to secrecy. This is not a test of friendship but a cry for help and must be treated as such.

Do not challenge, dare, or use verbal shock treatment: It is fallacious to think that telling an ambivalent suicidal person to commit suicide will shock him or her into rational thinking. This should not be tried; it may precipitate an irreversible tragedy. Instead, acknowledge the person's feelings, and reassure them that help is available and that the situation can be resolved. If the crisis is acute, DO NOT LEAVE THE PERSON ALONE.

Seek professional help: Do not try to handle the problem alone. Get in touch with a professional immediately. Encourage the person to see a physician or mental health professional for evaluation. Start with the person's family doctor, a local hospital, or mental health center. You may also wish to seek help from a local suicide prevention or crisis intervention center, the clergy, or even the police.

Make a contract: If you find yourself with a person who is obviously suicidal, and you need time to develop a plan of action, make a contract with that person. That is, get a commitment or promise, preferably in writing, from the suicidal person stating that he/she will not attempt suicide before you are able to get together again to talk it over.

Beware of elevated moods and quick recoveries: Elevated mood can sometimes be misleading. Individuals may wrestle with the idea of suicide and, after having made a decision to kill themselves, behave as though they have had a heavy burden lifted from their shoulders. They proceed to kill themselves, leaving everyone stunned who had assumed they were on the road to recovery.

Quick recoveries: On the other hand, there are individuals who experience psychological relief after sharing their problems with an empathetic listener and erroneously feel that the crisis is over. Subsequently, the crisis flares again. Followup is critical to any prevention effort.

In the words of one expert: "You can help best by taking the problem seriously, assuring the person that something can be done, encouraging the acceptance and use of professional help, being a good friend to talk to when you are needed, and getting advice from an expert. Your friendship and your actions could save a life." . . .

Further Reading _____

Farberow, N. *The Many Faces of Suicide: Indirect Self-Destructive Behavior.* New York: McGraw-Hill, 1979.

Hendin, H. *Suicide in America.* New York: Norton, 1973.

Hoff, L. *People in Crisis: Understanding and Helping.* 2d ed. Reading: Addison Wesley, 1984.

Robins, E. *The Final Months: A Study of the Lives of 134 Persons Who Committed Suicide.* New York: Oxford Press, 1981

Shneidman, E., Farberow, N., and Litman R. *The Psychology of Suicide.* New York: Aronson, 1983.

45

MENTAL HEALTH PROFESSIONALS AND THE BEREAVED

Marian Osterweis
Jessica Townsend
Institute of Medicine, National Academy of Sciences
Washington, D.C.

INTRODUCTION

Every year an estimated 8 million Americans suffer the death of an immediate family member, and an unknown number experience the death of other important relatives and close friends. Every year, there are 800,000 new widows and widowers. Suicide occurs in at least 27,000 families each year (and probably many more since suicide is underreported). Each year, approximately 400,000 children under the age of 25 die. Only those who die young escape the pain of losing someone they love through death. Just as each type of relationship has special meaning, so too does each type of death carry with it a special kind of pain for those who are left behind.

Bereavement is usually considered to have the most powerful impact of all stressful life events. In addition to feelings of grief and emotional distress, perturbations in physiologic functioning and interpersonal relations are very common. To be bereaved has been likened to being an immigrant in a foreign country—social relationships are altered, expectations for behavior are unclear, and one is generally disoriented. The established rhythms of everyday life are likely to be upset.

As with many other stressors, the consequences of bereavement are not uniform; many factors can modify that stress and affect long-term outcomes. The sudden and unexpected suicide of a young husband and father, for example, is likely to have much more profound effects on surviving family members than the long anticipated death of a beloved and elderly grandparent.

Although clearly not unique, some aspects of loss through death are distinctive. Even superb cop-

ing abilities cannot alter the finality of death. The survivors' helplessness and total inability to control the event may make bereavement particularly stressful. Understanding the nature of the bereavement process and why it is so long and difficult may help those who are experiencing it to cope, and help those who wish to assist the bereaved be more effective. . . .

IS GRIEF A DISEASE?

The typical early manifestations of grief—crying and sorrow, anxiety and agitation, sleeplessness, lack of interest in things, and loss of appetite—are similar in nature and intensity to the manifestations of clinical depression.

Whether grieving individuals with these depression-like symptoms are ill has been the subject of some controversy. In his classic paper, *Mourning and Melancholia*, Freud (1917) distinguishes between grief and depression. Grieving people feel a loss or emptiness in the world around them, while depressed patients feel empty within. The current consensus is that although individuals experiencing grief are distressed, they are not sick.

As is true of some mental disorders, the line between "normal" and "abnormal" bereavement reactions can be difficult to draw. The American Psychiatric Association's *Diagnostic and Statistical Manual—III* includes a category called "Uncomplicated Bereavement" that offers some guidance:

A full depressive syndrome frequently is a normal reaction to such a loss, with feelings of depression and such associated symptoms as poor appetite, weight loss, and insomnia. However, morbid preoccupation with worthlessness, prolonged and marked functional

[Editor's Note: This material has been adapted from an Institute of Medicine, National Academy of Sciences, study report *Bereavement: Reactions, Consequences, and Care,* edited by Marian Osterweis, Fredric Solomon, and Morris Green in 1984. It is an excerpt from a Department of Health and Human Services Publication No. (ADM) 88-1554, 1988.]

impairment, and marked psychomotor retardation are uncommon and suggest that the bereavement is complicated by the development of a Major Depression.

In Uncomplicated Bereavement, guilt, if present, is chiefly about things done or not done at the time of the death by the survivor; thoughts of death are usually limited to the individual's thinking that he or she would be better off dead or that he or she should have died with the person who died. The individual with Uncomplicated Bereavement generally regards the feeling of depressed mood as "normal," although he or she may seek professional help for relief of such associated symptoms as insommia and anorexia.

The reaction to the loss may not be immediate, but rarely occurs after the first two or three months. The duration of "normal" bereavement varies considerably among different subcultural groups.

Mental health professionals must judge whether an individual's grief has exceeded the bounds of normalcy to the point where it is pathologic and intervention is needed. Until the patterns of normal bereavement are understood, however, it is not possible to develop sound criteria for abnormal reactions. The sections that follow describe the range of reactions that have been observed in bereaved people by clinicians and researchers.

ADULT REACTIONS TO BEREAVEMENT

Everyone assumes that sadness accompanies the death of a loved one, but the bereavement experience contains a much broader range of emotional reactions and behaviors. Some may not only be surprising, but can be upsetting if they seem inappropriate to those who do not understand them. Knowledge about the various processes and outcomes associated with bereavement is likely to help avert some of the misunderstanding that can make the experience more difficult.

The first systematic study of bereavement was conducted by Erich Lindemann in 1944. He described uncomplicated grief as a syndrome with a predictable course and distinctive symptoms, including (1) somatic distress, (2) preoccupation with the image of the deceased, (3) guilt, (4) hostility, (5) loss of usual patterns of conduct, and in some people (6) appearance of traits of the deceased (such as mannerisms or symptoms associated with the final illness) (Lindemann 1944). Since that time, numerous clinicians and researchers have sought to corroborate these observations and to describe the grieving process in adults.

It is now generally agreed that:

The bereavement process is long, much longer than popular American notions would lead us to believe. Although, for many people, the worst is over within a year, evidence suggests that for some people the second year is more difficult than the first. For many people, the process may take several years.

The bereavement process does not necessarily progress in an orderly fashion, that is, people do not move systematically from one well-defined stage to another. Instead, they tend to move back and forth between what might be best described as overlapping and fluid phases.

Individual variation is substantial. People differ in how fast they recover and how they express their grief. Specific manifestations of grief depend on the personality and past experiences of the bereft person, cultural norms and expectations for behavior, the relationship with the deceased, the nature of the death, and the social milieu of the bereaved person.

Many emotions and behaviors that might be judged abnormal under other circumstances are common following bereavement. Nevertheless, some signs and symptoms may indicate serious problems that deserve the attention of a qualified mental health professional. However, the line between normal and abnormal (or pathological) is difficult to draw.

Anniversary reactions are common, even after the bereavement process is completed in the sense that one is again able to function and take pleasure in life. It is typical to experience new waves of grief around holidays, important family events, and the time of the year when the death occurred. These anniversary reactions may become briefer as time goes by, but they may never entirely disappear.

THE PHASES OF BEREAVEMENT REACTIONS

There is general agreement that forewarning of death permits the soon-to-be-bereaved to structure the event cognitively and to reconcile differences with the dying person in a way that can reduce some of the anger and guilt commonly felt after bereavement. There is disagreement, however, about whether anticipatory grieving allows people to begin to relinquish the relationship or whether attachment intensifies when a person is threatened with a loss (see, for example, Bowlby 1980; Parkes and Weiss 1983).

The most immediate response following death, even when the loss was anticipated, is shock, numbness, and a sense of disbelief. Because the reality of the death has not yet penetrated awareness, survivors can appear to others to be holding up well and to be quite accepting of the loss. This numbness usually turns to intense feelings of separation and pain in the days and weeks after the funeral. Beverly Raphael, a well-known Australian psychiatrist, describes this phase in the following way:

> The absence of the dead person is everywhere palpable. The home and familiar environs seem full of painful reminders. Grief breaks over the bereaved in waves of distress. There is intense yearning, pining, and longing for the one who has died. The bereaved feels empty inside, as though torn apart or as if the dead person had been torn out of his body (Raphael 1983).

During this phase, the bereaved frequently report illusions and misperceptions, such as seeing the dead person in the street and dreams in which the deceased is still alive. Eventually, these searching behaviors begin to decrease, but when the lost person fails to return, despair sets in. Symptoms such as depressed moods, difficulty in concentrating, anger at the deceased for dying and at the doctors who cared for him or her, guilt about what else might have been done to avoid death, irritability, anxiety, restlessnes, and extreme sadness then become common. Offers of comfort and support are often rejected because the grieving person is so focused on the deceased.

The bereaved may swing dramatically and swiftly from one feeling state to another, and avoidance of reminders of the deceased may alternate with deliberate cultivation of memories for some period of time. Gradually the death begins to be accepted. However, the bereaved may be intellectually aware of the finality of the loss long before they emotionally accept the truth. Depression and emotional swings are characteristic of most people for at least several months and often for more than a year following bereavement. Eventually, the survivor is able to recall memories of the deceased without being overwhelmed by sadness or other emotions, and is ready to reinvest in the world.

Accompanying these emotional changes are changes in physiologic functioning, behavior, and social relationships. The functioning of major bodily systems is likely to be altered during times of stress, including grief. Changes in the endocrine, immune, autonomic nervous system, and cardio-vascular system have been documented by many researchers, but the health consequences of these changes are not yet established.

Physiologic perturbations clearly represent reactions to a stressor—in this case, bereavement. However, just as psychosocial reactions may or may not presage mental disorder, physiologic reactions may or may not lead to documentable health consequences. They are probably adaptive physiologic responses that may become maladaptive and eventually deleterious to health if they continue for too long or become too extreme. That a normal physiologic adaptation to grief can become unregulated and lead to illness is consistent with modern views of the pathogenesis of some autoimmune diseases.

A number of case studies appear to link grief and specific diseases such as various forms of cancer, heart disease, and ulcers (see, for example, Schmale and Iker, 1965; Greene, 1965). Establishing causal connections is difficult because of statistical problems and the low base rate. It also seems more reasonable to consider bereavement a nonspecific stressor that triggers multiple changes which, in people who are vulnerable because of genetic predisposition, or past or current illness, might lead to disease.

Quite apart from actual disease, recently bereaved people frequently report a host of physical complaints. These include pain, gastrontestinal disturbances, sleep and appetite disturbances, lack of energy, and other vegetative symptoms that at another time might signal the presence of depression. Especially in the elderly, these grief-related symptoms may be misdiagnosed as organic dysfunction if health professionals are not aware of the nature of bereavement reactions and the history of the particular patient.

Behavioral changes accompany these physical complaints and emotional upset. Just as emotions may swing, so too may the bereaved person appear slowed down at one moment and restless and agitated the next. Crying and tearfulness are common. When emotional despair sets in, the bereaved may lose interest in the outside world and cease their normal activities including such relaxing pastimes as watching television or listening to music.

Certain risk-taking behaviors may intensify or appear for the first time. Smoking, drinking, and drug taking are common, especially among people who were already engaged in those behaviors to some extent before the bereavement. Altered eating habits (over-and under-eating and changes in the kinds of foods consumed) are also common expressions of depression that can be harmful, particularly for diabetics and others whose diets need to be carefully controlled. Behaviors such as these are an indirect expression of emotional distress that may eventually compromise a person's health.

Finally, bereavement often precipitates changes in interpersonal relationships in the family and in one's broader social network. Family roles and patterns of interaction are likely to shift after the death of a member. Bereft parents, for example, may be less emotionally available to their children because of their own grief, thus compounding the children's sense of loss.

Outside the family, the bereaved not only see themselves differently in relation to others, but are likely to be perceived in a new way. For example, suddenly thinking of another as a "widow" may evoke particular stereotypes or expectations, resulting in different qualities being arbitrarily ascribed to the person. The nature of these interpersonal changes is largely dependent on the relationship that was lost and sometimes on the nature of the death.

These changes are also powerfully influenced by the sociocultural context in which the person lives and by the bereaved person's age. For example, a middle-aged widow or widower may find social life greatly curtailed because people tend to socialize in couples. Elderly people may find that most of their friends and relatives have died, leaving few familiar people to be with. Especially when one is elderly and upset, making new friends can be difficult. Thus, social isolation and feelings of loneliness are common, often long after the bereavement.

THE END OF THE BEREAVEMENT PROCESS

When does the bereavement process end? What are the signs of a favorable outcome? There are no clearcut answers to these questions. Terms such as "recovery," "adaptation," and "completion" have been used to describe the end of the bereavement process. Each term has a somewhat different connotation and contributes to understanding, but no single term provides an adequate description.

A healthy bereavement process can be expected to end with recovery of lost functions (including taking an interest in current life, hopefulness, and the capacity to experience gratification), adaptation to new roles and statuses, and completion of acute grieving. Both favorable and unfavorable outcomes along several dimensions can be identified.

One of the most important dimensions is time. Despite the popular belief that the bereavement process is normally completed in a year or less, data from systematic studies and from clinical reports

confirm that the process may be considerably more attenuated for many people and still be considered normal. The length of time per se does not distinguish normal from abnormal grief, but the quality and a quantity of reactions over time. Thus, a precise endpoint cannot be specified.

Just as individuals vary in their reactions to bereavement, so, too, do they vary in outcomes. What may signal a healthy recovery for one individual may be a sign of continuing difficulty for another. For example, readiness to invest in new relationships does not invariably indicate completion of or recovery from bereavement. A seemingly quick remarriage or a decision to have another child after one has died may reflect a sense of hope or strength in one case, whereas in another such actions may stem mainly from a wish to escape from painful emotions.

For some, bereavement provides an opportunity for personal growth that might not otherwise have occurred. Widows who had very traditional marriages, for example, may be forced to take on new roles and acquire new skills following the death of a husband. Being able to rise to these challenges successfully may leave a widow with a greater sense of competence and independence than when she was married (Silverman 1982). Some have observed that bereavement can lead to heightened creativity, noting that numerous successful artists, writers, and musicians have experienced painful losses.

Among the unfavorable outcomes of the bereavement process, it has commonly been noted that 10–20 percent of the bereaved continue to exhibit depressive symptoms after 1 year (see, for example, Bornstein et al., 1973; Clayton and Darvish, 1979). Some people appear to be particularly vulnerable to poor outcomes in terms of their mental or physical health.

THOSE WHO MAY BE AT RISK FOLLOWING BEREAVEMENT

Because of their particular life situations or personal characteristics, some people have been found to be more vulnerable than others following the death of someone close. In general, children are more vulnerable than adults. The gender and age of bereaved individuals, the nature of the relationship with the deceased, the nature of the death, and certain behaviors and social situations that appear soon after the death may affect how well the bereaved person ultimately fares.

In the months and years following the death of a spouse, widowers are more likely to die than men the same age who have not lost their wives. This increased risk for premature death, which is characteristic for men up to age 75, seems to persist for at least six years unless the men remarry. Among widowers who remarry, their likelihood of dying prematurely is no greater than for non-widowed married men of the same age. It is not clear, however, whether marriage itself protects against ill health or whether good health is a factor that permits remarriage.

Increased risk of premature death in the first year after their husbands' deaths does not seem to characterize widows, although there is evidence for higher death rates in the second year following bereavement. Widows are much less likely than widowers to remarry because fewer single men are available (Helsing et al., 1981, 1982; Clayton, 1982). This may heighten widows' vulnerability to some other stresses, including social isolation and financial problems, that may require major alterations in lifestyle.

BEREAVEMENT AND CHILDREN

An estimated 5 percent of children in the United States lose one or both parents by the time they are 15 years old. The many children who lose a sibling, friend, or grandparent must also confront the reality of death, and the painful and often frightening emotions associated with bereavement. Bereaved children may be particularly vulnerable to physical and psychological sequelae in both the immediate mourning period and over the longer term. Specific reactions are likely to be influenced by the child's level of cognitive and emotional development when the death occurred.

To avoid misunderstanding bereaved children's behavior, it should be remembered that, although they share some similarities with adults, children's reactions to loss often do not look like adults' reactions. Many differences in behavior, as well as the special vulnerability of children, are due to immaturity and lack of well-developed coping mechanisms. For example, a child who plays games of death or funerals, one who tells strangers on the street "my sister died," or one who resumes play as if nothing distressing has happened, is not behaving inappropriately. Rather, the child is trying to master the loss, test others' reactions to the event, or protect himself from emotions so strong that they can be endured only for brief periods. Feelings that are expressed through misbehavior or angry out-bursts

may not appear to be, but often are, grief related. Furthermore, children are likely to exhibit these behaviors for many years after the loss occurred.

In the only prospective study of previously normal children who suffered bereavement, Kaffman and Elizur (1983) followed Israeli children who lost their fathers in 1973. Behavioral problems in these children peaked in the second year, and 40 percent of the children still showed maladaptive behavior in the third year after the father's death. Evaluations at 6, 18, and 42 months after the death showed nearly 70 percent of the children with signs of severe emotional disturbance in at least one followup period such that they were handicapped for at least 2 months in their everyday lives with their families, school, and peer groups.

The data also suggested that children with pre-existing emotional difficulties and those from unstable homes were at greater risk of serious pathologic problems than other children. Interestingly, when bereaved kibbutz children were compared with bereaved urban children 18 months after their fathers' deaths, the differences were insignificant (48 percent of kibbutz and 52 percent of urban children exhibited symptoms of persistent pathological grief) suggesting that the social supports and less central role of parents in a kibbutz did not supply much protection (Elizur and Kaffman, 1982; Kaffman and Elizur, 1983).

Children's ability to work through bereavement and complete their mourning depends in part on their ability to distinguish between death and temporary separations. Before the age of 6 or 7, children do not generally grasp the notion that death is irreversible. After that age, most children understand the finality of death but may not regard it as inevitable, universal, or of immediate relevance to them. By age 11, nearly all children understand that death is inevitable and represents the end of the life cycle. Only at this point does the child begin to conceptualize the future in terms of potential losses (Koocher 1973). These ages will vary for children who are intellectually precocious or retarded. In addition, children with previous bereavement experience and those who are facing their own deaths are likely to have greater understanding at an earlier age.

There is some theoretical disagreement about the implication of these stages of understanding for the outcome of childhood bereavement. In the past, some experts asserted that because very young children do not understand death and lack the capacity to mourn in a manner analogous to adults, they are unable to complete the process and are likely to have problems for the rest of their lives. A substantial body of research literature now demonstrates that even very young children are able to grieve and use family supports to cope with loss.

The chief difference between bereft children and adults is in the ways they manifest their grief and the need of children to rework and reintegrate understanding of the loss as they develop and are then able to comprehend the event at new levels. Thus, although bereavement may render young children vulnerable, long-term problems are neither as frequent nor as inevitable as was once thought. How a young child fares after sustaining a major loss will depend in large part on the adequacy and availability of supportive adults. . . .

References

Beck, A.; Rush, J.; Shaw, B.; and Emergy, G. *Cognitive Therapy of Depression.* New York: Guilford Press, 1979.

Birtchnell, J. The relationship between attempted suicide, depression, and parent death. *British Journal of Psychiatry* 116:307–313, 1970.

Black, D. What happens to bereaved children? *Proceedings, Royal Society of Medicine* 69:842–844, 1974.

Bornstein, P.E.; Clayton, P.J.; Halikas, J.A.; Maurice, W.L.; and Robins, E. The depression of widowhood after thirteen months. *British Journal of Psychiatry* 122:561–566, 1973.

Bowlby, J. *Attachment and Loss.* Vol.III *Loss.* New York: Basic Books, 1980.

Caplan, G. Emotional crisis. In: Deutsch, A., and Fishman, H., eds. *Encyclopedia of Mental Health,* Vol. 2 New York: Franklin Watts 1963.

Clayton, P.J. Bereavement. In: Paykel, E.S., ed. *Handbook of Affective Disorders.* London: Churchill Livingstone, 1982.

Clayton, P.J., and Darvish, J.S. Course of depressive symptoms following the stress of bereavement. In: Barrett, J.E., ed. *Stress and Mental Disorder.* New York: Raven Press, 1979.

Elizur, E., and Kaffman, M. Children's bereavement reactions following death of the father: II. *Journal of the American Academy of Child Psychiatry* 21:474–480, 1982.

Freud, S. *Mourning and Melancholia (1917).* In: Strachey, J., ed. *The Standard Edition of the Complete Psychological Works of Sigmund Freud,* Vol. 14 London: Hogarth Press and Institute for Psychoanalysis, 1957.

Greene, W.A. Disease response to life stress. *Journal of the American Medical Women's Association* 20:133–140, 1965.

Helsing, K.J.; Comstock, G.W.; and Szklo, M. Causes of death in a widowed population. *American Journal of Epidemiology* 116:524–532, 1982.

Helsing, K.J., and Szklo, M. Mortality after bereavement. *American Journal of Epidemiology* 114:41–52, 1981.

Helsing, K.J.; Szklo, M.; and Comstock, G.W. Factors associated with mortality after widowhood. *American Journal of Public Health* 71:802–809, 1981.

Hollister, L. Psychotherapeutic drugs in the dying and bereaved. *Journal of Thanatology* 2:623–629, 1972.

Horowitz, M.; Wilner, N.; Marmar, C.; and Krupnick, J. Pathologic grief and the activation of latent self-images. *American Journal of Psychiatry* 137:1157–1162, 1980.

Kaffman, M., and Elizur, E. Bereavement responses of kibbutz and non-kibbutz children following the death of a father. *Journal of Child Psychology and Psychiatry* 24:435–442, 1983.

Koocher, G. Childhood, death, and cognitive development. *Developmental Psychology* 9:369–375, 1973.

Lifshitz, M. Long range effects of father's loss. *British Journal of Medical Psychology* 49:189–197, 1976.

Lindemann, E. Symptomatology and management of acute grief. *American Journal of Psychiatry* 101:141–149, 1944.

Lloyd, C. Life events and depressive disorders reviewed: Events as predisposing factors. *Archives of General Psychiatry* 37:529–535, 1980.

Lopata, H. Self-identity in marriage and widowhood. *The Sociological Quarterly* 14:407–418, 1973.

MacMahon, B., and Pugh, T.F. Suicide in the widowed. *American Journal of Epidemiology* 81:23–31, 1965.

Morgan, D. Not all sadness can be treated with antidepressants. *West Virginia Medical Journal* 76(6):136–137, 1980.

Osterweis, M.; Solomon, F.; and Green, M., eds. *Bereavement: Reactions, Consequences and Care. A Report of the Institute of Medicine.* Washington, DC: National Academy Press, 1984.

Parkes, C.M., and Weiss, R.S. *Recovery from Bereavement.* New York: Basic Books, 1983.

Ramsay, R.W. Bereavement: A behavioral treatment of pathological grief. In: Sioden, P.O.; Bates, S; and Dorkens, W.S., eds. *Trends in Behavior Therapy.* New York: Academic Press, 1979.

Raphael, B. Preventive intervention with the recently bereaved. *Archives of General Psychiatry* 34:1450–1454, 1977.

Raphael, B. *The Anatomy of Bereavement.* New York: Basic Books, 1983.

Schmale, A., and Iker, H. The psychological setting of uterine cervical cancer. *Annals of the New York Academy of Sciences* 125:794–801, 1965.

Silverman, P.R. Transitions and models of intervention. *Annals of the Academy of Political and Social Science* 464:174–188, 1982.

PART IX

THEORIES OF HUMAN BEHAVIOR
AND DEVELOPMENT

INTRODUCTION

This final section of the anthology is quite different from all the others in that it presents brief overviews of several major theories that guide much of social services by helping professionals. In this introductory section, I would like to discuss how to translate theory into practice. Whatever theory a practitioner chooses to use in describing, explaining, and predicting the course of events in a client's situation, there remains the task of translating that system of abstract concepts and propositions into specific guides to action. Or, to put the matter more picturesquely, theorists build castles in the sky, but practitioners pay the rent and have to do any remodeling necessary to fit everyday life. So, select your theories wisely since you are the one who has to live with the results.

At its most helpful, theory

- describes some portion of the world with clarity and distinctness;

- explains in abstract and general terms how these events come into being, maintain themselves, and possibly go out of existence;

- predicts how these events will change (when, where, and in what form).

All of these kinds of information are helpful for different practical purposes. The practitioner needs to know what it is that is energizing the client to seek help for a problem to be resolved, or an objective to be attained. (This is important: Clients probably seek problem resolution and the attainment of desired objectives in every service situation; hence, practitioners are effectively involved in treatment and primary prevention at the same time.) The practitioner has the verbal description of the presenting problem from the client's perspective, but such a set of words, even added to the nonverbal information (posture, dress, other symbols of need), does not constitute a full description of the problem because it is from only the one person's point of view. We know that any social reality contains the perspectives of all the significant parties, and that by judicious questioning and further explorations, the practitioner often attempts to capture a more nearly well-rounded description of the situation.

Theories may guide that search for a more nearly complete description of a situation, if only to lead practitioners to ask additional questions and seek answers from different perspectives. As a basic assumption of any theory, we take for granted the notion that the complexity of life is more nearly understood by obtaining the views of all the participants. Yet, the corollary to this assumption is that we can be flooded with information to the point of immobilization, so that what we seek is a theoretical closure, that we have enough information from the parties involved to identify most of the outline of events, even if every detail is not known. We have the sense that what we know hangs together in an intelligible way, and thus provides the basis for the next level of action—explanation or understanding.

Our first level of descriptive information is often presented in the lay language, the words used by clients and collateral. In order to understand events, we have to move from the level of particular happenings to the abstract level of concepts and their interrelationships. This is so because understanding the pattern of events of others requires that we enter into their lives and situations so as to see events from their perspectives. We cannot do this literally, but we can use the tools of language (which are abstractions) in order to put ourselves in their places. ''I can understand how you must have felt when x occurred.'' In order to feel the client's feelings, we have to translate their particular experiences into the categories of like experiences we have known. These categories are concepts.

We can also enter into another life, that of a theorist, in order to comprehend how that person views certain categories of experience. In this case, the theorist's words are abstract, and we understand these concepts and propositions because we personalize them. ''Category x is the general situation of which I experienced the particular instance, x.'' Thus, we enter two separate worlds in different ways in order to connect the experiences of client and theorist. Practitioners are the site of that connection; indeed, they are the connection of theory and life experiences.

When we say that we understand a client's situation, it means in effect that we have connected the abstract system of ideas from a theorist who has offered a logical package of ideas for how some aspect of reality works, with the raw events from a client whose experiences seem to be instances of the categories described by the theorist. By using the abstract system of logically interrelated and flowing ideas—often in the form that x causes y, and y causes z, therefore x is a causal factor in the existence of z—we can get ideas about what is driving the events in the life of a given client. We look for instances of x and y and z, and check to see whether there is any concrete evidence that in fact the particular events x, y, and z in the client's life are related in the way the theory describes.

Prediction, the third level of theoretical activity, is crucial for helping professionals because, having a hunch as to what causes what in a particular situation, we have a suggestion about what events we might change so as to change the flow of events in a desired direction. Notice that practitioners are here imposing values on events, saying in effect that a given client situation is "bad," and that the client and we have worked out what is "desirable" in this context. Then we have to make plans to help that client achieve a situation with its components rearranged in such a way that the client's problem is resolved or his or her need fulfilled, and that no new problems are created for others. All of these value choices involve the impositions of values onto the abstractions of the theorist and the realities of the client. When I spoke earlier of the fact that practitioners put pieces of dissected actions back together again, I might have added that values are the glue.

Some theories are easy to grasp, which means that it is easy to link concrete instances of client behaviors and circumstances to theoretical terms, and then to follow the predictions within the logical package of the theory, and finally, to return to the client's level of concrete behaviors with specific guides on what to do to affect those desired changes. For example, the behavioral theory as described by Bruce Thyer, includes the concept of positive reinforcment, which states that behaviors followed by consequences viewed as positive by the person will likely be repeated. If we have a client whose behavior we seek to change for whatever reason, then this part of behavioral theory suggests that we should ar-

range the consequences of that client's behavior so that whenever he or she behaves in a desired way, he or she receives the reward that that person views as positive. (Not everyone will find the same consequences as reinforcing.)

The art of professional practice involves translating these abstract statements into concrete events. What particular behaviors (feelings, thoughts, and/or actions) in what particular environments (social, cultural, and physical) constitute the client's problems? What particular behaviors would constitute movement toward a more nearly desirable situation? What particular consequences could be practically and feasibly arranged that the client would find satisfying? No theory tells us exactly what these particulars are—that is not the function of theory. But any theory worth its salt gives us directions about the categories involved and their interrelationships, and then we are to make the specific translations based on our training and life experience.

Evaluation of our ongoing practice informs us immediately about how successful we have been in making these choices. This is why the ongoing evaluation of practice is a critical aspect of any service program. Evaluation is science in the support of art, the art of helping.

The theories or frames of reference presented here are among the major conceptual perspectives in use today. (I have included other theories as parts of other papers in this anthology where they focused on some specific substantive concern. See the alternative table of contents for a list of theories discussed in this book, page ix.)

Carel Germain's many contributions to an ecological perspective provide a contemporary view of systems thinking, how components of the person, primary and secondary groups, culture and the physical environment are to be viewed together in understanding any given situation. When the ecological model is used as a tool to think about human development, some very interesting and surprising results emerge.

Bruce Thyer's account of the behavioral position summarized some of the key concepts, but refocused them as a contribution to developmental thinking. How does the powerful behavioral theory account for features of human development? Thyer is careful to note that the behavioral theory does not support any underlying notion of universal stages of development—nor does Germain's ecological approach. But he is able to describe some common human experiences using the behavioral vocabulary, without assuming any cognitive or mental concepts as explanatory mechanisms.

Sophie Freud takes on the difficult task of explaining the current views of psychodynamic theory derived primarily from the writings of Sigmund Freud. There have been several major paths taken from Freud's original writings, and in this paper, Sophie Freud describes some of the newer thinking that remains grounded in the basic assumptions of unconscious conflicts and adaptive behaviors.

This book ends as it began, discussing theory-for-use in real world situations. Each of the forty-eight papers in this anthology presents some perspective on human functioning and development. These papers are stimuli, points of departure in a lifelong venture for seeking understanding of human behavior and development so as to be able to help others help themselves when needed. As you study these papers, their ideas become part of your ideas. The configuration of your knowledge has greatly expanded to include the provocative and informative ideas of many others. Now it is your turn to use these and other ideas in your professional practice, and perhaps to add new ideas to our growing knowledge base.

46

A CONVERSATION WITH CAREL GERMAIN ON HUMAN DEVELOPMENT IN THE ECOLOGICAL CONTEXT

Martin Bloom

School of Social Work
Rutgers, The State University of New Jersey

MB: Carel, in a recent paper ["Human development in contemporary environments," *Social Service Review*, 1987 (December), 565–580], you probably shook up the social work education community at a 9.9 on the Richter Scale, had it been an earthquake. You raised serious questions about the theoretical underpinnings of the mainstays of human behavior courses, namely, the familiar fixed, sequential stages of development theories of Freud, Erikson, Levinson, and others. You pointed out that current theorizing and research suggests that the transactions between the developing persons and their environments is the predominant influence on what these persons become. However, in a rapidly changing time, each cohort of persons (those born at the same time and who are therefore exposed to the same sequence of social and historical changes at particular ages) will likely experience these transactions quite differently and thus may be expected to be different from earlier and later cohorts. The more there are cohort differences, the less likely are fixed, sequential stages of development to apply to all people.

CG: Yes, these cohort differences are very pronounced, and developmentalists have to pay attention to them. The epigenetic assumptions of psychosocial development of Erikson, borrowed from biology and embryology, were never valid in the social sphere. Levinson based his stage model on the life experience of 40 white, middle-class men of his time (which was more than a decade ago) and place. He tended to ignore such influences as culture, power/powerlessness, color differences, poverty/affluence, and health and illness. So his assumptions of universal, fixed, sequential stages were incorrect even for their own time. We have

only recently begun to look at the life development in women and in minorities.

MB: That's true. I read an interesting paper by Roberts and Newton [Priscilla Roberts and Peter M. Newton, "Levinsonian studies of women's adult development," *Psychology and Aging*, 1986, 2(2): 154–163], which reviewed four doctoral dissertations that used Levinson's theory to study women's development in the adult stage. Instead of 40 white, middle-class men, like Levinson used, the authors of these dissertations studied 39 women, including eight black women. These authors report that these women went through roughly the same developmental periods and tasks as did men, but that the ways they dealt with these tasks differed, and different kinds of outcomes were achieved. [See the paper by Gill, Coppard, and Lowther, "Mid-life career development theory and research: Implications for work and education" in this anthology, pages 368–376, for a brief overview of Levinson's theory.]

CG: It may be that if those dissertation writers started with the Levinson framework, then the questions they asked and how they interpreted the data would be affected by that framework.

Moreover, there are some interesting age and gender crossovers, meaning that the clear, fixed stages of the classical developmental theories may not be descriptive of the life experiences of current cohorts. For example, Bernice Neugarten made a startling observation:

> Ours seems to be a society that has become accustomed to 70-year-old students, 30-year-old college presidents, 22-year-old mayors, 35-year-old grandmothers, 50-year-old retirees, 65-year-old fathers of

This paper was constructed for this anthology with the kind cooperation of Carel Germain, 1990.

preschoolers, 60-year-olds and 30-year-olds wearing the same clothing styles. . . . [Bernice L. Neugarten and Gunhild O. Hagestad, "Age and the life course," in *Handbook of Aging and the Social Sciences*, edited by R.H. Binstock and E. Shanas (New York: Van Nostrand Reinhold, 1976), pp. 35–55.]

So it seems to be less and less clear what all people will experience in their life development and in what sequence. What appears to be most critical about these age/sex crossovers and in the changing family forms, norms, values, and roles in the family is that the context of infants' and children's development is being drastically changed with consequences that we cannot now foresee.

MB: Given this more fluid view of human development, what do you see as the most nearly appropriate model for our times?

CG: I would say that the ecological approach to people-environment transactions is probably the most encompassing metaphor. (It isn't a model in the technical sense of the term.) That is, the ecological perspective is an easier way of grasping the reciprocal influences of people and environments in human development and functioning. Applied to developmental theory, the ecological perspective supports the notions of varied developmental paths and inherent unpredictability of the life course.

MB: Could you summarize the major elements of your ecological perspective?

CG: The dimensions of this ecological perspective took shape over a period of years, but the key ideas might be expressed this way: First, human beings are conceived as evolving and adapting through their transactions with every aspect of their environments—the biological, psychosocial, and physical context of their lives. In these adaptive processes the human being and the environment reciprocally shape each other. People mold their environments in many ways and, in turn, they must then adapt to the changes they created. [See Carel Germain, "The ecological perspective in casework practice," *Social Casework*, June, 1973, 54: 223–230.]

There are some major life transitions, such as beginning kindergarten, going through puberty, taking the first job, and so forth, that most people in this society experience. These life transitions hold the potential for challenge and growth for the individuals involved and for their families and commu-

nities. But depending on the resources of the persons and the environments, and their exchanges, there is also the possibility of stress and retarded development. When physical or social environments are unresponsive to people's needs or goals, or when people are caught in difficult interpersonal relationships, they may not be able to make use of available environmental resources for developing, and may undergo great stress.

Social work practice involves various activities that are directed at releasing people's potential for growth and adaptive functioning, as well as to increasing the responsiveness of environments to people's needs, capacities, and aspirations. [See Carel Germain and Alex Gitterman, *The Life Model of Social Work Practice*. New York: Columbia University Press, 1980.]

MB: You've pointed out that the concern for persons in environments is the distinguishing feature and unifying characteristic of social work, but that environmental understanding or interventions have been given short shrift, with some important exceptions such as Pincus and Minahan [Allen Pincus and Anne Minahan, *Social Work Practice: Model and Method*. Itasca, Illinois: F.E. Peacock, 1973] and Siporin [Max Siporin, *Introduction to Social Work Practice*. New York: Macmillan, 1975]. The ecological perspective seems to be trying to redress this omission.

CG: Yes. I once described the ecological approach as a " . . . continous set of reciprocal processes between the person and all layers and textures of the environment. In addition to the innate adaptiveness that has been built into the genetic structure of human beings over evolutionary time, people use an almost infinite variety of learned capacities to reach and sustain an adaptive balance between their needs and goals and the properties of the environment." [Carel Germain. "The ecological approach to people-environment transactions," *Social Casework*, June 1981, 323–331.]

MB: And that infinite variety of learned adaptations would also make any fixed stage theory less applicable to all people.

CG: The same possibilities of learned adaptations also provide social work with its point of departure for practice. The interchanges between people and environments are rarely smooth, and the rough spots mark lack of good fit, or stress. What is perceived as stressful varies with age, sex, genetic endowments, and previous social and cultural experiences. [Carel Germain, "An ecological perspective on social work practice in health care." *Social Work in Health Care*, 1977, 3(1): 67–76.]

This perceived stress gives rise to a sense of imbalance and the development of coping responses as the person tries to deal with the challenges or crises of everyday life. Using this paradigm of human adaptiveness, the emergence of stress, and the response of coping mechanisms, we have the outlines for a model of practice, one that enters the picture at any or all of these aspects of the person's ecology.

MB: The life model is clearly a useful tool for addressing problems and challenges of living, but what does it say specifically about developmental considerations?

CG: The life model is a specific practice approach derived from the ecological perspective. I think the question might better be stated as what this ecological perspective lends to developmental considerations, which gets us back to the recent developments in thinking about persons in environments. Cohort theory involves looking at particular groups of persons born at a particular time and thus exposed to the same sequence of social and historical events as they all developed. Cohorts are clearly very different in their life experiences, and so we might expect that they developed differently from other cohorts of persons.

MB: So this would throw into question the universal stages of development of theories like Freud's and Erikson's. I recall that you quoted Margaret Mead's observation on social change and the inevitable differences between generations:

> The paths by which today's adults came into the present can never again be traversed. Children today face a future that is so deeply unknown that it cannot be handled. [Margaret Mead. *Culture and Commitment: A Study of the Generation Gap.* New York: Natural History Press, 1970.]

Thus, for the first time ever, parents can't visualize the world their children will enter as adults, and cannot advise them how to prepare for it. Nor do children understand the world from which their parents emerged.

CG: Yes, this view on contemporary life fits well with the new concept of life course, which refers to the unique paths of development people take and their diverse life experiences in the various environ-

ments in which they live. The life course model accommodates the new research information about human development. The self-regulating, self-determining nature of human beings and the indeterminate nature of non-uniform pathways of psychosocial development and social life are acknowledged in this concept. [Carel B. Germain. Life forces and the anatomy of practice. *The Smith College Studies in Social Work,* March 1990.]

Hareven defined the term "life course" as being

> " . . . concerned with the timing of life events in relation to the social structures and historical changes affecting them. It thus takes into account the synchronization of individual life transitions with collective family configurations under changing social conditions." [Tamara K. Hareven. "The life course and aging in historical perspective," in *Aging and Life Course Transition: An Interdisciplinary Perspective,* edited by T. Hareven and K.J. Adams. New York: Guilford Press, 1982.]

MB: But if everything is changing in relation to everything else, are there no islands of universality, developmental points onto which we can anchor our understanding of human nature—as Freud and Erikson attempted to do?

CG: There are, of course, certain biologically predetermined stages in maturation (standing, walking, fine motor coordination, etc.) that are universal in the species. The stages occur despite individual variations in age and degrees of influence exerted by culture, nutrition, and other enviromental elements. However, this does not mean that emotional and social developments follow a fixed timetable and are thereby associated with universal age-specific life tasks at certain critical points. Developmental issues and life tasks may appear and reappear at almost any point over the life course, depending on many variables, and without following a predetermined, sequential order. [Carel Germain, "Human development in contemporary environments." *Social Service Review,* December 1987, 565–580.]

MB: Your quotation of Neugarten illustrates the crossovers in traditional age roles. You also made the point that there are changes in gender roles, such as women working in occupations that were once exclusively male. Likewise, men have been taking on tasks, such as being the homemaker, when their wives are the breadwinners, and are also taking positions as nurses, flight attendants, and other jobs that were once defined as female occupations.

CG: Also, the feminist writings of Carol Gilligan and others have reconceptualized human development. For example, the theory of the development of self-identity in contemporary writings is essentially a male-oriented version of what was important in life. For men, it was power, competitive success, and independence, and so their self-identities were formed around these concepts. But the life experiences of women tended to favor attachment, caring, and interdependence, and so their self-identity was shaped around these concepts. These kinds of differences in the life course experiences of persons of different ages, genders, as well as differences by races and life styles continue to raise question about the fixed, sequential stages of development in adulthood. [See the papers that discuss the Piaget/Kohlberg/Gilligan concepts of development in this anthology, chapters 10, 23.]

MB: Yet, if I am reading you correctly, you do quote with approval the recent work of Bowlby with regard to his concepts of an inborn capacity for affectional ties, which means that infants and parents form affectional bonding and caretaking behaviors necessary to the healthy development of the child. [John Bowlby, "Affectional bonds: Their nature and origin." in *Loneliness: The Experience of Emotional and Social Isolation,* edited by R.S. Weiss, Cambridge, Mass.: MIT Press, 1973.] It seems that this universal affectional trait is later expressed in adulthood by pair formation and sexual bonding, as well as affectional bonding with a small circle of others. You cite current research that tends to support these ideas [Germain, *Social Service Review, 1987*]. But doesn't this take us back to Freud's universal stages?

CG: I don't think so, because there is no necessary timing for affectional bonding, and more importantly, Bowlby views affectional bonding as occurring throughout adulthood. It is quite normal to form dependencies on friends, neighbors, coworkers—and they with us. There are appropriate occasions to be independent and occasions to be dependent, regardless of age, whereas the universal and one-directional theories of writers like Freud don't account for this ecological adaptation to environmental contexts.

MB: You also quote Robert White's concept of effectance, an inborn motivation to explore one's environment, which, if one receives satisfactory responses, leads to a sense of competence, that one

can affect one's environment. Then, in connection with recent research that demonstrates how active the very young infant is in establishing contact with his or her environment, you suggest that some traditional concepts such as Mahler's "normal autism" [a belief that normal newborns go through a stage of normal autism in which they are uninterested and non-registering of stimuli from the environment] simply are not accurate.

CG: Yes, research demonstrates that infants are interested in and responsive to their environment from the first days of life. Moreover, Stern criticizes Mahler's concept of the stage of "normal symbiosis," in which the infant was supposedly not able to distinguish him or herself from the environment. Again, infant research shows that infants are aware of their separateness from the caregivers. [Daniel Stern. *The Interpersonal World of the Infant.* New York: Basic Books, 1982.]

MB: I get the sense that you view the growing individual as extremely flexible and adaptive to environments, and that rather than present a universal scheme of individual stages, you are suggesting a view of patterned environmental experiences as being more descriptive of what happens to most individuals. You go on to describe some non-stage total life course models, such as Bronfenbrenner's ecological model. [Urie Bronfenbrenner. *The Ecology of Human Development.* Cambridge, Mass.: Harvard University Press, 1979.] But I wonder whether this will be enough of a conceptual handle for practitioners to be guided in helping clients through those crisis transitions, or for the researcher to hypothesize what factors may be significantly related to what other factors.

CG: That is a difficult question but an important one. I have been working on a related set of issues in my current writing [Carel B. Germain. *Human Behavior in the Social Environment: An Ecological View.* New York: Columbia University Press, 1991] and perhaps I will be able to suggest some answers for your quest for more developmental structure even as developmental openness appears to be emerging as the dominant picture of human experience.

MB: We will all be looking forward to your new book in hopes that you will be able to put all these complex pieces together. Thank you and best wishes for this current writing project.

47

A BEHAVIORAL PERSPECTIVE
ON HUMAN DEVELOPMENT

Bruce A. Thyer

School of Social Work, University of Georgia
Department of Psychiatry and Health Behavior,
Medical College of Georgia

From the perspective of the behavior analyst, human development is largely a function of *selection by consequences* (Skinner, 1981). Such selection has occurred phylogenetically (over the course of the development of the human species) through the processes of evolutionary biology. Those ancestors of ours who, through random variation or mutations, possessed physical or behavioral characteristics which promoted their ability to survive and reproduce, over many thousands of generations passed on such characteristics to you and me. The ontogenic (those occurring during an individual's lifetime) processes analogous to the effects of natural selection on the structure and behavior of entire species are known as the principles of operant conditioning.

The contemporary behavior analyst primarily focuses upon operant mechanisms, with a due regard for the role of respondent learning, our genetic endowment, and other biological variables, in an attempt to account for many of those phenomena we label human development across the life span. Specifically, the interest of the behavior analyst is in the role of present and past environmental transactions among person, behavior and the consequences of behavior provided by one's psychosocial environment. Biological variables are not ignored. Rather the distinctive feature is that of a rigorous emphasis upon seeking as complete an *environmental* account of human development as possible, prior to exploring potential biological, cognitive or intrapsychic mechanisms. The merits of the work of the physiologist, brain scientist, biochemist, geneticist, or neurologist are certainly recognized as valuable contributions that have yielded many significant discoveries concerning human development. Those areas of inquiry, however, are the subject matter of different disciplines. It is as unreasonable to criticize the behavior-

ist for purportedly ignoring a person's genes in developing a behavior-analytic account of a given behavioral phenomena as it is to criticize the geneticist for ignoring operant factors in explaining the same events.

THE BEHAVIOR ANALYTIC ALTERNATIVE TO STAGE THEORIES

A promising alternative to traditional stage theories of human development is the approach currently labeled behavior analysis. Based upon the principles of contemporary social learning theory, the behavior analyst attempts to arrive at explanations for the phenomena labeled human development. The term "behavior" refers to what a person *does,* regardless of the observable nature of the phenomena. Modern day behaviorists *do not* limit themselves to the study of publicly observable behavior. Although such was the position of the founder of behavioral psychology, John Watson (1913), subsequent formulations such as those of Skinner (1953, 1957) attempt to explain both overt (publicly observable) and covert behavior (those events which transpire beneath the skin and are labeled private events). In terms of their causes, private events are not held to be fundamentally different from observable actions, and relatively sophisticated behavioral accounts are being developed for inner phenomena such as hallucinations and delusions, thought, speech, and creativity (e.g., Skinner, 1957; Layng and Andronis, 1984), all without recourse to metaphysical constructs such as cognition or mental structures. The behavior analytic alternatives to these latter explicatory mechanisms consist of respondent conditioning, operant conditioning, and observational learning. Each of these will be briefly summarized.

This paper was written for this anthology, 1990.

RESPONDENT CONDITIONING

Respondent conditioning is the most fundamental mechanism by which all humans and other animals learn to adapt to their environment. The work of Pavlov was the major stimulus in bringing respondent processes to the attention of developmental and other psychologists concerned with learning and behavior change. Pavlov and his associates demonstrated how a neutral stimulus, if presented one or more times immediately prior to the occurrence of an event (unconditioned stimulus or UCS) which produced an innate reflexive response (unconditioned response or UCR), the previously neutral stimulus could come to elicit a similar response. After such conditioning trials, the neutral stimulus which now elicits such responses is called a conditioned stimulus (CS) and the involuntary response to the CS is called a conditioned response (CR). The types of bodily responses involved in such conditioning processes are called respondent behaviors, and the learning process has been labeled respondent conditioning. This is also known as Pavlovian or classical conditioning and has been referred to as S-R psychology (for stimulus-response).

The focus in respondent conditioning is how certain environmental stimuli come to evoke relatively automatic reactions over which the person has little control. All humans are born with an innate capacity to learn (i.e., change behavior) by means of respondent conditioning and the processes involved have been demonstrated to be valid in virtually every species of animal tested. This is not surprising since recent experimental evidence indicates that individual animal nerve cells can be affected through classical conditioning (Walters and Bryne, 1983), suggesting that these processes represent a fundamental property of all animal life, ranging from one-celled organisms to human beings.

Respondent learning seems implicated in our acquisition of a number of behavioral phenomena including relatively simple overt reflexive behaviors and affective responses. Significant components of sexual behavior, emotional reactions, and even glandular secretions can be modifiable through the processes of respondent conditioning (e.g., Nesse et al., 1985). Not only may adult humans learn by means of respondent conditioning, but children, infants, neonates, and unborn fetuses have been shown to develop conditioned responses to intentionally presented conditioned stimuli (Bernard and Sontag, 1947; DeCasper and Fifer, 1980; DeCasper and Spence, 1986). One example was provided by Lipsitt

and Kaye (1964), who demonstrated that the sucking response of newborns could be classically conditioned to occur following the presentation of a tone, previously paired with the presentation of a nonnutritive nipple.

A more complex example of the possible role of respondent learning processes was provided by Sainato, Maheady and Shook (1986). Three children in a kindergarten class who had been empirically identified as socially withdrawn and isolated from their peers were sequentially assigned by the teacher to a highly evaluated social role as the classroom manager. This manager was responsible for leading selected members of the class in completing highly desired activities, such as feeding the class guinea pig, collecting milk money, handing out keys and ringing bells. Repeated measures were taken of each child's social interactions prior to, during and after their assignment as the class manager. Both during and after such two week assignments it was found that the formerly isolated children experienced an increase in the quality and quantity of their social interactions, had many more friends, and were rated more positively by their peers. These improvements were maintained even after the formerly withdrawn students no longer served as the classroom manager. The authors hypothesized that by having the regular students observe their socially isolated peers engaging in highly prestigious activities and leadership positions, the affective reactions of the regular students towards their less socially valued classmates improved. Similarly, it is possible that social anxieties of the withdrawn students became desensitized through serving in the role of manager, thus enabling them to display more effective prosocial skills after they left the leadership role.

A further example involved the use of college students as subjects (Gale and Jacobson, 1970) in an experimental study demonstrating that verbal social comments can be respondently conditioned. In this study the subjects exhibited marked physiological reactions (galvanic skin response measures) when listening to tape-recorded insults. The authors concluded that social comments can be effective conditioned stimuli and suggest that similar respondent learning processes account for related behavioral and affective phenomena in real life contexts (e.g., becoming emotionally upset when verbally abused).

It is difficult to ascribe the phenomena associated with respondent conditioning in humans to cognitive or mental processes because similar phenomena occur in other animals lacking the extensive cerebral cortex which humans possess. To the extent that animal models are similar to human behavior, it seems more parsimonious to ascribe the human phenomena to processes similar to those employed in accounting for the animal behavior, rather than postulating the existence of complex cognitive events, processes and mechanisms whose only evidence for their existence is the very behavior they are presumed to cause. This latter difficulty, by the way, is a serious logical fallacy inherent in virtually all mentalistic models of human behavior, representing the philosophical error of circular reasoning.

OPERANT LEARNING

Although the distinction is often ignored by the critics of the behavioral position, the processes of operant conditioning are entirely different from the S-R psychology associated with respondent learning. In the latter framework, the focus is on how environmental events (stimuli), which occur *before* a behavior, come to automatically elicit relatively simple reflexive acts. In operant conditioning, the focus is on how *consequences* which *follow* a behavior come to influence the future probability of that behavior occurring.

In the operant model developed by Skinner there are four major types of consequences (outlined in Figure 1). An instance of a positively reinforcing event would be where a behavior occurs, is followed by a consequence that is *presented,* and the likelihood of that behavior occurring in the future *increases.* A negatively reinforcing event is where a behavior occurs, the consequence of which consists of the *removal* of something aversive, which also has the effect of *increasing* the likelihood of that behavior occurring in the future. Note that both positive and negative reinforcement processes are rewarding. We like it when we get nice things or when nasty things are removed, hence we tend to engage in actions which produce such results.

The opposite effects occur in both types of punishment. Positive punishment may be said to have taken place when a behavior occurs, is followed by the *presentation* of an aversive event, which *reduces* the likelihood of such behavior occurring in the future. In negative punishment, when a behavior occurs and is followed by something pleasant being *removed,* such behavior similarly becomes *less likely* in the future. Some specific examples of these four types of consequences are presented in Table 1. Persons not familiar with correct behavioral terminology often confuse the process of negative reinforcement with the operations of punishment. It helps to remember that terms "positive" and "negative" refer to whether or not a consequence represents something presented or taken away, that "reinforcement" (both positive *and* negative) strengthens behavior, and punishment (of either type) weakens it.

All behaviors which are affected by their consequences are said to "operate" on their environment, and thus are collectively labeled "operants." Operant conditioning occurs as a natural learning process whereby in everyday environments infants, children, teenagers and adults learn from the consequences of their actions and modify their subsequent comportment accordingly.

A considerable amount of experimental research has demonstrated both in laboratory contexts and in natural environments that much human behavior is operant in nature. This is even true for newborns. Bijou and Baer (1967) provide an early review of such fascinating studies, and include reports demonstrating that even extremely young children can alter their behavior in order to produce reinforcing consequences. Examples include the turning of one's head (Siqueland and Lipsitt, 1966), sucking responses, and crying or other vocalizations (Rheingold, Gewirtz and Ross, 1959).

As the infant grows older, more complex behavior is shaped through operant processes. An in-depth

FIGURE 1. The Four Major Categories of Consequences Which May Affect Behavior

| | | **Effect on Behavior** | |
| | | *The Behavior Is Likely to* | |
		Increase	Decrease
A	Presented	Positive Reinforcement	Positive Punishment
Stimulus Is	Removed	Negative Reinforcement	Negative Punishment

TABLE 1. Examples of Reinforcement and Punishment

Positive Reinforcement

1. A child opens a cabinet door and finds interesting things to play with. Exploratory behavior becomes more likely.
2. A child offers to share her toys with a friend, and is praised by her parents. Sharing behavior increases in likelihood.

Negative Reinforcement

1. A child who tantrums finds that parents will cease making aversive demands on him or her. Tantruming behavior becomes more probable in future similar circumstances.
2. A person complies with the nagging and aversive demands made by their spouse. Nagging immediately ceases and future compliance becomes more likely.

Positive Punishment

1. Taunting a peer results in being painfully struck. Taunting decreases.
2. A child is caught cheating on a test and receives a failing grade. Cheating is reduced.

Negative Punishment

1. Exceeding the speed limit results in a traffic fine, and the removal of something pleasant (money). Speeding decreases.
2. A teenager stays out past the time he was due home. Car privileges are taken away for one week and tardiness becomes less likely in subsequent weeks.

review is not possible in this chapter, but a limited summary is presented in Table 2 which outlines a variety of operant behaviors that develop in childhood and later years. These behaviors have been shown in well-designed experimental studies to be manipulable through contingency management programs in laboratory settings and in natural environments. Although such evidence does not provide conclusive proof that analogous behavior develops through identical processes experienced by children in real life contexts, similar operant factors are the most parsimonious explanations of these forms of human development.

One recently published example on the role of operant contingencies in acquiring and maintaining reasonably complex behavior may be found in Whitehurst and Valdez-Menchaca (1988). These authors used a sample of monolingual American $(n = 20)$ and Mexican $(n = 12)$ 2- and 3-year-old children attending preschool in their respective countries. Children were randomly assigned to two groups: group 1 was differentially reinforced by their bilingual teacher for using foreign vocabulary words; the children in group 2 received equivalent amounts of reinforcement on a noncontingent basis. Both groups received equal amounts of didactic education in the foreign language. After several weeks, the children in group 2 began receiving reinforcement for their accurate use of foreign vocabulary words. The children in group 1 acquired and utilized their foreign vocabulary, when formally tested as well as spontaneously, to a much greater extent than those in group 2. When the differential reinforcement procedure was applied to group 2 their use of foreign words quickly caught up to that found in group 1. The authors interpret their results as supporting the hypothesis that operant factors are strongly involved in the acquisition and use of language skills. This is not an implausible account. Common sense tells us that words or phrases which produce desired

TABLE 2. Examples of Behavior Shown to be a Function of Operant Factors*

Age Range of Subjects	Behavior	Supportive Citation
3 months	Simple Vocalizations	Rheingold et al. (1959)
9 months	Interacting with Peers	Becker (1977)
2–3 yrs.	Using Newly Taught Words	Whitehurst and Valdez-Menchaca (1988)
3–4 yrs.	Praising Peers/Sharing Toys	Charlesworth and Hartup (1967)
4 years	Playing with Peers	Allen et al. (1964)
3–6 yrs.	Improvising Tools	Parsonson and Baer (1978)
3–6 yrs.	Improving Racial Attitudes/Behavior	Spencer and Horowitz (1973)
7 years	Hitting Others	Walters and Brown (1963)
6–7 yrs.	Sharing Toys with Peers	Presbie et al. (1971)
6–9 yrs.	Sharing Food with Peers	Midlarsky and Bryan (1967)
9–10 yrs.	Self-Control in School	Drabman et al. (1973)
9–10 yrs.	Asking Questions	Ladd (1981)
7–12 yrs.	Cooperative Play	Azrin and Lindsley (1956)
18 yrs. +	Cooperative Work	Schmitt (1976)

*This table *does not* present the sequence in which these behaviors necessarily develop in human beings.

consequences are likely to be repeated by a child, while those which failed to yield useful results will extinguish.

A number of increasingly sophisticated variations on the basic contingency operations which comprise operant conditioning (outlined in Table 1) include the processes of extinction and shaping, and the distinctions between contingency shaped and rule-governed behavior. *Extinction* refers to the eventual decrease in the frequency or strength of a behavior, if the reinforcing consequences which have been maintaining the behavior cease. *Shaping* refers to the natural or planned development of complex behavioral repertoires through the selective reinforcement of successive approximations of the desired terminal response. Skinner (1953) provides an excellent introduction to these topics.

Rule-governed behavior is a more complex form of operant learning which occurs as human beings develop receptive and expressive verbal behavior. We acquire the ability to alter our behavior in response to instructions to the extent that such instructions serve as reliable discriminative stimuli, events which signal the presence of reinforcing or punishing consequences if certain behavior occurs. If instructions are provided to a child (e.g., "Don't touch the stove, it is hot!"), and he disobeys and is subsequently burned, noncompliance behavior is likely to decrease in the future (it was positively punished by the pain of a burn). If an instruction is given, obeyed, and a reinforcing consequence follows, the operant class which could be labeled "following directions" is generally strengthened. As a child grows up, he or she is exposed to literally thousands of such learning trials which, in most cases, produce people who as a general rule comply with instructions. This is because following instructions or rules has been regularly reinforced, initially by intentional reinforcers provided by caregivers and later by the naturally occurring consequences the rule-governed behavior generates.

In adolescents and adults, complex behavior is *not* seen as contingency-shaped, but rather is viewed by the behavior analyst as rule-governed. Rules may be viewed as verbal substitutes for actually experiencing contingencies. One early experimental demonstration of rule-governed behavior was reported by Risley and Hart (1968). In this series of studies, 12 black children aged 4- to 5-years-old attending a preschool were provided with reinforcers for stating that they had engaged in certain activities during the day. Unobtrusive observations were made to determine the truthfulness of the childrens' reports. In the initial phase of the study, rewards were provided regardless of the accuracy of the childrens' reports. Not surprisingly the numbers of children reporting, at the end of the day, that they had engaged in selected behaviors (e.g., playing with blocks, or painting) rapidly increased to near 100 percent. In reality however, it was found that their actual engagement in the selected activities was quite low. In other words, the children did not tell the truth. The next phase of the study provided similar reinforcers to the children but only if they actually had engaged in the activities they stated they performed that day. In other words, only truthful reports produced reinforcers. The children's engagement in the selected activities greatly increased and the accuracy of their verbal account of their actions soon approached 100 percent. In effect, the children were taught that verbal and nonverbal behavior should correspond. In a subsequent study, when the same children were reinforced for *saying* that they had engaged in a previously unreinforced activity, the children actually began *performing* the reported behavior even though such performance was not required in order to obtain reinforcement. In other words, the children may be said to have been taught to "tell the truth," a very important rule necessary for the establishment of functional social relationships in everyday life. This is an extremely complex topic which cannot be given justice in the small space provided here. The reader is referred to the recent text by Hayes (1989) for a more complete account.

Operant explanations avoid the difficulties inherent in the teleological explanations associated with psychodynamic and cognitive theories, which claim that certain behaviors have a "purpose" or are goal-oriented. The behavior analyst examines the influences of actual past events on present behavior, not the role of future events. People do not engage in behavior *in order to* get reinforcement; rather they behave in certain ways now because such actions have been reinforced in the past. In this manner an operant analysis avoids inferring the existence of traits, dispositions, mental events, and similar processes, and thus escapes the difficulties associated with reification and circular reasoning in explaining behavior. This approach to developing explanations for behavior is identical to that found in the natural sciences. Astronomers no longer look for the "purpose" of the solar system and evolutionary biologists no longer claim that a species develops a certain physical characteristic *in order* to be more competitive. Members of a species which have more of an adaptive trait will be more successful at reproducing and over time such adaptive traits become the norm. The unobtrusive hand of natural selection is the causative mechanism for the development of all physical and some behavioral features of a species. In a similar manner, the subtle influence of naturally occurring consequences is seen as gradually shaping an individual's comportment throughout life.

It is important to note that the behavior analyst *does not* deny the existence of the private events which are labeled as purpose, intentions, traits, beliefs, wishes, feelings, and so forth. These things exist, of course, and are an important part of the life experiences of all of us. Such phenomena, however, are considered ultimately explicable through social learning processes and are viewed as the by-products of one's learning history, *not the causes* of one's comportment. Othello did not kill Desdemona because he was jealous. He was jealous *and* he killed her because of the actions of Iago. The stock market does not rise because of an increase in investor confidence. Rather, *both* investor confidence and the purchasing of stocks are seen as the result of some favorable economic event. It is tempting to attribute our personal actions to the feeling states which may immediately precede our behavior, but temporal relations of this type are a poor form of evidence for inferring causality.

This reluctance to attribute causal influences to inner states is perhaps the critical distinction between radical behaviorism and other versions of contemporary social learning theory such as the cognitive behaviorism of Bandura (1977). Cognitive behaviorism, while incorporating the phenomena of respondent, operant and observational learning, also postulates the crucial nature of cognitive mechanisms which purportedly mediate these learning processes. Experimental studies of cognition, of course, are handicapped because they are limited to the study of actual behavior from which these inner, supposedly causal, states are inferred. Nevertheless, a large number of useful practice innovations have been developed from such cognitive-behavioral perspectives. Future experimental work will reveal which approach, radical behaviorism or its cognitive variants, most closely approximates nature's truth. In the interim the social work student or practitioner will find it useful to become familiar with the treatments derived from the broad spectrum of social learning theories.

OBSERVATIONAL LEARNING

From the perspective of radical behaviorism observational learning is primarily a complex form of operant behavior. Baer, Peterson and Sherman (1967) note that imitation is characterized by two features: "(1) relatively novel behavior can be developed before direct shaping, merely by providing an appropriate demonstration by a model, and (2) some imitative responses can be maintained, although unreinforced, as long as other imitative responses are reinforced (p. 407)." The fact that we can acquire new behavior through imitation alone, and in the absence of any apparent supportive reinforcing consequences, has lead some theorists such as Bandura (1977) to postulate the existence of cognitive mediating variables as causally implicated in observational learning. To the extent that observational learning may be accounted for through the noncognitive processes of respondent and operant learning, less parsimonious accounts such as Bandura's may be unnecessary.

One early attempt at such a purely operant account is described by Baer et al. (1967). Three severely/profoundly retarded children aged 9–12 years old did not possess any apparent capacity for imitative learning. The researchers used shaping techniques and food reinforcement paired with verbal praise to teach the children to imitate simple behaviors modeled by an instructor. Examples of such behaviors included touching various body parts, stand, sit, walk, manipulate various toys and tools, etc. Over 125 discrete behaviors were demonstrated to the children. Each child rapidly acquired the ability to imitate modeled behavior, but only after imitation was followed with reinforcement. In the early stages of this study, behaviors modeled by the instructor were not imitated by the children. The researchers faded out the reinforcers by asking the children to imitate various activities previously reinforced, and then gradually omitting planned reinforcement. Each child continued to display imitation of nonreinforced modeled behaviors, as long as some instances of imitation of other modeled behaviors continued to be rewarded. The generalization of the childrens' newly established capacity for observational learning was further examined by having the instructor model completely novel behaviors, activities without any history of reinforcement. The children accurately imitated these new behaviors as well. Throughout the study the childrens' abilities to accurately reproduce modeled behaviors gradually improved, and the use of shaping procedures, physical prompts and reinforcement became unnecessary as their skill in observational learning came under purely instructional (i.e., rule-governed) control. The children also displayed the capacity to imitate behaviors modeled by new instructors and began acquiring simple language skills, an ability they had previously lacked.

An observer naive to the childrens' complex learning history who watched their imitative abilities at the end of the study would be understandably tempted to ascribe their skills in observational learning to cognitive factors, as do many social learning theorists, rather than the sophisticated operant training procedures they had undergone. The radical behaviorist is reluctant to entertain such causal explanations based on internal mediating mechanisms due to the difficulties in scientifically testing such accounts, and because of the explanatory power of more parsimonious operant processes.

As is the case with all operants, human beings come with a phylogenetic history that has shaped, through the principles of evolutionary selection, the capacity to acquire new behavior through the imitation of others. There is now reasonable evidence suggesting that imitative capacities exist in human newborns (Field et al., 1982) and these initial efforts at imitative behavior produce consequences for the infant. Anyone watching the pleasure of parents playing with their babies is aware of the reciprocal nature of *behavior-imitation-reinforcement behavior* which supports this perspective. To the extent that one's imitative behaviors are reinforced, two processes simultaneously occur: the imitated behavior is itself strengthened, *and* the generic operant called "imitation" is strengthened as well.

Over the course of time the child learns that reproducing behaviors modeled by others, behaviors which appear to generate reinforcing consequences for the model, is likely to yield reinforcement for oneself as well (Liebert and Fernandez, 1970). The adaptive significance of this proposed analysis is obvious, both from the phylogenic and ontogenic perspectives. Deguchi (1984) and Baer and Deguchi (1985) provide expanded operant analyses of the phenomenon of imitation as a means for human beings to acquire new and often complex behavior.

TOWARDS A SYNTHESIS?

The capacity of human beings to imitate the behavior of others undoubtedly has adaptive significance in an evolutionary sense. By observing a peer engaging in a certain behavioral repertoire (using a stick as a tool, or tasting a novel fruit) and observing the consequences thereof (obtaining more succulent grubs, or dying a painful death from poisoning), our early ancestors who altered their behavior through this vicarious exposure to reinforcing or punishing contingencies were more likely to survive than those who failed to learn from observation. Thus, contemporary people may have come to be born with the genetically mediated capacity to imitate the actions of others. Such observational learning is strongly influenced by the consequences an individual receives during the course of his or her life as a result of imitation. Although the mechanisms of observational learning are usually explicated in terms of cognitive-behavioral theory, radical behaviorists have made a strong case that the phenomena we label as imitation or observational learning may be viewed as complex instances of operant learning (e.g., Deguchi, 1984; Baer and Deguchi, 1985).

The traditional distinctions made between respondent and operant learning are not as clear cut as was once thought, and some behavior analysts contend that fundamentally similar processes may be invoked to account for both types of learning (Pear and Eldridge, 1984). It is possible that the social work student of 50 years hence may be exposed to a theory of human development which is the equivalent of the grand unified theory sought for decades by physicists. In this unified approach to human behavior and development, respondent, operant and observational learning phenomena may have come to be seen as manifestations of more fundamental learning processes.

SUMMARY

Human development is seen as a lifelong process which is not readily divided into conceptually sound stages that are clearly distinguishable from one another. Our behavior is viewed as a function of complex and ongoing interactive processes between the person and environment, interactions which for practical purposes only cease at the death of the person. The mechanisms of respondent, operant and observational learning are a part of our genetic endowment, thus the behavior analytic perspective may be properly categorized as both a biological theory and a psychological one. Many of the phenomena labeled as human development seem to emerge at predictable times within the life of a person. Such behavior may occur in certain sequences because of general similarities in the learning experiences a culture provides to its young, the fact that certain complex activities are only possible if simpler behaviors have been mastered first, and as a function of the physical maturation of the person.

The behavior analytic perspective on human growth and development across the lifespan is obviously an incomplete account. However, by rigorously pursuing a person-in-environment analysis based upon psychosocial events (the antecedents and consequences of behavior), the study of human development is placed squarely within the domain of natural science. Slow but progressive increases in our knowledge base have occurred during the past three decades to the point where contemporary social learning theory is now a major approach to the study of behavioral development which provides accounts for overt activities, cognitive phenomena and affective responses.

References

Allen, K. E., Hart, B., Buell, J. S., Harris, F. R., and Wolf, M. M. (1964). Effects of social reinforcement on isolate behavior of a nursery school child. *Child Development, 35*, 511–518.

Azrin, N. H., and Lindsley, O. R. (1956). The reinforcement of cooperation in children. *Journal of Abnormal and Social Psychology, 2*, 100–102.

Baer, D. M. and Deguchi, H. (1985). Generalized imitation from a radical-behavioral viewpoint. In S. Reiss and R. R. Bootzin, (eds.). *Theoretical issues in behavior therapy* (pp. 179–217). New York: Academic Press.

Baer, D. M., Peterson, R. F., and Sherman, J. A. (1967). The development of imitation by reinforcing behavioral similarity to a model. *Journal of the Experimental Analysis of Behavior, 10*, 405–416.

Bandura, A. (1977). *Social learning theory.* Englewood Cliffs, NJ: Prentice-Hall.

Becker, J. M. (1977). A learning analysis of the development of peer-oriented behavior in nine-month old infants. *Developmental Psychology, 13*, 481–491.

Bernard, J. and Sontag, L. W. (1947). Fetal reactivity to tonal stimulation: A preliminary report. *Journal of Genetic Psychology, 70*, 205–210.

Bijou, S. W. and Baer, D. M. (1967) (eds.). *Child development: Readings in experimental analysis.* New York: Appleton-Century-Crofts.

Charlesworth, R., and Hartup, W. W. (1967). Positive social reinforcement in the nursery school peer group. *Child Development, 38*, 993–1002.

DeCasper, A. J., and Fifer, W. P. (1980). Of human bonding: Newborns prefer their mother's voice. *Science, 208,* 1174–1176.

DeCasper, A. J., and Spence, M. J. (1986). Prenatal maternal speech influences newborn's perception of speech sounds. *Infant Behavior and Development, 9,* 133–150.

Deguchi, H. (1984). Observational learning from a radical-behavioristic viewpoint. *The Behavior Analyst, 7,* 83–95.

Drabman, R. S., Spitalnik, R., and O'Leary, K. D. (1973). Teaching self-control to disruptive children. *Journal of Abnormal Psychology, 82,* 10–16.

Field, T. M., Woodson, R., Greenberg, R., and Cohen, D. (1982). Discrimination and imitation of facial expressions by neonates. *Science, 218,* 179–181.

Gale, E. N., and Jacobson, M. B. (1970). The relationship between social comments as unconditional stimuli and fear responding. *Behaviour Research and Therapy, 8,* 301–307.

Hayes, S. (1989) (ed.). *Rule-governed Behavior: Cognition, contingencies and instructional control.* New York: Plenum.

Ladd, G. W. (1981). Effectiveness of a social learning method for enhancing children's social interaction and peer acceptance. *Child Development, 52,* 171–178.

Layng, T. V., and Andronis, P. T. (1984). Toward a functional analysis of delusional speech and hallucinatory behavior. *The Behavior Analyst, 7,* 139–156.

Liebert, R. M., and Fernandez, L. E. (1970). Effects of vicarious consequences on imitative performance. *Child Development, 41,* 847–852.

Lipsitt, L. P., and Kaye, H. (1964). Conditioned sucking in the human newborn. *Psychonomic Science, 1,* 29–30.

Midlarsky, E. and Bryan, J. H. (1967). Training charity in children. *Journal of Personality and Social Psychology, 5,* 408–415.

Nesse, R. M., Curtis, G. C., Thyer, B. A., McCann, D. S., Huber-Smith, M., and Knoph, R. (1985). Endocrine and cardiovascular responses during phobic anxiety. *Psychosomatic Medicine, 47,* 320–332.

Parsonson, B. S., and Baer, D. M. (1978). Training generalized improvisation of tools by preschool children. *Journal of Applied Behavior Analysis, 11,* 363–380.

Pear, J. J., and Eldridge, G. D. (1984). The operant-respondent distinction: Future directions. *Journal of the Experimental Analysis of Behavior, 42,* 453–467.

Presbie, R. J., and Coiteux, P. F. (1971). Learning to be generous or stingy: Imitation of sharing behavior as a function of model generosity and vicarious reinforcement. *Child Development, 42,* 1033–1038.

Rheingold, H. L., Gewirtz, J. L., and Ross, H. W. (1959). Social conditioning of vocalizations in the infant. *Journal of Comparative and Physiological Psychology, 52,* 68–73.

Risley, T. R., and Hart, B. (1968). Developing correspondence between the non-verbal and verbal of preschool children. *Journal of Applied Behavior Analysis, 1,* 267–281.

Sainato, D. M., Maheady, L., and Shook, G. L. (1986). The effects of a classroom manager role on the social interaction patterns and social status of withdrawn kindergarten students. *Journal of Applied Behavior Analysis, 19,* 187–195.

Schmitt, D. R. (1976). Some conditions affecting the choice to cooperate or compete. *Journal of the Experimental Analysis of Behavior, 25,* 165–178.

Siqueland, E. R., and Lipsitt, L. P. (1966). Conditioned head-turning in human newborns. *Journal of Experimental Child Psychology, 3,* 356–376.

Skinner, B. F. (1953). *Science and human behavior.* New York: Free Press.

Skinner, B. F. (1957). *Verbal behavior.* Englewood Cliffs, NJ: Prentice-Hall.

Skinner, B. F. (1981). Selection by consequences. *Science, 213,* 501–504.

Spencer, M. B., and Horowitz, F. D. (1973). Effects of systematic social and token reinforcement on the modification of racial and color concept attitudes in black and white preschool children. *Developmental Psychology, 9,* 246–254.

Walters, E. T., and Byrne, J. H. (1983). Associative conditioning of single sensory neurons suggests a cellular mechanism of learning. *Science, 219,* 405–408.

Walters, R. H. and Brown, M. (1963). Studies of reinforcement of aggression: III. Transfer of responses to an interpersonal situation. *Child Development, 34,* 563–571.

Watson, J. B. (1913). Psychology as the behaviorist views it. *Psychological Review, 20,* 158–177.

Whitehurst, G. J. and Valdez-Menchaca, M. C. (1988). What is the role of reinforcement in early language acquisition? *Child Development, 59,* 430–440.

48

PSYCHODYNAMIC THEORIES:
A FRAME FOR DEVELOPMENT

Sophie Freud
School of Social Work
Simmons College

The activity of being a person is the activity of meaning making.

(Kegan, 1982, p. 12)

All of us approach other people, family members, friends, teachers and clients with certain assumptions regarding human nature, motivations,
causes and effects, important values and the nature
of change. These ideas have become part of our ongoing effort to make meaning in the process of
growing up in a particular family which was embedded in a particular network of subcultures. Many of
the concepts to be presented might already be part of
your assumptive world, because psychodynamic theories have become to some extent an integral part of
our Western culture. Other ideas may be new and
intriguing and expand or modify your meaning-
making options.

In this chapter, I shall avoid writing about
truths and "discoveries." Instead, I shall present
you with a particular frame, or lens, or perhaps a
filter, through which you can view and make meaning of your own and other people's behavior. You
will need to decide for yourself, leaning on your ongoing experiences, whether this particular frame is
compatible with your most important values and
whether it enhances your effort to help people who
come to you with their problems in living.

The use of the word "psychodynamic" has
changed over time. It referred initially to theories
dealing with the psychic energy created by sexual
and aggressive drives called upon by Freud to explain the mainsprings of human behavior. I shall use
"psychodynamic" in its current meaning, as referring to any framework which postulates unconscious
forces as a major explanation for human motivation.
Such unconscious forces may be viewed as innate
and "instinctual" or established in childhood

through certain developmental experiences, or as a
combination of both, as Freud viewed them. The
framework to be described selects Sigmund Freud,
founder of psychoanalysis, as a somewhat arbitrary
starting point. It distinguishes at least three branches
growing out of Freud's original ideas. One branch
known as Ego Psychology remained most faithful to
Freud's original hypotheses, in terms of acceptance
of drive theories. It was carried forward by his
daughter Anna Freud, Heinz Hartmann, Edith Jacobson, Erik Erikson, Margaret Mahler and many
other psychoanalysts, social workers and psychologists. A second branch, the Object Relations School,
replaced drive theory with the quality of the mother-
infant relationships as a major frame for explaining
human development. While Anna Freud may be
known as the mother of ego psychology, Melanie
Klein inspired the object relations school, associated
with the British school of psychoanalysis and with
such names as Ronald Fairbairn, Donald Winnicott,
Michael Balint, and Harry Guntrip, and, with a
somewhat different orientation, John Bowlby, again
mentioning only some of the outstanding names of
its founders. A third, perhaps less distinct, branch
growing out of Freud's original ideas could be the
one that focused on the more expanded interpersonal
life of the individual taking place in different contexts, including his or her culture, and also extended
formative influences through the life cycle. We can
consider Harry Stack Sullivan, founder of the Interpersonal School of Psychiatry as pioneering this
focus, adding Alfred Adler, Erich Fromm and
Karen Horney as three other early thinkers who
also paid respect to the all important sociocultural
environment.

While these three branches could be distinguished for the sake of a historical orientation, their
early convergences are as noteworthy as their differ-

This paper was written for this anthology, 1990.

[Editor's note: Dr. Freud uses distinctive capitalizations and placement of italicized words to emphasize key concepts.]

ences. Alfred Adler was viewed as a "heretic" by Freud, yet he could be viewed as the first ego psychologist, and Erikson's interest in the impact of culture was entirely compatible with the views of Sullivan or Fromm. Mahler's view of early development resembled those of object relations theorists in important respects. A relatively recent branch of psychoanalysis, Self Psychology, founded by Heinz Kohut, could be considered a creative combination of ego psychology and object relations theory. I believe it is the convergence of these three branches that has guaranteed the vitality and usefulness of what has come to be called the "psychodynamic" framework. In this latter use "psychodynamics" is defined by an object relationist as

> the study of the motivated and meaningful life of human beings, as persons shaped in the media of personal relationships which constitute their lives and determine to so large an extent how their innate gifts and possibilities will develop, . . . in the "facilitating" or so often "unfacilitating environment" of the other important human beings (Guntrip, 1971, p. 17).

It is difficult to present a theory that is so tightly interrelated in all its parts, that any one component can only be appreciated in the light of all other parts of the theory. I shall try to draw your attention to the first time a New Concept is mentioned, by capitalizing it. Let us take as arbitrary starting point Freud's view of

the Psychic Apparatus.

A core aspect of Freud's thinking was that many of the causes of our behavior are unknown to us, outside of our awareness, Unconscious. Freud saw this conscious/unconscious dimension of the mind as so central to its understanding, that he conceived of the mind as a layered structure, with the unconscious at its bottom, the Preconscious (that which could be brought into awareness at any time) in the middle and the Conscious on the surface. Although Freud later discarded this Topographical theory, our reference to Depth Psychology continues to conjure up a spatial image.

Later Freud preferred to think of the mind as divided into three components that transcended the conscious/unconscious dichotomy—the Id, Ego, and Superego. The id was equated with the unconscious, a reservoir of instinctual energies which were the fuel for psychic activity. The ego was a person's executive agent and the superego was the person's conscience, the internalized cultural and family values and moral beliefs that the child had incorporated from his or her parents. Both superego and ego were

counterweights to the id. While the id was entirely unconscious and could be equated with that concept, Freud viewed the ego and superego as partially conscious and partially unconscious. I shall now briefly discuss each of these three Structures of the Mind, remembering that the concept of structure is here no more than a metaphor that directs us to think in a particular way about our psychic life. Freud thought of

the Unconscious, or *the Id,*

as a dangerous force, a veritable subterranean cauldron of incestuous and aggressive childhood desires that needed to be Repressed, meaning kept out of conscious awareness. Yet, at times the Psychic Energy needed for such repression was insufficient, and unconscious wishes would escape, leak out, in the form of dreams, slips of the tongue, forgetting, errors or symptomatic behavior. Freud was particularly interested in dreams and called them "the royal road to the unconscious." Freud saw much of psychic life as a struggle between id forces insisting on some form of expression and ego and superego forces bent on modulating or suppressing those socially forbidden impulses. Freud saw the conflict and veritable war between psychic structures as the reason and essence of all forms of pathology. He even thought that the very price of civilization was a measure of suppression of our instinctual life. In this view, the focus of therapy will not be a particular piece of disturbed or disturbing "symptom" but the psychic conflict that is presumed to cause it and without which the undesirable behavior is presumed to disappear.

It is a central aspect of Freud's theory that Sexuality, (also known as Libido) either in direct or in some Sublimated or distorted forms, is a major human motivation. A constructive sublimation might be the transformation of infantile sexual curiosity into scientific research activities, or the love of money might be an indirect expression of interest in feces, a fixation on Anality, an immature form of sexual expression. Other psychodynamic theorists have postulated different major motivations. Sullivan thought that people's primary goal was an effort to avoid anxiety and promote security. Object relationists pointed to the wish for human connectedness as being the most important human goal, while self psychology emphasized the need for wholeness. The belief in an overriding need for self-regard which leans on relatedness, a firm sense of self, and competence combines some of these orientations. Freud's drive theories are also in other ways among those of his ideas that have not withstood the test of time. We now think of being alive as similar to being active, and the need for a "fuel" in the form of drives, to explain activity has become unnecessary. Guntrip has redefined the "sexual drive" as a bodily appetite that is usually interpersonally expressed and therefore leads to many human dramas and conflicts. Currently we have learned to appreciate the interpersonal nature and ensuing conflicts of all bodily appetites, including hunger and the need for sleep. Aggression, rather than an instinct, could be viewed as a defensive reaction of the self against physical, social or psychological phenomena that a particular culture has defined as dangerous.

Yet, the idea that we are frequently unaware of at least some of the reasons, perhaps even the "truest" reasons for our behavior continues to be anchored as a major conviction of our Western culture and to be confirmed by research in several disciplines. The unconscious has currently several meanings, all of them different from that of a place, a structure or even a childhood remnant. In one sense we think of it as the process of warding off, sometimes called Splitting off or Disowning, aspects of ourselves or our interpersonal world that would cause us too much pain. The second meaning refers to cognitive factors. The "Cognitive Unconscious" could be viewed as all our unexamined beliefs, premises and assumptions that constitute our taken for granted world. Some of these beliefs may come from our cultural learnings, others from particular childhood experiences, including traumatic events which have left a lasting and perhaps partly conscious and partly unconscious trace. Such traumatic events that shape our dreams, expectations, fears and wishes need not only occur in childhood, it now appears, but our vulnerability to Post-Traumatic Stress Disorders continues through adulthood.

The third meaning leans on a large body of social-psychological research on unconscious learning that refers to subliminal messages to which we are constantly exposed and which also influence our behavior outside our conscious awareness. Recognition of such influences is very important, since it points to our vulnerability to being manipulated by advertisements, politicians and the media in general. Consciousness-raising is the activity of taking stock of our cognitive unconscious.

I mentioned above that "ego psychology" was the natural heir to Freud's "id psychology." In the latter, the focus of therapy was on bringing the contents of the unconscious, the id, up to the surface, sometimes referred to as an "archeological dig" method, in the hope of dealing and making peace with unacceptable drives, decreasing irrational behavior, increasing self awareness and enlarging the ego at the expense of the id.

The ego

was defined as a psychic structure in charge of regulating, integrating and synthesizing our sensory-motor capacities; our cognitive skills; our social relationships; as well as our conscious emotional life. Moreover, the ego was to mediate between id desires and superego prohibitions, insuring some instinctual satisfactions without serious social transgressions. Ego strength was assessed in terms of intactness of the above mentioned ego functions, as well as the ego's mediating skills. A person with a defective memory, for example, would have an ego weakness in the cognitive area, an ego function. An ego that prohibits all instinctual pleasure, or an ego that allows free expressions of impulses would be judged as weak or defective in its mediating task.

In ego psychology, the focus of interest and therapeutic intervention focused on the ego, its functions and functioning, with the hope of strengthening both. Clinicians paid special attention to the ego's adaptive and defensive tasks. Psychoanalysis in its typically "noun language" called the means by which we learn to ward off too much psychic pain

Defense Mechanisms.

In the original theory, defenses were brought into play when sexual or aggressive wishes threatened to emerge. Others have enlarged and modified this creative concept and tied it primarily to our self-esteem. They postulate that we attempt to distort or at least reframe reality to ward off more guilt, shame, anguish, grief, helplessness or hopelessness than we think we can bear.

Many noun words have been invented to describe these self-protective processes. We speak of Denial, Reaction Formation which hides true feelings through opposite behavior, Fantasy, Delusions, Displacement of feelings from a forbidden object to a safer object, Conversion of feelings into actual or imaginary bodily symptoms, Splitting as already referred to, Avoidance, Projection and countless other "mechanisms." Each of these self-deceiving devices may be adaptive in certain situations, such as *denying* a terminal illness by making the best of the rest of one's life, or maladaptive in another context in which denial or neglect of a problematic situation can lead to disaster.

The concept of Projective Identification can be singled out as being particularly useful in clinical practice. In Projection we attribute our own self-doubts to others and accuse them of having contempt for us. In Projective Identification we are said to assign split-off and disowned aspects of the self to an intimate other, for example a spouse or a child, thus staying in touch with this part of ourselves and punishing, enhancing or even cherishing it in the other person. The other person is induced through various maneuvers to exhibit the disowned (mis)behavior while the projecting person remains blameless. This process has also been called Irrational Role Assignment. Such processes can also be viewed on the social level, where a group in power can project their undesired Shadows (a metaphor introduced by Carl Jung) onto a weaker, vulnerable group which then gets persecuted or oppressed for their "despised attributes." Racism and Homophobia are examples of such projective identification.

Psychoanalytic theory postulates that Anxiety signals to us that we are about to be in psychic danger, so we can set defenses into motion, anxiety thus functioning like pain which signals physical danger to our bodies. The theory of defense thus suggests that one part of the self can deceive another part. This whole process must proceed unconsciously if the purpose of emotional self-protection is to be achieved. However, if we think of lying as a conscious deception and denial as an unconscious one, this distinction between conscious and unconscious maneuvers may not be airtight since some people end up believing their own lies.

While defenses are considered an integral aspect of coping with the stresses of daily life, ego strength is judged by the degree of reality distortion of a particular defense, whether a defense promotes constructive problem solving, how quickly defenses are used to avoid even a small degree of anxiety, and how readily defensive behavior is given up when the psychic danger has passed. Maladaptive defenses that become "stuck" are considered symptoms. The concepts of "defense mechanisms" were neither new inventions, nor even based on new observations. We meet the fox and his "sour grapes" already in Aesop's fables. Neither did Freud "discover" or even "invent" the unconscious, or the formative nature of childhood which is already mentioned in the Bible. Rather, he integrated his clinical observations and ideas, into a coherent theoretical framework in which all the different pieces of the puzzle fit well together and result in a meaningful whole.

The lack of interest in drives as useful explanatory concepts, within psychodynamics, does not only diminish our interest in the id, but also raises questions about the concept of ego. Many clinicians have started to prefer the concept of Self to that of the ego, since the ego is only *part* of the self. We thus see the evolution and acceptance of Kohut's Self Psychology and increasing reference in the literature to self and Identity as focal concepts.

In line with his focal interest Freud hypothesized that young children went through *Psychosexual Stages of development,* in which their basic personality was formed. He distinguished the oral, anal, and immature genital stages, in which the focus of sexual feelings was transferred from one erotogenic zone to the next, the mouth, the anus and the immature genitals. As children grew through these stages, they might be overindulged or deprived at one stage or another, making for a Fixation at that period and for later problems with the issues that were to be resolved at that stage. The need to smoke or abuse substances might be considered an oral fixation. Moreover if stages were not well negotiated, a vulnerability might remain, with the danger of Regression to a particular stage under the stresses of adult life. These concepts of fixation and regression have pervaded all of psychodynamic theory in one form or another.

Freud believed that people had a need to repeat early conflicts over and over, perhaps in an effort to master them, calling this need Repetition Compulsion. His ideas about child development were not based on direct observations, but were reconstructions, derived from the behavior and accounts of his adult patients. He also felt that the need for and tendency to repeat early experiences meant that patients, given the situation of helpseeking and dependency induced by therapy, repeat with their therapist the problematic relationships and conflicting emotions of love and hate that they had with their parents. He called this Transference, establishing a central clinical concept. The therapist's own irrational response, presumably also based on his or her childhood conflicts, Freud called Countertransference, to be carefully controlled lest it interfere with the therapist's "objective" attitude.

Other psychoanalysts further developed the idea that certain character styles were developmental fixations, and the literature describes greedy, dependent "oral characters", or rigid, obstinate "anal characters" who can't get off the pot, or exhibitionist, competitive "phallic characters". These were vivid images in which everyone could recognize their clients and themselves.

In spite of his interest in early childhood, Freud emphasized the family drama of the 3- to 5-year-old as the crux of development. He called the love of the child for the parent of the opposite gender and the envy, competition and hostility of the child for his, or her rival, the parent of the same gender,

the Oedipus Complex,

Oedipus being a figure in a Greek legend in which he kills his father and marries his mother. Freud thought these loving and hating feelings towards one's parents had to be resolved at that point in development, for proper gender development and for the formation of the superego, identification with the values the parents represented, to proceed. Freud introduced such concepts as Castration Anxiety to explain the boy's readiness to make peace with his father, and Penis Envy to explain the little girl's angry disappointment with her mother and her turning towards her father in compensation. Once children had resolved the Oedipal crisis, they were ready to put aside their sexual urges and enter a period of Latency, with a chance to redirect their energy into intellectual development during the school years. Sexual urges were then revived with new urgency during adolescence, sometimes called a second Oedipal crisis.

Anna Freud was among those students of child development who emphasized the inevitably tumultuous nature of adolescence. Many of these ideas have now been elaborated or modified. For example Sullivan highlighted the juvenile and preadolescent period as one of major social development, both through their meeting with the adult world outside their own family and through their association with a peer group. Children of that age have to learn many social skills, they are evaluated by the social standards of the larger world, and hopefully they progress from exclusive self-interest to cooperation and eventual collaboration with others. Sullivan even thought that the preadolescent friendship with a child of the same gender, a Chum, was a very important development experience, preparing the way for adult intimacy. While adolescence continues to be seen as a major life transition, current research suggests that it is not necessarily tumultuous. Perhaps it is cultural expectations, including a measure of permission for rebellion, rather than biological urges that predicts adolescent behavior at any one period in history.

The particular ways in which love and hate towards parents are expressed at a particular developmental period continues to engage our interest, but

the concept of the Oedipus complex has been critiqued from many angles. Both castration anxiety and penis envy are now usually considered signs of troubled development, rather than inevitable. Penis envy, when it exists, is viewed either as the little girl's reaction to her brother's favored status and/or to the favored status of men in our society. Preoccupation with incestuous or aggressive feelings towards parents are thought to be the consequence of actual parental mishandling, rather than a developmental phase of the child's fantasy life. Gender development, it is pointed out, is well in place by age 3, and may merely be shaped rather than established through parental identifications.

The superego,

in Freud's thinking, is "heir to the Oedipus complex," and since boys, due to their castration anxiety had a more clearly defined Oedipus complex than girls, he thought they also had a superior superego. This was a bold assertion which has of course evoked women's indignation. Let me draw your attention to an alternate viewpoint which suggests that morality or a conscience is not a structure acquired at age 5, but that the roots of the capacity to care about others and a wish to be fair and just are acquired in infancy, during the attachment experience. These roots then need to be further developed through an increasing ability to take the perspective of another person and through an appreciation for the social community on which one depends. Most importantly, we have learned through history, that moral behavior is at all times defined by a social context and that few people have the moral independence to act against their own reference groups, on whom they rely for self-evaluation.

The Oedipus complex also lost its central organizing lens when the whole psychodynamic field in the 1950's followed the lead of object relationists in their focus on the infant rather than the preschool child. Thus, Freud's concept of

psychic determinism,

meaning that personality formation was "determined" by early experiences, was moved back to an even earlier time. Continuing Freud's thinking on fixations, early developmental experiences were seen as transforming into inner mental structures, including emotional and cognitive capacities, which were then the foundation of later development. The new emphasis was on the interpersonal nature of early experiences, such as mother-infant interactions, rather than on Freud's innate programs, but once the mental structures were built, at Critical Periods of development, personality was shaped and would be increasingly resistant to change. Defective early mothering would cause permanent fateful developmental deviations and become the source of adult pathology. The earlier and more faulty the inadequate mothering, the more severe was the adult disturbance. This has become such an axiom of psychodynamic theory that clinicians not only focus on early experiences in their assessment, but also infer early deprivations from their clients' problems, and often have hypotheses as to the exact time at which the earlier traumas and/or deprivations occurred. Kohut for example, just like Freud also formed a picture of early child development from the way his patients behaved in psychoanalysis, and concluded from the nature of his patients' transference what kinds of early experiences they MUST have had with their parents. He thought that the lack of admiration and due appreciation and affirmation, in the form of empathic mirroring by parents in early childhood, led to serious developmental deviations, such as excessive self-absorption usually known as Narcissism. Kohut thought that such serious disturbances were not caused by psychic conflict but by deficits in the early structure of the self.

Yet, starting in the 1950's a new interest in direct and increasingly sophisticated observations of children would revolutionize our understanding of *child development.*

Margaret Mahler was among these researchers and since she still worked within a drive theory framework she was accepted by ego psychologists. She thought that early development proceeded from a symbiotic oneness with the mother through a series of separation/individuation stages. Between the ages of 2 to 3, a well-developed child was thought to have acquired a firm sense of self and other, usually the mother, as a separate loved and loving nurturing person whose mental image could be evoked in times of separation and stress. Such an achievement is called Object Constancy, a sense that both the self and others, as well as physical things have an existence apart from the self, continuous over time. Mahler called the period between 18 months and 2 years the phase of Rapprochement, a time when the child's new awareness of a frightening and lonely self creates an acute ambivalent dependence/independence crisis. In line with the thinking described above, "borderline development" has been viewed, in this framework, as a non-resolution of the rapprochement crisis.

Mahler views the process as partially genetically preprogrammed, yet is also mindful of the mother's role as Auxiliary Ego and shaper of each stage. While she stresses the need to grow toward autonomy she bases that growth on firm bonding.

The object relations view
is complementary to Mahler's ideas, but with a somewhat different emphasis and without the encumbrance of drive language. The English pediatrician/child psychiatrist Donald Winnicott coined the felicitous term Good Enough Mother, one who is predictable, reliable, available, nurturant, a soothing container for the child's unregulated impulses. The good enough mother helps build optimal affective and cognitive structures and her soothing function is transformed into the ability for self-soothing. Cold, neglectful or harsh and abusive caretaking is thought to become transformed into a malignant introject, carried through life as an internal scolding hostile inner saboteur. One version of this theory is that we all learn about ourselves from the way we are treated (Sullivan's concept of Reflected Appraisals), and a small child naturally assumes that being maltreated means being bad. This feeling then becomes a persistent part of his or her self-concept. It is thought that the wish for parental approval is a deep longing and that some people who do not get such approval then spend their entire life in its pursuit, with their actual parents, with other people who come to stand for their parents, or with their internalized parents who can also never be satisfied.

We also owe to object relationists, particularly to Harry Guntrip the concept of a true and false self. The latter was thought to develop when demands for adaptation and conformity are premature, excessive and coercive. Children have to bury their spontaneous feelings of joy, grief, disappointment, anger, exhuberance, becoming good little girls or boys and later conforming, well-programmed adults who feel inauthentic, empty and despairing in their inner core.

John Bowlby, another important British theorist of human development started his work by describing the distressing results of early mother-infant separations, pioneering a large body of research dealing with Maternal Deprivation. Bowlby eventually synthesized both schools, combined them with ethological ideas and coined the concept of Attachment as an evolutionary survival mechanism. Once again, the idea that children need a secure attachment experience to thrive and develop their human potential, to learn to love and care about others, was elaborated in great detail. This important concept has set the stage for current research on such different forms of attachment as secure, anxious, avoidant and disorganized attachment. Longitudinal research is currently carried on to see the effects of different kinds of attachment on later development in a rigorous research effort to test the assumption of early determinism. It must also be remembered that development is Transactional, meaning snowballing and circular, leading optimally to upwards spirals or tragically to vicious cycles, or what Sullivan called Malevolent Transformations. Bowlby replaced ''introjects'' with the more cognitive concept of ''internal working models''. All of this research has set the stage for our new understanding of infants' needs, with a new emphasis on synchrony, attunement, attentiveness and self-regulation.

The belief in the fateful and perhaps irreversible importance of early life experiences does not lead to therapeutic optimism. It has seemed at times that only years of reparenting type treatments can build new structures and make up for early deficits. Social workers are however sometimes in a position where supportive interventions with young mothers and infants can get them off to a good start, enhancing the quality of a relationship that is considered such an essential building block of optimal development.

Developmental ideas were initially limited to childhood years, expanding from preschool years to adolescence and back to infancy, although Carl Jung had introduced quite early a focus on mid-life issues. It was, however,

Erik Erikson,

coming from a psychoanalytic tradition, who constructed in early 1950 a life-cycle chart of human growth and development that started an interest in the study of development throughout life. He followed Freud's example of thinking of development as progressing in Stages but he modified Freud's narrow focus on the development of sexuality, instead casting development in a psychosocial cultural context. He hypothesized that all human beings follow an Epigenetic, meaning biologically preprogrammed, groundplan that will naturally unfold with sufficient nurturance and guide all children through certain prototypical Crises. Such crises can be understood as periods of inner turmoil after which there is a shift in one's sense of self and one's relationships to others. Erikson called these successive crises: Trust versus Mistrust (infancy), Autonomy versus Shame and Doubt (toddler), Initiative versus Guilt (preschool child), Industry versus Inferiority (school child), Identity versus Identity Diffusion (adolescence), and the three stages of adulthood, In-

timacy versus Isolation, Generativity versus Stagnation, and Integrity versus Despair. These hypothesized crises had to be developed positively for optimal development. You can see that Erikson touched upon the most important aspects of mental health, such as ability to form important relationships (trust, intimacy), a sense of self-direction and control (autonomy) competence, mastery and self-esteem (industry, generativity) and a sense of wholeness (identity, integrity). All psychodynamic therapists would aim directly or indirectly at enhancing these capacities. Erikson's stage theory was accepted with enthusiasm by the mental health and even lay community. Indeed he had humanized, refined and expanded Freud's developmental ideas and his framework appealed to universal experiences. They formed for many years a yardstick against which a particular person's development could be measured. Thus, like all stage theories, and indeed all social science descriptions, it also became a prescription, setting certain norms and expectations for rate, sequence and the whole nature of development. Daniel Stern, an infant researcher, has made the suggestion, compelling to this writer, that Freud's, Mahler's and Erikson's ''stages'' could better be viewed as universal issues, such as orality, anality, attachment, autonomy, intimacy, identity, etc., that need to be negotiated at every phase of life.

Much research and theorizing has been done in the last twenty years on adult development, both in terms, once again, of describing and prescribing the ''predictable'' stages of adult life, as well as focusing in depth on the life tasks of adults in their many roles, at various ages, mindful of both similarity and diversity among people.

All psychodynamic theories depend for

therapy

on the talking cure, in the assumption that a verbal discussion of one's difficulties with an attentive, caring listener will be helpful. There are however different assumptions about the goals of therapy and different ways it is conducted. The time frame may vary from daily sessions over years, to a planned period of eight to twelve sessions, and sometimes even a single encounter can be conducted within such a framework and prove helpful. In classical psychoanalysis the therapist sits behind the patient who lies on a couch, promoting regression and the emergence of unconscious material through Free Associations, while most other dynamic therapies are conducted face to face. Therapeutic activities also vary in different theoretical frameworks, as has already been mentioned in the course of this chapter. If the assumption is that the patient's troubles are due to irrational unconscious wishes and conflicting goals and desires, the goal of therapy can be viewed as helping the patient understand his or her unconscious, meaning expanding self-awareness, self-knowledge, and therefore self-direction. This might be done through occasional Interpretations of the patient's dreams or by connecting puzzling self-defeating behavior with unconscious material. The promotion of Insight is a goal in most other psychodynamic therapies. Social workers have traditionally been wary of bringing the unconscious to the surface, yet the strengthening of the ego has been an important goal and we habitually deal with defenses, hoping to confront or modify maladaptive ones, or else shoring up weak defenses that might help people cope with difficult situations. If the unconscious is seen as a "split-off" part of the self, a goal might be to work toward greater cohesiveness of the self, an important concept in self psychology.

All psychodynamic therapies rely on the concept of transference but there has been much controversy on how actively caring or impersonal a therapist should be. Classical psychoanalysis held the theory that the more neutral and unknown the therapist remains, the more she or he can become a mirror for the patient's projections. Since it is pre-

sumed that irrational interpersonal feelings also enter the patient's daily relationship, and are only more condensed and visible in therapy, it is expected that addressing, understanding, and working through such feelings will help a person become more reasonable and emotionally open in all their human relationships. Other schools promoted the view that such "neutral" therapists can appear uncaring and that improvement in patients was due at least as much to an accepting, nonjudgmental, caring relationship, as to new insights. Indeed if the goal of therapy is to reproduce a more optimal parenting experience, as is true for objects relationists and self psychologists, treatment will be long-term and the therapist will be an empathic companion. The most important ingredient for improvement in therapy still has not been firmly established.

Social workers are in the fortunate position of not being beholden to any one of these schools. We can adapt our stance to particular clients, their needs and the context in which we work. We can create different meanings from a variety of theoretical perspectives and can borrow the best theoretical and clinical ideas from each school, or choose the perspective that is most suitable for a particular client. This is precisely the reason why this chapter has been written.

References and Suggested Background Readings

Baker, H. S. and Baker, M. N. (1987). Heinz Kohut's Self Psychology: an overview. *American Journal of Psychiatry, 144,* 1–9.

Blanck, G. and Blanck, R. (1974). *Ego Psychology.* N.Y.: Columbia U. Press.

Blanck, G. and Blanck, R. (1979). *Ego Psychology II.* N.Y.: Columbia U. Press.

Bowers, K. S. and Meichenbaum, D. (eds.) (1984). *The Unconscious Reconsidered.* New York: John Wiley.

Bowlby, J. (1988). Developmental psychiatry comes of age. *American Journal of Psychiatry,* 145 (1), 1–10.

Erikson, E. H. (1959). Identity and the Life Cycle. *Psychological Issues, 1.*

Freud, Anna. (1936). The Ego and the Mechanisms of Defense. *The Writing of Anna Freud, Vol. II.* New York: International Universities Press, 1966.

Freud, Sigmund. (1933). New Introductory Lectures on Psychoanalysis. *Standard Edition of the Complete Works of Sigmund Freud, Vol. 22.* London: Hogarth Press, 1953–1974.

Freud, Sigmund. *A General Selection from the Works of Sigmund Freud.* Edited by J. Rickman. (1989). New York: Doubleday Anchor.

Greenberg, J. and Mitchell, S. (1983). *Object Relations in Psychoanalytic Theory.* Cambridge, Mass: Harvard University Press.

Guntrip, H. (1971). *Psychoanalytic Theory, Therapy and the Self.* New York: Basic Books.

Kegan, R. (1982). *The Evolving Self.* Cambridge, Mass: Harvard University Press.

Offer, D. and Sabshin, M. (1984). *Normality and the Life Cycle.* New York: Basic Books

Sroufe, L. A. (1988). The role of infant-caregiver attachment in development. In J. Belsky and T. Nezworski (eds.), *Clinical Implications of Attachment.* Hillsdale, New Jersey: Erlbaum.

Stafford-Clark, D. (1967). *What Freud Really Said.* Penguin Books.

Stern, D. (1986). *The Interpersonal World of the Infant.* New York: Basic Books.

Stern, R. (ed.) (1987). *Theories of the Unconscious and the Self.* Hillsdale, New Jersey: The Analytic Press.

Sullivan, H. S. (1953). *The Interpersonal Theory of Psychiatry.* New York: Norton.

Stafford-Clark, D. (1967). *What Freud Really Said*. Penguin Books.

Stern, D. (1986). *The Interpersonal World of the Infant*. New York: Basic Books.

Stern, R. (ed.) (1987). *Theories of the Unconscious and the Self*. Hillsdale, New Jersey: The Analytic Press.

Sullivan, H. S. (1953). *The Interpersonal Theory of Psychiatry*. New York: Norton.